Prehistoric Man
in the New World

CONTRIBUTORS

PEDRO ARMILLAS

IGNACIO BERNAL

HENRY B. COLLINS

CAREY CRONEIS

GORDON F. EKHOLM

CLIFFORD EVANS

JAMES B. GRIFFIN

ROBERT F. HEIZER

JESSE D. JENNINGS

ALFRED KIDDER II

ALEX D. KRIEGER

BETTY J. MEGGERS

ERIK K. REED

IRVING ROUSE

WILLIAM H. SEARS

MORRIS SWADESH

ROBERT WAUCHOPE

WALDO R. WEDEL

Prehistoric

Man

in the

New World

Edited by
JESSE D. JENNINGS
EDWARD NORBECK

THE UNIVERSITY OF CHICAGO PRESS

CHICAGO & LONDON

ISBN: 0-226-39738-6 (clothbound); 0-226-39739-4 (paperbound)
Library of Congress Catalog Card Number: 63-18852

THE UNIVERSITY OF CHICAGO PRESS, CHICAGO 60637
The University of Chicago Press, Ltd., London

Foreword

THE PAPERS published in this volume are lengthier versions of addresses delivered at Rice University on November 9 and 10, 1962, in a symposium entitled "Prehistoric Man in the New World." This symposium formed part of the festivities celebrating the fiftieth year (1962) since the opening of Rice University.

As director of the symposium and co-editor of this volume, I wish to express my gratitude to many people for valuable aid in planning and conducting the symposium and in preparing this book for publication. First, I wish to give hearty thanks to the eighteen contributors and to say that their cheerful co-operation made our tasks easy. Special thanks for aid of many kinds are due to Jesse D. Jennings, senior editor of this book and participant in several important ways in the symposium; Carey Croneis, Chancellor of Rice University, who served admirably in multiple roles connected with the symposium and this book; and Mrs. Deni Seinfeld, who cheerfully bore the burden of many of the most tedious chores. Others to whom I am thankful for encouragement and aid of various kinds include President and Mrs. Kenneth S. Pitzer and Dean and Mrs. William H. Masterson, of Rice University; Thomas N. Campbell, Frank Hole, and Albert C. Spaulding, who graciously served as chairmen of the symposium; Mr. and Mrs. Dan E. Bloxsom, Mrs. Mimi Cohen, Miss Karren Cowdin, Miss Lenora Detering, Mr. and Mrs. Albert Fay, Dr. and Mrs. Richard J. Gonzalez, Mrs. W. C. Hardy, James A. Hilburn, Miss Mary Frances Harris, Dr. and Mrs. Gaylord Johnson, Mr. and Mrs. John T. Jones, Jr., Mrs. Konstantin Kolenda, Mrs. Lucybeth Rampton, Howard A. Thompson and his staff, Mr. and Mrs. Gail Whitcomb, Leslie A. White, Gordon Willey, Mr. and Mrs. Willoughby Williams, Mrs. Roy E. Willie, members of the Houston Archeological Society, and my wife. We are deeply thankful to Lucybeth Rampton for her unflagging efforts in the trying task of preparing the detailed Index.

We express our thanks to the University of Oklahoma Press for permission to use illustrations (Wedel, Figs. 1 and 2) from Waldo R. Wedel, *Prehistoric Man on the Great Plains* (1961) and illustrations (Wauchope, Figs. 2*a*, 3*b*, and 3*c*) from J. Eric S. Thompson, *The Rise and Fall of Maya Civilization* (1954); to the Yale University Press for the use of illustrations (Rouse, Figs. 1 and 2) from Irving Rouse and J. M. Cruxent, *Venezuelan Archeology* (in press); to the Southwest Museum, Los Angeles, for the use of illustrations (Wauchope, Figs. 1*d* and 4*a*) from George W. Brainerd, *The Maya Civilization* (1954); to Stanford University Press for the use of illustrations (Wauchope, Figs. 2*b*, 3*a*, and 4*d*) from Sylvanus G. Morley and George W. Brainerd, *The Ancient Maya*, 3d ed. (1956); to the Carnegie Institution of Washington for the use of illustrations (Wauchope, Figs. 1*a*, 1*c*, and 4*c*) from Tatiana A. Proskouriakoff, *An Album of Maya Architecture* (1946), Alfred V. Kidder, J. J. Jennings, and E. M. Shook, *Excavations at Kaminaljuyú, Guatemala* (1946), and Alfred V. Kidder, *The Artifacts of Uaxactun, Guatemala* (1947); to Centro de Investigaciones Antropológicas de México for the use of illustrations (Wauchope, 2*c*) from Alberto Ruz in Carmen Cook de Leonard (ed.), *El Esplendor de México Antiguo* (1959); and to the Encyclopaedia Britannica for the use of illustrations (Griffin, Figs. 1, 2, 3, and 4).

We are indebted to the Wenner-Gren Foundation for Anthropological Research for a grant-in-aid that allowed us to increase the number of topics and participants in the symposium.

EDWARD NORBECK

EDWARD NORBECK, professor of anthropology and chairman of the Department of Anthropology and Sociology, Rice University, received his doctoral degree from the University of Michigan. He is the author of books and many articles on Japanese and Hawaiian culture, religion, and various other ethnological subjects. Although his principal professional research and publications have been in cultural anthropology, he has maintained an interest in archeology and served as organizer and director of the symposium from which this volume is derived.

Contents

INTRODUCTION   1
Jesse D. Jennings and Edward Norbeck

OPENING ADDRESS
    GEOANTHROPOLOGY   13
    Carey Croneis

EARLIEST TIMES
    EARLY MAN IN THE NEW WORLD   23
    Alex D. Krieger

THE NORTH
    THE ARCTIC AND SUBARCTIC   85
    Henry B. Collins

WESTERN NORTH AMERICA
    THE WESTERN COAST OF NORTH AMERICA   117
    Robert F. Heizer

    THE DESERT WEST   149
    Jesse D. Jennings

    THE GREATER SOUTHWEST   175
    Erik K. Reed

    THE GREAT PLAINS   193
    Waldo R. Wedel

ix

EASTERN NORTH AMERICA

THE NORTHEAST WOODLANDS AREA   223
James B. Griffin

THE SOUTHEASTERN UNITED STATES   259
William H. Sears

MESOAMERICA

NORTHERN MESOAMERICA   291
Pedro Armillas

SOUTHERN MESOAMERICA   331
Robert Wauchope

SOUTH AMERICA

THE CARIBBEAN AREA   389
Irving Rouse

LOWLAND SOUTH AMERICA   419
Clifford Evans

SOUTH AMERICAN HIGH CULTURES   451
Alfred Kidder II

SPECIAL STUDIES

TRANSPACIFIC CONTACTS   489
Gordon F. Ekholm

NORTH AND SOUTH AMERICAN CULTURAL CONNECTIONS AND
CONVERGENCES   511
Betty J. Meggers

LINGUISTIC OVERVIEW   527
Morris Swadesh

CLOSING ADDRESS

CONCLUDING REMARKS   559
Ignacio Bernal

INDEX   567

Introduction

Introduction

D URING 1962, in celebration of its semicentennial year, William Marsh Rice University sponsored many events of scholarly and scientific interest. Among these was a symposium in anthropology, conducted on November 9 and 10, that bore the same title as this volume.

Most scholarly symposia deal in concentrated detail with specialized topics. After consultation with professional colleagues in various parts of the country, the decision was made to conduct a colloquium of a much broader nature. The symposium subsequently planned and conducted was deemed to be a project within the field of anthropology appropriate and informative for an educated lay audience. We hoped at the same time that the symposium would be valuable to professional anthropologists and that it would serve to stimulate scholarship in the field of anthropology. The principal direct aim of the symposium was to present a review and appraisal of facts and theories concerning the prehistoric peoples and cultures of North and South America. No summing-up of this scope has been attempted for many years, during which archeological and ethnological research has presented a rapidly growing body of information.

To achieve the objectives of the symposium, distinguished scholars were invited to distil their knowledge into short general papers in which both fact and theory would be presented. Participants were requested to avoid heavy emphasis on the development of particular theories to the exclusion of alternate or conflicting interpretations current in professional circles. Our goal was, then, a series of papers written in simple, non-technical language that presented the major outlines of knowledge of the prehistory of the two continents of the New World.

The audience was first conceived as being educated laymen. It soon became clear, however, that a second audience composed of students of prehistory, both amateur and professional, could also be served. In this age of rapidly accumulating knowledge and increasing specialization, even the specialist finds it hard to keep informed of developments in fields closely related to and having important bearing upon his own interests. With these considerations in mind, we asked contributors to the symposium to set down "knowledge common to specialists in the particular fields and areas" and, in doing so, to use "simple language that any educated reader might follow."

The eighteen papers that follow come closer to meeting our expectations than we had dared hope, and they reflect both the caliber and the co-operative spirit of the writers. As any scholar knows, a simple paper that takes a large view is harder to prepare than a thesis focusing on a highly specialized subject. We were gratified and encouraged to find that the participants agreed with our notion of the desirable, and, on behalf of the readers of this book as well as ourselves, we wish to express our gratitude to the eighteen scholars who have made our notions a reality.

We wish to present here a number of brief explanatory notes that we hope will make the volume easier to understand.

Planning of the subjects to be covered by the symposium was, of course, influenced by considerations of time and funds available and the state of knowledge of the subjects and geographical areas concerned. North America and Mesoamerica receive the major emphasis because those are the areas of which knowledge is the greatest. Unevenness of coverage within those areas stems in part from the same circumstances. Variation in the length of papers is also partly a reflection of the archeological wealth or poverty of the areas in question. It is not possible or desirable, for example, to present in a few pages a rounded discussion of the elaborate Indian civilizations of the Valley of Mexico or the Yucatan Peninsula. The varying size of the geographic areas covered by the papers also influenced the amount of details that could be reported. We think, however, that all areal papers contain enough information to allow readers to gain some notion of aboriginal cultures from period to period and area to area from their beginnings. Descriptive details are indispensable, but in this volume they have been held subordinate to interpretation. We believe that the flow of culture history is the overriding concern of the authors of this book. We shall restate ourselves by saying that we see archeology as a branch of study presenting an interpretation of cultural development. As such, archeology is an integral part of cultural anthropology, and one of its principal objectives is to formulate observations on the nature of culture and the manner in which it grows and changes. We hope and think that the present volume will be useful to readers, amateur or professional, who are interested in questions of this kind.

Editorial changes in the original writings of the authors have been held to a minimum. In retaining the individual styles of the authors, we believe that we have preserved an important although intangible quality of the symposium as we and other members of the audience experienced it. No effort has been made to reconcile divergent interpretations of data or differences in the authors' conceptions of the nature of culture. These differences of opinion seem to us healthful and to point up the present state of knowledge and the many unsolved problems in American archeology. The few instances of overlapping discussions in the papers have been left unchanged, since the passages are useful or necessary to the individual author's exposition.

Archeological terms used by the contributors are not always uniform. An editorial effort to impose uniformity was abandoned because it soon became clear that conformity would require drastic revision of some of the papers. To aid the reader in understanding terms with varied meanings and certain seemingly ordinary words that have special meanings in archeology, explanatory notes are included in this Introduction.

Although we have prepared no general bibliography, we consider the specialized bibliographies accompanying each essay among the most important parts of the book because they provide for the reader a key to further knowledge. Bibliographic citations follow standard anthropological convention; only author and year are given in the text, but full references appear at the close of each chapter. Some bibliographies include all works cited in the essay; others comprise a selected list of readings on the subject in question.

With the thought that these remarks will have value for the reader, we give below in the order of their appearance brief introductions to the sixteen papers dealing with geographical areas and specialized topics. The introductory and concluding articles by Croneis and Bernal seem to us fully self-explanatory and need no editorial comment.

In handling the topic of early man, Krieger faces a morass of old and new data. He has chosen to review previous work, add new data, and then establish a hemispheric classification. Although seemingly critical of the latest systematic effort by Willey and Phillips (1958; see bibliography following article by Krieger) to order by cultural stages the welter of cultures of the Western Hemisphere, Krieger actually revises and extends, and thus increases the usefulness of their scheme. He also usefully systematizes available data by classifying hundreds of sites and cultural complexes under categories representing developmental stages. For those who wish to read details concerning the excavation of sites of early man, reference may be made to the essays that follow Krieger's, many of which discuss typical early sites of human habitation in the areas of their concern. It is useful to note that Krieger's estimate of the antiquity of man in the New World as exceeding 30,000 years does not represent a consensus among archeologists, many of whom regard man's arrival in the Western Hemisphere as occurring 10,000 or more years later.

Collins' discussion concerns principally the Arctic for the reason that reliable data on the Subarctic are scant. Published writings on the broad area lying between the fiftieth and sixty-fifth parallels of latitude are limited to a few surveys and reports on site tests. Thus most of Canada south of the Eskimo-Arctic strip is essentially unknown archeologically. Literature on the Arctic is relatively abundant and, for the beginner, very confusing. Collins' chronological classes and accompanying descriptions of representative cultures bring order to the data and present a clear account.

In dealing with the west coast of North America, Heizer also faces a confusing collection of data. He balances his account between an evaluation of putatively ancient sites and discussion of the cultures of the region from early to recent times. Using the same evidence as Krieger, but interpreting it differently, Heizer regards the arrival of man in this area as occurring much later than the time suggested by Krieger. Heizer's paper is also noteworthy as the first publication to relate to each other the full range of coastal cultures and to point to cultures of the neighboring Great Basin, from which they may be derived.

Jenning's essay on the intermontane region of western North America shows that his interpretation of data on early man in this area generally agrees with that of Krieger. Although Jennings recognizes that evidence from individual sites is inconclusive, he clearly believes that the cumulative evidence makes it seem probable that man first lived in the New World 30,000–40,000 years ago. Discussing cultures of later times, Jennings tends to discount local differences in artifacts as evidence of markedly different ways of life. He argues that the fundamental manner of life, which he calls the "Desert Culture," dominated the region unchanged for nearly ten thousand years until historic times. Jennings maintains that aboriginal American cultures were fundamentally stable for long periods and that this stability is seen most clearly in the Desert West. This view contrasts with Heizer's interpretation of the cultural history of the adjoining coastal region.

The opening pages of Reed's paper on the Greater Southwest overlap part of Jennings' discussion, since these passages describe the Desert Culture of the region. Reed, with great care, then shows the richness and variety of the later Anasazi, Mogollon, and Hohokam cultures, pointing out and highlighting regional differences without obscuring board similarities among these three cultures.

Wedel's clear and systematic review of Great Plains archeology emphasizes evidence indicating that man occupied this area continuously for many millenniums until historic times, a view that archeologists first began to consider seriously only about three decades ago. In Wedel's paper the reader first encounters the use of a taxonomic system to organize archeological data. In discussing the culture called "Plains Woodland," Wedel shifts from the chronological categories he uses in ordering the simpler earliest cultures to the classification called the "Midwestern" or "McKern" system. This system of classification of culture traits is identical in principle with the taxonomic scheme used by biologists in classifying forms of life. It consists of a series of increasingly large and generalized categories, beginning with the cultural inventory of a single level in the earth at a single site, which is called a "component." Two or more closely similar components form a "focus." Successively larger categories are called "aspect" and "phase." The most useful of these classes has been the focus. Cultural inventories similar enough to be classified together as a focus occur close together geographically, and the focus then denotes a local variety of culture of a geographical range that is defined to the extent that components have been revealed by archeological excavation. When archeologists have recognized a number of components (i.e., when they have excavated a number of sites having essentially the same cultural materials), the possibility of assigning the focus an assured placement in time is increased, since the stratigraphic positions of the components are ordinarily known and cross-checks are possible. Although opinion is divided regarding the usefulness today of the McKern classification, there is no doubt of its usefulness in the past. Application of the system in the 1930's and 1940's to the mass of unorganized data from the eastern two-thirds of North America resulted in almost instantaneous perception of both spatial and chronological relationships previously unnoticed in a century of study. As a tool for understanding, it was revolutionary and spectacularly successful, a fact to which its present reduced importance attests.

In his detailed account of northeastern North America, Griffin gives primary attention to the sequence of cultural development, supporting his views with succinct factual data. The relationship between the Adena and Hopewell cultures is a problem of central concern and one in which Griffin has long been interested. He has here given the best extant analysis of it. Rejecting as inaccurate radiocarbon dates assigned to certain sites, he is able to clarify the developmental sequence and present a systematic interpretation of the history and spread of these cultures. Contrary to some views, Griffin sees Adena as preceding and being partly ancestral to Hopewell, an opinion he has consistently held. He identifies certain historically known tribes as descendants of peoples known only archeologically and supports this view with considerable archeological evidence. In this respect he goes further than most other scholars have been willing to go. Griffin appropriately uses the McKern system to present data, since he deals with the area where the system was most widely applied and achieved the greatest success.

In reviewing data on the southeastern United States, Sears suffered a serious handicap. Relevant publications are reasonably extensive and include some factual material, but scholarly interest in the area has been weighted in a way that makes interpretation of its complete prehistory extremely difficult. Until recently, attention was directed principally to the huge sites of the Mississippian culture of this area, which are rich in colorful material culture. Little effort was given to the more mundane tasks of attempting to learn the long story behind the flamboyant but recent Mississippian. The state of present knowledge of the area is revealed by Sears's essay, which indicates how incomplete the facts now available are. Despite this handicap, Sears has been able to give an account of the prehistory of the region by inferences drawn chiefly from the nature and distribution of pottery, of which fairly abundant collections exist. Sears recognizes several ceramic "traditions," classes of pottery that are broadly similar and have developmental continuity. His use of the terms "culture" and "cultural tradition" is sometimes, for lack of other information, essentially synonymous for "ceramic tradition." Sears's usage of the term "horizon" differs from those of Evans and Kidder, which we shall later explain. As used by Sears, "horizon" may be equated with what Krieger, Griffin, and Jennings have called "culture stage." Sears's classificatory scheme is essentially chronological, since the terms he uses describe stages of cultural growth, either implied or specified.

Armillas' paper changes the scene to northern Mesoamerica, where the richness of archeological material has long attracted those who romanticize archeology. The remains of ancient cultures are numerous and most impressive, and it is here that we find the center of dispersal of many important innovations that influenced the cultures of both North and South America. Rather than being a descriptive account, Armillas' essay is primarily an interpretation of economic, social, and political evolution. Following the tradition of Lewis Henry Morgan and other early cultural evolutionists, Armillas sees the cultures of this area passing through evolutionary stages of savagery and barbarism and finally reaching civilization. The key to development is a shift from hunting wild animals and gathering vegetable foods to the practice of plant husbandry, which permits the emergence of civilization about four thousand years after the time of the earliest attempts to raise plants.

In dealing with southern Mesoamerica, the area dominated in Precolumbian times by the Maya, Wauchope has chosen to follow the chronological-descriptive approach in general use among students of Mayan culture. Stages of the developmental sequence are summarized in a table and discussed in detail. Because other data suitable for this purpose are lacking, Wauchope must rely upon ceramic styles and types to give dates to archeological sites and to present hypotheses concerning their relationships.

Rouse, discussing the Caribbean area, and Evans, treating lowland South America, have at their disposal few archeological materials except pottery. Like Sears, they are forced to draw inferences chiefly from data on its distribution, features of style, and other characteristics. The geographic areas covered by these papers are vast, and little systematic excavation has been done in them.

Kidder organizes his summary of Andean culture around a scheme of cultural stages in general use. As with the categories used by Wauchope, these stages bear names that are brief descriptions of the cultures of the times. Kidder, and also Evans, use the terms "horizon" and "horizon style" to designate distinctive art motifs or techniques of manufacture of artifacts that achieved popularity and can be readily recognized over a wide area. A "horizon-marker" is usually a ceramic object, but the term may be applied to other items of material culture.

Ekholm's essay is the first of three on special topics of relevance to an understanding of the prehistory of both continents. Ekholm's subject can be stated as a question: Are the elaborate Indian cultures of Central and South America primarily indigenous developments, or were many of the most outstanding traits, such as pottery, architecture, and masonry, introduced from Asia by crossing or girdling the Pacific Ocean? Ekholm is one of a number of scholars who have come to believe that the important innovations that led to the emergence of the Indian civilizations of the New World are indeed Asiatic in origin. Others oppose this idea with fervor. Both groups will devote more than a superficial glance at Ekholm's paper, in which he gives particular attention to a comparison of Mesoamerican and Southeast Asian culture traits. Not only is Ekholm's paper an essay on Asiatic cultural influence; it is also an examination of the general concept of cultural diffusion, a subject of long-continued interest to anthropologists.

Meggers' paper is less a description of North and South American cultural similarities than it is a discussion of theories anthropologists use in attempting to explain these similarities. She extends Ekholm's discussion of diffusion, adding ideas concerning convergence and parallelism of cultural development. Both Meggers and Ekholm till ground that has seldom felt the plow. Their cautious conclusions are perhaps best seen as expressions of probabilities and as suggested avenues of necessary and fruitful research.

Swadesh, who is a linguist rather than an archeologist, uses information on the native languages of the New World to shed light on the questions of the origins, interrelationships, and movements of the indigenous peoples. Some of his views concerning the dynamics of culture and the nature of American archeology do not agree with those expressed elsewhere in this volume. Various scholars will also disagree with the suggestions he offers in conclusion. His essay is, however, more than a linguistic discussion of the New World. It presents theories about world-wide language relationships, a subject that has long interested Swadesh, and offers a good illustration of the ways in which comparative linguistics may contribute to an understanding of the prehistory of the world.

It seems to us that a major contribution of the papers on special topics by Ekholm, Meggers, and Swadesh lies outside their most obvious aims. Together, they provide comments on New World culture that have important bearing on theories of cultural evolution and threaten some current views regarding cultural developments in the New World.

The volume as a whole makes many explicit comments on the course of cultural development in the Americas. One noteworthy inference it allows is that American culture as a whole was simple and stable for long periods. There seems to be no reason to doubt that Mesoamerica was the primary source of important cultural innovations that spread north and south, but it is uncertain how the ideas and material objects spread. Whatever the form of the stimuli emanating from this center, the peripheral cultures retained evidence of their simpler previous states. The ultimate source of the invention of agriculture and other important innovations remains unclear, but we shall note that the accumulation of data suggesting diffusion from the Old World continues to grow more impressive. From the essays in this volume it is also possible to infer for both continents a development of culture, uneven and locally variable, that proceeds through several definable stages. The earliest men in the New World were hunters of big game, who brought with them from Asia crude stone tools resembling those of the Paleolithic cultures of Eurasia. The highest development of culture follows much later in the civilizations based on agriculture of Mesoamerica and northern South America. We believe that these essays contribute substantially to our understanding of the complex skein of events occurring in the interval between these stages in this vast area of the earth and that they do much to point out avenues of useful future research.

Finally, we wish to say that we regard as a privilege our roles as editors of this volume.

JESSE D. JENNINGS
EDWARD NORBECK

Opening Address

CAREY CRONEIS

Geoanthropology

THE PROPER STUDY of mankind is man." This authoritarian statement —from Alexander Pope's *Essay on Man*—has always given the anthropologists aid and comfort, particularly in those earlier days when many academic administrators were not quite certain that anthropology was an important intellectual discipline. The growing recognition of the significance of the subject and the upsurge of public preoccupation with both anthropology and archeology, however, suggest that Pope's dictum, accurately restated today, would read: "The *popular* study of mankind is man." Certainly the great and gratifying interest in this meeting devoted to the subject, "Prehistoric Man in the New World," confirms such a view. Therefore, on behalf of the President, Faculty and Board of Governors of Rice University, I am happy to welcome all those in attendance and to extend warm thanks to the distinguished participants and to Professor Edward Norbeck, who have made this notable symposium possible.

The explosive burst of interest in prehistory is not entirely new, even if the base of that interest is still constantly broadening. Strong (1935) stated:

Owing to the increasing interest in prehistoric research in this country, the number of amateur archeologists is growing rapidly. Encouraging as this rising interest in archeology undoubtedly is, it must frankly be admitted that inasmuch as it is often unaccompanied by technical knowledge, it is both a potential and an actual danger. This is demonstrated by the rapidly increasing destruction of important archeological sites, either by enthusiastic but untrained amateurs

CAREY CRONEIS, chancellor of Rice University, has had two distinguished academic careers, as geologist and as educator. After receiving the doctorate in geology and paleontology from Harvard University, he taught at several universities and engaged in extensive geological research. Leaving the post of professor of geology at the University of Chicago, he became president of Beloit College in 1944, and went to Rice University in 1954. He is the recipient of several honorary degrees and many other recognitions of outstanding scholarship and distinguished service awarded him by colleges, universities, and professional societies. His numerous activities at Rice University include organizing and directing the festivities celebrating the university's semicentennial year, which this volume memorializes.

or by persons who are frankly mere collectors or relic hunters. . . . Persons of the first type may be scientific archeologists in the making; those of the second type uselessly destroy the very stuff of human history.

I am afraid that I may fall in the second category. Long ago (Croneis 1939) I said:

The writer . . . has for a decade been sporadically investigating various geological features of a wide-mouthed cavern in Ste. Genevieve County, Missouri. Because of the character of the cave's outer chamber diligent search has been made for evidences of early habitation by man. During the 1939 field season there was discovered calcareous tufa containing not only both vertebrate and plant remains, but also numerous charcoal fragments. Inasmuch as the tufa occurs in a geological position suggesting some antiquity, and at a cave location unfavorable to the possible inclusion of charcoal resulting from fires not made by man, the suggestion of "early" human occupancy is reasonably strong. Results of a preliminary examination of the associated fossils at least do not weaken the other evidence supporting the thesis that the tufa cannot be very recent.

I am particularly apologetic that I did not continue this investigation because, not long after it was dropped, radiocarbon dating became possible and the study might well have turned out to be one of significance. Instead, as Strong suggested, some of the very stuff of human history may have been lost or destroyed.

The previous quotation was thrown in partly to demonstrate my long-standing, and very considerable, interest in archeology. Actually, as early as 1923 I introduced and taught a course in anthropology as a part of the geology curriculum at the University of Arkansas. Thus, when Edward Norbeck made the one mistake of which he has been guilty in arranging this symposium—that is, asking me to make an opening address rather than to say a few works of welcome—I seized upon the opportunity to offer a few gratuitous bits of advice to the entire anthropological fraternity, professional and amateur. Perhaps the remarks will seem a little less gauche if I point out that my own field, geology, is, like anthropology, largely based on a group of sister disciplines that are, if no more important, at least more fundamental.

In geology we have for many years suffered considerably from not paying the strictest attention to basic training in mathematics, chemistry, physics, astronomy, and biology, and we have found that gradually some of the major geologic problems were being solved by other scientists who saw the geological applications of their disciplines. Happily, important solutions were also being arrived at by geologists who were particularly well trained in the supporting sciences. As two pertinent and contrasting cases in point, the coveted Penrose Medal in Geology will be awarded at the Geological Society of America Annual Dinner to Alfred S. Romer, who is actually a biologist, but the Day Medal in Geophysics will go to Hatton Yoder, who is a geologist highly trained in physics and chemistry.

I have attempted, through a most cursory review of some anthropological-archeological literature and curricula, to ascertain whether anthropologists generally were aware of the problem that the geologists have encountered and whether they were taking steps to minimize it. I found some evidence pro and con.

Frank C. Hibben (1958), an active "popularizer" of the subject of anthropology, says,

The roles of professions other than history and anthropology cannot be overemphasized in the process of discovering the foundations of civilization. Biology, anatomy, geology, chemistry, physics, mathematics, the new science of atomic fission, and a host of other lines of research have all contributed to the whole. We may truly say now that all the sciences are aiding in the revelation of the beginnings of man.

This statement, which is perfectly true, is the most clean-cut pronouncement on the subject discovered in my brief search of the literature. It demonstrates a sharp awareness of the situation that apparently is shared by a growing number of anthropologists and archeologists. Nevertheless, a perusal of the entire Hibben volume shows little evidence that the awareness itself is translated directly into the discussion. In fact, the most direct approach to the contributions of the supporting sciences elsewhere in the book is found on page 87, where Hibben states:

To the pollen-analysis studies and the geological delineation of water bodies, shore lines, river terraces, and the like may be added most recent information dated by the Carbon 14 method. Dates derived from a careful examination of the radioactive carbon content of these specimens agree generally with pollen analysis and glacial studies. The Mesolithic period presumably began about twelve thousand years ago, lasting for perhaps six millenniums.

This sort of situation, that is, a statement of awareness of the value of the supporting sciences to anthropological researches, followed by only limited translation of that awareness into the body of the discussion, characterizes a number of anthropological and archeological papers. A rather noted contrast, however, is seen in the serious attention given to the sister scientific disciplines by Jennings (1957).

I also sought out anthropological papers of approximately a decade ago in order that a judgment might be made regarding changes in anthropological attitudes during the last ten to twenty years. A great volume dealing with the archeology of eastern United States, published in honor of Dr. Fay-Cooper Cole, admirably serves this purpose (Griffin 1952). Most of the papers showed the typical, and probably proper, preoccupation with cultures rather than chronology—in the geological sense. For example, the contribution, "Archeological Chronology of Middle Atlantic States," by the late Karl Schmitt, is concerned with the Early, Middle, or Late Woodland cultures. There is much information about this or that "focus" or "site" or "component" but literally no acceptable chronology.

As early as 1934, however, Fay-Cooper Cole, who was my colleague and close friend in those days, set up a dendrochronology laboratory at the University of Chicago. A paper by Robert E. Bell (Griffin 1952) dates the Kincaid site of southern Illinois, on the basis of dendrochronological data, as after A.D. 1523 and prior to A.D. 1613. This is one of a number of evidences of the anthropological interest in precision dating a score of years ago. Another may be found in a seemingly wry comment by Jennings in the same volume:

The welter of conflicting ideas regarding the dating of aboriginal cultures have in part been precipitated by Carbon 14 analyses. . . . Suffice it to say that I have been consistently guilty of extreme conservatism in my assignment of guess dates.

Dr. Griffin, as editor of the Cole memorial volume, was then in the forefront of those who recognized the importance of the new geochronological methods. In an appendix to the book, he included a number of radiocarbon dates, and stated: "One of the major tasks of the archeologist is to understand the chronology or time sequence of the cultural events with which he deals." He went on to say flatly that, in the past, "time scales [have] been erected without any sound foundation." He said, further, that by the time the Cole volume was written, "there was a definite trend among archeologists to lengthen the estimates of the duration of the various major archeological periods."

Dr. Griffin's concluding words were,

Radiocarbon dates have been of great value . . . for they have demonstrated a considerably greater antiquity than the prehistorians had been willing to recognize. . . . The present apparent discrepancies between archeologists' interpretations and the available dates will gradually be resolved by improvements in the technique of radiocarbon measurement, by more carefully controlled selection of specimens, and by time which heals all wounds.

The wounds are not yet healed! Some at present inexplicable anomalies in radiocarbon dating of cultures still bother anthropologists. Several competent glaciologists and a number of keen students of rhythmites and varves are similarly disturbed by certain radiocarbon dates; and the radiocarbon experts themselves are refining their laboratory procedures and, thus, their data.

As recently reported by Godwin (1962), the Fifth International Conference on Radiocarbon Dating was held at the University of Cambridge, England, during July, 1962, with archeologists, geologists, botanists, physicists, and chemists in attendance. The investigators from some thirty dating laboratories discussed new developments in counting techniques, problems with reference to the initial radiocarbon activity, atmospheric and hydrospheric problems, results of geochemical researches on radiocarbon climatic and oceanic changes, and Neolithic archeology.

The conference also adopted the following resolution:

We commend the three groups of research workers on their new determinations of the half-life of carbon-14. . . . We agree that . . . the mean of the values given, 5,730 ± 40 yr. is now the best value available.

Inasmuch as further experiments may lead to an even more reliable result, we recommend, as a temporary expedient, that radiocarbon age results continue to be reported on the basis of the "Libby half-life" 5,568 yr., used heretofore. . . . published dates can be converted to the basis of the new half-life by multiplying them by 1.03, without appreciably altering the standard errors as quoted.

The delay in revising the basis of reporting will also allow time for evaluation of the carbon-14 content of dendro-chronologically and historically dated samples.

The conference also confirmed the practice of using A.D. 1950 as the reference year of "zero age B.P." for purposes of reporting radiocarbon measurements.

Even as the geochronology made possible by radiocarbon analyses has awkwardly revolutionized some anthropological thought, it has also been most helpful to all researches into relatively recent prehistory. So, too, could be the application to anthropological studies of a large group of geological concepts that we might group under the heading "Geoanthropology." A perusal of the abstracts of this symposium reveals that there are already some movements in that direction.

Through the years I have found, however, that too few anthropologists and archeologists are really familiar with the subjects of—let alone the philosophies behind—glacial geology and stratigraphy, which are actually and potentially of such sharp pertinence to them. This lack can readily be ascertained by asking a group of the students of prehistory whether they have read Flint (1957) or Weller (1960). Few have. This is no carping criticism. Few geologists know anything about archeological or anthropological literature, but it would help them scientifically and humanistically if they did. It would also greatly increase the effectiveness of most archeologists if they were thoroughly familiar with the geological facts and theories presented in just the two volumes mentioned. Interestingly enough, I have just discovered that Professor Irving Rouse, of this symposium, conducts a graduate seminar at Yale with Professor Flint on geological and anthropological problems of the Pleistocene and the Recent. This is an admirable joint venture of the type that should be inaugurated at other universities.

Time does not permit me to make a number of detailed, and possibly similarly inappropriate, suggestions. I am certain, however, that important new anthropological and archeological "gold mines" can be, and will be, staked out by those anthropologists and archeologists who make skilful use of geological data. Let me, in conclusion, cite a few examples of types of geological studies of potential anthropological interest out of the many that could be brought to bear on the subject:

1. Radiocarbon dates for various recent peats (Fisk 1960).
2. Time controls for the various loesses already determined[1] (Frye, Glass, and Willman 1962).
3. Pleistocene and Recent physiographic history of various valleys. See Leonard and Frye (1962).
4. Soil origin, classification, and time rates of development. For a good, brief review, consult Simonson (1962).
5. The ramifications of speleology in the modern rather than the exploratory sense. See Curl (1962).
6. The general use of micropaleontology, including such forms as fresh water ostracodes and charophytes, as well as pollen. See, for example, Gutentag and Benson (1962).
7. The examination of the unconformable surfaces beneath relatively "recent" volcanic strata, particularly late Pleistocene ash falls, the age of the biotite in which deposits can be determined roughly by the potassium-argon method.
8. Geochronological methods of growing precision used in combination, through "shingling" of data, and field evidence, from relatively "recent" to relatively "ancient."

Let me also suggest for your consideration, essentially as a *non sequitur*, that demographic studies of prehistoric man are very skimpy, or nonexistent. He who establishes, on a firm basis, a subdiscipline of anthropology, which we might call "paleodemography" will make a name for himself and put many scholars in his debt.

I conclude with another apology. I realize that I do not really know what I have been talking about. Although this is a common enough trait within fields, and is thus expected if not forgiven, it is considered particularly bad taste to display such ignorance when one presumes to advise outside the area of his competence. I am well aware of this situation because in geology we are commonly irritated beyond words by chemists, mathematicians, astronomers, and physicists who tell us how to run "our show," when their very words are likely to demon-

---

[1] In a privately distributed rejoinder entitled "Preliminary Appraisal of the Recently Proposed Classification of Wisconsin Loess," M. M. Leighton (1962) challenges the validity of a number of the data and conclusions of Frye *et al*. Especially is Dr. Leighton critical of radiocarbon dates determined on the basis of the shells of terrestrial pulmonate gastropods "which lived in the calcareous loess environment and doubtless used in part the 'dead' cadbonate for their shells."

strate that, in the particular topic at hand, they are uninitiated. But, though commonly wrong because uninformed, they are embarrassingly often right, because they have a new and pertinent viewpoint. We, then, forgive them.

Perhaps you will forgive me.

BIBLIOGRAPHY

CRONEIS, CAREY
    1939   "Possible Evidence of 'Pre-Historic' Man in Southeastern Missouri."
        Bull. Geol. Soc. America, 50:1963.
CURL, RANI L.
    1962   "Speleology." *Science*, 137:285–87.
FISK, H. N.
    1960   "Recent Mississippi River Sedimentation and Peat Accumulation."
        *Compte rendu du quatrième Congrès pour l'advancement des études de
        stratigraphie et de geologie du carbonifère, Heerlen, 1958.*
FLINT, RICHARD FOSTER
    1957   *Glacial and Pleistocene Geology.* New York: John Wiley & Sons.
FRYE, JOHN C., H. D. GLASS, and H. B. WILLMAN
    1962   *Stratigraphy and Mineralogy of the Wisconsinan Loesses of Illinois.* (Ill.
        State Geol. Surv. Circ. 334.)
GODWIN, H.
    1962   "Radiocarbon Dating: Fifth International Conference." *Nature*, 195:
        943–45.
GRIFFIN, JAMES B. (ed.)
    1952   *Archeology of Eastern United States.* Chicago: University of Chicago
        Press.
GUTENTAG, EDWIN, AND RICHARD H. BENSON
    1962   *Neogene (Plio-Pleistocene) Freshwater Ostracodes from the Central High
        Plains.* (State Geol. Surv. Kan. Bull. 157, Part 4.)
HIBBEN, FRANK C.
    1958   *Prehistoric Man in Europe.* Norman: University of Oklahoma Press.
JENNINGS, JESSE D.
    1957   *Danger Cave.* ("Univ. Utah Anthrop. Paps.," No. 27.) Salt Lake
        City.
LEONARD, A. BYRON, AND JOHN C. FRYE
    1962   *Pleistocene Molluscan Faunas and Physiographic History of Pecos Valley
        in Texas.* (Univ. Tex. Bur. Econ. Geol. Rpt. Invest., No. 45.)
SIMONSON, ROY W.
    1962   "Soil Classification in the United States." *Science*, 137:1027–37.
STRONG, W. DUNCAN
    1935   *An Introduction to Nebraska Archeology.* ("Smithsonian Misc. Coll.,"
        Vol. 93, No. 10.) Washington, D. C.
WELLER, J. MARVIN
    1960   *Stratigraphic Principles and Practice.* New York: Harper & Bros.

Earliest Times

ALEX D. KRIEGER

Early Man in the New World

EVERY FIELD of archeological research has its problems, great and small, but that dealing with America's earliest inhabitants is one of the most difficult to discuss comprehensively and convincingly. There are many reasons for this.

1. The territory involved is so immense that it is virtually impossible for any one person to see the field situations and examine the cultural evidence at even the most important sites.
2. The archeologists of the United States seem to be convinced that the oldest cultures of America include well-made projectile points, and, because a number of radiocarbon dates on sites with the oldest-known types of projectile points reach no further back than about 13,000 years, such a "date line" automatically gives us the maximum age of New World cultures.
3. There is very little detailed literature on what may be "pre–projectile point" cultural remains. What there is, is written from many

ALEX D. KRIEGER, research professor of anthropology at the University of Washington, Seattle, received the degree of Doctor of Science from the Universidad Nacional de México. He has conducted extensive field research in the western United States and Mexico and in recent years has specialized in research on the earliest human inhabitants of the Western world. His many publications include outstanding writings dealing with problems of method and presenting synthetic interpretations of data gathered in the field. He is presently preparing for publication a full-length book on early man in the New World. In recognition of his contributions to archeology, Dr. Krieger was awarded the Viking Fund Medal in Archaeology in 1948.

AUTHOR'S NOTE: This article was written while I held a fellowship from the Bollingen Foundation, to which I express my gratitude. I also wish to express profound thanks to Dr. Angel Palerm, director, and Theo Crevenna, subdirector, of the Department of Social Affairs, Pan American Union (Organization of American States), for arranging a travel grant that allowed me to visit museums, universities, and private collectors in Mexico and ten South American countries in the first quarter of 1962. This research tour enabled me to see a very large amount of preceramic material in Latin America, about which I would never have known otherwise, as well as that which has been published. I also want to thank the many persons in each country who extended every courtesy and in many cases arranged transportation to examine actual sites. None of them, of course, is to be held responsible for the ways in which I have interpreted this material.

different points of view. If the layman is puzzled by the general ineffectiveness of professional discussions of this critical problem, he need only bear in mind that the professionals themselves are just as puzzled as he is by what can be "accepted" and what should be "rejected." It may be added that, by and large, the "acceptances" and "rejections" are made by scholars who have never seen the sites involved or examined the artifacts and other cultural evidences from them.

4. Surface collections are commonly regarded as of no consequence "because they cannot be dated," whereas they often can be of real importance for plotting the distribution of various levels of technological development even if their dates are unknown.

5. Many discoveries are likewise rejected because association with geological formations and/or extinct Pleistocene fauna have not been proved to everyone's satisfaction. In such cases, one must realize the limitations of extremely small samplings, and, rather than reject them, one should hope that more information will be gained in some way.

6. An incredible confusion exists regarding the terms with which artifacts themselves should be described, so that artifacts of the same form are designated by different names in different regions (or even by different individuals in the same region), and, conversely, the same terms are used for many artifact forms that are obviously different.

Other difficulties exist that cannot be explained here, but I wish to comment on the claim that hyperconservative notions on the age of American cultures can be blamed on the influences of Holmes and Hrdlička—especially the latter—from the 1890's to the 1930's and even later. It is often said that Hrdlička insisted on a "maximum" antiquity for man in America of some 6,000 years. Those who hold this view have failed to read his most important surveys of supposedly ancient material in North and South America (Hrdlička, 1907, 1912). His contention was that "American Indians" were all of postglacial age, that none of the claims had proved that "Indians" were present in America during any *glacial* stage. Yet, on the advice of geologists of his time, Hrdlička allowed from *20,000 to 60,000 years for postglacial time.* It so happens that our modern radiocarbon datings have reduced postglacial time to something like 10,000–11,000 years (using rise in sea-level as the main criterion rather than minor advances and retreats of the ice fronts); but it is interesting to note that, even now, human remains in the New World cannot be shown to exceed (or even equal) the 60,000 years or so that Hrdlička might have allowed for postglacial time in the crude estimates prevalent when he wrote.

Other, more serious, factors seem to have escaped Hrdlička's modern critics. First, although he had his own peculiar ideas about how "American Indian" remains should be dated, he carefully and exhaustively compiled observations and opinions on the various discoveries he discussed; these opinions ranged from reasonable to ridiculous, but he nevertheless included all of them in his surveys so that the reader could consider a wide range of interpretations. Second, his stubborn and constant insistence that field work was too poorly controlled to support the associations claimed was not only undoubtedly true in many or most cases, but in the long run it served to make archeologists more conscious of their obligations to conduct well-controlled excavation in place of random burrowing and removal of evidence before it could be properly recorded. At any rate, field methods are now incomparably advanced over the crude work of Hrdlička's time, and no purpose is served in alluding to his "stultifying" influences. What is needed is objective appraisal of the great amount of data available now that will lend historical perspective to the perennial question of how long man has occupied the American continents. The conservative skepticism that still prevails can no longer be charged to the dire influences of Hrdlička but must be due to some other causes. I suspect that the chief of these is lack of perspective. Scholars simply do not know how much material there is on both American continents that bears on the earliest cultures; instead, they try to discuss the problem on the basis of a few selected and widely scattered localities which have been mentioned most frequently in the *North American* literature.

Thus, what I primarily hope to accomplish in this short survey is to make the reader aware of the *quantity of material* available on the two continents, without discussing any of it in detail. To do this, I offer an outline of very general stages of preceramic culture development, each of which is of immense distribution in the New World, even though none can be said to occur everywhere. The chief criteria for each stage will be given, followed by a list of some important sites and complexes that, in present knowledge, seem to illustrate best the nature of each stage on both continents. Finally, some brief comments will be made on certain sites that have been the subject of considerable misunderstanding. Undoubtedly, some of my assignments to these stages will be found faulty, through either errors in judgment or insufficient data or both. It must be realized that stages, no matter how they are formulated, can never be perfect, even when plenty of information is available; furthermore, they are never to be regarded as end products of research: they are no more than conveniences or devices by which large amounts of data can be organized in some way to facilitate discussion.

Another aim of this study is to simplify the language used by archeologists to discuss these discoveries. Such terms as "culture," "stage," "tradition," "phase," "complex," "industry," and so on, are used in many different ways by different archeologists, and even the same author will use them interchangeably. Here, I will try to use "stage" as the broadest cultural unit, more or less continental in scope; "culture" will be used for similar material that is found over great regions and may indicate certain kinds of adaptation to specific geographical conditions; "complex" will be used for material that shows a high degree of unity in smaller areas, sometimes only a part of one state but, at other times, over two or three states (or provinces, or departments, as they are called in some Latin American countries); "site" will be used only for single localities, such as camp sites or kill sites, even though they may be stratified and contain material that belongs to more than one "complex."

When material is listed by stages, it is often necessary to make some change in the language used by the original authors, such as changing "stage" or "phase" to the word "complex" when that appears more appropriate. "Tradition," often used as a synonym for "culture," will not be used in that sense here; rather, it will refer only to a technological practice that may be traced through different kinds of cultural assemblages. For example, a *fluted-point tradition* can be recognized for its technological unity whether it is part of a *complex*, a *culture*, or even a *stage*. An "industry" is also technological but refers to a range of artifact forms made of the same material; examples would be a "chipped-stone industry," "polished-stone industry," "bone industry," "shell industry," and so on.

Throughout this study, emphasis will be placed on what may be termed a "pre–projectile point" stage of culture, although a better name should be found for it. This is not only because many archeologists (in the United States, at least) find it difficult to believe that there is any general technological stage that precedes the appearance of the first projectile points, but especially because *the question of man's antiquity in the New World cannot be discussed intelligently until the presence or absence of such a stage can be settled.* The writer believes that such a stage does exist, represented by a surprising amount of material in both North and South America. Precise datings for this stage are almost non-existent, except for a few radiocarbon dates. At the moment, it seems more important to recognize such a stage than to try to date it in every region. As with other stages, the matter of dating must be kept distinct from the matter of recognition through content. The failure of most writers to maintain this distinction has led to many confusions that seem to me largely unnecessary; obviously, a level of technological development can be recognized for what it is, even in undatable surface collections, provided that the sampling is adequate.

RECENT LITERATURE

We cannot trace here the history of ideas on the antiquity of man in the New World or the nature of the earliest cultures. There are, however, a number of surveys and interpretive schemes that can be mentioned briefly if only to show how widely divergent are the ideas on the extent of the problem and how it should be approached. The first general surveys in North America were those by Wormington in 1939 and Roberts in 1940, the latter having coined the term "Paleo-Indian" in previous papers. Since then, the term has gained wide acceptance, but there is also an increasing uncertainty over what it should embrace. Some tend to refer to the Paleo-Indians every discovery involving association with now-extinct Pleistocene mammals; some use the term for all discoveries that include the earliest known projectile-point types, whether extinct animals are present or not; some extend it backward to include assemblages of artifacts that seem to be older than those with any projectile points, but others do not; and some extend it forward to include somewhat more complex and later cultures with different projectile-point forms because these also are sometimes associated with extinct fauna.

In general, the references cited below begin approximately in 1950, when radiocarbon dating was becoming well enough established to force many revisions in the previous guesses as to the age, not only of archeological remains and associated fauna, but also of the times of advance and retreat of the last great Pleistocene ice sheets, fluctuations in sea-level, and climatic changes as seen in pollen profiles and geological formations. Revisions in dating have had to be made in both directions: much preceramic archeological material proved to be considerably older than anyone had suspected (for example, the beginnings of Archaic culture in the eastern United States, previously placed confidently at about 500 or 1000 B.C., were shown to have occurred by 5000 B.C. in some areas!); the Wisconsin glacial period proved to be much shorter than was previously estimated, and its end was brought up to approximately 10,000 years ago instead of 25,000. As age determinations changed, correlations between archeological remains and climatic or environmental fluctuations had to be revised constantly during the 1950's, and, of course, more revisions are in store. This latter point is mentioned because so many of the works to be cited contain correlation charts that rapidly became obsolete. Even now, those applied to local situations are the most reliable; those designed to apply to whole continents or based on assumptions of world-wide climatic changes are for the most part quite useless.

The most important general works that assemble data on "early man" in the New World as a whole are those by Macgowan (1950),

Canals Frau (1950), Sellards (1952), Martínez Del Río (1953), Wormington (1953), Menghin (1957a, 1957b), Willey and Phillips (1955, 1958), Macgowan and Hester (1962), and the great encyclopedic volume of Pericot y Garcia (1962). Most of these are devoted to general culture origins in America, of which early man is only a part. Sellards' well-known book is the only major work devoted exclusively to this subject, but it is concerned chiefly with validity of evidence for the primary association of artifacts and various now-extinct late Pleistocene mammals. The book gives no plan of cultural development, and it contains only those instances which Sellards regarded as valid, whereas there are numerous other situations that require discussion, even though they may not be capable of proof without further work.

Books and articles dealing with early man in North America alone include those of Hurt (1953), Daugherty (1956b), Wormington (1957), Mason (1962), and Miller (1962). The first two were not intended to be complete for the continent. Wormington's book (1957), as were its three earlier editions, is widely used as a convenient secondary source, consisting mainly of summaries and paraphrasings of published material on a great many discoveries, not all of which would ordinarily be classed as "early man." Mason's article, followed by solicited comments of fourteen other authorities, contains many interesting insights, but the diverse and often contradictory views of the author and commentators may confuse rather than enlighten the general reader.

For South America alone, only two recent works are complete enough to provide valuable surveys of preceramic cultures, including Paleo-Indian. These are the article by Lanning and Hammel (1961) and the monograph by Rex González (1960). The former is comprehensive as far as it goes but contains some errors and uncritical treatment of material that the authors had not examined personally; and, as do nearly all publications by archeologists trained in the United States, it assumes that no American cultures are older than those which contain stone projectile points. The superb monograph by Rex González, while dealing only with southern South America, is probably the most detailed and most analytical publication yet produced on preceramic cultures in the New World.

It may be noted that, with the exception of the publications of Menghin (1957a, 1957b) and Willey and Phillips (1955, 1958), none of those cited above presents an organizational scheme by which one can trace historical developments. Some minor articles present such schemes, but they are concerned primarily with terms and do not include enough archeological data to constitute actual historical reconstructions. For example, Krieger (1953) suggested four principal stages for the New World: "early hunting," "food-gathering," "food-producing," and "urban life," but this is far too simple and should be withdrawn. Suhm, Krieger, and Jelks (1954) organized the data from Texas and surrounding areas into four stages: "Paleoamerican," "Archaic," "Neo-american," and "Historic," but this also is too simple for comprehensive treatment of preceramic cultures. Smith (1957) objected to the use of "American" and "Archaic" in the scheme just mentioned and suggested instead, for the sake of uniformity in language, the terms "Paleo-Indian," "Meso-Indian," "Neo-Indian," and "Historic." [EDITORS' NOTE: Rouse, this volume, uses the same scheme.]

Beardsley *et al.* (1956) presented a unique scheme of historical ordering in stages based on both archeological and ethnological data that can be applied to all parts of the world; this is done through definition of population units ranging from wandering bands to permanent cities and discussion of their relative mobility according to means of exploiting environmental resources. Willey suggests three stages for the New World: "big-game hunting," "gathering-collecting," and "cultivation," then discusses them briefly in terms of relative population density and mobility, more or less following the definitions presented by Beardsley *et al.* (1956).

There are also some scores of general works in anthropology that contain a few pages on the antiquity of man in the New World, beginning with some such platitude as, "It has now been proved that man entered the New World at the end of the Pleistocene." After mentioning perhaps half a dozen of the more famous discoveries, such works drop the subject as though it were of no consequence when compared with the long history of early cultures in the Old World.

Returning to the works of Menghin mentioned above, we see that he employs six culture stages applied to both Old and New Worlds, namely, (1) Protolithic, (2) Epiprotolithic, (3) Miolithic, (4) Epimiolithic, (5) Neolithic, and (6) Chalcolithic. The first two are more or less equivalent to Lower Paleolithic as used by Old World archeologists; the next two to Upper Paleolithic; and the last two to stages of the same names in the Old World. Menghin is careful to avoid any implications that such stages in the New World are of an age equal to those of the Old World; even his Protolithic in America may not be more than twenty thousand years old (in his opinion), as against several hundred thousand years in the Old World. His Protolithic and Epiprotolithic are said to be "hand-axe cultures" on a crude technological level that lacks projectile points and other artifacts of comparable refinement. The Miolithic and Epimiolithic stages include projectile points and other technological advances, but on the whole I am puzzled by the criteria used for all these preceramic stages and believe that Menghin has been mistaken in a number of assignments of sites or complexes to each of them.

Willey and Phillips (1955, 1958) have performed the most comprehensive definition of culture stages applicable to both American continents and have gone to considerable length in explaining their theory and method of analyzing cultural material. In their two publications they have changed the terms, as follows:

1955	1958
Postclassic	Postclassic
Classic	Classic
Formative	Formative
Preformative	
Archaic	Archaic
Early Lithic	Lithic

Here we are concerned only with the preceramic stages, "Lithic" and "Archaic." In 1955 Willey and Phillips defined an "Early Lithic"

as embracing two major categories of stone technology: (1) unspecialized and largely unformulated core and flake industries, with percussion the dominant and perhaps only technique employed, and (2) industries exhibiting more advanced "blade" techniques of stone-working, with specialized fluted or unfluted lanceolate [projectile] points the most characteristic artifact types.

In 1958 these authors explained that they had previously hesitated to set up two separate stages on the basis of the two technologies just cited because

The evidence is still inconclusive, although the case for a distinct and earlier core and flake stage is somewhat stronger than it was . . . [and we] will refer hereinafter to this earliest New World stage simply as "Lithic," *allowing for future separation into "upper" and "lower" lithic stages, if such a course seems advisable.* [Italics mine.]

This conception is clear enough and avoids some of the awkwardness caused by vague, undefined uses of the term "Paleo-Indian." Yet Willey and Phillips continued to feel very unsure about the reality of a pre–projectile point or "lower Lithic" stage anywhere in America, and when they stated in 1958 that the case for it "is somewhat stronger than it was" (in 1955), they were not referring to new discoveries but to their own willingness to provide for such an initial stage in American prehistory. They state that "an immense corpus of Lithic stage data is available in the literature but has not so far been subjected to effective integration and synthesis," which is certainly true; but they do not specify whether they mean both "lower" and "upper" Lithic or mainly the latter. Their discussion of a "lower Lithic" (1958) is still extremely hesitant, incomplete, and somewhat inaccurate in the list of sites that they assign to this stage. To a few discoveries that they aver were either "accepted" or "rejected" by me at a meeting of nine archeologists at Andover in 1956, they add a few inexplicable decisions of their own. The only site that has been rejected by a number of competent archeologists is the now-famous Texas Street site in San Diego, California (Carter 1957; reviews by Johnson and Miller 1958, Krieger 1958).

Among other discoveries, Willey and Phillips reject, for their lower Lithic stage, the Tolchaco complex found on some seventy sites in northeastern Arizona (Bartlett 1942), and the Farmington complex, found in the gravels of some sixty-five sites in central California (Treganza 1952; Treganza and Heizer 1953). Their reason is of considerable theoretical interest, for in both cases they state that "confirmatory evidence of an early date is lacking." This confusion of the *content* of a culture stage and its *age* occurs repeatedly in the Willey and Phillips book and is common in other archeological writings. Actually, there is no necessity for confusion on this point; any stage can and should be recognized by its diagnostic traits, including its technological and economic level, whether its age is known or not. If and when datings can be determined or estimated, so much the better. Meanwhile, it can be taken for granted that stages of any kind will begin and end at different times in different regions; an early or simple one may survive in proximity to a more developed one.

Conversely, an age determination or estimate does not necessarily provide assignment to a particular stage. An example occurs in the excellent study of southern Californian cultures by Meighan (1959), wherein he assigns the Topanga culture (here called a complex) to the Paleo-Indian stage, apparently on the basis of an estimated age of "more than 7000 B.P. [Before Present]." With its common occurrence of food-grinding implements and some other traits, the Topanga complex agrees very well with many others in North and South America that I would place in a Protoarchaic stage (see below) with datings from 6000 or 7000 to more than 9000 years ago; but in no case would they suggest affiliation with Paleo-Indian, for their culture content is quite distinct. [EDITORS' NOTE: Krieger, as does Heizer in a later chapter, prefers to cite ages as "years ago." The other authors herein tend to use B.C. and A.D. dates.]

In their upper Lithic (which they often term simply "Lithic"), Willey and Phillips include two distinct technological traditions. The first is characterized by several well-known types of fluted, lanceolate-shaped projectile points like Clovis, Folsom, Cumberland, and perhaps others that have been named but are not clearly distinct from the three just mentioned. The peculiar Sandia points, which are basically of lanceolate shape with a slight incut of one edge, are also now commonly included with the fluted points in a general stage, despite the fact that they are usually unfluted (although a few fluted examples are known). The second tradition is marked by a larger range of projectile-point styles, all unfluted, that includes such types as Plainview, Meserve, Agate Basin, Milnesand, Lerma, Browns Valley; the long, slender, and beautifully chipped Eden points; and the broader Scottsbluff points, which have stems formed by right-angle incuts. The last two types, Eden and Scottsbluff, are often said to be characterized by a "parallel-flaking" technique. This is not quite accurate because, while the Eden points seemingly always have this technique in two forms (parallel scars running obliquely across the blade, or pairs of short scars meeting along a central ridge), the Scottsbluff points do not always have it; moreover, other types may sometimes have it, such as Plainview and Agate Basin. The parallel-flaking technique, furthermore, is almost entirely confined to the Great Plains and even to the western or "High Plains" part of this region.

These matters are mentioned here because Willey and Phillips designate this second tradition as "Eden-Scottsbluff." The term is not well chosen, for it omits the several other types belonging to the same culture horizon and thus is not likely to be used in areas or sites where Eden or Scottsbluff points do not happen to occur.

The two traditions are combined into an upper Lithic stage by Willey and Phillips because of their belief that the peoples who made all these projectile-point forms followed essentially the same pattern of economic life, namely, the hunting of late Pleistocene big-game animals. It is also true that many archeologists regard both these horizons or traditions as Paleo-Indian for the same reason. However, it must be noted that a number of new traits appear with the second tradition, such as drills or perforators, bone awls, eyed bone needles, projectile points with corner notches, shaft smoothers of sandstone, the first-known instances of human burials in North America, the first *intensive* occupation of caves and rockshelters, and other traits that need not be itemized here. The most important new trait, however, is that of *food-grinding* with stone implements: basin-shaped milling stones and manos. Food-grinding implements do not always occur in sites of this tradition, mainly because many of these sites are places where hunters killed such animals as bison, somewhat larger than the modern ones, and several species of horses, camels, and ground sloths. In other words, kill sites would not be expected to contain such household articles as food-grinding implements.

This widespread appearance of food-grinding has great economic implications; not only is it perfectly clear that Pleistocene big game was by now rapidly disappearing all over North America (and probably South America as well), with only lingering members of a few species still being hunted, but the milling stones and manos are *concrete evidence that collection and preparation of vegetal foods had begun, undoubtedly to provide sustenance to replace the dwindling game herds.* This is not to say that vegetal foods—seeds, nuts, berries, roots, etc.—were not consumed in earlier times too; but now they must have become more important, and the archeologist, moreover, has objective proof of it in the form of stone implements that not only are imperishable but can be recognized by anyone.

It may not be exaggerating to say that this situation gives evidence of a true economic revolution in American prehistory. Moreover, it can be seen over immense areas in South as well as North America. It was this revolution as well as the appearance of many traits not found in the cultures characterized by fluted points that led Griffin (1953) to break from tradition and apply the term "Early Archaic" rather than "Paleo-Indian" to the far-flung archeological material that appears immediately after the general (if not complete) disappearance of fluted points in North America, approximately 10,000 years ago. I prefer the term "Protoarchaic" over the term "Early Archaic." The prefix "proto" more definitely expresses the idea of introducing or leading up to a different situation. With the Protoarchaic we have the appearance not only of manos and milling stones over great expanses of the New World (and the Old World) but also, more locally and on the whole somewhat later, of mortars and pestles. The technique of making these implements, known as pecking, is also new. In the course of using these implements, their surfaces automatically became partly smoothed, but without specific intent. Later, during the "full" Archaic stage in the New World (and in the Old World, if we use the original meaning of Neolithic stage), many kinds of implements, ornaments, and artistic or ceremonial objects were shaped by pecking and other methods, then finished by intentional grinding and polishing. Thus it is easy to imagine that the partial and unintentional smoothing of food-grinding implements eventually suggested the entire finishing of many artifacts by grinding and polishing. Not only that, but the suggestion could have occurred independently in different parts of the world, both processes being of such general distribution.

In additon to this technological progression there was an economic one as well. Peoples of the Protoarchaic stage, being gatherers as well as hunters, were able to inhabit more permanent locations than were the pure hunters. Innumerable caves and rockshelters, as well as open sites, give evidence of intensive occupation during this stage; and the settlement pattern of the full Archaic is merely an intensification of this more settled existence, doubtless leading also to favorable prior conditions for the establishment and diffusion of agriculture.

A good example of the number and the variety in shape of manos in the stage under consideration in the Great Plains may be seen in Roberts' report on the San Jon site in eastern New Mexico (Roberts 1942). The recent survey by Farmer of what he calls "metates" and "mullers" gives a round figure of "some 10,000 years ago" for their appearance in the United States, a date that is probably quite close to the truth (although he is in error in stating that these implements have been found in Folsom levels, not to mention pre-Folsom levels). The term "metate" is still widely used for implements of many kinds for grinding vegetal materials, whereas the early ones, either flat or with shallow oval basins in which the mano (or muller) was used with *rotary motion*, are better designated as "milling stones." The true metates were used with a back-and-forth motion and are much later in time as well as much more restricted in distribution, principally among agricultural peoples of the southwestern United States and Middle America.

If a date of approximately 10,000 years ago (or a little less) is correct for the first appearance of milling stones and manos in the United States, it is of great interest that they appear as far away as central Argentina—even Tierra del Fuego—not less than 8000 years ago, as shown by radiocarbon dates at Intihuasi Cave in San Luis Province, Argentina (Rex González, 1952, 1960), and several caves in Magallanes Province in extreme southern Chile (Bird, 1938). This speaks for extremely rapid diffusion over immense areas within a space of only about 2000 years, although the point of origin of this trait in the New World is as yet unknown.

Jennings (1955), referring only to the Great Plains region in general, was, as was Griffin, aware of the considerable differences between the makers of fluted points and those who came soon after. Sellards (1952) had defined a Portales complex in eastern New Mexico, but, as defined, this concept was not of wide application. Jennings improved on this by defining a "Plano Culture," a term that seems eminently suitable. Quimby (1960) used the term "Aqua-Plano" for the Upper Great Lakes region, and Mason (1962) extended the idea of a Plano Culture from the Great Plains to much of the eastern United States. There is no conflict here with what Griffin (1953) called "Early Archaic" (and which I call "Protoarchaic") because Griffin and I are referring to a very broad and more or less continental culture *stage*, whereas Plano *Culture* refers to a regional expression of this stage.

In the arid regions west of the Rocky Mountains and in northern Mexico, a different kind of general culture has been recognized for some years, also characterized by food-grinding implements, with their economic implications. This is the Desert Culture. Kelley (1959) states that he used this concept (in the plural: "Desert cultures") as long ago as 1947. [EDITORS' NOTE: Probably the first published use of the term "Desert cultures" was by Vaillant in 1944.] But Jennings and Norbeck (1955) and the symposium edited by Jennings (1956) gave this concept more precise formalization, with detailed trait lists and a map of its distribution. They conceived of the Desert Culture as a neat adjustment of hunting and gathering peoples in the Great Basin and surrounding areas to an environment that, over nearly all the postglacial period, offered such scanty food resources that neither the gross population nor the size of population units (small, semisedentary bands) could be increased notably without some new means of exploiting the environment, that is, with agriculture.

Jennings and Norbeck (1955) defined three kinds of Desert cultures: Peripheral Big-Game Hunting, lasting from about 11,000 to 3000 years ago; Horticulture, lasting from about 3000 years ago to the Spanish intrusions; and Historic. The term "Peripheral Big-Game Hunting" is not ideal here, for the authors state that by this time the late Pleistocene game animals still being hunted in the Great Plains were already absent from the Great Basin.

In the 1955 seminar (Jennings [ed.] 1956), the concept of a Desert Culture was divorced from that of agricultural development (as it should have been); the far-reaching significance of food-grinding implements as the hallmark of this culture was emphasized; and it was said that there was a "geographic separation between Desert Culture and Paleo-Indian hunters, the former being the primary western culture, while the latter is more characteristically eastern and northern." However, the statement that the Desert Culture is "apparently of an antiquity equal to the Plains big-game hunters (Folsom and comparable cultures)" is not quite accurate; it was based on the premise that Great Basin caves, which were open to occupancy by 11,000 years ago, when the huge interior lakes had lowered enough (in response to climatic change) to expose them, would contain Desert Culture material from the beginning of occupancy. But, if we accept milling stones and manos as characteristic of this culture, it can be seen that these implements were not present as soon as the exposed caves began to be occupied; they came somewhat later, perhaps between 10,000 and 9000 years ago.

In other words, the *beginning* of Desert Culture west of the Rocky Mountains was contemporaneous not strictly with the fluted-point cultures of the Great Plains but with the Plano Culture. It is true that fluted points are found in all states west of the Rocky Mountains too, but for the most part they are surface finds and have not yet been connected with any particular culture pattern. The Clovis points associated with mammoths and other extinct animals at the Naco and Lehner Ranch sites in extreme southeastern Arizona are certainly directly related to finds where Clovis points are recovered with mammoths in the Great Plains and precede the Desert Culture. Clovis points with many other artifacts, including food-grinding implements, at the Borax Lake site in northern California (Harrington 1948) cannot possibly be regarded as pre-Folsom but must constitute either a local survival of fluted points or perhaps a revival of the fluting principle stimulated by their having been found by later Indians in the vicinity (Meighan 1959). Otherwise, Clovis points in western states are few, widely scattered, and of unknown affiliation. In southern Idaho, true Folsom points are found in some numbers, undoubtedly as an extension of their diffusion through the Great Plains, but they too are surface finds (Swanson, personal communication).

In the northwestern United States and southern British Columbia, a new concept of great importance is taking shape in the recognition of an Old Cordilleran Culture (Butler 1961). The diagnostic projectile-point type is known as the Cascade point and resembles the Lerma type of the Great Plains and Mexico, the El Jobo type of Venezuela, and even the Ayampitín type of Argentina, in that it is shaped like a long and narrow leaf, pointed at both ends. The Cascade point is sometimes serrated. In many caves, rockshelters, and open sites in the Northwest it is the only projectile-point type in the lowest levels; and in some of these it occurs without food-grinding implements but with heavy scrapers and choppers. When food-grinding does appear, the Cascade points may continue for a while, but other forms of projectiles, stemmed and notched, appear too. The last retreat of Pleistocene ice sheets in the Northwest, the Vashon, occurred about 13,500 years ago, at least 2000 years earlier than the last retreats in the Midwest. The Old Cordilleran Culture is thought to have become established soon after the Vashon retreat, or about 13,000 years ago, and to have ended with the appearance of food-grinding implements and other new traits some 10,000–9000 years ago. *This culture, then, appears to have been a western equivalent of the fluted-point cultures of the Great Plains.* It is not known to include any fluted points, although, as stated above, some do occur in the general region; and it precedes, on the whole, the appearance of food-grinding implements. Moreover, there are indications that it precedes the Desert Culture in the Great Basin and the Southwest, and there is a possibility that it may eventually be traced through immense areas in Latin America; but research is needed before anything more definite can be said. The characteristic Cascade point may also be traced far into Canada, even into the Yukon and Northwest Territories.

In central and western Texas and northeastern Mexico, another cau-ture pattern may be traced that, as in the Desert and Plano cultures, is characterized by food-grinding implements and many other traits not known in the fluted-point cultures. This is the Balcones Phase described by Kelley (1959). On the west, as in Frightful Cave in Coahuila (Taylor 1956), this Phase may be difficult to distinguish from the Desert Culture; but in western and central Texas it is sufficiently distinct from the Plano Culture, and it may be considered as a third major culture in a general Protoarchaic stage. While Kelley terms it a phase (in the midwestern system of terminology) it may be legitimate to call it a "Balcones Culture" in the sense used in this article.

In Mexico, Central America, and South America *all the way to Tierra del Fuego*, this Protoarchaic stage—featured by the first appearance of food-grinding implements as well as by other traits that distinguish it from earlier stages—may be seen quite clearly. However, since regional *cultures* have not yet been defined, in the sense used here, in Latin American countries, important sites and complexes are grouped in the lists below by regions rather than by cultures.

With regard to the stages defined by Willey and Phillips (1958), it should be reasonably clear that their upper Lithic consists of two very distinct stages, each of vast extent and great significance in the early culture history of both American continents. That part characterized by fluted points is, of course, valid only for the Great Plains region and eastern United States, since the few examples of fluted points found in the western United States, Canada, Alaska, Mexico, and Central America have not yet been found in circumstances that permit their assignment to specific stages. In these other regions, however, the level of technological development is similar to that connected with fluted points—in each case, the projectile points, though unfluted, are of lanceolate shape and seem to be the first ones. The rest of the cultural inventory consists of a few simple forms of chipped-stone and bone artifacts and of hearths; extinct Pleistocene mammals are often in association; and food-grinding implements are absent. *For this situation I suggest that the old term "Paleo-Indian" should be retained and extended over both continents and, by implication, should not be used for the "Pre–Projectile Point" stage that precedes this or for the Protoarchaic that follows.*

Some culture names within this Paleo-Indian stage may be suggested for certain regions. Sellards' term "Llano complex" for material associated with Clovis points in New Mexico, southern Arizona, and the Texas Panhandle (Sellards 1952) can be expanded into a much more widespread *Llano Culture*, reaching from the Naco and Lehner Ranch sites in southern Arizona through most of the Great Plains and into large portions of the eastern United States, that is, wherever Clovis points are an obvious diagnostic trait. The term *Lindenmeier Culture* could be coined to embrace the many sites in which Folsom points are the obvious diagnostic trait, most of which are in the Great Plains region. (The word "Folsom" would then be confined to a projectile-point type, as it should have been in the first place). The *Old Cordilleran Culture*, mentioned briefly above, would be a third regional expression of the Paleo-Indian stage, west of the Rocky Mountains. Other cultures in this broad regional sense have yet to be worked out, particularly in Latin America, and until this is done we can only speak of sites and complexes that appear to belong to this Paleo-Indian stage. Sandia points and artifacts of proved association, incidentally, do not provide grounds for a separate culture, but there may be a Sandia complex which can be included in the more general Llano Culture.

The second division of Willey and Phillips' upper Lithic stage, which they symbolize with the expression "Eden-Scottsbluff tradition," would also become incorporated in a vastly more extensive stage on both American continents, for which I have suggested the term "Protoarchaic." Some late Pleistocene mammals continue to appear here and there, but it is clear that most of them had become extinct. Exceptions would be the large bison, still fairly numerous, found in kill sites in the Great Plains region; ground sloths, as at Gypsum Cave in Nevada; and some lingering mastodons in the eastern United States, as shown by Williams (1957). In South America, the horse and ground sloth apparently survived into this stage in the vicinity of the Strait of Magellan (Bird 1938).

After this stage, another of vast extent may be seen on both continents, featured by a still richer inventory of artifacts of chipped, pecked, and polished stone as well as bone and shell; more permanent settlements; cemetery areas (rather than isolated burials); and many other new traits, which must have included effective water transportation in the form of dugout canoes. Characteristic late Pleistocene mammals had by now completely disappeared except for such anomalies as survival of ground sloths in Cuba. This stage, the full Archaic, is outside the subject of "early man."

Another theoretical proposition for analysis of early-man material in North America should be mentioned. Wormington (1957), following the suggestion of Quimby (1954), organized her book around a Paleo-eastern tradition, which emphasized big-game hunting, and a Paleowestern tradition, which placed a greater emphasis on food-gathering. To these, Wormington added a Paleonorthern tradition, to be "characterized by specially prepared cores, the prismatic flakes struck from them, small tools made from these flakes, and sometimes a special type of grooving implement called a burin." In theory this vertical arrangement (in contrast to a horizontal scheme of stages) has intriguing possibilities but works out in confusing ways. The Paleoeastern tradition extends far over the western states as well (west of the Rocky Mountains), and the Paleowestern tradition extends over large parts of the Plains and eastern United States. The word "tradition" implies that all these occurrences are historically connected and therefore the result of diffusion in both directions across the United States. Moreover, many of the sites and complexes discussed are not Paleo-Indian at all but are much too late for this designation as usually used. Eight sites and complexes are discussed under another heading, "Non–Projectile Point Assemblages," but several others that should come under this heading appear instead in the Paleowestern and Paleoeastern sections. The features intended to characterize the Paleonorthern tradition are by no means limited to northern Canada and Alaska; burins are found at least as far south as Central Mexico, and implements made from prismatic flakes removed from prepared cores are found as far south as Patagonia in the Casapadrense complex. The Paleonorthern tradition, as defined by Wormington, is not of great time depth in the extreme north; on the other hand, there are occurrences in the Arctic regions of such projectile-point types as Clovis (often erroneously called Folsom), Plainview, Agate Basin, and perhaps others, which *might* be called Paleo-Indian but are outside Wormington's definition. Their occasional appearance among indigenous Arctic cultures may be interpreted as the result of early hunting peoples moving northward after game herds as the great ice sheets melted away, but their mere presence does not make the indigenous Arctic cultures Paleo-Indian (Collins 1954).

In Mexico, terminology for early-man material has for many years followed (or, I should say, has attempted to follow) that in the United States, but it has been badly handicapped by the vagaries, changes, individual preferences, and constant use—without any precise definitions—of terms in the United States. An astonishing number of discoveries has just been compiled by Aveleyra Arroyo de Anda (1962) from seventy localities in Mexico and five in Central America. He assigns these to two cultural phases: Paleo-Indian hunters, and "advanced collectors and protoagricultural Meso-Indians." Some discoveries designated indeterminate are also, so far as is known, preceramic.

STATEMENT ON STAGES

There are many anthropologists and historians who see no particular need for any system of stages for the reconstruction of history. They say that stages are artificial constructs that hinder rather than aid the tracing of cultural continuities, particularly in any given region. Swanson (1959), for example, objects to the stages of Willey and Phillips as being a forced and artificial *classification* of cultural units rather than a history. The present study is open to the same criticism, for I have not even attempted to trace developments in any area from the apparent beginnings up to the appearance of ceramics; nor have I traced the way influences of one area produced changes in another. Nevertheless, the definition of a series of stages (all preceramic in this case) does serve a purpose; it reduces a great mass of material to a fairly simple form, which lends perspective for the general reader, without which he would become so bogged down in detail—meaning such a multiplicity of culture names and listing of artifact forms—that he would lose sight of the main trends of history. The stages, then, are not meant to constitute history; they are no more than a convenience by which some organization of the material can be gained—in other words, a framework that will aid in gaining perspective and on which the actual history with all its details and speculations can be written. In a larger work that I have been preparing for some years, the detailed contents of many sites and cultural units, ample illustrations of artifacts and other cultural evidence, speculations on the flow of history through time and space, and so on, will be treated comprehensively. In a short study like this one, it would be useless to try this. The best I can hope for is that the reader of this article will be familiar with some of the material cited and will take the time to look up the references on items that are new to him. [EDITORS' NOTE: Many of the papers that follow do provide a few details concerning the better-known sites.]

One of the greatest weaknesses of archeology is inadequacy of sampling. When new cultures are mentioned in print, there is rarely any attempt to discover how much field work was done to back up the claims, the amount of ground excavated, the number of artifacts found, or the portion of the site examined. Consequently, some extremely weak cases have been accepted and repeated in the literature, then repeated again by others until they become so firmly embedded in the minds of scholars that it is impossible to convince them that the original claim was based on no solid evidence. Sampling, however, is variable with different kinds of sites. A site deeply buried in alluvium, for example, is very difficult to explore, and even a small amount of material may be of great value. Some surface collections, on the other hand, may give a very large sampling because the sites were never buried; examples may be seen in collections taken from the shores of extinct lakes. Even the expression "surface collection" needs to be examined critically at times, for I have seen many situations in North and South America where material was literally picked up on the surface, but only because of erosion of the covering material. In some cases it is possible to find nearby locations where the cultural zone disappears under an overburden of sand, silt, or soil. In the following sections on specific stages, I have tried to make evaluations that consider both the problems of sampling and the problems of once-buried surface collections. Undoubtedly, either through further work or through defects in my reasoning about what has been found so far, some of my assignments will prove to be wrong.

Each of the stages covers several thousand years. Hence it is not to be thought that all the sites and complexes listed under each stage existed contemporaneously; indeed, some of them quite likely followed one another in time while still remaining in the same general stage. It is also possible—even likely—that two stages existed side by side in limited areas in some cases. We have examples of this in different parts of the world in historic times, where one cultural or ethnic group continues to live in a very primitive state, while its neighbors are regarded as more advanced. There is no reason to doubt that this happened in the distant past as well.

In the following lists I have given greatest emphasis to complexes when these have been described, although they may have been called "phases," "cultures," "industries," "foci," or even "stages" in the literature. If nothing equivalent to "complexes" has yet been worked out, sites are listed by name. In most cases, "site" refers to an open location, while closed or protected locations are called "caves" or "rockshelters." When one considers that a complex may be based on anything from one to more than one hundred known localities, it is apparent that several thousand localities are represented in the lists. This will come as a surprise to those anthropologists (even archeologists) who still think of early man in the New World as a minor problem concerned with one or two dozen discoveries of artifacts associated with now-extinct Pleistocene animals. Even at that, the reader must realize that the lists are very incomplete; they are only *indicative* of what may be included in each stage in major regions. I do not intend to slight authors who have done valuable work on sites or complexes not mentioned; but, on the whole, I have entered those items about which I feel most confident because I have seen the localities or artifacts (or both). This is particularly true of items in the South American lists, for their interpretations are often quite mystifying (to me, at least), and I have placed the items where they would seem to belong after examining the artifacts and, in some cases, the localities themselves.

The references are for the most part primary, although they are not always the first publications on a particular discovery; if not, they are improvements on the preliminary reports. Some references are secondary because their authors have drawn together some valuable comparisons between original reports. "Author's notes" could have been added to perhaps 80 per cent of the references, but it seemed best to refrain from this except in a few cases. A *complete* list of references would run to three or four times the length of the present one.

Rowe (1962) has discussed two kinds of stages: simple (based on a single criterion) and complex (based on several criteria). The present stages are complex, in Rowe's terms. All of them together would constitute one simple stage that could be called "preceramic," but it is clear that a simple preceramic stage must be subdivided into at least four complex stages.

The dangers of morphological dating have been ably discussed by Stewart (1949). It should be clear that my approach is of opposite nature: I am assuming, not that cultural material can be dated by its morphology, but that form and technology *indicate* a stage of development, while dating is a separate problem. Dates may or may not be available, and stages may begin and end at different times in different regions.

PRE–PROJECTILE POINT STAGE

OTHER NAMES

Lower Lithic stage (Willey and Phillips 1958), Percussion stage (Andover seminar 1956), Protolithic stage (Menghin 1957*a*, 1957*b*), and Paleolithic or Lower Paleolithic stage (several authors).

Defining characteristics. There was a low level of stone-working technology similar to that of the Lower Paleolithic stage in the Old World. All objects were made by percussion only; they might be called core and flake tools but this distinction is often hard to make. Often, but not always, they are quite large and heavy. Pebble tools are also present but vary greatly in frequency. The fact of percussion does not adequately describe the technology; more important is the apparent inability of peoples of this stage to *flatten and thin* the artifacts enough to produce what would be called projectile points and knives of thin, bifaced form. Bone implements are occasionally present in the form of splinters of leg bones of large mammals, with wear at one or both ends as though used for perforating; splinters also occur that may have been cut or beveled; and in two or three cases the leg bones of small animals have been cut into tubes. In some sites, shallow, basin-shaped hearths are found, but never, so far as is known, lined with stones. Such hearths may have been dug, in some cases, or they may have been shallow natural depressions, or both. No human burials in dug graves are known.

Discussion. I have already stated that Willey and Phillips (1958) have credited me with a number of rejections. The following list (Table 1, p. 44) should correct that impression to some degree, and it also contains some discoveries made since that time. A few additional notes are in order. (See also Krieger 1962.)

Fig. 1.—Some sites and complexes assigned to a "Pre–Projectile Point" stage in North America. Single sites, or several closely related sites for which no "complex" has yet been defined, are marked by ✕. Recognized complexes, or equivalent cultural units, are placed in their approximate locations and underscored. In some cases very little cultural material is known (see text). The map does not include numerous instances of "Paleolithic" implements in Baja California and other Mexican states, Guatemala, midwestern and northeastern United States, and Kansas, which, with the exception of the last-mentioned, were reported in the nineteenth and early twentieth centuries.

TABLE 1

Important Sites in North America	References
*Lewisville site, north-central Texas, with two dates greater than 38,000 years	CROOK and HARRIS 1957, 1958; KRIEGER 1957
*Friesenhahn Cave, central Texas, with rich late Pleistocene fauna	KENNERLY 1956; LUNDELIUS 1960; EVANS 1961
*Tule Springs site, southern Nevada, with one date greater than 28,000 years	HARRINGTON and SIMPSON 1961
*American Falls site, southern Idaho, with bones of very large bison (*latifrons?*) in which round holes were punched, probably with wooden spears, and pelvic bone cut with sharp tool; one date of greater than 30,000 years and possibly 43,000 years	HOPKINS and BUTLER 1961
*Santa Rosa Island sites, southern California, with dates ranging from about 10,000 to 29,500 years on charcoal and burned bone of dwarf mammoth in basin-shaped hearths	ORR 1956, 1960a, 1960b, 1962
*Scripps Campus site, La Jolla, southern California; one date of about 21,500 years	CARTER 1957; author's notes
*Tequixquiác locality, state of Mexico, central Mexico	DE TERRA, in DE TERRA, ROMERO, and STEWART 1949; MALDONADO-KOERDELL and AVELEYRA 1949; AVELEYRA 1950; author's notes
*Valsequillo localities, state of Puebla, central Mexico	ARMENTA CAMACHO, manuscripts in preparation; personal communications; author's notes
*Reports of "Paleolithic" implements in Baja California, central Mexico, Campeche, and Guatemala	For sources and comments see AVELEYRA A. DE ANDA 1950, 1962
Lake Chapala Basin, central Baja California, sites with "elongate-biface assemblage"	ARNOLD 1957
*Lake Manix complex, Mojave Desert, southern California	SIMPSON 1958, 1960
Coyote Gulch sites, Mojave Desert	SIMPSON 1961
Playa I complex, southern California and western Arizona	ROGERS 1939, 1958
Farmington complex, central California	TREGANZA 1952; TREGANZA and HEIZER 1953
Black's Fork complex ("culture"), southwestern Wyoming	RENAUD 1938, 1940
Tolchaco complex, northeastern Arizona	BARTLETT 1942
Los Encinos complex, northern New Mexico	BRYAN 1939
Imlay Channel sites, southern Michigan (a possibility; not yet well described)	BAGGERLY 1954; author's notes
Sheguiandah site, level V, Manitoulin Id., Ontario, Canada	LEE 1957
Kelley complex ("phase"), New England	BYERS 1959b
Various reports of "Paleolithic" artifacts in northeastern and midwestern states in late nineteenth and early twentieth centuries, including the gravels at Trenton, N.J. (This material should be re-examined; it cannot all be set aside as insignificant.)	For sources, excerpts, and comments see HRDLIČKA 1907; SELLARDS 1952
*Malakoff locality, east-central Texas	SELLARDS 1941, 1952
Kogruk complex, Anaktuvuk Pass, Alaska	CAMPBELL 1961

* Associated extinct fauna.

The Lewisville site, some twenty miles northwest of Dallas, Texas, yielded not only a Clovis fluted point from Hearth No. 1 but also two radiocarbon dates on charred vegetal material that were reported as "greater than 37,000 years" (Crook and Harris 1957, 1958) and have recently been remeasured as "greater than 38,000 years." This astonishing age has puzzled many archeologists, who, unable to believe that a Clovis point (or any kind of stone projectile point) can be that old, have chosen to reject the radiocarbon dates as hopelessly inaccurate (e.g., Hester 1960). However, as I pointed out soon after the discovery (Krieger 1957), there are alternative explanations, among them the distinct possibility that the Clovis point was planted in the hearth by someone not connected with the excavation or that, by some incredible accident, machinery used to excavate the huge borrow pit in which this and other hearths were exposed somehow caused the point to be dragged or lowered to this position. Sellards (1960) expressed the same view. At any rate, *those who reject the dates completely ignore the geology and paleontology of the hearths and their contents, which are in full accord with the radiocarbon dates.* If, then, the Clovis point is set aside as an unsolvable problem, Lewisville remains one of the most exciting and important archeological discoveries ever made in America.

At Friesenhahn Cave in Bexar County, central Texas, the enormously rich fossil fauna is believed to represent one or more stages of the Wisconsin glacial period (Kennerly 1956). As at least thirty genera and species of now-extinct fauna have been identified there, it may be said that this was a flourishing Wisconsin-age fauna in which extinctions had not begun to be evident. Sellards (1952) illustrated one flint artifact that he called a scraper, but he did not mention several small bone sections with square-cut ends and polished surfaces, which I had long thought to be artifacts. Evans (1961) offers another explanation: that the squared ends were sheared off by carnivores like the saber-toothed cats found in the same deposit and that polishing was caused by retention of the bone fragments in the intestines of these or other carnivores. The Swiss archeologist H. Müller-Beck has assured me that polishing of "green" bone can be accomplished in that way. Despite this illustration of extreme caution, Evans states that "several objects found in the excavations suggest that he [man] either entered the cave occasionally or lived in the immediate vicinity of its entrance." In November, 1962, I decided to look again at the flints and possible bone artifacts found in Friesenhahn Cave in the excavations of 1949, stored in the Texas Memorial Museum in Austin. To my utter amazement, the collection, which was being catalogued at the time Sellards selected the scraper illustrated in 1952, contains at least forty flints that show a crude but nonetheless definite pattern of chipping, resulting in steep, almost vertical edges with small, protruding "beaks." These artifacts are plano-convex and cannot be accidental; all come from zones 2 and 3 in the cave, the same zones that contained the bulk of the Pleistocene fossils and that were not disturbed by the erosion channel, zone 4.

The famous site of Tule Springs in southern Nevada had produced one radiocarbon date of "more than 23,800 years" at the time Willey and Phillips wrote. Harrington and Simpson (1961) published many more details on what seemed to be hearths with split and burned bones of such extinct mammals as horse, camel, and sloth, and some nineteen artifacts of stone and bone. A new date of at least 28,000 years and perhaps as much as 32,000 years had been obtained by that time. Since a huge excavation project is in process as this is written, it would be best not to comment further until its results are known.

On the northwest shore of Santa Rosa Island in southern California, numerous concentrations of charcoal and the split and burned remains of dwarf mammoth bones have been found exposed in cliffs of alluvium facing the ocean and in steep-sided arroyos leading to the beach. It is difficult to discuss this situation until mapping and excavation of these concentrations can be accomplished, a formidable task because of the height and steepness of the cliffs. There is no question that the alluvium was deposited several miles out from the present cliffs while the ocean was lower—that is, during a glacial stage—and that a rising ocean cut the alluvium back to where it is now. During a visit in 1960 with other archeologists and geologists, I saw no particular reason to doubt that the concentrations of charcoal and burned bones in basin-shaped depressions were due to the activities of man or that the range of radiocarbon dates from some 10,000 to 29,500 years would be valid. The absence of artifacts from these localities, so far, can be explained by the fact that no former land surfaces have been exposed horizontally.

At the Scripps Campus site on the California mainland near La Jolla, the physical situation is much like that on Santa Rosa Island, a rising postglacial sea having cut back extensive alluvial deposits and exposed burned areas (Carter 1957). A date of about 21,500 ± 700 years ago on this locality agrees with the alluvium having been deposited while the sea was lower during the last major glaciation. This site is more convincing (to me, at least) than the Texas Street site in nearby San Diego, because it does have some thin lenses of char and burned earth which contain bits of charred bone and shell, and small flakes, indicating a camp site.

The Tequixquiác locality on the north rim of the Valley of Mexico proved a rich source of late Pleistocene vertebrate fossils as early as 1870. The only artifact found at that time, so far as I know, was the famed sacrum of an extinct llama carved (and there is no doubt about the fact of carving) to resemble the face and snout of an animal: a coyote, wolf, or possibly a peccary. It was not until the late 1940's that simple stone scrapers and splinters of mammoth(?) leg bones sharpened at the tip began to be found by Aveleyra and Maldonado-Koerdell. Willey and Phillips mention radiocarbon dates of "earlier than 6000 B.C." obtained from the "top few inches of the Becerra formation" in this connection (1958), but these dates come from other parts of the Valley of Mexico and have nothing to do with Tequixquiác, where the artifacts are recovered from near the base of the Becerra formation, obviously far older than 6000 B.C. and probably too old for projectile points.

The work at the Valsequillo reservoir in the state of Puebla, Mexico, conducted by Juan Armenta Camacho and Cynthia Irwin, is best known for the now-famous fragment of proboscidean bone on which are carved rough depictions of many animals, at least one of which (an extinct horse?) has four spears driven into its body. Excavations here in 1962 revealed artifacts, including a large burin, associated with at least two mastodons. Geologically, the several stations in the Valsequillo area would seem to present problems like that of Tequixquiác and to be older than the uppermost part of the Becerra formation.

At Malakoff, in Henderson County, Texas, three human heads carved from large sandstone boulders were found on bedrock by paleontologists in the 1930's (Sellards 1941). They lay under twenty-six feet of gravels containing fossils of several Pleistocene animals, some of them partly articulated. Willey and Phillips state that this discovery is "not generally accepted by archeologists," which is true and another instance in which so many of them feel free to pass judgments without examining the field situation or circumstances of discovery. I am quoted as believing that the heads are "probably" of human workmanship, whereas this cannot be doubted for two of them, although the third bears only some vague incisions. There are no other artifacts or evidences of a camp at this locality, but, as a guess, I have added this discovery to the list of "pre–projectile point" items given above.

The Potter Creek Cave locality in northern California has been omitted from the list, although I am not convinced that the presence of man can be completely discounted. The cave was excavated by paleontologists (Sinclar 1904), with excellent vertical and horizontal controls. It was the paleontologists who presented a number of bone objects to anthropologists at the University of California, stating that some of them must have been modified by man. Some anthropologists agreed (Putnam 1906), but others were violently opposed when they learned that the associated fauna was "middle Pleistocene," and the matter gradually subsided. Now that the fauna is regarded as late Pleistocene, with anomalies that occur along the Pacific littoral, the matter does not seem so unreasonable. Müller-Beck has explained to me that he does not believe that most of the bone fragments are artifacts, but for reasons that California archeologists had not thought of before. However, this still leaves one small, polished-bone tube with square-cut ends; a large stone chip with sharp edges; and deposits of charcoal found deep in the cave in 1904, which can hardly be ignored.

Discussion. During my visit in 1962 to South America, I learned several things of great importance. The first is that there is a large amount of material that must be termed "pre–projectile point" for the same reasons that this term is used in North America: a *low level of technology*. Many artifact forms differ from those in North America, but there are some artifacts that show similarities. Second, only a small amount of this material, which ranges from some fifty to one hundred specimens to as many as eight thousand specimens from a single site, has been published, and the publications contain far too few illustrations to show the range of artifact forms. Third, the methods of analysis, as in North America, are not uniform so that each person gives names to the artifacts without much regard to what other workers call them. Fourth, on the Atlantic side of the continent, the material I call "pre-projectile point" is, with few exceptions, made from quartzitic rocks, while that on the western or Pacific side is almost without exception made from black or brown basalt. In short, there is a huge amount of material that requires analysis according to some common principles.

It may be argued that many of the sites and complexes are survivals of simple cultures into rather recent times. This may be true of some of them, but many are found in areas where a whole sequence of development can be traced, with increasing complexity, to the ceramic cultures and advanced civilizations. Objective datings have not been obtained for any of this material, but it should be remembered that radiocarbon dates have been obtained on complexes that contain well-made projectile points and other artifacts over 10,000 years ago as far south as Tierra del Fuego (see below). Therefore, this much cruder material, which has often been called Paleolithic by South American archeologists, should be considerably older than the first projectile points. Moreover, it contains many differences from one complex to another, even in limited areas, so that, if datings could be determined, a long history of changes might be revealed before projectile points appeared.

Cruxent (1962) mentions Paleo-Indian artifacts from the *barrio* of Manzanillo in Maracaibo, western Venezuela, and states that there are comparisons with the El Jobo complex described by Cruxent and Rouse (1956) in the state of Falcón. Actually, the Manzanillo complex consists

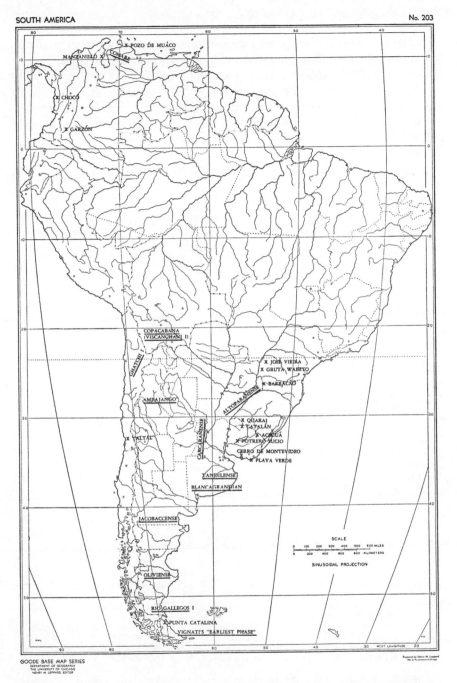

Fig. 2.—Some sites and complexes assigned to a "Pre–Projectile Point" stage in South America. Single sites, or several closely related sites for which no "complex" has yet been defined, are marked by ×. Recognized complexes, or equivalent cultural units, are placed in their approximate locations and underscored. In many cases the South American sites and complexes have produced much more material than those in North America assigned to the same stage.

of many thousands of extremely crude implements made from petrified wood with veins of flint that, when chipped with "sinuous edges," make effective chopping tools or hand axes. The terms "knives" and "prismatic flakes," used by Cruxent, are not well chosen, for the implements are much too crude to correspond with objects described by these terms in the United States. There is nothing even faintly suggesting projectile points, whereas the El Jobo complex has many of these, very well made

TABLE 2

Important Sites in South America	References
Manzanillo complex, Maracaibo, state of Zulia, Venezuela	CRUXENT 1962; author's notes
Camare complex in El Jobo district, state of Falcón, Venezuela (not to be confused with El Jobo complex in same area)	CRUXENT, personal communications; author's notes
* Pozo de Muaco site (La Vela de Coro site), state of Falcón, Venezuela	ROYO Y GÓMEZ 1961; CRUXENT, personal communication; author's notes
José Vieira site, state of Paraná, Brazil (lower levels)	LAMING and EMPERAIRE 1959
Barracão site, state of Paraná, Brazil	Author's notes
Gruta de Wabeto, state of Paraná, Brazil	Author's notes
Quarai site, state of Rio Grande do Sul, Brazil	Author's notes
Cerro de Montevideo site, Uruguay	Author's notes
Playa Verde site, department of Maldonado, Uruguay	Author's notes
Catalán Chico and Catalán Grande sites, department of Artigas, Uruguay	Author's notes
Aceguá site, department of Cerro Largo, Uruguay	Author's notes
Potrero Sucio site, central Uruguay	Author's notes
Altoparanense complex, province of Misiones, Argentina	MENGHIN 1955–56
Tandilense complex, province of Buenos Aires, Argentina	MENGHIN and BÓRMIDA 1950
Blancagrandian complex, province of Buenos Aires, Argentina	BÓRMIDA 1960
Carcarañense complex, province of Santa Fe, Argentina	REX GONZÁLEZ and LORANDI 1959
Oliviense complex, Santa Cruz Territory (Patagonia), Argentina	MENGHIN 1952
* Río Gallegos I complex, Santa Cruz Territory (Patagonia), Argentina	MENGHIN 1957b; author's notes
Jacobaccense complex, Rio Negro Territory (Patagonia), Argentina	CASAMIQUELA 1961
Argentine coast of Tierra del Fuego, "earliest phase"	VIGNATI 1927
Punta Catalina site, Tierra del Fuego, Chile	Author's notes on Reichnel collection in Lima, Peru
Ampajango complex, province of Catamarca, northwestern Argentina	CIGLIANO 1961; author's notes
Ghatchi I complex, province of Antofagasta, Chile	LE PAIGE 1958, 1960; author's notes
Copacabana complex, department of Potosí, southern Bolivia (also known as Viscanchani I complex)	H. MÜLLER-BECK, personal communication
* Garzón site, department of Huila, Colombia	BÜRGL 1958
Site in central part of department of Chocó, Colombia	Collected by G. REICHEL-DOLMATOFF; author's notes

* Associated extinct fauna.

and pointed at both ends, and many plano-convex scrapers. Manzanillo compares in some ways with another complex in the El Jobo *district* that Cruxent now calls Camare (personal communication), consisting of large bifacially chipped artifacts and large flake tools, but lacking anything as refined as projectile points or thin, bifacially chipped knives. I therefore include the Manzanillo and Camare complexes in a Pre–Projectile Point stage, and El Jobo proper in Paleo-Indian.

In the barren deserts and high mountain basins in the contiguous portions of Chile, Bolivia, and Argentina, a considerable body of similar material, crudely chipped by percussion and invariably of basalt, has often been called Paleolithic. In Chile it is called the Ghatchi I complex (Le Paige 1958, 1960; Barfield 1961); in Bolivia the Copacabana complex (Müller-Beck, personal communication) or Viscanchani I; and in northwestern Argentina the Ampajango complex (Cigliano 1961). It should form a distinctive *culture*, with perhaps some minor regional differences. Very similar, if not identical, material was recognized long ago at Taltal on the Chilean coast by Uhle (1917) and Capdeville (1921–22; 1922). Taltal was also one of the chief sites where Bird (1943) defined a "Shell Fishhook Culture" characterized by beautifully chipped artifacts of flint, chalcedony, and jasper, many objects of polished stone, shell fishhooks, bone harpoon points, etc. Although Bird could not find any stratigraphic separation of the chipped-basalt industry and the incomparably richer "Shell Fishhook Culture" at Taltal, it is perfectly clear that the crude artifacts of basalt are closely similar to those of the Ghatchi I, Copacabana, and Ampajango complexes and have little relation, if any, to the "Shell Fishhook Culture."

PALEO-INDIAN STAGE

OTHER NAMES

Early American Hunters (Krieger 1947); Paleo-American stage (Suhm, Krieger, and Jelks 1954), Fluted-Point stage (Andover seminar 1956), and Upper Lithic stage, in part (Willey and Phillips 1958).

Defining characteristics. Percussion chipping of stone artifacts continues but is much better controlled, so that the surfaces are worked down to produce the relatively thin and flat artifacts that can be called projectile points and/or knives. (Despite these categorical terms, usually used with great confidence, it is often impossible to distinguish them.) Although it is often assumed that pressure chipping was needed to produce any kind of projectile point or biface knife, experiments have shown that Clovis fluted points, for example, can be made entirely by percussion, but such delicately made objects as the true Folsom points require pressure (Wormington, personal communication). The projectile points are usually of lanceolate or leaf shape (Sandia points with a single slight shoulder can be included), but stemmed points with shallow incuts are also known. Of whatever shape, the projectile points and thin knives are usually (if not always) the first to appear in any given region. The range of chipped-stone and bone artifacts is still quite narrow when compared with later stages but varies with the kinds of sites known. In the Great Plains most of the known localities are kill sites, where Pleistocene mammals were butchered, so they contain little more than projectile points and cutting or scraping tools. The Lindenmeier site in Colorado is an exception in that it was a true camp site and has a wider range of both stone and bone artifacts. In the eastern United States, on the other hand, most of the localities are camp sites, not kill sites, and remains of extinct Pleistocene mammals have yet to be found. In other regions, associated extinct fauna is sometimes found, sometimes not. Hearth pits are known, usually (if not always) unlined with stones. No human burials in dug pits are known. Food-grinding implements, if not absent, are exceedingly rare.

The term "Llano Culture" is here used for sites characterized by Clovis fluted points and extinct mammals in the Southwest and Great Plains. Another term should be coined for sites in the eastern United States that have Clovis fluted points, Cumberland fluted points, and perhaps other types, as well as a wider range of artifacts. "Lindenmeier Culture" is used for sites in the Great Plains region characterized by Folsom fluted points. "Old Cordilleran Culture" is used for sites in the Pacific Northwest characterized by Cascade points. Otherwise, sites and complexes are listed by major regions, but not by cultures, for these have still to be worked out. The lists are by no means complete. Many discoveries are lumped under the headings to conserve space.

Discussion.   The problem of dating the Paleo-Indian stage must be discussed very briefly. Crane (1956) has published dates of about 20,000 years and "greater than 28,000 years" on fossil bone and charcoal supposed to have been obtained from the Sandia level of Sandia Cave in New Mexico; but Crane himself and several others have pointed out that there is no proof that these dates apply to *cultural material* in the cave. There are also some serious questions about the provenience of Sandia points themselves and the stratigraphy of Sandia Cave, but, since new work is being done there by Haynes and Agogino, it is best to set aside this problem until their conclusions are available. It may be that Sandia points are not much older than Clovis fluted points.

Clovis points have been dated at 9250 ± 300 years ago at the Naco site in Arizona, and seven radiocarbon measurements at the Lehner site nearby range from 7022 ± 450 to 12,000 ± 450 years ago (Haury, Sayles, and Wasley 1959). These authors regard the youngest dates as

FIG. 3.—Some sites and complexes assigned to a "Paleo-Indian" stage in North America.
Single sites, or several closely related sites for which no "complex" has yet been defined,
are marked by ×. Recognized complexes, or equivalent cultural units, are placed in their
approximate locations and underscored. In sites of more than one level it is usually the deepest
that has been assigned to this stage. For names and locations of many additional fluted-point
sites, especially in the eastern United States, see Wormington (1957) and Mason (1962);
for Mexico and Central America see Aveleyra (1962).

TABLE 3

Important Sites of the Llano Culture	References
* Sandia Cave, northern New Mexico	HIBBEN 1941
* Lucy site, central New Mexico	ROOSA 1956
* Blackwater Draw ("Clovis") site, eastern New Mexico; "Gray sand stratum" only	SELLARDS 1952
* Naco site, southeastern Arizona	HAURY 1953
* Lehner site, southeastern Arizona	HAURY, SAYLES, and WASLEY 1959
* Scharbauer ("Midland") site, western Texas	WENDORF et al. 1955; WENDORF and KRIEGER 1959
* Other sites in the Great Plains and contiguous areas, often associated with mammoths and sometimes with other extinct animals	For sources and comments see SELLARDS 1952 and WORMINGTON 1957

Fluted-Point Sites in the Eastern States	
Great Lakes region	QUIMBY 1958, 1960; MASON 1962
Northeastern region	RITCHIE 1953, 1957; BYERS 1954, 1955, 1959b; WITTHOFT 1952, 1954
Midwest, Southeast, etc.	WORMINGTON 1957; BYERS 1959b; MASON 1962 and commentators; MILLER 1962

Important Sites of the Lindenmeier Culture	
* Lindenmeier site, northeastern Colorado	ROBERTS 1935, 1936, 1940; HAYNES and AGOGINO 1960
* Blackwater Draw ("Clovis") site, eastern New Mexico; "diatomite stratum" only	SELLARDS 1952 and other sources therein
* Lubbock site, Texas Panhandle; "diatomite stratum" only	SELLARDS 1952
* Other sites in the Great Plains and contiguous areas, often associated with bison and occasionally with other extinct animals	ROBERTS 1940; SELLARDS 1952; WORMINGTON 1957

Important Sites of the Old Cordilleran Culture (Tentative List)	
Olcott and seven other sites, western Washington	THOMSON 1961
Ash Cave, eastern Washington; lowest level	BUTLER 1958
Indian Well site, Washington side of Columbia River gorge; level 1	BUTLER 1959
Five-Mile Rapids site, Oregon side of Columbia River gorge, lowest level	CRESSMAN 1960
Cougar Mountain Cave, central Oregon; lowest level	COWLES 1960
Fort Rock Cave, central Oregon; lowest level	CRESSMAN 1942
Crane Creek sites on Weiser River, western Idaho	SWANSON and BUTLER, personal communications; author's notes
Yale site, Fraser River, British Columbia; lowest levels	BORDEN 1957, 1961
Fort Liard complex, southern Yukon, Canada	MACNEISH 1959
Flint Creek complex ("tradition"), northern Yukon, Canada	MACNEISH 1959

Miscellaneous Sites and Complexes in Western United States and Mexico	
Danger Cave, Utah; lowest level	JENNINGS 1957
Death Valley I complex ("phase"), eastern California	HUNT 1960
Lake Mohave complex, southern California	CAMPBELL and CAMPBELL 1937; WALLACE 1954; MEIGHAN 1959; HUNT 1960; EBERHART 1961; WARREN and TRUE 1961
San Dieguito complex, southern California	ROGERS 1939, 1958; WARREN and TRUE 1961
Playa II complex, California and Arizona	ROGERS 1939, 1958; WARREN and TRUE 1961
Lerma complex, Tamaulipas, Mexico	MACNEISH 1958
* Santa Isabel Iztapan sites 1 and 2, Valley of Mexico	AVELEYRA and MALDONADO-KOERDELL 1953; AVELEYRA 1956, 1962
* San Juan complex ("industry"), Valley of Mexico	DE TERRA, in DE TERRA, ROMERO, and STEWART 1949

* Associated extinct fauna.

unreasonable and believe that 11,000–12,000 (or 12,500) years is closer to the truth. The famous mammoth near Dent, Colorado, with Clovis points, has recently been dated at 11,200 years (Agogino, personal communication). While these measurements are intriguing, archeologists are inclined to believe that the beginning of Clovis points must be pushed back to something like 15,000 years ago because of the immense distribution of this type in North America. There is considerable speculation on where this fluted principle was invented. For example, Mason (1962) favors the central part of the eastern United States because Clovis points are most frequent there, and Witthoft (1954) believes that the oldest examples may be from Pennsylvania. I have argued (Krieger 1954) that no one can say with any confidence where the fluting technique originated but that the old idea of its having reached North America from Asia via the Alaska steppingstone must be abandoned because it is not found in Asia. In other words, it is an American invention, but the place of origin cannot yet be determined.

Folsom points and associated artifacts have been dated at three places, all in the Great Plains. A measurement of 9883 ± 350 years ago at the Lubbock site in the Texas Panhandle (Sellards 1952) is well known and can be rounded off to about 10,000 years. (A second date of 9700 ± 200 years ago on pond-snail shells from the *top* of the same deposit at Lubbock does not apply to cultural material.) At the Lindenmeier site in Colorado, excavated by Roberts in the 1930's, Haynes and Agogino (1960) obtained a dating on charcoal of 10,780 ± 375 years ago; and, at the Brewster site in eastern Wyoming, a date on the "Folsom level" is 10,375 ± 700 years ago (Agogino, personal communication). Since true Folsom points (in contrast to the larger and heavier Clovis points) are virtually limited to the Great Plains, these dates indicate that they were made between approximately 10,000 and 11,000 years ago, and, as might be expected, are somewhat younger than Clovis (and probably Sandia) points.

An interesting new development is the recognition of Hell Gap points in Wyoming, with a radiocarbon date of 10,850 ± 550 years ago (Agogino 1961). These points are unfluted and have long, slightly incut stems, which, like nearly all the early types, were ground smooth along the edges to prevent cutting of the sinews that bound them to their shafts. This apparent contemporaneity with the totally different Folsom points in the same area suggests distinct ethnic groups but not necessarily that they permanently occupied the same area together.

A number of radiocarbon dates have been obtained on sites of the Old Cordilleran Culture in the Pacific Northwest and on the earliest levels of caves in the Great Basin that appear to precede the introduction of food-grinding implements. It must suffice here to say that they range

Fig. 4.—Some sites and complexes assigned to a "Paleo-Indian" stage in South America. Single sites, or several closely related sites for which no "complex" has yet been defined, are marked by ✕. Recognized complexes, or equivalent cultural units, are placed in their approximate locations and underscored. In the Lauricocha and Lagoa Santa caves only the lowest levels are assigned to this stage; the other sites are not stratified.

from some 9500 to 12,000 years ago and thus agree in age with fluted points—both Folsom and Clovis, so far as these have been dated—in the Great Plains, New Mexico, and Arizona. The Lerma complex in Tamaulipas has one date of 9270 ± 500 years ago (MacNeish 1958), and I suppose that approximately the same date would apply to the artifacts associated with mammoths at Santa Isabel Iztapan, as well as the San Juan complex, in the Valley of Mexico.

Discussion. I have no idea why sites that I would assign to a Paleo-Indian stage as here defined would be so rare in South America in comparison with North America, whereas in the Pre–Projectile Point stage a very large number of sites and complexes is found on both continents. Perhaps it is an accident resulting from what I saw and did not see in the various universities and museums visited.

TABLE 4

Important Sites in South America	References
El Jobo complex, state of Falcón, Venezuela	Cruxent and Rouse 1956; Rouse and Cruxent 1957
* Lagoa Santa Caves, state of Minas Gerais, eastern Brazil	Hurt 1962
* Mylodon Cave, province of Magallanes, Chile	Bird 1938
El Totoral complex, province of La Rioja, Argentina	Rex González 1960; author's notes
Ghatchi II complex, province of Antofagasta, Chile	Le Paige 1958, 1960
Zuniquena sites, Salar de Atacama, province of Antofagasta, Chile	Author's notes
Quebrado de Camarones sites, province of Tarapacá, Chile	Author's notes
Lauricocha caves, department of Huánuco, central highlands of Peru; level 1	Cardich 1958; author's notes

* Associated extinct fauna.

The El Jobo complex in Venezuela most definitely belongs to this stage, with its characteristic lanceolate projectile points, very thick and pointed at the proximal end as well as the distal end, at some eighty sites, all of which lack food-grinding implements. The dating of this complex has been widely misunderstood. A radiocarbon date of 16,375 ± 300 years ago was obtained on fossil mammal bone at the site of Muaco, well to the east of the El Jobo area (Cruxent, in Royo y Gómez 1961). The black organic muck at Muaco, formed in a small swamp, contained a fantastic array of late Pleistocene mammals, a fragment of a typical El Jobo point, a fragment of a typical El Jobo scraper with remains of a mastodon, and a number of other simple artifacts. While the spring that fed this swamp long ago was active, the muck must have been constantly churned by large animals walking around in it, so the date, and another of about 14,000 years ago, do not necessarily apply to the El Jobo point and scraper. They could be several thousand years later, for all one can tell.

Hurt (1962) has just published revised radiocarbon dates from his excavations in rockshelters in the vicinity of Lagoa Santa, Brazil. Those from levels 2 and 3 average 9311 ± 120 years ago, and those from levels 6 and 7 average 10,024 ± 127 years ago. There is a great amount of literature on the famed caves and rockshelters at Lagoa Santa, which contain extinct fauna, artifacts, and human skeletal remains, but their association has been a knotty problem since Peter Lund worked there in the 1830's, nearly 130 years ago (see Hrdlička 1912 for extensive source material). Hurt states about Rockshelter No. 6:

Apparently, this shelter was occupied by a small band of hunters about 10,000 years ago. Although no bones of extinct animals were found in the human occupational deposits, it is possible, on the basis of the time periods and unconfirmed finds made by other investigators in the region, that the hunters of Lagoa Santa were acquainted with giant forms of cave bear and armadillos [glyptodons?]. The hunters used projectiles tipped with square-stemmed projectile points. The presence of pitted hammerstones in the caves indicates that they probably cracked vegetal products such as small palm nuts with these utensils.

At Mylodon Cave in the Patagonian part of southern Chile, Bird (1938) found cultural material associated with remains of extinct ground sloths and later obtained a date of 10,832 ± 400 years ago on sloth dung. I am not sure that either projectile points or mano-like stones were found in this cave with such an age, but they were at the Fell's and Palli Aike caves farther east (see Protoarchaic Stage, below).

The Totoral, Ghatchi II, and Zuniquena material in northwestern Argentina and northern Chile contains rather crudely made lanceolate-shaped projectile points of black basalt, presumably chipped by percussion (pressure chipping is probably impossible on basalt), but food-grinding implements are absent, and the other artifacts do not seem to differ from the material listed under "Pre–Projectile Point" in this region.

The Quebrado de Camarones material and that from level 1 (bottom) of the Lauricocha Caves do not seem to include definite projectile points, but in both cases there was sufficient control of percussion chipping to produce relatively thin and flat artifacts that could be called bifacially worked knives, technologically equivalent to projectile points; food-grinding is again absent. The material in these sites is mainly flint and chert rather than basalt. Lauricocha 1 has a radiocarbon date of about 9525 years ago (Lanning and Hammel 1961; margin of error not given), which Rex González (1960) regards as very satisfactory because Lauricocha 2 and 3 contain many lanceolate points like those of Ayampitín and Intihuasi in central Argentina, where there are two dates of about 8000 years ago and where both manos and milling stones are common.

In recent years there have been several reports of Sandia, Clovis, and Folsom points from South American countries, which, if true, would be exciting indeed. I was able to examine some of these artifacts and do not believe that they are even projectile points, let alone the types just mentioned.

Protoarchaic Stage

OTHER NAMES

Early Archaic (Griffin 1953), Upper Lithic stage, in part (Willey and Phillips 1958).

Defining characteristics. The problem of distinguishing this stage from Paleo-Indian and from the rest of Willey and Phillips' upper Lithic stage has already been mentioned. It is marked mainly on both American continents by the appearance of food-grinding implements, such as manos and milling stones; to a lesser extent, by mortars and pestles; and by occasional instances of similar objects probably used for pulverizing pigments. When these objects were shaped, this was done by the pecking process, and their surfaces subsequently became partly smoothed by use rather than intent. Such implements are not found everywhere, being notably absent from Alaska, Canada, and some of the most northerly United States, and from areas where any kind of stone artifacts are rare. They may also be absent from kill sites where household implements would not be expected. In such cases, other artifacts that belong neither to Paleo-Indian nor to the full Archaic stage marked by intentional grinding and polishing may take the place of food-grinding implements as indicators of this stage. Some lingering species of Pleistocene mammals were still being hunted, notably bison in the Great Plains and perhaps mastodons in the eastern United States. Fluted points may survive in small numbers in some areas, but in general they have given way to a number of unfluted lanceolate forms; several forms with stems or corner notches; such new techniques as beveling and parallel flaking by pressure; and a far greater range of stone and bone artifacts than had been known before. Burials in dug graves appear, as in Minnesota (Jenks 1937), Wisconsin (Mason and Irwin 1960), and the Topanga complex in California (Meighan 1959).

In the list of Desert Culture sites given in Table 5, many well-known localities will not appear because they are not involved in problems of early man.

Discussion. Many radiocarbon dates that cannot be cited here permit rather close estimates as to when this stage began in different parts of North America. They show not only that there is an amazing amount of agreement but also that this stage followed very closely on the gen-

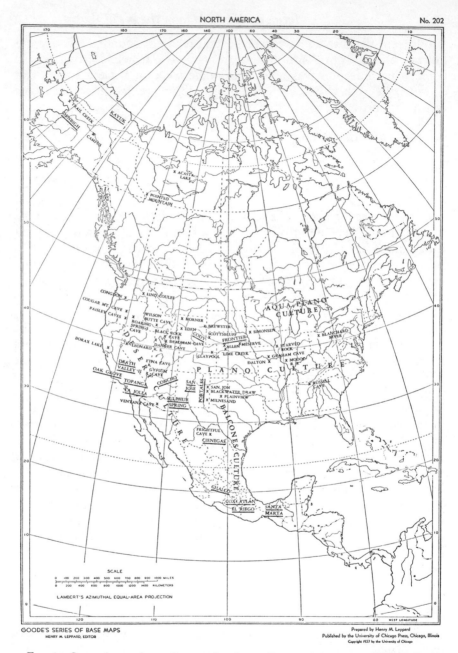

Fig. 5.—Some sites and complexes assigned to a Protoarchaic stage in North America. Single sites, or several closely related sites for which no "complex" has yet been defined, are marked by ×. Recognized complexes, or equivalent cultural units, are placed in their approximate locations and underscored. In stratified sites it is usually, but not always, the lowest level that is assigned to this stage, and in some cases more than one level is so assigned. For lack of space, the following have been omitted: the Chiricahua complex, in the same area as the Sulphur Spring complex in southeastern Arizona; the Sisters Hill site near the Brewster site in Agate Basin, eastern Wyoming; and the Red Smoke site near the Allen and Lime Creek sites in the Medicine Creek Reservoir basin, southern Nebraska. For additional sites, particularly in the eastern United States, see Mason (1962).

eral disappearance of fluted points in the regions where these points are characteristic of the Paleo-Indian stage. For example, Plainview points have been dated at the Plainview site at 9800 ± 500 years ago (Wendorf and Krieger 1959), at the Lime Creek site in Nebraska at 9524 ± 450 years ago (Davis and Schultz 1952), and at the Allen site in Nebraska at 8274 ± 500 years ago and 10,493 ± 1500 years ago. The last date has such a large margin of error that the actual date may well be between 9000 and 10,000 years ago rather than about 10,500 years. Agate Basin points in Wyoming and South Dakota range from 9350 ± 450 to 9990 ± 450 years ago (Roberts and Agogino, personal communications). Corner-notched points at the Simonsen site in western Iowa bear a date of 8430 ± 520 years ago (Frankforter and Agogino 1960). At Graham Cave, Missouri, and Modoc Rockshelter in Illinois, points of "Plano" types also range from about 8830 ± 500 to 10,651 ± 650 years ago. (Another date of 11,200 ± 800 years ago comes from the bottom of Modoc Rockshelter and seems to be considerably out of line from the others.) These and other dates apply only, of course, to the *beginnings* of a Plano Culture; the ending dates vary in different areas from about 7000 to perhaps 5000 or 4000 years ago.

Datings on Desert Culture material are of about the same magnitude if we consider the levels in which manos and milling stones first occur. Danger Cave in Utah has dates of 8960 ± 250 and 9789 ± 630 years ago on Level II; in Level I (bottom) the dates are earlier, but grinding stones are not certainly present. At Gypsum Cave there are two dates obtained on dung of ground sloths, 10,455 ± 340 and 8527 ± 250 years ago, but it has not been demonstrated that both dates apply to food-grinding implements from the general deposits containing sloths and other artifacts.

The well-known Cochise Culture in southeastern Arizona, originally consisting of three "stages" (Sulphur Spring, Chiricahua, and San Pedro), has been described in detail (Sayles and Antevs 1941). Later, a fourth "stage," Cazador, was revealed by excavations at the Double Adobe site, but is unpublished. (In accord with terms used here, these cultural units can be considered complexes, with Sulphur Spring, Cazador, and Chiricahua falling within a widespread Desert Culture rather than a localized Cochise Culture, a conversion favored by other authors as well.) San Pedro, involved in early agricultural and ceramic developments in the Southwest, is irrelevant here. By 1950 or so, radiocarbon dates of 6210 ± 450 and 6343 ± 250 years ago were available for what was then called Sulphur Spring, but may be the Cazador complex now, and 4006 ± 270 years ago for Chiricahua. Other dates are now available from the Double Adobe site. One, measured at 8200 ± 260 years ago for the Sulphur Spring complex by the solid-carbon method

TABLE 5

Important Sites of the Desert Culture	References
Danger Cave, Utah; most levels	JENNINGS 1957
Black Rock Cave, Utah	STEWARD 1937
Deadman Cave, Utah	SMITH 1941, 1952
* Etna Cave, Nevada	WHEELER 1942
* Gypsum Cave, Nevada; except top levels	HARRINGTON 1933
Leonard Rock Shelter, Nevada; except lowest level on lake gravel	HEIZER 1951
Death Valley II complex, California	HUNT 1960
Topanga complex ("culture"), California	HEIZER and LEMERT 1947; TREGANZA and MALAMUD 1950
La Jolla complex, California	ROGERS 1945; MORIARTY, SHUMWAY, and WARREN 1959; WARREN and TRUE 1961
* Ventana complex, Ventana Cave, Arizona	HAURY et al. 1950
* Sulphur Spring complex ("stage"), southeastern Arizona	SAYLES and ANTEVS 1941; HAURY 1960
Chiricahua complex ("stage"), southeastern Arizona	SAYLES and ANTEVS 1941
Cienegas complex at Frightful Cave, Coahuila	TAYLOR 1956
Concho complex, northeastern Arizona (peripheral to Desert Culture)	WENDORF and THOMAS 1951
San Jose complex, northern New Mexico (peripheral to Desert Culture)	BRYAN and TOULOUSE 1943

Important Sites in the Pacific Northwest	
Paisley caves 1 and 2, Roaring Springs Cave, eastern Oregon	CRESSMAN 1942
Cougar Mountain Cave, eastern Oregon; except lowest level	COWLES 1960
* Lind Coulee site, eastern Washington	DAUGHERTY 1956a
Congdon site, Washington; lowest level	BUTLER 1959
* Wilson Butte Cave, southern Idaho	GRUHN 1961

Important Sites in Alaska and Canada	
Campus site, central Alaska	RAINEY 1940
Trail Creek site, central Alaska	LARSEN 1951
Denbigh Flint complex, western Alaska	GIDDINGS 1951, 1954
Kayuk complex, Brooks Range, Alaska	CAMPBELL 1959
Pointed Mountain site, Northwest Territories	MACNEISH 1954, 1959
Acasta Lake site, Northwest Territories	FORBIS 1961

Important Sites of the Plano Culture in the Great Plains	
* Cody complex at Horner site, Wyoming	JEPSEN 1953a, 1953b
* Cody complex at Eden site, Wyoming	HOWARD, SATTERTHWAITE, and BACHE 1941; SATTERTHWAITE 1957
* Cody complex at Claypool site, Colorado	DICK and MOUNTAIN 1960
* Brewster and Sisters Hill sites in Agate Basin, eastern Wyoming	ROBERTS and AGOGINO, personal communications
* Meserve site, Nebraska	SCHULTZ 1932
* Scottsbluff site, Nebraska	BARBOUR and SCHULTZ 1932; SCHULTZ and EISELEY 1935
* Red Smoke and Lime Creek sites, Nebraska	SCHULTZ and FRANKFORTER 1948; DAVIS 1953; DAVIS and SCHULTZ 1952
* Frontier complex at Allen site, Nebraska	HOLDER and WIKE 1949
* Simonsen site, western Iowa	AGOGINO and FRANKFORTER 1960; FRANKFORTER and AGOGINO 1960
* Portales complex at Blackwater Draw site, top level, eastern New Mexico	SELLARDS 1952
* Portales complex at Milnesand site, eastern New Mexico	SELLARDS 1955
* San Jon site, eastern New Mexico	ROBERTS 1942
* Plainview site, Texas Panhandle	SELLARDS et al. 1947

TABLE 5—*Continued*

Important Sites of the Plano Culture in the Eastern United States	References
Graham Cave, Missouri; lowest levels	LOGAN 1952
Dalton site, Missouri; lowest levels	LOGAN 1952
Modoc Rockshelter, Illinois; lowest levels	FOWLER 1959*a*, 1959*b*
Starved Rock site, Illinois; lowest levels	MAYER-OAKES 1951
Russell Cave, Alabama; lowest levels	MILLER 1956
* Several sites in Missouri and Midwest where mastodons may be associated with this stage	WILLIAMS 1957
"Aqua-Plano Culture" in Great Lakes region	QUIMBY 1960
Blanchard River sites, northwestern Ohio	JOHNSON and NEILL 1961
For these and other sites see	MASON 1962 and commentators

Important Sites in Central and Southern Mexico	
Chalco complex ("culture"), central Mexico	DE TERRA, in DE TERRA, ROMERO, and STEWART 1949
Coxcatlán and El Riego complexes in lowest levels of many caves in State of Puebla, Mexico; and Santa Marta complex, Chiapas	MACNEISH 1961*a*, 1961*b*, 1961*c*

* Associated extinct fauna.

in 1957, has been remeasured at 9350 ± 160 years ago by conversion to carbon dioxide (Damon and Long 1962). Ages of 8270 ± 250 and 8240 ± 960 years ago on charcoal from the Sulphur Spring and Cazador complexes, respectively, and of 4960 ± 300 years ago on organic soil from the Chiricahua have also been obtained (Damon and Long 1962). While the Sulphur Spring complex is the only one in the sequence to reveal extinct late Pleistocene mammals (mammoth, horse, and dire wolf) in some quantity, all the complexes show common use of manos and milling stones for grinding vegetal foods. Haury (1960), presumably writing before the remeasured date of 9350 ± 160 years ago was available, estimated that the Cochise sequence began about 9000 years ago and that some Pleistocene fauna, including mammoth, was still extant in southern Arizona by 7000 or 8000 years ago. Unlike many authors, Haury is not disturbed by longer survival of such fauna in some parts of western North America than in others, even to overlapping a well-established food-grinding economy. Needless to say, I agree completely with Haury's flexible interpretation of such situations, this being only one of many in which *some* lingering Pleistocene mammals continued into what is here called a Protoarchaic stage marked by food-grinding implements.

Frightful Cave in Coahuila, Mexico (Taylor 1956), has a date of 7300 ± 370 years ago from its *bottom* level but 8023 ± 350 and 8870 ± 350 years ago from the *middle* level. Caves, unfortunately, often present confused stratigraphic order, resulting, probably, from the activities of the people who lived in them, digging fire pits, graves, or cache pits and thereby bringing older objects up to higher levels.

The Ventana complex, based on the two bottom levels in Ventana Cave in southwestern Arizona (Haury *et al.* 1950), has usually been regarded as unquestionably Paleo-Indian because of cultural material associated with abundant remains of late Pleistocene mammals, namely, horse (by far the most frequent), four-horned antelope, dire wolf, ground sloth, bison, and extinct forms of tapir and jaguar. The basal stratum, termed the "conglomerate," produced only two artifacts, a scraper and a possible hammerstone. Overlying it was the "volcanic debris" containing ninety artifacts, only two of which are projectile points. One of these, called "Folsom-like" by Haury although unfluted, has always seemed to me closer to the Plainview type; the other is a broad object with a short stem which does not resemble anything else from an early context. The volcanic debris also produced a circular mano with parallel faces, strikingly like those found by Bird (1938) in Patagonian Chile. Moreover, the hammerstone from the conglomerate, also circular, resembles this mano in shape. Recently, charcoal from a "lower member" of the volcanic debris bears a radiocarbon date of $11,300 \pm 1200$ years ago (Damon and Long 1962). In standard parlance for this method, there are two chances out of three that the true age of the charcoal lies between 12,500 and 10,100 years ago. Assignment of the Ventana complex to a Protoarchaic stage because of the manos is therefore open to question; it might just as logically be considered Paleo-Indian with a provision that food-grinding implements had begun to be used in that stage but were exceedingly rare.

The establishment of chronological ordering in a great deal of archeological material in southern California has been a nightmare for many years. Wallace (1954) began to unravel this with his definition of an Early Milling Stone Culture, which, as the name implies, requires food-grinding implements as a major criterion. Eberhart (1961) and Warren and True (1961) have published further interpretations of chronology that make good sense, so there seems no doubt that complexes like La Jolla, Topanga I, Oak Grove, Little Sycamore, etc., all belong in a Protoarchaic stage, while Lake Mohave is Paleo-Indian because it lacks food-grinding. These authors tend to set a date of about 9000 years ago for the dividing line, which may be approximately correct. There is no need to confuse this southern California material with the Old Cordilleran Culture of the Pacific Northwest, as Warren and True (1961) have shown. Whether or not it should also be clearly separated from the Desert Culture is a moot question: milling stones and manos are held in common, but there are also differences, not only in artifacts but in environmental adaptations, for the Pacific littoral in California is a very distinct geographical region from the far more arid interior deserts.

In summary, food-grinding implements were almost certainly well established over great areas of North America by 9000 years ago. There are indications that the date should be about 10,000 years ago rather than 9000, which means that they follow directly on the disappearance of fluted-point cultures and may even overlap them in some areas, but this remains to be demonstrated more precisely.

Discussion. Table 6 is only a sampling. The reader will find many more localities of comparable material in the monograph of Rex González (1960) and the article by Lanning and Hammel (1961). The dating centers on two situations. At Intihuasi Cave in San Luis Province, there are two radiocarbon dates on level IV, the lowest:

TABLE 6

Important Sites in South America	References
Lauricocha Gaves, Department of Huánuco, Peru; levels II and III	CARDICH 1958; author's notes
Ichuña Rockshelter, department of Puno, Peru	MENGHIN and SCHROEDER 1957
El Inga site, near Quito, Ecuador	MAYER-OAKES and BELL 1960; BELL 1960; author's notes
Viscanchañi complexes II and III, Bolivia	MENGHIN 1953–54
Ayampitín complex, province of Córdoba, central Argentina	REX GONZÁLEZ 1952, 1960; author's notes
Intihuasi Cave, province of San Luis, central Argentina	REX GONZÁLEZ 1952, 1960
Ongamira Cave, province of Córdoba, central Argentina; lowest levels	REX GONZÁLEZ 1952; author's notes
* Toldense complexes I and II, Los Toldos caves, territory of Santa Cruz, Argentina	MENGHIN 1952; author's notes
Casapadrense complex, Los Toldos caves; upper levels	MENGHIN 1952; author's notes
* Magellan Period I, Palli Aike and Fell's caves, Province of Magallanes, Chile	BIRD 1938
Magellan Periods II and III, same caves	BIRD 1938

* Associated extinct fauna.

7970 ± 100 and 8068 ± 95 years ago (Rex González 1960), which make it certain that manos and milling stones were established in central Argentina by 8000 years ago, along with bifacially chipped projectile points of lanceolate shape and/or knives and other artifacts. Virtually identical points and/or knives are characteristic of the Ayampitín site in Córdoba Province, which Rex González regards as closely related and contemporaneous with Intihuasi Cave, level IV, and with Lauricocha II and III in the Peruvian highlands, where a date of about 8000 years ago is also postulated because Lauricocha I, beneath them, has one date of about 9500 years ago.

Rex González also relates the Huancayo and Ichuña rockshelters of Peru, the Viscanchani complexes II and III in Bolivia, Toldense complexes I and II, and Bird's Magellan period III to Ayampitín and Intihuasi, lowest level (IV), in their common possession of lanceolate and triangular projectile points, food-grinding implements, and other arti-

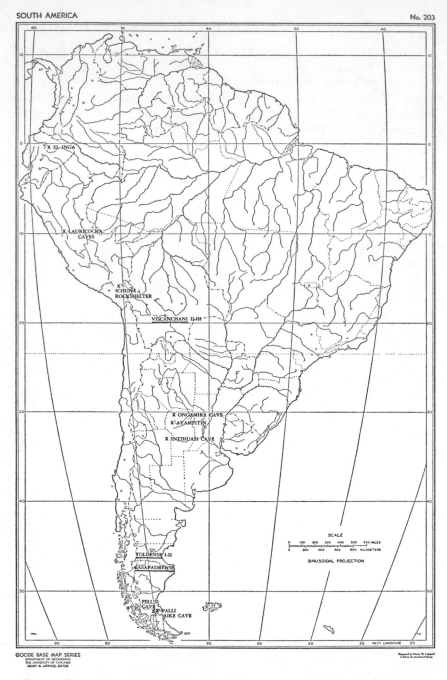

GOODE BASE MAP SERIES
DEPARTMENT OF GEOGRAPHY
THE UNIVERSITY OF CHICAGO
HENRY M. LEPPARD, EDITOR

FIG. 6.—Some sites and complexes assigned to a Protoarchaic stage in South America. Single sites, or several closely related sites for which no "complex" has yet been defined, are marked by ✕. Recognized complexes, or equivalent cultural units, are placed in their approximate locations and underscored. In stratified sites it is usually, but not always, the lowest level that is assigned to this stage, and in some cases more than one level is so assigned. For additional sites in southern South America see Rex González (1960); for western and southern South America see Lanning and Hammel (1961).

facts, so that a very widespread *culture* should be named from these and other sites. Ongamira Cave and the Casapadrense complex, also in Argentina, are later estimated as beginning about 6000 years ago.

The second dating situation is posed by Bird's Magellan I period in Palli Aike and Fell's caves near the Strait of Magellan in Chile. The lowest level of Palli Aike has one date of 8639 ± 400 years ago obtained on burned bone, while charcoal from a fire pit in "the oldest occupation layer" of Fell's Cave measured 10,720 ± 300 years ago. For these dates and for the one from Mylodon Cave, Chile, see Rubin and Berthold (1961). The interesting thing is that Bird (1938) illustrates, not only a number of *stemmed* projectile points, one lanceolate point very much like the Plainview type in North America, and bone implements, but also two very well made, circular "rubbing stones" with flat faces. If the rubbing stones are not manos, at least they were shaped by pecking. Both caves had remains of extinct horse and ground sloth in their lowest levels. Unfortunately, no exact provenience data are given in Bird's publication, hence I am a little doubtful that the date of 10,720 ± 300 years ago positively applies to the stemmed points, the rubbing stones (manos?), and the Plainview-like point. The date of 8639 ± 400 years ago from Palli Aike would seem more in keeping with such traits in Argentina and also in North America.

While North America would seem to be too far away to have any direct bearing on cultures or their dates in extreme southern South America, I must mention my astonishment at seeing, in the museum of the Universidad Nacional de Córdoba, several dozen projectile points from that province, as well as the territories of Neuquén and Chubut in Patagonia, which would be very difficult to distinguish from such types in the Plano Culture of the Great Plains and Texas as *Plainview*, *Lerma*, and *Angostura*, not only in shape, but in the smoothing of their basal edges. Rex González (1960) also illustrates triangular points with beveled edges and thinned bases that seem identical to the *Tortugas* type in Texas, and others like the *Gary* type in eastern Texas and the eastern United States in preceramic cultures. All the above-named types are described in Suhm, Krieger, and Jelks (1954).

A lithic complex from the Huancayo rockshelters, department of Junín, central highlands of Peru, was described as preceramic by Tschopik (1946). On the basis of controlled excavations, however, Lanning and Hammel (1961) deny that this material can be isolated from ceramic horizons, hence it is omitted from Table 6.

The El Inga site in Ecuador (Bell 1960; Mayer-Oakes and Bell 1960) contains stemmed projectile points resembling those from Bird's Period I in Fell's and Palli Aike caves, some of which have crude fluting in the stems. The fragmentary artifacts that Bell and Mayer-Oakes call bases of Clovis points are plainly broken-off stems of the kind of projectiles just mentioned. Their estimate of 10,000 years or more for the El Inga material seems excessive to me, for some artifact forms are present that do not seem to appear in either of the older stages discussed above for South America, and the entire complex labeled "El Inga" consists of obsidian, a material not used in South America until relatively late preceramic times. Lanning and Hammel (1961) offer two positions for El Inga in their chronological chart; my guess is that the younger one, at about 3000 B.C., is about right.

CONCLUSIONS

I have by no means discussed all the available material bearing on early man in the New World. I have done little more than indicate the scope of the problem through a system of culture stages, intended to provide a framework or basis of organization for both continents and try to simplify that organization by using a minimum of technical terms, with consistency.

The most surprising result of this study is that all three of the preceramic stages outlined here not only are of vast extent on both continents but reach all the way to the southern tip of South America. So does a fourth stage, the Archaic or Full Archaic, which is characterized by intentional shaping of stone artifacts by grinding and polishing and many other new traits but which I have not attempted to discuss under the heading of "early man."

It seems clear enough that on both continents, even to Tierra del Fuego, projectile points and knives of equivalent technology occur throughout postglacial time, some 10,000 or 11,000 years. In North America some forms appeared even earlier, some 13,000 years ago or more. This is possible in South America, too, but evidence is lacking for want of objective datings.

What can be said of the age of the Pre–Projectile Point stage? In North America only a few of the many localities have been dated, but those that have suggest a beginning far back in the Wisconsin glacial period, possibly as long as 35,000 or 40,000 years ago. An assumed diffusion from north to south would mean that South American localities are somewhat younger, but how much? In the Paleo-Indian and Proto-archaic stages, datings in both North and South America are amazingly similar, even to Patagonia and Tierra del Fuego, so possibly there is not much difference in the Pre–Projectile Point stage either.

BIBLIOGRAPHY

AGOGINO, GEORGE A.
  1961 "A New Point Type from Hell Gap Valley, Eastern Wyoming."
        Amer. Antiquity, 26:558–60.

AGOGINO, GEORGE A., and W. D. FRANKFORTER
 1960   "A Paleo-Indian Bison-Kill in Northwestern Iowa." *Amer. Antiquity*, 25:414–15.
ARNOLD, BRIGHAM A.
 1957   *Late Pleistocene and Recent Changes in Land Forms, Climate, and Archaeology in Central Baja California*, pp. 201–318. (Univ. Calif. Pub. Geog. 100.)
AVELEYRA ARROYO DE ANDA, LUIS
 1950   *Prehistoria de Mexico*. Mexico, D.F.: Ediciones Mexicanas, S.A.
 1956   "The Second Mammoth and Associated Artifacts at Santa Isabel Iztapan, Mexico." *Amer. Antiquity*, 22:12–28.
 1962   *Antigüedad del hombre en México y Centroamerica: Catalogo razonado de localidades y bibliografia selecta (1867–1961)*. (Cuadernos del Instituto de Historia "Serie Antropológica," No. 14.) Mexico, D.F.: Universidad Nacional Autónoma de México.
AVELEYRA ARROYO DE ANDA, LUIS, and MANUEL MALDONADO-KOERDELL
 1953   "Association of Artifacts with Mammoth in the Valley of Mexico." *Amer. Antiquity*, 18:332–40.
BAGGERLY, CARMEN
 1954   "Waterworn and Glaciated Stone Tools from the Thumb District of Michigan." *Amer. Antiquity*, 20:171–73.
BARBOUR, E. H., and C. BERTRAND SCHULTZ
 1932   *The Scottsbluff Bison Quarry and Its Artifacts*. (Neb. State Mus. Bull. 34.) Lincoln.
BARFIELD, LAWRENCE
 1961   "Recent Discoveries in the Atacama Desert and the Bolivian Altiplano." *Amer. Antiquity*, 27:93–100.
BARTLETT, KATHERINE
 1943   "A Primitive Stone Industry of the Little Colorado Valley, Arizona." *Amer. Antiquity*, 8:266–68.
BEARDSLEY, RICHARD K., *et al.*
 1956   "Functional and Evolutionary Implications of Community Patterning." Pp. 129–57 in ROBERT WAUCHOPE (ed.), *Seminars in Archaeology, 1955*. (Soc. Amer. Arch. Mem. 11.) Salt Lake City.
BELL, ROBERT E.
 1960   "Evidence of a Fluted Point Tradition in Ecuador." *Amer. Antiquity*, 26:103–6.
BIRD, JUNIUS B.
 1938   "Antiquity and Migrations of the Early Inhabitants of Patagonia." *Geog. Rev.*, 28:250–75.
 1943   "Excavations in Northern Chile." *Amer. Mus. Nat. Hist. Anthrop. Paps.*, 38:171–318.
BORDEN, CHARLES E.
 1957   "DjRi 3, An Early Site in the Fraser Canyon, British Columbia." Pp. 101–18 in *Contribs. to Anthrop., 1957*. (Nat. Mus. Canada Bull. 162, "Anthrop. Ser.," No. 4.) Ottawa.
 1961   "Fraser River Archaeological Project." *Nat. Mus. Canada Anthrop Paps.*, No. 10, pp. 1–6. Ottawa.

Bórmida, Marcelo
    1960   *Investigaciones paleontológicas en la region de Bolivar (Pcia. de Buenos Aires).* ("Comisión de Investigación Científica," Vol. 1.) La Plata, Argentina.

Bryan, Kirk
    1939   "Stone Cultures near Cerro Pedernal and Their Geological Antiquity." *Tex. Arch. & Paleont. Soc. Bull.*, 11:9–42.

Bryan, Kirk, and Joseph H. Toulouse, Jr.
    1943   "The San Jose Non-Ceramic Culture and Its Relation to a Puebloan Culture in New Mexico." *Amer. Antiquity*, 8:269–80.

Bürgl, Hans
    1958   "Artefactos paleolíticos de una tumba en Garzón (Huila)." *Revista Colombiana de Antropología*, 6:7–28. Bogotá.

Butler, B. Robert
    1958   "Ash Cave (45WW61): A Preliminary Report." *Wash. Archaeologist*, 2 (No. 12): 3–10.
    1959   "Lower Columbia Valley Archaeology: A Survey and Appraisal of Some Major Archaeological Resources." *Tebiwa: Jour. Idaho State Coll. Mus.*, 2:6–24.
    1961   *The Old Cordilleran Culture in the Pacific Northwest.* ("Idaho State Coll. Mus. Occ. Paps.," No. 5.) Pocatello.

Byers, Douglas S.
    1954   "Bull Brook—a Fluted Point Site in Ipswich, Massachusetts." *Amer. Antiquity*, 19:343–51.
    1955   "Additional Information on the Bull Brook Site, Massachusetts." *Ibid.*, 20:274–76.
    1959a   "An Introduction to Five Papers on the Archaic Stage." *Ibid.*, 24: 229–32.
    1959b   "The Eastern Archaic: Some Problems and Hypotheses." *Ibid.*, pp. 233–56.

Campbell, Elizabeth W. Crozer, and William H. Campbell
    1937   "The Lake Mohave Site." Pp. 9–24 in Campbell *et al.*, *The Archology of Pleistocene Lake Mohave: A Symposium.* ("Southwest Mu Paps.," No. 11.) Los Angeles.

Campbell, John M.
    1959   "The Kayuk Complex of Arctic Alaska." *Amer. Antiquity*, 25:⁵ 105.

Campbell, John M.
    1961   The Kogruk Complex of Anaktuvuk Pass, Alaska. *Anthropolo* n.s., 3 (No. 1):3–20. The Canadian Research Center for Anth U. of Ottawa, Canada.

Canals Frau, Salvador
    1950   *Prehistoria de America.* Buenos Aires: Editorial Sudamericana.

Capdeville, Augusto
    1921–22   "Notas acerca de la arqueología de Taltal." *Boletín de la Ac Nacional de Historia*, 2:1–16, 256–61; 3:229–33. Quito.
    1922   "Apuntes para la arqueología de Taltal." *Ibid.*, 4:115–18. Q

CARDICH, AUGUSTO
  1958 *Los yacimientos de Lauricocha, nuevas interpretaciones de la prehistoria peruana.* (Centro de Estudios Prehistoricos, "Studia Praehistorica," Vol. I.) Buenos Aires.
CARTER, GEORGE F.
  1957 *Pleistocene Man at San Diego.* Baltimore: Johns Hopkins Press.
CASAMIQUELA, RODOLFO M.
  1961 "Dos nuevos yacimientos patagónicos de la cultura Jacobaccense." (Universidad Nacional de La Plata [Facultad de Ciéncias Naturales y Museo, Sección de Antropología], 5:171–78.) La Plata.
CIGLIANO, EDUARDO MARIO
  1961 "Noticia sobre una nueva industria precerámica en el valle de Santa María (Catamarca): el Ampajanguense." *Anales de Arqueología y Etnología. Universidad Nacional de Cuyo*, 16:169–79. Mendoza, Argentina.
COLLINS, HENRY B.
  1954 "Archaeological Research in the North American Arctic." Pp. 184–94 in *Arctic Res.* (Arctic Inst. North America Spec. Pub. 2.)
COWLES, JOHN
  1960 *Cougar Mountain Cave.* Rainier, Ore.: Privately printed.
CRANE, H. R.
  1956 "University of Michigan Radiocarbon Dates I." *Science*, 124:664–72.
CRESSMAN, L. S.
  1942 *Archaeological Researches in the Northern Great Basin.* (Carnegie Inst. Wash. Pub. 538.) Washington, D.C.
  1960 "Cultural Sequences at the Dalles, Oregon." *Amer. Phil. Soc. Trans.*, 50:1–108.
CROOK, WILSON W., JR., and R. K. HARRIS
  1957 "Hearths and Artifacts of Early Man near Lewisville, Texas, and Associated Faunal Material." *Bull. Tex. Arch. Soc.*, 28:7–97.
  1958 "A Pleistocene Campsite near Lewisville, Texas." *Amer. Antiquity*, 23:233–46.
CRUXENT, JOSÉ M.
  1962 "Artifacts of Paleo-Indian Type, Maracaibo, Zulia, Venezuela." *Amer. Antiquity*, 27:576–79.
CRUXENT, JOSÉ M., and IRVING ROUSE
  1956 "A Lithic Industry of Paleo-Indian Type in Venezuela." *Amer. Antiquity*, 22:172–79. (See also ROUSE and CRUXENT.)
DAMON, PAUL E., and AUSTIN LONG
  1962 "Arizona Radiocarbon Dates III." *Radiocarbon*, 4:239–49. Published by the American Journal of Science, Yale University, New Haven, Conn.
DAUGHERTY, RICHARD D.
  1956a "Archaeology of the Lind Coulee Site, Washington." *Amer. Phil. Soc. Proc.*, 100:223–78. Philadelphia.

DAUGHERTY, RICHARD D.
1956b *Early Man in the Columbia Intermontane Province.* ("Univ. Utah Anthrop. Paps.," No. 24.) Salt Lake City.
DAVIS, E. MOTT
1953 "Recent Data from Two Paleo-Indian Sites on Medicine Creek, Nebraska." *Amer. Antiquity,* 18:380–86.
DAVIS, E. MOTT, and C. BERTRAND SCHULTZ
1952 "The Archaeological and Paleontological Salvage Program at the Medicine Creek Reservoir, Frontier County, Nebraska." *Science,* 115:288–90.
DE TERRA, HELMUT, JAVIER ROMERO, and T. D. STEWART
1949 *Tepexpan Man.* ("Viking Fund Pub. Anthrop.," No. 11.) New York.
DICK, HERBERT, and BERT MOUNTAIN
1960 "The Claypool Site: A Cody Complex Site in Northeastern Colorado." *Amer. Antiquity,* 26:223–35.
EBERHART, HAL
1961 "The Cogged Stones of Southern California." *Amer. Antiquity,* 26:361–70.
EVANS, GLEN L.
1961 *The Friesenhahn Cave.* (Tex. Mem. Mus. Bull. 2.) Austin.
FARMER, MALCOLM F.
1960 "A Note on the Distribution of the Metate and Muller." *Tebiwa: Jour. Idaho State Coll. Mus.,* 3:31–38.
FORBIS, RICHARD G.
1961 "Early Point Types from Acasta Lake, Northwest Territories, Canada." *Amer. Antiquity,* 27:112–13.
FOWLER, MELVIN L.
1959a "Modoc Rock Shelter, an Early Archaic Site in Southern Illinois." *Amer. Antiquity,* 24:257–69.
1959b *Modoc Rock Shelter: A Summary and Analysis of Four Seasons of Excavations.* (Ill. State Mus. Rpt. Invest., No. 8.) Springfield, Ill.
FRANKFORTER, W. D., and GEORGE A. AGOGINO
1960 "The Simonsen Site: Report for the Summer of 1959." *Plains Anthropologist,* 5:65–70.
GIDDINGS, J. L., JR.
1951 "The Denbigh Flint Complex." *Amer. Antiquity,* 16:193–202.
1954 "Early Man in the Arctic." *Scient. American,* 190:82–89.
GRIFFIN, JAMES B.
1953 *United States and Canada: Indigenous Period.* (Instituto Panamericano de Geografía e Historia, Comisión de Historia Pub. 51.) Mexico, D.F.
GRUHN, RUTH
1961 *The Archaeology of Wilson Butte Cave, South-Central Idaho.* ("Idaho State Coll. Mus. Occ. Paps.," No. 6.) Pocatello.
HARRINGTON, MARK RAYMOND
1933 *Gypsum Cave, Nevada.* ("Southwest Mus. Paps.," No. 8.) Los Angeles.
1948 *An Ancient Site at Borax Lake, California.* ("Southwest Mus. Paps.," No. 16.) Los Angeles.

HARRINGTON, MARK RAYMOND, and RUTH DeETTE SIMPSON
1961   *Tule Springs, Nevada: With Other Evidences of Pleistocene Man in North America.* ("Southwest Mus. Paps.," No. 18.) Los Angeles.

HAURY, EMIL W.
1953   "Artifacts with Mammoth Remains, Naco, Arizona." *Amer. Antiquity*, 19:1–14.
1960   "Association of Fossil Fauna and Artifacts of the Sulphur Spring Stage, Cochise Culture." *Ibid.*, 25:609–10.

HAURY, EMIL W., KIRK BRYAN, EDWIN H. COLBERT, NORMAN E. GABEL, CLARA LEE TANNER, and T. F. BUEHRER
1950   *The Stratigraphy and Archeology of Ventana Cave, Arizona.* Albuquerque: University of New Mexico Press.

HAURY, EMIL W., E. B. SAYLES, and WILLIAM W. WASLEY
1959   "The Lehner Mammoth Site, Southeastern Arizona." *Amer. Antiquity*, 25:2–30.

HAYNES, VANCE, and GEORGE AGOGINO
1960   "Geological Significance of a New Radiocarbon Date from the Lindenmeier Site." *Denver Mus. Nat. Hist. Proc.*, No. 9. Denver.

HEIZER, ROBERT F.
1951   "Preliminary Report on the Leonard Rockshelter Site, Pershing County, Nevada." *Amer. Antiquity*, 17:89–97.

HEIZER, ROBERT F., and EDWIN M. LEMERT
1947   "Observations on Archaeological Sites in Topanga Canyon, California." *Univ. Calif. Pub. Amer. Arch. & Ethnol.*, 44:237–58.

HESTER, JIM J.
1960   "Late Pleistocene Extinction and Radiocarbon Dating." *Amer. Antiquity*, 26:58–77.

HIBBEN, FRANK C.
1941   *Evidences of Early Occupation in Sandia Cave, New Mexico, and Other Sites in the Sandia-Manzano Region.* ("Smithsonian Misc. Coll.," Vol. 99, No. 23.) Washington, D.C.

HOLDER, PRESTON, and JOYCE WIKE
1949   "The Frontier Culture Complex: A Preliminary Report on a Prehistoric Hunters' Camp in Southwestern Nebraska." *Amer. Antiquity*, 14:260–66.

HOPKINS, M. L., and B. ROBERT BUTLER
1961   "Remarks on a Notched Fossil Bison Ischium." *Tebiwa: Jour. Idaho State Coll. Mus.*, 4 (No. 2):10–18.

HOWARD, EDGAR B., LINTON SATTERTHWAITE, JR., and CHARLES BACHE
1941   "Preliminary Report on a Buried Yuma Site in Wyoming." *Amer. Antiquity*, 7:70–74.

HRDLIČKA, ALEŠ
1907   *Skeletal Remains Suggesting or Attributed to Early Man in North America.* (Bur. Amer. Ethnol., Bull. 33.) Washington, D.C.
1912   "The Skeletal Remains of Early Man in South America." Chap. 7 in HRDLIČKA *et al.*, *Early Man in South America* (Bur. Amer. Ethnol. Bull. 52.) Washington, D.C.

HUNT, ALICE
   1960   *Archeology of the Death Valley Salt Pan, California.* ("Univ. Utah An-throp. Paps.," No. 47.) Salt Lake City.
HURT, WESLEY, R., JR.
   1953   "A Comparative Study of the Preceramic Occupations of North America." *Amer. Antiquity*, 18:204–22.
   1962   "New and Revised Radiocarbon Dates from Brazil." *Museum News* (W. H. Over Mus., State Univ. of South Dakota), 23 (Nos. 11, 12): 1–4.
JENKS, ALBERT E.
   1937   *Minnesota's Brown's Valley Man and Associated Burial Artifacts.* (Amer. Anthrop. Assoc. Mem. 49.) Menasha, Wis.
JENNINGS, JESSE D.
   1955   *The Archeology of the Plains: An Assessment.* Salt Lake City: Depart-ment of Anthropology, University of Utah, and the National Park Service.
   1957   *Danger Cave.* (Soc. Amer. Arch. Mem. 14.) Salt Lake City: The Society and University of Utah Press.
JENNINGS, JESSE D. (ed.)
   1956   "The American Southwest: A Problem in Cultural Isolation." Pp. 59–127 in ROBERT WAUCHOPE (ed.), *Seminars in Archaeology, 1955.* (Soc. Amer. Arch. Mem. 11.) Salt Lake City.
JENNINGS, JESSE D., and EDWARD NORBECK
   1955   "Great Basin Prehistory: A Review." *Amer. Antiquity*, 21:1–11.
JEPSEN, GLENN L.
   1953a   "Ancient Buffalo Hunters of Northwestern Wyoming." *Southwestern Lore*, 19:19–25.
   1953b   "Ancient Buffalo Hunters." *Princeton Alumni Weekly*, 53:10–12.
JOHNSON, FREDERICK, and JOHN P. MILLER
   1958   *Review of* G. F. CARTER, *Pleistocene Man at San Diego. Amer. Antiq-uity*, 24:206–10.
JOHNSON, FREDERICK, and O. J. NEILL
   1961   "Some Ancient Sites in Greensberg and Ottawa Townships, Putnam County, Ohio." *Amer. Antiquity*, 26:420–26.
KELLEY, J. CHARLES
   1959   "The Desert Cultures and the Balcones Phase: Archaic Manifesta-tions in the Southwest and Texas." *Amer. Antiquity*, 24:276–88.
KENNERLY, T. E.
   1956   "Comparisons between Fossil and Recent Species of the Genus *Perog-nathus.*" *Tex. Jour. Sci.*, 8:74–86.
KRIEGER, ALEX D.
   1947   "Certain Projectile Points of the Early American Hunters." *Tex. Arch. & Paleont. Soc. Bull.*, 18:7–27.
   1953   "Basic Stages of Cultural Evolution." Pp. 247–50 in SOL TAX *et al.* (eds.), *An Appraisal of Anthropology Today.* Chicago: University of Chicago Press.

1954 *Comment on* John Witthoft, "Fluted Point Relationships." *Amer. Antiquity*, 19:273–75.
1957 "Notes and News: Early Man." *Ibid.*, 22:321–23.
1958 *Review of* George F. Carter, *Pleistocene Man at San Diego. Amer. Anthropologist*, 60:974–78.
1962 "The Earliest Cultures in the Western United States." *Amer. Antiquity*, 28:138–43.

Laming, Annette, and José Emperaire
1959 *A jazida José Vieira: Um sitio Guaraní e pre-cerámico do interior do Paraná.* (Universidade do Paraná, Departmento do Antropología, "Communicaçãos Avulsas," No. 1.) Curitiba, Paraná, Brazil.

Lanning, E. P., and E. A. Hammel
1961 "Early Lithic Industries of Western South America." *Amer. Antiquity*, 27:139–54.

Larsen, Helge
1951 *De Dansk-Ameríkanske Alaska-Ekspeditioner, 1949–1951.* ("Saetryk af Geografisk Tidsskrift," Vol. 51.) Copenhagen.

Lee, Thomas E.
1957 "The Antiquity of the Shequiandah Site." *Canadian Field-Naturalist*, 71:117–37. Ottawa.

LePaige, Gustavo R. P.
1958 "Antiguas culturas atacameñas en la cordillera chilena." *Revista Universitaria, Universidad Católica de Chile*, 43:139–65. Santiago.
1960 "Antiguas culturas atacameñas en la cordillera chilena." *Ibid.*, 44–45:191–206.

Logan, Wilfred D.
1952 *Graham Cave, an Archaic Site in Montgomery County, Missouri.* (Mo. Arch. Soc. Mem. 2.) Columbia.

Lundelius, Ernest L., Jr.
1960 *Mylohyus nasutus: Long-nosed Peccary of the Texas Pleistocene.* Tex. Mem. Mus. Bull. 1.) Austin.

Macgowan, Kenneth
1950 *Early Man in the New World.* New York: Macmillan Co.

Macgowan, Kenneth, and Joseph A. Hester, Jr.
1962 *Early Man in the New World.* New York and Garden City: American Museum of Natural History and Doubleday & Co.

MacNeish, Richard S.
1954 "The Pointed Mountain Site near Fort Liard, Northwest Territories, Canada." *Amer. Antiquity*, 19:234–53.
1958 "Preliminary Archaeological Investigations in the Sierra de Tamaulipas, Mexico." *Amer. Phil. Soc. Trans.*, 48:1–210.
1959 "Men Out of Asia; as Seen from the Northwest Yukon." *Univ. Alaska Anthrop. Paps.*, 7:41–70.
1961a *Tehuacán Archaeological-Botanical Project, No. 1.* Andover, Mass.: Robert S. Peabody Foundation for Archaeology.
1961b "Recent Finds Concerned with the Incipient Agriculture Stage in Prehistoric Mesoamerica." Pp. 91–102 in *Homenaje a Pablo Martínez*

del Río, en el 25° aniversario de la primera edición de "Los Orígenes Americanos." Mexico, D.F.

1961c   *Restos precerámicos de la cueva de Coxcatlán en el sur de Puebla.* (Instituto Nacional de Antropología e Historia, "Publicaciones del Dirección de Prehistoria," No. 10.) Mexico, D.F.

MALDONADO-KOERDELL, MANUEL, and LUIS AVELEYRA ARROYO DE ANDA
1949   "Nota preliminar sobre dos artefactos del Pleistoceno superior hallados en la region de Tequixquiác, Mexico." *El Mexico Antiguo*, 7:154–61. Mexico, D.F.

MARTÍNEZ DEL RÍO, PABLO
1952   *Los Orígenes Americanos.* (Tercera edición. Páginas del Siglo XX. Mexico, D.F.)

MASON, RONALD J.
1962   "The Paleo-Indian Tradition in Eastern North America." *Cur. Anthropology*, 3:227–78.

MASON, RONALD J., and CAROL IRWIN
1960   "An Eden-Scottsbluff Burial in Northeastern Wisconsin." *Amer. Antiquity*, 26:43–57.

MAYER-OAKES, WILLIAM J.
1951   "Starved Rock Archaic: A Prepottery Horizon from Northern Illinois." *Amer. Antiquity*, 16:313–24.

MAYER-OAKES, WILLIAM J., and ROBERT E. BELL
1960   "Early Man Site Found in Highland Ecuador." *Science*, 131:1805–6.

MEIGHAN, CLEMENT W.
1959   "Californian Cultures and the Concept of an Archaic Stage." *Amer. Antiquity*, 24:289–305.

MENGHIN, OSVALDO F. A.
1952   "Fundamentos cronológicos de la prehistoria de Patagonia." *RUNA* (*Archivo para las Ciéncias del Hombre*), 5:23–43. Buenos Aires.

1953–54   "Culturas precerámicas en Bolivia." *Ibid.*, 6:125–32.

1955–56   "El Altoparanense." *Revista Ampurias*, 17–18: 171–200. Barcelona.

1957a   "Vorgeschichte Amerikas." Pp. 162–218 in *Abriss der Vorgeschichte*. Munich: Verlag von R. Oldenbourg.

1957b   "Das Protolithikum in Amerika." *Acta Praehistorica* (*Centro Argentino de Estudios Prehistóricos*), 1:5–40. Buenos Aires.

MENGHIN, OSVALDO F. A., and MARCELO BÓRMIDA
1950   "Investigaciones prehistóricas en cuevas de Tandilia, Provinc a de Buenos Aires." *RUNA* (*Archivo para las Ciéncias del Hombre*), Vol. 3, Parts 1, 2. Buenos Aires.

MENGHIN, OSVALDO F. A., and GERD SCHROEDER
1957   "Un yacimiento en Ichuña (Dep. Puno, Peru) y las industrias precerámicas de los Andes centrales y septentrionales." *Acta Praehistorica* (*Centro Argentino de Estudios Prehistóricos*), 1:41–56. Buenos Aires.

MILLER, CARL F.
1956   "Life 8,000 Years Ago Uncovered in an Alabama Cave." *Nat. Geog. Mag.*, 110:542–58.

1962 "Early Man in Virginia." Pp. 38–109 in *Archeology of the John H. Kerr Reservoir Basin, Roanoke River, Virginia–North Carolina.* (Bur. Amer. Ethnol. Bull. 182.) Washington, D.C.

MORIARTY, JAMES R., GEORGE SHUMWAY, AND C. N. WARREN
1959 "Scripps Estates Site 1 (SDi-525): A Preliminary Report on an Early Site on the San Diego Coast. Pp. 187–216 in *U.C.L.A. Arch. Surv. Ann. Rpt. 1958–59.* Los Angeles.

ORR, PHIL C.
1956 *Radiocarbon Dates from Santa Rosa Island, I.* (Santa Barbara Mus. Nat. Hist., Dpt. Anthrop. Bull. 2.) Santa Barbara, Calif.
1960a "Late Pleistocene Marine Terraces on Santa Rosa Island, California." *Geol. Soc. America Bull.,* 71:1113–19.
1960b *Radiocarbon Dates from Santa Rosa Island, II.* (Santa Barbara Mus. Nat. Hist., Dpt. Anthrop. Bull. 3.) Santa Barbara, Calif.
1962 *On New Radiocarbon Dates from the California Channel Islands.* (Santa Barbara Mus. Nat. Hist., Dpt. Anthrop. Bull. 8) Santa Barbara, Calif.

PERICOT Y GARCIA, LUIS
1962 *América Indigena.* Vol. I. *El hombre americano, los pueblos de América.* 2d ed. Barcelona, Madrid, Buenos Aires, Mexico, D.F., Caracas, Bogota, and Rio de Janeiro: Salvat Editores, S.A.

PUTNAM, F. W.
1906 "Evidence of the Work of Man on Objects from Quaternary Caves in California." *Amer. Anthropologist,* n.s., 8:229–35.

QUIMBY, GEORGE I.
1954 "Cultural and Natural Areas before Kroeber." *Amer. Antiquity,* 19: 317–31.
1958 "Fluted Points and Geochronology of the Lake Michigan Basin." *Ibid.,* 23:247–54.
1960 *Indian Life in the Upper Great Lakes, 11,000 B.C. to A.D. 1800.* Chicago: University of Chicago Press.

RAINEY, FROELICH
1940 "Archaeological Investigations in Central Alaska." *Amer. Antiquity,* 5:299–308.

RENAUD, E. B.
1938 *The Black's Fork Culture of Southwest Wyoming.* (Univ. Denver Arch. Surv. Western High Plains Rept. 10.) Denver.
1940 *Further Research in the Black's Fork Basin, Southwest Wyoming.* (Univ. Denver Arch. Surv. Western High Plains Rept. 12.) Denver.

REX GONZÁLEZ, ALBERTO
1952 "Antiguo horizonte precerámico en las sierres centrales de la Argentina." *RUNA (Archivo para las Ciéncias del Hombre),* 5:110–33. Buenos Aires.
1960 "La estratigrafia de la gruta de Intihuasi (Prov. de San Luis, R.A.) y sus relaciones con otros sitios precerámicos de Sudamérica." *Revista del Instituto de Antropología, Universidad Nacional de Córdoba,* Vol. I. Cordoba, Argentina.

Rex González, Alberto, and A. M. Lorandi
1959   "Restos arqueológicos hallados en las orillas del Río Carcareñá, Provincia de Santa Fe." *Revista del Instituto de Antropología, Universidad Nacional del Litoral,* 1:161–222. Rosario, Argentina.

Ritchie, William A.
1953   "A Probable Paleo-Indian Site in Vermont." *Amer. Antiquity,* 18:249–58.
1957   *Traces of Early Man in the Northeast.* (N.Y. State Mus. & Sci. Serv. Bull. 358.) Albany.

Roberts, Frank H. H., Jr.
1935   *A Folsom Complex: Preliminary Report on Investigations at the Lindenmeier Site in Northern Colorado.* (Part 4, pp. 1–35, in "Smithsonian Misc. Coll.," Vol. 94.) Washington, D.C.
1936   *Additional Information on the Folsom Complex: Report of the Second Season's Investigations at the Lindenmeier Site in Northern Colorado.* (Part 10, pp. 1–38 in "Smithsonian Misc. Coll.," Vol. 95.) Washington, D.C.
1940   "Developments in the Problem of the North American Paleo-Indian." Pp. 51–116 in *Essays in Historical Anthropology.* ("Smithsonian Misc. Coll.," Vol. 100.) Washington, D.C.
1942   *Archeological and Geological Investigations in the San Jon District, Eastern New Mexico.* (Pp. 1–30 in "Smithsonian Misc. Coll.," Vol. 103.) Washington, D.C.

Rogers, Malcolm J.
1939   *Early Lithic Industries of the Lower Basin of the Colorado River and Adjacent Desert Areas.* ("San Diego Mus. Paps.," No. 3.) San Diego.
1945   "An Outline of Yuman Prehistory." *Southwestern Jour. Anthrop.,* 1:167–98.
1958   "San Dieguito Implements from the Terraces of the Rincon-Pantano and Rillito Drainage System." *Kiva,* 24:1–23. Tucson, Arizona.

Roosa, William B.
1956   "The Lucy Site in Central New Mexico." *Amer. Antiquity,* 21:310.

Rouse, Irving, and José M. Cruxent
1957   "Further Comment on the Finds at El Jobo, Venezuela." *Amer. Antiquity,* 22:412.

Rowe, John Howland
1962   "Stages and Periods in Archaeological Interpretation." *Southwestern Jour. Anthrop.,* 18:40–54.

Royo y Gómez, José
1961   "El yacimiento de vertebrados pleistocenos de Muaco, estado Falcón, Venezuela, con industria lítica humana." *Internat. Geol. Cong., 21st Sess., Norden,* Part 4. Copenhagen.

Rubin, Meyer, and Sarah M. Berthold
1961   "U.S. Geological Survey Radiocarbon Dates VI." *Radiocarbon,* 3:86–98. New Haven, Conn.: Yale University.

Satterthwaite, Linton
1957   *Stone Artifacts at and near the Finley Site, near Eden, Wyoming.* (Univ. Mus., Philadelphia, Monog.) Philadelphia.

SAYLES, E. B., and ERNST ANTEVS
1941 *The Cochise Culture.* ("Gila Pueblo Medallion Paps.," No. 29.) Globe, Ariz.

SCHULTZ, C. BERTRAND
1932 "Association of Artifacts and Extinct Mammals in Nebraska." *Neb. Mus. Bull.*, 33:171–83.

SCHULTZ, C. BERTRAND, and L. C. EISELEY
1935 "Paleontological Evidence of the Antiquity of the Scottsbluff Basin Quarry and Its Associated Artifacts." *Amer. Anthropologist*, 37:306–19.

SCHULTZ, C. BERTRAND, and W. D. FRANKFORTER
1948 "Preliminary Report on the Lime Creek Sites: New Evidence of Early Man in Southwestern Nebraska." *Univ. Neb. State Mus. Bull.*, 3:43–62.

SELLARDS, E. H.
1941 "Stone Images from Henderson County, Texas." *Amer. Antiquity*, 7:29–38.
1952 *Early Man in America: A Study in Prehistory.* Austin: University of Texas Press.
1955 "Fossil Bison and Associated Artifacts from Milnesand, New Mexico." *Amer. Antiquity*, 20:336–44.
1960 "Some Early Stone Artifact Developments in North America." *Southwestern Jour. Anthrop.*, 16:160–73.

SELLARDS, E. H., GLEN L. EVANS, GRAYSON E. MEADE, and ALEX D. KRIEGER
1947 "Fossil Bison and Associated Artifacts from Plainview, Texas." *Geol. Soc. America Bull.*, 58:927–54.

SIMPSON, RUTH D.
1958 "The Manix Lake Archeological Survey." *Masterkey*, 32 (Part 1): 4–10.
1960 "Archeological Survey of the Eastern Calico Mountains." *Ibid.*, 34 (Part 1):25–35.
1961 *Coyote Gulch: Archeological Investigations of an Early Lithic Locality in the Mohave Desert of San Bernardino County.* ("Arch. Surv. Assoc. Southern Calif. Paps.," No. 5.) Los Angeles.

SINCLAIR, W. J.
1904 *The Exploration of the Potter Creek Cave.* ("Univ. Calif. Pub. Amer. Arch. & Ethnol.," Vol. 2.) Berkeley.

SMITH, A. G.
1957 "Suggested Changes in Nomenclature of the Major American Time Periods." *Amer. Antiquity*, 23:169.

SMITH, ELMER R.
1941 *Archaeology of Deadman Cave, Utah.* (Univ. Utah Bull. 32.) Salt Lake City.
1952 *The Archaeology of Deadman Cave: A Revision.* ("Univ. Utah Anthrop. Paps.," No. 10.) Salt Lake City.

STEWARD, JULIAN H.
1937 *Ancient Caves of the Great Salt Lake Region.* (Bur. Amer. Ethnol. Bull. 116.) Washington, D.C.

STEWART, T. D.
   1949   "The Development of the Concept of Morphological Dating in Con-
            nection with Early Man in America." *Southwestern Jour. Anthrop.*,
            5:1–16.
SUHM, DEE ANN, ALEX D. KRIEGER, and EDWARD B. JELKS
   1954   *An Introductory Handbook of Texas Archeology. Tex. Arch. Soc. Bull.*
            25. Austin.
SWANSON, EARL H., JR.
   1959   "Theory and History in American Archaeology." *Southwestern Jour.
            Anthrop.*, 15:120–24.
TAYLOR, WALTER W.
   1956   "Some Implications of the Carbon-14 Dates from a Cave in Coahuila,
            Mexico." *Tex. Arch. Soc. Bull.* 27:215–34. Austin.
THOMSON, JACK
   1961   "Preliminary Archaeological Survey of the Pilchuck River and South
            Fork of the Stillaguamish River." *Wash. Archaeologist*, 5 (Part 3):4–
            10.
TREGANZA, ADAN E.
   1952   *Archaeological Investigations in the Farmington Reservoir Area, Stanislaus
            County, California.* ("Univ. Calif. Arch. Surv. Rept.," No. 14.)
            Berkeley.
TREGANZA, ADAN E., and ROBERT F. HEIZER
   1953   *Additional Data on the Farmington Complex: A Stone Implement As-
            semblage of Probable Early Postglacial Date from Central California.*
            ("Univ. Calif. Arch. Surv. Rept.," No. 22.) Berkeley.
TREGANZA, ADAN E., and C. G. MALAMUD
   1950   "The Topanga Culture: First Season's Excavation of the Tank Site,
            1947." *Univ. Calif. Anthrop. Records*, Vol. 12, No. 4. Berkeley.
TSCHOPIK, HARRY, JR.
   1946   "Some Notes on Rock Shelter Sites near Huancayo, Peru." *Amer.
            Antiquity*, 12:73–80.
UHLE, MAX
   1917   "Sobre la estación paleolítica de Taltal." *Pub. Museo de Etnología y
            Antropología de Chile*, 1:31–50. Santiago.
VAILLANT, GEORGE C.
   1944   *The Aztecs of Mexico.* New York: Doubleday, Doran.
VIGNATI, M. A.
   1927   "Arqueología y antropología de los conchales fueginos." *Revista del
            Museo de La Plata*, 30:79–143. Buenos Aires.
WALLACE, WILLIAM J.
   1954   "The Little Sycamore Site and the Early Milling Stone Cultures of
            Southern California." *Amer. Antiquity*, 20:112–23.
WARREN, CLAUDE N., and D. L. TRUE
   1961   "The San Dieguito Complex and Its Place in California Prehistory."
            Pp. 246–91 in *U.C.L.A. Arch. Surv., Ann. Rept., 1960–61.* Los An-
            geles.

WENDORF, FRED, and ALEX D. KRIEGER
  1959 "New Light on the Midland Discovery." *Amer. Antiquity*, 25:66–78.
WENDORF, FRED, ALEX D. KRIEGER, CLAUDE C. ALBRITTON, and T. D.
  STEWART
  1955 *The Midland Discovery: A Report on the Pleistocene Human Remains
  from Midland, Texas.* Austin: University of Texas Press.
WENDORF, FRED, and TULLY H. THOMAS
  1951 "Early Man Sites near Concho, Arizona." *Amer. Antiquity*, 17:107–
  14.
WHEELER, S. M.
  1942 *Archeology of Etna Cave, Lincoln County, Nevada.* Carson City: Nevada State Park Commission.
WILLEY, GORDON R., and PHILIP PHILLIPS
  1955 "Method and Theory in American Archaeology. II. Historical-Developmental Interpretation." *Amer. Anthropologist*, 57:723–819.
  1958 *Method and Theory in American Archaeology.* Chicago: University of
  Chicago Press.
WILLIAMS, STEPHEN
  1957 "The Island 35 Mastodon: Its Bearing on the Age of Archaic Cultures in the East." *Amer. Antiquity*, 22:359–72.
WITTHOFT, JOHN
  1952 "A Paleo-Indian Site in Eastern Pennsylvania: An Early Hunting
  Culture." *Amer. Phil. Soc. Proc.*, 96:464–95.
  1954 "A Note on Fluted Point Relationships." *Amer. Antiquity*, 19:271–
  73.
WORMINGTON, H. M.
  1939 *Ancient Man in North America.* (Denver Mus. Nat. Hist. [2d ed.,
  Popular Series, No. 4].) Denver.
  1953 *Origins.* (Instituto Panamericano de Geografía e Historia, Comisión
  de Historia Pub. 51 ["Programa de Historia de América," Vol. 1,
  No. 1].) Mexico, D.F.
  1957 *Ancient Man in North America.* 4th ed. (Denver Mus. Nat. Hist.,
  Popular Series, No. 4.) Denver.

The North

HENRY B. COLLINS

The Arctic and Subarctic

Two of the most important problems of American anthropology have their setting in the Arctic—the original entry of man into America and the origin of the Eskimo and his peculiar form of culture. It may be said at once that there are as yet no indisputable finds in the Arctic that throw light on the larger problem, though pre-Eskimo remains of some antiquity have been found, and the probability grows that it will eventually be possible to trace the Arctic path of the first human migrants to the New World. With regard to the second problem we are on firmer ground. It may fairly be stated, I think, that archeology has at least shown us the direction in which we must search and some of the basic factors to be taken into account in seeking a solution to the much discussed question of the origin of Eskimo culture.

The archeological sites that reveal the record of prehistoric man in the American Arctic and Subarctic are of two kinds: (1) hundreds of sites in Alaska, Canada, and Greenland from a few centuries to three thousand years old that may be attributed to the ancestors of the present Eskimo and (2) numerous recently discovered pre-Eskimo sites containing mainly chipped-stone implements, some of which are comparable typologically to those from Paleo-Indian sites to the south. [EDITORS' NOTE: See Plano of Krieger, p. 34.] These early Arctic sites contain projectile points identical with or closely similar to Angostura, Agate Basin, Fluted, Plainview, Milnesand, Browns Valley, and Scottsbluff, and side-notched forms [EDITORS' NOTE: See Griffin, pp. 227–28] resembling Old Copper and other Archaic manifestations (Rainey 1939; Johnson 1946; Skarland and Giddings 1948; Solecki and Hackman 1951; Irving 1953, 1957; MacNeish 1956, 1959a, 1959b; Skarland and Keim 1958;

HENRY B. COLLINS, principal anthropologist, Bureau of American Ethnology, Smithsonian Institution, received his doctoral degree from Millsaps College. Since 1927 his chief interest as a research scholar has been Arctic North America. Earlier he did pioneer archeological work in Mississippi and Louisiana. The author of numerous writings on the Eskimos, he was awarded the Gold Medal of the Royal Danish Academy of Sciences and Letters for his research on the origin of Eskimo culture. He played a key role in establishing the Arctic Institute of North America and in planning and supervising the *Arctic Bibliography*.

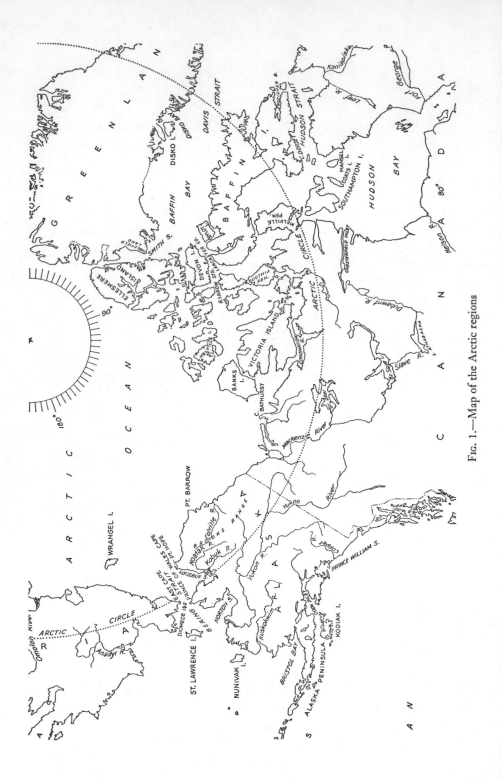

Fig. 1.—Map of the Arctic regions

Campbell 1959, 1961*a*, 1961*b*; Giddings 1961; Harp 1961). MacNeish (1959*a*, *b*) has described the often scanty finds at the interior Arctic sites and discussed their age and relationships. The sites are described as representative of five "traditions," which are, from oldest to youngest, the British Mountain, Cordilleran, Northern Plano, Northwest Microblade, and Arctic Small Tool.

PRE-ESKIMO SITES

Two of the Arctic sites give hints, but hints only, of real antiquity: the lowest level—British Mountain—at the Engigstciak site on Firth River near the Arctic Coast, Yukon Territory (MacNeish 1956), and the Kogruk site at Anaktuvuk Pass in the Brooks Range of northern Alaska (Campbell 1961*a*). Here were found, among other types, crude choppers, flake scrapers, and a few Mousterian-like points suggestive of the Levalloisian technique. However, the Kogruk material came from an unstratified surface site, and at Engigstciak the stratigraphy was affected by soil slipping caused by solifluction. A third site for which great age has been suggested is Palisades I at Cape Krusenstern on the Arctic Coast of Alaska (Giddings 1961, n.d.), but this also is a surface site and its principal claim to antiquity is that the stone implements assigned to the complex are chemically altered from their original state. None of these sites, therefore, presents the kind of evidence needed to demonstrate an age commensurate with the typological appearance of the implements themselves.

Since radiocarbon dates are lacking for most of the Arctic sites containing Plano-type projectile points, there is as yet no way of determining their age in relation to the sites far to the south. What is needed in the north, in addition to radiocarbon dating and stratigraphic control, is indisputable evidence of the association of specific types of implements with extinct fauna. It is of interest to recall in this connection that the first artifacts of Paleo-Indian (Plano) type described from the Arctic may actually have been found in such association (Rainey 1939). These were two projectile points of Angostura and Agate Basin form, and accompanying them were a thin lozenge-shaped blade with the general shape of a Solutrean laurel leaf and two long, slender bone points like those frequently found at Paleolithic sites in the Old World. These artifacts were reported to have been found in gold-dredging operations near Fairbanks, in frozen silt deposits overlying the gold-bearing gravels at depths from 12 to 20 meters, and some of them were further reported to have been in direct association with mammoth, mastodon, bison, and horse bones. This of course cannot be accepted as a record. No archeologist was present, and there is no way of checking on the authenticity of the finds; for that reason these first potential clues to the presence of Pleistocene man in Alaska have been largely ignored or forgotten. It should be noted, however, that the two projectile points that we would now identify as Angostura and Agate Basin (Rainey 1939) were found as early as 1933 (before even the Clovis type had been described in print) and 1936–37, which would seem to speak in favor of their authenticity. The same might be said of some of the accompanying artifacts—the Solutrean-like blade and the slender bone points (Rainey 1939). Bone points of similar form, but with beveled instead of conical bases, were found at the Clovis site in New Mexico, in association with mammoth bones, and also at early sites in Florida and Oregon. Cotter (1962) has commented on the significance of bone points of this type as a link between the early American cultures and the Upper Paleolithic cultures of Eurasia.

Despite the uncertainties attending the Fairbanks finds, it may well be that these bone and stone artifacts were found, as claimed, deep in the frozen muck in association with Pleistocene mammals. If so, they would be the only Arctic materials comparable in age to those from early sites in the south. The generally prevailing view is that artifacts of Plano type in the Arctic are later than their southern counterparts, indicating either a south-to-north culture drift or the northward movement of big-game hunters from the Plains. The Fairbanks finds, however, suggest the possibility of an alternative explanation, namely, that artifacts of this kind found in interior Alaska and Canada are part of a local cultural continuum extending from a Pleistocene base in Alaska itself.

The Arctic coast sites tell another story, that of the late persistence of typologically ancient forms in this area. At Kotzebue Sound on the Arctic Coast of Alaska there is clear evidence from Giddings' excavations that Plano and Archaic types continued in use to as late as 1000 B.C. From his work at Cape Krusenstern, Kotzebue Sound, Giddings (1961, n.d.) has defined several culture stages that include in their inventories projectile points resembling Angostura, Scottsbluff, Browns Valley, and Old Copper. The sites are found on a long succession of old beach lines, 114 in number, extending far back from the present shore. The series of old beaches reveals a record of continuous, successive occupation by sea mammal and caribou hunters over a period of some five thousand years as the beaches were gradually built up by the scouring action of storm waves and sea ice. The oldest cultural remains, on beach 105, were the small, delicate end blades, side blades, microblades, and burins of the Denbigh Flint complex. Next came the Old Whaling culture, characterized especially by side-notched blades, on beach 53, followed in turn by Choris, Norton (on beach 35), Near Ipiutak, Ipiutak (beach 29), Thule, and, finally, at the present shore line, recent Eskimo.

On about beach 45 was found a cache of thirty-six complete and eight broken points, which in size, shape, and flaking technique are to be identified as Angostura (Wormington 1957), the only difference being that the tips are somewhat more narrow and tapering. The beach on which the cache was found lay between the Choris beaches, radiocarbon dated at around 1000 B.C., and those of the Old Whaling culture, radiocarbon dated from 2000 to 1500 B.C., indicating a date of no earlier than 1500 B.C. for the Angostura-like implements. A few implements of similar type were found also at the Choris site, dated at 1000 B.C., from which Giddings (n.d.) concludes: "The Angostura form appears to have continued, almost without change, from the time of the Denbigh Flint complex to that of pre-Choris and Choris, and even to late Choris phases of culture." The finds at Cape Krusenstern indicate, therefore, that projectile points like those used on the Plains 9000 years ago were used by caribou hunters on the Arctic Coast of Alaska as late as 3500 years ago, and that some of them were deposited on a beach that was probably not even in existence 4000 years ago.

This great disparity in age is not surprising but, rather, is consistent with everything that Arctic archeology has taught us for the last twenty years. It is merely another, striking example of what should be recognized as a generalization of Arctic archeology, the phenomenon of "Arctic retardation." There is, of course, nothing new or novel in the idea that the Arctic should have been a refuge area. Because of distance and geographical considerations, culture traits and influences from the south, whether emanating from America or the Old World, are late in reaching the Arctic; more important, once received, they are likely to persist there for a surprisingly long time. Herein we have an explanation for the seeming paradox that the Eskimos, whose history in America probably does not extend beyond several thousand years, are the one American people whose culture, on the basis of specific trait resemblances, can be traced in substantial part to the Mesolithic and Upper Paleolithic cultures of the Old World.

The cultural and environmental factors that have fostered stability and relative uniformity in Eskimo culture, but without inhibiting culture change, have been discussed elsewhere (Collins 1940). Later discoveries in Alaska, Canada, and Greenland have provided more striking evidence of the truly marginal character of Arctic cultures, both Eskimo and pre-Eskimo, and of the long persistence there of culture traits and life patterns inherited from earlier times (Collins 1943, 1951, 1953*a*, *b*, 1957, n.d.*a*, *b*). Some examples of culture lag and retention in the Arctic might be mentioned. The Ipiutak culture, radiocarbon dated at around A.D. 300, possessed a stone industry that was in large part a continuation from the five-thousand-year-old Denbigh Flint complex. It also has bone and ivory arrowheads and lances equipped with inset stone side blades, implements remarkably similar to those of the early Siberian Neolithic and the Mesolithic of northern Europe. As a technique, the side-blading of weapons had a more widespread distribution in Eskimo culture—on harpoon heads (Okvik–Old Bering Sea, Birnirk, and Ipiutak) and on harpoon lances (Dorset). An early stage of Dorset culture, represented by the T 1 site on Southampton Island in Hudson Bay (675–100 B.C.) exhibits an impressive array of implement types like those of the Old World Mesolithic: microblades, burins, burin spalls, end blades, oval and rectangular side blades, as well as triangular-sectioned knives similar to Paleolithic backed blades but struck from the outer edges of prepared cores. Burins, which are several thousand years later in the American Arctic and Siberia than in Europe, were used by the Dorset Eskimos as late as 100 B.C., while the burin tradition, through a series of changing forms, continued into modern Eskimo culture. The Arctic Small Tool tradition, especially as represented by the Denbigh Flint complex, was characterized by such important Mesolithic and/or Paleolithic traits as burins, side blades, microblades, and cores, but was probably no more than five thousand years old; its implement typology suggests that it was essentially an American variant of the much older Eurasian Mesolithic. And the later Eskimo cultures to which it gave rise not only continued to follow a Mesolithic *way* of life but, in so doing, continued to employ specific Mesolithic types of implements that had gone out of use thousands of years earlier in other parts of the world. And now we have this final example of Plano-type projectile points like those used thousands of years earlier by hunters of extinct animals in the Plains and Southwest still being used by caribou hunters in the Arctic as late as 1500 B.C.

ESKIMO SITES—NORTHERN MARITIME TRADITION

Among the Eskimo sites, the oldest that has been dated by radiocarbon is one representative of the southern variant of Eskimo culture. This is the Chaluka site, a large midden on Umnak Island in the Aleutians, for which a date of 1000 B.C. was obtained (Laughlin 1952*a*). Next in age is a site on Yukon Island, Cook Inlet, Alaska, excavated by de Laguna (1934); here a date of 748 B.C. was obtained for the earliest culture stage, called Kachemak Bay I (Rainey and Ralph 1959). The earliest culture stage on St. Lawrence Island, Okvik–Old Bering Sea, has been dated at 250 B.C. (Arnold and Libby 1951). The Norton culture at Cape Denbigh dates from around 100 B.C., and the Choris culture at Kotzebue Sound at around 1000 B.C. (Giddings 1961, n.d.). In the eastern Arctic an early stage of Dorset culture, from the

T 1 site on Southampton Island, has dates ranging from 675 B.C. to 100 B.C. (Rainey and Ralph 1959).

If viewed in broad perspective, prehistoric Eskimo culture exhibits several contrasting regional patterns that may be described as traditions (Giddings 1960; Collins 1960). The principal traditions are (1) the northern maritime, a series of closely related, sequential culture stages— Okvik–Old Bering Sea–Birnirk–Punuk–Thule–Inugsuk—forming a cultural continuum that began in northeastern Siberia near Bering Strait more than 2000 years ago and later spread eastward to Greenland, to form the principal basis for modern Eskimo culture in northern Alaska, Canada, and Greenland; (2) that of South Alaska in what de Laguna (1956) has called the Pacific Eskimo–Aleut province, a distinctive culture pattern ancestral to that of the Prince William Sound and Kodiak Island Eskimos and the Aleuts on the Aleutian Islands; (3) the prehistoric Dorset culture of the eastern Canadian Arctic and Greenland and the earlier stages from which it developed; and (4) the Choris, Norton, and Near Ipiutak cultures extending from Point Hope and Kotzebue Sound on the Arctic Coast south to Bristol Bay, a pattern of culture that was ancestral in large part to that of the modern Bering Sea Eskimos.

As the first of these traditions or configurations is the one that has been most fully documented and that has provided a basic chronology for the largest section of the Arctic, we may begin by examining its culture stages and the record of culture change and development that they reveal in the area around Bering Strait. The first excavations in this area were made by Diamond Jenness (1928*a*, *b*; 1933) in the summer of 1926. At Cape Prince of Wales and the nearby Diomede Islands in Bering Strait, Jenness excavated harpoon heads and other artifacts showing that the Thule culture, discovered by Therkel Mathiassen in 1922 and 1923 (Mathiassen 1927) in the central Canadian Arctic, had also existed in Alaska. Moreover, Jenness obtained from the Eskimos several ivory harpoon heads and other objects decorated with the graceful curvilinear designs of what he described as the Bering Sea culture, now called Old Bering Sea. These objects, which were deeply patinated and dark brown in color, had been dug up by the Eskimos at the Little Diomede village, and one of the harpoon heads was known to have been found at a depth of eight feet. In the same year Aleš Hrdlička and Otto W. Geist obtained similar artifacts on St. Lawrence Island; these also had been excavated by Eskimos at old village sites. Although the pieces he had were few in number, Jenness immediately recognized their significance. He saw in them evidence of an early, pre-Thule stage of culture, of Asiatic origin, that had existed around Bering Strait probably more than 2000 years ago. Jenness' conclusions as to the origin and nature of the Old Bering Sea culture and its role in the development of

Eskimo culture in general, based on a mere handful of artifacts, have been in no sense altered but rather extended and confirmed by later, more intensive excavations in the area, particularly those on St. Lawrence Island, 150 miles south of Bering Strait.

At Gambell (Sevuokok), at the northwest end of St. Lawrence Island, excavations at five old village sites, each of different age, brought evidence of a long succession of culture changes that came about as one village after another had been established and then abandoned (Collins 1932, 1935, 1937*a*). The resulting chronology, revealing an unbroken continuity of Eskimo culture for a period of over two thousand years, was based on (1) direct stratigraphy in midden deposits, (2) seriation (overlapping of implement types from one site to another), (3) the positions of the several old villages in relation to former beach lines and the present beach, and (4) continuous changes in art and implement types consistent with the interpretations implied by the foregoing.

Four of the Gambell sites were situated on a gravel spit half a mile wide and three-quarters of a mile long (Fig. 2). This gravel foreland had been formed by wave and ice action, as shown by a series of old beach lines extending westward from the base of the Gambell mountain to the present village at the far end of the spit. The oldest of the four sites, known to the Eskimos as Miyowagh, the "climbing-up place," lay at the base of the mountain on the first two, the oldest, beach lines. Two hundred yards to the north and separated from it by four beach lines was Ievoghiyoq, the next oldest site, with six additional beaches between it and the present shore. At the far end of the spit, near the present village of Gambell, was the next oldest site, Seklowaghyaget, and adjacent to it the ruins of underground houses occupied as late as 1890.

The fifth, and oldest, site lay on the lower slope of the mountain just back of Miyowagh. Completely buried beneath the sod and fallen rocks, it blended perfectly into the hillside, and its presence had not been suspected by modern Eskimos, though the trail to the top of the mountain which they and their ancestors had followed for generations passed directly over a part of it. The three-foot-deep midden and two house ruins at this hillside site yielded some six hundred artifacts in addition to large quantities of animal bones; potsherds; stone chips; fragmentary objects of wood, bone, ivory, baleen; and other refuse, all in a good state of preservation owing to the frozen ground. As on the Diomede Islands, the ivory objects were all deeply patinated. The incised designs on the decorated ivory objects were either those of the graceful Old Bering Sea style 2 or those of a simpler, more linear style (Old Bering Sea style 1). Most of the style 1 artifacts were found between or below the floor stones of the houses, indicating that they were older than those decorated in style 2. At a third house ruin at the Hillside site, excavated by Louis Giddings in 1939, the decorated objects were all of style 1 (Rainey 1941; Giddings 1960). This style of art is now generally referred to as Okvik, from a pure site of the period excavated in 1934 by Otto W. Geist and Ivar Skarland on Punuk Island off the east end of St. Lawrence (Rainey 1941). The large number of decorated ivory artifacts from this site revealed three substyles of Okvik art, probably of different age, the latest and most elaborate of which developed into Old Bering Sea style 2 (Collins 1960, 1962).

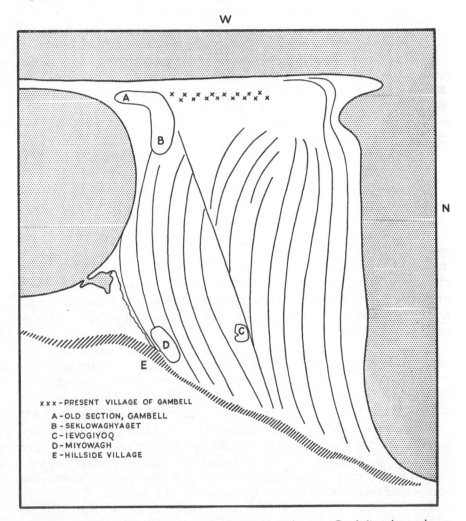

xxx – PRESENT VILLAGE OF GAMBELL
A – OLD SECTION, GAMBELL
B – SEKLOWAGHYAGET
C – IEVOGIYOQ
D – MIYOWAGH
E – HILLSIDE VILLAGE

Fig. 2.—Outline map showing location of old Eskimo sites near Gambell at the northwest end of St. Lawrence Island, Alaska.

Miyowagh, the second oldest of the Gambell sites, was a midden roughly oval in shape, with an average diameter of 100 yards. Artifacts from the lower levels of the midden were in general like those from the Hillside site but included no examples of Old Bering Sea style 1 (Okvik) art. Instead, all the harpoon heads and decorated objects were those of Old Bering Sea styles 2 and 3. Overlying this older material were the distinctive artifacts and simplified art of the Punuk culture that had been previously described from Punuk Island (Collins 1929). The 164 harpoon heads from Miyowagh showed a gradual transition in form and decoration from Old Bering Sea to early Punuk (Fig. 3).

The next oldest midden, Ievoghiyoq, was a pure Punuk site. Harpoon heads of early Punuk type from the lower levels showed a linkage with Miyowagh, but the bulk of the two thousand artifacts from Ievoghiyoq were those characteristic of the later, developed stage of Punuk culture. The site had been established just before Miyowagh was abandoned and had continued to be occupied for many years thereafter. At the two most recent sites, Seklowaghyaget and the old section of Gambell, further changes in harpoon heads and other implements carried the developmental sequence through the protohistoric to the modern stage of St. Lawrence culture.

The Gambell sequence, based on a stratigraphic linkage of one site to another, was duplicated at Kukulik, a huge 20-foot midden on the north coast of St. Lawrence Island, where Otto W. Geist found a direct stratigraphic sequence of Old Bering Sea styles 2 and 3, Punuk, and modern material at this one site (Geist and Rainey 1936). Changes in artifacts at the Gambell sites were correlated in some degree with changes in house construction. Five types of houses were found, four of them semisubterranean and one a surface type, all of them different from the modern dome-shaped, skin-covered house that came into use only in recent times.

Animal bones from the houses and middens showed that the prehistoric St. Lawrence Eskimos of all periods subsisted mainly on sea mammals—hair seals, walrus, bearded seals, and whales—supplemented by birds and fish, mainly cod. Whaling, as indicated by the number of whaling harpoon heads, was of far more importance in Punuk and later times than in the Old Bering Sea period. The same was true of bird hunting, for the Punuk sites contained much larger quantities of bird bones, and of more species, than did the older sites. This might be correlated with the use of the bird bolas, for bone and ivory bolas weights were common at the later sites but absent at the earlier.

The harpoon with which the Eskimo captures the sea mammals on which his livelihood depends is also a tool that greatly aids the archeologist in his task of establishing regional chronologies and tracing cul-

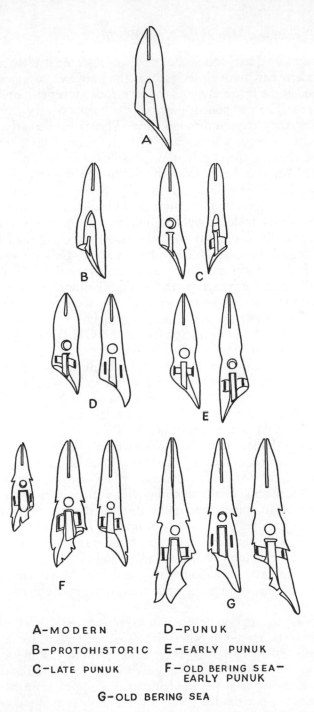

A—MODERN   D—PUNUK

B—PROTOHISTORIC E—EARLY PUNUK

C—LATE PUNUK   F—OLD BERING SEA—
                 EARLY PUNUK

G—OLD BERING SEA

FIG. 3.—Chart showing developmental changes in harpoon heads at Gambell, St. Lawrence Island, Alaska, beginning with the elaborate older forms (G) and ending with the simple modern type (A).

ture change. The harpoon is a composite implement consisting usually of a wooden shaft with an ice pick at the butt end, a finger rest at the center, and at the fore end a socket piece, loose foreshaft, and detachable toggle head. The component parts of the harpoon vary from region to region, and they change through time. This is particularly true of the toggle harpoon head, which, more than any other Eskimo artifact, possesses the characteristics essential for a "time indicator."

The 417 harpoon heads from the Gambell sites were found to have undergone continuous change from Old Bering Sea to modern times (Fig. 3). The older examples, from the Hillside site and the lower levels of the Miyowagh midden, were complicated and highly variable in form and were usually decorated with the elaborate designs of Old Bering Sea art. Beginning with the early Punuk stage, they became gradually simpler, both in form and decoration, and evolved finally into the one simple utilitarian form used by the modern Eskimos (Collins 1937a, b).

Paralleling these changes in harpoon heads were those which occurred in the curious butterfly-shaped ivory "winged objects." These objects (Fig. 4), which are so characteristic of the Old Bering Sea and Punuk cultures, were probably attached to the butt end of a harpoon or dart used with a throwing board, the purpose being to provide a "wing," as on some Greenland harpoons, and also a counterweight for the heavy toggle head and socket at the opposite end of the harpoon. Beginning in Okvik (Old Bering Sea style 1) with a small winged form, they developed in later Old Bering Sea times into a larger, more graceful form resembling an Indian banner stone. Later, in early Punuk, as the wings became narrower and inclined upward instead of outward, they gradually assumed the form of a trident, which in turn developed into a "turreted" form, and finally into one with a shape suggestive of a bottle. These objects are almost invariably decorated with the designs of Old Bering Sea styles 1, 2, or 3 or early, middle, or late Punuk, the decoration in every case being consistent with the form. Many other artifacts, such as needle cases, box handles, knife handles, and scrapers, also bore incised decorations, beginning with the graceful and elaborate designs of Old Bering Sea and ending with the simple straight-line patterns of laet Punuk.

In addition to harpoon heads, winged objects, and art, developmental changes may be traced in other classes of artifacts: needle cases, bird darts, bone and ivory arrowheads, fishline sinkers, knives, adzes, and ivory runners for the small hand-drawn sled. At the Hillside site there were almost twice as many implements of chipped stone as there were of rubbed slate, but the Eskimos of the Punuk stage used rubbed slate almost exclusively.

Outside St. Lawrence Island, Okvik and later Old Bering Sea are

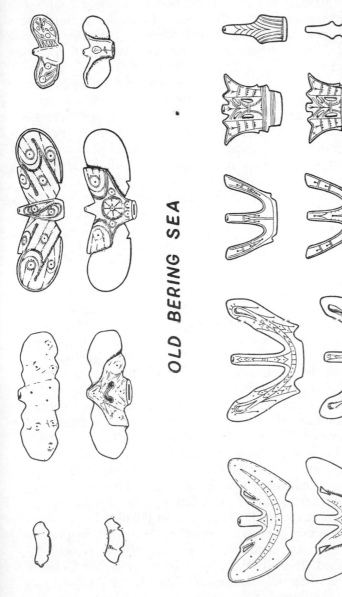

OLD BERING SEA

PUNUK

Fig. 4.—Examples of ivory "winged objects" from St. Lawrence Island and the Arctic Coast of Alaska illustrating stages in their development from the Okvik form (*upper left*) to those of late Punuk (*lower right*).

known to have existed as cultural entities only on the Diomede Islands and the opposite Siberian shore, particularly Uelen at East Cape. However, typical Okvik artifacts and art occur at sites of the Ipiutak culture at Point Hope, Kotzebue Sound, and Seward Peninsula in northern Alaska, and Okvik influence may have extended much farther in the opposite direction. This is suggested by the presence of Okvik art motifs in the Bristol Bay–Aleutian area and by the finding of a typical Okvik artifact at an old Eskimo site near the mouth of the Kuskokwim. Old Bering Sea artifacts and art have been found on the Alaskan mainland only at Point Hope and Point Barrow (Ford 1959), but there are no indications that the culture existed there except in a form blended with Ipiutak. The Punuk culture existed on the northeastern coast of Siberia, on the Diomede Islands, and at Cape Prince of Wales on the Alaskan side of Bering Strait. A single house containing Punuk art and artifacts was excavated by Ford at Nunagiak, seventy-five miles south of Point Barrow. At the Nukleet site, in Norton Sound, a few Punuk-type artifacts have been reported (Giddings 1960), and Punuk influence may have extended farther down the coast, since the art of the Bering Sea Eskimos as far south as Bristol Bay shows rather close resemblances to Punuk.

The St. Lawrence Island Eskimos are members of the Yuit or Siberian group, and from the earliest known times they have maintained close relations with Siberia, only forty miles away, rather than with the more distant Alaskan mainland. It is not surprising, therefore, that recent archeological work in northeastern Siberia should have borne out previous indications that the prehistoric St. Lawrence cultures had originated in this area. Excavations by Soviet archeologists have shown that the Okvik, Old Bering Sea, Punuk, and later St. Lawrence culture stages, as well as Birnirk and Thule, are represented at a number of old sites in northeastern Siberia (Machinskii 1941; Rudenko 1947; Chard 1955, 1960; Levin 1958, 1960; Sergeev 1959; Levin and Sergeev 1960). The most important of the Siberian sites is that at Uelen, near East Cape, where an abundance of Okvik material was found, including harpoon heads, knife handles, and other artifacts typical of what appears to have been the oldest stage of Okvik culture on Punuk Island. Moreover, the presence of an early type of arrowhead, slotted at both ends like those from the Siberian Neolithic, the absence of pottery, and the near absence of rubbed slate all confirm the impression that Uelen is the oldest known site of the Okvik culture (Rudenko 1947).

Two of the Alaskan cultures of the northern maritime tradition—the Birnirk of the Point Barrow region and the Thule culture of the Canadian Arctic—were not represented as distinct culture stages at Gambell. However, Birnirk and Thule harpoon heads were found at the Gambell and other St. Lawrence sites—and in contexts that clearly indicated their relative age. The most distinctive of the Thule harpoon heads (Thule type 2), along with a number of other typical Thule artifacts, occurred only at sites representative of the fully developed Punuk culture, while Birnirk heads were restricted to sites of the early Punuk stage.

Although direct stratigraphic evidence was lacking, typological and other considerations indicated that the Birnirk was an outgrowth of Old Bering Sea; that the Thule culture of the central Arctic was not only coeval with, but in large part equivalent to, the Punuk stage on St. Lawrence; that Thule harpoon heads, wherever found in Alaska, were later than Birnirk; and that they and the Thule culture as a whole had developed out of Birnirk (Collins 1929, 1937a).

Excavations in 1936 at Kurigitavik, an old Eskimo site at Cape Prince of Wales, Bering Strait, produced stratigraphic evidence of the postulated Birnirk-to-Thule sequence and more precise information on the status of the Thule culture in Alaska. Kurigitavik proved to be a site that was essentially Thule in character, the first such to be found in Alaska, or, as it might better be called, Thule-Punuk, for typical Punuk art and artifacts formed an integral part of the implement complex. The material excavated at Kurigitavik corresponded in general with that described by Mathiassen (1927) from Thule sites in the Canadian Arctic. Significantly lacking, however, were a number of Thule traits that are commonly found at recent and protohistoric Alaskan sites but never at the earlier sites—traits that indicated a recent return flow of Thule culture into northern Alaska from the central Arctic within the past few centuries. Kurigitavik was slightly older and contemporaneous with the Punuk stage on St. Lawrence Island and had been occupied during the time, somewhat prior to A.D. 1000, when other groups of Eskimos, probably between Point Barrow and the Mackenzie, were moving eastward, carrying the Thule culture to the Canadian Arctic and Greenland (Collins 1937b, 1940). Several radiocarbon determinations fall within this general time range: A.D. 607 and A.D. 727 for the upper middle (Thule-Punuk) deposits at Kurigitavik, A.D. 637 for the lower deposits (Birnirk), A.D. 477 for the Birnirk levels of the nearby beach midden at Wales, and A.D. 887 and A.D. 1047 for Ievoghiyoq, the pure Punuk site at Gambell, St. Lawrence Island (Rainey and Ralph 1959).

The nature of the Birnirk-Thule relationship at Kurigitavik was shown principally by the distribution of the Thule type 2 and related forms of harpoon heads in the 7–9-foot-deep midden. Typical Thule type 2 heads were restricted to the upper and middle levels of the midden. Below these were harpoon heads that had some of the characteristics of the Birnirk type. Finally, at the base of the midden, at a depth of 86 inches, a typical Birnirk harpoon head was found. Potsherds showed a similar distribution, with curvilinear stamped sherds of Birnirk type in the lower levels and plain ware above (Collins 1940).

Until recently our information on the Birnirk culture was limited to brief descriptions by Wissler (1916), Mason (1930), Mathiassen (1930*a*), Beregovaia (1953), and Chard (1955). Ford's excavations at Birnirk and other sites around Point Barrow in 1931–32 and 1936 have now provided full information on the Birnirk culture and on the Thule and later culture stages that followed it in this part of Alaska (Ford 1959). Ford's extensive collection of bone, ivory, stone, wood, skin, and baleen artifacts revealed in detail, even to items of clothing, the material possessions and way of life of the Eskimos who occupied the Point Barrow region from Birnirk to modern times.

Ford's (1959) analysis of the constituent elements of the Birnirk culture leads to the following conclusions:

> It is immediately apparent that the Birnirk has more traits in common with the Okvik and Old Bering Sea periods of St. Lawrence Island and Siberia than with the geographically closer Ipiutak Culture of Point Hope. . . . In conclusion, it may be stated briefly that the Birnirk cultural phase seems to have been derived from the Okvik and Old Bering Sea cultural complexes of the Bering Strait Region. The Thule Culture of Central Canada was, in turn, primarily derived from Birnirk. . . . The postulated late return migration of Thule people into Alaska is also supported by the evidence presented here.

The principal significance of the Thule culture is its key role in the formation of modern Eskimo culture from north Alaska to Greenland. The first Thule Eskimos to move eastward from Alaska seem to have taken the far northern route, along the coasts of the northern islands of the Canadian Arctic archipelago and then on to northwestern Greenland. This is suggested by the fact that the eastern Thule remains showing the closest similarity to early Alaskan Thule have been found in this area—in Inglefield Land, Northwestern Greenland (Holtved 1944), and on Cornwallis Island, north of Barrow Strait (Collins 1952) —whereas the Thule sites in the Hudson Bay region excavated by Mathiassen show closer resemblances to later Alaskan Thule culture. The latest culture stage of the northern maritime tradition was the Inugsuk, a modified form of Thule that developed in western Greenland partly under the stimulus of the Greenlandic Norse culture of the thirteenth and fourteenth centuries (Mathiassen 1930*b*).

As mentioned before, there is clear evidence of a late return movement or movements of Thule peoples and culture into northern Alaska, north of Norton Sound, some centuries after the original eastward spread of the Thule culture. These eastward and westward Thule movements have a particular significance as providing insight into the development and patterning of historic Eskimo culture (Collins 1937*a*, 1940, 1954). They appear to have been the mechanism primarily responsible for the remarkable uniformity of Eskimo language and culture throughout the northern Arctic, a phenomenon that in the past was often interpreted as evidence of a deep-seated, innate conservatism on the part of the Eskimo but which Stefansson (1914) and Sapir (1916) correctly recognized as more likely to have been the result of relatively recent contacts and movements. As Jenness (1928*b*) first pointed out, the Alaskan Eskimo dialects spoken north of Norton Sound were closer to those of far away Labrador and Greenland than to those of the Bering Sea Eskimos immediately to the south. It is highly significant that Norton Sound was also the dividing line between two generally dissimilar forms of culture, as indicated by pronounced differences in house types, lamps and cooking pots, ceremonialism, art, and many other features. Here, again, it is the northern pattern of culture that shows the closest resemblance to the eastern Eskimo, and mainly for the same reason—that Thule influences, so strong in the north, were much less pronounced south of Norton Sound. What has been said of language and culture is also true to some extent of physical type, the Bering Sea Eskimos south of Norton Sound having low and relatively broad heads in contrast to the longer, higher-headed type to the north and east. Since the Thule skulls from the Canadian Arctic excavated by Mathiassen are virtually identical with those of the modern Point Barrow Eskimo, it would appear that actual movements of people were in part responsible for the cultural resemblances that have been mentioned.

ESKIMO SITES—SOUTHERN AND OTHER TRADITIONS

The two other Alaskan cultural configurations or traditions, the Pacific Eskimo–Aleut and the Choris-Norton–Near Ipiutak, appear to have been in some degree related and represent the bases from which Eskimo culture south of Norton Sound developed. The lines of continuity, however, are less clear, and the record for the most part less complete, than in the case of the series of successive culture stages forming the Okvik to Inugsuk or northern maritime tradition.

The only areas in southern Alaska where prehistoric Eskimo culture has been fully described are Cook Inlet and Prince William Sound at the southern periphery of the Eskimo territory. Here Frederica de Laguna not only has published detailed descriptions of the materials she excavated in 1930 and 1933 but has presented equally detailed and extensive analyses of individual culture traits and their distribution as a basis for reconstructing culture development in southern Alaska in relation to that in other parts of the Arctic (de Laguna 1934, 1940, 1947, 1956).

At Cook Inlet, de Laguna (1934, 1956) has described three stages of prehistoric Eskimo culture called Kachemak Bay I, II, and III and in Prince William Sound a relatively late phase of Chugach Eskimo culture corresponding in the main to Kachemak Bay III. Kachemak Bay I, with a radiocarbon date of 748 B.C., is seen to be several centuries older than Okvik, the oldest known Eskimo culture at Bering Strait. Chipped-stone implements, including those of slate, were more abundant in the earlier stages, rubbed slate in the later. The early Kachemak Bay culture was more Eskimoid than were the later stages, which were influenced by Indian cultures to the south. Cultural connections with Asia are indicated by a number of traits that occur in the Kachemak Bay and Aleutian cultures and also in Kamchatka and Japan (de Laguna 1934).

Excavations at prehistoric sites on Kodiak and the Aleutian Islands have revealed a form of culture generally similar to that of Cook Inlet and Prince William Sound (Jochelson 1925; Hrdlička 1944, 1945; Quimby 1945a, b, 1946, 1948; Laughlin 1951, 1952a, b; Laughlin and Marsh 1951, 1954, 1956; Bank 1953; Spaulding 1953; Heizer 1956). A radiocarbon date of 1000 B.C. for the Chaluka midden on Umnak Island (Laughlin 1952b) is the oldest recorded for southern Alaska. The lower levels of the midden contained microblades like those found in association with cores at a site on Ananiuliak (Anangula) Island, near Umnak (Laughlin 1951; Laughlin and Marsh 1954). To judge from the preliminary reports thus far published, there was considerable variation in implement typology from island to island, and some evidence of culture changes through time. On the whole, however, culture changes appear to have been much less frequent and less pronounced than in the northern Eskimo area.

Although basically Eskimo, the culture of southern Alaska has few traits, other than the art motifs already noted, that are specifically like those of the northern maritime tradition, and it contains numerous other features that are foreign to that tradition. There is, in fact, a sharper contrast between Pacific Eskimo–Aleut culture and that of Bering Strait than between Bering Strait and Greenland. The traits and tendencies of prehistoric and modern southern Alaskan culture that set it apart from the northern Eskimo pattern include oval and round stone lamps, whaling with poisoned lance, the detachable barbed dart with hole in tang more important than the toggle harpoon head, composite fishhooks and stone sinkers, specialized forms of slate blades, emphasis on decoration of clothing and the person, high development of woodworking, painting, and especially of weaving. Such trait resemblances as exist between southern Alaska and the north are mainly with the Ipiutak culture and the third western Eskimo tradition, the Choris-Norton–Near Ipiutak, described below.

Of the Eskimo cultures in northern Alaska not included in the northern maritime sequence, only two, Ipiutak and Near Ipiutak, have been described in full (Larsen and Rainey 1948). In many respects, however, Ipiutak remains a puzzle. This remarkable site at Point Hope on the Arctic Coast of Alaska was discovered in 1939 by Froelich Rainey, Helge Larsen, and Louis Giddings. Containing over six hundred houses, it is the largest Eskimo site known in the Arctic. The houses, made of driftwood, were semisubterranean and from 3 to 6 meters square. They were arranged in long rows, none of them overlapping or superimposed, and the refuse deposit on the floors was so thin as to suggest a very short occupancy, probably no more than a single season. Despite the huge size of the site, there was little variation in house structures, and the cultural material found in them and with the burials was remarkably uniform (Larsen and Rainey 1948). An average of several radiocarbon samples gave a date of A.D. 339 ± 210 for the site (Rainey and Ralph 1959). The one hundred and thirty-eight Ipiutak burials contained a rich array of artifacts, including elaborate non-functional arrowheads of antler, ivory chains, and curious openwork ivory carvings in a wide variety of forms, some resembling pretzels and others non-functional swivels. These may have been part of shamans' regalia—ivory imitations of iron chains and other ornaments that Siberian shamans attach to their clothing. An engraving tool with iron point of Siberian origin and ivory animal carvings and design motifs like those of Scytho-Siberian art are further evidence of a cultural linkage with northern Eurasia (Larsen and Rainey 1948). There are also affinities with Okvik–Old Bering Sea, prehistoric Pacific Eskimo–Aleut culture, and modern Eskimo culture of the Bering Sea region from Norton Sound south to Bristol Bay.

Ipiutak artifacts of ivory, bone, and antler are more elaborate, both in form and ornamentation, than those of any other Eskimo culture. The resemblances of Ipiutak art to that of Okvik–Old Bering Sea carry over to the implements, including specialized forms of harpoon heads, socket pieces and foreshafts, arrowheads, salmon-spear barbs, side- and end-bladed knives, adz heads and blades, engraving tools, cup-shaped scrapers of ivory, mattocks, shovels, cannon-bone scrapers, picks, flint flakers, flaking hammers, ivory hooks, buttons, brow bands, snow goggles, ivory chains, marlinspikes, side and end scrapers, knife blades, gravers, and burin-like slate implements with rubbed edges. However, there are also pronounced differences between Ipiutak and Okvik–Old Bering Sea, as shown by the absence at Ipiutak of such typical Eskimo features as rubbed-slate blades, float plugs and bars, float mouthpieces and stoppers, harpoon finger rests, wound plugs, meat or boat hooks, fishhooks, fishline sinkers, pottery, lamps, bow drills, needle cases, combs, drum handles, ice creepers, ivory sled runners, and implements made of baleen.

One of the most striking features of the Ipiutak culture is its stone industry, and it is this that provides a clue to its origin. Chipped-stone knives, scrapers, and end and side blades for arrows and harpoons occur in large numbers, and many of them, particularly the missile blades, closely resemble those of the Denbigh Flint complex and the Siberian Neolithic. Moreover, Ipiutak arrowheads and lances with inset side blades are very similar to those of the Siberian Neolithic and the European Mesolithic. It is highly probable that the Ipiutak stone industry was derived from the Denbigh Flint complex, which in turn had close ties with the Old World Neolithic and Mesolithic.

A related but somewhat older form of culture at Point Hope called "Near Ipiutak" was characterized by somewhat different types of arrowheads, harpoon heads, and other implements and, in addition, possessed whaling harpoon heads, stone lamps, pottery, and rubbed-slate implements, none of which were present at Ipiutak (Larsen and Rainey 1948).

While the cultural position of Ipiutak is not clear, Near Ipiutak appears to be related to Norton, a culture discovered by Giddings (1949, 1951) at the Iyatayet site at Cape Denbigh, Norton Sound. Radiocarbon dated at around 250 B.C., it lay above the basal Denbigh Flint complex and below Nukleet, a Thule-Punuk manifestation. Norton artifacts have not been illustrated or described in detail, but Giddings (1960) provides the following summary:

Village sites of square houses with short entrance passages contain hard, thin, sand-tempered pottery; extensive flint work including small, bifaced side blades and end blades, flake knives, and several scraper forms; polished hard stone, but rudimentary scraped and ground slate; many stone net sinkers, drill bits, stone lamps and stone dishes; large medial labrets of stone; crude toggle harpoon heads, some lacking line hole; and heavy stone tools. Engraving art appears negligible. Affinities are with Near Ipiutak culture and Pacific sites.

The Norton culture is also included in the remarkable beach-ridge sequence discovered by Giddings (1960, 1961, n.d.) at Cape Krusenstern, Kotzebue Sound, to which we referred earlier. Preceding Norton was Choris, radiocarbon dated at around 1000 B.C. (Giddings 1957, 1960, 1961). Choris has been described as follows (Giddings 1960):

Closely related to the southern Norton culture, but lacking many of the elements of Norton, such as net sinkers, polished adz blades, oval lamps, and side blades, this culture has some points of resemblance in flint work to the Denbigh Flint complex. Large weapon points, for example, are flaked diagonally with skill, and in styles recalling those of the western United States. Almost wholly lacking, however, is the "small tool" combination, including the microblade technique, burin-making, and the practice of insetting side blades. Choris people etched on ivory sparingly, but with extremely fine-line designs. They kept no dogs, and they appear to have preferred caribou to sea mammals as food. Scapulimancy is strongly indicated. Their sealing dart heads were elegant, but their knowledge of the toggle harpoon appears to have been rudimentary.

There seems to be little connection between Choris-Norton and two earlier cultures at Cape Krusenstern—Old Whaling (2000 B.C.) and Palisades II, both of which are characterized by side-notched blades resembling those of the Old Copper culture. Until further evidence is available, the meaning and significance of these two cultures must remain in doubt.

It seems clear, on the other hand, that Norton, Near Ipiutak, and to some extent Ipiutak had strong cultural ties with southern Alaska and in all probability represent the principal base from which modern Eskimo culture in the intervening Bering Sea region developed (Larsen and Rainey 1948; Larsen 1950; Collins 1954, 1962). The cultural evidence is paralleled by that of physical anthropology. Debetz (1959), in a preliminary report on the Ipiutak skeletal material, finds that the Ipiutak cranial type could not have been ancestral to northern Eskimo but resembled rather closely that of the early inhabitants of the Aleutian Islands whom Hrdlička called "Pre-Aleut." I should say, on the basis of the measurements presented, that there was an even closer resemblance to the modern Bering Sea Eskimos. Debetz also noted resemblances between Ipiutak and Yukaghir crania. The somatological evidence thus seems to point to a physical relationship between the Ipiutak Eskimos and peoples in areas where Ipiutak cultural affinities are strongly indicated—northern Siberia, the Bering Sea Coast south of Norton Sound, and southern Alaska—a situation parallel to that in the north where the longheaded specialized Eskimo physical type is found over thousands of miles of the Arctic Coast from Bering Strait to Greenland, where another cultural configuration, the northern maritime tradition, prevailed.

The radiocarbon dates at present available indicate that the more southern alignment—Choris, Norton, Near Ipiutak, southern Alaska— is some centuries older than the northern. However, it would be premature to accept this as conclusive evidence of the relative age of the two traditions. Okvik, the oldest known stage of culture at Bering Strait, is a fully developed, highly specialized Eskimo culture, obviously the result of many centuries of growth. Earlier stages leading up to Okvik must exist, and it seems highly probable that the Battle Rock site north of Cape Krusenstern represents just such a stage, one that was ancestral to both Okvik and Ipiutak. Giddings (1961) places the Battle Rock phase between Old Whaling (1800 B.C.) and Choris (1000 B.C.). The slender, delicately chipped end and side blades are much like those Giddings found on the oldest Krusenstern beaches (Giddings, 1961):

The Battle Rock phase of culture rests on an enormous collection from a single multiple burial discovered a few miles north of Cape Krustenstern last season. The flint work appears to fall midway between Denbigh and Ipiutak and the projectile heads and other artifacts anticipate Ipiutak (Fig. 11), while perhaps giving us an idea of what Denbigh art may prove to be. The engraving style depends upon precision-made long gashes tastefully done on antler artifacts (Fig. 12). Its elements, though much larger, anticipate those of both Okvik and Dorset.

One of the antler arrowheads illustrated, with slot for a side blade, is an Ipiutak type, but I would say that the other three anticipate or, perhaps better, duplicate Okvik as well as Ipiutak. Arrowheads like these—with conical tang and end-blade slit, some with sharp, low-lying barbs just above the tang—occur at the Hillside site and Miyowagh on St. Lawrence Island (Collins 1937a), at the Okvik site on Punuk Island (Rainey 1941), and at Okvik and Old Bering Sea sites in Siberia (Rudenko 1947). And, if the thick, bold designs on the antler object from Battle Rock (Giddings 1961) give us a preview of what Denbigh art will prove to be, it will be Okvik. These deeply incised, straight and curving lines, with long, sharp spurs attached, are characteristic of what appears to have been the oldest style of Okvik art (Giddings 1960; Collins 1960). It occurs at the Hillside site (Collins 1937a), at the Punuk Island Okvik site (Rainey 1941), and at Uelen, the Okvik site at East Cape, Siberia (Rudenko 1947). This association of Okvik and Ipiutak features at a site apparently older than other known sites of these cultures is further evidence of a genuine relationship between Okvik and Ipiutak and casts additional doubt on the often expressed view (Larsen and Rainey 1948; Giddings 1960) that Okvik–Old Bering Sea art and artifacts at the Point Hope site were merely the result of trade or contact. The Battle Rock site carries the further implication that the Denbigh Flint complex may have been the primary source not only of Ipiutak and the Choris-Norton–Near Ipiutak sequence but also of Okvik, the oldest stage of the northern maritime tradition as well as of the Dorset tradition of the eastern Arctic—a series of cultural configurations that at first sight would seem to have had little in common.

Eskimo Sites—Dorset Culture

For many centuries before the arrival of the Thule people from Alaska, the central and eastern Arctic had been occupied by the Dorset Eskimos, whose culture was markedly different from Thule but significantly similar in some respects to earlier stages of Alaskan culture. The

Dorset culture was first described by Jenness (1925, 1928*b*, 1933) on the basis of material excavated by Eskimos at Cape Dorset on Hudson Strait and on Coats and Mansell Islands. Since then Dorset sites have been discovered at many localities from Newfoundland north through eastern Canada to Greenland (Wintemberg 1939–40; Rowley 1940; Leechman 1943; Holtved 1944; Collins 1950, 1952, 1956, 1957; Harp 1951, 1953; Knuth 1952, 1954; O'Bryan 1953; Meldgaard 1955, 1960*b*, *c*; Larsen and Meldgaard 1958; Mathiassen 1958; Taylor 1959; Lowther 1960; Maxwell 1960).

The Dorset Eskimos lived in underground houses built of stones and turf, and they hunted seals, walrus, polar bear, caribou, fox, hares, birds, and fish. Their harpoon heads and other implements of bone, ivory, and stone were small and delicately made in contrast to those of the Thule culture. They lacked such typical Thule traits as whale-bone mattocks, snow shovels, bone arrowheads, harpoon sockets and finger rests, bow drills, and ulus, and they had no dogs. The fate of the Dorset Eskimos, curiously enough, is more of a mystery than their origin. They lived in the eastern Arctic for over two thousand years, and small groups of them continued to occupy their old territory for some centuries after the Thule people had taken possession of the area. They should have left some imprint on the Thule-derived modern Eskimo culture, but as yet the only modern Eskimo traits for which a Dorset origin can be proved are the harpoon heads commonly used in the central Arctic, the side-bladed lance, and the peculiar art of the Angmassalik Eskimos of eastern Greenland (Collins 1954, 1957, 1962; Meldgaard 1960*a*).

Indications of a cultural relationship between Dorset and the much older Denbigh Flint complex (Collins 1951, 1953*a*, *b*, 1955*b*; Harp 1953; Giddings 1956) became clearer with the discovery of many pre-Dorset sites in Canada and Greenland with radiocarbon dates ranging from 400 B.C. to 2000 B.C. (Knuth 1952, 1954; Meldgaard 1952; Giddings 1956; Harp 1958, 1961; Larsen and Meldgaard 1958; Mathiassen 1958; Taylor 1959; Maxwell 1960). These sites, along with the Denbigh Flint complex and related microlithic phases in the western Arctic, constitute what Irving (1953) has called the Arctic Small Tool tradition.

The problem of the origin of the Dorset culture was further clarified by discovery of the T 1 site on Southampton Island, representing an early stage of the culture (675 B.C.) with substantially different inventory from that of classic Dorset (Collins 1956, 1957). Older than other known Dorset sites and lacking many of the traits of later Dorset culture, it exhibited several significant parallels with the early Neolithic of Siberia and Mongolia (microblades; oval and rectangular side blades; small, delicate end blades; and triangular-sectioned flakes similar to European backed blades but struck from the outer edges of prepared cores or blades) and others that provided a firm linkage with the Arctic Small Tool tradition—microblades, oval side blades, burins, and tiny implements made from burin spalls. The Dorset culture is clearly an outgrowth of the Arctic Small Tool tradition, and, as noted above, there are strong indications that the same is true of the oldest stages of culture in Arctic Alaska. The fact that the Arctic Small Tool tradition has close affinities with the Old World Mesolithic thus reinforces previous indications of the Mesolithic origin of Eskimo culture as a whole.

Bibliography

Arnold, J. R., and W. F. Libby
  1951 "Radiocarbon Dates." *Science*, 113:111–20.
Bank, Theodore P., II
  1953 "Cultural Succession in the Aleutians." *Amer. Antiquity*, 19:40–49.
Beregovaia, N. A.
  1953 "Harpoon Heads from Ancient Settlements at Cape Baranov." *Materialy i Issledovaniia po Arkheologii SSSR*, 39:421–45. (In Russian.)
Campbell, John M.
  1959 "The Kayuk Complex of Arctic Alaska." *Amer. Antiquity*, 25: 94–105.
  1961a "The Tuktu Complex of Anaktuvuk Pass." *Univ. Alaska Anthrop. Paps.*, 9:61–80.
  1961b "The Kogruk Complex of Anaktuvuk Pass, Alaska." *Anthropologica*, n.s., 3:3–20.
Chard, Chester S.
  1955 "Eskimo Archaeology in Siberia." *Southwestern Jour. Anthrop.*, 11: 150–77.
  1960 "Recent Archaeological Work in the Chukchi Peninsula." *Univ. Alaska Anthrop. Paps.*, 8:119–30.
Collins, Henry B., Jr.
  1929 *Prehistoric Art of the Alaskan Eskimo.* ("Smithsonian Misc. Coll.," Vol. 81, No. 14.) Washington, D.C.
  1932 "Prehistoric Eskimo Culture on St. Lawrence Island." *Geog. Rev.*, 22:107–19.
  1935 "Archaeology of the Bering Sea Region." Pp. 453–68 in *Smithsonian Inst. Ann. Rpt., 1933.* Washington, D.C.
  1937a *Archaeology of St. Lawrence Island, Alaska.* ("Smithsonian Misc. Coll.," Vol. 96, No. 1.) Washington, D.C.
  1937b "Archaeological Excavations at Bering Strait." Pp. 63–68 in *Smithsonian Institution Explorations and Field-Work, 1936.* Washington, D.C.
  1940 "Outline of Eskimo Prehistory." Pp. 533–92 in *Essays in Historical Anthropology.* (Smithsonian Misc. Coll.," Vol. 100.)
  1943 "Eskimo Archaeology and Its Bearing on the Problem of Man's Antiquity in America." *Amer. Phil. Soc. Proc.*, 86:220–35.

1950 "Excavations at Frobisher Bay, Baffin Island, Northwest Territories." Pp. 18–43 in *Nat. Mus. Canada Ann. Rpt. 1948–59.* (Nat. Mus. Canada Bull. 118.) Ottawa.

1951 "The Origin and Antiquity of the Eskimo." Pp. 423–67 in *Smithsonian Inst. Ann. Rpt., 1950.* Washington, D.C.

1952 "Archaeological Excavations at Resolute, Cornwallis Island, N.W.T." Pp. 48–63 in *Nat. Mus. Canada Ann. Rpt., 1950–51.* (Nat. Mus. Canada Bull. 126.) Ottawa.

1953a "Recent Developments in the Dorset Culture Area." Pp. 32–39 in MARIAN W. SMITH (ed.), *Asia and North America: Transpacific Contacts.* (Soc. Amer. Arch. Mem. 9.) Salt Lake City.

1953b "Radiocarbon Dating in the Arctic." *Amer. Antiquity,* 18:197–203.

1954 *Comment on* MORRIS SWADESH, "Time Depths of American Linguistic Groupings." *Amer. Anthropologist,* 56:364–72.

1955a "Archaeological Research in the North American Arctic." *Arctic,* 7:296–306.

1955b "Excavations of Thule and Dorset culture sites at Resolute, Cornwallis Island, N.W.T." *Nat. Mus. Canada Ann. Rpt., 1953–54,* pp. 22–35. (Nat. Mus. Canada Bull. 136.)

1956 "The T 1 Site at Native Point, Southampton Island, N.W.T." *Univ. Alaska Anthrop. Paps.,* 4:63–89.

1957 "Archaeological Work in Arctic Canada." Pp. 509–28 in *Smithsonian Inst. Ann. Rpt., 1956.*

1960 *Comment on* J. L. GIDDINGS, "The Archaeology of Bering Strait." *Cur. Anthropology* 1:131–36.

1962 "Eskimo Cultures." Pp. 1–28 in *Encyclopedia of World Art,* Vol. 5. New York: McGraw-Hill Book Co., Inc.

n.d. *a* "Paleo-Indian Artifacts in Alaska: An Example of Cultural Retardation in the Arctic." *Univ. Alaska Anthrop. Paps.* (In press.)

n.d. *b* "Recent Trends and Developments in Arctic Anthropology." *Proc. 6th Internat. Cong. Anthrop. & Ethnol. Sci., Paris, 1960.* (In press.)

COTTER, JOHN L.
1962 *Comment on* RONALD J. MASON, "The Paleo-Indian Tradition in Eastern North America." *Cur. Anthropology,* 3:250–52.

DEBETZ, G.
1959 "The Skeletal Remains of the Ipiutak Cemetery." Pp. 157–64 in *Actas del 33° Congreso Internacional de Americanistas, San José, Costa Rica, 1958.*

FORD, JAMES A.
1959 "Eskimo Prehistory in the Vicinity of Point Barrow, Alaska." *Amer. Mus. Nat. Hist. Anthrop. Paps.,* Vol. 47, Part 1.

GEIST, OTTO W., and FROELICH G. RAINEY
1936 *Archaeological Excavations at Kukulik, St. Lawrence Island, Alaska.* ("Univ. Alaska Misc. Pub.," Vol. 2.) Washington, D.C.

GIDDINGS, J. L.
1949 "Early Flint Horizons on the North Bering Sea Coast." *Wash. Acad. Sci. Jour.,* 39:85–90.

GIDDINGS, J. L.
1951 "The Denbigh Flint Complex." *Amer. Antiquity*, 16:193–203.
1952 *The Arctic Woodland Culture of the Kobuk River.* (Univ. Pa., Univ. Mus. Monog.) Philadelphia.
1956 "A Flint Site in Northernmost Manitoba." *Amer. Antiquity*, 21: 255–68.
1957 "Round Houses in the Western Arctic." *Ibid.*, 23:121–35.
1960 "The Archaeology of Bering Strait." *Cur. Anthropology*, 1:121–30.
1961 "Cultural Continuities of Eskimos." *Amer. Antiquity*, 27:155–73.
n.d. "Some Arctic Spear Points and Their Counterparts." *Univ. Alaska Anthrop. Paps.* (In press.)

HARP, ELMER, JR.
1951 "An Archaeological Survey in the Strait of Belle Isle Area." *Amer. Antiquity*, 16:203–20.
1953 "New World Affinities of Cape Dorset Eskimo Culture." *Univ. Alaska Anthrop. Paps.*, 1:37–54.
1958 "Prehistory in the Dismal Lake Area, N.W.T., Canada." *Arctic*, 11:219–49.
1961 "The Archaeology of the Lower and Middle Thelon, Northwest Territories." *Arctic Inst. North America Tech. Pap.*, No. 8, pp. 5–74.

HEIZER, ROBERT F.
1956 "Archaeology of the Uyak Site Kodiak Island, Alaska." *Univ. Calif. Anthrop. Records*, Vol. 17, No. 1. Berkeley.

HOLTVED, ERIK
1944 "Archaeological Investigations in the Thule District." *Meddelelser om Grønland*, Vol. 141, Nos. 1–2. Copenhagen.

HRDLIČKA, ALEŠ
1944 *The Anthropology of Kodiak Island.* Philadelphia: Wistar Institute of Anatomy and Biology.
1945 *The Aleutian and Commander Islands and Their Inhabitants.* Philadelphia: Wistar Institute of Anatomy and Biology.

IRVING, WILLIAM N.
1953 "Evidence of Early Tundra Cultures in Northern Alaska." *Univ. Alaska Anthrop. Paps.* 1:55–85.
1957 "An Archaeological Survey of the Susitna Valley." *Ibid.*, 6:37–52.

JENNESS, DIAMOND
1925 "A New Eskimo Culture in Hudson Bay." *Geog. Rev.*, 15:428–37.
1928a "Archaeological Investigations in Bering Strait." Pp. 71–80 in *Nat. Mus. Canada Ann. Rpt.*, 1926. (Nat. Mus. Canada Bull. 50.)
1928b "Ethnological Problems of Arctic America." *Amer. Geog. Soc. Spec. Pub.*, No. 7, pp. 167–75.
1933 "The Problem of the Eskimo." Pp. 373–96 in *The American Aborigines, Their Origin and Antiquity.* Toronto: University of Toronto Press.

JOCHELSON, WALDEMAR
1925 *Archaeological Investigations in the Aleutian Islands.* (Carnegie Inst. Wash. Pub. 367.) Washington, D.C.

JOHNSON, FREDERICK
  1946   "An Archaeological Survey along the Alaska Highway, 1944." *Amer. Antiquity*, 11:183–86.
KNUTH, EIGIL
  1952   "An Outline of the Archaeology of Peary Land." *Arctic*, 5:17–33.
  1954   "The Paleo-Eskimo Culture of Northeast Greenland Elucidated by Three New Sites." *Amer. Antiquity*, 19:367–81.
LAGUNA, FREDERICA DE
  1934   *The Archaeology of Cook Inlet, Alaska.* Philadelphia: University of Pennsylvania Press.
  1940   "Eskimo Lamps and Pots." *J. Roy. Anthrop. Inst. Great Britain and Ireland*, 70:53–76.
  1947   *The Prehistory of Northern North America as Seen from the Yukon.* (Soc. Amer. Arch. Mem. 3.) Menasha, Wis.
  1956   *Chugach Prehistory: The Archaeology of Prince William Sound, Alaska.* Seattle: University of Washington Press.
LARSEN, HELGE
  1950   "Archaeological Investigations in Southwestern Alaska." *Amer. Antiquity*, 15:177–86.
LARSEN, HELGE and JØRGEN MELDGAARD
  1958   "Paleo-Eskimo Cultures in Disko Bugt, West Greenland." *Meddelelser om Grønland*, Vol. 161, No. 2. Copenhagen.
LARSEN, HELGE, and FROELICH RAINEY
  1948   "Ipiutak and the Arctic Whale Hunting Culture." *Amer. Mus. Nat. Hist. Anthrop. Paps.*, Vol. 42.
LAUGHLIN, WILLIAM S.
  1951   "Notes on an Aleutian Core and Blade Industry." *Amer. Antiquity*, 17:52, 54–55.
  1952a "The Aleut-Eskimo Community." *Univ. Alaska Anthrop. Paps.*, 1:25–46.
  1952b "Contemporary Problems in the Anthropology of Southern Alaska." Pp. 66–84 in *Science in Alaska: Selected Papers on the Alaskan Science Conference.* (Arctic Inst. North America Spec. Pub. 1.)
LAUGHLIN, WILLIAM S., and GORDON H. MARSH
  1951   "A New View of the History of the Aleutians." *Arctic*, 4:75–88.
  1954   "The Lamellar Flake Manufacturing Site on Anangula Island in the Aleutians." *Amer. Antiquity*, 20:27–39.
  1956   "Trends in Aleutian Stone Artifacts." *Univ. Alaska Anthrop. Paps.*, 5:5–21.
LEECHMAN, DOUGLAS
  1943   "Two New Cape Dorset Sites." *Amer. Antiquity*, 8:363–75.
LEVIN, M. G.
  1958   "Field Work on Chukotka in 1957." *Sovetskaia Etnografiia*, 6:128–34. (In Russian.)
  1960   "Ancient Eskimo Cemetery in Uelen." *Ibid.*, 1:139–48. (In Russian.)
LEVIN, M. G., and D. A. SERGEEV
  1960   "Contribution to the Problem of the Date of Arrival of Iron in the Arctic." *Sovetskaia Etnografiia*, 3:116–22. (In Russian.)

LOWTHER, G. R.
1960 "An Account of an Archaeological Site on Cape Sparbo, Devon Island." *Contribs. to Anthrop.*, pp. 1–19. (Nat. Mus. Canada Bull. 180.)

MACHINSKII, A. V.
1941 "The Old Eskimo Culture on the Chukotsk Peninsula." (Institut Istorii Material'noi Kul'tury.) *Kratkie Soobshcheniia*, 9:80–89.

MACNEISH, RICHARD S.
1956 "The Engigstciak Site on the Yukon Arctic Coast." *Univ. Alaska Anthrop. Paps.*, 4:91–111.
1959a "Men Out of Asia: As Seen from the Northwest Yukon." *Univ. Alaska Anthrop. Paps.*, 7:41–70.
1959b "Speculative Framework of Northern North American Prehistory as of April 1959." *Anthropologica*, n.s., 1:7–23.

MARINGER, JOHN
1950 *Contribution to the Prehistory of Mongolia.* (Sino-Swedish Expedition Pub. 34.) Stockholm.

MASON, J. ALDEN
1930 "Excavations of Eskimo Thule Culture Sites at Point Barrow, Alaska." Pp. 383–94 in *Proc. 23d Internat. Cong. Americanists, New York, 1928.*

MATHIASSEN, THERKEL
1927 "Archaeology of the Central Eskimos." *Report of the Fifth Thule Expedition, 1921–24*, Vol. 4, Pts. 1 and 2. Copenhagen.
1930a "Archaeological Collections from the Western Eskimos." *Ibid.*, Vol. 10, No. 1. Copenhagen.
1930b "Inugsuk, a Mediaeval Eskimo Settlement in Upernivik District, West Greenland." *Meddelelser om Grønland*, Vol. 77. Copenhagen.
1958 "The Sermermiut Excavations 1955." *Ibid.*, Vol. 161, No. 3. Copenhagen.

MAXWELL, MOREAU S.
1960 "The Movement of Cultures in the Canadian High Arctic." *Anthropologica*, n.s., 2:177–89.

MELDGAARD, JØRGEN
1952 "A Paleo-Eskimo Culture in West Greenland." *Amer. Antiquity*, 17:222–30.
1955 "Dorset kulturen." Pp. 158–77 in Kuml. *Arbog for jysk arkaeologisk Selskab.* Aarhus.
1960a *Eskimo Sculpture.* London: Methuen & Co.
1960b "Prehistoric Culture Sequences in the Eastern Arctic as Elucidated by Stratified Sites at Igloolik." Pp. 588–95 in *Sel. Paps., 5th Internat. Cong. Anthrop. & Ethnol. Sci., Philadelphia, 1956.*
1960c "Origin and Evolution of Eskimo Cultures in the Eastern Arctic." *Canadian Geog. Jour.*, 60:64–75.

O'BRYAN, DERIC
1953 "Excavation of a Cape Dorset Eskimo House Site, Mill Island, West Hudson Strait." Pp. 40–57 in *Nat. Mus. Canada Ann. Rpt., 1951–52.* (Nat. Mus. Canada Bull. 128.)

QUIMBY, GEORGE I.
1945*a* "Pottery from the Aleutian Islands." *Fieldiana: Anthropology*, 36: 1–13. Chicago.
1945*b* "Periods of Prehistoric Art in the Aleutian Islands." *Amer. Antiquity*, 11:76–79.
1946 "Toggle Harpoon Heads from the Aleutian Islands." *Fieldiana: Anthropology*, 36:15–23.
1948 "Prehistoric Art of the Aleutian Islands." *Fieldiana: Anthropology*, 36:72–92.
RAINEY, FROELICH G.
1939 "Archaeology in Central Alaska." *Amer. Mus. Nat. Hist. Anthrop. Paps.* 36:351–40.
1941 "Eskimo Prehistory: The Okvik Site on the Punuk Islands." ("Amer. Mus. Nat. Hist. Anthrop. Paps.," Vol. 37.)
RAINEY, FROELICH, and ELIZABETH RALPH
1959 "Radiocarbon Dating in the Arctic." *Amer. Antiquity*, 24:365–74.
ROWLEY, GRAHAM
1940 "The Dorset Culture of the Eastern Arctic." *Amer. Anthropologist*, 42:490–99.
RUDENKO, S. I.
1947 "The Ancient Culture of the Bering Sea and the Eskimo Problem." Trans. PAUL TOLSTOY. Arctic Inst. North America, *Anthropology of the North: Translations from Russian Sources*, No. 1, 1961. HENRY N. MICHAEL (ed.).
SAPIR, EDWARD
1916 *Time Perspective in Aboriginal American Culture: A Study in Method.* (Canada Geol. Surv. Mem. 90; "Anthropol. Ser.," No. 13.) Ottawa.
SERGEEV, D.
1959 "The First Old Bering Sea Burials on Chukotka." *Institut Etnografiia Kratkie Soobshcheniia*, 31:68–75. (In Russian.)
SKARLAND, IVAR, and J. L. GIDDINGS, JR.
1948 "Flint Stations in Central Alaska." *Amer. Antiquity*, 14:116–20.
SKARLAND, IVAR, and CHARLES H. KEIM
1958 "Archaeological Discoveries on the Denali Highway, Alaska." *Univ. Alaska Anthrop. Paps.*, 6:79–88.
SOLBERG, O.
1907 *Beitrage zur Vorgeschichte der Osteskimo.* Videnskabs-Selskabets Skrifter. II. Hist.-Filos. Klasse. Christiania.
SOLECKI, RALPH S.
1951 "Notes on Two Archaeological Discoveries in Northern Alaska, 1950." *Amer. Antiquity*, 17:55–57.
SOLECKI, RALPH S., and ROBERT J. HACKMAN
1951 "Additional Data on the Denbigh Flint Complex in Northern Alaska." *Wash. Acad. Sci. Jour.*, 41:85–88.
SPAULDING, ALBERT C.
1953 "The Current Status of Aleutian Archaeology." Pp. 29–31 in MARIAN W. SMITH (ed.), *Asia and North America: Transpacific Contacts.* (Soc. Amer. Arch. Mem. 9.) Salt Lake City.

STEFANSSON, VILHJALMUR
  1914   *Prehistoric and Present Commerce among the Arctic Coast Eskimo.* (Canada Geol. Surv. Mus. Bull. 6; "Anthrop. Ser.," No. 3.) Ottawa.
TAYLOR, WILLIAM E.
  1959   "Review and Assessment of the Dorset Problem." *Anthropologica*, 1:1–23.
VAN STONE, JAMES W.
  1955   "Archaeological Excavations at Kotzebue, Alaska." *Univ. Alaska Anthrop. Paps.*, 3:75–155.
WINTEMBERG, W. J.
  1939–40   "Eskimo Sites of the Dorset Culture in Newfoundland." *Amer. Antiquity*, 5:83–102, 309–33.
WISSLER, CLARK
  1916   "Harpoons and Darts in the Stefansson Collection." *Amer. Mus. Nat. Hist. Anthrop. Paps.*, 14:397–443.
WORMINGTON, H. M.
  1957   *Ancient Man in North America.* 4th ed. (Denver Mus. Nat. Hist. "Pop. Ser.," No. 4.) Denver.

Western North America

ROBERT F. HEIZER

The Western Coast of North America

T HE PACIFIC COAST of North America north of Mexico (Fig. 1) may
be defined physiographically as a narrow coastal plain bounded by a
more or less continuous series of mountain ranges running closely parallel to the shore (Kroeber 1939, Map 7). From Prince William Sound in
the north (lat. 60° N.) to Los Angeles in the south (lat. 34° N.), the
coast could be reached from the continental interior only by crossing
substantial mountain barriers. Free access along this coastal border was
available to boat-using groups,[1] but the main population accretions of the
past were presumably provided by small contingents moving westward
across the mountains. Level access to the Pacific rim from the east was
provided only in the south through the Basin-and-Range province across
what is now southern Nevada, southern Arizona, and the southern California desert, or from the south out of Mexico, by way of the west-
coast corridor known as the Sonoran Desert.

The western continental fringe clearly has not been an area into which
massive population movements or major culture complexes have flowed
and spread out as they have east of the Rockies but, rather, has been
a marginal area, generally difficult of access, into which many small
groups have been pushed or found their way over a long period of time,
with the result that extraordinarily complex series of local cultures have
taken root, developed, and interinfluenced their neighbors over the past
several thousand years.[2] Although Kroeber (1962) warned against too

ROBERT F. HEIZER, who is professor of anthropology at the University of California,
Berkeley, received his doctoral degree from the same institution. His extensive field research
has ranged from Alaska to Veracruz and centered upon California and Nevada. His numerous
writings include many outstanding publications on the archeology of these areas and also
important contributions on the subject of field techniques in archeology. He has also contributed to archeology as an outstanding teacher; the ranks of young archeologists include
many who received their training under him.

[1] The distribution of boat types along the Pacific Coast does not encourage the view that
they served to transport migrating groups (Heizer and Massey 1953; Durham 1960).

[2] Lest this statement appear to imply flatly that no external influences have helped modify
and shape California cultures, the reader is reminded that Southwestern ("Pueblo") influ-

easy acceptance of the "fish-trap theory, according to which the multiplicity of languages in California is due to the successive crowding, into
this more desirable habitat, of waves or bands of unrelated immigrants
from less favorable territories, to which none of them were ever willing
to return," a considerable body of evidence and opinion indicates that
acceptance of the fish-trap theory helps to account for some of the

ARCHAEOLOGICAL AREAS OF THE WESTERN COAST OF NORTH AMERICA

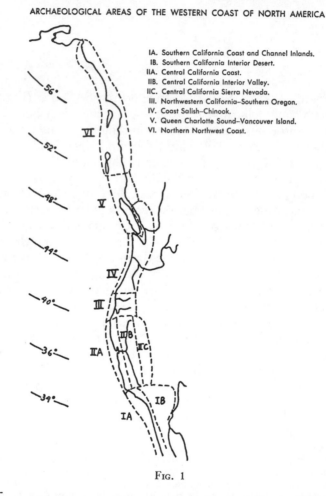

IA. Southern California Coast and Channel Inlands.
IB. Southern California Interior Desert.
IIA. Central California Coast.
IIB. Central California Interior Valley.
IIC. Central California Sierra Nevada.
III. Northwestern California–Southern Oregon.
IV. Coast Salish–Chinook.
V. Queen Charlotte Sound–Vancouver Island.
VI. Northern Northwest Coast.

FIG. 1

ences were fairly strong (Heizer 1946), that the Northwest Coast proper significantly shaped
the basic features of northwestern California (Kroeber 1920), and that California and Great
Basin peoples share a basic cultural substratum (Lowie 1923). Oceanian elements also may
have been received, but conclusions on this score depend upon whether such features as
curved shell and bone fishhooks, the plank canoe (Heizer 1938), and Polynesian-style cos-
mogonic myths (Kroeber 1925) are independent parallels or are ascribable to transpacific
diffusion.

considerable linguistic, cultural, and somatic variability on both the ethnographic and the prehistoric time levels of the west-coast region (Heizer 1952*b*; see also Dixon 1905; Putnam 1880). Only in this way can we reasonably account for the high degree of linguistic diversity and cultural fractionation exhibited anciently as well as ethnographically along the Pacific Coast.

Reconstructing the histories of linguistic stocks (through computing the sequence and time of splitting-off of dialects) by the method of lexicostatistics and glottochronology (Hymes 1960) has come in for some attention in the area discussed in this paper. The reader may refer, as an introduction, to the works of Baumhoff and Olmsted (1963), Cressman (1960), Kroeber (1917, 1935, 1955), Swadesh (1956), and Taylor (1961) for views (all tentative) on the homelands and migrations of groups belonging to the language families represented on the Pacific Coast.

Although the subject of ancient man is surveyed by Krieger in this volume, I wish to refer to some aspects of the matter as regards California. In recent years we have been presented with a number of claims of the finding of evidence of man's presence in California at a time so early, and with proofs so vague, that most American archeologists have taken the position that they would wait to see more evidence before they accepted the proposals. I refer here to G. Carter's (1959) claims and to their critical assessment by Haury (1959), Johnson and Miller (1958), and Krieger (1958, 1959). Carter's "artifacts" have been judged by a number of archeologists to be natural forms and not man-made implements. Recent discussions of value on the subject of fractured flint or chert pieces that could be taken for artifacts but that were produced by natural means are by Bourdier (1953), Clark (1961), Harner (1956), and Watanabe (1949).

In this same vein, I wish to state here my opinion that the several bone fragments from Potter Creek Cave, believed by Putnam (1906; see also Merriam 1906) to be tools made by man, are *not* artifacts. A few bone scraps that have features suggesting artificial modification, found in the midst of thousands of bone fragments that are clearly not artifacts, make their fortuitous production the most probable explanation. Nature can, on occasion, cause certain features in bone pieces that make them appear to be the result of the hand of man, and in these instances our usually workable (but not infallible) test criteria give us the wrong answer. Instances of this sort are presented in detail by Nelson (1928), Pei (1938), and Koby (1943). Krieger (1953) accepts the Potter Creek bones as artifacts and suggests (1951) that there may have been, on a very early time level, a bone-tool industry in North America. Hurt (1953) has indicated his doubts about the tenability of this proposition, but it is apparently a persistent idea (cf. Menghin 1957). If we were to accept Sellards' (1960) proposition that the earliest men in the New World were so poorly equipped that stone tools were rare or lacking, we should be coming very close to the concept of a Prelithic, or Protolithic, or Eolithic (cf. Greenman 1957), or possibly Osteodontokeratic culture level—for none of which I see any support at all.

A new series of alleged ancient evidences of man has been proposed by P. C. Orr on the basis of his findings on Santa Rosa Island. I have already expressed my inability to accept these claims as they are stated (Heizer 1962), for the reason that we are not given the detailed evidence of occurrence. Orr may be correct in stating that he has found evidence of man's presence on Santa Rosa Island dating back to 30,000 or more years ago, but until his findings are published in detail the claims cannot be accepted.

A similar degree of obscurity, which necessitates withholding acceptance, surrounds the age of artifacts associated with former beach lines in southern California lake basins such as Lake Mohave and Lake Manix (Roberts 1940). A radiocarbon age (LJ-200) for fresh-water mussel shells from the high shore line of Lake Mohave of 9640 years[3] may indeed date the lake stand, but it does not answer the problem of whether the stone artifacts occurring on the surface of that beach are the same age as the molluscan remains imbedded in the beach deposit. The same hazard in applying the date for some event in nature to an assumed contemporaneity of surface artifacts obtains also in the radiocarbon age of Lake Manix tufa (UCLA-121) of 19,300 years. In view of the known fact that in the very brief historic period some of these lakes have filled with water, which has remained for many months (Rogers 1939; Thompson 1921), we may assume that a number of these temporary fillings have occurred in the last 10,000 years and would have attracted aboriginal settlement. In 1938, for example, Lake Mohave filled in a thirteen-day period and formed a body of water 16 miles long, 2.5 miles wide, and 10 feet deep. Thus, artifacts lying on the surface of these beaches may or may not date from the time the beaches were formed. Regardless of how persuasive and detailed the reasoning, it is not possible to be convinced that the dry lake basins of southern California have produced datable evidence of early man or that the

[3] While I have suggested (Heizer 1958b; see also Bird 1961) that radiocarbon ages be suffixed not with B.P. (Before Present) but with an indication of the year in which the laboratory determination was made, e.g., B-61 (= Before 1961), in order that all conversions to calendar dates may be accurate and consistent, regardless of when they are calculated or who makes the calculations, only the central age determination is given in this paper. By noting the sample number in parentheses, the reader can easily refer to the published age determination.

"cultures" or "complexes" that have been proposed are probably contemporaneous aggregates of artifacts (i.e., industries).[4] If one argues
that water is necessary in the southern California desert for Indians to
be present, one might first ponder Julian Steward's observation (1937;
see also Wallace 1958):

In the southern end of Eureka Valley, near the northern end of Death Valley,
California, there is a site bordering a playa and extending several miles. Thousands of flint flakes with relatively few artifacts mark it as predominantly a
workshop, though the source of the flints is several miles distant in the mountains. The nearest water is a spring 3 to 5 miles away. There is no apparent
reason why anyone should choose a place lacking water, having virtually no
vegetation, and, in fact, devoid of anything of apparent use to man or beast, for
a workshop or other purpose. Nevertheless, the presence here of large spherical
stone mortars of the type used by Death Valley Shoshoni and at least one arrow
point of the Shoshonean type is presumptive evidence that the Shoshoni visited
the site, though it does not, of course, prove that they used it as a workshop.
Although Mr. and Mrs. Campbell have never found a camp site more than 3
miles from a water hole in southern California (1935:26), the writer has
repeatedly received accounts from Shoshoni and Paiute informants of camps
maintained by entire families and groups of families for days at a time 10 and
even 20 miles from water when seeds, salt, flint, edible insects, or other important supplies made it worth-while to do so. Water is used sparingly and
when the ollas in which it is transported are empty one or two persons make
the long trip to replenish them. Remoteness from present water, then, is not
per se, the slightest proof that a site dates from the pluvial period.

While the Santa Rosa Island, Lake Mohave, and Lake Manix materials may be ancient, they have not been adequately demonstrated to
be so. The most persuasive indication to date that the Lake Mohave
materials may predate 7000 years ago come from the recent excavation
of the Harris site near San Diego (Warren and True 1961). The lower

---

[4] One wonders what thinking lies behind the use of such familiar terms applied to American materials as "Paleolithic-like assemblages," "Clactonian," and the like, by a few workers. Simpson (1961), referring to the Coyote Gulch locality in San Bernardino County,
proposes that the "Coyote Gulch artifact assemblage may be assigned to a stage typologically
similar to the later portion of the Old World Lower Paleolithic." Elsewhere she states that
she employs European terms and period names because "it indicates the stage reached in the
evolution of lithic workmanship." Carter has suggested that there is a New World Paleolithic. Willey and Phillips (1958) review some of these proposals and remain unconvinced.
What we are asked to believe is that America went through stages of cultural development
parallel to those of the Old World Paleolithic, that is, the lithic "industries" labeled by
European terms are *homotaxial* (cf. Peake 1940; Childe 1956).
A recent article by Wormington (1962) discusses in a way that I believe quite acceptable
the problem of flaking techniques in the New World that are similar to those of the Old
World Paleolithic. Wormington, although she thinks it possible that "bifacial flaking developed independently in America from a base that included Mousterian traits and those of
the chopper-chopping tool industries," does not suggest a homotaxial culture sequence in
the New World.

levels of the site, which was excavated earlier by M. J. Rogers, produce materials of the San Dieguito I culture, named by Rogers (1939) and equated by him on the basis of shared traits with the Lake Mohave–Playa cultures of the interior lake basins of southern California.[5] The San Dieguito culture inventory is limited to chipped-stone forms including scraper planes, a wide variety of scrapers (keeled, flake, snubnose, side, end, etc.), heavy bipointed blades or knives, eared crescents, leaf-shaped projectile points, choppers, pebble hammerstones, and hammerstones made from cores or nuclei. If we accept the Harris site materials from the bottom level as providing an adequate sample of material culture of the San Dieguito culture, the absence of grinding tools is worthy of comment. Wallace (1958) has discussed the lack of seed-grinding tools in the Death Valley I culture and points out that it appears to be a non-seed-using culture whose primary economy rested upon hunting and that these characteristics do not permit its classification in the "Desert Culture" tradition. Warren and True (1961) suggest that the San Dieguito culture may represent evidence of an early "Western Hunting Culture," different from and older than the Desert Culture, and that the Lake Mohave–Playa cultures of the interior lake basins are manifestations of this hunting culture. Although manos were found at Lake Mohave, they incline to accept Amsden's explanation (1937) that these are attributable to the later Pinto Basin culture. Absence of portable stone mortars or metates at camp or village sites does not necessarily prove that a group did not grind seeds, since the site may have been occupied for reasons or at times when seed-grinding was impossible or inappropriate. Alternatively, the wooden mortar (Kroeber 1925) in wide use in southern California in ethnographic times (and in central California prehistorically in the Middle Horizon period), if used, would leave no archeological vestiges. Clearly, we should be careful not to decide too hastily that we are dealing only with hunters when we fail to find, in a very small series of sites producing very few material objects, familiar forms of seed-grinding implements. Indeed, to prove that a prehistoric culture group avoided seeds and subsisted on hunting

[5] M. J. Rogers' chronology (1939) is much too short. He has revised this several times, most notably in Haury (1950), to give it a greater time range. The revision is critically discussed by Warren and True (1961). The complicated terminology is summarized in the following table:

Rogers 1929	Rogers 1939, 1945	Rogers 1939	Rogers 1958 Haury 1950	Warren and True 1961
Shell Midden Scraper-Maker	La Jolla San Dieguito	Playa II Playa I Malpais	San Dieguito III San Dieguito II San Dieguito I	Yuman La Jolla San Dieguito I

requires direct evidence of the latter pursuit. Incorrect deductions of prehistoric economic practices are very common (Heizer 1960).

Rogers (1958) and Wallace (1954) propose a derivation of the San Dieguito from the Cochise Culture of southern Arizona, a proposal made originally by E. B. Sayles (1937). The suggestion of an early (pre-7000 years ago) simple and widespread hunting-based culture in the Pacific Coast area, exemplified by the San Dieguito–Lake Mohave–Playa–Death Valley cultures, must be, for now, only a possibility, which later work will support or deny. No reliable radiocarbon dates have been determined for the San Dieguito culture. One radiocarbon determination (LJ-136) of *Chione* shell, 4720 years old, believed at one time to refer to this culture, is rejected by Warren and True (1961) as reliably dating the San Dieguito culture level at the Harris site.

Between about 7000 and 4000 years ago, we have a number of radio-carbon-dated sites from the southern California coast region extending from Santa Barbara to San Diego. From Santa Rosa Island an age determination of midden shell (M-1133) gave an age of 7350 years for what is apparently the Dune Dweller culture (Orr 1956), and for the later Highland culture on Santa Rosa Island there are two determinations —4790 (UCLA-105) and 5370 (L-446B) years old. On the mainland there is the Topanga site, as yet undated (Heizer and Lemert 1947; Treganza and Bierman 1958); Zuma Creek site (Peck 1955) dated 4950 years old (LJ-77); Malaga Cove site at Redondo Beach (Walker 1951) with an age of 6510 years (LJ-3); the undated Little Sycamore site (Wallace 1954); the undated Oak Grove culture (D. B. Rogers 1929); the Pauma complex (True 1958); and the Scripps Estate site (Shumway, Hubbs, and Moriarty 1961), which is radiocarbon-dated as occupied between 5460 and 7370 years ago (samples LJ-79, LJ-109, LJ-110, LJ-221). All or most of these sites can be construed as manifestations of the La Jolla culture, which is more generally subsumed under what has been called the "Milling Stone Horizon" (Wallace 1955). The trait inventory of the sites listed varies somewhat and may thus reflect regional subphases of a fairly simple and uncomplex culture type. The culture is generally characterized by the following: abundance of deep-basined metates; manos; scraper planes; flake scrapers; choppers; pebble hammerstones; pitted hammerstones; lesser frequency of bone tools (awls, punches); "cogstones" (cf. Eberhart 1961); flexed burials (at Little Sycamore site, Scripps Estate site); prone extended burial, usually covered with a cairn of metates (Oak Grove sites, Topanga site); and reburial (Little Sycamore site, Topanga site). The economy was based on seed-gathering, which was supplemented with hunting and shellfish-collecting. The Milling Stone Horizon sites lack cremation, pottery, and C-shaped shell fishhooks. Use of ocean resources is limited and apparently secondary to economic pursuits of the hunting-catching-gathering order.

The abundant presence of stone mortars on the ocean bottom off La Jolla (Tuthill and Allanson 1954) is difficult to explain. No means of dating these has been found, and it may be that they are evidence of a marked change in sea level, which occurred after the shore had been occupied by man, although one senses that the artifacts are of later rather than earlier types. Only more investigation will help explain these ocean-floor concentrations of artifacts.

Meighan (1962) proposes that on Santa Catalina and San Nicolas Islands there was occupation in the fourth millennium B.C. by peoples who practiced a sea-hunting economy.[6] Curved shell fishhooks are radio-carbon-dated on San Nicolas Island at 400 years old (UCLA-164), but they must be rather older in the general Channel area (cf. Heizer 1949c).[7] The oldest archeological dates for the Channel Islands (omitting Santa Rosa) are 3300 (UCLA-165), 3980 (UCLA-147), and 5070 (W-981) years for San Nicolas Island; 3880 years (M-434) for Santa Catalina Island; 450 years (LJ-259) for San Clemente Island; 2120 (LJ-218) and 1750 years (LJ-25) for San Miguel Island. These dates do not, of course, necessarily mark the earliest occupation of any of the islands.

For the southern California coastal area, a series of what Wallace (1955) terms "Intermediate Cultures" occupies the two millenniums between 2000 B.C. and the beginning of the Christian Era (or perhaps to A.D. 500). These are little known in detail and include the poorly defined Hunting Culture of the Santa Barbara region (D. B. Rogers 1929) and the La Jolla II phase in the San Diego region (Rogers 1945; Harding 1951). The basket- or hopper-mortar makes its appearance,

[6] I am citing an unpublished paper and therefore do not wish to criticize a view that may be altered before it is in print. The proposal is an extremely interesting one, but because of its significance it will need pretty solid evidence to warrant acceptance. Presence of bones of cetaceans (*Delphinus, Lissodelphis*), pinnipeds (*Otariidae* and *Phocidae*), and aquatic carnivora (*Enhydra*) in coastal sites does not prove that these animals were hunted in open water. All these forms are known to be stranded dead on shore and could have been secured in this way without leaving dry land (cf. Meighan 1959b). Occupation of the offshore islands does, of course, prove presence of some form of watercraft, but whether sea hunting was practiced with these crafts is another matter.

[7] Meighan (1962) briefly discusses Polynesian parallels to the curved shell hooks and believes that if a historical connection exists between these areas in shell hooks, the diffusion may have been from California to Polynesia. The means of transference, if this did occur, need not have been by human carriers or drift canoes but could have been by live fish, carrying hooks in their mouths. Thus, the oceanic skipjack (*Katsuwonus pelamis* L.), albacore (*Germo alalunga* Gmelin), yellowfin tuna (*Neothunnus albacares* Bonnaterre), and swordfish (*Xiphias gladius* L.), according to Dr. W. I. Follett (California Academy of Sciences), are all migrants which might have carried imbedded hooks to or from the American coast as far west across the Pacific as Japan. On transportation of artifacts by live migratory animals see Heizer (1944).

perhaps indicating the institution of the acorn-preparation process (hulling, grinding, winnowing, warm-water leaching, and stone-boiling in baskets), a greater variety of flaked implements occurs, flexed primary burial is the standard method of disposal of the dead, and hunting and shellfish gathering are the main economic pursuits. Larger villages and more sedentary patterns indicate this period as developmental and anticipatory to the appearance of the late prehistoric period of cultural climax, which ends with the appearance of the Spanish explorers and missionaries in the mid-sixteenth century (Heizer 1958a).

The late prehistoric period in southern California is marked by the clear emergence of local culture varieties as a result of large population numbers, and their separation is registered culturally through local ecological accommodations and political independence (cf. Meighan 1954; Wissler 1958; Orr 1943; Olson 1930). This is clearest in the Santa Barbara region, where local mainland-shore culture subtypes are apparent, as well as accentuated mainland-island differentiations. The bow and arrow is clearly by now the dominant weapon. Steatite is a common material for cooking vessels, except where pottery is the alternative for direct-fire cooking. The essentially exclusive distribution of steatite and pottery indicates the latter as a recent acquisition in desert and coastal southern California (cf. Kroeber 1925), the source lying to the east across the Colorado River in Arizona (Harner 1958). The circular shell fishhook, while it may make its appearance in the Intermediate culture period so far as is known, is most characteristic of the later period (Olson 1930; Robinson 1942; Heizer 1949c; Wissler 1958), and by this time an undoubted maritime orientation of the coastal peoples has been effected (cf. Beals and Hester 1960; Olson 1930; Wallace 1955; Heizer 1938). An abundance of stone and shell-bead and shell-ornament types (cf. Heye 1921), bone artifacts (Gifford 1940), burins and bladelets presumably used in woodworking (Heizer and Kelley 1962; Kowta 1961), circular thatch-covered houses, complicated painted pictographs (True 1954; Grant 1961), and flexed burial or cremation are characteristic. Wallace (1955) has summarized the site inventories for the southern coast for this period.

The interior of southern California is, culturally speaking, an extension of the Great Basin area toward the Pacific. Artifact materials associated with shore-line features of extinct lakes (Lake Mohave, Pinto Basin, Lake Manix) have been mentioned earlier. The cultural adaptation to the rather confining way of life imposed by a water-deficient land has prevailed from the earliest times. An uncomplicated technology, which manifests material expression in seed-grinding tools, flaked knives, points and scrapers, and little else in open sites (Rogers 1939, 1945; Davis 1962), with the addition of some perishables in the form of basketry and cordage (Peck and Smith 1957; Smith *et al.* 1957) in cave or shelter sites, provides us with a picture of the Desert Culture (Jennings and Norbeck 1955) that has endured in relatively stable form for several thousand years. Petroglyphs are abundant, are of several styles that are widely distributed throughout the Great Basin, and served as a ritual accompaniment to hunting (Heizer and Baumhoff 1962). Names and sequences of cultures are summarized in Bennyhoff (1958) and in Meighan (1959*a*).

To the south of San Diego, on both shores of the northern peninsula of Baja California, there is evidence of the La Jolla culture (e.g., at Puertas Minitas, where a radiocarbon age of midden shell is 7020 years old, sample LJ-231). The later archeology of the peninsula has strong ties with that of southern desert and coastal California, although these have not been worked out in detail. Reference to the publications of Massey (1947, 1961) and Massey and Osborne (1961) will provide the reader with a summary of recent work in the peninsular area. Aschmann's (1959) superlative monograph on the historic aboriginal demography and ecology of Baja California provides the ethnographic time-level continuum to the prehistoric archeology.

Central California, defined here as the region lying between Tehachapi (where the Sierra Nevadas join with the Coast Range) in the south to the head of the Sacramento Valley in the north, and the ocean coast on the west to the Sierra Nevada crest on the east, may be divided into three zones: (1) coastal (i.e., shore plus Coast Range section), (2) interior valley (the combined Sacramento and San Joaquin valleys), and (3) Sierran (western slopes of the Sierra Nevada). The complicated sequence of cultures has been summarized by Heizer (1949*a*) and Beardsley (1954), with more recent amplifications by Meighan (1959*a*).

The most carefully worked-out sequence is for the lower Sacramento Valley region (Lillard, Heizer, and Fenenga 1939; Heizer and Fenenga 1939; Belous 1953). Here occur sites of the Early Horizon characterized by rigid adherence to disposal of the corpse lying on the face and fully extended (i.e., prone); "charm stones" of various forms (including phallic shapes) and almost invariably drilled at one end; large, heavy projectile points; shell beads and ornaments of several types; flat slab metate and bowl mortar; fiber-tempered baked clay balls (surrogates for rocks used in cooking by stone-boiling); rare bone awls; twined (but not coiled) basketry (evidenced by impressions in baked clay); the atlatl as the chief weapon (Heizer 1949*a*); fairly clear indications that strong development of individual accumulation of wealth did not exist and some indications that warfare was uncommon. For additional details see Heizer (1949*a*) and Beardsley (1948). The age of the Early Horizon, which is now known from seven sites, derives from a series of radiocarbon dates based on charcoal from site SJo-68, which are 4052, 4100, and 4350 years old (samples C-440, C-522, M-645, M-646, M-647, discussed in Heizer 1958*b*).

The Oak Grove–Topanga–La Jolla–Milling Stone Horizon is probably related to the culture disclosed in the lowest levels of the sites reported on by Wedel (1941) at Buena Vista Lake in the southern San Joaquin Valley, where mullers and extended burials occur, and the connection may be traced farther north to the Cosumnes Valley near Sacramento in the Early Horizon sites (Heizer 1939, 1949*a*). The Tranquillity site in the San Joaquin Valley (Hewes 1946) appears to be ancient on the grounds of fossilization of animal and human bone (Heizer and Cook 1952), but the apparently associated cultural materials seem more recent.

The Middle Horizon, which follows in time and is in part an outgrowth of the Early Horizon culture, falls in the time period from about 2000 B.C. to A.D. 300. Emphasis on materials and types has changed from the earlier period. Burial position is now regularly tightly flexed; cremation occurs (though rare, and usually with a rich accompaniment of grave goods); offerings with primary interments are minimal or absent; and bones are fairly frequently found with weapon points imbedded—an indication that warfare (or at least violent death) has become more developed since the preceding period. Sparing use of grave offerings may indicate emphasis on wealth accumulation and reluctance of heirs, through greed, to "waste" such goods, a situation having an ethnographic parallel among the Yurok of northwestern California. Coiled basketry (as indicated by abundance of bone awls) was manufactured, a large variety of abalone-shell bead and ornament types is present, and bone is now used more as an industrial material (for making sweat-scrapers, punches, whistles, and tubes). The slab metate carries over, but the deep wooden mortar (with stone pestle) is the most important seed-grinding tool. Charm stones or plummets continue to be made, though in forms different from earlier types, and the phallic form is lacking. Barbed harpoons and a peculiar blunt-tipped bone or antler point, probably for taking fish, appear in this period (Bennyhoff 1950). The bow, as well as the atlatl, was apparently used, perhaps each devoted to special purposes in hunting or war. Sites are larger, and the population was obviously greater than in the Early period.

The Late Horizon, which is dated from A.D. 300 to the opening of the historic period in the late eighteenth century (see Cook and Heizer 1962 for dates of the five phases of this horizon), can be pretty certainly identified as the prehistoric culture of the Penutian-speaking tribes of central California (Heizer 1941*a*). The Middle Horizon culture carries over in essence, but, again, specific material forms are distinctive. Thus, this period is characterized by a new set of varieties of shell beads; a bewildering array of ornaments made of abalone shell; small obsidian arrowpoints (often with deep edge serration) for use with the bow and arrow; large stone mortars (bowl and slab form with basketry hopper attached); long, tubular steatite smoking pipes; bird-bone tubes with extremely detailed and complicated fine-line incised decoration; and increased use of cremation and sacrifice by burning grave offerings in the grave pit just prior to placing the corpse in the grave. Based on both archeological and ethnographical evidence, central California seems to have come under fairly strong influence from the Southwest over the last millennium, the line marked by the territories of the Pomo, Wintun, and Maidu tribes appearing to represent the northwestern frontier of the "greater Southwest." The archeological evidence for Southwestern influence on California is given in detail elsewhere (Heizer 1946; cf. Haekel 1958; Taylor 1961).

In the southern San Joaquin Valley, the work of Gifford and Schenck (1926), Kroeber (1910), Walker (1947), and Wedel (1941) has shown a long sequence of cultures that go back to the same period as the Early Horizon culture and continue into the historic period. The Late period shows influence from the Santa Barbara coast, as well as from the Colorado River region.

On the coast of central California south of San Francisco Bay, shell mounds are the characteristic type of site (Pilling 1955). At the mouth of Willow Creek (Monterey County), the base of a shore-line midden has been dated by radiocarbon as 1879 and 1840 years old (C-628, C-695). Curved shell fishhooks in this level help to date this form, which is more abundant (but undated) in the Santa Barbara region to the south. At this time level a fully developed coastal culture was operating, as indicated by evidence of fishing, mollusk collecting, and taking of shore-frequenting sea mammals (seal, sea lion), as well as oceanic forms (sea otter). On the shores of San Francisco Bay a number of large shell mounds have been excavated and dated. The bottom levels of these cluster around the age of 3000 years[8]—for example, site Ala-328 (Davis and Treganza 1959) with an age of 2588 years (C-690), site SMa-77 (Heizer 1958*b*) with dates of 2700 and 3150 years old (L-187A, L-187B), site Ala-307 with a series of inconsistent radiocarbon dates whose maximum for the mound base probably should read about 3500 years old (Heizer 1958*b*), and the base of site Ala-309 (Schenck 1926) with an age of 2310 years (LJ-199).

Thus far, the earliest occupation of the well-favored shore of San

---

[8] Kroeber (1925) believed that the lower levels of the San Francisco Bay mounds dated "from 3000 or more years ago." This view, which is essentially correct, derived from the efforts of Nelson and Gifford to compute age by rate of refuse accumulation (cf. Cook 1946).

Francisco Bay seems to have occurred in early Middle Horizon times; the Early Horizon sites, if ever present, have either escaped detection or were situated in locations where subsidence of the shore of the bay has led to their encroachment by the water (cf. Beardsley 1954 and Greengo 1951 for detailed discussion). Generally speaking, allowing for local ecologic adjustments to tidal shore (as against valley riverine locale), the Middle and Late sequence on the bay conforms to that already sketched for the Interior Valley.

The general picture of the coast and valley sections of central California is, in summary, one of a change from peaceful egalitarianism in Early Horizon times to warlike wealth-consciousness in the following Middle Horizon. One can read the Late archeological evidences as conformable to the political units outlined by Kroeber (1962). Beardsley (1948) has perceptively characterized the industrial materials upon which greatest attention was lavished—Early Horizon on stone, Middle Horizon on bone, and Late Horizon on shell. The major shore-line occupation of the central California coast seems to have occurred from 3000 to 3500 years ago, although traces of earlier settlement almost certainly remain to be discovered. The first clear indication of dense populations goes back to Middle Horizon times, and, with improving economic exploitative techniques, the population numbers increased until, by the opening of the historic period, California, comprising about 1 per cent of the total land area of North America north of Mexico, contained not less than 10 per cent of the total Indian population of that region. This density of population led to very large villages in some districts (actual counts run as high as fourteen hundred persons), and there was a notable development of craft specialization. Willey and Phillips (1958) class California as Formative in their system of developmental stages; Meighan (1959a) calls California an area of Archaic cultures; and Heizer (1958a) has shown that late prehistoric California can be ranked in climax locations (southern San Joaquin Valley, Sacramento River, and Santa Barbara Channel) as Preformative or incipiently Formative in the revised classification system of Willey and Phillips (1958). The failure of California Indians to accept agriculture is ascribed to cultural resistance based on the well-established and complicated technology of the acorn economic complex (Kroeber 1917:394; Heizer 1958a).

In the Coast Ranges and along the coast north of San Francisco Bay, there was substantial inhabitation in Middle Horizon times (cf. Beardsley 1954, Heizer 1953, sections dealing with sites Nap-1 and Nap-32), the cultural materials being similar to those found farther east in the interior valley. On an earlier time level is site Nap-131 (Meighan 1953), which produced flaked basalt and obsidian implements similar to some from the Borax Lake site in Lake County (Harrington 1948), whose proper position in time has never been satisfactorily agreed upon, even though it has yielded a number of Clovis fluted points. Surveys carried out since 1949 have led to the location of eight additional sites,[9] characterized by manos; heavy, short, concave-base projectile points with basal-thinning flakes; and heavy flake scrapers and scraper planes, which are coming to light in the Coast Range valleys north of San Francisco Bay. It is tempting to lump these together as evidence of an old seed-using–hunting culture that is coeval with, or possibly antedates, the Early Horizon culture of the lower Sacramento Valley, whose age is 4000 and more years old. What are called the Mendocino and Borax Lake complexes (Meighan 1955) are probably both to be included in this proposed category, as well as some sites to the north in Shasta County (Treganza and Heicksen 1960). A definite tendency to use flint and basalt rather than obsidian for flaked implements appears to be characteristic of this time level (cf. Heizer and Elsasser 1953). However, until more investigation is carried out and some dating of these sites can be secured, this suggestion of an early hunting-collecting culture should be considered only a hypothesis. Late Horizon sites in the northern Coast Ranges are abundant, though little archeology has been carried out in the region (Treganza, Smith, and Weymouth 1950). Just west of the head of the Sacramento Valley, in the Coast Range section, salvage archeology in reservoir areas has yielded an abundance of late materials that are basically central Californian in type but are modified by influences reaching southeast from the distinctive culture development of northwestern California (Treganza 1954; Treganza and Heicksen 1960).

In the Sierra Nevada Mountains, which rise to the east of the Sacramento and San Joaquin valleys, the history of human occupation probably begins with the same metate-using collectors and hunters whose presence has been dimly perceived in the northern Coast Ranges. This possibility derived from the numerous discoveries in the last half of the nineteenth century of artifacts in the auriferous gravel deposits. Evaluation of these older finds cannot be done at this date, nor can Holmes's (1901) critical review be improved upon. Dating of the artifacts recovered in the past century from the gravels is not possible at this remove, and the best that can be said is that some may date from middle postglacial times—say 5000–6000 years ago. It was thought that similar materials had been found recently *in situ* at the Farmington site (Sta-44) (Treganza and Heizer 1953), but radiocarbon ages of 1660 and 1170 years old (UCLA-132, UCLA-133) from the gravels at Farmington

[9] For purpose of reference I list sites Lak-261, Nap-242, and six other Napa County sites (Heizer and Elsasser 1953).

seem effectively to dispose of this site as ancient. The Farmington gravels have been judged to be much older than the radiocarbon dates secured, and further age determinations should be made before a final decision is reached on the antiquity of the implements that are incorporated in the lower gravels. Middle Horizon materials (presumably dated by the chronology cited for the valley area) occur in the Sierran limestone caverns, usually in association with human bones, this association resulting from throwing corpses and burial offerings down the natural shafts (Wallace and Lathrap 1952; Wallace 1951*a*, 1951*b*). Some of the bones have thick incrustations of travertine, which led Orr (1953) to compute their age at 12,000 years, but this has now been reduced by radiocarbon tests to 1400 years (L-530A, L-530C) by Broeker, Olson, and Orr (1960). Probably equivalent in time to the limestone cavern ossuaries is the Martis complex of the High Sierra (Heizer and Elsasser 1953) in the Lake Tahoe region, which is characterized by heavy basalt points (stemmed and side-notched forms), scrapers and drills, "boatstones" (atlatl weights?), slab metate and portable mortar, and economic emphasis directed to seed-collecting and hunting. The Martis complex is succeeded in this region by the Kings Beach complex, which is late in time and is believed to refer to the late prehistoric Washo tribe. It is characterized by use of obsidian; bedrock mortar; small, light Desert side-notched projectile points (used with the bow and arrow); and economic emphasis on fishing and seed-collecting. That this same general sequence of cultures occurs through the central and southern Sierra is indicated by the more recent work of Bennyhoff (1956), Elsasser (1960), Hindes (1962), and Lathrap and Shutler (1955). Northeastern California has been neglected by archeologists, but recent work by Baumhoff and Olmsted (1963) shows that the Pit River area is a transition cultural zone between central California and the Great Basin. Smith and Weymouth (1952) have described the Late-period archeology in the Shasta Dam area, Treganza (1954) found Late-period sites in the Redbank Reservoir area in Tehama County, and Baumhoff (1955, 1957), on the basis of excavations in Payne's and Kingsley caves in Tehama County, identifies two archeological complexes: (1) Mill Creek, which is similar to the Late Horizon of the Sacramento Valley area, and (2) Kingsley, which seems to have a close similarity to the Martis complex, whose recently determined Sierran distribution is shown by Elsasser (1960). In the southern Sierras, pottery (Owens Valley Brown Ware) was introduced about A.D. 1300 by diffusion across the Great Basin through Shoshonean-speaking peoples, its source perhaps being in the Woodland pottery of the western Great Plains or possibly in the Southwest (Gruhn 1961). Its known distribution in California is shown by Elsasser (1960). Cross-dating through trade items (basketry and shell beads) of central Californian and trans-Sierran sites on the western fringe of the Great Basin is on a fairly firm basis (Bennyhoff and Heizer 1958; Baumhoff and Heizer 1958; Lanning n.d.).

Moving now farther north, we will review the scanty evidence of prehistoric occupation of the coastal area from Cape Mendocino in northern California to Prince William Sound in southern Alaska. It will be convenient to follow the cultural subareas or "provinces" defined by Drucker (1955a), which are in part derived from his earlier ethnographic and archeological investigations (Drucker 1943, 1955b) and which, in their aggregate, comprise what Kroeber (1939) called the Northwest Coast culture area.

Northwestern California north of Cape Mendocino and the southern coast of Oregon south of the Coquille River are believed to form an identifiable prehistoric cultural subarea. This conclusion is supported by the relatively small amount of work done in this coastal area by Schumacher (1874) and Berreman (1944) at Chetco; Leatherman and Krieger (1940) on the lower Coquille River; Newman (1959) at site Cu-47 on the Oregon coast; Mills (1950), Heizer and Mills (1952), and Loud (1918) in a series of coastal sites in northwestern California. Most of the sites excavated thus far are shell-mound deposits, which appear to be fairly late in time. Few radiocarbon dates have been secured. There is a determination for site Cs-23 on the lower Coquille River of 350 years old (L-189B) discussed by Cressman (1952) and Newman (1959), a radiocarbon age of 1050 years (M-938) for the base of the Gunther Island site in Humboldt Bay (Loud 1918), a guess date for the Patricks Point shell mound to the south of the mouth of the Klamath River of 600–1000 years old (Mills 1950), and a "date" of A.D. 1620 calculated as the age of the Tsurai site at Trinidad Bay (Heizer and Mills 1952). Some cultural change has occurred in northwestern California in the last thousand years, evidenced mainly by small variations in projectile point forms and bone harpoons (Bennyhoff 1950), and the late appearance of the wooden smoking pipe with inset steatite bowl. The archeological practice, evidenced in the lower levels of Gunther Island, of lavish burning of grave goods in the grave pit with the corpse laid on top of the still-burning embers, was succeeded in late prehistoric times by extended primary interment without burned offerings, which is the ethnographic mode of disposal of the dead. Also in the Gunther Island site were curved bone fishhooks (Heizer 1949c), grooved clay balls (sinkers?), pottery female figurines (Heizer and Pendergast 1955), and slate zoöform clubs inaptly labeled "slavekillers" by Loud (1938), which were pretty clearly a distinctive form of wealth object whose vogue had passed before the opening of the historic period.

Surveys on the southern Oregon coast have failed to produce evidence of occupation older than 500 years ago, and the roster of archeological traits is interpreted as late prehistoric manifestations of the cultures of the ethnographic people (Tututni). About the same situation, though with a longer period of settlement, obtains in northwestern California, where we are obviously dealing with the archeological manifestations of historic groups (Tolowa, Yurok, and Wiyot). Whether the origin of these coastal peoples lies farther north along the shore or in the interior from which they came downriver is not known; as a guess, a southward coastal drift seems most likely. On the upper Klamath River, just south of the Oregon boundary, Leonhardy (1961) has excavated a late site (radiocarbon-dated at 554 years old) that manifests a basically northwestern California type of culture; the same situation holds for a small late shelter (site Sis-13) nearby, excavated by Wallace and Taylor (1952). Some work has been done in the interior of Oregon, notably at Gold Hill on the Rogue River (Cressman 1933), which has produced flexed burials and large obsidian blades of northwestern California type, and in the Willamette Valley (Heizer 1941b; Laughlin 1941, 1943), where flexed burials were associated with drilled antler camas-digging-stick handles, flat whalebone clubs, large obsidian blades of northwestern California type, shallow stone mortars, antler wedges, and extensive use of bone as an industrial material for small tools and ornaments. These interior sites are late in time and evidence the same general type of culture as those on the coast to the west.

Next along the Pacific shore to the north lies the Coast Salish–Chinook area, comprising the upper Oregon and Washington coasts, Straits of Juan de Fuca, and the Gulf of Georgia. Somewhat more archeology has been carried out here, and there is an abundance of hypotheses in the literature to account for archeological sequences disclosed by excavation. On the Oregon coast, excavation by Newman (1959) of site Ti-1, in the territory of the ethnographic Tillamook, is late in time (three radiocarbon age determinations were 150, 280, and 550 years old—M-805, M-806, M-904), and evidences a culture fully adapted to the coast in the form of antler wedges, adzes, composite harpoons, rectangular plank-walled houses, and economic exploitation of shore mollusks and sea mammals (sea lion, otter, seal), as well as land mammals (elk, deer). On the Columbia River at the Dalles, work by Cressman (1960) in site Ws-4 produced evidence of a riverine adaptation 8000 or more years old that included the taking of sea mammals. Thus, the basic elements of the coastal culture appear to date back to the Paleo-Indian period, and the hypothesis of a downriver movement to the coast, which H. I. Smith (1907), Kroeber (1939), and others proposed long ago, appears to be supported by the Dalles evidence. For the Columbia River below Portland archeological information is almost lacking, an amateur's book (Strong 1960) being at this time the best source. Late-period materials from sites along the lowermost reaches of the Columbia show materials with affiliations, both to the south (stone zoöform clubs) and to the north, with the Salish area (sculptured stone bowls). A brief summary of Lower Columbia Valley prehistory has been made by Butler (1959).

King (1950) interprets the history of a site on San Juan Island as evidencing initial occupation by people with an inland economy that changed through time in the direction of increasing maritime adaptation. Carlson (1960) revises and expands the archeological perspective in the San Juan Islands. Borden (1950, 1951, 1954) has reported briefly on a series of important excavations in sites in the delta of the Fraser River and interprets the oldest ("Early Maritime") culture disclosed in the Locarno Beach and Whalen Farm sites, with radiocarbon ages of 2430, 1580, and 2450 years old (Daugherty 1958), as "Eskimoid" and of northern derivation. The traits which, to Borden, warrant drawing this conclusion are one- and two-piece toggling harpoon heads, ground-slate knives and blades, figurines, labrets, and, by inference, skin-covered boats. Drucker (1955a, b) and M. W. Smith (1956) accept Borden's general proposition but, largely on the basis of ethnographic traits, suggest some modification of it (cf. M. W. Smith, 1950). Questions about Borden's interpretation of the Eskimoid early base and subsequent development of the coastal adaptation have also been raised by Osborne *et al.* (1956) in argumentation that is particular and complicated. Borden's Intermediate period, which is known from four sites in the Fraser River Delta, is interpreted as marking the advent of interior cultures, which came down the rivers from the Plateau to the coast and there underwent accommodation to what becomes in the Late period (by radiocarbon dating about A.D. 1300) the fully developed southern aspect of Northwest Coast culture that can be identified with the ethnographic Coast Salish tribes of the Gulf of Georgia. The Late-period inventory includes antler wedges, stone mauls and adze blades, barbed antler harpoons, developed fishing and sea-mammal hunting economy, and elaborate stone sculpture (cf. M. W. Smith 1956; Duff 1956). Also probably belonging to this Late period are elaborate wood-carving and petroglyphs (Heizer 1947; M. W. Smith 1946). Full details on the Late period may be found in Borden's publications (cited above), Drucker (1955a), and M. W. Smith (1956).[10]

[10] Since this paper was written, C. E. Borden has published a very important paper ("West Coast Crossties with Alaska." In *Prehistoric Cultural Relations between the Arctic and Temperate Zones of North America.* Arctic Institute of North America, Tech. Paper No. 11, 1962, pp. 9–19) in which he examines carefully the evidence for Eskimo culture connections.

The Queen Charlotte Sound and Vancouver Island region, which was the historic homeland of the Nootkan, Kwakiutl, and Bella Coola tribes, is judged by Drucker (1955a) to have long been the most isolated, least influenced, and therefore "purest" local culture type on the Northwest Coast. Nothing highly unusual occurs in the artifacts from the sites so far tested, and the picture is one of shore-living, dugout-traveling, fish-eating, wood-carving peoples much resembling the recent tribes as far back in time as the limited archeological evidence takes us.

The last and most northerly of the cultural subareas is called by Drucker "Northern" and ranges from Queen Charlotte Island to Prince William Sound, covering the historic domains of the Tsimshian, Haida, and Tlingit tribes. From this locale we have only the archeological reconnaissance of Drucker (1955a) and excavation of two late sites at Angoon in Tlingit territory by De Laguna (1960). Eskimo influence is apparent in this region on the ethnographic level (evidenced by use of the spear-thrower, umiak, and oil lamp), and a basically similar archeological petroglyph style (Heizer 1947; Keithahn 1940; de Laguna 1960) ranges as far north and west as Kodiak Island (cf. de Laguna 1956, specimens from Prince William Sound). The list of material traits in this northern Northwest Coast region includes abundant ground-slate blades, points, and knives; barbed harpoons; splitting adzes; grooved maul heads; hand mauls; celts; stone vessels; and T-shaped labrets. We quite lack any appreciable time depth in the few archeological sites thus far tested and can observe only that nearly everything yet remains to be learned of the prehistory of the Northwest Coast north of Vancouver Island.

Earlier summaries or chronological charts of California prehistory have been published by Kroeber (1909, 1936), Baumhoff and Elsasser (1956), Bennyhoff (1958), and Meighan (1959a), and a bibliography (now being revised) of California archeology exists (Heizer 1949b). No attempt at a detailed synthesis of the prehistory of the Oregon, Washington, British Columbia, and southeast Alaskan coasts has yet been done; the closest approach to this is in papers by M. W. Smith (1956), Drucker (1955b), and de Laguna (1947).

The present survey attempts merely to give an idea of the general succession and nature of the prehistoric cultures of the Pacific Coast littoral, and the reader is supplied with references with which to flesh the bare bones offered. Considering the area treated as a whole, we may divide into it two major sections in which historical continuities can be seen. In the north is the Northwest Coast section, ranging from Prince William Sound in Alaska (lat. 60° N.) to Cape Mendocino in California (lat. 40° N.). Willey and Phillips (1958) affirm the distinctiveness of the Northwest Coast, of which they say, "one senses here the presence of forces . . . definitely outside the range of the more familiar patterns of New World cultural development." This uniqueness was pointed up first by Kroeber (1923), and the concept was sharpened by M. W. Smith (1956). The very distinctiveness of the culture(s) of this area makes for difficulty in readily classifying it by the measures that have served reasonably well for the rest of North America, as Willey and Phillips (1958) point out in answer to McKern's (1956) objections to their earlier placement of this area in the Archaic stage. Along this coastal region we may predict that, as more work is done, a connected series of local prehistoric events will be reconstructed. South of here, and extending into the still little known peninsula of Lower California, another connected series of local prehistories can be seen, and it should be the large aim of local workers to indicate affiliations with areas adjoining those in which they concentrate their attention so that the historical continuities and correlations can be drawn more sharply than we are at present able to do.

On finishing this survey, I am impressed with the large amount of published material now available, but depressed by learning how many sizable areas are still archeologically unknown along the Pacific Coast. In addition, a number of important papers remain in manuscript in default of an opportunity to publish them. To me it is obvious that another of our great archeological needs is more funds for publication.

The slightly pessimistic view expressed here should not be taken too seriously because, as Meighan (1961) points out, 90 per cent of our useful information on Pacific Coast prehistory has been accumulated in the last twenty-five years. We are probably approaching the point that archeology in the eastern United States had reached when Ford and Willey wrote the first broad synthetic review of the area in 1941.

BIBLIOGRAPHY

AMSDEN, CHARLES
 1937 "The Lake Mohave Artifacts." Pp. 51–98 in CAMPBELL *et al., The Archaeology of Pleistocene Lake Mohave: A Symposium.* ("Southwest Mus. Paps.," No. 11.) Los Angeles.
ASCHMANN, HOMER
 1959 *The Central Desert of Baja California: Demography and Ecology.* ("Ibero-Americana," No. 42.) Berkeley.
BAUMHOFF, M. A.
 1955 "Excavation of Teh-1 (Kingsley Cave)." *Calif. Arch. Paps.* No. 33, pp. 40–73. ("Univ. Calif. Arch. Surv. Rpt.," No. 30.) Berkeley.
 1957 *An Introduction to Yana Archaeology.* ("Univ. Calif. Arch. Surv. Rpt.," No. 40.) Berkeley.

BAUMHOFF, M. A., and A. B. ELSASSER
  1956 *Summary of Archaeological Survey and Excavation in California. Calif. Arch. Paps.*, No. 37, pp. 1–27. ("Univ. Calif. Arch. Surv. Rpt.," No. 33.) Berkeley.
BAUMHOFF, M. A., and R. F. HEIZER
  1958 "Outland Coiled Basketry from the Caves of West Central Nevada." Pp. 49–59 in *Current Views on Great Basin Archeology.* ("Univ. Calif. Arch. Surv. Rpt.," No. 42.) Berkeley.
BAUMHOFF, M. A., and D. OLMSTED
  1963 "Palaihnihan: Radiocarbon Support for Glottochronology." *Amer. Anthropologist*, 65:278–84.
BEALS, R. L., and J. A. HESTER
  1960 "A New Ecological Typology of the California Indians." Pp. 411–19 in *Acts Internat. Cong. Anthrop. & Ethnol. Sci.*, Vol. 5. Philadelphia.
BEARDSLEY, RICHARD K.
  1948 "Culture Sequences in Central California Archaeology." *Amer. Antiquity*, 14:1–29.
  1954 Temporal and Areal Relationships in Central California Archaeology. 2 parts. ("Univ. Calif. Arch. Surv. Rpt.," Nos. 24, 25.) Berkeley.
BELOUS, RUSSELL E.
  1953 "The Central California Chronological Sequence Re-examined." *Amer. Antiquity*, 18:341–53. Salt Lake City.
BENNYHOFF, JAMES A.
  1950 "California Fish Spears and Harpoons." *Univ. Calif. Anthrop. Records*, 9:295–337. Berkeley.
  1956 *An Appraisal of the Archaeological Resources of Yosemite National Park.* ("Univ. Calif. Arch. Surv. Rpt.," No. 34.) Berkeley.
  1958 "The Desert West: A Trial Correlation of Culture and Chronology." Pp. 98–112 in *Current Views on Great Basin Archaeology.* ("Univ. Calif. Arch. Surv. Rpt.," No. 42) Berkeley.
BENNYHOFF, J. A., and R. F. HEIZER
  1958 "Cross-dating Great Basin Sites by Californian Shell Beads." Pp. 60–92 in *Current Views on Great Basin Archaeology.* ("Univ. Calif. Arch. Surv. Rpt.," No. 42.) Berkeley.
BERREMAN, J. V.
  1944 *Chetco Archaeology: A Report of the Lone Ranch Creek Shell Mound on the Coast of Southern Oregon.* ("Gen. Ser. Anthrop.," No. 11.) Menasha, Wis.
BIRD, J. B.
  1961 "B.P.: Before Present or Bad Policy?" *Amer. Antiquity*, 26:557–58.
BORDEN, CHARLES E.
  1950 "Preliminary Report on Archaeological Investigations in the Fraser Delta Region." *Anthrop. British Columbia*, No. 1, pp. 13–27.
  1951 "Facts and Problems of Northwest Coast Prehistory." *Ibid.*, No. 2, pp. 35–52.
  1954 "Some Aspects of Prehistoric Coastal-Interior Relations in the Pacific Northwest." *Ibid.*, No. 4, pp. 26–32.

BOURDIER, F.
1953 "Pseudo-industries humaines sur galets de quartzite glaciaires." *Bull. la Soc. Préhist. Franç.*, 50:436. Paris.

BROECKER, WALLACE S., EDWIN A. OLSON, and PHIL C. ORR
1960 "Radiocarbon Measurements and Annual Rings in Cave Formations." *Nature*, 185:93–94.

BUTLER, B. ROBERT
1959 "Lower Columbia Valley Archaeology: A Survey and Appraisal of Some Major Archaeological Resources." *Tebiwa: Jour. Idaho State Coll. Mus.*, 2:6–24.
1961 *The Old Cordilleran Culture in the Pacific Northwest.* ("Idaho State Coll. Mus. Occ. Paps.," No. 5.) Pocatello.

CAMPBELL, ELIZABETH W., and WILLIAM H. CAMPBELL
1935 "The Pinto Basin Site." ("Southwest Mus. Paps.," No. 9.) Los Angeles.

CARLSON, ROY L.
1960 "Chronology and Culture Change in the San Juan Islands, Washington." *Amer. Antiquity*, 25:562–86.

CARTER, GEORGE F.
1959 "Man, Time and Change in the Far Southwest." *Assoc. Amer. Geog. Ann.*, 49:8–30. Washington, D.C.

CHILDE, V. GORDON
1956 *Piecing Together the Past: The Interpretation of Archaeological Data.* New York: F. Praeger.

CLARK, J. D.
1961 "Fractured Chert Specimens from the Lower Pleistocene Bethlehem Beds, Israel." *Brit. Mus. Nat. Hist. Bull.* (Geol., Vol. 5, No. 4.) London.

COOK, S. F.
1946 "A Reconsideration of Shellmounds with Respect to Population and Nutrition." *Amer. Antiquity*, 12:50–53.

COOK, S. F., and R. F. HEIZER
1962 *Chemical Analysis of the Hotchkiss Site (CCo-138).* ("Univ. Calif. Arch. Surv. Rpt.," No. 57, Part 1.) Berkeley.

CRESSMAN, L. S.
1933 *Contributions to the Archaeology of Oregon: Final Report on the Gold Hill Burial Site.* (Univ. Ore. Pub., Vol. 4, No. 3.) Eugene.
1952 "Oregon Coast Prehistory." Pp. 256–60 in *Amer. Phil. Soc. Yrbk., 1952*, Philadelphia.
1960 "Cultural Sequences at the Dalles, Oregon." *Amer. Phil. Soc. Trans.*, Vol. 50, Part 10. Philadelphia.

DAUGHERTY, RICHARD D.
1958 "Notes and News: West Coast and Great Basin." *Amer. Antiquity*, 23:453–54.

DAVIS, J. T.
1962 *The Rustler Rockshelter Site (SBr-288), a Culturally Stratified Site in the*

Mohave Desert. ("Univ. Calif. Arch. Surv. Rpt.," No. 57, Part 2. Berkeley.

DAVIS, J. T., and A. E. TREGANZA
  1959 *The Patterson Mound: A Comparative Analysis of the Archaeology of Site Ala-328.* ("Univ. Calif. Arch. Surv. Rpt.," No. 47.) Berkeley.

DIXON, RONALD B.
  1905 *The Northern Maidu.* (Amer. Mus. Nat. Hist. Bull., Vol. 17, No. 3.) New York.

DRUCKER, PHILLIP
  1943 "Archaeological Survey on the Northern Northwest Coast." *Anthrop. Paps.*, Nos. 19–26, pp. 17–132. (Bur. Amer. Ethnol. Bull., 133.)
  1955a "Sources of Northwest Coast Culture." Pp. 59–81 in *New Interpretations of Aboriginal American Culture History: Seventy-fifth Anniversary Volume of the Anthropological Society of Washington.* Washington, D.C.
  1955b *Indians of the Northwest Coast.* (Amer. Mus. Nat. Hist. Anthrop. Handbook No. 10.) New York.

DUFF, WILSON
  1956 "Prehistoric Stone Sculpture of the Fraser River and Gulf of Georgia." *Anthrop. British Columbia*, No. 5, pp. 15–151.

DURHAM, BILL
  1960 *Canoes and Kayaks of Western North America.* Seattle: Copper Canoe Press.

EBERHART, HAL
  1961 "The Cogged Stones of Southern California." *Amer. Antiquity*, 26: 361–70.

ELSASSER, A. B.
  1960 *The Archaeology of the Sierra Nevada in California and Nevada.* ("Univ. Calif. Arch. Surv. Rpt.," No. 51.) Berkeley.

FORD, J. A., and G. R. WILLEY
  1941 "An Interpretation of the Prehistory of the Eastern United States." *Amer. Anthropologist*, 43:325–63.

GIFFORD, E. W.
  1940 "Californian Bone Artifacts." *Univ. Calif. Anthrop. Rec.*, Vol. 3, No. 2. Berkeley.

GIFFORD, E. W., and W. EGBERT SCHENCK
  1926 "Archaeology of the Southern San Joaquin Valley." *Univ. Calif. Pub. Amer. Arch. & Ethnol.*, Vol. 23, No. 1. Berkeley.

GRANT, CAMPBELL
  1961 "Ancient Art in the Wilderness." *Pacific Discovery*, 14:12–19.

GREENGO, ROBERT E.
  1951 *Molluscan Species in California Shell Middens.* ("Univ. Calif. Arch. Surv. Rpt.," No. 13.) Berkeley.

GREENMAN, EMERSON F.
  1957 "An American Eolithic?" *Amer. Antiquity*, 22:298.

GRUHN, R.
  1961 *The Archaeology of Wilson Butte Cave, South-Central Idaho.* ("Idaho State Coll. Mus. Occ. Paps.," No. 6.) Pocatello.

HAEKEL, JOSEF
  1958 "Zur Frage alter Kulturbeziehungen zwischen Alaska, Kalifornien und dem Pueblo-Gebiet." Pp. 88–96 in *Proc. 32d Internat. Cong. Americanists, 1956.* Copenhagen.
HARDING, M.
  1951 "La Jollan Culture." *El Museo,* 1:10–11, 31–38.
HARNER, M. J.
  1956 "Thermo-Facts vs. Artifacts: An Experimental Study of the Malpais Industry." *Calif. Arch. Paps.,* Nos. 37–43, pp. 39–43. ("Univ. Calif. Arch. Surv. Rpt.," No. 33.) Berkeley.
  1958 "Lowland Patayan Phases in the Lower Colorado River Valley and Colorado Desert." Pp. 93–97 in *Current Views on Great Basin Archaeology.* ("Univ. Calif. Arch. Surv. Rpt.," No. 42.) Berkeley.
HARRINGTON, M. R.
  1948 *An Ancient Site at Borax Lake, California.* ("Southwest Mus. Paps.," No. 16.) Los Angeles.
HAURY, EMIL W.
  1959 *Review of* G. F. CARTER, *Pleistocene Man at San Diego. Amer. Jour. Arch.,* 63:116–17.
HAURY, EMIL W., with KIRK BRYAN, EDWIN H. COLBERT, NORMAN E. GABEL, CLARA LEE TANNER, and T. E. BUEHRER
  1950 *The Stratigraphy and Archaeology of Ventana Cave, Arizona.* Tucson and Albuquerque: University of Arizona Press and University of New Mexico Press.
HEIZER, ROBERT F.
  1938 "The Plank Canoe of the Santa Barbara Region, California." *Etnologiska Studier,* 7:193–229. Göteborg.
  1939 "Some Sacramento Valley–Santa Barbara Archaeological Relationships." *Masterkey,* 13:31–35.
  1941*a* "The Direct Historical Approach in California Archaeology." *Amer. Antiquity,* 7:98–122.
  1941*b* "Oregon Prehistory—Retrospect and Prospect." *Commonwealth Rev.,* 23:30–40.
  1944 "Artifact Transport by Migratory Animals." *Amer. Antiquity,* 9:395–400.
  1946 "The Occurrence and Significance of Southwestern Grooved Axes in California." *Ibid.,* 11:187–93.
  1947 "Petroglyphs from Southwestern Kodiak Island, Alaska." *Amer. Phil. Soc. Proc.,* 91:284–93. Philadelphia.
  1949*a* "The Archaeology of Central California. I. The Early Horizon." *Univ. Calif. Anthrop. Records,* Vol. 12, No. 1. Berkeley.
  1949*b* *A Bibliography of the Archaeology of California.* ("Univ. Calif. Arch. Surv. Rpt.," No. 4.) Berkeley.
  1949*c* "Curved Single-Piece Fishhooks of Shell and Bone in California." *Amer. Antiquity,* 15:89–97.
  1952*a* "Incised Slate Figurines from Kodiak Island, Alaska." *Ibid.,* 17:266.
  1952*b* "A Review of Problems in the Antiquity of Man in California." Pp.

3–17 in *Symposium on the Antiquity of Man in California.* ("Univ. Calif. Arch. Surv. Rpt.," No. 16.) Berkeley.

1958*a* "Prehistoric Central California: A Problem in Historical-Developmental Classification." *Calif. Arch. Paps.*, No. 66, pp. 19–26. ("Univ. Calif. Arch. Surv. Rpt.," No. 41.) Berkeley.

1958*b* "Radiocarbon Dates from California of Archeological Interest." ("Univ. Calif. Arch. Surv. Rpt.," No. 44, Part 1.) Berkeley.

1960 "Physical Analysis of Habitation Residues." Pp. 93–124 in *The Application of Quantitative Methods in Archaeology.* ("Viking Fund Pub. Anthrop.," No. 28.) Chicago.

n.d. "Comments on the Broad Archaeological Picture in Southwestern United States." Paper read at U.C.L.A. Radiocarbon Conf., February 28, 1962.

HEIZER, ROBERT F. (ed.)
1953 "Archaeology of the Napa Region." Pp. 225–358 in *Univ. Calif. Anthrop. Records*, Vol. 12, No. 6. Berkeley.

HEIZER, ROBERT F., and M. A. BAUMHOFF
1962 *Prehistoric Rock Art of Nevada and Eastern California.* Berkeley: University of California Press.

HEIZER, ROBERT F., and S. F. COOK
1952 "Fluorine and Other Chemical Tests of Some North American Human and Fossil Bones." *Amer. Jour. Phys. Anthrop.*, 10:289–304.

HEIZER, ROBERT F., and ALBERT B. ELSASSER
1953 *Some Archaeological Sites and Cultures of the Central Sierra Nevada.* ("Univ. Calif. Arch. Surv. Rpt.," No. 21.) Berkeley.

HEIZER, ROBERT F., and FRANKLIN FENENGA
1939 "Archaeological Horizons in Central California." *Amer. Anthropologist*, 41:378–99.

HEIZER, ROBERT F., and H. KELLEY
1962 "Burins and Bladelets in the Cessac Collection from Santa Cruz Island." *Amer. Phil. Soc. Proc.*, 106:94–105. Philadelphia.

HEIZER, ROBERT F., and E. M. LEMERT
1947 "Observations on Archaeological Sites in Topanga Canyon, California." *Univ. Calif. Pub. Amer. Arch. & Ethnol.*, Vol. 44, No. 2. Berkeley.

HEIZER, ROBERT F., and WILLIAM C. MASSEY
1953 "Aboriginal Navigation off the West Coasts of Upper and Baja California." *Anthrop. Paps.*, No. 33–42, pp. 285–311. (Bur. Amer. Ethnol. Bull. 151.) Washington, D.C.

HEIZER, ROBERT F., and J. E. MILLS
1952 *The Four Ages of Tsurai: A Documentary History of the Indian Village on Trinidad Bay.* Berkeley: University of California Press.

HEIZER, ROBERT F., and D. M. PENDERGAST
1955 "Additional Data on Fired Clay Human Figurines from California." *Amer. Antiquity*, 21:181–85.

HEWES, G. W.
1946 "Early Man in California and the Tranquillity Site." *Amer. Antiquity*, 11:209–15.

HEYE, G. G.
1921 *Certain Artifacts from San Miguel Island, California.* ("Indian Notes and Monographs," Vol. 7, No. 4.) New York.

HINDES, M. G.
1962 *The Archaeology of the Huntington Lake Region in the Southern Sierra Nevada, California.* ("Univ. Calif. Arch. Surv. Rpt.," No. 58.) Berkeley.

HOLMES, W. H.
1901 "Review of the Evidence Relating to Auriferous Gravel Man in California." *Smithsonian Inst. Ann. Rpt., 1899*, pp. 419–72. Washington, D.C.

HURT, WESLEY R., JR.
1953 "A Comparative Study of the Preceramic Occupations of North America." *Amer. Antiquity*, 18:204–22.

HYMES, D. H.
1960 "Lexicostatistics So Far." *Cur. Anthropology*, 1:3–39. Chicago.

JENNINGS, J. D., and E. NORBECK
1955 "Great Basin Prehistory: A Review." *Amer. Antiquity*, 21:1–11.

JOHNSON, FREDERICK, and JOHN P. MILLER
1958 *Review of* G. F. CARTER, *Pleistocene Man at San Diego. Amer. Antiquity*, 24:206–10.

KEITHAHN, E. L.
1940 "The Petroglyphs of Southeastern Alaska." *Amer. Antiquity*, 6:123–32.

KING, ARDEN R.
1950 *Cattle Point: A Stratified Site in the Southern Northwest Coast Region.* (Soc. Amer. Arch. Mem. 7.) Salt Lake City.

KOBY, F. E.
1943 "Les soi-disant instruments osseux du paléolithique alpin et le charriage à sec des os d'ours des cavernes." *Verhandlungen der Naturforschenden Gesellschaft in Basel*, 54:59–95.

KOWTA, M.
1961 "Excavations at Goleta: Artifact Description; Chipped Lithic Material." Pp. 349–83 in *U.C.L.A. Arch. Surv. Ann. Rpt., 1960–61*, Los Angeles.

KRIEGER, ALEX D.
1951 "Notes and News: Early Man. *Amer. Antiquity*, 17:77–78.
1953 "New World Culture History: Anglo-America." Pp. 238–64 in A. L. KROEBER *et al.*, *Anthropology Today*. Chicago: University of Chicago Press.
1958 *Review of* GEORGE F. CARTER, *Pleistocene Man at San Diego. Amer. Anthropologist*, 60:974–78.
1959 *Comment on* GEORGE F. CARTER, *Man, Time, and Change in the Far Southwest. Assoc. Amer. Geog. Ann.*, 49:31–33. Washington, D.C.

KROEBER, A. L.
1909 "The Archaeology of California." In *Putnam Anniversary Volume*, pp 1-42. New York: G. E. Stechert & Co.

1910   "At the Bedrock of History: Remarkable Discovery of Human Remains in Kern County, California." *Sunset Mag.*, 25:255–60.
1917   "The Tribes of the North Pacific Coast of North America." Pp. 385–401 in *Proc. 19th Internat. Cong. Americanists.* Washington, D.C.
1920   "California Culture Provinces." *Univ. Calif. Pub. Amer. Arch. & Ethnol.*, Vol. 17, No. 2, pp. 151–69. Berkeley.
1923   "American Culture and the Northwest Coast." *Amer. Anthropologist,* 25:1–20.
1925   *Handbook of the Indians of California.* (Bur. Amer. Ethnol. Bull. 78.) Washington, D. C.
1935   *Preface to* S. KLIMEK, "The Structure of California Indian Culture." *Univ. Calif. Pub. Amer. Arch. & Ethnol.*, Vol. 37, No. 1. Berkeley.
1936   "Prospects in California Prehistory." *Amer. Antiquity*, 2:108–16.
1939   "Cultural and Natural Areas of Native North America." *Univ. Calif. Pub. Amer. Arch. & Ethnol.*, Vol. 38. Berkeley.
1955   "Linguistic Time Depth Results So Far and Their Meaning." *Internat. Jour. Amer. Linguistics*, 21:91–104.
1962   *Two Papers on the Aboriginal Ethnography of California.* ("Univ. Calif. Arch. Surv. Rpt.," No. 56.) Berkeley.

LAGUNA, FREDERICA DE
1947   *The Prehistory of Northern North America as Seen from the Yukon.* (Soc. Amer. Arch. Mem. 3.) Menasha, Wis.
1956   *Chugach Prehistory.* Seattle: University of Washington Press.
1960   *The Story of a Tlingit Community.* (Bur. Amer. Ethnol. Bull. 172.) Washington, D.C.

LANNING, E. P.
n.d.   "Archaeology of the Rose Spring Site (Iny-372)." *Univ. Calif. Pub. Amer. Arch. & Ethnol.*, Vol. 46, No. 2. (In press.) Berkeley.

LATHRAP, DONALD W., and DICK SHUTLER, JR.
1955   "An Archaeological Site in the High Sierra of California." *Amer. Antiquity*, 20:226–40.

LAUGHLIN, W. S.
1941   "Excavations in the Calapuya Mounds of the Willamette Valley, Oregon." *Amer. Antiquity*, 7:147–55.
1943   "Notes on the Archaeology of the Yamhill River, Willamette Valley, Oregon." *Ibid.*, 9:220–29.

LEATHERMAN, KENNETH E., and ALEX D. KRIEGER
1940   "Contributions to Oregon Coast Prehistory." *Amer. Antiquity*, 6: 19–28.

LEONHARDY, F. C.
n.d.   "The Cultural Position of the Iron Gate Site." University of Oregon, Department of Anthropology, 1961. Mimeographed. Eugene.

LILLARD, J. B., R. F. HEIZER, and F. FENENGA
1939   *An Introduction to the Archaeology of Central California.* (Sacramento Junior Coll. Bull. 2.) Sacramento.

LOUD, L. L.
1918   "Ethnogeography and Archaeology of the Wiyot Territory." *Univ. Calif. Pub. Amer. Arch. & Ethnol.*, Vol. 14, No. 3. Berkeley.

LOWIE, R. H.
    1923   "The Cultural Connection of Californian and Plateau Shoshonean Tribes." *Phoebe Apperson Hearst Memorial Volume, Univ. Calif. Pub. Amer. Arch. & Ethnol.*, 20:145–56. Berkeley.
McKERN, W. C.
    1956   *Comment on* WILLEY AND PHILLIPS, *Method and Theory in American Archaeology. Amer. Anthropologist*, 58:360–61.
MASSEY, WILLIAM C.
    1947   "Brief Report on Archaeological Investigations in Baja California." *Southwestern Jour. Anthrop.*, 3:344–59.
    1961   "The Cultural Distinction of Aboriginal Baja California." Pp. 411–22 in *Homenaje a Pablo Martínez del Río en el 25o aniversario de la primera edición de "Los Orígenes Americanos."* Mexico, D.F.
MASSEY, WILLIAM C., and CAROLYN M. OSBORNE
    1961   "A Burial Cave in Baja California: The Palmer Collection, 1887." *Univ. Calif. Anthrop. Records*, 16:339–64. Berkeley.
MEIGHAN, C. W.
    1953   "Archaeology of Sites Nap-129 and Nap-131." Pp. 315–17 (Appendix 3) in R. F. HEIZER (ed.), *The Archaeology of the Napa Region. Univ. Calif. Anthrop. Records*, Vol. 12, No. 6. Berkeley.
    1954   "A Late Complex in Southern California Prehistory." *Southwestern Jour. Anthrop.*, 10:215–27.
    1955   "Archaeology of the North Coast Ranges, California." *Calif. Arch. Paps.*, No. 32. ("Univ. Calif. Arch. Surv. Rpt.," No. 30.) Berkeley.
    1959a   "Californian Cultures and the Concept of an Archaic Stage." *Amer. Antiquity*, 24:289–305.
    1959b   "The Little Harbor Site, Catalina Island: An Example of Ecological Interpretation in Archaeology." *Ibid.*, pp. 383–405.
    1961   "The Growth of Archaeology in the West Coast and the Great Basin, 1935–1960." *Ibid.*, 27:33–38.
    n.d.   "Some Radiocarbon Dates from California's Channel Islands." Paper read at U.C.L.A. Radiocarbon Conf., February 28, 1962.
MENGHIN, O. F. A.
    1957   "Das Protolithikum in America." *Acta Praehistorica, Centro Argentina de Estudios*, 1:5–40. Buenos Aires.
MERRIAM, JOHN C.
    1906   "Recent Cave Exploration in California." *Amer. Anthropologist*, n.s., 8:221–28.
MILLS, J. E.
    1950   *Recent Developments in the Study of Northwest California Archaeology. Calif. Arch. Paps.*, Nos. 1–5, pp. 21–25. ("Univ. Calif. Arch. Surv. Rpt.," No. 7.) Berkeley.
NELSON, N. C.
    1928   "Pseudo-Artifacts from the Pliocene of Nebraska." *Science*, 67:316–17. Washington, D.C.
NEWMAN, T. M.
    1959   *Tillamook Prehistory and Its Relation to the Northwest Coast Culture Area*. Eugene: University of Oregon, Department of Anthropology.

OLSON, RONALD L.
1930 "Chumash Prehistory." *Univ. Calif. Pub. Amer. Arch. & Ethnol.*, 28:1–21. Berkeley.

ORR, P. C.
1943 *Archaeology of Mescalitan Island and Customs of the Canaliño.* ("Santa Barbara Mus. Nat. Hist. Occ. Paps.," No. 3.) Santa Barbara.
1953 "Speleothem Age Dating." *Tex. Arch. Soc. Bull.*, 24:7–17.
1956 *Radiocarbon Dates from Santa Rosa Island*, I. (Santa Barbara Mus. Nat. Hist., Anthrop. Bull. 2.) Santa Barbara.

OSBORNE, D., W. W. CALDWELL, and R. H. CRABTREE
1956 "The Problem of Northwest Coastal-Interior Relationships as Seen from Seattle." *Amer. Antiquity*, 22:117–28.

PEAKE, H. J. E.
1940 "The Study of Prehistoric Times." *J. Roy. Anthrop. Inst. Great Britain and Ireland*, 70:103–46. London.

PECK, STUART L.
1955 "An Archaeological Report on the Excavation of a Prehistoric Site at Zuma Creek, Los Angeles County, California." *Arch. Surv. Assoc. Southern Calif. Pap.*, No. 2. Los Angeles.

PECK, STUART L., and G. A. SMITH
1957 *The Archaeology of Seep Spring.* ("San Bernardino Mus. Scient. Ser.," No. 2 [Quarterly, Vol. 4, No. 4].) San Bernardino.

PEI, W.-C.
1938 "Le rôle des animaux et des causes naturelles dans la cassure des os." *Paleont. Sinica*, New Scr. D, No. 7; Whole Ser., No. 118. Peiping.

PILLING, ARNOLD R.
1955 "Relationships of Prehistoric Cultures of Coastal Monterey County, California." *Kroeber Anthrop. Soc. Paps.*, No. 12, pp. 70–87. Berkeley.

PUTNAM, F. W.
1880 "The Indians of California." *Bull. Essex Inst.*, 12:4–6. Salem, Mass.
1906 "Evidence of the Work of Man from Quaternary Caves in California." *Amer. Anthropologist*, 8:229–35.

ROBERTS, F. H. H., JR.
1940 "Developments in the Problem of the North American Paleo-Indian." Pp. 51–116 in *Essays in Historical Anthropology of North America.* ("Smithsonian Misc. Coll.," No. 100.) Washington, D.C.

ROBINSON, E.
1942 *Shell Fishhooks of the California Coast.* ("Bishop Mus. Occ. Paps.," Vol. 17, No. 4.) Honolulu.

ROGERS, D. B.
1929 *Prehistoric Man of the Santa Barbara Coast.* Santa Barbara: Santa Barbara Museum of Natural History.

ROGERS, MALCOLM J.
1929 "The Stone Art of the San Dieguito Plateau." *Amer. Anthropologist*, 31:454–67.
1939 *Early Lithic Industries of the Lower Basin of the Colorado River and Adjacent Desert Areas.* ("San Diego Mus. Paps.," No. 3.) San Diego.

ROGERS, MALCOLM J.
1945 "An Outline of Yuman Prehistory." *Southwestern Jour. Anthrop.* 1: 167–98.
1958 "San Dieguito Implements from the Terraces of the Rincon-Patano and Rillito Drainage System." *Kiva*, 24:1–23.

SAYLES, E. B.
1937 *An Archaeological Survey of Texas.* ("Gila Pueblo Medallion Paps.," No. 17.) Globe, Ariz.

SCHENCK, W. EGBERT
1926 "The Emeryville Shellmound (Final Report)." *Univ. Calif. Pub. Amer. Arch. & Ethnol.*, 23:123–46. Berkeley.

SCHUMACHER, PAUL
1874 "Remarks on the Kjökken-möddings on the Northwest Coast of America." Pp. 354–62 in *Smithsonian Inst. Ann. Rpt., 1873.* Washington, D.C.

SELLARDS, E. H.
1960 "Some Early Stone Artifact Developments in North America." *Southwestern Jour. Anthrop.* 16:160–73.

SHUMWAY, G., C. L. HUBBS, and J. R. MORIARTY
1961 "Scripps Estate Site, San Diego, California: A La Jolla Site Dated 5460 to 7370 Years before the Present." *N.Y. Acad. Sci. Ann.*, 93: 37–132. New York.

SIMPSON, RUTH D.
1956 "An Introduction to Early Western American Prehistory." *Southern Calif. Acad. Sci. Bull.*, 55:61–71. Los Angeles.
1961 "Coyote Gulch." *Arch. Surv. Assoc. Southern Calif. Pap.*, No. 5. Los Angeles.

SMITH, C. E., and W. D. WEYMOUTH
1952 *Archaeology of the Shasta Dam Area, California.* ("Univ. Calif. Arch. Surv. Rpt.," No. 18.) Berkeley.

SMITH, G. A., W. C. SCHUILING, L. MARTIN, R. J. SAYLES, and P. JILLSON
1957 *Newberry Cave, California.* ("San Bernardino County Mus., Scient. Ser.," No. 1 [Quarterly, Vol. 4, No. 3].) San Bernardino.

SMITH, HARLAN I.
1907 "Archaeology of the Gulf of Georgia and Puget Sound." ("Amer. Mus. Nat. Hist. Mems., Vol. 4, Part 6.) New York.

SMITH, M. W.
1946 "Petroglyph Complexes in the History of the Columbia-Fraser Region." *Southwestern Jour. Anthrop.* 2:306–22.
1950 *Archaeology of the Columbia-Fraser Region.* (Soc. Amer. Arch. Mem. 6.) Menasha, Wis.
1956 "The Cultural Development of the Northwest Coast." *Southwestern Jour. Anthrop.*, 12:272–94.

STEWARD, J. H.
1937 *Ancient Caves of the Great Salt Lake Region.* (Bur. Amer. Ethnol. Bull. 116.) Washington, D.C.

STRONG, EMORY M.
1959 *Stone Age on the Columbia River.* Portland: Binfords & Mort.
SWADESH, MORRIS
1956 "Problems of Long-Range Comparison in Penutian." *Language,* 32: 17–41.
TAYLOR, WALTER W.
1961 "Archaeology and Language in Western North America." *Amer. Antiquity,* 27:71–81.
THOMPSON, D. G.
1921 Pleistocene Lakes along Mohave River, California. *Wash. Acad. Sci. Jour.,* 11:423–24.
TREGANZA, ADAN E.
1954 *Salvage Archaeology in the Nimbus and Redbank Reservoir Areas, Central California.* ("Univ. Calif. Arch. Surv. Rpt.," No. 26.) Berkeley.
1958 *Salvage Archaeology in the Trinity Reservoir Area, Northern California.* ("Univ. Calif. Arch. Surv. Rpt.," No. 43, Part 1.) Berkeley.
1959 *Salvage Archaeology in the Trinity Reservoir Area, Northern California —Field Session 1958.* ("Univ. Calif. Arch. Surv. Rpt.," No. 46.) Berkeley.
TREGANZA, A. E., and A. BIERMAN
1958 "The Topanga Culture: Final Report on Excavations, 1948." *Univ. Calif. Anthrop. Records,* 20:45–86. Berkeley.
TREGANZA, A. E., and M. H. HEICKSEN
1960 *Salvage Archaeology in the Whiskeytown Reservoir Area and the Wintu Pumping Plant, Shasta County, California.* ("San Francisco State Coll. Occ. Paps. Anthrop.," No. 1.) San Francisco.
TREGANZA, A. E., and R. F. HEIZER
1953 "Additional Data on the Farmington Complex, a Stone Implement Assemblage of Probable Early Postglacial Date from Central California." *Calif. Arch. Paps.,* Nos. 21–26, pp. 28–38. ("Univ. Calif. Arch. Surv. Rpt.," No. 22.) Berkeley.
TREGANZA, A. E., C. E. SMITH, and W. D. WEYMOUTH
1950 "An Archaeological Survey of the Yuki Area." *Univ. Calif. Anthrop. Records,* 12:113–28. Berkeley.
TRUE, D. L.
1954 "Pictographs of the San Luis Rey Basin, California." *Amer. Antiquity,* 20:68–72.
1958 "An Early Complex in San Diego County, California." *Ibid.,* 23: 255–63.
TUTHILL, CARR, and A. A. ALLANSON
1954 "Ocean-Bottom Artifacts." *Masterkey,* 28:222–32.
WALKER, EDWIN F.
1947 *Excavation of a Yokuts Indian Cemetery.* Bakersfield, Ore.: Kern County Historical Society.
1951 *Five Prehistoric Archaeological Sites in Los Angeles County, California.* (Publications of the F. W. Hodge Anniv. Pub. Fund, Vol. 6.) Los Angeles: Southwest Museum.

WALLACE, W. J.
1951a "The Mortuary Caves of Calaveras County, California." *Archaeology*, 4:199–203. New York.
1951b "The Archaeological Deposit in Moaning Cave, Calaveras County." *Calif. Arch. Paps.*, Nos. 13–16, pp. 29–41. ("Univ. Calif. Arch. Surv. Rpt.," No. 12.) Berkeley.
1954 "The Little Sycamore Site and the Early Milling Stone Cultures of Southern California." *Amer. Antiquity*, 20:112–23.
1955 "A Suggested Chronology for Southern California Coastal Archaeology." *Southwestern Jour. Anthrop.*, 11:214–30.
1958 "Archaeological Investigations in Death Valley National Monument, 1952–1957." Pp. 7–22 in *Current Views on Great Basin Archaeology*. ("Univ. Calif. Arch. Surv. Rpt.," No. 42.) Berkeley.

WALLACE, W. J., and D. LATHRAP
1952 "An Early Implement Assemblage from a Limestone Cave in California." *Amer. Antiquity*, 18:133–38.

WALLACE, WILLIAM J., and EDITH S. TAYLOR
1952 "Excavation of Sis-13, a Rockshelter in Siskiyou County, California." *Calif. Arch. Paps.*, No. 18, pp. 13–38. ("Univ. Calif. Arch. Surv. Rpt.," No. 15.) Berkeley.

WARREN, C. N., and D. L. TRUE
1961 "The San Dieguito Complex and Its Place in California Prehistory." Pp. 246–91 in *Arch. Surv. Ann. Rpt. 1960–61*. Los Angeles: Department of Anthropology and Sociology, University of California at Los Angeles.

WATANABE, H.
1949 "Natural Fracture of Pebbles from the Fossil-bearing Pleistocene Deposits near Akashi." *Zinruigaku Zassi*, 60:121–42. Tokyo.

WEDEL, WALDO R.
1941 *Archeological Investigations at Buena Vista Lake, Kern County, California.* (Bur. Amer. Ethnol., Bull. 130.) Washington, D.C.

WILLEY, G., and P. PHILLIPS
1958 *Method and Theory in American Archaeology.* Chicago: University of Chicago Press.

WISSLER, MILDRED
1958 A Canaliño Site near Deer Canyon, Ventura County, California. *Masterkey*, 32:73–87.

WORMINGTON, H. M.
1962 "The Problems of the Presence and Dating in America of Flaking Techniques Similar to the Paleolithic in the Old World." *Atti del VI Congresso Internazionale delle Scienze Preistoriche ed Protostoriche.* Vol. 1, Relazioni Generali, pp. 273–83. Rome.

JESSE D. JENNINGS

The Desert West

THIS PAPER is concerned with that physiographic area usually called the Intermontane or Basin Plateau province. This larger region has also been called, for purposes of archeological description, the Desert West. Central to this wide, peak-studded trough between the Rockies and the Sierra is the Great Basin, a vast triangular region characterized by a lack of outward drainage. While its extent can be quite precisely delineated, it is a distinctive natural area *only* in the physiographic sense; in its biotic assemblage, it is part of a larger province. The region is elevated and is one of abrupt parallel mountain ranges with long, narrow valleys between the sometimes very tall peaks. The valleys are themselves often without external drainage; even those with an outlet will, however, show an occasional or even a series of shallow, dry lake beds or playas, where water briefly stands after flash runoffs. Such lakes as are in any sense permanent are normally brackish or saline.

The entire Intermontane area (which includes the Great Basin, the Columbia Plateau, and a part of the Colorado Plateau) has been described as a steppe or, more often, as a desert, but these terms do not tell the whole story. While the desert designation implies the dominance of sagebrush and the associated flora, the region has such contrasts in relief that several floral zones are repeated endlessly as one moves from valley to mountain. Despite the desert classification, one can properly describe the full floral assemblage as sagebrush, juniper-piñon-pine-spruce. Or, for those more accustomed to the life-zone concept, the Intermontane region can be described as including typical life-zone assemblages from lower Sonoran to Arctic-Alpine. These of course are a function of altitude and moisture. Both Kroeber (1939) and Steward

JESSE D. JENNINGS, professor of anthropology, University of Utah, received his Ph.D. degree from the University of Chicago. His many writings include works resulting from his field researches in Guatemala, the southeastern United States, the Great Plains, and the Great Basin. He has served as editor of *American Antiquity* and as president of the Society for American Archeology. In 1958 he was awarded the Viking Fund Medal in Archaeology in recognition of his contributions to the field.

(1938) deal in detail with the overriding cultural significance of this compressed range of biotic resource.

The present ecology of the region is as described above, and the evidence (Jennings 1957) is conclusive that no significant change in Great Basin environment has occurred for some 10,000 or more years, although climatic change in the Columbian Plateau may have been greater. Hence, the prehistory of the Desert West—whatever human activity there was —can be generally understood as having occurred in about the same climatic and biotic setting as is familiar to us today. Rainfall is everywhere scanty; nowhere would it exceed twenty-five annual inches, while for the most of the area it comes to ten inches or less. Deserts are usually regarded as harsh, as environments hostile to man and difficult of mastery. Survival probably requires special knowledge in contrast to lusher woodlands or savannas, where abundance and variety of species is characteristic. The Desert West, by any set of standards, qualifies as difficult. Aside from the Arctic zone, it is as difficult as any other area of human occupancy in America. Human survival in such an environment must be organized around some fully exploitive gathering-collecting-hunting scheme involving great mobility and special food-getting techniques. And, fortunately for interpretation, the historic tribes of the West provide living analogies for many of the inferences derived from archeological finds (e.g., Jennings 1957; Steward 1938).

Since the 1930's, the standard interpretations of the prehistoric ecology of all western North America have partially been rooted in the climatologic reconstruction made by Bryan and Antevs, with Antevs' work the more frequently consulted. Antevs' ideas of recent western climate are based on a complex correlation or reconciliation of diverse data—such as temperature, rainfall, storm paths, palynological findings, strand lines on fossil lakes, recent sediments, fossil watercourse histories—and theories about runoff rates and erosional patterns, combined with extrapolated findings from other parts of the world as to time spans. These studies lead Antevs to postulate three sets of recent climatic *conditions*, which, being sequential, have come to be regarded and utilized as *periods* of time. These conditions, covering about 10,000 years' time, he calls (1) Anathermal—a time of cooler temperatures and more moisture than now that marked the end of the significant ice advances— beginning in 9000 or 8000 B.C. Gradual increase in temperature progressed until, by 5000 B.C., conditions were hotter than now, aridity was increased, and the descriptive term (2) Altithermal summarizes the situation. By 2500 B.C. a cooling trend toward something resembling modern conditions was achieved and is called the (3) Medithermal. The scheme of course recognizes short-term cyclic variations within these general trends.

Aschmann (1958) and Martin *et al.* (1961) have successfully questioned Antevs' core hypotheses, using new data not available to Antevs. The similar conclusions of Aschmann and Martin (neither knew of the work of the other) simply deny the existence of the condition of aridity implied by Antevs' definition of the Altithermal. The work of Martin, with data from palynology, geology, and hydrology, actually demonstrates for a sizable province in Arizona that there was actually more, rather than less, precipitation during the period of time that Antevs' Altithermal was thought to have prevailed. The biota (the same species as today exist there) would in fact have been more abundant than now. The erosional pattern was different, Martin thinks, because the period of rainfall changed. There were probably more summer rains during the Altithermal, and the runoff pattern was sharply different from that resulting from winter precipitation. Aschmann's treatment, concerned with the entire West, uses meteorological and other findings merely to question, on theoretical grounds, any great variation in precipitation or temperature. Since the problem for human survival would be not temperature but aridity, we can perhaps safely discard any notion of an Altithermal with conditions of aridity markedly greater than now. It will be assumed, however, that there were the usual rhythmic, cyclical annual variations in both precipitation and temperature such as are seen in modern times. (See Antevs [1962] for his response to Martin.)

The importance of the challenge to Antevs' key concept, the arid Altithermal, is that, if it is supported by further work, there will be need for sweeping revisions in interpretation of western prehistory. Virtually every author of recent years has seen culture change and variation as resulting in part or in whole from rather drastic climatic change. Now it seems that, while the fact of culture change can still be shown, explanation based merely on Altithermal conditions cannot be supported. Hence, on the empirical grounds of archeological findings of modern species, and findings from other disciplines of both empirical and theoretical nature, a stable environment very like that of today is assumed as the setting for the human story that we can piece together in the Desert West after 7000–6000 B.C.

As Krieger has already reminded us, man has been in the Western world for perhaps 40,000 years. In the Desert West the evidences of the earliest phases of human life are rarer than in other parts of the Americas. Save for possibly Gypsum Cave, the Lind Coulee, and one or two other sites, not the slightest evidence of early man has yet been found in the whole vast area. Nonetheless, in this account I accept as given the presence of a chopper-scraper stage or culture stratum antecedent to both the Desert Archaic and the Big Game/Llano/Fluted Point traditions of the Plains. In fact, in the absence, save peripherally, of any well-documented evidence of big game hunters in the Desert West (Sandia, Naco, Lehner, the earliest Cochise, Ventana Cave), it is assumed here that the Desert Culture actually followed close upon the Paleolithic stratum, with occasional evidence (Ventana Cave, Borax Lake, Level I at Danger Cave) of an intervening Llano or other Big Game hunting population (see also Meighan 1959). It is further supposed that a significant percentage of the scrapers, planes, and choppers

FIG. 1

of any Desert Culture artifact complex are tools that developed from earlier pre-Lithic prototypes or, more properly, are merely ancient tool types carried over into the Archaic context. [EDITORS' NOTE: Here Jennings and Krieger are in essential agreement.]

The coverage of this paper can then be seen as largely restricted to the manifestation labeled the Desert Culture, an Archaic stage, found within the Desert West, and the occasional transformations of the Desert Culture up to historic times. As explained earlier, the environmental context throughout will be regarded as essentially constant. The archeological Desert Culture is seen as evidence of a specialized, successful way of life geared to the rigor and apparent biotic parsimony of the Desert West. The term must be understood as a *general* one, implying *not* an unvarying complex of archeological traits or a period of time but a culture *stage* wherein wide exploitation of available species is a diagnostic attribute. True, there are artifacts of specific sorts from region to region, but the concept has ecological and culture-focal implications as well as strictly artifactual ones. As a result of stimulus and increment from areas outside the Desert West, the several Southwest cultures and the historic tribes of the Basin and Plateau have developed from the Desert Culture base. In their development these later culture forms sometimes masked, but never entirely obscured, the artifact and subsistence pattern contributed by the basic Archaic stratum.

Before introducing the regional variations in the culture, or culture changes, the generalized base should be synthesized and exemplified. The full range of even material culture objects of the Desert Culture cannot be fully known. Many of the artifact series available for study come from open sites or are even surface finds and comprise only stone, providing little basis of comparison with the collections from caves where perishable items have been preserved and often constitute the bulk of the collections. Stratigraphy is also rare, with some notable exceptions.

The Desert Archaic during the period 6000–7000 B.C. until 2000 B.C. (and much later in some places) is seen as a stable, successful adjustment to a special environment, an environment characterized by chronically deficient moisture. The several typical sites located in the Great Basin proper are Danger, Paisley, Fort Rock, Levels II, III, and IV, Promontory, Lovelock, Level I, Roaring Spring, Gypsum, Fishbone, and Etna caves, among others. Open sites include Karlo, Concho, and Stahl. The Desert Culture was also dominant in the Plateau area during this time. In the High Plains sites like Birdshead, Pictograph II, Laramie and Ash Hollow caves and open sites—Signal Butte, McKean I, perhaps the upper levels of Angostura, and others—represent an eastward extension of the Desert Archaic during the 5000–3000 B.C. time period.

Slight local differentiation begins to be noticed after 2000 B.C. Basin sites like Humboldt, Lovelock, Gypsum (upper levels), and Danger (Level V) caves typify this stage in the Basin. In the Plateau are sites that show this same trend. Probably by A.D. 1000, and certainly by historic times, the variations of the Basin and Plateau tribes had become marked, with local linguistic diversity and evidence of contact and social organizational influence from adjacent areas being far more noticeable than are changes in subsistence or material culture.

The core cultural assemblage to be described in this paper is, thus, the Desert Archaic. Although Kroeber, Lowie, Krieger, and others recognized during the 1920's an "ancient culture stratum" in the Great Basin, it remained for Zingg (1933) to isolate a cluster of characteristic traits for what he called a "Proto-Uto-Aztecan" culture. Because the term Zingg applied was one usually reserved for linguistic classification, and because some of his conclusions were unpalatable, Zingg's perceptive study was largely ignored. Later, Cressman and Krieger (1940) and Cressman (1942) solidly demonstrated that a quite early culture stage could not be denied; at the same time, Steward (1940) was defending the view that all the Great Basin cultures were derivative from a Pueblo base and would fall entirely within the Christian Era.

It was possible for students to ignore the implications of the first finds, and for Steward to deny any antiquity to the western sites, largely because of the reluctance scholars sometimes have in abandoning old ideas and because there was actually no *demonstrable* time depth. Even so, there was ample inferential evidence for thousands of years' time lapse in Steward's material from Utah caves and in Cressman's Oregon studies. But, until 1950, when radiocarbon dating was developed, there was no way to prove that 8000–12,000 years of age could be ascribed to certain of the remains that were being recovered in the Desert West.

Zingg's first formulation of the Proto-Uto-Aztecan cultural substratum listed the following traits, both general and specific: twisted-fur blankets, tanned buckskin, fiber apron skirt, sandals, moccasins, olivella and abalone shell, twined bags, hoop cradle, coiled trays, coiled bowls, coiled carrying basket, seed-beater, earth oven, digging stick, simple fire-drill hearth, metate-mano, atlatl, dart-arrow, rabbit net, rabbit clubs, hafted knives, horn sizer-wrench, figure-4 stick and string trap, deer-net noose, *Nicotina attenuata*, tubular pipe, double bone handle for rattle, feather wands, bunches of feathers, medicine bags, bone dice, stick dice, kicking football. He also lists some non-material traits of ancient origin.

Jennings *et al.* (1956), after radiocarbon dating and renewed excavation had re-established an interest in the problem, listed some generalized traits for the Desert Archaic lifeway: cave and overhang locations for settlement, bark or grass beds, seasonal gathering, intensive exploitation of resources, small-seed harvesting and special cooking techniques, basketry (twined predominant), netting and matting, fur cloth, tumpline, sandals (moccasins rare), atlatl, pointed hardwood dart shafts, varied (relatively small) projectile points, preferential use of glassy textured stone, flat milling stone and mano, a high percentage of crude scraper and chopper tools, digging stick, firedrill and hearth, bunt points, wooden clubs, horn-shaft wrenches, tubular pipes, use of olivella and other shells, vegetable quids. Heizer (1956; see also Heizer and Krieger 1956) went further and listed a series of core traits, both material and inferred, and began an isolation of nuclear traits for the several centers that developed later. Note that with additional data, and with an altogether different thesis, Heizer's list of core traits corresponds with

Zingg's in many details: deer-hoof rattles, medicine bags or pouches, twined-tule matting, scapula grass-cutter, horn or antler wrench, bird-bone whistle, compound arrow (with foreshaft), wooden-handled knife, L-shaped scapula awl, digging stick, solid-shaft fire drill–wooden hearth, game darts, caves for shelter, caching supplies in caves.

The distribution of these traits was by no means restricted to the Desert West; it has been found archeologically deep into Mexico and in Gulf Texas and in the High Plains. Jennings *et al.* (1956) would include the western one-third of continental United States, some of Canada, and most of the Mexican Plateau in the area once covered by the Desert Culture. [EDITORS' NOTE: Krieger would perhaps agree; see pp. 59 ff.]

Perhaps the most famous of the Desert Culture sites are the cluster in Oregon reported by Cressman and Krieger (1940) and Cressman (various). Especially important are Roaring Spring and Fort Rock caves. At Roaring Spring, sealed under a pumice fall, were atlatl darts, a distinctive series of small triangular side- and end-notched projectile points, along with basketry. At nearby Fort Rock Cave, again under an ash seal, there were twined basketry, many scrapers of several types, a fire drill, and projectile points like those from Roaring Spring. Most important was a collection of well-woven fiber sandals of excellent design. One of these sandals, charred by hot volcanic ash, yielded a radiocarbon date of over 7000 B.C. From above the pumice, hence later in time, Cressman recovered from several sites a varied inventory. Basketry, matting, netting, and cordage occurred in variety; Catlow Twined is one basketry technique that Cressman sees as quite distinctive. Fur strips, perhaps for weaving into blankets, were seen. There were fire-drill fragments, thin milling stones, L-shaped scapula awls, bone beads, bone bars for chipping flint, more sandals, moccasins, antler tools and knife handles, olivella shell, a variety of bone awls and other tools, and, of course, scraps of bone and other food debris.

At Gypsum Cave, one of the earliest of the reported sites, Harrington found evidence of the association of man with the giant sloth. The most spectacular find here was a collection of darts and atlatls (which have not yet been radiocarbon-dated). Some of the sloth dung has been dated at 8500 B.C.; this date seems too recent. The cave also contained hafted knives, cane flageolets, deer-hoof jinglers or tinklers, compound arrows, bone bars, thin-slab milling stones with manos, basketry, scapula cutting or seed-harvesting tools, digging sticks, and an assortment of choppers and scraper tools. Several characteristic projectile points or knives of the "lozenge" shape now called the Gypsum point were used on the compound darts. In the presence of the darts the use of the atlatl is assumed.

Another important site, not yet fully reported, is Frightful Cave in Coahuila. Here, from a rich site, Taylor (1956) records material of ages ranging older than 7000 B.C.: atlatls and darts, fire drills and hearths, fire tongs, grooved clubs, pegs, awls, and over five hundred woven sandals. All the fauna and flora were of modern species.

At Danger, Promontory, Stansbury, and other Utah caves, large collections have been made. At Danger Cave the deposits were quite deep, covering a radiocarbon-dated time span from about 8300 B.C. until the Christian Era. There were many perishable items, especially basketry, cordage, and bone, along with thousands of flint specimens, one thousand slab milling-stone fragments, and much food scrap. Most of the fill in Danger Cave consisted of chaff from pickleweed or burroweed. Presumably, this was the seed crop being harvested by the foraging bands and is one reason for the periodic visits to the area. At this site twining was the earliest of the basketry techniques, being the only style found on the first level of intensive human occupancy (Danger Cave II). All fauna and flora in the Utah caves were modern, except for one horse bone in Juke Box.

As to open sites, the Cochise sequence of Arizona is perhaps the best known. Here Sayles and Antevs (1941), through a series of excavations at several locations and some pioneer stratigraphic work in correlating stream deposits, unfolded a story of a three-stage developmental sequence. The oldest Cochise stage is the Sulphur Spring stage—radiocarbon-dated at about 5000 B.C. The artifacts of chipped stone included knives, scrapers, and choppers. The mano and milling stone were there. Most important was the presence of food animals now extinct. These were the native American horse, dire wolf, and mammoth. (Bones of modern bison, pronghorn antelope, and coyote were also represented.) These finds of bones of extinct animals are at variance with the contents of other Desert Culture sites. Either the dates ascribed are too young, or the extinct fauna are incorrectly associated, or there was here in southeast Arizona a province where the big beasts of the waning ice ages survived longer than elsewhere in the West.

Above the Sulphur Spring level were the Chiricahua and San Pedro stages. Stone artifact types continued, with the addition of several projectile-point types, on into the appearance of the Mogollon culture (e.g., Martin *et al.* 1952). The artifact assemblage for the Cochise sequence is meager because only stone tools survived in the open locations. Material comparable to Cochise is found in the Rio Grande Valley, at Concho, Arizona, and in many other open sites over the West. At Ventana Cave, where a complex geological history made interpretation difficult, the Cochise series was also observed. Haury (1957), from Cienega Creek at Point of Pines, reports a developmental sequence from Chiri-

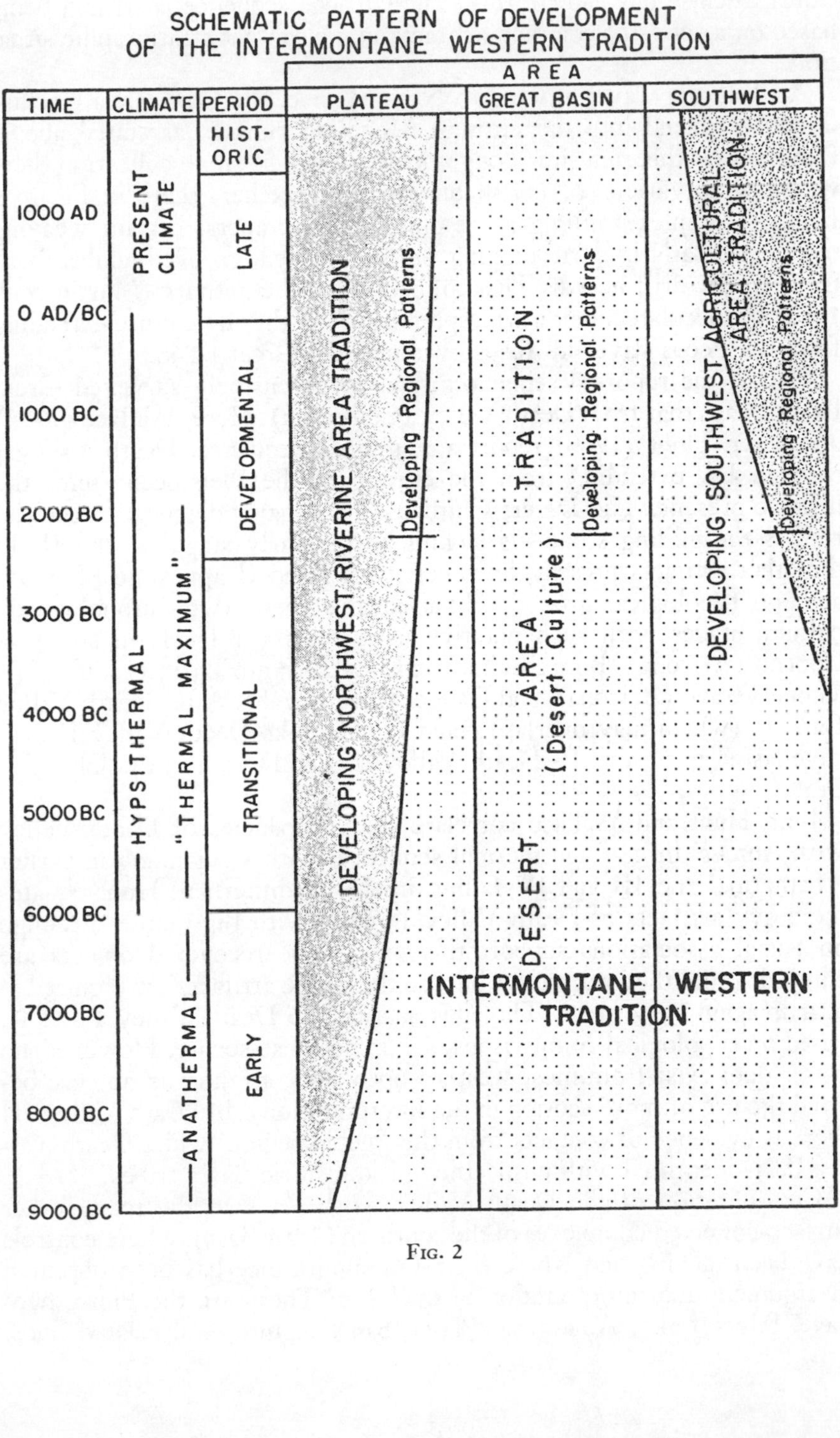
SCHEMATIC PATTERN OF DEVELOPMENT
OF THE INTERMONTANE WESTERN TRADITION
AREA
TIME
CLIMATE
PERIOD
PLATEAU
GREAT BASIN
SOUTHWEST
1000 AD
0 AD/BC
1000 BC
2000 BC
3000 BC
4000 BC
5000 BC
6000 BC
7000 BC
8000 BC
9000 BC
PRESENT CLIMATE
HYPSITHERMAL
ANATHERMAL
"THERMAL MAXIMUM"
HISTORIC
LATE
DEVELOPMENTAL
TRANSITIONAL
EARLY
DEVELOPING NORTHWEST RIVERINE AREA TRADITION
Developing Regional Patterns
DESERT AREA TRADITION
(Desert Culture)
Developing Regional Patterns
DEVELOPING SOUTHWEST AGRICULTURAL AREA TRADITION
Developing Regional Patterns
INTERMONTANE WESTERN TRADITION

Fig. 2

cahua Cochise into later forms. The Cienega sequence is strong, being based on a series of common artifacts in a clean-cut stratigraphic situation.

At Tularosa Cave, in western New Mexico, the Chiricahua Cochise is seen to blend into the farming Mogollon culture, as stated above. However, at this rich site, along with the Cochise stone collection there was a wide variety of perishable items. Together, these make up a familiar complex: milling stone and mano, scrapers, certain weaving techniques, atlatl, dart, digging sticks, curved grooved clubs, bark trowels, fire-drill hearth. This collection led the authors (Martin *et al.* 1952) to speculate about a widespread early gathering culture extending from the Pecos River in Texas over into the Great Basin.

One of the reported sequences from an intensively surveyed Great Basin area is that from Death Valley (California). Here, Wallace (1958) and, later, Hunt (1960) report a four-stage sequence, Death Valley I through IV, extending from the closing of the Pleistocene until the historic present. The Desert Culture—if its major diagnostic material trait is the milling stone—is lacking in the early stages, I and II. In the other artifacts present, however, both I and II appear to be early, and, on typological ground, Hunt equates these two chronological/cultural stages with such putative early sites (or levels in sites) as Concho (Arizona), Borax Lake, Little Lake, Pinto Basin (California), Ventana Cave (Arizona), and Danger Cave (Utah). After Death Valley I and II (which may overlap)—and Hunt thinks Death Valley II may have lasted until A.D. 1—Death Valley III and IV fall in the Christian Era.

Both Hunt and Wallace correlate the occupancies of Death Valley with Antevs' three-stage thermal sequence, with I beginning in earlier Anathermal and III and IV falling in the Medithermal. Hunt equates the heavy artifacts of Death Valley I and II with Big Game, although no faunal associations support this view. The recovered objects are chipped stone; the interpretive burden that stone artifacts are required to bear is again very great. The ages ascribed to Death Valley I and II, based on typological comparisons, are in no sense secure. However, no better data exist from most western open sites, so there is no cure beyond the use of more caution in the interpretations. In Death Valley III there is evidence of contacts from the Pueblo region, while Death Valley IV is identified with unspecified protohistoric Basin tribes.

Consideration of the Death Valley work leads to the many other surface-collected complexes of the southern Great Basin, where controls have been lacking and where their full significance has been obscured in argument and interpretation of evidence. These are the Pinto, Mohave, Silver Lake, Amargosa, Playa, San Dieguito, and related finds.

These collections have never been adequately assessed. Usually associated with fossil waterways, terraces, or beaches and often heavily patinated, the remains are widely regarded as ancient. They seem to fit, on the basis of stone types, into the Desert Culture tradition, but, as in Death Valley I, the milling stone and mano are not always present in the complex or, if present, are not common. But, because of surface locations, it has never been possible to be certain just what the several sequent complexes were. Their segregation into complexes was perforce made on subjective grounds, as was also the assignment to chronological niches. The problems of understanding the value of these data have been intensified by vacillation and terminological changes without full explanation of the revisions or what these were based on.

Recent studies, however, are making the matter much clearer. Perhaps the most useful one is that of Warren and True (1961) as they report the C. W. Harris site; the site is not actually in the Great Basin but provides perhaps the best control over these "floating" complexes yet available. C. W. Harris is a stratified site in which the lowest level yielded a congeries of artifacts comparable to San Dieguito I of Rogers (e.g., 1958), a complex extending from the West Coast to central Arizona. Warren and True are properly cautious in their comparisons and conclusions and stop short of including all the Western Desert cultures in Rogers' San Dieguito I, II, and III scheme, even though this procedure would have been justifiable, and the few radiocarbon dates derived from C. W. Harris and other sites make the ascription of the 7000 B.C. date to San Dieguito I acceptable. Typologically, all these complexes are seen as similar and related. Blanketing all the Desert industries into the San Dieguito series, as I do here, seems at least a step toward reduction of confusion and a move toward understanding, a step rooted in typology, stratigraphy, and radiocarbon dates.

Although the cultures subsumed under these terms have been included by some in the Desert Culture, the rarity (or lack) of milling stones has been seen by others as negating this ascription. Perhaps it does. It is entirely possible that the Death Valley I—San Dieguito I *et al.* complexes are tools left by Big Game hunting peoples, with a technology little changed from the chopper-scraper base, and that the Desert Culture orientation to the full biotic offering is of northern origin (as has often been averred). Perhaps San Dieguito I, then, can be viewed as a terminal Big Game stage transitional to the Desert lifeway. Its apparent contemporaneity with Desert Culture sites to the north is not important at this point. Either this could result from the facts of geography— Desert traits had not yet moved this far south—or the entire San Dieguito complex may be older than True and Warren think. It may, in fact, be the Intermontane tradition of Daugherty and antecedent to the Desert Archaic.

At one other location, the Stahl site (California), Harrington (1957) reports a site yielding a large series of the indented-base Pinto points from a buried, rather than a surface, location. At Stahl, also, there were evidences of rounded or elliptical houses (or, more properly, there was a series of post-mold patterns). No prepared floors or fire areas or other of the usual archeological criteria for identifying dwellings were present, because the old surface where the houses originated was evidently eroded or scoured away before the deposition of the fill that later sealed over the post-mold patterns. By means of a tenuous cross-dating (a typological correlation of projectile points from Stahl and those from a cave near Moapa, Nevada, the latter having two associated radiocarbon dates of 4050 ± 300 B.C. and 3870 ± 250 B.C.) and an identification of the complex geological data with the "little pluvial," Harrington places the Stahl site at about 2000–1000 B.C.; but, despite inadequate data regarding the houses, the site is important as showing most of the stone artifact attributes of the Desert Culture and in the possibility of houses early in Great Basin history. The association/co-occurrence of Pinto Basin projectile points with Silver Lake and other types in buried strata seems to show that these several associated types can be regarded as a valid complex of artifacts normally found together as a local variant of the Desert Culture. The site tends to confirm or strengthen the validity of the associated occurrence of all these types in surface collections. The date ascription of 2000–1000 B.C. may be correct, but the site could equally well be earlier.

In the Humboldt area the specialization toward lake resources seems to have begun early. The sites there form an important cluster in the heart of the Great Basin. Of these, Lovelock is the first to have been studied (Loud and Harrington 1929). Its contents have been divided into three stages based on presence or absence of a small complex of artifacts. All the cave sites of the region yield a wide variety of perishable objects and give the best available inventory of the later prehistoric phases of the Desert Culture. The sites supply ample evidence in such artifacts as duck decoys, nets and fishhooks, of a concentration upon the animal resources of a shallow lake. Other objects and tools show the same old concern with other species. There are twined and coiled baskets of several types, flexible twined bags, matting and one "wallet," sandals, feather robes, and many examples of cordage, including snares. All these were made from vegetable fibers. From bone and horn were made awls, sickles, grass-cutters, and other objects. Wood was used in a variety of ways—arrow and dart foreshafts, knife handles, fire drills and hearths, and some unidentified pieces. Stone included chipped-flint knives and points, tubular pipes, scrapers, and hammer-stones. None was numerous, but, since the sites are not midden or habitation zones, there would have been no reason for this kind of debris to accumulate.

Of the two sites (Lovelock and Humbodt caves), Lovelock was the richer in specimens and appears to have been the older. Dating back to about 2000 B.C., the early Lovelock deposits are characterized by some traits that disappear after A.D. 1—long, triangular, stemmed points, flexible twined basketry, two types of haliotis shell ornaments, atlatl and darts, L-shaped awls, horn pendants and sickles, and one olivella bead type. In Late Lovelock, some artifact types not found earlier are carved-stone art, mats with cordage wefts, and combined fur and feather robes. Exclusive early traits number fifteen. There are twenty-eight transitional and late traits. Seventeen occur throughout all the deposits (Grosscup 1960).

More important are the Lovelock traits that also characterize the historic northern Paiute. These are shredded-fiber aprons, mats, hoof pendants or rattles, nets, fur blankets, feather blankets, pointed wooden foreshafts and slings, moccasins, stone pipes, duck decoys, bow and arrow, twined tule bags. (Not all these Paiute traits occur on every level in either Lovelock or Humboldt, but all are found in the full range of artifacts in the inventory.) Heizer and Krieger, after considering the possibility, conclude that the Humboldt Cave collection (allocated to Late Lovelock stage) is not clearly antecedent to, or related to, historic Paiute. It seems to me that the material similarity of the Lovelock culture to the Paiute is perhaps closer than the restricted inventory of objects from specialized cache (Humboldt and Lovelock) sites could possibly reveal. It should be pointed out in passing that the basketry techniques most common at Humboldt were *not* known to the northern Paiutes, although the latter are skilled in other basketry work.

While other examples could be adduced, the facts are that one can argue for a cultural continuum, with increasingly marked regional variation in technological details, in the Great Basin up until historic times. In fact, at least three regional centers can be seen diverging by 3000 B.C. These regional centers and variants are now labeled as (1) Oregon-Utah (2) California-Nevada, and (3) Southern California–Southern Arizona.

Because of more and vigorous extra-areal influences, the Plateau remains show a greater change after A.D. 1 than can be demonstrated for the Great Basin. A case in point is seen in the interpretations of the Tommy Tucker Cave collection. When first reported, it was adjudged to be protohistoric northern Paiute, but a later reassessment allocates it to the Late Lovelock level. On artifactual grounds both ascriptions could obviously be correct, or the specimens could perhaps be earlier.

The matter of late change in the Great Basin is further complicated by the fact that virtually no identified historic village sites have been excavated (Riddle 1951); if excavated, the material and observed data are so nondescript or non-diagnostic as to provide no help in clarifying the conception either of culture change or of stability. About all that can be said for the basin is that pottery (Owens Valley Brown), the small side-notched point (Desert side-notched), and certain types of shell beads are all diagnostic traits of recent date and are usually dated as protohistoric or historic. Also, in many parts of the basin the flat milling stone has given way to the mortar and pestle. The basket mortar is also common. The use of mortars by many groups is a corollary of specialization toward larger seeds—acorns and pine nuts—with a reduced concern with grass seeds.

Scholars are generally agreed that the changes seen in Basin traits in the past few centuries in such things as pottery, different basketry traditions, and use of wickiup shelters result from the gradual spread, from the south, of the Shoshoni speakers. There is not yet enough data to argue linguistics from archaeology or vice versa, but both Romney (1957) and Lamb (1958) aver that the linguistic evidence supports a southern origin and a recent northward Basin-Plateau dispersal of the historic Shoshoni speakers. Taylor (1961) has gone further than anyone else in an attempt to correlate the data of linguistics, ethnology, and archaeology. In a persuasive paper, he suggests a hypothesis (not necessarily contrary to the conclusions of Lamb) that the Utaztecan stock, of which the Shoshoni speakers are members, is of quite ancient northern origin, having entered the Desert West from the north as early as six thousand years ago, following the western slopes of the Rockies south, and ever south, until the present distribution was achieved. In the process they spilled out into the Plateau and Basin to displace the even earlier Hokaltecan speakers, also of northern origin, who made the original cultural adaptation to the Desert West. Taylor's imaginative statement makes consistent and economical use of the archeological data and the present distribution of the aboriginal linguistic stocks. The southern origin of the Shoshoni is not challenged by Taylor's hypothesis.

Turning now to the Columbia Plateau and Idaho, we find that research has been slow, but certain trends can be determined. Several students have recently opined that a Desert Archaic stage was characteristic of the Plateau for a period followed what has been called the Old Cordilleran Culture (which is identified by the double-pointed Cascade point), regarded as coeval with the Llano stage of the Plains. [EDITORS, NOTE: See Krieger, p. 52.]

After the Cordilleran the Desert Archaic lifeway was dominant over the Intermontane area, including the Columbia River drainage, for most of the period from about 6000 B.C. to A.D. 1. Systematic archeological work in the Plateau area is barely begun, but it is evident that local variant cultures will be sorted out for the periods since Christ. One difficulty with the fast-growing literature is that there is less descriptive material than one could desire. Instead, much interpretation, often with an ecological slant, is being offered, but on scant evidence or on evidence all too briefly summarized. The culture differences of the later (post–A.D. 1) remains seem to be more readily perceptible in other than artifactual data. I think that perhaps unwittingly the prehistorians (who well know the cultural diversity of the historic Plateau) may perhaps be pressing too hard in their efforts to discover, in earlier and earlier levels, evidences of incipient change, when in fact the evidence, if it exists, is not yet available through archeological study. The literature of the Plateau is further blurred by extensive debate about the origin of Plateau culture and the origins of the coastal cultures as these two may overlap. The arguments are easy to keep going because of the paucity of controlled and firmly dated archeological materials that are available to the contestants.

All the same, one can accept the statements of the several authors that there are transitional periods in the Plateau, but the evidence is of a restricted sort. One can sense a change more easily than he can demonstrate it from archeological specimens because the changes are generally those resultant from partial adaptation to a specialized subsistence base, but without an abandonment of earlier practices. This specialization, moreover, is usually associated with the adoption of a lacustrine- or riverine-based economy. The accretions to the artifact inventory are not numerous, nor are they very dramatic. One is astounded at the small size of the reported collections that support the assertions about Plateau prehistory. Chipped-stone tools are again the major class of artifacts recovered. This single class of artifacts makes detailed cultural interpretation more than hazardous. I incline still to defend the idea that the Desert Archaic as a culture stage persisted in the Intermontane region until the coastal influences—such as mat and plank houses, wood and bone carving, cremation, and scaffold burial—penetrated the interior.

At the Dalles, Cressman (1960) reports a sequence of unusual cultural remains. The basalar stratum, dated by radiocarbon at about 7000 B.C. or slightly earlier, yields quantities of chipped-stone, bone, and antler artifacts. Found also were coarse stone tools, burins or gravers, and grooved stone balls, which he calls bolas. The food remains included bones of both land and marine animals, large birds, and fish. This assemblage is represented only in the lowest level. Except for some general similarities to the Pointed Mountain (McNeish) complex, the early Dalles material stands as different from that found elsewhere in the Columbia drainage and shows an early adaptation to riverine resources.

The Dalles has, however, one way and another, provided a vast amount of material for study. Much has been recovered by amateurs and is relatively uninformative because of poor controls. Butler (1959), however, has attempted to analyze some of the amateur reports and has set up a sequence of complexes covering several thousand years. These complexes rest on his segregation of associated materials as reported by the amateur diggers.

At the basal level Butler places the Congdon I complex—peripherally flaked pebble choppers, cobble choppers, flat grinding slabs, shallow basin-type mortars, scrapers, large triangular side-notched points, some stemmed points, and little else. These, at the Congdon site, were recovered from a midden deposit.

Later in time, in Congdon II, the same tools occur, but to them is added a long list of new types. Included are beads of several kinds of stone (jet, steatite, serpentine, etc.), atlatl weights of galena and stone, tubular and elbow pipes of stone, pendants, crescentic stones, fish gorges, abraders, shaft-smoothers, whetstones, two- and four-notch pebble net sinkers, long conical pestles, basalt adzes, deep mortars, zoömorphic (sheep) sculpture, and numerous projectile points of basin type. This complex was found in a deposit containing many fire-cracked basalt fragments. Associated with Congdon II was an extensive burial area. The nearby Maybe and Big Leap sites evidently equate with Congdon II. At Indian Well (Level I) the sequence of occupation and general nature of the artifacts fits well with the lower levels of Congdon, as well as with the finds of Cressman in the earliest Dalles sequence. Indian Well II includes some cremated burials and the associated artifacts. Lamellar flake knives or burins are present. The collection contains small disc beads of stone, steatite rings and pendants with zoömorphic sculptures on them, nephrite celts, wide-flanged mauls, pipes of stone, stone vessels, a stone club, and a variety of chipped-stone points.

On the basis of his survey, Butler opines that cremation is earlier in the Plateau than has been previously believed. He emphasizes, along with others, that parts of the Congdon II assemblage—atlatl weights, gorgets, etc.—bespeak contact with either an eastern or a boreal Archaic.

The dates ascribed by Butler cover the presumed range of human use of the area. To Indian Well I and its counterparts he allows a period of 8000–5500 B.C.; to Congdon I, II, and other such levels, from 5500 B.C. to A.D. 500, with the time of arrival of boreal traits estimated as 1500–

1000 B.C. By A.D. 500 the Wakemup mound series takes over. Wakemup I is characterized by excellent carving in antler and wood, rectangular houses with mat siding, and special fishing equipment. In Wakemup II there are additions. Particularly important are stick dice (a late time-marker in the Plateau) from the Southwest, and a clay figurine cult. Whalebone clubs and "slave-killer" clubs or hammers, as well as very sophisticated sculpture, mark the onset of the historic period. Butler sees the Columbia Plateau as being influenced by coastal peoples after about A.D. 500. Others would date the coastal contacts as even earlier.

At Klamath Lake, Cressman (1956) excavated a series of sites and has put together a local sequence which he thinks carries the prehistory of the Klamath area back to 7500 (or even 10,000) years ago. Whether all the conclusions are valuable is of no great importance here. What should be mentioned is that Cressman thinks that he can see the earliest levels as affiliated with (or representing) the Desert Archaic, with an early trend away from the Desert lifeway toward a specialized pattern resultant from a richer and more stable lake and forest environment. This specialization is seen in the early exploitation of fish and mussels. The original foraging exploitive techniques of the Desert Archaic can be noted, however, in the continued heavy reliance on tubers and seeds down into historic time. In the years since Christ, the earth lodge was introduced, and an intensive use of *Wocas* (water lilies) for food marks a final local food specialization that characterized the historic Klamath. The two-handed horned mano is a diagnostic Klamath artifact used in the grinding of *Wocas* seeds.

As exemplifying the later evidence for the Plateau region, and as exemplification of the extent of the evidence at hand, I use the work of Shiner (1961) at McNary Reservoir in southeast Oregon on the Columbia River. Shiner describes a series of occupations that reflect a simple economy not particularly specialized. At Hat Creek, the earliest site Shiner describes, a typical archaic assemblage occurred. Several choppers, made either from flat pebbles or from large flakes from such cobbles, are characterized as crude. There were a few well-made projectile points and some flake scrapers. Bone was confined to two tubular beads (cross-sections of bird bones), a couple of splinters, and some unidentifiable fragments. The deposit containing these was a midden yielding land mammal (rabbit and deer) bones, and some salmon bone. Considerable use was made of red ocher. At nearby Cold Springs, Shiner reports the same inventory but perceives an improvement in the techniques used in the manufacturing of all artifacts. Notched stones identified as net weights or sinkers appear for the first time. These were simply small pebbles, notched, grooved, or perforated for use with nets. Nets themselves were found, of course. Among the examples, a lanceolate basalt knife becomes more numerous. However, there were many more fishbones in the midden. Side-notched projectile points of several types appear in the Cold Creek deposits. In the later deposits at this site, marine shell and carved stone (a steatite pendant and a tubular pipe) were found, and a chipped discoid chopper was added. And shallow houses, built over saucer-like excavations, are reported. The houses (interpreted from ethnographic analogy) were light frameworks of wood covered with mats. No real archeologic evidence of superstructure was noted. The circular depressions were about three feet deep and from twenty-five to forty feet in diameter.

House form later shifted to an oval shape, and the size was somewhat reduced; some of the later houses were built of plank. At some time prior to historic contact the characteristic stone club or mallet, carved fetishes, sandstone shaft-smoothers, ornaments made from teeth and claws, and antler digging-stick handles were added to the inventory. Stone bowls and adzes for woodworking appear to be late, as are pestles, shell beads, antler wedges, and beads of stones. These items are recovered from graves at historic sites (e.g., Wallula), where European trade goods were common. At other places in the Plateau, antler wedges are found earlier; they are, in fact, deemed to be quite an old and general North American trait. Roasting ovens and large quantities of burned rock are fairly standard phenomena at most Plateau sites.

Plateau chronology is still shaky. Radiocarbon dates are rare; many dates are derived from geological events, soil studies, and other phenomena for which firm dates are entirely lacking. The chronologies inferred therefrom are equally dubious. It seems clear that the Plateau is less differentiated in broad outline from cultures either to the north or to the south than the language of some of the reports would suggest.

Although there have been continuing researches in Idaho since about 1958, only Wilson Butte is recorded in great detail; the sequence is the familiar one. Here Gruhn (1961c) was able to separate six accretional levels over an estimated 10,000 years of time. After comparative study, she sees early Plano affiliations for the Wilson Butte collections, but thereafter the analogies are greatest with the Desert Culture until protohistoric times, when late Plains traits are noted.

SUMMARY

The Desert Culture concept, though only recently expressed, is an old one. Many authors concerned with the ethnology of the West have postulated an ancient cultural substratum or base from which the later cultures had evolved. Archeology eventually caught up when a long radiocarbon-dated record of a stable lifeway adapted to a land of sparse resources was discovered and reported. Upon the evidence from Danger

Cave, the Desert Culture (Archaic) was suggested as a theoretical device for ordering the many "floating" collections of data excavated or collected over the Great Basin.

As originally defined, the Desert Culture was seen as a widespread uniform culture existing from about 8000 B.C. to 3000 B.C. Certainly, after 2000 B.C. some changes and specializations can be noted and regionally variant artifact inventories and techniques of manufacture can be isolated. While there may be regional differentiation prior to 2000 B.C., it is more readily perceived in the later sequences. The local sequences have been correlated as to time (Bennyhoff 1958) at a conference of local specialists, but no artifact inventories accompany this summary.

The significant point that has developed in this article is that the Desert Archaic can evidently be recognized from archeological materials over an area much larger than the Great Basin. By some it has been seen as a corollary of a set of climatic/environmental factors. Daugherty (1962) has extended the coverage of the Desert Culture and incorporated it into what he calls the Intermontane tradition. This he sees as early, stable, and uniform over a wide band from British Columbia to Mexico (cf. Jennings *et al.* 1956). The tradition shows regional change through five periods—Early, Transitional, Developmental, Late, and Historic forms as early as 9000 B.C. in the Plateau and by 4000 B.C. in the Southwest. The core area, modified only in riverine or lacustrine specializations, continues to be the Basin, where a pattern or tradition persists with least change into historic times. Artifacts from the earliest levels of Danger and Gypsum caves are akin to Big Game hunter artifacts of comparable age, and the Desert Culture may have succeeded a western, and as yet unidentified and undescribed, version of the Big Game (lithic) hunters. Lind Coulee would suggest the same thing, and San Dieguito I (as used in this paper) is also thus interpreted.

Obviously, interpretation of data differs from student to student, depending on many factors: a scholar is influenced by the simple facts of location of work. He sees more clearly the nuances of the data he himself collects, and, moreover, he strives to make these data meaningful in a wider framework. Too, he is influenced by what he deems important. If one believes that each little valley sheltered a human group, which was in some detailed way culturally distinct from contemporary but nearby groups, then a single new material trait spells a separate and distinctive culture. If, on the other hand, one's concern is with the inferable lifeway, its subsistence base, technology, presumed social structure, and world view, these are seen as a complex to which a few artifacts, either present or absent, are not always especially relevant.

Of course, material objects reflect culture contact and even culture change, but I know of no rule to follow as to when a culture with deep roots and a stable history of increment can be said to be new (see Heizer [1956]; Jennings [1957]).

The range of data available for analysis and inspection also affects the view of the reporter and his conclusions. If, as is unfortunately so often the case in the Desert West, one recovers only chipped stone and worked bone, these objects dominate the interpretation. But sometimes, in cave situations, the lithic evidence is augmented by large collections of perishable items and materials that are often more amenable than stone to modification in form or technique of manufacture. In this latter situation an altogether different set of comparisons and conclusions is possible.

Actually, I do not see important differences between the Plateau and the Great Basin until after A.D. 1. In both areas, by that time, we find lacustrine and riverine specialization in subsistence and increasing coastal contacts, but in no case do we find abandonment of the full exploitive round until quite late in historic times, when some Plateau tribes took on a patina of Plains horse culture. On the other hand, the differences after A.D. 1 from the preceding cultures are greater in the Plateau than in the Basin. I therefore suggest that the minor but perceptible changes of the past two thousand years in the material culture of the Basin tribes argue less for change than for stability.

As conclusion to this chapter, a chart (Fig. 1) summarizing the preliminary views of Daugherty (1962) is provided as being a useful current statement of the sequence of events in the Desert West. I find that his proposal does not alter the original conception of the Desert Culture or its postulated distribution (Jennings 1956, 1957; Bennyhoff 1958). He has described the Intermontane tradition and then isolated the diagnostic (but generalized) traits that distinguish the subsequent cultures that are based on it. He defines the tradition as extending from British Columbia to Northern Mexico, based on diversified economy with local big-game emphasis, showing strong similarity in artifact tradition and even specific types, and having great cultural stability. Changes from early to historic times are described as accretions on the older base. Interestingly, and probably correctly, he sees the early period—prior to 7000–8000 B.C.—as more locally diversified than any later ones except possibly the historic.

As, perhaps, a commentary on Daugherty's ideas, I mention the work of Swanson (1962) on the identification of early cultures in the Northwest. He postulates a sequence of Old Cordilleran, Mountain-Plains, and Bitterroot, each characterized by one or more associated flint forms: Cascade points, Plano forms, and northern side-notched, respectively.

However, each of these types tends to persist in time, and in some cases the data imply continuity rather than "layer-cake" evidence of cultural change, and the chronology is therefore difficult to establish. There are not yet enough data to sustain all Swanson's views (as he is first to point out). However, the Swanson paper takes its importance from the closely argued effort to align archeological finds with postulated Late Pleistocene ecological situations. While the presentation seems to me to weight hypothetical climate and resources far too heavily, the entire

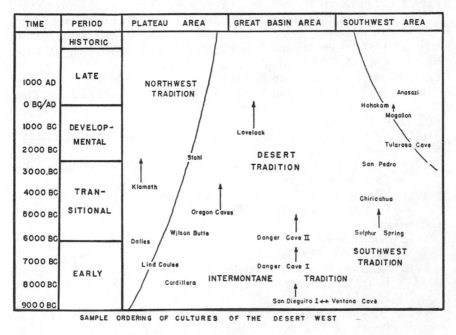

SAMPLE ORDERING OF CULTURES OF THE DESERT WEST

F𝗂ɢ. 3

paper is valuable, as is Daugherty's, in that it establishes another theoretical framework, utilizing the pitifully scant data now available, in some sort of broad general interpretation. Whether Swanson's scheme survives testing is unimportant; the existence of the several partially conflicting interpretations will speed understanding and prevent the shortsightedness that poring over flint scraps invites.

B𝗂ʙʟɪᴏɢʀᴀᴘʜʏ

Aɴᴛᴇᴠs, Eʀɴsᴛ

   1962   "Late Quaternary Climates in Arizona." *Amer. Antiquity*, 28:193–99.

ASCHMANN, H. H.
  1958 "Great Basin Climates in Relation to Human Occupance." Pp. 23–40 in *Current Views on Great Basin Archaeology.* ("Univ. Calif. Arch. Surv. Rpt.," No. 42.) Berkeley.
BAUMHOFF, M. A.
  1958 "History of Great Basin Ethnography." Pp. 1–6 in *Current Views on Great Basin Archaeology.* ("Univ. Calif. Arch. Surv. Rpt.," No. 42.) Berkeley.
BENNYHOFF, J. A.
  1958 "The Desert West: A Trial Correlation of Culture and Chronology." Prepared from data submitted and discussed by participants at a seminar proceeding, the Fourth Annual Great Basin Conference, August, 1957. Pp. 98–113 in *Current Views on Great Basin Archaeology.* ("Univ. Calif. Arch. Surv., Rpt.," No. 42.) Berkeley.
BRYAN, ALAN L., and DONALD R. TUOHY
  1960 "A Basalt Quarry in Northeastern Oregon." *Amer. Phil. Soc. Proc.,* 104:485–510. Philadelphia.
BUTLER, R. ROBERT
  1958 "The Prehistory of the Dice Game in the Southern Plateau." *Tebiwa: Jour. Idaho State Coll. Mus.,* 2:65–71.
  1959 "Lower Columbia Valley Archaeology: A Survey and Appraisal of Some Major Archaeological Resources." *Ibid.,* pp. 6–24.
  1961 *The Old Cordilleran Culture in the Pacific Northwest.* ("Idaho State Coll. Mus. Occ. Paps.," No. 5.) Pocatello.
CRESSMAN, LUTHER S.
  1942 *Archaeological Researches in the Northern Great Basin.* (Carnegie Inst. Wash. Pub. 538.) Washington, D.C.
  1956 "Klamath Prehistory: The Prehistory of the Culture of the Klamath Lake Area, Oregon." *Amer. Phil. Soc. Trans.,* n.s., Vol. 46, Part 4. Philadelphia.
  1960 "Cultural Sequences at the Dalles, Oregon: A Contribution to Pacific Northwest Prehistory." *Amer. Phil. Soc. Trans.,* n.s., Vol. 50, Part 10. Philadelphia.
CRESSMAN, LUTHER S., and ALEX D. KRIEGER
  1940 "Atlatls and Associated Artifacts from South-Central Oregon." Pp. 16–52 in CRESSMAN *et al., Early Man in Oregon: Archeological Studies in the Northern Great Basin.* (Univ. Ore. Monogs., "Studies in Anthrop.," No. 3.) Eugene.
CRESSMAN, LUTHER S., HOWEL WILLIAMS, and ALEX D. KRIEGER
  1940 *Early Man in Oregon: Archeological Studies in the Northern Great Basin.* (Univ. Ore. Monogs., "Studies in Anthrop.," No. 3.) Eugene.
DAUGHERTY, RICHARD D.
  1952 "Archaeological Investigations in O'Sullivan Reservoir, Grant County, Washington." *Amer. Antiquity,* 17:374–83.
  1956 *Early Man in the Columbia Intermontane Province.* ("Univ. Utah Anthrop. Paps.," No. 24.) Salt Lake City.
  1962 "The Intermontane Western Tradition." *Amer. Antiquity,* 28:144–50.

ELSASSER, ALBERT B., and E. R. PRINCE
 1961 "II. Eastgate Cave." Pp. 139–49 in *The Archaeology of Two Sites at Eastgate, Churchill County, Nevada.* ("Univ. Calif. Anthrop. Records," Vol. 20, No. 4.) Berkeley.
GROSSCUP, GORDON L.
 1960 *The Culture History of Lovelock Cave, Nevada.* ("Univ. Calif. Arch. Surv. Rpt.," No. 52.) Berkeley.
GRUHN, RUTH
 1960 "The Mecham Site: A Rockshelter Burial in the Snake River Canyon of Southern Idaho." *Tebiwa: Jour. Idaho State Coll. Mus.*, 3:3–19.
 1961a "A Collection of Artifacts from Pence-Duerig Cave in South-Central Idaho." *Ibid.*, 4:1–24.
 1961b "Notes on Material from a Burial along the Snake River in Southwest Idaho." *Ibid.*, pp. 37–39.
 1961c *The Archaeology of Wilson Butte Cave, South-Central Idaho.* ("Idaho State Coll. Mus. Occ. Paps.," No. 6.) Pocatello.
HARRINGTON, MARK R.
 1933 *Gypsum Cave, Nevada.* ("Southwest Mus. Paps.," No. 8.) Los Angeles.
 1948 *An Ancient Site at Borax Lake, California.* ("Southwest Mus. Paps.," No. 15.) Los Angeles.
 1957 *A Pinto Site at Little Lake, California.* ("Southwest Mus. Paps.," No. 17.) Los Angeles.
HAURY, EMIL W.
 1950 *The Stratigraphy and Archaeology of Ventana Cave, Arizona.* Albuquerque and Tucson: University of New Mexico Press and University of Arizona Press.
 1957 "An Alluvial Site on the San Carlos Indian Reservation, Arizona." *Amer. Antiquity*, 23:2–27.
HEIZER, ROBERT F.
 1951 "Preliminary Report on the Leonard Rock Shelter, Pershing County, Nevada." *Amer. Antiquity*, 17:89–98.
 1956 "Recent Cave Explorations in the Lower Humboldt Valley, Nevada." *Calif. Arch. Paps.* Nos. 37–43, pp. 50–57. ("Univ. Calif. Arch. Surv. Rpt.," No. 33) Berkeley.
HEIZER, ROBERT F., and M. A. BAUMHOFF
 1961 "I. Wagon Jack Shelter." Pp. 119–38 in *The Archaeology of Two Sites at Eastgate, Churchill County, Nevada* ("Univ. Calif. Anthrop. Records," Vol. 20, No. 4.) Berkeley.
HEIZER, ROBERT F., and ALEX D. KRIEGER
 1956 "The Archaeology of Humboldt Cave, Churchill County, Nevada." *Univ. Calif. Pub. Amer. Arch. & Ethnol.*, 47:1–190. Berkeley.
HUNT, ALICE B.
 1953 *Archeological Survey of the La Sal Mountain Area, Utah.* ("Univ. Utah Anthrop. Paps.," No. 14.) Salt Lake City.
 1960 *Archeology of the Death Valley, Salt Pan, California.* ("Univ. Utah Anthrop. Paps.," No. 47.) Salt Lake City.

HUNT, CHARLES B.
1956 "A Skeptic's View of Radiocarbon Dates." Pp. 35–46 in FAY-COOPER COLE *et al., Papers of the Third Great Basin Archaeological Conference.* ("Univ. Utah Anthrop. Paps.," No. 26.) Salt Lake City.

JENNINGS, JESSE D.
1957 *Danger Cave.* ("Univ. Utah Anthrop. Paps.," No. 27.) Salt Lake City.

JENNINGS, JESSE D. (ed.)
1956 "The American Southwest: A Problem in Cultural Isolation." Pp. 59–128 in *Seminars in Archaeology, 1955.* (Soc. Amer. Arch. Mem., 11.) Salt Lake City.

JENNINGS, JESSE D., and EDWARD NORBECK
1955 "Great Basin Prehistory: A Review." *Amer. Antiquity,* 21:1–11.

KROEBER, A. L.
1939 *Cultural and Natural Areas of Native North America.* ("Univ. Calif. Pub. Amer. Arch. & Ethnol.," Vol. 38.) Berkeley.

LAMB, SYDNEY M.
1958 "Linguistic Prehistory in the Great Basin." *Internat. Jour. Amer. Linguistics,* 24:95–100.

LATHRAP, DONALD W., and DICK SHUTLER, JR.
1955 "An Archaeological Site in the High Sierra of California." *Amer. Antiquity,* 20:226–39.

LEHMER, DONALD J.
1960 "A Review of Trans-Pecos Texas Archeology." Pp. 109–44 in *A Review of Texas Archeology,* Part I. (Tex. Arch. Soc. Bull., Vol. 29.) Austin.

LOUD, L. L., and MARK R. HARRINGTON
1929 "Lovelock Cave." *Univ. Calif. Pub. Amer. Arch. & Ethnol.,* 25: 1–183. Berkeley.

MACNEISH, RICHARD S.
1954 "The Pointed Mountain Site near Fort Liard, Northwest Territories, Canada." *Amer. Antiquity,* 19:234–54.

MARTIN, PAUL S., JOHN B. RINALDO, ELAINE BLUHM, HUGH C. CUTLER, and ROGER GRANGE, JR.
1952 "Mogollon Cultural Continuity and Change: The Stratigraphic Analysis of Tularosa and Cordova Caves." *Fieldiana: Anthropology,* Vol. 40. Chicago.

MARTIN, PAUL S., JAMES SHOENWETTER, and BERNARD C. ARMS
1961 *The Last 10,000 Years.* Tucson: Geochronology Laboratories, University of Arizona.

MEIGHAN, CLEMENT W.
1959 "Varieties of Prehistoric Cultures in the Great Basin Region." *Masterkey,* 33:46–58.

MULLOY, WILLIAM
1954 "The McKean Site. . . ." *Southwestern Jour. Anthrop.,* 10:432–60.

OSBORNE, DOUGLAS
  1958 "Western American Prehistory—An Hypothesis." *Amer. Antiquity*, 24:47–52.
OSBORNE, DOUGLAS, ALAN BRYAN, and ROBERT H. CRABTREE
  1961 "The Sheep Island Site and the Mid-Columbian Valley." *River Basin Surv. Pap.*, No. 24. (Bur. Amer. Ethnol. Bull. 179.) Washington.
OSBORNE, DOUGLAS, WARREN W. CALDWELL, and ROBERT H. CRABTREE
  1956 "The Problem of Northwest Coastal-Interior Relationships as Seen from Seattle." *Amer. Antiquity*, 22:117–28.
RIDDELL, F. A.
  1958 "The Eastern California Border: Cultural and Temporal Affinities." Pp. 41–48 in *Current Views on Great Basin Archaeology*. ("Univ. Calif. Arch. Surv. Rpt.," No. 42.) Berkeley.
RIDDELL, HARRY S.
  1951 "The Archaeology of a Paiute Village Site in Owens Valley." *Calif. Arch. Paps.* Nos. 13–16, pp. 14–28. ("Univ. Calif. Arch. Surv. Rpt.," No. 12.) Berkeley.
ROGERS, MALCOLM J.
  1958 "San Dieguito Implements from the Terraces of the Rincon-Pantano and Rillito Drainage System." *Kiva*, 24:1–23.
ROMNEY, A. K.
  1957 "The Genetic Model and Uto-Aztecan Time Perspective." *Davidson Jour. Anthrop.*, 3:35–41. Seattle.
SAYLES, E. B., and ERNST ANTEVS
  1941 *The Cochise Culture*. (Gila Pueblo "Medallion Paps.," No. 29.) Globe, Ariz.
SCHUETZ, MARDITH K.
  1961 "An Analysis of Archaic Material from Three Areas of North America." *Tex. Arch. Soc. Bull.*, 30:163–82.
SHINER, JOEL L.
  1961 "The McNary Reservoir: A Study in Plateau Archeology." *River Basin Surv. Pap.*, No. 23 (Bur. Amer. Ethnol. Bull. 179.) Washington, D.C.
SMITH, MARIAN W.
  1956 "The Cultural Development of the Northwest Coast." *Southwestern Jour. Anthrop.*, 12:272–94.
STEWARD, JULIAN H.
  1937 *Ancient Caves of the Great Salt Lake Region*. (Bur. Amer. Ethnol. Bull. 116.) Washington, D.C.
  1938 *Basin-Plateau Aboriginal Socio-political Groups*. (Bur. Amer. Ethnol. Bull. 120.) Washington, D.C.
  1940 "Native Cultures of the Intermontane (Great Basin) Area." Pp. 445–502 in *Essays in Historical Anthropology*. ("Smithsonian Misc. Coll.," Vol. 100.) Washington, D.C.
STRONG, W. DUNCAN, W. EGBERT SCHENCK, and JULIAN H. STEWARD
  1930 "Archaeology of the Dallas-Deschutes Region." *Univ. Calif. Pub. Amer. Arch. & Ethnol.*, 29:1–154. Berkeley.

SWANSON, EARL H., JR.
  1961 "Preliminary Report on Archaeology in the Birch Creek Valley, Eastern Idaho." *Tebiwa: Jour. Idaho State Coll. Mus.*, 4:25–28.
  1962 "Early Cultures in Northwestern America." *Amer. Antiquity*, 28: 151–58.
SWANSON, EARL H., JR., DONALD R. TUOHY, and ALAN L. BRYAN
  1959 *Archeological Explorations in Central and South Idaho, 1958.* I. *Types and Distributions of Site Features and Stone Tools.* ("Idaho State Coll. Mus. Occ. Paps.," No. 2.) Pocatello.
TAYLOR, WALTER W.
  1956 "Some Implications of the Carbon-14 Dates from a Cave in Coahuila, Mexico." *Tex. Arch. Soc. Bull.*, Vol. 27. Austin.
  1961 "Archaeology and Language in Western North America." *Amer. Antiquity*, 27:71–81.
TUOHY, DONALD R., and EARL H. SWANSON, JR.
  1960 "Excavation at Rockshelter 10-AA-15, Southwest Idaho." *Tebiwa: Jour. Idaho State Coll. Mus.*, 3:20–24.
WALLACE, W. J.
  1958 "Archaeological Investigations in Death Valley National Monument 1952–1957." Pp. 7–22 in *Current Views on Great Basin Archaeology.* ("Univ. Calif. Arch. Surv. Rpt.," No. 42.) Berkeley.
WARREN, CLAUDE N.
  1960 "Housepits and Village Patterns in the Columbia Plateau and Southwestern Washington." *Tebiwa: Jour. Idaho State Coll. Mus.* 3:25–28.
WARREN, CLAUDE N., and D. L. TRUE
  1961 "The San Dieguito Complex and Its Place in California Prehistory." Pp. 246–91 in *Arch. Surv. Ann. Rpt. 1960–1961.* Los Angeles: University of California at Los Angeles.
ZINGG, ROBERT MOWRY
  n.d. "A Reconstruction of Uto-Aztecan History." Ph.D. diss., University of Chicago, 1933.

ERIK K. REED

The Greater Southwest

THE ARCHEOLOGICAL Southwest extends approximately from Durango, Colorado, to Durango, Mexico, and from Las Vegas, New Mexico, to Las Vegas, Nevada, and from the Pecos River to the lower Colorado River and central Utah. The term "greater Southwest" includes the intermontane arid region south of about Great Salt Lake, as well as the deserts of southern California and Baja California. Actually, however, in this necessarily brief discussion I shall treat only casually and in passing these latter areas, because in this paper they are of peripheral interest.

In the Southwest proper we are concerned archeologically with change and progress, specifically with a series of impulses, a discontinuous but continual emanation of influence from centers of advanced culture in Mexico. In practice, we tend to stop at the international boundary and recognize only in theory that Sonora and Chihuahua really are "Southwest" rather than "Mexican." All the Southwest was, after all, part of New Spain for some three hundred years, and, if the Gadsden purchase had not been made in 1854, all the Hohokam cultural material south of the Gila River would still be Mexican legally and politically as well as Mexican in cultural affiliation.

The other major archeological groups of the Southwest proper, the Puebloan Anasazi and Mogollon, likewise but differently and less manifestly, represent the northern frontier provinces, outlying rural offshoots, of Mesoamerican civilization. Of course, each has its own local developments and special modifications. And on beyond, in the surrounding regions, with still greater modifications, we see the final glim-

ERIK K. REED, regional chief of the Southwest Region, Division of History and Archeology, National Park Service, received his doctoral degree from Harvard University. His archeological research has centered chiefly on the southwestern United States, and he is the author of outstanding analytic writings on the prehistory of this area. Dr. Reed has also done archeological research in Peru and the Galapagos and Mariana Islands. He has held many editorial and advisory positions in scientific organizations and institutions.

mering of these reflections of Mexico, with continuation from millenniums of an Archaic desert way of life.

The Archaic Desert Culture, traceable from at least nine thousand years ago at sites like Danger Cave in westernmost Utah (Jennings 1957), was observable essentially unmodified in modern Paiutes of the Great Basin and in Baja California, where the spear-thrower still was used in historic times (Massey 1961). On the eastern side, arid Coahuila and most of trans-Pecos Texas did not participate to any perceptible degree in the rapid, steady advance from Archaic or Basketmaker-like status. In most of the Southwest proper, however, a complicated process of cultural history led to stable and essentially successful permanent sedentary agricultural societies, simply but subtly organized, advanced or even sophisticated in arts and crafts, but never quite attaining the urban level of civilization.

To return momentarily to definition of the area under discussion— when I say "the Southwest proper" I am thinking of the Pueblo and Hohokam region, that is, central and northern and eastern Arizona and western and southern New Mexico, northwestern Chihuahua, and southwesternmost Colorado, southern Utah, and the Virgin River or Moapa Valley district of southernmost Nevada. There are three major natural geographic divisions of this country: (1) the high plateau land of the Anasazi canyons and mesas with piñon-juniper woodland and sagebrush, the "Upper Sonoran" zone, fairly arid (with, however, a growing body of evidence to indicate that very likely much more of this region was covered by ponderosa pine a thousand years ago than at present; cf. Reed 1962); (2) the higher, comparatively well-watered mountain zone, correlating to a considerable extent with Mogollon culture, with extensive "Transitional" forest cover of yellow pine; (3) the desert of western and southern Arizona and much of southern New Mexico, with creosote brush and yucca, with saguaro cactus in the Hohokam area of southern Arizona, and with other distinctive plants of the "Lower Sonoran" arid zone.

We may safely assume that the cultural inventory of the Archaic people of the arid intermontane West, and even of their fairly remote ancestors, comprised several virtually world-wide items: the throwing spear and its throwing stick or atlatl, domestic dogs, implements of bone and wood and chipped stone, utensils of bark and wood and basketry. Sandals and basketry are known from as early as 7000 B.C. (Wormington 1962). In general, only the stone objects have survived to undergo typological analysis—dartpoints, knives and scrapers, grinding stones. The last of these items is perhaps the most interesting, since it clearly suggests considerable utilization of wild-plant seeds, along with partial dependence on hunting—in fact, undoubtedly, highly intensive exploitation for subsistence of all the varied but relatively sparse biological resources of the desert and the semiarid regions. Milling stones are present at least by 8000 B.C.

This cultural group contrasts with the other more spectacular and somewhat better known, partially contemporaneous, Upper Paleolithic Early Man or Paleo-Indian complex concentrated on hunting of large animals—notably elephants in the very early period, then primarily *Bison antiquus* later on—and represented, above all, by skilfully made large parallel-flaked and/or channel-fluted stone points. I see no sufficient reason for hesitating to call this material Upper Paleolithic. No time assignment is thereby implied; the term implies only a technological stage.

In much of the Southwest proper, the Big Game hunters do not seem to have been present in any number. Sandia Cave, two elephant kills in southernmost Arizona, Gypsum Cave, and a few isolated finds of single points of known types (occurring scattered from Durango and Baja California northward, but rare within the Southwest proper, except perhaps northern Chihuahua)—this almost exhausts the list. The recent discovery of a fluted-point site in Monument Valley, north of Comb Ridge, in northernmost Arizona or southernmost Utah, has been reported. In addition, there is the unreported (so far as I am aware) surface find in 1950 of a Sandia point on a mesa a few miles northwest of Shiprock, New Mexico.

In the region to the west, a number of important Early Man sites fall within the Greater Southwest, as far north as Danger Cave. But the Big Game hunters—and presumably the big game—were concentrated, it appears, on the Great Plains from eastern New Mexico and the Texas panhandle and eastern Colorado north and eastward. Very possibly the great beasts of the Late Pleistocene did not range normally or in any great numbers into the mountain and mesa country of the central Southwest. But neither are very early Desert Archaic remains known from the central and southern Colorado Plateau, and the preagricultural Basketmaker I period still is a postulated necessary assumption in what theoretically should be its home range, though its equivalents are found almost all around—particularly in the Cochise sequence of southern Arizona and southwestern New Mexico.

To the small scattered bands of Desert Archaic food-collectors, specifically to those of the Cochise group, there came a series of new and, eventually, revolutionary traits. First, and ultimately the most important, maize—appearing in southwestern New Mexico more than four thousand years ago, and coming, whatever its original source, from somewhere in central or southern Mexico so far as we are concerned, very likely in a continuous diffusion from one group to the next all the way along, quite possibly up the Sierra Madre rather than through the lower-lying inhospitable deserts.

Strangely, the introduction of maize apparently brought about no significant cultural change or conspicuous population increases; nor, a millennium later, did the addition of squash and beans (which enter the record in southwestern New Mexico by 1000 B.C., reaching the northern Southwest only much later). Maize, though it must have been cultivated, must have been, in effect, simply another item added to the list of wild plant foods, requiring different handling and special attention, but producing no radical effects for the first two thousand years or more. The same was evidently true, though even more surprising and puzzling, of the first cultivated beans for one thousand years. For the squashes-pumpkins I find this less incomprehensible, since they might conceivably have been valued for the gourds rather than for the flesh, or even the seeds, as food.

The preceramic agricultural (or semiagricultural or, we might say, crop-using) people of the late Cochise horizons in the south and of Basketmaker II of the Anasazi, in the San Juan River region of the northern Southwest, still were essentially Archaic or Mesolithic foragers of the Desert Culture, subsisting in considerable part on wild plants and game animals, and consequently living in small and scattered bands, probably still moving about a good bit, at least seasonally. But permanent or semipermanent habitations had come in by this time—how early, we do not know, but certainly before the time of Christ in the San Pedro stage of the Cochise lithic sequence, and, by the first century of our era in the Anasazi, seen in the Basketmaker II site near Durango, Colorado (Morris and Burgh 1954).

Other known traits for Basketmaker II in the northern Southwest proper include: storage cists; inhumation of the dead (in caves for the most part, so far as is known, tightly flexed and wrapped in blankets and woven bags, accompanied by baskets and other offerings); chipped-stone drills, knives, scrapers and dart points; manos and flat metates; stone pipes; atlatl and throwing spear; grooved, curved club ("rabbit stick" or "fending stick"); digging stick; bone implements; horn blades, horn wrenches; wooden scoops, small wooden boxes; unfired clay vessels; coiled basketry with black and sometimes also red ornament; twined bags and matting; sandals woven of yucca cord; woven straps or sashes; women's aprons; fur-cloth blankets; human hair cordage; some use of deerskin for shoulder robes; beads and ornaments of seashell, wood, seeds, lignite, hematite, and other minerals (not, so far as is known, turquoise); tobacco—and the lack of pottery; bow and arrow or stone axe; stone construction or surface houses; occipital cradleboard deformation; the domestic turkey; and apparently cultivation of beans (Morris 1939; Morris and Burgh 1954).

Elsewhere, little material other than stonework has survived. In a few dry caves of southern New Mexico, remains are found comparable to San Juan Basketmaker and presumably representing preceramic late Cochise, perhaps to be legitimately called "Basketmaker II" in a broad sense (Cosgrove 1947). Materials found in early levels of Tularosa Cave, in the Reserve District of southwestern New Mexico (Martin *et al.* 1952), preceramic and Pine Lawn phase, offer a list of traits from between 500 or 300 B.C. and A.D. 500 or so, more or less broadly comparable to the Anasazi Basketmaker inventory summarized above (those appearing only in Pine Lawn times, probably about 150 B.C., are starred with an asterisk)—storage pits, shallow pit houses*; flexed burial, half-seated, wrapped; chipped-stone drills, knives, scrapers, and projectile points; manos and metates, mortars*, stone pipes*; reed flutes, dice; both the atlatl and spears *and* the bow and arrow (including preceramic occurrence!); digging stick; bone implements, antler tools; unfired clay vessels (rare), unpainted well-made brownware*; coiled basketry, twined matting*, fur-cloth and feather-cloth blankets*, wickerwork sandals, leather sandals, and moccasins (!); shell bracelets* (?) and wooden pendants, bone tube beads; cultivated beans (as well as maize and cucurbits), tobacco, various wild plants utilized. Stone axes and turkey remains are not mentioned.

Not reported from Tularosa Cave are: the curved grooved club (known from the Upper Gila, further south, however; Cosgrove 1947); the small wooden "feather boxes," human-hair cordage, twined soft bags, variety of beads and pendants (Martin *et al.* 1952). The significant differences between Anasazi and Mogollon at this early period are few. Broadly similar material, of uncertain antiquity for the most part, is found in caves of trans-Pecos Texas and Coahuila and also right across Oklahoma, here and there, to the Ozarks, as well as north to Oregon and beyond. [EDITORS' NOTE: Compare the above lists with Jennings, pp. 153–55.]

The distinctively Southwestern developments begin with the introduction of pottery (from further south in Mexico) and the occurrence for the first time *so far as we now know* of definite clustered villages, presumably more or less permanent, of large and small pit houses. These two clear indications of sedentary farming, of completing the transition from food-collecting to food-producing village life, seem to appear pretty much together; and some factor as yet not convincingly identified must finally have brought about full primary dependence on agriculture and the many deep changes thereby entailed. I do not believe that this phenomenon is mere coincidence of discovery caused by the fact that we find sites more easily when they are marked by surface potsherds. Sites of the earliest ceramic horizons in each area of the Southwest are also rather few and far between, and the great increase of population manifests itself only later on.

Before continuing on the theme, at last reached, of pottery—the devoted Southwesternist's favorite subject—let us consider briefly the other and somewhat earlier item of pit houses. Here is an important element that does *not* come out of the south; true pit houses are unknown, I believe, or at least unimportant, in Mexico generally. The typical Southwestern pit houses resemble broadly various Eurasian structures of different places and times, as early as Upper Paleolithic Moravia and as late as eighteenth-century Kamchatka. Across the intervening region of northwestern America, few occurrences bridge the enormous gap, since comparisons with the Northwest Coast and the Eskimo areas are not satisfactorily close; in fact, the pit house appears in the Plateau area of the northwestern United States only later than in the Southwest. Nevertheless, the pit-house idea must be of northern derivation somehow (Roberts 1929; Daifuku 1952, 1961). And yet one of the oldest (probably) known in the Southwest is the very large, deep four-post-roof pit house of the earliest period (the Vahki phase, estimated date around the time of Christ) at Snaketown, the type site of the Hohokam area, on the lower Gila River in southern Arizona (Gladwin *et al.* 1937).

By then, however, pottery had become well established in the southern parts of the Southwest. The first ceramic phases are not yet well known in Durango and Chihuahua but surely must date back equally far; probably also in Sonora likewise. In any case, pottery—not crude experimentation, but well-made polished brownware—had been introduced to the southern Mogollon area before the time of Christ, in fact by at least 200 B.C., according to radiocarbon dates of recent finds. The same general kind of ceramics appeared in southern Arizona by A.D. 300.

The idea, and actual vessels of southern brownware, reached the Anasazi of the San Juan region about a hundred and fifty years later, evidently stimulating the local development there of a different and quite distinctive ware, the plain gray pottery of Basketmaker III. Recent work, as yet unpublished, in the vicinity of the confluence of the Piedra and Pine rivers with the San Juan has for the first time produced still earlier occurrences of brownware in the north—first about A.D. 150, seemingly, in small quantity; then a gap, a phase with no pottery; and then reappearance of brownware somewhere between, I gather, A.D. 300 and 450.

In another direction, meanwhile, in the western Arizona desert and along the lower course of the Colorado River below the Grand Canyon, people who are suspected of being ancestors of the historic Yuman-speaking tribes of that same region had also received agriculture and pottery, likewise incorporating these activities into a basic food-collecting Desert Culture way of life. The names Patayan and Hakataya apply to the proto-Yumans upon the receipt of the ceramic art.

For about A.D. 475–775, it is possible to describe various communities in different parts of the Southwest with reasonably adequate comprehension—selected examples of Basketmaker III or initial Pueblo I in the San Juan Anasazi group, such as Alkali Ridge in southeastern Utah, Jeddito 264 in northeastern Arizona, Mesa Verde sites in southwestern Colorado, and Shabik'-eschee in Chaco Canyon, New Mexico; known sites of the Mogollon culture in the plainware-redware period of the Pine Lawn and Georgetown phases (and with broad-line red-on-brown painted pottery appearing); and the Snaketown and Gila Butte phases of the Hohokam sequence at Snaketown.

By this time not only pit houses and fired pottery had reached the northern Southwest (probably from opposite directions); the bow and arrow, with small stone points, and the stone axe (presumably from opposite directions) and cultivation of cotton—from the south—and domestication of the turkey (possibly stimulated from an outside source?) also came in during this period. Another cultural trait that spread into the northern Southwest toward the end of this period was artificial cranial deformation (occipital flattening resulting from the use of a hard, rigid cradleboard)—among the Anasazi taking the unique form of a high-angle "lambdoid" deformation (Reed 1949). Occipital deformation of a milder form, producing a more or less vertical flattened area on the back of the head, appeared in the Pine Lawn phase of the southern Mogollon by A.D. 500, or perhaps earlier. In the early Mogollon pit-house villages in the Forestdale Valley of eastern Arizona, occipital flattening may have occurred as early as A.D. 320, and extreme deformation (of the vertical type) was present by *ca.* A.D. 700 (Haury 1940; Haury and Sayles 1947).

Most of the "Basketmaker" traits previously listed continued in use, except those which were superseded by new introductions—for example, the atlatl and throwing spear and the large flaked-stone dart points. In at least the north (San Juan Anasazi), feather-cloth superseded fur-cloth blankets after domestication of turkeys came in. But the great majority of implements of stone, bone, and wood; basketry containers; sandals; and various textile items carried right on with only minor changes. In fact, virtually all continued up to the late prehistoric Pueblo periods with rather slight modifications and very few losses or disappearances. The story is one of continuous addition of new elements, some locally developed and some introduced. The same is essentially true for Mogollon as well as Anasazi and, to at least a considerable extent, for Hohokam.

All the groups mentioned above shared a generally similar way of life at the time—about A.D. 500–750 or 800, with only the Hohokam being radically different in any important manner. At this period the Anasazi and Mogollon groups actually diverge only in very minor details, except in ceramics—polished brownware in the south, predominance of gray pottery, largely unpolished, in the San Juan. Distinctive features of the contemporaneous horizons at Snaketown, however, include oblong surface-cleared houses (not actually pit houses); ball courts; cremation of the dead; distinctive buff pottery, shaped with paddle and anvil; slate palettes, carved-stone bowls; abundance of shell ornaments; well-made $\frac{3}{4}$-grooved stone axes; mosaic plaques; and irrigation ditches.

Several of these are definitely Mexican traits, the ball court most notably and unquestionably so. In fact, recent opinion has begun to swing toward the concept of arrival in southern Arizona, among Yuman or Mogollon folk, of an actual group of colonists (or even conquerors?) from farther south.

These preliminary or transitional phases at the end of the Pioneer period at Snaketown crystallized into the fully developed Hohokam culture of the eighth to twelfth centuries—the Santa Cruz (Colonial) and Sacaton (Sedentary) periods. Hohokam villages exemplified by Snaketown consisted of irregularly scattered huts or jacales in shallow excavations, hardly more than surface leveling, built of perishable materials and broadly resembling both recent Pima and Papago houses and the ordinary houses of southern Mexican Indian groups. Only the adobe floors have survived—oval to oblong, about 6 by 3 meters, with entranceway at the middle of one of the long sides, bowl-shaped fire pit in front of it, postholes around the rim, few other floor features.

In addition, Hohokam villages included ball courts, sometimes an earthen platform mound (a truncated-pyramid substructure, likewise extremely Mexican in principle, though crude in detail and execution), trash mounds (great heaps of rubbish and soil, which must have been deliberately accumulated), cremation burial areas, irrigation systems, undoubtedly extensive fields of corn and cotton, and presumably also beans and cucurbits. Wild plants and game animals were also utilized; the turkey was evidently not domesticated by the Hohokam.

Specific material culture traits included red-on-buff and plain buff pottery, a variety of shell ornament—including carved and etched shell —shell trumpets; mosaic plaques and slate palettes; copper bells from the region of Michoacan (after about A.D. 900); clay figurines; $\frac{3}{4}$-grooved axes of diorite; long, slender barbed projectile points and side-notched triangular points; small carved or plain stone bowls; manos and trough metates; pestles and mortars; reamers; whetstones; rings of vesicular basalt; flake knives; hammerstones; earplugs and labrets or nose buttons; turquoise pendants; incised bone tubes; and painted antlers.

Very few remnants of textiles have survived in the Hohokam area proper, but it is safe to assume that an advanced weaving industry flourished, and it is possible to surmise that the varied and marvelous textiles found in surrounding regions may have been of Hohokam inspiration or even actual origin. Hohokam colonies occupied not only the Tonto Basin but the Verde Valley, with one offshoot as far north as Winona, fourteen miles east of Flagstaff. The cultural inventory, the kind of settlement, and the indicated way of life set off the Hohokam very sharply from all Puebloan groups, Anasazi or Mogollon, and align them with central and even southern Mexico—specifically, the Chalchihuites culture of Durango and Zacatecas and the Tula-Mazapan horizons (see discussion, primarily by J. Charles Kelley, in Jennings *et al.* 1956). [EDITORS' NOTE: See also Armillas, pp. 314 ff.] Contact with Mexican cultures to the south cannot, however, have been very close or continuous, for there are many cultural elements known in Mexico that never spread north to our area, such as chili peppers, legged (tripod) metates, polished-stone celts, dental mutilation, to name a few. Others—for example, biconical spindle whorls (Haury 1945)—have only a very limited Southwestern occurrence.

During the period of Hohokam rise and florescence, the various Puebloan groups went through a series of complicated phases of change and advance, an evolution that appears to have been very largely a local development, with relatively little outside influence. Certain traits, however, evidently were of Hohokam derivation or inspiration, and some of the features that appeared earlier in the south, among the Mogollon Puebloans, may very probably have originated still farther south in Mexico. A large and rapid increase in population is clearly indicated by the great number of sites, often quite large, of this period.

The major steps involved in the transition to fully developed Pueblo culture included (1) surface masonry buildings of contiguous rooms, developing from the Basketmakers' storage cists, with the pit house becoming the kiva (a distinctive ceremonial chamber, usually subterranean and, in the north, among the San Juan Anasazi, circular); (2) crystallization of a definite type of site plan in the Anasazi consisting of compact surface pueblo residential structure, then kiva or kivas, then refuse mound with burials, along a northwest-southwest axis (with, at least in some districts, pit houses continuing in use until much later); (3) development of the particularly specialized large circular ceremonial structure called the Great Kiva; and (4) virtually universal production, in

San Juan Anasazi, of indented corrugated gray utility pottery; distinct local styles of black-on-white painted ware and, in some areas, black-on-red and polychrome. The circular kiva and the definitely oriented site plan along a single axis are distinctively Anasazi traits; so are the gray corrugated pottery and, originally, the black-on-white; so is whatever style of cradleboard arrangement produced the "lambdoid" type of occipital deformation; so are notched-pebble or full-grooved stone axes, domestication and eating of turkeys, and perhaps also other features.

More generalized, or at least somewhat less distinctive and more conservative, the southern brownware or Mogollon Pueblo groups retained polished brown utility ware and successively developed red-on-brown, red-on-white, and black-on-white painted pottery, and emerged only later and even more gradually from pit houses into surface pueblos with rectangular kivas. The differences between Mogollon sites of around A.D. 500 and of A.D. 1000–1100 are few: painted pottery (by about A.D. 1000, black-on-white in most areas); cotton cloth; the pit houses almost all rectangular, generally with a fairly long entrance-ramp passageway, instead of predominantly roundish with few long entrance passages, with a four-post arrangement of main roof supports more nearly standard and ubiquitous than in early phases; full-trough metates, along with the older basin and slab types; a few stone axes, full-grooved and $\frac{3}{4}$-grooved, probably intrusive, as well as the widespread full-grooved maul, which occurs throughout; only very minor changes or trends in other categories of material (Wheat 1955).

Finally, about A.D. 1100–1150, the building of pueblos (stone surface structures of contiguous rooms) spread across the Mogollon area. These, however, are generally merely agglomerations of rooms with no definite town plan such as the northern sites had. Nor did the distinctive circular kiva of the Anasazi accompany the idea of stone pueblos built at ground level southward. In the Mogollon pit-house villages of A.D. 500–1000, there frequently are exceptionally large ones, usually with some distinctive features, which generally have been considered probable ceremonial structures; in most of the later Mogollon pueblos, rectangular kivas occur, including very large ones with ramp entrances in the Tularosa–Upper Little Colorado area (Hough 1914; Martin *et al.* 1962). In the Sinagua culture of the Flagstaff district and the Verde Valley, no recognizable kivas are found in many of the sites.

In the time between about A.D. 1150, or shortly after, and A.D. 1275 or 1300, several well-defined patterns are known in various parts of the Southwest: the Mesa Verde phase or culture in southwesternmost Colorado, southeastern Utah, most of northwestern New Mexico, and northeasternmost Arizona; the Largo phase in the Gallina River area

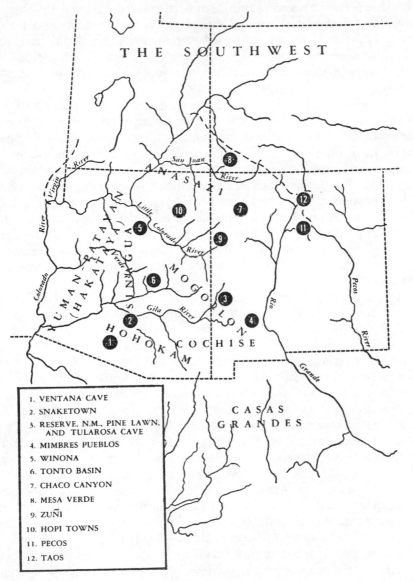

1. VENTANA CAVE
2. SNAKETOWN
3. RESERVE, N.M., PINE LAWN, AND TULAROSA CAVE
4. MIMBRES PUEBLOS
5. WINONA
6. TONTO BASIN
7. CHACO CANYON
8. MESA VERDE
9. ZUÑI
10. HOPI TOWNS
11. PECOS
12. TAOS

FIG. 1

of north-central New Mexico; the Tularosa phase in west-central New Mexico; a distinctive culture on the Mimbres River in southwestern New Mexico; the Kayenta culture of northeastern Arizona; the Sinagua development of central Arizona; and a poorly known transitional stage in the Hohokam area of southern Arizona in which polished redware, inhumation of the dead, and other new traits (presumably from the north) appear, along with platform substructure mounds (presumably Mexican).

The most striking occurrence at this time is the fact that two kinds of conspicuous large, distinctive ceremonial structures went out of use: the Hohokam ball court and the Anasazi Great Kiva. Why this happened we do not know. What precisely superseded the ball court in southern and central Arizona we do not know. In the eastern San Juan region in this period, instead of continued functioning of the Great Kiva, we find triple-walled "towers" and other structures of bizarre ground plan. A number of detailed architectural features that appeared in the San Juan after A.D. 1050 seem to be of Mexican derivation and may well represent the arrival in the northern Southwest of the cult of Quetzalcoatl (Ferdon 1955), by what mechanism of transmission we do not know.

Again, these various local groups or cultural subdivisions of Pueblo III times—the period A.D. 1150–1300—share most of the basic aspects of their way of life and many detailed features. Common to all of them are settled agricultural life in large and small villages, with primary dependence on maize, with cultivation also of beans and curcurbits and cotton, supplemented by hunting of deer and rabbits and other animals and by utilization of wild plants, with no definite indications of true urbanization, extensive occupational specialization, or social stratification—in other words, practically everyone living the same way, virtually all farmers, with a number of priests and perhaps a few outstanding craftsmen or craftswomen who were excused from the normal round with its varied work load. Common to all of them, likewise, are the manufacture and use of pottery vessels, bow and arrow, stone and bone tools, baskets and matting, cotton fabrics and textiles of wild plant materials, use of animal skins, sandals, and many other fairly generalized traits, and many types of specific items—kinds of stone tools, use of turquoise, use of tobacco, and presence of macaws and parrots from Mexico. Differences appear in settlement patterns and details of architecture, in religious structures, in many features of the ceramic art, in certain other artifactual categories, and in methods of burial of the dead.

Contrast, for example, the Mesa Verde period of the Anasazi of the upper San Juan and the Sinagua group of central Arizona from the Flagstaff vicinity south:

1. *Residential architecture.* Mesa Verde: very large to very small pueblos, well built of selected and worked stone, arranged consistently in a front-oriented plan. Sinagua: pueblos of generally inferior masonry with no particular orientation, no front and back.

2. *Ceremonial structures.* Mesa Verde: specialized kivas, quite distinct from domiciliary rooms, generally circular, with standard features; also various peculiar buildings. Sinagua: none definitely recognizable (in a few pueblos, for example Tuzigoot, a rectangular chamber larger than other rooms, with a few special features, and very possibly a kiva).

3. *Utility (culinary) pottery.* Mesa Verde: gray, all-over indented corrugated, scraped (no use of paddle and anvil), unpolished. Sinagua: polished, smooth brown- and redware, finished with paddle and anvil.

4. *Painted pottery.* Mesa Verde: a distinct type of fine black-on-white. Sinagua: none locally made; imported Anasazi vessels.

5. *Stone axes.* Mesa Verde: full-grooved for a wrapped haft, only the cutting edge ground, made on river pebbles. Sinagua: well-made, polished $\frac{3}{4}$-grooved (for a J-shaped haft), worked all over, of hard volcanic rock.

6. *Artificial (cradleboard) deformation of the skull.* Mesa Verde: both lambdoid and vertical occipital types. Sinagua: exclusively vertical.

7. *Burial of the dead.* Mesa Verde: both flexed and extended inhumation, the former predominating. Sinagua: uniformly extended inhumation.

8. *Turkeys.* Mesa Verde: domesticated, or at the very least kept and eaten. Sinagua: wild turkeys occasionally hunted (or captured for feathers?), probably not eaten.

At the same time, during the climax of classic Pueblo culture in the San Juan and Little Colorado and Upper Gila drainages, the western and northwestern frontiers of Anasazi expansion began to collapse. The generalized "Pueblo II" culture, of the period A.D. 850 or thereabouts to A.D. 1100 or 1200, in southernmost Nevada and southwestern Utah is not followed by classic Pueblo III developments anywhere north and west of the Colorado River but, instead, by decline and disappearance. It has been widely thought that possibly this was regression to the old Desert Archaic way of life, that Puebloized Shoshoneans became the historic Paiutes. It also has been thought that perhaps the Pueblos west of the Colorado River gave way before Paiute expansion and retired toward the Kayenta-Hopi districts of northeastern Arizona.

In any case, the process of Pueblo withdrawal, or disappearance as such, and abandonment of extensive areas gathered sudden momentum in the last quarter of the thirteenth century. Rather abruptly and rapidly, so far as the available evidence indicates, the Anasazi vanished from the entire San Juan River drainage toward A.D. 1300; the Flagstaff district was abandoned, and apparently also the Tularosa River and Upper Little Colorado valleys in west-central New Mexico.

For the period A.D. 1300–1450, or early Pueblo IV, we have Pueblo Indians known only in the following areas: (1) the Rio Grande area, where a very scanty early occupation suddenly became tremendously expanded in the thirteenth century; (2) the Acoma district; (3) the Zuni country, as far east as the Ramah area, with numerous large four-teenth-century pueblos; (4) a few sites in the Petrified Forest; (5) the Hopi villages, with a mixture of elements from several directions; (6) the Verde Valley (a good number of large Sinagua pueblos) and the Tonto Basin; (7) the White Mountains–Upper Salt drainage, many large sites from Pinedale and Showlow to Point of Pines; (8) south-eastern Arizona; (9) the classic Casas Grandes culture or the Ramos phase of northwestern Chihuahua, finally becoming known beyond its polychrome pottery through the recent excavations there of Charles C. DiPeso; and (10) the so-called "Classic" stage of the Hohokam area; Gila Polychrome pottery and also red-on-buff, both inhumation (ex-tended) and cremation, wattle-and-daub jacales and adobe compounds, and the Casa Grande, the last item possibly representing another Mexi-can intrusion (Ferdon 1955).

Two notable innovations in pottery decoration occurred in the north about or soon after A.D. 1300: (1) use of a metallic glaze paint, evidently a local invention in east-central Arizona, soon carried to the Rio Grande, where lead replaced copper as the key constituent, and (2) in the Hopi country, where the glaze paint never was introduced, appearance on Sikyatki Polychrome of a new realistic—or, rather, fantastic represen-tational—style of design (possibly of Mexican derivation), superseding the old geometric motives (Brew 1944). Another idea that does not seem to occur widely and regularly in the Southwest before about A.D. 1300 is the formal arrangement of a town around a central plaza or several plazas, an inward-facing hollow-square type of layout. The source of, and reasons for, this change are unknown.

Further mass abandonments of large pueblos and entire districts oc-curred between 1450 and 1540. When the Spaniards arrived in the sixteenth century, bringing still another set of new cultural elements to the Southwest from southern Mexico, the only areas still occupied by Pueblo Indians were the Rio Grande, from Taos down to about San Marcial and from Pecos to the lower Chama and the lower Jemez; Acoma, isolated and picturesque; the six historic Zuni pueblos; and the half-dozen villages of the Hopi, including Awatovi (but evidently not Kawaioku or Sikyatki). The wide expanse of high country from Pine-dale to Point of Pines had been relinquished, and the Sinagua had com-pletely disappeared; the great houses of Chihuahua were abandoned; and there seem to have been only comparatively rude settlers left in much of the Hohokam region of southern Arizona. In at least certain localities, however, continuity of occupation—and even, apparently, of Gila Poly-chrome pottery—into the historic period (meaning, in Sonora, the late seventeenth century) has been clearly indicated (DiPeso 1953, 1956, 1958).

In the western Arizona desert and along the lower Colorado River, the Patayan or Hakataya had continued to exist with little change and enter the historic scene as Yuman-speaking tribes. A little farther north, the Southern Paiute were already at hand. Finally, in the plains of eastern New Mexico, we encounter for the first time the Apache— known from documentary sources, not from archeology, beginning in 1540. It is now generally recognized that the Apache, including the ancestral Navajo, evidently moved southward along the High Plains and just east of the Rocky Mountains not long before the Spaniards entered the Southwest from the opposite direction and that they spread westward into eastern Arizona only during the historic period.

Under the two pressures of the less civilized Apaches—hunting and fighting Plains Indians who only gradually and partially accepted certain aspects of Pueblo culture—and the technically advanced and politically dominant Spaniards, the Pueblos, especially along the Rio Grande, crystallized into withdrawn conservatism and succeeded, largely through a kind of secretive passive resistance, in preserving the essence and structure of their way of life during three hundred and fifty years of European control and missionary efforts (Eggan 1950; Reed 1944). In southern Arizona, the Pimans reacted somewhat differently under similar pressures, beginning later and applied less strongly (Spicer 1954; Ezell 1961). The Apache tribes were for the most part never really conquered by the Spanish or converted to Catholic Christianity, but they—particularly the Navajo—acquired and utilized many traits of European or Mexican origin as well as features of Pueblo culture.

A new and perhaps final period in aboriginal Southwestern history, which might be called Pueblo VI, began sixteen years ago. The young men returning from the war, from associating with other Americans and with other nationalities, did not settle back easily and readily into the traditional beliefs and patterns; witchcraft persecutions at Zuni increased sharply, and factional dissension came into the open at several other pueblos as the painful transition to twentieth-century life in the United States began. For the Apache tribes, and particularly the Navajo, an outstanding characteristic of the current period and the last fifteen years has been the emergence of independent handling of affairs by the tribal councils.

BIBLIOGRAPHY

BREW, J. OTIS
1944   "On the Pueblo IV and Katchina-Tlaloc Relations." *El Norte de Mexico y el Sur de los Estados Unidos.* (Report of Tercera Reunion de la Mesa Redonda.) Mexico, D.F.

Cosgrove, C. B.
  1947 *Caves of the Upper Gila and Hueco Areas in New Mexico and Texas.*
        ("Peabody Mus. Amer. Arch. & Ethnol. Paps.," Vol. 24, No. 2.)
        Cambridge, Mass.
Daifuku, Hiroshi
  1952 "The Pit House in the Old World and in Native North America."
        Amer. Antiquity, 18:1–7.
  1961 *Jeddito 264.* ("Peabody Mus. Amer. Arch. & Ethnol. Paps.," Vol.
        33, No. 1.) Cambridge, Mass.
DiPeso, Charles C.
  1953 *The Sobaipuri Indians of the Upper San Pedro River Valley, Southeastern
        Arizona.* ("Amerind Foundation Paps.," No. 6.) Dragoon.
  1956 *The Upper Pima of San Cayetano de Tumacacori: An Archaeohistorical
        Reconstruction of the Ootam of Pimeria Alta.* ("Amerind Foundation
        Paps.," No. 7.) Dragoon.
  1958 *The Reeve Ruin of Southeastern Arizona: A Study of a Prehistoric Western
        Pueblo Migration into the Middle San Pedro Valley.* ("Amerind Foun-
        dation Paps.," No. 8.) Dragoon.
Eggan, Fred R.
  1950 *Social Organization of the Western Pueblos.* Chicago: University of
        Chicago Press.
Ezell, Paul H.
  1961 *The Hispanic Acculturation of the Gila River Pimas.* (Amer. Anthrop.
        Assoc. Mem. 90.) Menasha, Wis.
Ferdon, Edwin N., Jr.
  1955 *A Trial Survey of Mexican-Southwestern Architectural Parallels.* (Sch.
        Amer. Res. Monog. 21.) Santa Fe.
Gladwin, Harold S., Emil W. Haury, E. B. Sayles, and Nora Gladwin
  1937 *Excavations at Snaketown: Material Culture.* ("Medallion Paps.," No.
        25.) Globe, Ariz.
Haury, Emil W.
  1940 *Excavations in the Forestdale Valley, East-Central Arizona.* (Univ. Ariz.
        Soc. Sci. Bull. 12.) Tucson.
  1945 *The Excavation of Los Muertos and Neighboring Ruins in the Salt River
        Valley, Southern Arizona.* ("Peabody Mus. Amer. Arch. & Ethnol.
        Paps.," Vol. 24, No. 1.) Cambridge, Mass.
Haury, Emil W., and E. B. Sayles
  1947 *An Early Pit House Village of the Mogollon Culture: Forestdale Valley,
        Arizona.* (Univ. Ariz. Soc. Sci. Bull. 16.) Tucson.
Hough, Walter
  1903 "Archaeological Field Work in Northeastern Arizona." *Smithsonian
        Inst. Ann. Rpt. 1901; U.S. Natl. Mus. Rpt.,* pp. 279–358. Washington.
  1914 *Culture of the Ancient Pueblos of the Upper Gila River Region, Arizona
        and New Mexico.* (U.S. Natl. Mus. Bull. 87.) Washington.
Jennings, Jesse D.
  1957 *Danger Cave.* (Soc. Amer. Arch. Mem. 14.) Salt Lake City.

JENNINGS, JESSE D. (ed.)
1956   "The American Southwest: A Problem in Cultural Isolation." In
ROBERT WAUCHOPE (ed.), *Seminars in Archaeology, 1955.* (Soc. Amer.
Arch. Mem. 11.) Salt Lake City.

MARTIN, PAUL S., JOHN B. RINALDO, ELAINE BLUHM, HUGH B. CUTLER, and
ROGER GRANGE
1952   *Mogollon Cultural Continuity and Change: The Stratigraphic Analysis of
Tularosa and Cordova Caves.* ("Fieldiana: Anthropology," Vol. 40.)
Chicago.

MARTIN, PAUL S., JOHN B. RINALDO, WILLIAM A. LONGACRE, CONSTANCE
CRONIN, LESLIE G. FREEMAN, JR., and JAMES SCHOENWETTER
1962   *Chapters in the Prehistory of Eastern Arizona,* I. ("Fieldiana: Anthropology," Vol. 53.) Chicago.

MASSEY, WILLIAM C.
1961   "The Survival of the Dart-Thrower on the Peninsula of Baja California." *Southwestern Jour. Anthrop.,* 17:81–93.

MORRIS, EARL H.
1939   *Archaeological Studies in the La Plata District: Southwestern Colorado
and Northwestern New Mexico.* (Carnegie Inst. Wash. Pub. 519.)
Washington, D.C.

MORRIS, EARL H., and ROBERT F. BURGH
1954   *Basket Maker II Sites near Durango, Colorado.* (Carnegie Inst. Wash.
Pub. 604.) Washington, D.C.

REED, ERIK K.
1944   "Aspects of Acculturation in the Southwest." *Acta Americana,* 2:
62–69.
1949   "The Significance of Skull Deformation in the Southwest." *El Palacio,*
56:106–19.
1962   "Pine Trees, Pollen, and Recent Climatic History of the Southwest."
(Region Three Research Abstract, No. 292. Southwest Regional
Office, National Park Service.) Santa Fe.

ROBERTS, FRANK H. H., JR.
1929   *Shabik'eshchee Village: A Late Basketmaker Site in the Chaco Canyon,
New Mexico.* (Bur. Amer. Ethnol. Bull. 92.) Washington, D.C.

SPICER, E. H.
1954   "Spanish-Indian Acculturation in the Southwest." *Amer. Anthropologist,* 56:663–78.

WHEAT, JOE BEN
1955   *Mogollon Culture Prior to A.D. 1000.* (Amer. Anthrop. Assoc. Mem.
82.) Menasha, Wis.

WORMINGTON, H. MARIE
1962   "A Survey of Early American Prehistory." *Amer. Scientist,* 50:230–
42.

WALDO R. WEDEL

The Great Plains

THE PLAINS REGION, as herein recognized (Fig. 1), lies between the Rocky Mountains on the west and the ninety-fourth degree of west longitude on the east. It extends northward to the Saskatchewan River Basin and southward nearly to the Rio Grande. Stretching thus some 1500 miles through twenty degrees of latitude and eastward from 400 to 700 miles, it encompasses an area of more than 800,000 square miles. Not all this, to be sure, belongs to the Great Plains of the geographer or physiographer or plant specialist, however these or others choose to define the region for their particular purposes, but, in general terms, the region may be said to possess the major characteristics of what Webb (1931) has appropriately termed the "Plains environment." That is to say, the landscape is generally marked by flatness or moderate relief of its surface, by a predominantly grassland rather than a woodland or desert flora, and by a semiarid to subhumid climate of continental nature, with warm, dry summers and cold, dry winters and a highly variable precipitation and temperature regimen.

Within their limits as here set, the Plains include at least two major geographic subdivisions, with significantly different environmental characteristics. On the west are the short-grass plains, or steppes, a 300–400-mile-wide belt fronting on the Rockies and having an annual precipitation average of 10–20 inches. On the east are the tall-grass prairies, with precipitation ranging between 20 and 40 inches annually. In historic times, the short-grass plains were the habitat of Wissler's "typical" Plains tribes, among which were the horse-using, bison-hunting Assiniboin, Blackfeet, Dakota Sioux, Crow, Cheyenne, Arapaho,

WALDO R. WEDEL, who received his doctorate from the University of California, is head curator, Department of Anthropology, United States National Museum. He has devoted over three decades to the systematic study of the archeology of the Great Plains. In recognition of his contributions toward an understanding of the human ecology of this region in prehistoric times, he was the recipient in 1947 of the award for distinguished service in the biological sciences of the Washington Academy of Sciences. He is the author of the recently published book *Prehistoric Man on the Great Plains* and many other writings.

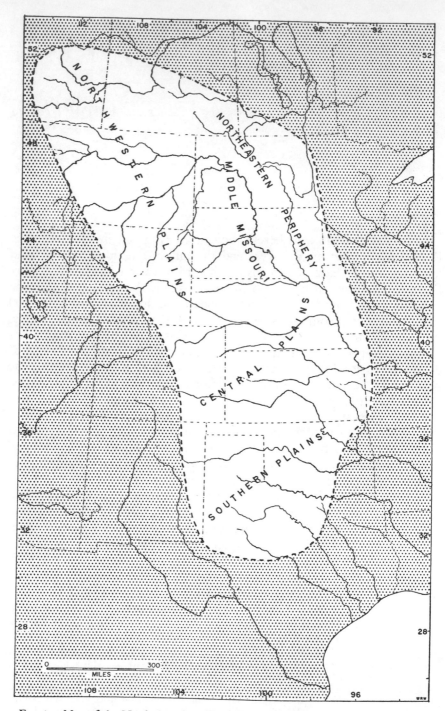

Fig. 1.—Map of the North American Plains area and its subareas. (From Wedel, *Prehistoric Man on the Great Plains*, University of Oklahoma Press.)

Comanche, and Kiowa. Generally east of these were the less "typical" semisedentary Siouan and Caddoan Village tribes, whose villages and cornfields, like those of their ancestors and precursors, stood for some hundreds of years prior to the coming of the white man along the timbered banks of the perennial streams in the Prairie Plains. It should be noted that neither the geographic subdivisions here indicated nor the two divergent lifeways that broadly characterize them can be sharply delimited on a map, since, like most natural and cultural boundaries in the region, these are transitional rather than abrupt.

The environmental characteristics of the Plains region, as they presented opportunities or limitations to aboriginal occupancies, have been outlined in some detail elsewhere (Wedel 1941, 1953, 1961) and need not be further considered here. It is perhaps sufficient to observe that its contrasts to the regions farther east not only caused marked changes in men's ways of living as they moved west but also strongly influenced anthropological thinking until a quarter of a century ago. The direction of that thinking is clear from the following sample quotations spanning a century:

The prairie is not congenial to the Indian, and is only made tolerable to him by the possession of the horse and the rifle [L. H. Morgan in White (ed.) 1959].

. . . the largely negative results of archeology indicates the Plains as only sparsely or intermittently inhabited for a long time [Kroeber 1928].

. . . nowhere [in Canada's Prairie Provinces] have archeologists found evidence of other inhabitants than those of the present day, or traces of even their occupation earlier than a century or two before the arrival of the white man [Jenness 1932].

But even as these later words were being written, the spade of the archeologist was uncovering evidence on the margins of the Plains to indicate that men had lived and hunted in the region some thousands of years ago. And in the last thirty years the record has been vastly expanded, so today the question is, not whether native man adjusted his lifeways to the Plains environment, but how he did.

There are, of course, various ways in which a review of Plains prehistory can be presented. Here I propose to approach the task according to a fourfold scheme based on what seem to be broad-scale and significant changes through time in lifeways or subsistence economies. The categories are (1) the Early Big Game Hunters; (2) the Hunters and Gatherers, or Foragers; (3) the Woodland People, or Incipient Agriculturists; and (4) the Plains Village Indians. The scheme is not without serious difficulties, and it undoubtedly oversimplifies what is becoming an increasingly complex picture, but, in the absence of a better and generally accepted system, it will perhaps serve our purposes adequate-

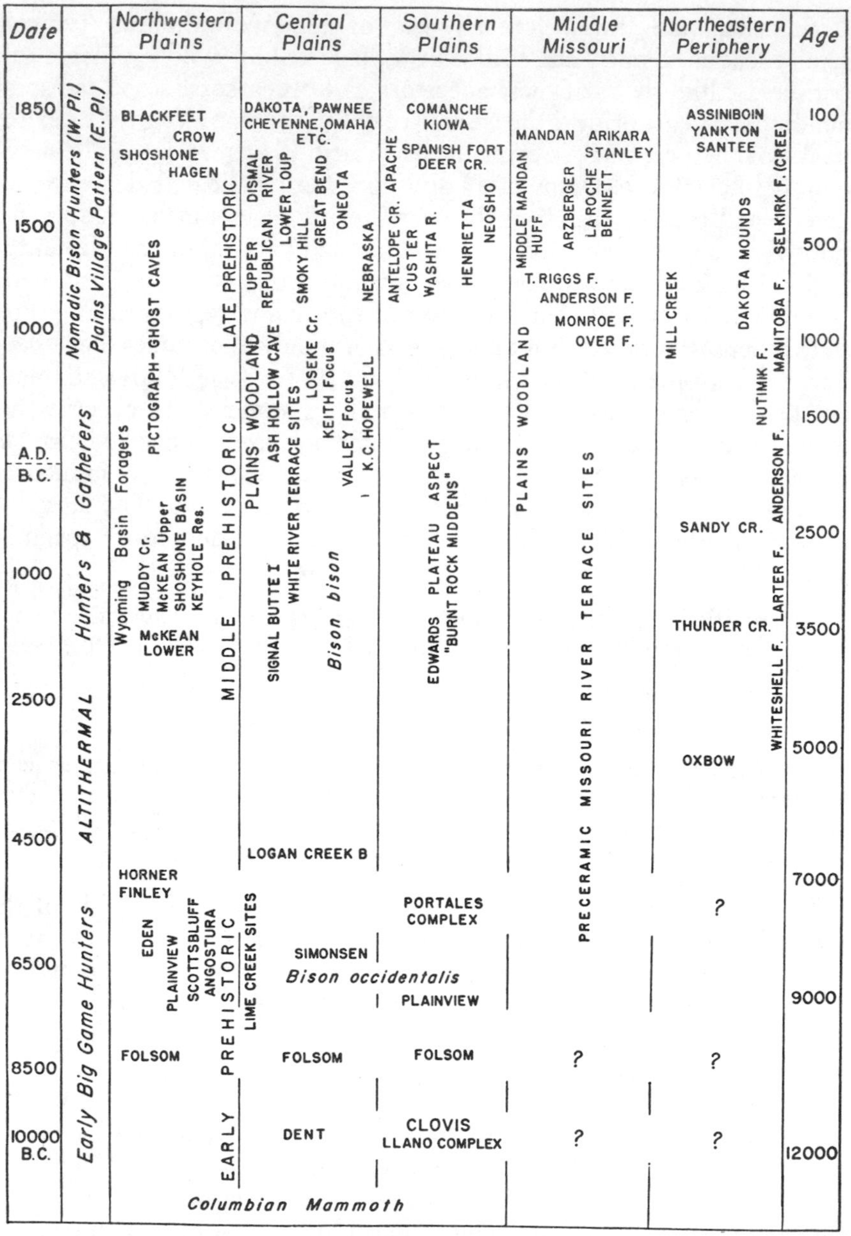
Date
Northwestern Plains
Central Plains
Southern Plains
Middle Missouri
Northeastern Periphery
Age
1850
1500
1000
A.D.
B.C.
1000
2500
4500
6500
8500
10000 B.C.
Nomadic Bison Hunters (W. Pl.)
Plains Village Pattern (E. Pl.)
Hunters & Gatherers
ALTITHERMAL
Early Big Game Hunters
BLACKFEET
CROW
SHOSHONE
HAGEN
PICTOGRAPH-GHOST CAVES
Wyoming Basin Foragers
MUDDY Cr.
McKEAN Upper
SHOSHONE BASIN
KEYHOLE Res.
McKEAN LOWER
HORNER
FINLEY
EDEN
PLAINVIEW
SCOTTSBLUFF
ANGOSTURA
FOLSOM
LATE PREHISTORIC
MIDDLE PREHISTORIC
EARLY PREHISTORIC
DAKOTA, PAWNEE
CHEYENNE, OMAHA
ETC.
UPPER REPUBLICAN
DISMAL RIVER
LOWER LOUP
SMOKY HILL
GREAT BEND
ONEOTA
NEBRASKA
PLAINS WOODLAND
ASH HOLLOW CAVE
WHITE RIVER TERRACE SITES
LOSEKE Cr.
KEITH Focus
VALLEY Focus
K.C. HOPEWELL
SIGNAL BUTTE I
Bison bison
LOGAN CREEK B
LIME CREEK SITES
SIMONSEN
Bison occidentalis
FOLSOM
DENT
Columbian Mammoth
COMANCHE
KIOWA
APACHE
SPANISH FORT
DEER CR.
ANTELOPE CR.
CUSTER
WASHITA R.
HENRIETTA
NEOSHO
EDWARDS PLATEAU ASPECT
"BURNT ROCK MIDDENS"
PORTALES COMPLEX
PLAINVIEW
FOLSOM
CLOVIS
LLANO COMPLEX
MANDAN
ARIKARA
STANLEY
MIDDLE MANDAN
HUFF
ARZBERGER
LA ROCHE
BENNETT
T. RIGGS F.
ANDERSON F.
MONROE F.
OVER F.
PLAINS WOODLAND
PRECERAMIC MISSOURI RIVER TERRACE SITES
?
?
ASSINIBOIN
YANKTON
SANTEE
SELKIRK F. (CREE)
MILL CREEK
DAKOTA MOUNDS
MANITOBA F.
NUTIMIK F.
ANDERSON F.
SANDY CR.
LARTER F.
THUNDER CR.
WHITESHELL F.
OXBOW
?
?
?
100
500
1000
1500
2500
3500
5000
7000
9000
12000

Fig. 2.—Suggested time relationships of certain archeological sites and complexes in the North American Plains area. (From Wedel, *Prehistoric Man on the Great Plains*, University of Oklahoma Press.)

ly. It should not be necessary to add that here, as in other matters, the several lifeways are not sharply separated either in time or in space but often intergrade (Fig. 2).

THE EARLY BIG GAME HUNTERS

So far as we now have acceptable archeological evidence, human history in the Plains begins with the Early Big Game Hunters, usually designated the Paleo-Indians. Such information as we have comes mostly from game kills and butchering grounds, where these people took and processed the large herbivorous game animals on which they seem principally to have subsisted. There are also a few camp sites and occupation areas where stays of some duration or on a recurrent basis have given us more abundant and varied materials and thus a somewhat more complete picture (Roberts 1940; Sellards 1952; Wormington 1957).

The earliest of these hunter folk were those who preyed upon the terminal Pleistocene fauna, notably, of course, the mammoth and its contemporaries. Their remains are manifested at Blackwater Draw, New Mexico; Dent, Colorado; Miami, Texas; and a few other localities. Possibly the recent mammoth finds near Cooperton and Stecker, Oklahoma, and Rawlins, Wyoming, should be included here, but the records are still incomplete. At the first three locations listed, the large distinctively shaped Clovis spear points and sometimes cutting, scraping, and chopping tools of non-diagnostic character have been found in association with partially dismembered skeletons of the Columbian mammoth. None of the mammoth kill sites in the Plains proper has as yet been dated, but, since the radiocarbon date for the U. P. Mammoth kill near Rawlins, Wyoming, at 9330 B.C. correlates satisfactorily with four dates from the Lehner mammoth site in southern Arizona, it seems safe to infer that the mammoth hunters were active in the Plains some eleven to twelve thousand years ago. By how much their occupation of the region may have preceded and followed that span of time, we do not yet know from any reliable "absolute" dates.

In later sites, dating from about 8000 B.C. and after, the mammoth is absent and the prime quarry of the hunters was the bison. Here are included the Folsom (Roberts 1935, 1936) and Plainview (Sellards, Evans, and Meade 1947) complexes, marked, respectively, by characteristically shaped fluted and unfluted points, and perhaps such other complexes or assemblages as are indicated at Lime Creek (Holder and Wike 1949) in southwestern Nebraska, Angostura in South Dakota, and at Hell Gap and Agate Basin (Roberts 1961) in Wyoming. The excavations at Lime Creek and Lindenmeier, particularly, have supplied data for a more extended artifact inventory than we have for the earlier elephant hunters. These comprise a varied assortment of chipped and ground stone tools, including projectile points, end and side scrapers, knives, large blades and choppers, gravers, grooved abraders, and bolas weights or sinkers. The presence of some antler and bone objects, including, particularly, needles, awls, and simple ornaments and/or gaming pieces, is noteworthy.

Perhaps in part contemporaneous with the immediately foregoing and continuing into a later time level are the complexes marked by Eden and Scottsbluff points and the Portales complex of Sellards. Some, at least, of these artifacts may be associated with bison of essentially modern type, though conclusive identification is impossible from the evidence now at hand. Radiocarbon dates from the Horner site, where classic Eden points were directly associated with Scottsbluff points, fall at about 5000 B.C., and one date for the Portales complex would place this at about 4500 B.C. For present purposes, the period of the Early Big Game Hunters is considered to have ended at or soon after *ca*. 5000 B.C.

At none of the Early Big Game Hunter sites yet examined is there evidence of structural remains, of posthole patterns, or of food storage pits, such as are usually associated in the later Plains with fairly stable subsistence economies. Hearths sometimes occur, but usually in small numbers, and they seldom give evidence of prolonged use. There is no indication of the dog. Inferentially, these early hunters were free-ranging, moving wherever the large game animals were available and perhaps not regularly returning to reoccupy earlier camping locations.

That the earliest hunters carried on their way of life in an environmental setting somewhat unlike that of the present is indicated, of course, by the kinds of game on which they subsisted. Though we cannot be certain of the dietary and other habits of the mammoth, it is certain that proboscideans would find survival difficult or impossible in the sort of short-grass and semidesert environment that today characterizes most of the localities in which their known remains occur. A wetter and cooler climate presumably prevailed at that time, with a much more lush natural vegetation.

It is perhaps worth noting that many of the cutting, scraping, and chopping tools of eight to ten thousand years ago differ little from those found on Plains Indian sites of the last five hundred years, and this is true also of such bone tools as awls, needles, etc. These similarities suggest that the skin-working techniques so well developed among the Plains Indians of early white-contact days were probably characteristic of, or at least had their counterparts among, the ancient hunters of the Plains. They do not support the idea that native human residence in the Plains was a recent or posthorse phenomenon.

Although we know most about the ancient hunters in the western

Plains, it is now evident that there were contemporary Big Game Hunters in the eastern Plains as well. The recent discoveries at the Simonsen site in northwestern Iowa, where notched spear points were associated with *Bison occidentalis* in a 6471 B.C. setting (Agogino and Frankforter 1960), strongly suggest that further work will bring to light equally early kill sites west of the Missouri that may equate in time with Eden-Scottsbluff and perhaps with even earlier cultural complexes to the west. It will be interesting to see how these early complexes with eastern affiliations interdigitate with the better-known western ones as investigations intensify in the Nebraska region and to the north and south in the present mixed and short-grass country.

Here we must take note of a recent suggestion by Mayer-Oakes (1959) that certain of the complexes I have considered as Early Big Game Hunters, to wit, the Frontier complex at Lime Creek, Plainview, Scottsbluff, Angostura, and Portales, though Early Hunter in time, may represent a merging of an ancient Plains hunting (Clovis-Folsom fluted point) tradition and the less specialized Eastern Archaic, out of which developed a Plains Archaic stage. This view has been received in some quarters with rather less than whole-hearted enthusiasm, and even the term "Plains Archaic" seems now to be acquiring increasingly controversial connotations. The increasing time depth now demonstrable for Eastern Archaic materials from Missouri and Illinois eastward, and their evident contemporaneity at least in part with the western Plains Paleo-Indian materials, makes a long-continued contact between the two lifeways in the eastern Plains and Prairie region seem highly likely. Such contacts would probably have affected the degree to which big game animals were utilized as the major subsistence item in the western tradition, and I should think might well have deflected some of the erstwhile Plains hunting groups toward a more diversified subsistence base not unlike that of the early Archaic hunting-gathering-fishing groups farther east. In any case, there is an interesting set of problems involved here, and it is imperative that we have more sustained and systematic investigations whenever and wherever the opportunity arises.

[EDITORS' NOTE: Compare the foregoing passages with Krieger's treatment, pp. 51–57.]

THE HUNTERS AND GATHERERS

The period between *ca.* 5000 and 2000 B.C. is, for most of the Plains region, one about which almost nothing is known so far as direct archeological evidence is concerned. The Early Big Game Hunters were no longer present; pottery-making and the semisedentary lifeways that accompanied or followed its introduction were not yet here. In the western Plains, where dated sites are virtually absent, this time span

appears to correspond rather well with the estimated time of the Altithermal, and it is tempting to suggest that the heightened temperatures
and reduced precipitation of this period had forced abandonment by
man of what is now the short-grass plains and compelled its erstwhile
bison hunters to betake themselves elsewhere, perhaps into the mountain
valleys to the west or, alternatively, toward the better-watered grasslands to the east and north in their search for large game. That some
such exodus took place is entirely possible, but, until we have additional
proof that the High Plains really lack hunting-culture sites of this period,
I have some reservations about Jennings' otherwise plausible suggestion
that the Desert Culture "was the dominant one throughout the Plains
at the height of the Altithermal (probably 5000 B.C.) until perhaps 2000
or 3000 B.C." (Jennings 1957).

That influences from the eastern Archaic notched-point traditions
were operating in the eastern Plains during this time period is indicated
by the recent finds at Logan Creek, Nebraska, where two occupational
levels, with an abundance of bison bone and with side-notched points,
have been radiocarbon dated at 4674 B.C. and 5300 B.C. The points are
typologically quite close to those from the Simonsen site dated at 1000
years before. Closely similar point forms have since been recognized in
surface collections from widely scattered localities throughout the Nebraska Sandhills and may also be present in a still undated buried occupation zone at Redwillow Reservoir in southwestern Nebraska. Other
artifacts with strong eastern affinities on an apparently early level come
from northeastern Kansas and elsewhere on the eastern margin of the
Plains area as herein defined. Their relationships seem to be with
Archaic manifestations in Missouri, eastern Oklahoma, and elsewhere
in the deciduous forest areas of the eastern United States. It thus appears probable that man was in the region frequently, if not continuously, during the period in question. But, until such materials are found
in situ and can be collected under acceptable scientific controls, their
significance lies primarily in what they suggest rather than in anything
that we can build on.

In the western Plains, this brings us to a series of complexes assigned
by Mulloy (1952, 1954a, 1954b, 1958) to the Middle Prehistoric period.
Archeologically, this is represented by a number of sites widely scattered throughout Wyoming and Montana, apparently extending eastward as far as the Black Hills of South Dakota and with a still undetermined eastern limit elsewhere in the region. Reported sites include
Pictograph and Birdshead caves (Bliss 1950), the McKean and Shoshoni
Basin camp sites, and Signal Butte I (Strong 1935).

The projectile points are usually much cruder than those of the Early
Big Game Hunters and include the McKean-Duncan-Hanna series, as

well as other less well-known forms. In addition to other cutting and scraping tools, the sites commonly have milling stones, from which it is inferred that seeds, roots, and other vegetal foods were more extensively relied upon than was large game. The bone refuse includes a higher proportion of small game, including rodents, reptiles, etc., perhaps because bison and other large mammals were scarcer than previously. This "forager" lifeway, inferentially much like that which characterized the Great Basin for thousands of years, was thus typified by a much more thorough exploitation of the environment, in which all edible resources, not alone the big game, were utilized.

It is likely that this lifeway, along with some of the artifact types by which it is recognized archeologically, spread eastward into the short-grass lands of Wyoming from the Great Basin. That it did not wholly overspread the northern Plains is suggested by the fact that at Signal Butte, in some of the Montana sites, and apparently in southern Canada, milling stones are less characteristic of this time horizon, whereas projectile points, skin-working tools, and bison bones sometimes occur in such relative abundance as to justify the conclusion that a strongly developed bison-hunting Plains economy rather than one oriented primarily toward foraging, as in the Great Basin, was practiced. The Powers-Yonkee bison trap (Bentzen 1962) in Powder River County, Montana, dated at 2500 B.C., and Signal Butte I at 2600 B.C., are illustrative. So also is the roughly contemporaneous Oxbow culture at Long Creek in southern Saskatchewan (Wettlaufer, Mayer-Oakes, *et al.* 1960), where a bison-hunting complex with side-notched projectile points is dated at *ca.* 2600–2800 B.C. In the Colorado Rockies west of Denver, Complex D at the LoDaisKa site, dated at 2880 B.C., is regarded by the investigators as a manifestation of the Desert Culture (Irwin and Irwin 1959, 1961). The "burnt-rock middens" of the Edwards Plateau aspect in central Texas, estimated to range from 4000 or 5000 B.C. to A.D. 500 or 1000, apparently represent a southern Plains specialization of this hunting-gathering, or foraging, lifeway (Suhm, Krieger, and Jelks 1954).

THE WOODLAND PEOPLES

At some time still undetermined, but possibly preceding the opening of the Christian Era, pottery-making reached the Plains. The earliest wares of which we now have evidence are clearly related to some of the widely spread Woodland pottery of the Mississippi and Ohio valleys, and the local complexes to which they belong are thus subsumed under the general designation of Plains Woodland cultures. Woodland wares are most plentiful in the eastern Plains from the Dakotas southward to Oklahoma, and their distribution evidently extends westward to the Front Range of the Rockies. Their stratigraphic position, where directly determinable, is below all other currently known pottery horizons.

The Plains Woodland peoples are best known from investigations in the Central Plains of Nebraska and northern Kansas. A fairly long occupation or series of occupations is inferred, even if we discount as improbable the validity of a radiocarbon date of 1872 B.C. for a Valley focus Woodland site; and the variations in pottery styles, in projectile-point forms, and in other particulars are sufficiently consistent to permit recognition of several variants. These include a group of relatively advanced Hopewellian village and burial-mound sites in the Kansas City–Kansas River–eastern Oklahoma region (Wedel 1943, 1959; Bell and Baerreis 1951), plus a number of simpler culture complexes (Strong 1935; Hill and Kivett 1941; Champe 1946; Spaulding 1949; Hurt 1952; Kivett 1952, 1953; Wedel 1959) represented by many small, inconspicuous sites widely scattered throughout the region between the Missouri and the Rockies. At the moment, it seems reasonable to bracket the Woodland occupation of the Plains between *ca.* 500 B.C. and A.D. 1000.

The Hopewellian sites consist of fairly heavy, if areally limited, accumulations of village debris, numerous storage pits, and a relatively varied assortment of artifacts in pottery, stone, bone, and other materials. Pottery wares include plain, rocker-marked, and zone-decorated types, as well as a limited amount of cord-roughened ware, and there are clear-cut affinities in many respects with eastern Hopewellian manifestations. Imitation bear teeth of bone, conical or mammiform objects of clay and stone, native copper objects, and obsidian are other traits shared with the east, the last two indicating trade relations with distant groups. Grooved axes, large corner-notched projectile points, stemmed plano-convex scrapers, conical flint disks, and beaming tools made of deer pelvis bones and metapodials are other locally distinguishing traits. Burial was apparently in small mounds often erected over rectangular dry-masonry-walled inclosures, sometimes provided with vestibule entryways. The limited skeletal materials indicate a longheaded population. A fairly stable community life is indicated, and this was apparently based in part on hunting and gathering, with bison much less important than deer, and in part on the cultivation of maize and beans, which here make their earliest dated appearance in the general Plains region. Radiocarbon dates vary rather widely, but the Hopewellian occupation is probably safely assignable to the period *ca.* A.D. 200–400.

Other described Woodland complexes include the Sterns Creek focus in the Missouri Valley from above Omaha to northwestern Missouri; the Valley focus in central Nebraska; the widespread Keith focus in

Nebraska, northern Kansas, and eastern Colorado; and the Loseke Creek focus in eastern Nebraska. Thick, cord-roughened pottery characterizes the Keith and Valley focuses, with calcite tempering an important distinguishing feature of the former. Loseke Creek pottery frequently carries rim designs in single-cord patterns. The artifact inventory is less extensive than that for Hopewellian sites. Secondary ossuary pits unmarked by mounds are attributed to Keith focus; in eastern Kansas and Nebraska, mound burials are thought to be of Woodland origin. Most sites appear to be those of people following mainly a creek-valley hunting and gathering subsistence economy, with deer and small game seemingly favored over bison. The depth of refuse at some sites suggests some permanence of occupancy or else frequent return to favored locations. Corn has been found at Loseke Creek sites but radiocarbon dates are not available, though this complex seems to be somewhat later than Keith or Valley focus. [EDITORS' NOTE: See Introduction, p. 7, for a brief discussion of the term "focus."]

The Woodland period in the Plains is still very inadequately known, and a number of its local manifestations, including among others the Buick focus in eastern Colorado and caves with perishable material said to relate to this period in the same region, await full description and comparison with the better-known Central Plains variants. Still unclear are the interrelationships between Plains Woodland complexes and contemporaneous Southwestern cultures. The northern limits to which Plains Woodland culture spread are undetermined, but in southern Saskatchewan, Kehoe and McCorquodale (1961) have proposed that the Avonlea point, which occurs widely at bison kills and associated occupation sites and has been dated at *ca.* A.D. 460, appears to be a horizon-marker for a preceramic bison-hunting tradition, which thus must have been in part coeval with the Plains Woodland ceramic complexes farther south.

That the Plains Woodland period is an important one is indicated by the fact that it witnessed the first appearance of pottery in the region, and, more importantly, it apparently marks the time when the cultivation of crops was first attempted in what had previously been exclusively a region of hunting and gathering complexes. This change-over from a food-collecting to a food-producing way of life laid the basis for a far more efficient subsistence economy and a much surer hold on the land than was possible for any of the pre-Woodland groups about which we now know.

The burial mounds of the Northeastern Periphery and their extension westward to approximately the Missouri River in North and South Dakota are another interesting facet of the Woodland problem (MacNeish 1958; Neuman 1960; Wedel 1961). They occur most plentifully in the eastern portions of the Dakotas, east of the Coteau du Missouri, and, more scatteringly, northward into Manitoba and Saskatchewan. Most are relatively low and inconspicuous, but examples 80 or 90 feet in diameter and up to 10 or 12 feet high are known. In some localities, as at the Souris-Antler Creek junction and in the Devils Lake district, mounds may be joined by linear embankments or the embankments radiate outward in several directions from a central mound.

In and under these structures are burial pits, many of them apparently once covered with poles or split logs. Burials were both primary and secondary, and in many cases multiple burial was practiced. Bison skulls and/or skeletons have been reported from many of these burial mounds since early days, and recent investigations by the River Basin Surveys along the Missouri River have confirmed these associations. Cultural materials include spirally incised and other pottery, as well as articles of stone, bone, shell, native copper, and other materials. Small mortuary pots with spiral grooves running upward around the body are common from some sections, and these are unlike any pieces yet reported from village or camp-site explorations. There are also projectile points, spearheads, and knives of chipped stone; tubular catlinite and steatite pipes shaped like cigar-holders; incised catlinite tablets, and other objects of ground stone; thinly scraped armlets, unilaterally barbed spear points, whistles, and other objects of bone and antler; and occasional marine shell gorgets carved to represent the human face. Sewed birchbark containers suggest some recency, but iron, glass beads, and other items showing contact with Europeans are generally absent, except occasionally as associations with intrusive interments.

No comprehensive analysis of the mound complex or complexes of the Northeastern Periphery has yet been attempted, and their age, as well as the identity of their makers, remain unanswered questions. It has long been suspected that they were somehow, or in part, connected with the westward dispersal of Siouan-speaking peoples, and some support for this view may lie in the obvious resemblances between some of the mound materials and those of the Blackduck focus in Minnesota. MacNeish has assigned some of the southern Manitoba mounds to the Manitoba focus, which he suggests may represent the spread into the Plains of the Assiniboin, perhaps even before A.D. 1400. Other mounds in the Souris-Antler district have been designated the Melita focus; but neither this nor Griffin's (1946) Devils Lake focus have yet been adequately defined or characterized as to content.

As to their age, such items as catlinite, birchbark, and shell mask gorgets suggest a fairly late time level, and there is some reason to suspect that at least some of the mounds may have been approximately contemporaneous with the long-rectangular-house cultures of the Middle

Missouri. On the other hand, radiocarbon dates from a number of mounds recently investigated along the Missouri River by the River Basin Surveys show a surprisingly long time range, running from about 250 B.C. to A.D. 1000 or a bit later. I am not yet convinced of the validity of the earlier dates, but, in the absence of a detailed report on the content and nature of the dated materials, further speculation here seems pointless. It does not seem pointless, however, to suggest that mound-building in this region may have covered a longer span than most of us have suspected and that, in any case, there is here an interesting and important set of problems from which we must hope no competent student will be deterred by the fact that much of the extant information is of dubious quality and reliability because the early-day digging and reporting was sadly inadequate by present-day standards.

THE PLAINS VILLAGE INDIANS

In the ninth or tenth century of the Christian Era, if not before, the Woodland complexes in the eastern Plains were followed by others of markedly different cast, which are evidently assignable to peoples having a much more settled way of life. Their communities were concentrated principally along the rivers and creeks in the tall- and mid-grass country, but there is ample archeological evidence that some of them also ventured far to the west and for a time practiced corn-growing in the creek valleys along the margin of the High Plains. A dual subsistence economy was clearly followed, the people exploiting alike the agricultural potential of the fertile valley bottoms and the abundant game resources of the wooded bottomlands and the adjacent grassy uplands. These were the people who have been termed the Plains Village Indians (Lehmer 1954*a*, *b*) and who, until the nineteenth century, were to dominate the eastern Plains.

Common to the lifeway of practically all the Plains Village Indians were certain practices that also serve to distinguish their remains from those of the simpler hunters and gatherers, and the incipient maize-growers, who preceded them. These included the use of permanent multifamily habitations, often larger and much more substantially constructed than anything of which we have record from the Woodland period; residence for most of the year in fixed villages, which were sometimes protected by ditches and stockades, and with which there were usually associated large numbers of underground storage pits; abundant pottery of varied and distinctive character; and a greatly increased range of artifacts in stone, bone, horn, shell, and other materials. The bone hoe, varying in certain particulars but generally fashioned from the scapula of the bison, was one of the most characteristic items, persisting long after the introduction of iron hoes by the white man. Small triangular arrow points, with or without side notches, also distinguish these from most earlier Woodland complexes.

The Village Indian period may be conveniently divided into two stages, each characterized by the appearance of regional and local cultural variants. The earlier, which consistently lacks any evidence of white contacts and seems to be everywhere marked by square or rectangular house forms and grit-tempered pottery, predates, in general, A.D. 1550. On the Missouri River above the Niobrara, the remains of this period are represented by the Monroe, Anderson, Over, and Thomas Riggs focuses (Lehmer 1952, 1954*a*, *b*; Hurt 1951, 1953*b*). Collectively grouped in the Middle Missouri tradition, these carry radiocarbon dates ranging from A.D. 710 for the Breeden site (Monroe focus) to *ca*. A.D. 1300 for late Thomas Riggs focus sites; dendrochronology, on the other hand, places several Thomas Riggs components as late as the early 1500's. All foci are characterized by long-rectangular houses with deeply excavated floors, entrance ramps, and main fireplaces usually offset toward the entrance. Pottery includes plain-surfaced and cord-roughened wares, the latter being replaced above the Cheyenne River by simple-stamped surface treatment. Some of the villages show evidence of careful planning, with houses tending to be arranged in rows, and defensive works in the form of dry ditches and stockades, sometimes with regularly spaced bastions, are found at some sites.

In the Central Plains, manifestations of this period include the Upper Republican and Nebraska aspects (Strong 1935; Champe 1936; Hill and Cooper 1938; Cooper 1936, 1940; Wedel 1935, 1959, 1961), dated at *ca*. A.D. 1100–1450, with the still inadequately known Smoky Hill complex probably representing a third variant. These constitute the Central Plains tradition or phase. Here the communities were usually loosely arranged, unfortified, and small. Houses were basically square with rounded corners, had four primary roof supports set in a square around a central firepit, and were earth covered. The associated pottery was plain surfaced and cord roughened. Noteworthy is the appearance at this time level on the Missouri River above Kansas City of a Middle Mississippi complex, whence probably came the animal figures on pottery, effigy pipes, pottery "anvils," and shell tempering found occasionally in Nebraska aspect sites farther upriver (Wedel 1943).

In the Southern Plains, the Washita River and Custer focuses of Oklahoma, the former with at least two radiocarbon dates at A.D. 1000 and 1150, can be assigned to this time horizon, and their house types, pottery, and other material culture traits seem consistent with the cultural inventories we have from the Central Plains and Middle Missouri traditions (Bell and Baerreis 1951). The Antelope Creek and Optima focuses of the Panhandle aspect, although somewhat aberrant in such matters as architecture, also seem to find congenial company on this level (Krieger 1946; Bell and Baerreis 1951).

Broadly viewed, all these manifestations, from the Dakotas to northern Texas, suggest the former presence of many small, widely scattered communities whose inhabitants were exploiting much more fully than had any of their predecessors the resources of their environment. Subsistence was based on a creek-bottom, maize-bean-squash, hoe agriculture, with hunting important; fishing, with curved bone hooks and, along the Missouri, with toggle-head harpoons, was widely practiced; and undoubtedly there was much reliance also upon the wild fruits, roots, and berries available in all parts of the Plains. In the Central Plains, the Upper Republican peoples carried their semihorticultural way of life westward to or beyond the Colorado line—far beyond the limits of aboriginal corn-growing in historic times and about as far as climate and soils permitted bottomland gardening, or streams and springs could be depended on for year-round water, or timber for building purposes was obtainable. In the north, where long-rectangular-house villages are known as far as the Little Missouri River, agricultural practices seem likewise to have spread nearly or quite to the limits of reliability from the standpoint of climate.

There is little extant published information on the physical anthropology of these groups and of their relationships to one another, to contemporary peoples in the adjacent areas, or to later tribes in the region. Of their sociopolitical and ceremonial life we can say very little. In general, there seems to be little or no indication of social classes, of groups specializing extensively in particular arts and crafts, or of well-developed ceremonialism, and such specialized structures as temples and burial mounds are lacking. On the other hand, the scattered clustering of house sites in Upper Republican communities, for example, contrasts very strongly with such tight, well-laid-out Middle Missouri towns as the Huff site, and we may infer that in the latter, at least, there were strong social controls and a well-regulated society in which large-scale community efforts could be channeled toward a common end.

In late prehistoric times, shortly before the coming of the white man, notable changes in community settlement patterns took place among the Village Indians, and, at least in some areas, there were major readjustments in the distribution of the native populations. Thus, in the Central Plains the little hamlets of earth lodges, widely scattered from two to four hundred miles westward from the Missouri, were apparently abandoned, perhaps because of drought or of enemy attacks or for other reasons that we do not yet understand. And when the first Europeans arrived, the native peoples were concentrated in fewer but much larger towns farther to the east, mostly within a hundred miles or so of the main stem. Whereas the earlier villages had been strung along the lesser streams, where wood for fuel and building, arable land, water, game, and shelter were close at hand, the later settlements were usually on or near the larger waterways. Thus, the Lower Loup focus communities of the protohistoric Pawnee (Dunlevy 1936; Wedel 1938) were scattered principally around the confluence of the Loup and Platte rivers; in central and southern Kansas, the Great Bend aspect settlements of the Wichita stood on the Walnut and other major tributaries of the Arkansas River (Wedel 1942, 1959). In the Middle Missouri district, such large rambling communities developed as La Roche (Meleen 1948), the Bennett focus villages near the mouth of the Cheyenne River, the Shannon focus settlements below the Big Bend of the Missouri (Smith and Grange 1958), and others. Somewhat later, as indicated by white-contact materials, were the compact stockaded villages of the Stanley focus around Pierre (Lehmer 1954a), the Heart River focus in North Dakota (Will and Hecker 1944), and various other complexes in the Middle Missouri region. Some of these communities must have numbered their inhabitants in the many hundreds, even if we assume that not all portions of the sites were inhabited simultaneously. I am under the impression that most of these communities do not show defensive works.

There were notable changes in the material-culture inventory, as well. Thus, the earth-lodge–dwelling peoples of the Middle Missouri and Central Plains everywhere used circular structures, which, like the earlier square houses of the Central Plains, had a four-post primary foundation around a central hearth. From central Kansas southward, the earth lodge of prehistoric times gave way to a grass lodge or other structure, which left few or no archeological traces. The older cord-roughened pottery was giving way to simple stamped wares, often with incised or trailed shoulder decoration, or, in the Mandan area, to single-cord-impressed motifs. Stone artifacts were varied, plentiful, and well made, including small triangular arrow points, end scrapers, and various kinds of knives and other tools, and bone artifacts were present in much greater variety and numbers than formerly. Certain of these may be considered horizon-markers, for example, the rib-edge awl; transversely scored ribs or so-called musical rasps; wedge-shaped, cancellous-bone paint applicators; and stemmed projectile points, none of which have been reported from square or long-rectangular-house complexes north of the Arkansas River.

The archeological record suggests that many of the artifact types of the early round-house period were already in use among the earlier

Village Indians. But, until we have better chronological controls and access to substantial bodies of unpublished data, it is extremely hazardous to suggest the time and probable place of their origin or even to try to guess whether they are of northern or southern Plains derivation. At the moment, it still seems probable that the later Village Indian cultures from the sixteenth century on represent, at least in part, as Lehmer (1954*a*) has suggested, a fusion of earlier Central Plains and Middle Missouri traditions, whence we have the concept of a Coalescent tradition. The Arzberger site near Pierre, South Dakota (Spaulding 1956), may be one of the transitional manifestations of this fusion, but this interpretation has been strongly questioned by some observers; farther up the Missouri, the Huff site appears to be another.

Relations between the central and southern Plains at this level are less well known and will probably remain obscure until we acquire further data regarding the backgrounds of the Great Bend aspect and the grass-house–using peoples of southern origin who apparently spread over this region in late prehistoric times. Additional information from the Henrietta focus, and also from the Chilocco Historic sites in Oklahoma, would be helpful (Krieger 1946; Bell and Baerreis 1951). Glaze-paint pottery, turquoise, olivella beads, and perhaps other items found sporadically as far north as central Kansas and possibly southern Nebraska indicate trade or other contacts with the Southwest at least as far back as the fourteenth or the fifteenth century. Moreover, in a number of particulars, the late prehistoric and protohistoric cultures as far north as the Great Bend of the Arkansas River seem to have their closest affinities with the south, in contrast to the northerly linkages of the Lower Loup focus and contemporary manifestations in Nebraska. The nature and significance of this dichotomy, and its possible connection with climatic and other phenomena, require further study.

It seems likely that the climax of Plains Village Indian culture was achieved during the period between A.D. 1500 and 1750, with the peak probably occurring somewhat later in the north than in the south. Agriculture was practiced intensively as well as extensively, and, to judge from the size and profusion of storage pits in the villages, crops must have been large and the surplus for barter and storage considerable. Very likely it was this accelerated and improved food production, perhaps with heavier crop yields from improved varieties of plants, that made life possible in large communities, and this community life, in turn, stimulated a notable florescence of culture that probably involved non-material as well as material matters. Archeology suggests that these large communities were in existence even before introduction of the horse increased the mobility of their inhabitants and vastly expanded the available food sources.

Many of the late post–A.D. 1750 archeological complexes can be acceptably linked with named historic tribes, and it is now possible to speculate with some assurance on the earlier antecedents of several of the principal tribes. Thus, the Mandan are thought to be rooted through the Heart River and Huff focuses in the prehistoric Thomas Riggs focus; the Arikara probably derive in substantial part from the Bennett and La Roche focuses through the Stanley focus; the Pawnee, through Lower Loup, may have some connection with Upper Republican; and the Wichita are almost certainly represented, in part at least, by the Great Bend aspect. But in these matters we must guard against the danger of oversimplification and the tendency to set up simple linear courses of development that can scarcely reflect the true story. Who, actually, were the Arikara of 1650, for example, and how closely did they resemble, linguistically and somatologically, the Arikara of Lewis and Clark's day? Are their earlier manifestations to be included in one or several of the archeological complexes between the Niobrara and Grand rivers? Without much doubt, all these tribes, as we know them from history, were the end product of several or many converging lines of development that stemmed from more than one basic archeological complex.

Despite the fact that the Village Indian period has been more extensively and intensively worked than any other in the Plains region, perplexing problems still abound. Apart from the still imperfectly understood variations through time and space, the changing settlement patterns and, where they occur, the associated defensive systems, await analysis and interpretation. There are some curious trait distributions whose meaning eludes us. Thus, for example, the smooth-bladed metapodial digging-stick tip (or hide scraper?) and the bison frontal scoop with horn-core handle occur in the Middle Missouri region and southeastern South Dakota and again in the Oklahoma region, but appear to be absent, or at least extremely uncommon, in the Central Plains of Nebraska and Kansas. The unilaterally barbed bone spear or "harpoon" head has been reported in the eastern Dakota mounds and also at Pictograph Cave, Montana. Are the discontinuities here attributable to inadequate sampling, or do they reflect populational movements or diffusion? Is it possible that some of the typical skin-working bone tools that seem to appear earliest in the Middle Missouri tradition actually originated among, or were brought into the Plains region by, low-culture hunting tribes to the west, where their earlier history is beyond hope of recovery because of unfavorable conditions of preservation? These are but a few samples of the many questions to which the answers are not yet at hand.

During the closing decades of the eighteenth century and the first quarter of the nineteenth, the story of the Village Indians was essentially one of steady decline. Decimated by repeated smallpox and other epidemics brought on by white contact and under steadily increasing pressure from the mounted bison-hunters to the west and north, the Mandan, Arikara, and their neighbors on the Middle Missouri held closely to their compact, stockaded earth-lodge villages. The archeologist is able to confirm the deteriorating culture of the villagers in the shoddy pottery wares and the generally inferior work in bone, stone, and other native materials manifested at such sites as Leavenworth and Like-a-Fishhook. Farther south, the Pawnee and Wichita had also fallen on hard times, and, as did their northern contemporaries, they were supplementing the products of their own decadent crafts and industries with a growing variety of trade materials in iron, glass, and other materials obtained from the white man.

The decadent Village Indian cultures have received less attention than they deserve, for this involves the intriguing larger problem of trade relations during several centuries between the Plains natives and the Euro-Americans. A thoroughgoing study of this Indian trade, using all available documents and archeological materials critically, and integrating them in a chronological framework, would probably give us new insights into the cultural changes for which we already have abundant archeological indications.

More or less contemporary with the later Village Indians, if we restrict this appellation to the earth-lodge and grass-house peoples on and west of the Missouri, were the Oneota communities strung along the eastern edge of the Plains (Hill and Wedel 1936; Wedel 1959). None of these, so far as present evidence goes, is more than sixty miles west of the Missouri River, and all are in the Prairie rather than in the Plains proper. These are usually regarded as having a Siouan linguistic affiliation and are, of course, much more abundantly represented by many sites east of the Missouri. Their shell-tempered and trailed or incised pottery is readily distinguishable from practically all other Plains wares, though it seems to have influenced the technologies of certain groups still farther west. At such sites as Leary, Fanning, and Stanton, the artifact inventory other than pottery and the presumed house type show a great many similarities to those of the Village Indians. A subsistence economy based partly on hoe agriculture and partly on bison- and deer-hunting and on fishing seems to be indicated. Bison shoulder-blade hoes, snubnose or end scrapers, deep cache pits with constricted necks, and perhaps other traits suggest adaptations by an eastern or Prairie to a western or Plains culture.

None of the Oneota sites in the Plains has yet been convincingly assigned to a named tribal group, though it has been suggested that

Fanning may be of Kansa origin and Leary of Oto origin. Farther east, the evidence is good that the Iowa and Oto were carriers of Oneota culture (Mott 1938; M. M. Wedel 1959), as were the Missouri (Chapman 1952). The Osage, on the contrary, seem to have developed out of late prehistoric cultures widely distributed around the flanks of the Ozarks, who came in contact in early historic times with Oneota groups to the north (Chapman n.d.); so they look like a marginal Prairie people who acquired Plains hunting practices and other traits in relatively late times. I consider it likely that the Kansa, who used the bark- or mat-covered dwelling along with the earth lodge, similarly became plainsmen in late times and probably had little to do with prehistoric culture growth in the eastern Plains.

Concerning the native occupations of the steppe belt fronting the Rockies from Alberta to Texas, we are still ill informed for the period following the Woodland peoples. From historical and traditional data, it has long been thought likely that Shoshoneans once held the plains of Alberta and Montana, from which region they were forced by the Blackfeet and perhaps other tribes; this view still has strong adherents despite the adverse opinions of Kroeber, Lowie, and Steward, among others. Archeological evidence suggests that the Forager way of life that apparently had dominated much of the Wyoming region for perhaps two or three millenniums witnessed a return to bison-hunting subsistence economies in what Mulloy has designated the Late Prehistoric period, that is, after *ca.* A.D. 500.

As manifested in Pictograph Cave III and Ghost Cave, with additional but less abundant data from Birdshead Cave, Ash Hollow B–E (Champe 1946), and a few other localities, Wyoming groups of this time level shared a number of the material-culture traits possessed by the Village Indians. The serrate metapodial flesher; bird-bone whistle; thinly scraped antler or bone bow guard; narrow bone bracelets, pierced at one end and notched at the other for lashing into a curved shape; edge-slotted bone knife handles with chipped blade; and, in general, the forms of arrow points, end scrapers, drills, knives, and grooved shaft-smoothers, all have their essentially identical counterparts in the Village Indian cultures of the eastern Plains. Flat-bottomed pottery of the Intermontane tradition and steatite vessels apparently occur here, though it seems probable that earlier penetrations, for example, by Woodland and later by Village Indian pottery-makers, took place in eastern portions of Montana and Wyoming. Unfortunately, there are no radiocarbon dates for these cave deposits, so their exact correlation with eastern sites is at present impossible. Such dates would be of much interest, too, for their possible light on the significance of the unilaterally barbed bone spearheads, dentalium shells, and coiled-basket fragments found among the perishable materials in the cave deposits.

Farther south, the first white men who ventured into the High Plains in the mid-sixteenth century found them inhabited by apparently full-fledged pedestrian bison-hunters, whom they called the Querechos and who were very likely Plains Apache. How long these had been in the region is not yet clear, though Gunnerson (1956) has suggested their arrival in the southern Plains not long before Coronado's *entrada*. Archeological evidence of their passage through the Plains north of the Arkansas is still wanting; possibly they moved southward through the mountain valleys farther west, where, as has been pointed out long ago (Huscher and Huscher 1943), the environmental surroundings would have paralleled more closely those of the Canadian lands from which these Athabascan-speaking groups presumably came. On the other hand, pedestrian hunters unencumbered with pottery and corn-growing practices and possessed of a material culture no more elaborate than that described for the Querechos in 1541, would have left almost no traces of their passage if they did move southward through the High Plains to reach New Mexico by, or soon after, A.D. 1500.

Regarding Plains Apache culture of the sixteenth century, archeology has been able to contribute virtually nothing. However, from the Spanish documents (Thomas 1935; Schroeder 1959) we know that Apache peoples were practicing maize agriculture in northeastern New Mexico and southeastern Colorado during the seventeenth and eighteenth centuries, and archeological evidence of such an occupation in western Kansas, Nebraska, and elsewhere in the High Plains is well known to us as the Dismal River culture (Strong 1935; Champe 1949; Gunnerson 1960; Wedel 1959). Many of the stone and bone artifacts of this complex were shared with contemporary Village Indian groups; their pottery, the presumed house type, and baking pits—otherwise unreported from Plains sites—were regionally distinctive; and such items as bone flageolets, turquoise, olivella shell beads, incised pottery pipes, and obsidian were undoubtedly directly obtained from the Puebloan groups on the upper Rio Grande. The Dismal River materials have been acceptably dated by dendrochronology at *ca.* A.D. 1700; disappearance of the complex by the second quarter of the eighteenth century seems to coincide rather closely with the documented appearance of the Comanche, who, soon after 1700, are thought to have moved out of the mountains of Colorado and New Mexico onto the Plains and, quickly adopting the horse, swept away the unfortified settlements of the semi-agricultural Apache. More work needs to be done on the western Dismal River sites especially, since most of our present information comes from less than half a dozen sites in western Nebraska and Kansas. The relationships of the complex to Promontory materials in Utah and to contemporary Taos-Picuris materials on the Rio Grande also need further attention, particularly from students thoroughly familiar with late Pueblo cultures of the upper Rio Grande district.

Our brief and incomplete review of Plains prehistory will end here. There is much we have not touched on, for various reasons, but the broad outlines of the story have been indicated. We do not know when man first ventured into the region, but it is abundantly clear that peopling of the Plains was under way at least by 11,000 years ago and probably as early as twelve to fifteen thousand years ago, when the Early Big Game Hunters pursued the Columbian mammoth and, later, large bison in the western grasslands. Since there is dated evidence of bison-hunting peoples along the eastern edge of the Plains more than eight thousand years ago, I see no reason for assuming that any significant portion of the region was uninhabited, even if a sparse and widely scattered population is inferred.

By 5000 B.C., the Early Big Game Hunters and the animal species on which they mainly subsisted had disappeared from the western Plains, and other economies had replaced them. In the Wyoming region, possibly reflecting the climatic vicissitudes of the Altithermal, the population appears to have been one of foragers not unlike those of the Great Basin, and a similar dependence on hunting and on food-grinding seems to have been the case in the western part of the southern Plains. Along the eastern margin there were apparently hunters and gatherers related to eastern Archaic groups from the middle Mississippi-Missouri Valley region.

Hunting, or hunting and gathering, subsistence economies in which cultural development and population remained at relatively low levels until introduction of the horse two centuries or more ago, seem always to have been characteristic of the western Plains. In the eastern Plains, on the other hand, environmental conditions and proximity to more advanced cultures to the east permitted the addition perhaps 2000 years ago or earlier, of a food-producing economy. First manifested on the Woodland-Hopewellian level, but much more strongly evidenced after A.D. 800, maize agriculture provided a firm foundation for the development of a succession of semisedentary, pottery-making, village-dwelling cultures. These were characterized by steadily increasing population aggregates who drew much of their cultural heritage from the east and who shared the Plains in the final century or two of their existence with the equestrian bison-hunters.

In appraising Plains archeology as of today, I think it can be said that we have made progress in the last thirty years—not as much, perhaps, as some of us would like to see, but progress, nevertheless. We have reached the point at which specific problems, over and above those concerned with the reporting of sherd types and site content, should be accorded an increasing proportion of our energy. It is to a brief enumeration of some of the problems I consider especially important and promising that I should like to devote the remainder of my remarks.

There is great need for refinement and clarification of the systematics of Plains archeology through careful statistical manipulation of detailed and up-to-date trait lists from the many sites and complexes for which controlled data are now available. Radiocarbon dating, dendrochronology, and other techniques, critically applied, should make possible a more precise ordering of our data and interpretations as we acquire additional dates in sufficient numbers to permit cross-checking and a measure of verification. Insufficient attention has as yet been devoted to the highly important matter of interareal relationships on various time levels between Plains cultures and those in adjacent regions, for example, the Eastern Woodland, the Southwest, the Great Basin, and the Plateau. Comprehensive studies on the physical anthropology of the native Plains peoples to determine their interrelationships from area to area, from one time level to another, and to those in adjacent regions should be made available. Interdisciplinary attacks on problems of the aboriginal human ecology of the Plains are urgently needed to sharpen our insights into the ways in which various groups, coming into the region from other areas and different environments, adapted their ways of living to the peculiarities of the grassland setting. In this connection, I believe that further intensive work in the short-grass belt fronting the Rockies from Alberta to the Llano Estacado is highly desirable, despite their apparently limited archeological resources; for the relatively simple hunting folk who probably utilized this "low-culture" area throughout a very long span of time may have been a good deal more important in the development and history of the "high-culture" Village Indians on the east than we now realize.

BIBLIOGRAPHY

AGOGINO, G. A., and W. D. FRANKFORTER
    1960 "A Paleo-Indian Bison-Kill in Northwestern Iowa." *Amer. Antiquity*, 25:414–15.
BELL, ROBERT E., and DAVID A. BAERREIS
    1951 "A Survey of Oklahoma Archeology." *Tex. Arch. & Paleont. Soc. Bull.*, 22:7–100.
BENTZEN, RAYMOND
    1962 "The Powers-Yonkee Bison Trap." *Plains Anthropologist*, 7:113–18.
BLISS, WESLEY L.
    1950 "Birdshead Cave, a Stratified Site in Wind River Basin, Wyoming." *Amer. Antiquity*, 15:187–96.

CHAMPE, JOHN L.
1936   "The Sweetwater Culture Complex." *Chaps. Neb. Arch.*, 1:249–97. Lincoln.
1946   *Ash Hollow Cave: A Study of Stratigraphic Sequence in the Central Great Plains.* ("Univ. Neb. Studies," n.s., No. 1.) Lincoln.
1949   "White Cat Village." *Amer. Antiquity,* 14:285–92.

CHAPMAN, CARL H.
1952   "Culture Sequence in the Lower Missouri Valley." Pp. 139–51 in J. B. GRIFFIN (ed.), *Archeology of Eastern United States.* Chicago: University of Chicago Press.
n.d.   "The Origin of the Osage Tribe, an Ethnological, Historical, and Archaeological Study." Unpublished manuscript, Department of Anthropology, University of Michigan, 1959.

COOPER, PAUL
1936   "Archeology of Certain Sites in Cedar County, Nebraska." *Chaps. Neb. Arch.,* 1:11–145. Lincoln.
1940   "The Archeological Exploration of 1938." *Neb. Hist. Mag.,* 20:94–131.

DAVIS, E. MOTT
1953   "Recent Data from Two Paleo-Indian Sites on Medicine Creek, Nebraska." *Amer. Antiquity,* 18:380–86.

DUNLEVY, M. L.
1936   "A Comparison of the Cultural Manifestations of the Burkett and Gray-Wolfe Sites." *Chaps. Neb. Arch.,* 1:147–247. Lincoln.

GRIFFIN, JAMES B.
1946   "Cultural Change and Continuity in Eastern United States Archaeology." Pp. 37–97 in FREDERICK JOHNSON (ed.), *Man in Northeastern North America.* ("Robert S. Peabody Foundation for Arch. Paps.," Vol. 3.) Andover.

GUNNERSON, DOLORES A.
1956   "The Southern Athabascans: Their Arrival in the Southwest." *El Palacio,* 63:346–65.

GUNNERSON, J. H.
1960   "An Introduction to Plains Apache Archeology—the Dismal River Aspect." *Anthrop. Paps.,* No. 58, pp. 131–260. (Bur. Amer. Ethnol. Bull. 173.) Washington, D.C.

HILL, A. T., and PAUL COOPER
1938   "The Archeological Campaign of 1937." *Neb. Hist. Mag.,* 18:237–359.

HILL, A. T., and MARVIN F. KIVETT
1941   "Woodland-like Manifestations in Nebraska." *Neb. Hist. Mag.,* 21:147–243.

HILL, A. T., and GEORGE METCALF
1942   "A Site of the Dismal River Aspect in Chase County, Nebraska." *Neb. Hist. Mag.,* 22:158–226.

HILL, A. T., and WALDO R. WEDEL
  1936   "Excavations at the Leary Indian Village and Burial Site, Richardson County, Nebraska." *Neb. Hist. Mag.*, 17:2–73.

HOLDER, PRESTON, and JOYCE WIKE
  1949   "The Frontier Culture Complex, a Preliminary Report on a Prehistoric Hunters' Camp in Southwestern Nebraska." *Amer. Antiquity*, 14:260–66.

HUGHES, JACK T.
  1949   "Investigations in Western South Dakota and Northeastern Wyoming." *Amer. Antiquity*, 14:266–77.

HURT, WESLEY R., JR.
  1951   *Report of the Investigation of the Swanson Site 39BR16, Brule County, South Dakota.* (S.D. Arch. Comm., Arch. Studies Circ. 3.) Pierre.
  1952   *Report of the Investigation of the Scalp Creek Site 39GR1 and the Ellis Creek Site 39GR2, Gregory County, South Dakota.* (S.D. Arch. Comm. Arch. Studies Circ. 4.) Pierre.
  1953a   "A Comparative Study of the Preceramic Occupations of North America." *Amer. Antiquity*, 18:204–22.
  1953b   *Report of the Investigation of the Thomas Riggs Site 39HU1, Hughes County, South Dakota.* (S.D. Arch. Comm. Arch. Studies Circ. 5.) Pierre.

HUSCHER, BETTY H., and HAROLD A. HUSCHER
  1943   "The Hogan Builders of Colorado." *Southwestern Lore*, 9:1–92.

IRWIN, H. J., and C. C. IRWIN
  1959   "Excavations at the LoDaisKa Site in the Denver, Colorado, Area." *Denver Mus. Nat. Hist. Proc.*, No. 8. Denver.
  1961   "Radiocarbon Dates from the LoDaisKa Site, Colorado." *Amer. Antiquity*, 27:114–15.

JENNESS, DIAMOND
  1932   *Indians of Canada.* ("Anthrop. Ser.," No. 15; Nat. Mus. Canada Bull. 65.) Ottawa.

JENNINGS, J. D.
  1957   *Danger Cave.* (Soc. Amer. Arch. Mem. 14.)

KEHOE, ALICE B.
  1959   "Ceramic Affiliations in the Northwestern Plains." *Amer. Antiquity*, 25:237–46.

KEHOE, THOMAS F.
  1960   "Stone Tipi Rings in North-Central Montana and the Adjacent Portion of Alberta, Canada: Their Historical, Ethnological, and Archeological Aspects." *Anthrop. Paps.*, No. 62, pp. 417–73. (Bur. Amer. Ethnol. Bull. 173.) Washington, D.C.

KEHOE, THOMAS F., and BRUCE A. McCORQUODALE
  1961   "The Avonlea Point, Horizon Marker for the Northwestern Plains." *Plains Anthropologist*, 6:179–88.

KIVETT, M. F.
1949 "Archeological Investigations in Medicine Creek Reservoir, Nebraska." *Amer. Antiquity*, 14:278–84.
1952 *Woodland Sites in Nebraska.* ("Neb. State Hist. Soc. Pub. Anthrop.," No. 1.) Lincoln.
1953 "The Woodruff Ossuary, a Prehistoric Burial Site in Phillips County, Kansas. *River Basin Surv. Paps.*, No. 3. (Bur. Amer. Ethnol. Bull. 154.) Washington, D.C.
KRIEGER, ALEX D.
1946 *Culture Complexes and Chronology in Northern Texas, with Extension of Puebloan Datings to the Mississippi Valley.* (Univ. Tex. Pub. 4640.) Austin.
KROEBER, A. L.
1928 "Native Culture of the Southwest." *Univ. Calif. Pub. Amer. Arch. & Ethnol.*, 23:375–98. Berkeley.
LEHMER, DONALD J.
1952 "The Fort Pierre Branch, Central South Dakota." *Amer. Antiquity*, 17:329–36.
1954a "Archeological Investigations in the Oahe Dam Area, South Dakota, 1950–51." *River Basin Surv. Paps.*, No. 7. (Bur. Amer. Ethnol. Bull. 158.) Washington, D.C.
1954b "The Sedentary Horizon of the Northern Plains." *Southwestern Jour. Anthrop.*, 10:139–59.
MACNEISH, RICHARD S.
1958 *An Introduction to the Archeology of Southeast Manitoba.* ("Anthrop. Ser.," No. 44; Nat. Mus. Canada Bull. 157.) Ottawa.
MAYER-OAKES, WILLIAM J.
1959 "Relationship between Plains Early Hunter and Eastern Archaic." *Wash. Acad. Sci. Jour.*, 49:146–56.
MELEEN, E. E.
1948 *Report of an Investigation of the La Roche Site, Stanley County, South Dakota.* (Univ. S.D. Mus. Arch. Studies Circ. 5.) Vermillion.
MOTT, MILDRED
1938 "The Relation of Historic Indian Tribes to Archeological Manifestations in Iowa." *Iowa Jour. Hist. & Politics*, 36:227–314.
MULLOY, WILLIAM
1952 "The Northern Plains." Pp. 124–38 in J. B. GRIFFIN (ed.), *Archeology of Eastern United States.* Chicago. University of Chicago Press.
1954a *Archeological Investigations in the Shoshone Basin of Wyoming.* (Univ. Wyo. Pub., Vol. 18, No. 1.) Laramie.
1954b "The McKean Site in Northeastern Wyoming." *Southwestern Jour. Anthrop.*, 10:432–60.
1958 *A Preliminary Historical Outline for the Northwestern Plains.* (Univ. Wyo. Pub., Vol. 22, No. 1.) Laramie.
NEUMAN, ROBERT W.
1960 "The Truman Mound Site, Big Bend Reservoir Area, South Dakota." *Amer. Antiquity*, 26:78–92.

ROBERTS, F. H. H., JR.
  1935 *A Folsom Complex: Preliminary Report on Investigations at the Linden-meier Site in Northern Colorado.* ("Smithsonian Misc. Coll.," Vol. 94, No. 4.) Washington, D.C.
  1936 *Additional Information on the Folsom Complex: Report on the Second Season's Investigations at the Lindenmeier Site in Northern Colorado.* ("Smithsonian Misc. Coll.," Vol. 95, No. 10.) Washington, D.C.
  1940 "Developments in the Problem of the North American Paleo-Indian." Pp. 51–116 in *Essays in Historical Anthropology of North America.* ("Smithsonian Misc. Coll.," Vol. 100.) Washington, D.C.
  1961 "The Agate Basin Complex." Pp. 125–32 in *Homenaje a Pablo Mar-tínez del Río en el 25° aniversario de la primera edición de "Los Orígenes Americanos."* Mexico.

SCHROEDER, A. H.
  1959 *A Study of the Apache Indians.* Parts I–II. Santa Fe.

SELLARDS, ELIAS H.
  1952 *Early Man in America: A Study in Prehistory.* Austin: University of Texas Press.

SELLARDS, E. H., GLENN L. EVANS, and GRAYSON E. MEADE
  1947 "Fossil Bison and Associated Artifacts from Plainview, Texas." With description of artifacts by ALEX D. KRIEGER. *Geol. Soc. America Bull.,* 58:927–54.

SMITH, CARLYLE S., and ROGER T. GRANGE, JR.
  1958 "The Spain Site (39LM301), a Winter Village in Fort Randall Reservoir, South Dakota." *River Basin Surv. Paps.,* No. 11, pp. 79–128. (Bur. Amer. Ethnol. Bull. 169.) Washington, D.C.

SPAULDING, ALBERT C.
  1949 "The Middle Woodland Period in the Central Plains." *Proc. 5th Plains Conf. for Archeol.,* pp. 105–11. (Univ. Neb. "Lab. Anthrop. Note Book," No. 1.) Lincoln.
  1956 *The Arzberger Site, Hughes County, South Dakota.* (Univ. Mich. Mus. Anthrop. "Occ. Contrib.," No. 16.) Ann Arbor.

STRONG, W. D.
  1933 "The Plains Culture Area in the Light of Archaeology." *Amer. Anthropologist,* 35:271–87.
  1935 *An Introduction to Nebraska Archeology.* ("Smithsonian Misc. Coll.," Vol. 93, No. 10.) Washington, D.C.
  1940 *From History to Prehistory in the Northern Great Plains.* ("Smithsonian Misc. Coll.," Vol. 100.) Washington, D.C.

SUHM, DEE ANN, A. D. KRIEGER, and E. B. JELKS
  1954 *An Introductory Handbook of Texas Archeology.* (Tex. Arch. Soc. Bull., Vol. 25.) Austin.

THOMAS, A. B.
  1935 *After Coronado: Spanish Exploration Northeast of New Mexico 1696–1727.* Norman: University of Oklahoma Press.

WEBB, WALTER P.
  1931 *The Great Plains.* Boston: Ginn & Co.

WEDEL, MILDRED M.
   1959   "Oneota Sites on the Upper Iowa River." *Mo. Archaeologist*, Vol. 21, Nos. 2–4.
WEDEL, WALDO R.
   1935   "Contributions to the Archeology of the Upper Republican Valley, Nebraska." *Neb. Hist. Mag.*, 15:132–209.
   1938   *The Direct-Historical Approach in Pawnee Archeology.* ("Smithsonian Misc. Coll.," Vol. 97, No. 7.) Washington, D.C.
   1940   "Culture Sequence in the Central Great Plains." Pp. 291–352 in *Essays in Historical Anthropology of North America.* ("Smithsonian Misc. Coll.," Vol. 100.) Washington, D.C.
   1941   *Environment and Native Subsistence Economies in the Central Great Plains.* ("Smithsonian Misc. Coll.," Vol. 101, No. 3.) Washington, D.C.
   1942   *Archeological Remains in Central Kansas and Their Possible Bearing on the Location of Quivira.* ("Smithsonian Misc. Coll.," Vol. 101, No. 7.) Washington, D.C.
   1943   *Archeological Investigations in Platte and Clay Counties, Missouri.* (U.S. Natl. Mus. Bull. 183.) Washington, D.C.
   1953   "Some Aspects of Human Ecology in the Central Plains." *Amer. Anthropologist*, n.s., 55:499–514.
   1956   "Changing Settlement Patterns in the Great Plains." Pp. 81–92 in G. R. WILLEY (ed.), *Prehistoric Settlement Patterns in the New World.* ("Viking Fund Pub. Anthrop.," Vol. 23.) New York.
   1959   *An Introduction to Kansas Archeology.* (Bur. Amer. Ethnol. Bull. 174.) Washington, D.C.
   1961   *Prehistoric Man on the Great Plains.* Norman: University of Oklahoma Press.
WETTLAUFER, B., and W. J. MAYER-OAKES
   1960   The Long Creek Site. (Saskatchewan Mus. Nat. Hist., "Anthrop. Ser.," No. 2.) Regina.
WHITE, L. A. (ed.)
   1959   *Lewis Henry Morgan: The Indian Journals 1859–62.* Ann Arbor: University of Michigan Press.
WILL, GEORGE F., and THAD C. HECKER
   1944   "The Upper Missouri River Valley Aboriginal Culture in North Dakota." *N.D. Hist. Quart.*, 11:5–126.
WORMINGTON, H. M.
   1957   *Ancient Man in North America.* 4th ed. (Denver Mus. Nat. Hist., "Pop. Ser.," No. 4.) Denver.

Eastern North America

JAMES B. GRIFFIN

The Northeast Woodlands Area

THIS SUMMARY deals with a large area of North America that lies east of the Plains, north of the lower Missouri and Ohio drainage, and south of the tundra zone. A large part of this region was called the Eastern Woodland culture area by anthropologists over fifty years ago (Wissler 1922). The major linguistic groups were the Algonquin, Iroquoian, and Siouan. In the boreal forests of Canada at the time of the first European explorations there were hunting bands, while to the south were peoples who practiced agriculture and who taught the early colonists how to raise and subsist on native American crops. The degree of agricultural dependence and population density increased toward the southern border of the area because of more favorable climatic conditions. In general, the prehistoric cultural trends are similar to those in most of the Americas, namely, a gradual shift from the earliest primarily hunting peoples, through a period of gradual ability to exploit the available resources of local areas, to the development of fairly sedentary agricultural populations. (The compilation of data presented in this chapter is based on a much larger bibliography and other sources than has been directly cited in the references. Apologies are offered to those who have seemingly been ignored and also to those authorities who may feel that their ideas have been abused.)

THE FLUTED BLADE HUNTERS

The apparent earliest occupation by man is by small groups of people whose projectile points are similar to those of the Clovis and Folsom hunters of the western Plains. These Fluted Blade Hunters occupied all the states within this survey, the southwestern part of On-

JAMES B. GRIFFIN received his doctoral degree from the University of Michigan, where he is director and curator of archeology, Museum of Anthropology, and professor of anthropology. He has done extensive research in the United States and Mexico. Noted for his broad knowledge of American archeology and a specialist in the cultures of the Ohio Valley, he is also interested in the archeology of Northern Eurasia. Recipient in 1957 of the Viking Fund Medal in Archaeology, he is the author of numerous books and papers.

tario between Lake Erie and Lake Huron and as far to the northeast as Nova Scotia. There is a remarkable similarity in their stone implements over the entire area and, indeed, to other Fluted Blade Hunters in the Southeast and the Plains. Very few camp sites of this complex have been found, and the great majority of the fluted points are surface finds, usually without other artifacts of the complex. The distribution of the fluted points in the Great Lakes area suggests that the hunters who made them occupied the area within a few hundred miles of the ice border of the last major Wisconsin moraine, known as the Valders, about 9000 B.C. It is also strongly indicated that the distinctive fluting of the points had passed out of style by 8000 B.C. over most of the area, with, however, the possibility that on the northern and northeastern periphery the fluted-point style lasted a short time after this date.

We do not know exactly when these hunters first entered the northeast Woodland area, but evidence from the west and south and indications of minor cultural variations make it appear that they were present by at least 10,000 B.C. Their origins before that are even less certain, but their general way of life and technology must inevitably be traced back to northeastern Asia to advanced Paleolithic cultures that were adapted to an Arctic environment between 30,000 and 10,000 B.C. (Griffin 1960a). As a likely hypothesis, we can assume that the penetration into the Upper Mississippi, Great Lakes, and New England was from the south.

The varied environments in which these people lived in the Northeast were quite different from that of the grasslands of the Plains or even that of the Southeast. In the southern part of the Northeast area, by 10,000 B.C., the forest composition would have been primarily deciduous, merging gradually into a spruce-fir forest within a few hundred miles or less of the ice border. Presumably, their quarry included a variety of animals such as elk, deer, beaver, and in the north the moose, caribou, perhaps the mammoth, mastodon, or even the musk-ox. Smaller animals, birds, fish, and seeds and nuts would have been available and could have become part of their diet. If the Fluted Blade Hunters were responsible for the disappearance of the mammoth, mastodon and musk ox, they succeeded in destroying the evidence, for there is not a single valid association of man and behemoth in the whole area, in spite of the recovery of hundreds of late Glacial elephant forms. The restriction of the diet of these early hunters to "big game" animals has been by certain archeologists, not by the people of 10,000–8000 B.C.

The inventory of weapons and tools that we now have reflects their primarily hunting culture with fluted projectile points and knives; scrapers of a variety of shapes and types; prepared cores of flint from which bladelike sections were struck by hammerstones to obtain the blank for points and scrapers; flakes with small, sharp graving points and chisel-like points; and spurred end scrapers. To this known list of tools might be added, on the basis of western and southern evidence, beveled bone points, grinding stones, bone discs, awls and beads, heavy flint choppers and scrapers, and the use of red ocher for decoration.

A reasonable *reconstruction* of other aspects of their culture would include the use of a small temporary shelters; the preparation of skins for clothing, bedding, and shelter; a moderate amount of woodworking; a technique of fire production; an ability to cross major streams by logs, rafts, dugouts or skin boats; and the rather rapid dissemination of minor culture changes in spite of the distances involved. A further assumption is made that the physical type of this earliest population had a basic similarity to the longheaded groups of the Late Archaic to the historic period in the Northeast.

THE ARCHAIC CULTURE

Quite a few contributors to this volume may continue their discussion of Paleo-Indian cultures, or time period, well past 8000 B.C., but in this reconstruction the cultural complexes after that date in the Northeast will be referred to as Archaic. The Archaic complexes representing a variety of hunting, gathering, collecting, and fishing activities, will span a long time period up to about 1000 B.C. In the early part of this seven-thousand-year span there are few sites and not much material, so much of the interpretation is even more conjectural than normal in an archeological synthesis. In this paper, the term "Archaic" is not limited to a complex like that found at the Lamoka site in New York, which included ground- and polished-stone tools. It is, rather, a long period of gradual cultural change from the initial hunting cultures to the Woodland groups, who had a more stable economic basis and had become more sedentary.

The Archaic cultures of the Northeast include a wide range of technological skills, many of which could have been developed from the techniques known to the Fluted Blade Hunting cultures. The diverse regional environments influenced the Archaic cultural development in terms of available food, industrial raw materials, and the ability of the small bands to move from one area to another. Another environmental factor was the very gradual change in climate and in plant succession that moved ecological zones to the north. The increment in the ability of these people to exploit the environment came about slowly. New techniques or the development of new resources probably spread within a few hundred years over most of the territory suited to their employment. By approximately 3000–2000 B.C. the present ecological zones were essentially established and have been shifted only in minor degree

FIG. 1.—Some North American culture groups of about 8000 B.C.

by slight climatic oscillations since that time. It is a result of this north-ward shift, and the uneasy stabilization of the mixed deciduous and boreal forest, that major Archaic sites and cultural developments appear in the Great Lakes to New England area for the first time around 3000 B.C.

The ability of ideas, techniques, and tools to spread in prehistoric times exceeds the present ability of the archeologist to pinpoint their first appearance. Their development, speed, and direction of movement are difficult to identify, except as a vague and inevitably controversial judgment. While radiocarbon dates have been of great assistance, they are not accurate enough for many problems. We will need to have a great deal of work done with sites of short time span, or with levels accurately isolated, defined, and, above all, dated with precision, before we can confidently reconstruct the changing cultural complex of the Archaic peoples.

In the Plains area, following the disappearance of the fluted blades, many variations of a common leaf-shape projectile form appear. Some of these have distinctive ripple flaking, some are stemmed, but the majority are variants on a common theme. For some time I have referred to this primarily hunting adaptation on the Plains as the Plano cultures, following Jennings (1955). This term as a *cultural complex* should be limited to the Plains area, for there it was an adaptation to a particular environment. The distribution of some of the projectile-point forms is, however, a different story, for some of the forms in Plano sites are also found in the Northeast and about in the same chronological position as in the Plains.

The position taken in this review, that the Fluted Blade Hunters moved into the Northeast from the south or west, is one about which there is little controversy. The appearance of Plano-like forms in the Early Archaic of the Northeast may be, however, a result of a gradual stylistic change over wide areas in North America, and this interpreta-tion is favored here. The appearance of these forms may also be viewed as a result of a movement of people out of the Plains because of the depletion of grasslands and herds as the climate became warmer and dryer. This interpretation is not adopted here because the projectile points are known east of the grasslands long before the Plains are said to be uninhabitable. In fact, most, if not all, of the Plano forms have gone out of style long before the period of "maximum warmth" and/or dry-ness in the Plains, and after the same styles have disappeared in the east. The proponents of the migration school also fancy a cultural break be-tween the Fluted Blade Hunters and the Early Archaic, and apparently would depopulate the Northeast area for a fairly long period. Just as southeastern archeologists who are intimately working with Early

Archaic materials are recognizing a gradual shift from fluted blades to slightly later forms, there is in the Northeast a growing tendency to interpret the scanty available evidence as indicating gradual culture change from the technology of the fluted blades as the predominant theme of the Early Archaic.

The archeological sequence in the Upper Mississippi Valley, as in other areas of the Northeast, begins with the Fluted Blade Hunters, for such projectile points have been found in northern Illinois, southern and western Wisconsin, southern Minnesota, and Iowa. I am deliberately ignoring "Minnesota Man," for the excavation data, artifact association, and "probability" have never been satisfactory for assigning it to an 11,000 B.C. date. A radiocarbon assay made in 1957 (W-530), while not to be regarded as definitive, nevertheless suggests a temporal placement in Late Archaic. This is reasonable in view of the association of the burial with an *elk* antler dagger and a *Busycon perversa* perforated pendant, an incisor of the eastern timber wolf, a loon metatarsal, and carapace fragments of turtle. The shell pendant of Minnesota Man is a style known in Late Archaic shell heaps in Kentucky, and the use of marine shells becomes known only in Glacial Kame and other Transitional to Early Woodland cultures in the north-central United States.

Wittry (1959) has some evidence for human occupation at the Raddatz rock shelter in central Wisconsin between 8000 and 7000 B.C. This is approximately the period of the appearance of a cremation burial complex with Eden, Scottsbluff, and a side-notched point, from an Algonquin-stage beach of Lake Michigan in Brown County, Wisconsin (Mason and Irwin 1960). This Renier site provides a basis for an approximate time period for the extension into the upper Great Lakes, and as far east as Ohio, of projectile forms identified with the Plano groups of the Plains from 8000 to 5000 B.C. The Brohm site on a raised beach of about 7000 B.C., northwestern Lake Superior, and the George Lake and Sheguindah sites in northern Lake Huron of about the same age have connections in projectile-point styles to Plano forms. The latter two sites, along with Renier, also have large side-notched forms with concave bases similar to forms from as far south as the Tennessee Valley of about the same time and later.

It is a wise archeologist who can interpret the association of cultural material in Graham Cave (Logan 1952) in central Missouri with the radiocarbon dates (Crane 1956). The dates confirm occupation of the cave from about 7700 to 6000 B.C., while the upper levels come close to late prehistoric times. The lower levels represent the transition from Fluted Blade Hunters to the early projectile-point forms, such as the Dalton type, which are regarded as Early Archaic in this paper. Lanceolate points are most common in the lower levels, and side-notched forms in the middle level. The ground-stone mortars, hand stones, pestle, hematite adze, chipped adzes and choppers, and full-grooved ax from the lower levels represent a fairly early position for these tools of *ca.* 6000 B.C.

The earliest occupation, which can be adequately described, at the Modoc, Illinois, rock shelter, near St. Louis, is interpreted here as between 7000 and 6000 B.C. and has a few hammerstones, scrapers, perforators, choppers, a piece of worked antler, a side-notched projectile point, and a side-notched hafted scraper (Fowler 1959). The first major occupation level, Stratum III, is dated between *ca.* 6000 and 3500 B.C. and has a variety of stemless, side-notched and stemmed points, including Hidden Valley Stemmed, which is not regarded in this paper as at all close to the Gypsum Cave point. There is a wide range of faunal materials from this period, and presumably native vegetal materials were actively gathered. Of particular interest is the grooved ax at 5000 B.C. and of bannerstone fragments slightly later. This has been called the period of "local adaptation" and Modoc, as well as other sites of this time period in the southern part of the Northeast, have every indication of a wide variety of foods incorporated into the diet and of most of the basic manufacturing skills known in Late Archaic times. In the southern half of the lower peninsula of Michigan a series of sites has a high proportion of large, stemmed "argillite" and flint points. This Satchell complex probably can be attributed to a time period of about 4000 B.C., since they have disappeared by the time of the Late Archaic complexes in the same area.

A more complete view of Archaic development in southern Illinois will result from publication of the results of the Southern Illinois University study of that area. There are many sites representing a more diverse type of occupation, and particularly a more intimate connection with the Ohio-Tennessee-Cumberland drainage. Most of the known Archaic sites immediately north of the Ohio Valley fall into the Late Archaic period.

THE LATE ARCHAIC CULTURES

The Lamoka and Laurentian expressions of the Late Archaic in New York and southern Ontario have been described by Ritchie in a number of publications from 1932 to 1958. Because they are the earliest complexes that he has been able to recognize, following a Fluted Blade occupation, they are for him "Early" Archaic, even though their artifact types and radiocarbon dates place them on the same level with Late Archaic complexes in the Ohio Valley and farther south. It has been suggested that Lamoka projectiles are related to forms found in coastal Archaic sites, but they are also known in the upper levels of shell heaps in Kentucky and are known from surface sites in southwestern Ontario and from eastern Michigan. There are other connections between Lamoka and the Ohio Valley Archaic in bone implement and ornament types, so a strong element in the culture has southern affiliations. The beveled adze is a specialized (and later?) form of the ground adze and the presence of the ground-stone celt is a further suggestion of the relative lateness of Lamoka, within the increasing use of ground-stone woodworking tools. The major conclusion to be drawn from this data is that Lamoka does not date much earlier than 2500 B.C. (Crane and Griffin 1959) and was relatively short lived as a distinctive complex. Its major elements reached New York and the lower Great Lakes area as the result of diffusion or other movement of traits from various sources to the south.

Most of the discussions of the Laurentian culture of about 3000–1000 B.C. emphasize its presence in the New York, St. Lawrence Valley, and New England areas. There are a number of regional and chronological variants, but it will probably be some time before these are clearly delineated and their interaction understood. Since Laurentian was one of the first of the Archaic complexes to be recognized in the Northeast, there has been a natural tendency to regard it as an important center for the dissemination of Laurentian traits, even though Ritchie has at times looked to the west for Laurentian origins in the deciduous forest zone. Little or no attention is given in this paper to a possible "circumboreal" complex with northern Eurasian connections because many of the artifact types do not occur in the boreal or tundra zones of North America or over large areas of eastern Siberia. Some of the suggested artifact connections, such as the grooved ax, are as early or earlier in the eastern United States as they are from northwestern Europe to the Caucasus. There is an increasing awareness that many of the projectile forms that have been identified as Laurentian have a wide distribution, at least from the Ohio Valley north to the southern border of the spruce-fir forest in the Great Lakes area (Dragoo 1959) and even as far west as the eastern part of the northern prairies.

In New England there is recognized a southern or "Coastal" variant, divided into "Early" and "Late" complexes, although, as usual, the dividing line between them is not very clear. The primary affiliations are toward southeastern New York, New Jersey, and to the south, but strong trait resemblances are also seen in central New York in the several complexes called Laurentian by Ritchie, and there are also strong connections to the northern New England Early and Late "Boreal" Archaic. Probably the best-known site in southern New England is the Boylston Street Fishweir (Johnson *et al.* 1942, 1949), which has been dated by two radiocarbon assays on two of the fishweir stakes at about

2500 B.C. (Byers 1959). A village site of similar age in southeastern Massachusetts is Wapanucket No. 6, dated approximately 2300 B.C. (Robbins 1959). At this site, six house floors and post-mold patterns were uncovered. The houses are circular with an overlapping entrance-way and an average diameter of 35 feet. One of the lodges was nearly 65 feet in diameter and, because of other unusual features, is regarded as a ceremonial structure. Under the assumption that the houses are contemporary, it has been estimated that the population consisted of one hundred or more individuals leading a hunting, fishing, and food-gathering existence. Also significant is the presence of cremations at this site, some use of red ocher with the burials, and artifacts that link this village to the Maine Boreal Archaic and to other Late Archaic burial complexes north of the Ohio and east of the Mississippi. The tools, utensils, and weapons of Wapanucket No. 6 village include a number of forms of the gouge, the adze, knobbed and ringed plummets, bipennate bannerstones, semi-lunar knives, pestles, a grooved ax, anvil stones, a muller, stone-bowl fragments, and a number of other chipped- and ground-stone artifacts. The projectile forms are quite varied, with a number of different triangular forms, small stemmed, diamond, eared; a number of varieties of corner-removed points; and variant forms of spear or lance points. A rather large number of small scrapers of various forms testify to the importance of skin-working in the community. The presence of iron pyrites is interpreted as an indication of its use in making fire. It is difficult to believe that this varied cultural assemblage belongs to a single short-lived occupation.

In northeastern New England the Kelly phase, as reconstructed by Byers (1959), is composed of percussion-flaked, large and heavy scrapers similar to "pulper planes" of the west, core scrapers, hammerstones, and one large bipointed, bifacially flaked knife. This complex presumably has an estimated antiquity of before 3000 B.C. Byers does not regard this complex as part of the Archaic "stage" because it does not have ground-stone tools, but in this paper it will be included along with the older George Lake, Chickinising Creek, and some part of the Sheguindah sites, which are relatively early Archaic complexes in the Great Lakes area that precede the gradual spread of ground-stone Archaic forms from the south.

The characteristic artifacts of the Early Boreal Archaic of northern New England and the lower St. Lawrence Valley are known between 3000 and perhaps 2000 B.C. They include the chipped adze, ground and slightly beveled adzes, the gouge, grooved "bolas stones," knobbed plummets, shouldered slate points, stone rods, and narrow bifacially worked projectiles. The Late Boreal Archaic has a time range from approximately 2000 to about 1000 B.C., if the introduction of pottery at about

Fig. 2.—Some North American culture groups of about 2500 B.C.

the latter date may be said to represent the beginning of Early Woodland. Late Boreal is a development of the ground-stone forms of its predecessor, with an increase in the variety and quality of products, and also witnesses the introduction of bannerstones, semilunar knives, stone tubes, iron pyrites, red ocher in graves, and perhaps the pop-eyed birdstone. It also has an emphasis on medium-size, stemmed and side-notched points. There are a few scrapers, expanded-base and side-notched base drills, and small trianguloid stone pendants with an apical perforation. The lower levels of some shell mounds have bone barbed points, beaver incisors, and implements of the swords of swordfish. The Boreal Archaic is found in northern New England and into the Maritime Provinces, and some elements extend into Newfoundland and Labrador. Some artifacts of this complex seem to last well up into much later time periods.

THE OLD COPPER CULTURE

The Old Copper Culture has received considerable attention in the last decade or so, and its general temporal position and cultural relationships are becoming better known. The greatest number of copper tools of this culture unit are from sites from northern Illinois to Lake Superior. From this area, in all directions, may be found smaller amounts of copper implements, but the main distribution is in the Great Lakes drainage basin eastward into the Lower Peninsula of Michigan and Lower Ontario. Because of a black-carbon radiocarbon date (Libby 1955), some archeologists favor the beginning of Old Copper before 5000 B.C. In this paper a date of 3000 B.C. will be used, and most of the Old Copper Culture will be placed between 2000 and 1000 B.C. Some of the arguments for this time span have been presented in a recent publication (Griffin 1961*b*), and there seems to be no additional evidence that would call for a change of view in this paper. Some of the projectile points associated with Old Copper burials appear to correspond to corner-notched forms of Laurentian. Side-notched projectile forms, apparently associated, are a part of long tradition of such forms in the upper Mississippi Valley. Some of the Old Copper flint projectile points are identified as Larter Tanged of the preceramic Anderson focus of Manitoba. They are one form of Brewerton Side-Notched. For unknown reasons, the production of the large and varied copper utilitarian implements gradually declined, but the manufacture of small awls, knives, and a few other forms continued in the upper Great Lakes area to the historic period.

While there have been no pollen studies or an adequate analysis of faunal material from an Old Copper village site, we can still be confident that these first American "metallurgists" lived in the northern mixed-deciduous-spruce-pine zone and that their environment was not significantly different from what it is today in the area delineated. It was not a boreal forest environment, nor do the copper implements— either traded, carried, or copied—appear in any number in locations that would have been in the boreal forest. It is commonly accepted that the large copper implements have some interesting parallels in shape with those of slate forms of the Northeast that are now known to date primarily within the 2000–1000 B.C. period. Old Copper is regarded as an unusual development in Late Archaic times in the upper Great Lakes by Indian groups who discovered the strange "stone" that could be hammered and shaped into forms resembling bone, stone, and perhaps wood prototypes. There can be no direct connection between this copper industry and other world centers of the early development of metals for human use.

The Glacial Kame burial complex is distributed from southern Ontario across southern Michigan, northern Ohio, Indiana, and with some evidence of connections into northern Illinois and southeastern Wisconsin. The earliest attempts at chronological and cultural assessment of this burial complex, about 1940, were in error because of the reported association of a pottery vessel and a platform pipe with the burials. It was regarded as a north-central burial procedure related to Adena-Red Ocher and to Hopewell. Since then, it has rapidly become clear that Glacial Kame was preceramic, and now an age of roughly 1500 ± 500 B.C. would seem to be about the correct order of magnitude, because of the appearance of the diagnostic sandal-sole gorget in a Red Ocher mound in Illinois, an Old Copper site in Wisconsin, and at the Picton site in Ontario, where it is connected with a phase of Point Peninsula I. Sandal-sole gorgets are also found in a Late Archaic context in western Tennessee and in northern Alabama.

The Glacial Kame sites are usually located in high glacial features or sandy knolls away from the village. Various tools and ornaments were placed with primarily flexed burials. The importance of copper is represented by awls, beads, celts, gouge, repoussé plate, and a bar gorget. A birdstone, tubular stone pipes, celts, and a bell-shaped pestle are some of the ground- and polished-stone materials indicative of a very late Archaic placement. The most significant burial items, however, are the sandal-sole and rectangular gorgets from marine shell and the disk-shape 3-hole gorgets or pendants and shell beads also made from ocean shell. Red ocher is associated with the burials at a number of sites.

It should be observed that this burial complex is in the same geographical area as that of a more intensive use of red ocher and a somewhat different group of burial practices known from Red Ocher in Illinois across into New York and New England. It is partly for this reason that

Glacial Kame may also be viewed as an early form of the developing emphasis on burial ceremonialism that characterizes the Transitional and Early Woodland groups in the Great Lakes area.

TRANSITIONAL AND EARLY WOODLAND CULTURES

Just before and after 1000 B.C., from the Great Lakes to New England a widespread burial complex appears (Ritzenthaler and Quimby 1962). There is a definite overlap in the west with Old Copper and Glacial Kame and its copper utilitarian forms and with Laurentian–Late Boreal forms in the east. There is also a clear extension of these burial complexes into the ceramic-using northern Early Woodland cultures. Temporal and artifactual connections are also seen with other Early Woodland groups in the Ohio Valley. One of the distinctive features of these burial complexes is a marked increase in cremation, which is paralleled in the developing Ohio Valley Adena sites. Cremation has been present in the whole Northeast area since about 6000 B.C. and is known somewhat sporadically since that time. Red ocher with burials also has a long temporal span in the Northeast. The burial goods include items with a fairly long history, but new forms, particularly the trianguloid points in large caches, the turkey-tail forms, certain large stemmed forms, tubular pipes, gorgets, birdstones of distinctive types, mound burial in the west, and the use of galena cubes are indications of new cultural practices.

While there are some important items of this time period about 1000 B.C., which serve to link these burial sites, an equally significant fact is that in the several areas there are local materials and artifacts that demonstrate an essentially regional character for the sites. For example, the Orient burial complex of Long Island Sound is probably connected with the Late Archaic groups, whose culture at a slightly earlier period would be called Laurentian or Coastal Archaic. These northern burial practices are not a single functioning burial complex of a single group of related bands of people moving about the Northeast, but represent, instead, the interaction of localized populations among which various ideas of the time spread and were incorporated into their burial observances. There is certainly no push of a large number of new peoples into the Great Lakes–New England area from the area northwest of Lake Superior, even though the Sturgeon Triangular and Nutimik concave points of the Late Archaic focuses of Manitoba are part of the northern burial complex (MacNeish 1958).

Associated at this time period with the Red Ocher to Point Peninsula I (Ritchie 1955) burials are, occasionally, examples of Early Woodland pottery of the distinctive cord-marked exterior-and-interior style on simple jar forms. The distribution of this pottery is from eastern Minnesota to New England. It is not known in the Plains, or north of the upper Great Lakes. While it displays a marked similarity in construction, general tempering characteristics, form, and surface finish, we cannot yet state where this pottery first appears or how it spreads; nor, indeed, can we give a completely satisfactory explanation of its origin. That it is related to early cord-marked, fabric-impressed and plain wares along the Ohio drainage to the middle Atlantic states has been clear for twenty years. There are no specific prototypes for this Early Woodland pottery in the American arctic or boreal forest and certainly not in any excavated ceramics from northern Asia. It is assumed here that the best explanation for its origin is by spread of the concept of pottery-making from northwestern Canada by peoples with knowledge of the Choris-Norton ceramic complex of that area. How this was accomplished is unknown. Some archeologists have suggested an independent origin for northern pottery—that it developed out of steatite bowl forms in the Middle Atlantic area. Others have suggested that it developed from the earlier fiber-tempered pottery of the Southeast, but this is doubtful, and some will inevitably suggest an origin in Mesoamerica, where cord-marked pottery on the Pacific Guatemala coast is about 1000 B.C. Whatever its origin, the Early Woodland pottery becomes a utilitarian addition of relatively little importance in each of the several areas where it is found. The Ohio Valley types have greater variety of surface treatment; some are even decorated and, in southern Ohio, clearly show overlap in time with steatite bowls by the common possession of cylindrical lug handles and flat bases. The northeastern variant of this Early Woodland pottery, known as Vinette I, is, on the whole, thinner and does not have as coarse tempering material as do the western representatives. It is probably later in time.

The Adena development, climax, and demise, in the Ohio Valley, is one of the least understood of the northeastern cultural complexes in spite of the excavation of a large number of sites and some good comparative studies. One of the main difficulties is the lack of adequately documented radiocarbon dates that could aid in developing a sound reconstruction of the gradual growth of this culture from relatively simple, low mounds, with modest burial construction and offerings, to the large multistage structures, with many elaborate burials, which come into the period of Hopewell dominance in southern Ohio. The area of the Adena culture is in southern Ohio, adjacent Kentucky, Indiana, West Virginia, and Pennsylvania. It is the earliest of the burial-mound-building cultures of the Ohio Valley. Its time period is approximately from 1000 B.C. to perhaps A.D. 200. Many of the roots of the Adena culture are in the Late Archaic sites of its immediate area and in the

Red Ocher–Glacial Kame–Point Peninsula I burial elaboration, which has been briefly discussed above.

A number of students of the Adena culture, and of the Adena physical type, have strongly supported the hypothesis that both people and culture were migrants into the area from Mesoamerica. That no cultural complex remotely resembling any phase of Adena has ever been found in Middle America is ignored, as is the absence of any Adena sites, in terms of a complex of traits, in sites south of Kentucky, which could represent way stations on this prehistoric "Drang nach Norden." Adena and the other Early Woodland cultures of the Ohio–upper Mississippi drainage fall within the period in which some archeologists have postulated independent origins for such native plants as chenopodium, the sunflower, pigweed, ragweed, and marsh elder. None of the sites or complexes so far studied in connection with such an independent development predate the indicated, or probable, appearance of domesticated gourds, squash, and perhaps even corn, in the Mississippi Valley. The period from 1000 B.C. to A.D. 1 is about when we could expect to have infiltration of early simple agriculture in the eastern United States on the basis of its long residence in Tamaulipas and its presence in the Southwest and along the eastern slopes of the mountains in Colorado between 2000 and 1000 B.C. One must assume a fairly long period of gradual cultural adaptation to agricultural plants and practices. We must also assume a fairly wide geographical spread of agriculture before the possibility of between-harvest food storage for the people of any small area becomes practical. In other words, the view adopted in this paper is that the extraordinary cultural growth, population increase, and evidence of exchange of goods in both the Southeast and the Northeast between 3000 and 2000 years ago, was aided by the introduction of early agricultural plants.

The long time span of Adena means that the people of the earliest Adena sites who made the relatively simple burials in low mounds; circular-house forms with a single row of posts; barrel-shaped and straight cylinder pipes; early gorget forms; Fayette Thick pottery; grooved axes; stemmed and notched points, and leaf-shaped cache blades are participating in the general cultural growth of the eastern United States. The Early Woodland in southern and central Illinois also has rather simple burial customs and a group of flint, stone, and pottery material that goes through a gradual development. In the central Illinois and Mississippi Valley this development passes into the Early Hopewell Havana phase. The later and more elaborate Adena sites with circular earthworks and large complex conical and ovoid mounds, with effigy tubular pipes, use of mica, copper gorgets, bracelets, rings, and beads, engraved tablets, Adena Plain and Montgomery Incised pottery types, check and simple stamped pottery, circular paired post-mold house patterns, rectangular house patterns, a variety of cloth weaves, pearl beads, and an art style of Hopewellian character are reflections of increased population, a more sedentary life, and broadening of the cultural resources incorporated into the Adena culture.

While a strong case can be made for a movement of people with Adena traits to Chesapeake Bay about the time of the birth of Christ (Ritchie and Dragoo 1960), we do not know whether this movement took place as a single- or a multiple-group displacement or over a few months, decades, years, or a few hundred years. The same type of evidence used to support the hypothesis of a displacement of Adena populations into the New York area can also be found in sites in eastern Michigan and northern Lake Huron. The interpretation favored in this paper is that the appearance of specific Ohio Valley Adena materials in sites in the Great Lakes drainage and New York is more likely to have been the result of trade or contact carried out by a few individuals whose journeys may have been prompted by a variety of reasons. Many cultural traits of Adena in the Ohio Valley are shared with other Early Woodland groups.

In the lower Delaware Valley, early pottery equivalent to Vinette I of New York and steatite-tempered pottery of Marcey Creek type has been found in a number of sites. Unfortunately, the archeologists of this region have not been able to work out an Early Woodland complex or complexes because of the mixed occupations at most of the sites that have been systematically investigated. It should be noted that such Early Woodland pottery and associated materials are in the area before the spread of Ohio Valley Adena artifacts into the Chesapeake Bay area. There is a strong tendency among some New England archeologists to place their local equivalent of Vinette I at a substantially later date than it appears in adjacent New York, but there are no radiocarbon dates to support such an assignment. Most of the Early Woodland materials from New England should date before A.D. 1.

The increasing cultural complexity and intensity of Early Woodland produces evidence, from burial customs and ceremonial constructions, of status differentiation within the society. Such differentiation appears to be primarily of a magicoreligious nature, for the grave goods with individuals given special burial are still "personal" property and never rise to the symbolic level of the Southeastern Ceremonial complex of the later Mississippian cultures. While a certain degree of group co-operation is required in constructing the large mounds and circular earthworks, it is not of the order of social control that implies a tightly organized or directed society. Not only is the Adena culture, as presently defined, not adequately broken down into a sequential or dynamic developmental interpretation of the whole complex, but, also, little attempt has been made to differentiate or present local continuities. We need, for example, to recognize the influences on sites in the Miami River system of southwestern Ohio and to compare them with those in the Big Sandy of Kentucky or the Kanawha in West Virginia.

HOPEWELLIAN AND MIDDLE WOODLAND CULTURES

While much has been written about the Hopewellian cultures, there are few, if any, published comprehensive interpretations, and certainly this will not be one. Hopewell in the Illinois Valley may be said to begin with the early phase of Havana complex pottery as represented at Havana Mound 6. It is an arbitrary beginning because there is no break in ceramic continuity from the late Morton focus–Early Woodland complex that precedes Havana. The view that Illinois Hopewell begins with an intrusion or movement of people from Ohio, bringing exotic Hopewellian elements with them, is not supportable for a number of reasons. The Illinois Hopewell ceramic complex is not known in Ohio at any time. Early Illinois Hopewell begins while Adena is still dominant in southern Ohio and so does not have the specific Ohio Hopewell items, such as effigy platform pipes and copper ear spools, as part of its early traits. It is in the later Hopewellian sites in Illinois that we find these Ohio artifacts.

A few comments are in order concerning the temporal position of some of the Hopewellian communities. There is very good reason to be suspicious of the mussel-shell date (M-15) for the Poole site of 550 B.C. This is not only because of the charcoal date of A.D. 210 (M-183) from the same site but also because mussel shells from waters in limestone country are known to date considerably earlier than the true date. While I still retain some confidence in the Knight site Mound 8 date (M-164) on ocean shell of A.D. 250 ± 300, I am quite skeptical of the Ohio Hopewell site Mound 25 date (C-137) on ocean shell of 335 B.C. This is not only because bark from the same section of the mound gave a date of 94 B.C. (C-139) but because there is now good evidence that the large marine gastropods may also be unreliable according to the environment from which they obtained their carbon. Another date on mussel shell from Illinois is M-256, from the Weaver site, at 350 B.C., and this makes no sense in terms of the stratigraphical and developmental level of the Weaver complex. These interpretations have the result of raising a beginning date for Illinois Hopewell to around 300 B.C. and of placing the beginning of Ohio Hopewell at approximately 100 B.C. or later, on the basis of the few dates we have from that area. This would have the further effect of aligning the northern Hopewellian cultural climax closer in time to the obviously related lower Mississippi

Fig. 3.—Some North American culture groups of about 1 B.C.

Valley Marksville-Issaquena sites. Since my survey of Hopewellian dates was published (Griffin 1958), we have run an additional sample (M-928) from the West Mound in Highland County, Ohio, which came to A.D. 130 ± 200, and this conforms very well with the previously published date (M-650), which as A.D. 70 ± 200.

I am not aware of a published detailed listing or cataloguing of Ohio Hopewell sites. One partial list includes 27 sites, but the actual number should be at least 75–100 if relatively small sites near or adjacent to some of the major centers are included. At some of the major Ohio Hopewell earthworks, conical mounds and small circular earthworks are incorporated into the group. Some of these are Adena in construction and artifact content. While there is a strong resemblance of many features of Adena to Hopewell items, the relationship between them is not one showing contemporaneity but primarily one of continuity. Even the Adena sites in north-central Kentucky, which have a few Hopewell artifact forms, maintain their own cultural character.

One of the major reasons for the high development of the Ohio Hopewell complex is that it developed out of the seven hundred years of Adena growth, plus influences from Illinois Hopewell, from contemporary northern groups, and from the Southeast. There is a growing tendency to view Ohio Hopewell as a uniform cultural complex dominated by an elite class that marshaled its manpower for conquest and the establishment of outlying subject groups. Close students of Ohio Hopewell have, however, emphasized the considerable diversity in the materials from the major sites. While it is possible, perhaps even probable, that a single language stock was spoken in southern Ohio, it is also likely that there were minor dialect differences between the occupants of the lower Muskingum and of the area around Cincinnati. There must have been a clear recognition of a common cultural complex that would have enabled groups localized near Marietta to have participated freely in feasts, dances, and ceremonies near Chillicothe, but it may be doubted that they were ever bound together as an effective political unit. The same generalization is also valid in the Illinois Hopewell area, where a number of distinctive focuses and local traditions have been recognized.

When adequate interpretations of the functioning Hopewellian society are made, they should be done on the basis of considerable familiarity with the ethnography of the early historic Indian groups of the Northeast Woodlands area. It may be doubted that Hopewellian social or political organization was as advanced as that of the early historic Iroquois or of the Delaware and Shawnee. The Adena-Hopewell continuum represents the gradual shift from societies on a level that may be similar to northern Chippewa to ones approaching the southern Central and Coastal Algonkians of the historic period. The Adena-Hopewell economy or population did not reach the social level of the later Fort Ancient people, and their ceremonial and religious life is of a markedly different order, as an integrating force, from that of the Southeastern Ceremonial Complex of a thousand years later.

The growth of the importance of pipes in Adena-Hopewell suggests that tobacco-smoking rituals were being developed and became widely disseminated. There is, I believe, no specific identification of tobacco at this period, and it is an assumption that this domesticated plant (*Nicotiana rusticum*) was the one grown for smoking. The wide dissemination of this plant in eastern North America in early historic times and its importance in the ceremonial life is a guide to its possible antiquity. As a native South American plant, its appearance in eastern North America, and rarity in middle America, has not been adequately explained. Even MacNeish's valuable acquisitions of paleobotanical material have not aided us with this problem.

One of the surprising things about Ohio Hopewell is that, in spite of its vitality in ceremonial and artistic affairs and its widespread collection and distribution system, it does not seem to have operated as an effective, expanding social group into immediately contiguous territories. The scarcity of Hopewellian communities along the Lake Erie drainage, the weakness of the penetration into eastern Ohio, western Pennsylvania, southwestern New York, eastern Indiana, and northern Kentucky suggests that it was not politically or geographically aggressive. The raw materials brought into Ohio were gathered from areas and populations that did not effectively participate in the Hopewellian cultural level with the exception of the northwest coast of Florida. This latter area received its primary Hopewellian ceramic flavor as a result of interaction with the Lower Mississippi Valley. Certainly there was distribution of platform pipes of Ohio pipestone, into the Illinois Valley particularly, and these are regarded as items that could be readily integrated into existing ceremonial patterns. Probably copper ear spools were made in much greater numbers in Ohio than elsewhere, and there is a tendency to interpret their distribution to the west as trade items from Ohio. It is not certain or even probable that the Dakota chalcedony or Rocky Mountain obsidian projectile points and spear forms in Illinois, Iowa, and Wisconsin were distributed from Ohio. The source of these raw materials is much closer to the upper Mississippi Valley sites, and obsidian flint chips have been found on a number of Illinois sites. Implements of Flint Ridge flint, where these are certainly identified, are indicators of cultural exchange. The Ohio Hopewell acquisition of exotic raw materials was designed primarily for conspicuous local ceremonial consumption.

It is not necessary to review too extensively the evidence pro and con for Hopewellian agriculture. There is no question that they had some. It would not seem, however, that they were primarily agricultural or even close to the agricultural levels of the Mississippian cultures. The position adopted here is that there was a sufficient agricultural food supply to allow greater population concentration in relatively restricted areas and more rapid accumulation of village debris, at least in some areas, than is indicated for either Archaic or Early Woodland groups. It is difficult to interpret the Adena-Hopewellian efflorescence in any other terms than as resulting from the benefits of agriculture.

The Illinois Valley Hopewell complex had a definite expansive trend, which caused it to spread and/or influence Middle Woodland developments around it. It spread northeast along the Kankakee to the southern half of the Lower Peninsula of Michigan, producing resident Hopewellian cultures in the St. Joseph, Grand, and Saginaw valleys. The earliest of the ceramic types in Michigan clearly belongs to the Havana group of the Illinois Valley and probably indicates population movement. The location of these sites in the major river valleys with broad alluvial terraces and soils, paralleling the location of Illinois Hopewell sites, and the failure of this complex to penetrate very far north of the present dominantly agricultural area of the state is significant in terms of the probable agricultural activity of this group. Another northeastern push reached as far as southeastern Wisconsin.

Northern and northwestern expansion of Illinois Hopewell is known in eastern Iowa, northwestern Iowa, and the Minnesota-Wisconsin adjacent territory south of the mouth of the Minnesota River. In eastern Iowa there is ceramic evidence that the spread into that area took place during Middle Hopewell and that there was effective participation there in a series of cultural events leading to the gradual disappearance of Hopewell. The Trempealeau burial complex in southwestern Wisconsin is strongly reminiscent of the Illinois area, but most of the accompanying ceramic material does not belong to the Havana decorative incised and dentate styles. There is some indication that the most northern penetration comes about in relatively late Hopewellian times.

A further expansion of Illinois Hopewell is seen to the west across Missouri to the Kansas City area. There are a sufficient number of sites and enough variability within them to indicate that these areas were occupied for some time by resident groups participating in general Middle Woodland trends. The Renner site near Kansas City is clearly in the latter half of the Hopewellian complex, according to the ceramic features as well as other items. This is borne out by radiocarbon dating. South of St. Louis in western Illinois there are some sites along the Mississippi bottoms that have a strong element of Hopewellian styles in pottery, flint blades, and projectile points. In the tributary valleys, however, these are diluted and there is a much stronger flavor of Middle Woodland without the developed Hopewellian characteristics.

A significant area of Hopewell is in the lower Wabash Valley. This has a cast of its own that differentiates it from either Ohio or the other areas of Illinois. One of the most striking features is the presence in some quantity of early Swift Creek complicated stamp pottery at the Mann site in Posey County, where it is probably associated with cord-marked and Hopewell Zone Stamped pottery. Much of the Middle Woodland pottery in southwestern Indiana is clay tempered. This is the result of a spread of this type of temper along the Mississippi alluvial plain into the Ohio Valley. The type of temper is also fairly common along the Mississippi from Cairo to St. Louis.

The Hopewellian cultures occupied essentially the south-central part of the Northeast. To the north and northeast of them are a number of variants of Middle Woodland. The best-known one was originally called Point Peninsula in New York during the 1930's, but this has now been divided into three sequential temporal periods. The primary identifying material is a series of dentate stamped pottery types that are known from the Atlantic Coast across New York into southwestern Ontario, and around Lakes Huron and Superior into western Ontario, Alberta, and northern Minnesota, where such pottery is known as the Laurel complex. According to Canadian archeologists, the Laurel–Point Peninsula types are the first pottery to appear in the area along the north side of Lake Superior into Alberta. There is a remarkable similarity in the dentate stamp techniques and designs over this whole area, and it is a wise archeologist who can now tell where the Rainy River aspect of Minnesota-Manitoba fades out to the east and where Point Peninsula of New York–Ontario fades out to the west. This east-west cultural continuum represents another example of the effect of the Great Lakes on the transmission of cultural practices and ideas over a considerable area, which first became clearly recognizable in the Late Archaic. Recent work on Isle Royale has identified village occupations that were presumably there for the extraction of copper. Much of this copper eventually found its way into the hands of Hopewellian craftsmen. The Rainy River aspect of northern Minnesota and adjacent Manitoba and Ontario of *ca*. A.D. 1–500, in spite of burial mounds, dentate stamped pottery, and copper artifacts, shows little or no influence from the Hopewellian. The artifact and burial complex includes conical and perforated antler projectile points, beaver-teeth gravers, skulls with clay-filled sockets (part of a mask?), red ocher with skeletons, and stemmed points.

The Point Peninsula sequence (less Point Peninsula I) of Ontario–

New York has a congeries of pottery types and a welter of stations with an overlapping of artifact types and complexes known from Laurentian to Owasco. New York archeologists have had a tendency to interpret the appearance of the dentate stamp Point Peninsula series sometimes as the result of Hopewellian stimulus and at other times as the result of a movement out of Asia through the Canadian forests into Ontario. In this latter interpretation Point Peninsula becomes the migration of Algonkian Indians into the Northeast and is said to have been a stimulus to Hopewell development. An Asiatic connection for the pottery, not the Algonkian, has not yet been substantiated by American arctic finds but remains a reasonable hypothesis. The Algonkians have probably been in the Northeast since at least Laurentian times. There are relatively few mounds identified with Point Peninsula culture. The most interesting one is probably the Serpent Mound of Ontario, where charcoal associated with a partial cremation gave a radiocarbon date of A.D. 130 (M-850). The ceramic association begins with Point Peninsula II. Considerable attention was given to burial ceremonies, but there is less cremation and some tendency toward group burials of individuals who had been dead long enough to allow decomposition of the bodies. Burial goods of Point Peninsula, such as platform pipes, sharks' teeth, and pearl beads, reflect a temporal position within Middle Woodland with Hopewellian affinities. Other items of the culture, such as triangular projectiles of a number of forms, the obtuse-angle pipe of clay or stone, large combs, antler harpoons, and stone and bone gorgets, represent a more general northern Middle Woodland complex.

Point Peninsula II–IV pottery and other items of the complex are known not only in New England but also as far as New Brunswick and Nova Scotia. While some time lag may be recognized, one would expect a general contemporaneity with cultural events to the west. Throughout most of the area, either in a boreal forest or a mixed forest, the major food supply appears to be from hunting and fishing. Agriculture is not yet recognized or hardly even postulated for most sites of Point Peninsula affiliation. Initial agriculture may well, however, have begun in New York and southern New England in middle to late Point Peninsula.

LATE WOODLAND AND MISSISSIPPIAN CULTURES

If the Middle Woodland cultures of the Northeast are identified by various forms of cultural behavior associated directly or indirectly with the dominant Hopewellian culture, the Late Woodland complexes are identified both by the disappearance of Hopewellian traits and by the gradual development of different cultural forms. These gradual changes have been recognized over the whole area. A possible explanation for the decline of Hopewell may be climatic deterioration, which resulted

FIG. 4.—Some North American culture groups of about A.D. 1000

in a shortened and unreliable growing season (Griffin 1960*b*, 1961*a*). The majority of the resident cultural complexes from A.D. 400 or 500 to the historic period of A.D. 1600–1800 clearly show their development out of the preceding Middle Woodland; they vary from area to area according to the persistence of locally developed patterns, to the degree of importance of agriculture, and to the strength of influences from the developing Mississippian cultures of the Southeast. In the Ohio Valley and the southern part of its northern tributaries, and in the Mississippi Valley from Kansas City to Peoria, variants of the Mississippian cultures gradually become dominant from *ca.* A.D. 800 to the historic period.

In some areas, such as Illinois, it is clear, from both published and unpublished papers and excavations, that the culture products that identify Hopewellian gradually decline in quality and that the cultural intensity that produced excellent and distinctive art forms gradually fades into the production of drab and uninspired material. One of the changes is the abandonment of the construction of large, complex burial mounds in the valley floors adjacent to the village sites. Smaller mounds were placed on bluffs overlooking the streams. Another tendency is toward greater use of stone slabs in association with burials, as crypts or enclosures or as part of the mound construction. Another tendency is toward an increased amount of bundle and group-bundle burials and a decrease in cremation. These trends begin in late Hopewellian times. There is very little complex ceramic decoration, and the vessels are noticeably thinner. Most of the vessels have a simple jar form with a conoidal to rounded base. Their surfaces are plain or cord marked. The decoration is usually limited to modification of the lip by punching, crimping, and notching. There is a minor amount of incising and punctating on the outer rim. Projectile points become smaller in size and probably indicate a shift to the bow and arrow.

At a few sites a shift to a rectangular-house form is seen, but certainly the older circular or oval house is the dominant type during the early Late Woodland occupations of the entire area. The use of stone and bone gorgets continues, and pipes change from the platform style to the elbow form.

In the adjacent area of Iowa, Minnesota, Wisconsin, and Illinois the gradual shift out of Hopewell turns into a cultural complex known as Effigy Mound because of the large number of low mounds in the form of various birds, beasts, and even men. Long linear and conical mounds were also built. This area retained the custom of burial mounds up to the historic period, with both Algonkian and Siouan people participating. One of the earliest Late Woodland ceramic styles that develops out of late Hopewellian is known as Madison Cord-Impressed. Single-cord impressions were placed in parallel horizontal, or triangular, patterns on the outer rim. This style of decoration spreads from Lake Michigan to northeastern Nebraska and eastern South Dakota. There is a movement of people to the south carrying this complex into the area around Peoria, Illinois, where it merges with the local groups of the late Weaver focus.

In the northern half of Missouri, a Late Woodland complex known as the Boone focus develops out of the Hopewellian. It is connected on the east to such groups as Jersey Bluff and Raymond. Late Woodland representatives up the Missouri are known as Stearns Creek, the Missouri Bluff complex, Loeseke Creek, and Scalp Creek.

In the northern forest zone from Minnesota through the Great Lakes–St. Lawrence Valley and along the east as far as Washington, D.C., there is a series of interrelated ceramic complexes that have in common the use of a cord-wrapped element to apply decorative designs on the upper rim of conoidal and round-bottomed vessels. In Minnesota-Manitoba a series of local developments lead to the early historic northern Siouan tribes. Across Michigan and northeastern Wisconsin the minor but important complexes come into the historic period as the northern Central Algonkian groups. In the early part of Late Woodland, the northern border of Lake Superior seems to be abandoned by pottery-making peoples and is occupied during the latter half by probably Algonkian peoples, who are strongly influenced by ceramic styles more common to the west. Through time, there is an increasing complexity and variety of designs.

In lower Ontario and New York a series of gradual cultural changes lead from late Point Peninsula into Owasco and Owasco-like cultures. While there is gradual cultural change, there is no significant change in physical type. The size of villages increases, and some are palisaded. Most of the burials are flexed and are relatively poor in burial furniture. The normal hunting and combat weapon is the bow and arrow, tipped with triangular points. Corn and beans are increasingly important in the diet. Dwellings are of the wigwam type, and charred remains confirm the presence of mats, nets, and basketry. Some finds are highly suggestive of association with the bear cult. Flutes and rattles are other indications of ceremonial and social life.

The last major cultural development in the eastern United States is called Mississippian because its primary center was in the valley of the Mississippi River and along its major tributaries and in the Southeast. This predominantly agricultural complex was a marked cultural advance over earlier levels of development in the east. Its initial growth and expansion is at approximately A.D. 700–1000 in the area between St. Louis and Vicksburg. There is some evidence that the Mississippian development was stimulated by the introduction of concepts, ceremonial attitudes, and practices from Mexico. It was based on such improved agricultural procedures as the marked use of the flint hoe and probably of improved strains of corn, which resulted in large populations and a more sedentary societal organization. In certain favorable areas, such as the American Bottoms near St. Louis, this resulted in important cultural centers, which exerted a marked influence during the early part of Mississippian development.

The outstanding features of Mississippian centers were the earthen platform mounds upon which stood the main buildings of the community. These were council houses and "temples" and were the major political and ceremonial centers. The platform mounds were placed on the sides of plazas, which formed the nuclear centers for the important recurrent ceremonies or during times of unusual stress. The more important buildings, both family and community, were of wattle-and-daub construction and were usually rectangular in floor plan. In some centers burial was made in large cemeteries, but in many places burials were made in the floors of the houses, in refuse pits, or around the village. Some of the major Mississippian centers were walled by impressive log constructions which provide clear testimony to the growing importance of group aggression on a more intensive level than had been practiced earlier.

One of the most significant features of the Mississippian development was the considerable increase in village size to about 10–20 acres, and for the major centers to up to 100 acres, although it is difficult to assess the extent of the occupied area for any particular year. Another major feature was the pottery complex, which had a wide variety of specialized vessel forms for specific functions. Along with the other material-culture remains indicating marked cultural growth was the development over some hundreds of years of the Southeastern Ceremonial Complex. This is described in more detail in the chapter on the Southeast. The concepts and practices of the religious and magical activities were portrayed on pottery, engraved on shell, embossed and formed on copper, sculptured in stone, and reflected in burial practices and grave offerings. The individuals responsible for these ceremonies occupied a position of status in the society that was not achieved during Hopewellian times.

As a strongly agricultural society and with greater population density, the Mississippian culture was expansive and dominant. It expanded both by population movement, that is, migration, and by diffusion. Given time, it could well have dominated the entire agricultural area in the Northeast. One of the early areas of Mississippian development was in the American Bottoms from the mouth of the Illinois River to about the Jefferson Barracks bridge south of St. Louis. There are many sites on the alluvial flood plain on the east side of the Mississippi River. It had the largest concentration of platform mounds in the United States and was occupied from Late Woodland almost to the historic period. When

the University of Michigan was engaged in work in this area, we referred to the Late Woodland grit-tempered pottery as Canteen Cord-
Marked and Canteen Plain, named after a small creek that flows through
the Cahokia group. Other Late Woodland pottery, tempered with limestone or with clay, was given different names. In local areas there are
differing percentages of these, and some of the differences may reflect
temporal change. Certain areas had heavy or exclusive concentrations of
Late Woodland pottery, with little or no evidence of Mississippian
ceramic traits. One of these was the Pulcher site in the south end of the
American Bottoms, which also had four medium-sized mounds that had
been plowed. These may or may not have been platform mounds. In the
main area of the Cahokia site and on top of the bluffs to the east, there is
a considerable amount of Late Woodland pottery that may be either
Woodland developing into Mississippian forms or Woodland influenced
by Mississippian, or both. More recent field work by the Illinois State
Museum has fortunately uncovered a sequence of settlement patterns
and house forms to accompany the known ceramic sequence.

The Late Woodland occupation had small semisubterranean houses
without central fireplace and with no organized village plan (Warren
Wittry, personal communication). Corn was grown, and the population
was fairly large. The early Mississippian or "Old Village" occupation
continued to build a similar style of house, but the rectangular pattern
became more common. The early platform mounds, or inner portions
of some of the larger structures, were begun at this time and had an
orientation *ca.* 3 degrees east of true north. The Old Village pottery
is a distinctive Mississippian complex and has considerable importance
in the recognition of influences and actual migration from the major
area. One of the important factors in the primacy and importance of
Cahokia was the striking development of the flint hoe, both notched and
unnotched, which provided an excellent tool for working the flood-plain
soils. The corn was primarily the so-called "Eastern" type, which was
the dominant corn of the Mississippian complex.

From *ca.* A.D. 800 to 1100 the Old Village complex dominated the
American Bottoms and immediately adjacent areas. From Cahokia
there was a spread up the Illinois River to the Peoria area and north
into the upper Mississippi Valley, where it is known particularly from
the Aztalan site halfway between Madison and Milwaukee. The strong
influence of Old Village may be seen in the early Mill Creek levels in
northwest Iowa and adjacent South Dakota. Examples of Old Village–
style pottery, *ca.* A.D. 1100, have been found at the Straits of Mackinac,
near Memphis by about the same date, and as far south as the Lake
George site near Vicksburg. The northern and northwestern push of
Old Village culture and people into the upper Mississippi has been

interpreted as the movement of the ancestors of the Winnebago, Iowa, Oto, and Missouri tribes with a dominant agricultural economy during a relatively mild climatic period from *ca.* A.D. 700 to 1200 in the upper Mississippi Valley–Great Lakes and Northeast (Griffin 1960*b*). They moved north about as far as effective corn agriculture is possible at present and, for a time, seem to have maintained such an economy. While adequate stratigraphic and stylistic evidence is not at hand, it is possible, even probable, that the Oneota cultural complex of the late prehistoric period developed from this northern push of Old Village culture. In many cultural features Oneota is a regression, and this has been interpreted as a reflection of less favorable agricultural conditions from A.D. 1200 to A.D. 1700, which forced a shift to more dependence on hunting and on such local plants as wild rice. The Oneota culture comes into the early historic period as the Iowa, Missouri, Oto, and Winnebago tribes. A similar interpretation of culture change is possible in northwest Iowa, where there has been observed a gradual shift from an emphasis on agriculture in the lower levels of Mill Creek sites to an increasing reliance on bison as a source of food.

In Minnesota and southern Manitoba the resident Siouan groups continue as Late Woodland cultures into the historic period, as do the Menominee-Ottawa-Chippewa of the Superior and northern Lake Michigan and Huron basins. Following the spread of Laurel–Point Peninsula pottery north of Lake Superior, there is an absence of pottery and other evidence of occupation during the early part of the Late Woodland period. There is, however, a resurgence of ceramic-making peoples so that, by *ca.* A.D. 1100–1400, pottery of a Late Woodland Blackduck style is distributed along the north shore of Superior as far as the Pic River. At the mouth of Michipicoten River a Late Woodland pottery underlies late prehistoric and historic Huron-Petun material.

Along the Ohio River from its mouth to about Louisville and up the tributary streams, there are many Mississippian sites. The best known of these are Kincaid in southern Illinois (Cole *et al.* 1951) and Angel, near Evansville, Indiana (Black 1944). Both these are a part of the Tennessee-Cumberland varieties of Mississippian and, so to speak, face south. South of St. Louis, along both sides of the river, the Mississippian sites are closely connected to western Kentucky and southeastern Missouri. The historic tribal affiliations of these complexes are not known.

The early Late Woodland cultures of central Illinois are submerged by the Spoon River Late Mississippian complex. This complex is very similar to the Trappist phase at Cahokia, and there is some evidence indicating that the early historic Illini bands, such as the Peoria, Cahokia, and Tamaroa, are responsible for these sites. These are the most northern of the predominantly agricultural Mississippian cultures. In

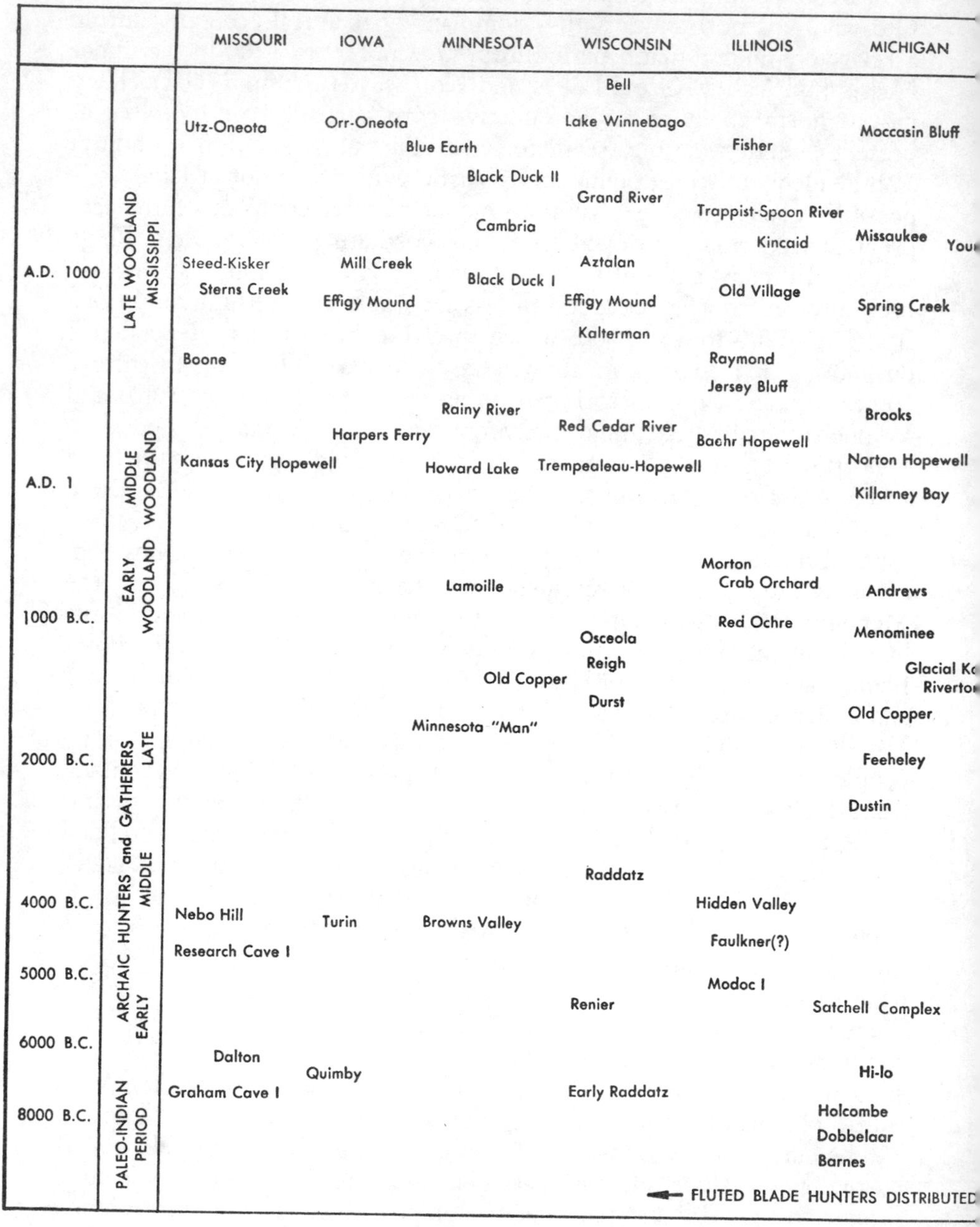

		MISSOURI	IOWA	MINNESOTA	WISCONSIN	ILLINOIS	MICHIGAN
					Bell		
	LATE WOODLAND MISSISSIPPI	Utz-Oneota	Orr-Oneota		Lake Winnebago		Moccasin Bluff
				Blue Earth		Fisher	
				Black Duck II			
					Grand River		
				Cambria		Trappist-Spoon River	
A.D. 1000						Kincaid	Missaukee You
		Steed-Kisker	Mill Creek		Aztalan		
		Sterns Creek		Black Duck I		Old Village	
			Effigy Mound		Effigy Mound		Spring Creek
					Kalterman		
		Boone				Raymond	
						Jersey Bluff	
				Rainy River			Brooks
	MIDDLE WOODLAND		Harpers Ferry		Red Cedar River	Bachr Hopewell	Norton Hopewell
A.D. 1		Kansas City Hopewell		Howard Lake	Trempealeau-Hopewell		
							Killarney Bay
						Morton	
	EARLY WOODLAND			Lamoille		Crab Orchard	Andrews
1000 B.C.						Red Ochre	Menominee
					Osceola		
					Reigh		Glacial K. Riverto
				Old Copper	Durst		Old Copper
	LATE			Minnesota "Man"			
2000 B.C.							Feeheley
							Dustin
					Raddatz		
4000 B.C.	MIDDLE	Nebo Hill	Turin	Browns Valley		Hidden Valley	
		Research Cave I				Faulkner(?)	
5000 B.C.	EARLY					Modoc I	
					Renier		Satchell Complex
6000 B.C.		Dalton					Hi-lo
	PALEO-INDIAN PERIOD	Graham Cave I	Quimby		Early Raddatz		
8000 B.C.							Holcombe
							Dobbelaar
							Barnes

◄── FLUTED BLADE HUNTERS DISTRIBUTED

FIG. 5.—Culture sequence and chronology

INDIANA	WEST VIRGINIA OHIO	ONTARIO	PENNSYLVANIA NEW YORK	NEW ENGLAND	NEW JERSEY	
	Madisonville Whittlesey	Pic River Huron-Iroquois	New York Iroquois	Clarks Pond		
Angel		Uren	Monongahela	Titicut	Rosenkrans Ferry	
	Fort Ancient		Owasco			
Albee		Pic River I	Clemsons Island	Oaklawn		1000 A.D.
Yankeetown	Newtown		Point Peninsula III			
La Motte				North Beach		
	Intrusive Mound Culture	Le Vesconte		Locust Spring	Abbott Farm	
Mann Late Adena	Hopewell	Serpent Mound	Point Peninsula II			A.D. 1
Petersen			Meadowood (Point Peninsula I)		Skunk Run	1000 B.C.
		Picton	Transitional	Late Boreal	Red Valley	
		Old Copper	Late Laurentian		Koens-Crispin	
Du Bois		Malcolm I	Lamoka	Early "Boreal"		2000 B.C.
	Raisch-Smith	Early Laurentian		Boylston Wapanucket I		
	Rohr I		Bare Island	Kelley(?)		4000 B.C.
	Sawmill					5000 B.C.
	McConnell					6000 B.C.
		Brohm				
		Sheguindah I George Lake	Reagan	Twin Rivers Bull Brook		8000 B.C.

OVER MOST OF THIS AREA ➝

for the Northeast Woodland Area

the northern Illinois Valley, the Kaskaskia, an Illini band, may be identified with the Fisher focus of about A.D. 1200 and with a number of
later archeological complexes.

The major archeological complex in the central Ohio Valley of the
Late period is the Fort Ancient culture, which extends from West
Virginia to southeastern Indiana and from northern Kentucky to central
Ohio (Griffin 1943). It is produced by a gradual cultural shift as the
Late Woodland cultures became increasingly agricultural and by strong
Mississippian influences moving up the Ohio, and also from eastern
Tennessee, perhaps by way of the Kanawha and Big Sandy. By A.D.
1400–1650 Fort Ancient was a dominantly agricultural and Missis-
sippian culture.

In the upper Ohio and Monongahela drainage, the Monongahela
Woodland culture is the last of the prehistoric cultures (Mayer-Oakes
1955). It had a strong agricultural base. While participating to a
minor degree in cultural developments of the Mississippian period,
they had not acquired the wattle-and-daub rectangular house or the
platform mound and plaza, nor did they participate in the Southeastern
Ceremonial Complex. The villages were relatively small and were surrounded by a circular or oval wooden palisade. Their houses were
wigwam type, about 20 feet in diameter. They had a rather close association with Fort Ancient people to the west, Iroquois to the north,
and down the Potomac to the Virginia coastal Algonquin groups.

The emphasis on agriculture that aided the growth of the Owascoid
cultures in the lower Great Lakes and New York areas continued, as
Owasco and its relatives developed into varieties of prehistoric Iroquoian and other Late Woodland archeological complexes. The distinctive ceramic and pipe styles of Iroquois, and archeological remains
of the long house, were known by *ca.* A.D. 1200. Indications of regional
"tribal" groupings can be recognized. Historical records show that some
Iroquois groups moved their main village about every ten years because
of soil and firewood depletion, and archeological work in New York
tends to substantiate this behavior for late prehistoric times. Some of
the Iroquoian sites have close to a hundred "houses," and a population
estimate of close to one thousand is reasonable for some of the villages.
Some population displacement took place, for at the time of Cartier, in
1534–40, Iroquoian groups, related to Mohawk-Onondaga, were in the
Montreal region and the lower St. Lawrence but had shifted to east-
central New York by *ca.* A.D. 1600. The Susquehannock also seem to
have gone down the river that bears their name not long before the
arrival of the early colonists. Iroquoian cultural development from archeological evidence does not seem to be unique in the Northeast or as
superior as the evaluation by ethnologists has suggested. It did not move

into the Northeast as a complex; it developed there. Adjacent Algonquin groups to the south and southeast were on the same general cultural level, but their cultural life had suffered much more from European contact than had that of the Iroquois.

As a result of some population displacement in Virginia and the Carolinas, owing to the expansion of Mississippian groups, some prehistoric cultures of this area moved north into southern New Jersey. The Middle Woodland groups of New Jersey and southern New England had gradually shifted into the late prehistoric complexes, some of which can be attributed to early historic tribes. Ceramic styles associated with Iroquoian tend to dominate much of the Ontario–New England coastal area as the historic period is reached. It is becoming clear that some part of "Iroquoian" pottery was not made by Iroquoian-speaking peoples.

SUMMARY

The interpretation presented above of some of the prehistoric cultures and events of the Northeast Woodlands has had a number of major themes. The earliest occupants were Fluted Blade Hunters, who entered and spread through the area from about 10,000 to 8000 B.C. At that time Plymouth Rock was not on the shore, for sea level was substantially lower. These early hunters were the first to explore and discover the area and to make the first human use of animal, vegetable, and mineral resources.

For descriptive and classificatory reasons, the long period of time between 8000 and 1500 B.C. is called the Archaic when the way of life of the people was gradually changing from a primarily, but not exclusively, hunting economy to a hunting-gathering-fishing way of life. This shift in emphasis was not caused by any major movement of new populations into the area but was one of slow adaptation and development along with the diffusion of techniques and ideas from adjacent areas. The most important of these areas was the Southeast, which possessed a more equitable climate, a wide variety of food resources, and throughout the Archaic probably had a larger population than was present in the Northeast. The greatest population density in the Archaic, as well as later, was in the southern part of the Northeast.

During middle to late Archaic times the effect of regional environments was reflected in cultural groupings located around the Great Lakes–upper St. Lawrence Basin, the southern New England and Middle Atlantic coastal area and drainage, the Ohio Valley, and the upper Mississippi Valley. Within each of these there were local areas with a strong tendency to preserve distinctive developmental traditions. But there were no major physiographic or climatic barriers in the Northeast that prevented the spread and exchange of significant technological advances, and no area, except the spruce-fir forest zone, lagged far behind.

The most important cultural introduction into the Northeast was the concept and practice of agriculture. Its source was, of course, the Mexican area, but the route, or routes, and the time of introduction are not known. This new source of food was gradually adopted and, along with the introduction or development of pottery, mound burial, increasing status differentiation, production of specialized ceremonial items, and increase of trade or exchange, resulted in a wide variety of local complexes that are called Woodland. While there are many unanswered questions about these increments, it can be confidently stated that they did not arrive from a single source and direction. Woodland culture did not move into the Northeast from Asia; it is a local growth and has no single center from which it spread. It is, instead, an intricate fabric of long-established Archaic activities, with an overlay of new characteristics. The relatively rapid cultural growth and dissemination during Early and Middle Woodland has as its most spectacular product the Hopewellian cultural explosion. There are a number of local expressions of Hopewell that represent the influences of areal traditions and differing external contacts. While there is certainly some archeological artificiality in regarding Hopewell as a "culture," such a concept has sufficient validity for its use. It was the common possession of a large number of cultural groups in the Northeast Woodlands, and archeologists recognize it as a distinctive way of life, which had not been known before and which was destined gradually to disappear. One possible influence that resulted in the cultural deterioration from Hopewell to the earliest of the Late Woodland units is, perhaps, a relatively minor climatic shift from about A.D. 200 to A.D. 700, which shortened the growing season and affected the stability of the agricultural food supply.

After A.D. 800 the dominant trend in the Northeast was the increase in the importance of agriculture and the development and spread of the Mississippian cultural adaptation. This was a period of marked population increase throughout the area, in terms of both the size of individual villages and the number of contemporary villages. It was the period of the highest cultural development in the Northeast.

BIBLIOGRAPHY

BLACK, GLENN A.
    1944   "Angel Site, Vanderburgh County, Indiana: An Introduction." Pp. 447–521 in "Prehist. Res. Ser.," Vol. 2. Indianapolis.
BYERS, DOUGLAS S.
    1959   "The Eastern Archaic: Some Problems and Hypotheses." *Amer. Antiquity*, 24:233–56.

COLE, FAY-COOPER, ROBERT BELL, JOHN BENNETT, JOSEPH CALDWELL, NORMAN EMERSON, RICHARD MACNEISH, KENNETH ORR, and ROGER WILLIS
1951 *Kincaid, a Prehistoric Illinois Metropolis.* Chicago: University of Chicago Press.

CRANE, H. R.
1956 "University of Michigan Radiocarbon Dates I." *Science,* 124:664–72.

CRANE, H. R., and JAMES B. GRIFFIN
1959 *University of Michigan Radiocarbon Dates IV. Amer. Jour. Sci.,* Radiocarbon Suppl. I.

DRAGOO, DON W.
1959 "Archaic Hunters of the Upper Ohio Valley." *Carnegie Mus. Ann.,* 35:139–246. ("Anthrop. Ser.," No. 3.) Pittsburgh.

FOWLER, MELVIN L.
1959 *Summary Report of Modoc Rock Shelter.* (Ill. State Mus. Invest. Rpt. 8.) Springfield.

GRIFFIN, JAMES B.
1943 *The Fort Ancient Aspect: Its Cultural and Chronological Position in Mississippi Valley Archaeology.* Ann Arbor: University of Michigan Press.
1958 *The Chronological Position of the Hopewellian Culture in the Eastern United States.* (Univ. Mich. Anthrop. Mus., "Anthrop. Paps.," No. 12.) Ann Arbor.
1960a "Some Prehistoric Connections between Siberia and America." *Science,* 131:801–12.
1960b "Climatic Change: A Contributory Cause of the Growth and Decline of Northern Hopewellian Culture." *Wis. Archeologist,* 41:21–33. Milwaukee.
1960c "A Hypothesis for the Prehistory of the Winnebago." Pp. 809–65 in STANLEY DIAMOND (ed.), *Culture in History: Essays in Honor of Paul Radin.* New York: Columbia University Press.
1961a "Some Correlations of Climatic and Cultural Change in Eastern North American Prehistory." *N.Y. Acad. Sci. Ann.,* 95:710–17.
1961b *Lake Superior Copper and the Indians: Miscellaneous Studies of Great Lakes Prehistory.* (Univ. Mich. Anthrop. Mus., "Anthrop. Paps.," No. 17.) Ann Arbor.

JENNINGS, JESSE D.
1955 *The Archaeology of the Plains: An Assessment.* Salt Lake City: University of Utah Department of Anthropology and the National Park Service.

JOHNSON, FREDERICK (ed.)
1949 *The Boylston Street Fishweir. II. A Study of the Geology, Palaeobotany, and Biology of a Site on Stuart Street in the Back Bay District of Boston, Massachusetts.* ("Robert S. Peabody Foundation Paps.," Vol. 4, No. 1.) Andover, Mass.

JOHNSON, FREDERICK et al.
1942 *The Boylston Street Fishweir.* ("Robert S. Peabody Foundation Paps.," Vol. 2.) Andover, Mass.

LIBBY, WILLARD F.
  1955   *Radiocarbon Dating*. 2d ed. Chicago: University of Chicago Press.
LOGAN, WILFRED D.
  1952   *Graham Cave, an Archaic Site in Montgomery County, Missouri*. (Mo. Arch. Soc. Mem. 2.) Columbia.
MACNEISH, RICHARD S.
  1958   *An Introduction to the Archaeology of Southeast Manitoba*. (Nat. Mus. Canada Bull. 157, "Anthrop. Ser.," No. 44.) Ottawa.
MASON, RONALD J., and CAROL IRWIN
  1960   "An Eden-Scottsbluff Burial in Northeastern Wisconsin." *Amer. Antiquity*, 26:43–57.
MAYER-OAKES, WILLIAM J.
  1955   "Prehistory of the Upper Ohio Valley." *Carnegie Mus. Ann.*, Vol. 34. ("Anthrop. Ser.," No. 2.) Pittsburgh.
RITCHIE, WILLIAM A.
  1932   "The Lamoka Lake Site, the Type Station of the Archaic Algonkin Period in New York." *N.Y. State Arch. Assoc. Res. & Trans.*, Vol. 7, No. 4. Rochester.
  1955   *Recent Discoveries Suggesting an Early Woodland Burial Cult in the Northeast*. (N.Y. State Mus. & Sci. Serv. Circ. 40.) Albany.
  1958   *An Introduction to Hudson Valley Prehistory*. (N.Y. State Mus. & Sci. Serv. Bull. 367.) Albany.
RITCHIE, WILLIAM A., and DON W. DRAGOO
  1960   *The Eastern Dispersal of Adena*. (N.Y. State Mus. & Sci. Serv. Bull. 379.) Albany.
RITZENTHALER, ROBERT E., and GEORGE I. QUIMBY
  1962   "The Red Ocher Culture of the Upper Great Lakes and Adjacent Areas." *Fieldiana: Anthropology*, 36:243–75. Chicago Natural History Museum, Chicago.
ROBBINS, MAURICE
  1959   *Wapanucket No. 6: An Archaic Village in Middleboro, Massachusetts*. (Cohannet Chap., Mass. Arch. Soc., Inc.) Middleboro.
WISSLER, CLARK
  1922   *The American Indian: An Introduction to the Anthropology of the New World*. New York: Oxford University Press.
WITTRY, WARREN W.
  1959   "The Raddatz Rockshelter, Sk 5, Wisconsin." *Wis. Archeologist*, 40:33–39. Milwaukee.

WILLIAM H. SEARS

The Southeastern United States

THE PRESENT STATES of Georgia, Alabama, Florida, Mississippi, Louisiana, and Tennessee form a neat unit, geographically, ecologically, and culturally, today and in the geologically recent past. These contemporary political units define the core of a prehistoric Southeastern culture area very well, but definition of the boundaries past the borders of these states necessitates use of a series of compromises, depending on culture history and our knowledge of it. In this discussion the borders of the Southeast will be allowed to waver back and forth, depending on our knowledge of definable prehistoric cultures.

The prehistory of the Southeast to be outlined and summarized here will utilize available knowledge for the erection of a space-time framework and for details concerning culture fact and change. However, I must here omit the fine details of description and analysis that have provided our information and proceed at a relatively abstract level. The outline and summary is intended to provide descriptions of particularly well-known and especially significant prehistoric cultures and to suggest, in terms of historical process, some of the major events of Southeastern prehistory.

THE ARCHAIC

The earliest occupation of the Southeast has been discussed by Krieger. I cannot here say a great deal about Krieger's Protoarchaic or "transitional" horizons or cultures that follow, and presumably develop from, the earliest cultures. We have little more for these early periods than specimens and collections that, on typological grounds, appear to

WILLIAM H. SEARS, curator of the Florida State Museum, University of Florida, Gainesville, and professor of anthropology, University of Florida, received his doctorate from the University of Michigan. His major field of interest has been the archeology of the southeastern United States. He is most noted for his work in excavating and interpreting the Kolomoki mounds in southern Georgia. He has held editorial and other posts in various professional societies and institutions.

259

fit into the "transitional" stage. There are also radiocarbon dates suggesting that these collections may actually belong to the early periods.

We are on firmer ground, around 5000 or 6000 B.C., with the Archaic horizon or culture type. Archaic culture, throughout the Southeast, has as diagnostic artifacts a series of long, heavy projectile points with stems, or less often, side notches. Bone hooks and stone weights for throwing sticks demonstrate that the points were used on short spears propelled with the growing stick. These and a series of other artifacts adapted to a hunting-gathering economy in essentially similar ecological situations, such as bone fishhooks, stone net-sinkers, grooved stone axes, and milling stones, are of importance in most local culture variants. Other flint artifacts are common on most Archaic sites but are not rigidly stylized. Heavy cutting tools are frequent, as are flakes modified in various ways to serve various scraping and cutting functions.

Archaic artifacts are found on sites of two kinds, primarily, indicative of two quite different adaptations to the environment. First, and best known, are the shell mounds, often very large. Quite clearly, the occupants of these sites had economies based on shellfish as the primary food source, and they were, as a result, sedentary. Permanent structures were not built, although light shelters or windbreaks appear to have been made. Second, in every part of the Southeast there are also dirt middens, yielding the same artifact complexes as do the shell middens. Certainly these sites were occupied by peoples deriving their food from the game animals of the forest, especially the deer, and from wild vegetable products. These two types of sites may reflect seasonal occupation, with the shell middens occupied during some part of the year and the forest sites during the other part. Yet some of the inland sites are of such size as to imply quite permanent occupancy.

Still a third kind of site is Poverty Point, a specialization that stands alone in the Southeast. Huge earthworks, and large populations, are simply not normal; nor can they be explained adequately until we know something about the economy at Poverty Point.

There are in this early period at least two major Southeastern styles of projectile points. Heavy, broad points dominate assemblages from the coastal plain, as far to the northeast as New Jersey. In the mountain areas, particularly the Tennessee River drainage, a slender type with an expanded stem is most frequent. Since culture history follows rather different courses in the two areas from this time on, the distinction appears to have some significance.

There are, of course, individual cultures with somewhat different artifact assemblages within each of these two broad style traditions. But with broad or narrow points, and with or without ground-stone tools, cultures throughout the Southeast from 5000 or 6000 B.C. until a few centuries before the birth of Christ had economies based on shell-fish and other gathering and on hunting. The characteristic weapon was a short spear with a large, rather heavy point, propelled by an atlatl. It is possible to trace continuities from Archaic cultures through successive, apparently in-place, developments in many of the subregions. Thus it appears quite possible that these early Southeasterners were the actual ancestors of most, but not all, later Southeastern cultures.

The end of the Archaic is herein marked, quite arbitrarily and by definition, by the advent of pottery. The kind of pottery varies, and the date of introduction varies through some fifteen hundred years. In some instances, no other changes in the cultures have been demonstrated; in others, usually the later cases, major culture changes coincide with the appearance of pottery.

The earliest pottery, dating about 2000 B.C., appeared nearly simultaneously in the shell-mound communities of the St. Johns River in Florida, the Savannah River and adjacent coast line in Georgia and South Carolina, and the Tennessee River. Vessel shapes and tempering fibers differed, but the idea was the same. Some hundreds of years later each of these cultures developed a different style of pottery decoration. Bands or rows of linear punctation were used on the Savannah, stamping of one kind or another on the Tennessee, and incising in rather elaborate patterns on the St. Johns.

During the thousand years or more of use of fiber-tempered pottery in these three rather small areas, cultures elsewhere, even quite near by, got along perfectly well without pottery. Possibly excepting certain Appalachian Mountain cultures, most Indians of the Southeast did not begin to make pottery until a few centuries before the birth of Christ. Then new techniques, vessel forms, and decorative styles appear, some of them growing out of fiber-tempered styles. The new varieties spread rapidly throughout the Southeast, either as the first pottery used or as replacements for the fiber-tempered pottery.

Thus, through a limited local development in the lower Savannah River area, the punctated fiber-tempered pottery developed into Deptford pottery, made in the form of small vessels, often with four legs, with check-stamped decoration. To the west, at the mouth of the Mississippi River, vessels of the same sizes and shapes were made in Tchefuncte pottery (the first pottery in the area) but derived their decoration both from the fiber-tempered styles and from contemporary midwestern styles. In some parts of the Tennessee area, a completely different pottery, decorated with heavy fabric or mat marking, either followed fiber tempering in time or was the first pottery made there.

Actually, we know next to nothing about most of the cultures of this period, a few centuries B.C., when distinctive pottery styles appeared all over the Southeast. I suspect that all this activity in pot-making, initiating traditions that in many instances continued on to the historic period, was the result of the pressure of ideas from the North and from Mesoamerica, many of them connected with religion and economy. As these cultures develop more specific characteristics, we can say more about them.

EARLY BURIAL MOUNDS

Shortly after the appearance of the new ceramic traditions, burial mounds began to be built in southeastern United States. All appear to be the product of ideas (a burial cult, a religion, or an economic system intertwined with these) that originated in the Hopewellian cultures of Illinois and Ohio. This is evident in the mounds themselves. There is evidence, as well, for contact among most Southeastern cultures and between many of them and midwestern Hopewell. Not only sacred or magical objects, such as pan pipes, platform smoking pipes, and copper ear spools, but also pottery vessels were traded from north to south and from east to west. Correlated with this activity was a tremendous increase in Southeastern population. Sites were larger and more abundant. Some of the cultures spread out and replaced others with great rapidity. This is the period, from a few centuries B.C. to a few centuries A.D., of the appearance of most Southeastern cultural traditions. Their ceramic styles, their economic, political, and religious systems, and their physical boundaries were all reasonably well established in this early period and remained relatively constant for a thousand to fifteen hundred years. For the next thousand years, particularly, the pattern in the Southeast was one of slowly shifting boundaries, continual slow shifts in ceramic styles, and, presumably, an accompanying slow shift in most aspects of culture. But, except in a very late period, there was modification, not replacement.

An outline of some of the major cultural traditions in this early Burial Mound period follows. Inevitably, I must stress pottery traditions, since this is all we have for most cultures, and they will continue to define culture types, changes, and areas.

Among the more interesting and important developments in Southeastern prehistory was the coeval but independent development of the Gulf and South Appalachian ceramic traditions and the eventual merging of these two prolific and attractive styles into the Weeden Island pottery complex.

The development of the Gulf ceramic and cultural tradition begins, for our purposes, with Tchefuncte, a culture found in the small area of the Mississippi Delta. Tchefuncte economy was based on shellfish, and the culture appears to have been much like that of the preceding, if little-known, Archaic. There are not a great many sites, and they are relatively small. Ceremonial structures were missing, possibly excepting one mound group. The atlatl and the stemmed stone point attest to Archaic-style hunting. Bone points are rather common, perhaps because of accidents of preservation, and there are a few Florida-like conch-shell tools. But, except for the new pottery, Tchefuncte was essentially another shellfish-gathering Archaic culture. The pottery, with the same four-footed-jar form as the contemporary Deptford, drew for its decoration on all the fiber-tempered styles, and on midwestern Hopewell for the rather common rocker stamping. All the fiber-tempered sources for Tchefuncte pottery decoration had gone out of existence before Tchefuncte appeared, and the mechanism for the spread of these styles into Tchefuncte is not understood at all. Hopewell, however, which provided the rocker stamping, is in a mid-to-late stage of development in the Midwest, and continues influential for some time.

While Tchefuncte appears full blown, with the steps in the development of its ceramic complex missing, a more gradual development took place five hundred miles to the east, around the mouth of the Savannah River. The Deptford pottery complex, with check- and simple-stamped decoration on the four-footed jars, developed gradually from the fiber-tempered ware. Owing largely to lack of publication, we know next to nothing about Deptford except for its pottery and some aspects of its ceremonialism. Most Deptford sites are shell middens, and projectile points appear to be for atlatl darts, once more indicating a hunting-and-gathering economy. There are inland Deptford sites in southern Georgia, which suggests that agriculture may have been of some significance in the culture.

Tchefuncte did not spread widely, but Deptford did. No sooner was the ceramic style developed and stabilized than the culture, or the ceramic style, spread, in just a few centuries, all the way west to Pensacola, inland to the middle of Georgia, and across the northern part of peninsular Florida. In most places in this area our interpretively inadequate test-pitting does demonstrate that Deptford pottery was the first pottery made.

Now, Tchefuncte shows little evidence of contact with the midwestern Hopewellian centers. The rocker stamping is perhaps the only reasonably certain evidence of such contact, although I think more may appear when some Tchefuncte burial mounds are located and excavated. There were, however, at least four Deptford burial mounds, one of them at a major ceremonial center, with other structures, on the lower Chattahoochee River. These large burial mounds were all of the type that was used over some centuries, with burials and artifacts added at intervals. They contained such classic Hopewellian artifacts as pan pipes,

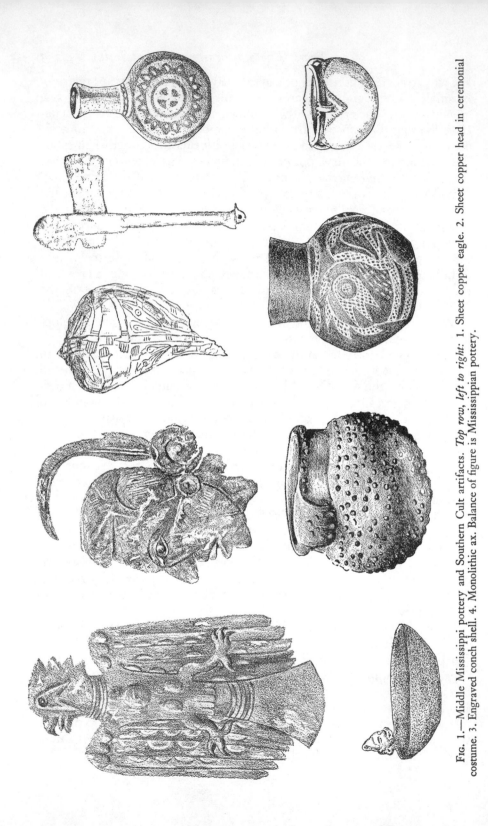

FIG. 1.—Middle Mississippi pottery and Southern Cult artifacts. *Top row, left to right:* 1. Sheet copper head in ceremonial costume. 3. Engraved conch shell. 4. Monolithic ax. Balance of figure is Mississippian pottery.

platform pipes, and copper ear spools, along with quantities of pottery, which was usually foreign or which was made in special, unique shapes or decorative styles. Examples are negative-painted vessels, a specimen in the shape of a doughnut with four spouts, a copy of a Tchefuncte vessel, and an import from northern Georgia. In the Midwest at the same time, we find Gulf Coast conch shells and Deptford pots. Quite certainly, then, some part of the Hopewellian culture—whatever religious system is manifested by pan pipes, platform pipes, bi-cymbal copper ear spools, and burial-mound interment for some part of the population—spread from Ohio and Illinois to the Gulf Coast. The coast, of course, was the source of Hopewellian conch shells. Since this evidence for intensive two-way contact on an esoteric level is coincident with the tremendous spread of Deptford, and just prior to the great spread of the cultures that developed from Tchefuncte, I think that a socioeconomic system, more efficient in exploitation of southeastern resources than anything that had existed previously, came south with the religious ideas as part of a total system. Certainly, from this time on, there were trade relationships as well as participation in some common elements of religion among most southeastern and midwestern cultures.

To continue with the Gulf Coastal Plain, our two major ceramic traditions, the Lower Mississippi Valley (represented at this early time by Tchefuncte) and the South Appalachian (with Deptford as its representative) continued their separate ways for some time. Although a merger took place shortly, there were always, from this point on to the historic period, some cultures that continued these traditions—the South Appalachian stamped ware and the Lower Valley, soon Gulf, tradition of incised, zone-decorated, and painted pottery.

The Tchefuncte culture developed into Marksville. Pottery acquired such distinctively midwestern Hopewellian features as crosshatched cambered rims and bird designs executed in an alternate-area technique. The culture center, however, moved from the coast to the mouth of the Red River. There are, if anything, fewer Marksville than Tchefuncte sites; but one of these, the Marksville site itself, is a great ceremonial center in the Hopewellian tradition, with large burial mounds and an encircling earthen embankment. Here, as in the Deptford mounds, such distinctly Hopewellian ceremonial artifacts as copper ear spools and platform pipes were interred with the dead. The size of the ceremonial center alone indicates an economic change, and we may presume that the move to better agricultural lands to the north is related to a greater emphasis upon agriculture.

A period of rapid development, centered in the Mississippi Valley around the mouth of the Red River, transformed Marksville into the

Troyville period and culture. Again, insofar as daily life is concerned, we can only make inferences. The pottery is well known and abundant. It was a development from Marksville pottery, changed by simplification of zoned rocker-stamped decoration and by diversification of incised designs. Vessel feet were no longer made; flat bases, which became a hallmark of Gulf Coastal Plain pottery, appeared instead. There were many more communities and many large ones; both facts indicate a stronger, more satisfactory economy than had previously existed. Some larger sites, still scattered around the mouth of the Red River, were ceremonial centers, and sometime in the period the truncated earthen pyramids or temple mounds began to be built.

It is quite clear that the Troyville culture had a firm, substantial economic base and a social and religious structure with Hopewellian foundations, apparently modified by new ideas represented by the temple mounds. This culture spread widely, far past the modest limits of its earlier Tchefuncte and Marksville stages. Troyville pottery, with variations and additions, is found at many sites from the Mississippi Delta to the Yazoo Basin and east across the Mississippi to the Tombigbee and Mobile rivers.

It appears from this that the Hopewellian influence, which I suggested had spurred the great spread of Deptford, did not achieve full effectiveness in the Mississippi Basin, since Troyville shows much contact with Early Swift Creek culture, which is a development out of Deptford. But, when the potentials of the Hopewellian system were realized, probably through Deptford rather than directly from the Midwest, the effect on Lower Valley culture was great.

Development continued in the South Appalachian culture area of southern Georgia, northwestern Florida, and southern Alabama. The ceramic style here featured elaborately carved, complicated-stamped designs, replacing the simple Deptford style. With the introduction of this new Swift Creek style of decoration, burial mounds became somewhat more common, although smaller on the whole. There appears to have been a major center in south Georgia, the Mandeville site on the Chattahoochee River. It was used through the Deptford–Early Swift Creek development, as is true of most Early Swift Creek sites. A platform mound is reported. Unfortunately, while we know of the existence of burial mounds, lack of excavation and publication prevents statements about any aspect of Early Swift Creek culture except the pottery.

The burial mounds in this period (all on the Florida northwest coast except for the Mandeville site) contained very few artifacts indicative of contact with the Midwest. The important artifacts were the same Early Swift Creek vessels found in sherd form in the middens and a few pieces that were Troyville or copies of Troyville vessels. Some secularization of ceremonialism seems apparent, coincident with a greater reliance on local resources. Ties with the Midwest weakened as relationships across the Gulf Coastal Plain became stronger. We can see here the emergence of a new social and religious tradition, exemplified in the burial mounds. Its sources were in Hopewell, but by this Troyville–Early Swift Creek period it was on its own, drawing on indigenous resources. The Gulf tradition, ceramic and cultural, dates from this time.

The area around Mobile Bay, particularly sites of the Porter complex, is critical in the study of the emergence of the Gulf tradition. These small sites, from well up on the Tombigbee to the island and sandbars at the mouth of Mobile Bay, contain a ceramic complex that is a thorough mixture of Early Troyville and Early Swift Creek. At least one unexcavated burial mound is known.

Starting with or just before the end of the manufacture of fiber-tempered pottery, fabric-marked pottery began to be made in the highland areas of the Southeast. Some of the sites are shell mounds; others appear to represent economies based on nuts or acorns. Fabric-marked pottery is replaced during the burial mound period by a variety of other pottery styles, some of them associated with burial mounds. Examples are check stamping, much like Deptford; complicated stamping, allied to Swift Creek; cord marking; and brushing. In northern Alabama and adjacent areas, the Copena burial-mound complex is associated with these post-fabric-marked ceramic complexes. Copena copper artifacts, such as ear spools, are distinctly Hopewellian, and characteristic large stone Copena effigy and elbow pipes have been found in classic Hopewellian burial mounds.

In northern Mississippi, and down the Tombigbee River for a hundred miles, a culture called Miller I is characterized by fabric-marked pottery. Except that they probably had houses, little else is known of this culture. We do know that a ceramic development took place, in which cord marking replaced fabric marking, and that the vessel forms and manufacturing techniques changed. By the end of the period, the Miller complex can be seen as the immediate source of the cord-marked pottery so common in some Troyville sites, once again documenting the interconnectedness of Southeastern culture in all its developing varieties. This point is further demonstrated by finds of South Appalachian and Troyville sherds on Miller sites. Burial mounds are particularly common on the more southern sites, with clusters of as many as seventy on a single lower Tombigbee site. Thus far, none of them has been properly excavated, but their presence, with that of the trade sherds, makes rather obvious the impact of such cultures as Deptford, Hopewell, and Troyville on these mountain cultures. Once the differentiation of

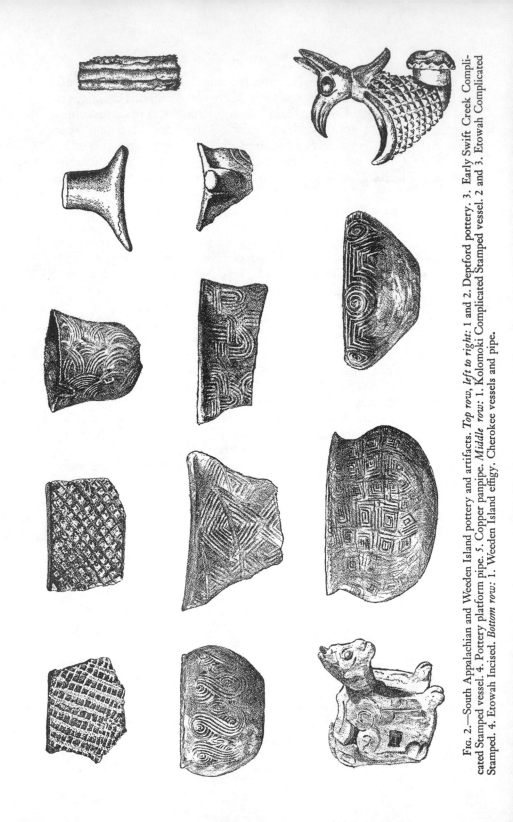

FIG. 2.—South Appalachian and Weeden Island pottery and artifacts. *Top row, left to right:* 1 and 2. Deptford pottery. 3. Early Swift Creek Complicated Stamped vessel. 4. Pottery platform pipe. 5. Copper panpipe. *Middle row:* 1. Kolomoki Complicated Stamped vessel. 2 and 3. Etowah Complicated Stamped. 4. Etowah Incised. *Bottom row:* 1. Weeden Island effigy. Cherokee vessels and pipe.

the basic culture type marked by fabric-marked pottery begins, however, they seem to become increasingly unlike as time goes on.

I should here at least mention the Caddoan culture. developing in southern Arkansas, northern Louisiana, and eastern Texas and Oklahoma, although it did not participate in or significantly contribute to Southeastern developments until later. With minor exceptions, about all we can say is that there was gradual, late acceptance of pottery from lower and central Mississippi Valley sources and that the area emerged slowly from the Archaic stage. Sites, both before and after the advent of pottery, are small, thin, and scattered, with an abundance of projectile points, indicating a continued emphasis on hunting and gathering, and only fringe participation in the new way of life spreading through the rest of the Southeast.

The Burial Mound I time period and the earlier part of Burial Mound II, with the transition from the Archaic, are covered in the Central Mississippi Valley by the Tchula and Baytown periods. The area appears to be one that received ideas from the north, south, and east in this period but formulated little of its own except plain clay-tempered pottery differing little from the plain ware of the Tchefuncte, Marksville, and Troyville periods to the south. There are burial mounds, as there are in most of the parts of the Southeast, but we cannot say much more than that they appear to reflect Hopewellian influence. Cultures in the Central Valley, like those in the Caddoan area, appear to have been minor participants in the events of this period; in later times, it was they who produced new culture types and exported them to other areas.

To summarize, three particularly significant cultural traditions emerged at the end of the Archaic and developed into and through the Burial Mound I period. All of them during this time greatly increased their populations, expanded to cover much wider areas, and continued to have great influence on Southeastern prehistory. All three were greatly influenced by the Hopewellian tradition, which reached them from the Midwest, and all participated in the new Southeastern synthesis of this tradition. The three were the South Appalachian tradition (Deptford and the subsequent Swift Creek complicated-stamped-pottery complexes); Tchefuncte and the lower Mississippi Valley (and later Gulf) tradition of zoned and incised wares, developing through Marksville and Troyville; and the Appalachian or fabric-marked-pottery tradition, which split during the period into a number of subdivisions.

I noted above that each of the three dominant cultures, after a period of incorporating Hopewellian concepts into local systems, spread very rapidly over large areas. These spreads, observed in terms of occurrence of everyday, utilitarian pottery, appear indicative of movement of people in the case of Deptford and of spread of ideas through an already homogeneous culture in the case of the fabric-marked pottery. This suggests, certainly, that the manifestations of religion or magic that we see in the burial mounds are but manifestations of a way of life, a total cultural pattern complete with economic and social components, which was new to the Southeast when it reached there a few centuries B.C. and which, when accepted, was economically far more successful than anything that had existed previously.

LATE BURIAL MOUNDS AND EARLY TEMPLE MOUNDS

The period from perhaps A.D. 500 to A.D. 1000 is of particular significance in Southeastern prehistory. In these five centuries the Southeast ceased to draw upon the North; in fact it began to send ideas back to the North. The patterns accepted from Hopewell were thoroughly integrated and transformed into new and distinctive patterns. Peculiarly Southeastern culture types solidified and, with only minor modifications, continued on into the historic period. As these distinctly Southeastern cultures developed, major ceremonial centers emerged and became larger and more complex during the period; states were probably organized around some of these centers.

I think we can demonstrate this most clearly by reviewing first, in their combinations and permutations, the lower Mississippi Valley and South Appalachian traditions and the development with and from them of the Gulf tradition.

From the Delta, and particularly from the mouth of the Red River, to the Yazoo Basin, the lower Mississippi Valley culture continued in all respects the growth and development it had started with Tchefuncte. Sites become larger, and ceremonial centers with temple mounds increased in size, number, and complexity.

There is no sharp marker for the end of the Troyville period and the emergence of Coles Creek, the latter being the period during which this growth reached something like its eventual limits. Instead, through late Troyville and into Coles Creek, the area occupied by the culture, all of it marked by the ceremonial centers, increased. The many sites throughout the area, and the number of large ones with platform mounds, point to increasing population density. In pottery, some types, such as the elaborately incised French Fork Incised (the local representative of a coastal-plain-wide style of zoned incision), dropped out of use. Other styles changed somewhat, usually in the direction of simplification of design, and a new style appeared, characterized by horizontal incised lines below the rim. This style—Coles Creek Incised—was presumably of local origin. It continued popular in the Lower Valley and to the west for a long time, but did not spread eastward as did other Lower Valley styles.

In the South Appalachian area, our data continue to be limited almost entirely to pottery, but we may review this, since we will refer to rather significant cultures later whose ceramic ties can be traced back to this time. In northern Georgia, a style of angular complicated stamping gradually replaced the check stamping, which in turn had replaced fabric marking. In the southern part of the state, style changes in stamped-pottery designs and in vessel form took place at a steady rate through the period. Apparently, insofar as ceramic development was concerned, there was very little difference throughout southern Georgia and most of southern Alabama. However, in a limited portion of this area, extending along the coast from the bend of the Florida peninsula to Mobile Bay and reaching inland about one hundred miles, a new culture emerged called Weeden Island. Its principal ingredients are Hopewellian in religious ceremonialism, with the general culture pattern coming in through Deptford and the Gulf ceramic traditions but ultimately deriving from the lower Mississippi Valley early Troyville culture with its temple mounds. Actually, there are only two ceremonial centers with temple mounds in the 300-mile-long Weeden Island area. One of these is Kolomoki in southern Georgia, a very large, multiple-mound site; the other is a smaller center in southern Alabama. When temple mounds appear, usually in a few centers in this period of their earliest development in Troyville and Weeden Island, they are probably indicative of another stream of ideas from Mesoamerica. They tie in, I am sure, with still another culture pattern and a new and very effective economic system, in view of the multiplication of sites and their increase in size. "Weeden Island" is a term used variously to mean a ceramic complex, a culture, and a cultural period. All these need some further examination. The basic ceramic series is composed almost entirely of pottery styles that originated in the lower Mississippi Valley and are, in fact, very similar to Troyville pottery. With this complex of incised and painted pottery, we find in village middens varying quantities of complicated-stamped ware and, either with or without the complicated-stamped sherds, varying quantities of check-stamped pottery.

Perhaps the most distinctive characteristics of northwestern Florida coast Weeden Island culture are to be found in the burial mounds. All these appear to be the products of a single ceremony, which started with the interment, in a pit or a log-lined grave, of one individual, who was often wearing copper ornaments and conch-shell beads. Later stages in the ceremonies included deposition of other bodies, some of them apparently persons killed at that time, as well as quantities of mica, conch-shell dippers and large quantities of pottery. The pottery, usually placed in a mass deposit at the east side of the mound during an early stage of construction, included both Gulf tradition of South Appalachian stamped

Fig. 3.—Lower Mississippi Valley pottery. Tchefuncte to Plaquemine and Natchez, from left to right

and check-stamped vessels, with the Gulf or complicated-stamped vessels sometimes being particularly numerous. Many of the Gulf-tradition vessels were made in effigy and other elaborate forms specifically for ceremonial function. Most vessels of any type are killed [EDITORS' NOTE: deliberately ruined by punching a hole in the bottom], often with the kill hole neatly cut through before firing. The middens associated with the mounds often emphasize the Gulf, check-stamped, or complicated-stamped wares to the exclusion of the others, and not always in the same proportions as are found in the cememonial caches. A highly stratified theocratically oriented society, with an upper class related to a solar deity, such as persisted to the historic period in such tribes as the Natchez and the Timucua, can be inferred from the contents of these mounds. In this Weeden Island area the Gulf-tradition cultures disappeared before the historic period. The vitality of the religious system, and presumably of the economic system with which it must have been associated, are attested by the spread of Weeden Island pottery through most of northern Florida in strictly ceremonial context. It is found in large numbers of cultures that appear to have differed greatly in other respects.

Ceramic styles originating in Coles Creek and possibly in the central Mississippi Valley were adopted in the Caddoan area sometime during the latter part of the Coles Creek period. As noted earlier, the adoption of Mississippi Valley styles in the Caddoan area began during the Troyville stage. As one moves north and west into the Caddoan area, the Mississippi Valley styles becomes less important and cruder in execution. At the same time, new elements appear in the Caddoan area during the latter part of Coles Creek, notably in the Alto focus, as represented by the Davis site. Here, one of the first large sites in the Caddoan area, there has been sufficient excavation to document a number of very interesting points. First, it was a major ceremonial center, with a large temple mound and other mounds. Second, it was also a major population center, with numbers of well-built houses. Third, it was fully agricultural. Corn has been found, and animal bones are very scarce. In all these respects it seems to resemble the many contemporary and earlier Coles Creek and Troyville sites and the inland Weeden Island centers. Contact with the Mississippi Valley is quite clearly demonstrated by some of the incised pottery, which has Mississippi Valley prototypes. However, a set of new ceramic elements also appears. Krieger has emphasized the engraved decorations, with the designs cut into fired vessel surfaces, and the new bottle form, both with Mesoamerican ancestries. I see the Alto focus, too, as the immediate Southeastern source for the carinated bowl and its characteristic incised or engraved scroll and meander decoration, a combination that gains in importance in the

Caddoan area and later becomes important in most historic Southeastern cultures. The bottles and engraving also are shortly exported to Mississippian cultures developing in the north-central part of the Mississippi drainage.

I might here make the point that Alto-focus pottery, as does the Weeden Island pottery in northern Florida, spreads in a ceremonial context in many instances. In most cases, away from the Davis site, it is found in mounds and graves on sites usually having plain pottery in the middens. A good example is the Harlan site in Oklahoma, a ceremonial center similar to, but smaller than, Davis. Here the midden produces almost entirely plain pottery like that of the Mississippi Valley, but Alto-focus pottery is important in a mound. The mound also produced a pair of copper "Long-Nosed God" masks—small, mask-shaped objects with extremely long noses. I think that a new culture synthesis takes place in the Caddoan area, starting in this Alto-focus period of scattered but populous, fully agricultural ceremonial centers. Quite probably it is this new synthesis of Hopewellian elements, entering through Troyville and Coles Creek, and modified Mesoamerican ideas, thoroughly stirred in a Southeastern pot, that produced the elaborate religious manifestation that we call the Southern Cult in the next time period. Certainly the standards set in the Caddoan area at this time became effective, because very shortly we see that Caddoan culture, ceremonial centers, and pottery proliferate. The area becomes full of people and sites, ceremonial and otherwise, and Caddoan ideas become available for export.

Returning to the central Mississippi Valley briefly, we come to the monotonous (from survey data, at least) Baytown period. Pottery is mostly plain, and we do not know a great deal else except that there are burial mounds and ceremonial centers with temple mounds. Presumably, here too we have large, constantly increasing populations, with economies based on effective agriculture. There seem to be no distinctive central Valley cultural innovations in this period, and the pottery even shows evidence of influence from the adjacent areas. Until the next period, the resident cultures of the central Valley seem to have served as a channel for the transmission of ideas developed by more vigorous and inventive peoples.

A brief look at a few other areas may be appropriate here, since it will help us to see what was going on in the Southeast as a whole. Back in peninsular Florida, people were still adding layers to shell mounds and making temperless pottery much like that made centuries earlier. Burial mounds were still present. Check-stamped pottery became important here about 1000 A.D., as elsewhere in the Southeast. This is a point of some interest, since it demonstrates rather nicely the level of communication reached at this time. Just at the time of this datable ceramic introduction, another of the pairs of "Long-Nosed God" masks was placed in the Grant mound in northern Florida. As Goggin and Williams demonstrated, all the data indicate simultaneous use of these ornaments or insignia over a wide area. Their use in Oklahoma, Florida, Louisiana, and Illinois in cultures that were very different in most respects, and their consistent association with special types of ear ornaments and with ceremonial stone axes and other ceremonial artifacts, suggest very closely related but widespread ceremonialism.

In the Tennessee River Valley burial mounds were certainly present and a few ceremonial centers may have been built. Pottery continued to be dominated by cord marking and check stamping, with variable elements of complicated-stamped and plain wares that entered from the west and the south. I suspect that some of the resident cultures of the Tennessee were strong and vigorous and were playing a greater part in the development of the Southeast as a whole than these vague statements imply, but the available data do not permit firm conclusions.

To recapitulate, the centuries between A.D. 500 and 1000 were, in much of the Southeast, a time of internal development and consolidation into distinctly Southeastern culture traditions. The Gulf tradition emerged from its small beginnings in Tchefuncte, continued its spread and effectiveness in the lower Mississippi Valley, and amalgamated or interacted with the South Appalachian tradition to form the vigorous Weeden Island culture. The South Appalachian complicated-stamped-pottery tradition is itself poorly known, but, to judge by events of the next period in southern Georgia, it continued its growth and development with its own resources, never to be greatly influenced by other traditions. Caddoan culture, now shared by a large and rapidly growing population, emerged from a long, little-known period of virtually Archaic culture to become a major, even dominant, influence in the Southeast. Other cultures, particularly those with a Woodland background, such as Miller and the Wilmington of the Georgia coast, only hung on, soon to change or be replaced by one of the more vital cultural traditions.

Meanwhile, just north of the Mason-Dixon Line, a new culture type, the Middle Mississippi, was emerging during the latter part of this period. In one way or another, it was vital and often dominant in Southeastern prehistory from this time on.

EARLY MIDDLE MISSISSIPPI AND ITS CONTEMPORARIES

Early Middle Mississippi culture appears to have been fully formed and to be setting out on a phenomenal growth and expansion by A.D. 1000. The most significant elements of this culture complex in its early phase are a series of pottery styles with plain or cord-marked globular

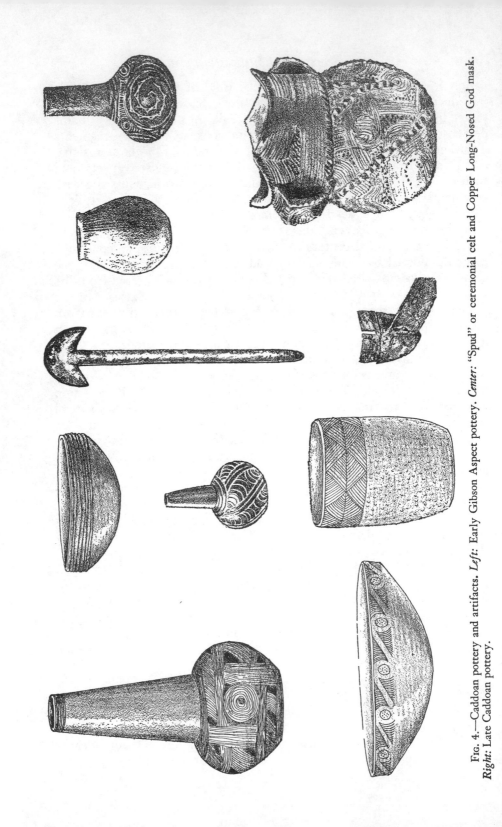

Fig. 4.—Caddoan pottery and artifacts. *Left:* Early Gibson Aspect pottery. *Center:* "Spud" or ceremonial celt and Copper Long-Nosed God mask. *Right:* Late Caddoan pottery.

pots, often with loop handles and usually shell tempered, and a series of bowl forms that often possess small rim effigies. Major sites are, compared to most earlier and/or non-Mississippi sites, very large, often fortified, and have one or more temple mounds. Ceremonial council houses, often semisubterranean and related to the Caddoan earth lodges, are common. When this culture dominates an area, satellite villages spread out over the favored river-bottom habitat from the major centers. Quite clearly, with the large fortified ceremonial centers, the very large populations, and the wholesale adoption of river-bottom habitat, a new way of life based on a new economic system associated with a new religion and a new, tightly organized social system are present here. Unfortunately, neither the Early Middle Mississippi ceramic complex nor the associated temple mounds are very good time-markers in the Southeast. Coles Creek, late Baytown, and late Weeden Island, among others, must have been contemporaneous with Early Middle Mississippi, and they all have their own distinctive ceramics. Temple mounds appeared earliest in Troyville and other Gulf Coast cultures.

I do not know where, or precisely from what, this culture originated. The general area of origin is certainly north of the Mason-Dixon Line in the great flat bottomlands of the Mississippi and the lower Ohio, Illinois, and Tennessee rivers. Influence from this developing culture reached Tennessee early, and the cultures there, such as Hiwassee Island, appear to have served at least as secondary centers of radiation. Early Mississippi cultures, with the characteristics listed above, are rare in the Southeast. The culture type is dominant only in parts of the Tennessee River Valley and to the north of it. We do have one good case of apparent invasion, a population movement into the Southeast of an Early Mississippi group to Macon Plateau in central Georgia. This huge site, with a large temple mound, earth lodges, a huge plaza, and other structures, was occupied by a large population. Seemingly, the invasion was not successful in the long run, since it is limited to this site and a very few nearby smaller sites. The culture type in surrounding areas remained South Appalachian.

Most established Southeastern culture traditions, in this period, beginning about A.D. 1000, showed individually only slight, if any, traces of Middle Mississippi influence. It was in the next, the late or mature Mississippi period, that the Mississippian culture type became so important. Nonetheless, certain events took place in the established Southeastern cultures and in Middle Mississippi at this time that laid the foundations for the more obvious happenings a century or two later. As suggested earlier, I do not think it accidental that temple mounds and "Long-Nosed God" masks appeared simultaneously, or nearly so, in the Caddoan area, along with ceramic styles of Mesoamerican origin and at the largest Middle Mississippi site, Cahokia, on the American Bottom near St. Louis, just when these two new culture types were beginning major expansions that resulted in their domination of the Southeast. Nor, I think, is it pure coincidence that semisubterranean ceremonial lodges, bottle forms, and engraving as a pottery-decoration technique (all Caddoan innovations as far as the Southeast was concerned) appeared in Middle Mississippi at about this time. It seems to me that the economic, social, and religious basis for Middle Mississippi, symbolized by the "Long-Nosed Gods" and temple mounds, reached Middle Mississippi from the Caddoan area. After integration with ideas and systems developed locally from Hopewellian bases, and adaptation to the local scene, they produced the most effective culture type yet seen in North America. It was so effective that in a few more years Middle Mississippi influenced Caddoan culture at least as much as the reverse and very strongly influenced most cultures in the southeastern United States.

This is of course hypothesis rather than demonstrated historical fact, but it fits all the facts I know. Ceremonial stone axes, ceremonial objects called "spuds," and copper or copper-covered stone ear spools are, among other things, consistently associated with the "Long-Nosed God" masks. These and the figure represented by the masks continue to be important and are elaborated in the mature or late Mississippi period. This may help us to understand the nature and later distribution of Southern Cult ceremonial centers and artifacts.

The Late Mississippi Period and the Southern Cult

The most striking and significant phenomenon of the period starting about A.D. 1400 is the great spread of the Mississippian culture type or its influence not only to the Southeast but over most of North America east of the deserts. This culture, in this late period, continues the essential characteristics of its earlier manifestation. Sites, both villages and ceremonial centers, grow larger in area, in depth of deposits, and in numbers and size of ceremonial structures. Some of them, such as Moundville in Alabama, are metropolitan centers in almost every sense.

The Mississippi ceramic complex is marked by tremendous quantities of plain, round-bottomed, often shell-tempered jars. Strap handles are quite common, as is a decoration consisting of four incised arches. Bowls are very common, and a number of unusual vessel forms, such as stirrup-spouts and tripods, appear. Most decorative techniques except stamping or paddling are used, including simple versions of incised, punctated, and modeled styles that had been common in the Southeast for centuries.

Any discussion of this period must include some consideration of the Southern Cult. Archeologically, as defined by Waring and Holder

(1945), the "Cult" is a complex of ceremonial artifacts, art styles, and representations ranging from ceremonial axes, through often elaborate ear spools, to representations of an eagle-being and other natural and symbolic motifs, executed in copper and conch shell. Most of the objects in or bearing these styles have been recovered from a few graves in a few structures in a few major ceremonial centers. Outstanding among these are Spiro, a Caddoan culture site in Oklahoma; Moundville, a Middle Mississippi site in Alabama; and Etowah, a northern Georgia center where the utilitarian ceramics were made in the native complicated-stamped, South Appalachian tradition. Several centers on the Tennessee, such as the Dallas stage at Hiwassee Island, might also be included. Lesser towns (in terms of size and number of ceremonial structures) produce smaller quantities of Cult material. Some elements of the Cult have appeared in the Southeast wherever Mississippian, Caddoan, or the Etowah variant of South Appalachian culture have been found. In all cases a single major ceremonial center appears to have functioned as the capital of a rather precisely definable state, throughout which the Cult served as the mechanism for social organization and control.

Waring and Holder suggest that a form of the Cult continues to the historic period as the Busk or Green Corn ceremonies of most Southeastern cultures. I agree, although all the historic tribes appear to have followed parallel courses of secularization and watering-down of the old ceremonial and political structure. Obviously, while the Cult is a major Southeastern phenomenon, a widespread form of ceremonialism in this Late Mississippi or Temple Mound II period, it is not a Middle Mississippi phenomenon. Its most elaborate expressions are at Spiro and Etowah.

I suggested earlier that the "Long-Nosed God" and temple mounds represented a new way of life, which first appeared in the Caddoan area. This was a way of life based on a new type of agriculture, perhaps with a new, more adaptable variety of corn—a lifeway that gave Mississippian as well as Caddoan cultures their great impetus and effectiveness. As Phillips, Ford, and Griffin suggest (1951), this Caddoan influence was not the only factor involved in the formation of Middle Mississippi culture. There was also the genius of the culture, the pool of ideas available from many cultures that had been in rather close and continued contact for centuries. Quite possibly there was also a continuation of Mesoamerican influence. Perhaps, too, the area of Mississippian origin was a particularly favorable region for the new agriculture.

The essential items in this tremendous new vitality apparent in Mississippian and Caddoan culture were, in addition to the as yet unreconstructed new economy, the religious and social organizations that made it culturally effective. These are manifest in the remains of ceremonial structures, objects, and their associations, first perceived at the beginning of their effectiveness in the "Long-Nosed Gods" and the temple mounds and carried on into the Southern Cult, which reached its peak in the sixteenth century. The continuity, over only a century or two, of the "Long-Nosed God" itself, let alone such insignia of rank and office as spuds and ear spools, is shown by such items in full Cult

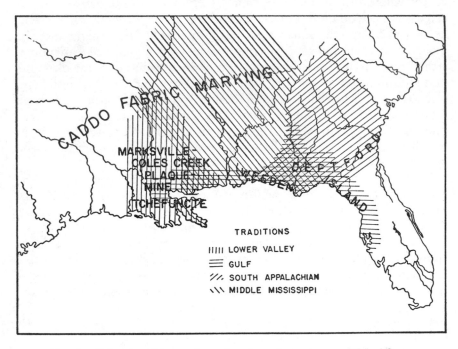

Fig. 5.—Cultural traditions and certain cultures in southeastern United States

association as the ear ornaments shown on a pipe from Spiro representing a personage in a feather robe and the copper-covered rattles from Etowah and Illinois representing this same being.

Etowah, a large community with temple mounds and other structures surrounded by a ditch and palisade, is neither Caddoan nor Middle Mississippi. The everyday ceramics are South Appalachian. Elements of Mississippian culture are certainly present, however, in that a great deal of the pottery at the Etowah site, just at and before the period of the Cult, is shell tempered. But this is true only at the Etowah site itself, not at the lesser Etowah communities. With very little data to work with, and virtually none of it published, it appears that the northern

Georgia variant of South Appalachian culture was not particularly strong. It was not representative of a very large population until temple mounds and the Cult reached it. Then, as with other cultures, it flourished. As suggested later, Etowah culture throughout its area ends up as Cherokee culture. The Cherokee were the major non-Muskhogean practitioners of Busk ceremonial. Etowah, then, represents the scene of their economic, social, and religious transformation and remained their major ceremonial center until early in the historic period.

There are three obvious kinds of culture in this period. First, the Middle Mississippian cultures themselves, in their several variants. Second, cultures in other traditions, strongly modified by Middle Mississippi. Third, cultures that continued old, established, indigenous traditions, with little or no modification attributable to Middle Mississippi. There are, in the Southeast, so many variants of Middle Mississippi culture, all adhering to the basic pattern but varying in comparatively minor details of ceramic complex, community pattern, and other details, that we cannot even list them here. A few representative examples might be briefly described.

Dallas may serve as an example of Mississippian Tennessee Valley cultures, since it has been adequately described. The large Dallas site had multiple temple mounds, semisubterranean ceremonial structures, and the Southern Cult. Shell-tempered utilitarian pottery was predominantly cord marked, as that of the preceding Early Mississippi Hiwassee Island stage had been. Such obviously Middle Mississippian ceramic features as strap handles on jars; effigy-head bowls; and plain, lobed, or negative-painted bottles were common.

Moundville, in Alabama, differed in many respects. Well known only from one very large site in west-central Alabama, with a great many temple mounds, this variant probably does not have many other sites. Moundville appears to represent the first penetration of a Mississippian people, perhaps from the Tennessee-Cumberland area, into the Alabama-Tombigbee drainage. The Southern Cult was well represented, with an emphasis here on cult symbols engraved on bottles that were used as grave furniture, a style of decoration and a vessel form with obvious Caddoan antecedents. Utility pottery was mostly plain, with strap handles on the large jars, often decorated with the common Mississippian incised arches.

In the central Valley, Early and Late Mississippi, readily distinguishable there, are probably successive steps within the Late Mississippi period. Multiple mound sites, some of them apparently fortified, are common. Most of the shell-tempered bowls and strap-handled jars are plain, although there are styles of decoration that may have some roots in older Gulf tradition styles. The presence of the Cult is indicated by a few specimens, such as the eagle from the Rose Mound (the eagle is sometimes described as a lance head when viewed upside down) and by occasional engraved pottery of Moundville inspiration.

Caddoan-area cultures have been divided by scholars into an earlier Gibson aspect, with isolated ceremonial centers and burial mounds, and a later Fulton aspect, with more temple-mound communities and fewer burial mounds. The pottery distinctions are subtle, but, in general, Gibson pottery is simpler and less varied, while the more complex and varied Fulton-aspect pottery often is shell tempered, has handles, or otherwise shows some signs of Mississippian influence. These components share such features as large ceremonial centers, temple mounds, burial mounds with graves dug into them and with large quantities of exceptionally well-made pottery in the graves, and varying manifestations of the Southern Cult. I would align the beginning of the Gibson aspect, represented by such sites as Davis and Harlan, with the beginning of Early Mississippi. The later Gibson-aspect components and focuses, such as Spiro, Haley, and Belcher, are coeval with rather Late Mississippi, around A.D. 1500 or slightly later. [EDITORS' NOTE: Many students of Southeastern prehistory would assign earlier dates to these sites. Caddoan prehistory is not yet well known; its interpretation probably involves more controversy than that of any other area in North America.]

A change in Caddoan ceramics that might be mentioned here is a progressive emphasis, through a local evolution, on brushed-surface treatment for jars and on incised or engraved carinated bowls. The latter appear to have originated in the early Alto-focus levels of the Gibson aspect. These become very important to the east in the full historic period, where they are taken over by Mississippian cultures.

In the lower Mississippi Valley, the process of culture change is sharply accelerated, at least as this can be observed in ceramics. Very strong influence from the Caddoan area is apparent in the suddenly achieved dominance of brushed pottery in the late-period Plaquemine culture. Engraving, again of obvious Caddoan inspiration, achieves some considerable popularity. Burial mounds continue to be built, apparently along Caddoan lines, with chambers dug back into mounds and with pottery offerings placed in the graves. Sites are often very large and show that they were carefully planned, with a large temple-mound–plaza complex and other ceremonial structures at some of them.

Perhaps one of the best examples of a culture that continued relatively unaffected, for a while, by these far-reaching developments in Caddoan and Middle Mississippi culture is the Weeden Island culture of the Florida Northwest Coast and its ceremonially associated relatives on the west coast of Florida. Actually, this about all we need say. Except for minor adjustments in ceramic complexes, Weeden Island communities remained on the same sites, with the same economies, and continued building burial mounds that appear to have reflected the same ceremonialism. It was not until after the period of the Southern Cult efflorescence, well up in the sixteenth century, that the Mississippian culture became important here.

The Early Historic Period: Mississippi and Mississippi Influence

The cultures of the Caddoan area and the central Mississippi Valley continued into the sixteenth and seventeenth centuries without any great changes until, sometime in this period, there was a great population decline apparently attributable to epidemics of European origin. In southern Alabama, northwestern Florida, and southern Georgia, however, a number of new developments did take place separating off an early historic period rather sharply from the general Late Mississippi period.

In southern Alabama the Pensacola culture—known only from the pottery complex, which is one with a great emphasis on carinated bowls with the characteristic scroll and guilloche designs—became prominent. The culture, derived from the Moundville variant of Middle Mississippi, suddenly expanded down to and along the coast. The huge shell-midden sites are found all the way to the Mississippi Delta and eastward to Pensacola. In the same period Fort Walton culture, with a ceramic complex very similar to that of Pensacola, quickly materialized through the area from the valley of the Chattahoochee and Apalachicola westward to the Pensacola area. There are many large coastal and inland Fort Walton sites, with multiple temple mounds and the other appurtenances of ceremonial centers. Coastal sites are shell middens, although I am sure that some agriculture was practiced. Inland sites represent almost fully agricultural economies. I am not at all sure where Fort Walton comes from, although Moundville pottery (and copies of it), which appears in the earliest sites on the Chattahoochee, are suggestive. I am, though, fully convinced that this widespread culture, found in precisely the area of documented eighteenth-century lower Creek occupation, does in fact represent the Creek invasion of the area.

Pensacola and Fort Walton completely and abruptly replaced the old Weeden Island culture and certain of its close Gulf-tradition relatives in the coastal plain between peninsular Florida and the Mississippi. This is, I am convinced, a clear case of invasion and complete expulsion of an old population by Middle Mississippian peoples. I would date the appearance of both as late sixteenth century, with continued existence through the seventeenth century. This is based on the continued association in graves and mounds of artifacts of both complexes with odds and ends of European materials dating from the earliest European contacts along the coast.

At this time, South Appalachian tradition cultures in Georgia emerged from a long static period and took the form of the Lamar horizon or style, a ceramic style marked by large jars with careless, overstamped complicated-stamped decoration and notched or pinched rim and by the carinated bowls so widespread at this time. We do not have adequate reports on any of the varied manifestations of this horizon, but we do know that such pottery occurs at many sites, many of which are very large and have temple mounds, all the way across southern Georgia from the contact zone with Fort Walton on the Chattahoochee to the Savannah. Demonstrated interaction with Fort Walton, and continued use of the pottery on into the historic period, indicate that the Lamar horizon is a post-1500, possibly even post-1600, phenomenon.

Through a series of developments, the complicated-stamped-pottery complex in northern Georgia associated with Etowah develops into a Lamar variant, too, and is identified as the pottery of the historic Cherokee.

The Full Historic Period and the Historic Decline

A number of distinct tribes or cultures can be definitely associated with specific archeological complexes of the eighteenth and early nineteenth centuries. The population decline in the Caddoan area and the central Mississippi Valley was noted in an early contact period, a situation that continued. Groups in the lower valley appear to have fared somewhat better. Historic Natchez culture here developed gradually from that of the Plaquemine period without sharp breaks. The Natchez are of some interest because their continued use of mounds and ceremonial structures, associated with a theocratic caste system and elaborate ceremonialism, is quite different from the culture of contemporary groups derived from the Middle Mississippi. It is, I believe, a last relic of the old Gulf tradition, and ultimately the Hopewellian, way of life.

In the areas occupied in the early contact period by the Pensacola and Fort Walton cultures, we now find the related Choctaw, Chickasaw, and Creek. I suggested earlier that the Creek invasion of their historic area was the Fort Walton invasion. The transition implied in ceramics is a very simple one, and the areas coincide quite well. A point of some potential importance is that, just as in the Caddo area a century or two earlier, the development in these Florida areas of a ceramic complex consisting of carinated bowls with simple incised decoration and brushed jars is coincidental with a breakdown of the old ceremonial centers and population dispersal to smaller towns and individual farmsteads. I cannot interpret this, but it does suggest that the pottery complex is symbolic of, and associated with, some basic cultural change, probably economic, which brought about a complete change in the religious and political structure of these two groups.

The same ceramic and social developments appear to have taken place in the upper Creek country from a Moundville base. This enables us to speak of "grit-tempered" and "shell-tempered" Creeks back to 1600 or so, terms that are at least no more confusing than "upper" and "lower" Creeks.

SUMMARY AND CONCLUSIONS

I have not been able in this paper to review all the known facts, sequences, sites, or pottery types and series of the Southeast. Some areas, periods, and cultures have in fact been slighted shamefully. I have tried to show the major themes of cultural development in the Southeast and the development of culture types that had the most far-reaching influence. This is provided as an outline or a frame of reference for the interpretation of Southeastern prehistory and culture change at many points in space and time.

Particularly important, I think, was the introduction of Hopewellian culture to the Southeast and its acceptance and reorganization by lower Mississippi Valley and South Appalachian cultures. This was followed by a continually more intimate relationship between these latter two so that through interchange and amalgamation of ideas the Troyville and Weeden Island cultures were produced. Both of these latter affected most other cultures in the Southeast to some degree. Perhaps the most significant event after this is the formation of the distinctive Caddoan culture, with roots in both the coastal Weeden Island–Troyville and the Mesoamerican traditions, and its exploitation of a new way of life symbolized by temple mounds and the "Long-Nosed God." The Caddoan was nearly contemporaneous with a similar development in the new Middle Mississippi culture in the Midwest. The development there of this vigorous culture is viewed as being in some part due to the introduction of the Caddoan-developed economic and interrelated political and religious systems to the Midwest area. From this horizon develops the Southern Cult. There is some continuity of a Middle Mississippi–Caddoan axis and an expansion and movement southward of the Middle Mississippi culture type. This southward expansion was accompanied by the exportation of ideas to other Southeastern cultures, such as the Etowah variant of the South Appalachian tradition. Development of all these cultures into the historic period is noted, with a secularization in the Caddoan area evidenced by an emphasis on brushed pottery and carinated bowls and the loss of the ceremonial centers. The same losses and increments are noted somewhat later in the Creek and other historically known cultures of the Middle Mississippi tradition.

BIBLIOGRAPHY

BURNETT, E. K.
   1945   *The Spiro Mound Collection in the Museum.* ("Contribs. Mus. Amer. Indian Heye Foundation," Vol. 14.) New York.
CALDWELL, JOSEPH R.
   1958   *Trend and Tradition in the Prehistory of the Eastern United States.* (Amer. Anthrop. Assoc. Mem. 88.) Springfield, Ill.
CALDWELL, JOSEPH R., and CATHERINE McCANN
   1941   *The Irene Mound and Village Site, Chatham County, Georgia.* ("Univ. Ga. Ser. Anthrop.," No. 1.) Athens.
COTTER, JOHN L.
   1952   "The Gordon Site in Southern Mississippi." *Amer. Antiquity*, 18: 110–25.
COTTER, JOHN L., and JOHN M. CORBETT
   1951   *Archaeology of the Bynum Mound, Mississippi.* (Nat. Park Serv., "Arch. Res. Ser.," No. 1.) Washington, D.C.
FAIRBANKS, CHARLES H.
   1942   "The Taxonomic Position of Stalling's Island, Georgia." *Amer. Antiquity*, 7:223–31.
   1946   "The Macon Earth Lodge." *Amer. Antiquity*, 12:94–108.
   1956   *Archaeology of the Funeral Mound—Ocmulgee National Monument, Georgia.* (Nat. Park Serv., "Arch. Res. Ser.," No. 3.) Washington, D.C.
FORD, JAMES A.
   1951   "Greenhouse: A Troyville-Coles Creek Period Site in Avoyelles Parish, Louisiana." *Amer. Mus. Nat. Hist. Anthrop. Paps.*, Vol. 44, Part 1. New York.
   1952   "Measurements of Some Prehistoric Design Developments in the Southeastern States." *Ibid.*, Part 3. New York.
FORD, JAMES A., and GEORGE I. QUIMBY, JR.
   1945   *The Tchefuncte Culture, an Early Occupation of the Lower Mississippi Valley.* (Soc. Amer. Arch. Mem. 2.) Menasha, Wis.
GOGGIN, JOHN M.
   1952   *Space and Time Perspective in Northern St. Johns Archeology, Florida.* ("Yale Univ. Pub. Anthrop.," No. 47.) New Haven, Conn.
GRIFFIN, JAMES B.
   1952   *Archeology of Eastern United States.* Chicago: University of Chicago Press.
HAMILTON, HENRY W.
   1952   "The Spiro Mound." *Missouri Archaeologist*, Vol. 14. Columbia, Mo.

JENNINGS, JESSE D.
1941   "Chickasaw and Earlier Indian Cultures of Northeast Mississippi."
       Jour. Miss. Hist., 3:135–226.
LEWIS, T. M. N., and MADELINE KNEBERG
1946   *Hiwasee Island: An Archaeological Account of Four Tennessee Indian
       Peoples.* Knoxville: University of Tennessee Press.
1958   *Tribes That Slumber: Indian Times in the Tennessee Region.* Knoxville:
       University of Tennessee Press.
NEWELL, H. PERRY, and ALEX D. KRIEGER
1949   *The George C. Davis Site, Cherokee County, Texas.* (Soc. Amer. Arch.
       Mem. 5.) Menasha, Wis.
PHILLIPS, PHILIP, JAMES A. FORD, and JAMES B. GRIFFIN
1951   "Archaeological Survey in the Lower Mississpipi Alluvial Valley,
       1940–1947." *Peabody Mus. Amer. Arch. & Ethnol. Paps.*, Vol. 25.
       Cambridge, Mass.
SEARS, WILLIAM H.
1956   *Excavations at Kolomoki: A Final Report.* ("Univ. Ga. Ser. Anthrop.,"
       No. 5.) Athens.
1958a "The Wilbanks Site (9CK-5), Georgia." *River Basin Surv. Paps.*,
       No. 12, pp. 129–94. (Bur. Amer. Ethnol. Bull. 169.) Washington,
       D.C.
1958b "Burial Mounds on the Gulf Coastal Plain." *Amer. Antiquity*, 23:
       274–84.
1960   "The Gulf Coastal Plain in North American Prehistory." Pp. 632–38
       in *Sel. Paps. 5th Internat. Cong. Anthrop. & Ethnol. Sci.*, Philadelphia.
SWANTON, JOHN R.
1946   *The Indians of the Southeastern United States.* (Bur. Amer. Ethnol. Bull.
       137.) Washington, D.C.
WARING, A. J., JR., and PRESTON HOLDER
1945   "A Prehistoric Ceremonial Complex in the Southeastern United
       States." *Amer. Anthropologist*, 47:1–34.
WEBB, CLARENCE H.
1959   *The Belcher Mound: A Stratified Caddoan Site in Caddo Parish, Louisi-
       ana.* (Soc. Amer. Arch. Mem. 16.) Salt Lake City.
WILLEY, GORDON R.
1949   *Archaeology of the Florida Gulf Coast.* ("Smithsonian Misc. Coll.,"
       Vol. 113.) Washington., D.C.
WILLEY, GORDON R. (ed.)
1956   *Prehistoric Settlement Patterns in the New World.* ("Viking Fund Pub.
       Anthrop.," No. 23.) New York.

Mesoamerica

PEDRO ARMILLAS

Northern Mesoamerica

T HE TERM "Mesoamerica" has been defined by Kirchhoff (1943, 1952) to refer to the culture area comprising the Mexican and Mayan civilizations. This concept rightly emphasizes the fundamental unity of these developments, notwithstanding the diversity of regional expressions. The area included a large part of Mexico; the whole of Guatemala, British Honduras, and El Salvador; western Honduras, the Pacific side of Nicaragua; and northwestern Costa Rica. Its northern frontier at the time of the Spanish Conquest ran from the mouth of the Sinaloa River in northwestern Mexico eastward over the Sierra Madre Occidental and along the edge of its piedmont in the plateau to the Bajío (middle Lerma River valley). From there it followed downstream the course of the Moctezuma River across the eastern escarpment of the uplands and, describing an arc around the lowland sections of the drainages of the Tamuín and Tamesí rivers, ended on the Gulf Coast about at the mouth of the Soto la Marina River (on the northeastern *terminus* see MacNeish 1958). Along most of this frontier—between the Sierra Madre Occidental and the Gulf of Mexico—a cultural chasm set apart the Mesoamerican farmers from their nomadic hunting-gathering northern neighbors; the historic limit of farming settlement roughly coincided with the border line between the climates of savanna, on the one hand, and of steppe, on the other. The southern boundary was less sharply defined, either ecologically or culturally. It can be traced from the

PEDRO ARMILLAS, associate professor, Department of Anthropology, and curator of Mesoamerican archaeology, The Museum, Southern Illinois University, is a graduate of the University of Barcelona and pursued advanced studies at the Escuela Nacional de Antropología in Mexico. His major interest has been the rise of civilization and patterns of land use in ancient Mexico. He has conducted excavations in Mexico and Central America. Before joining Southern Illinois University he taught at the Escuela Nacional de Antropología in Mexico, and at Bowdoin College and the University of Michigan in the United States. He is the author of numerous published contributions on his subjects of research and of a Program of the History of the American Indians, prepared under the auspices of the Commission on History of the Pan American Institute of Geography and History (OAS) and the Rockefeller Foundation.

mouth of the Ulúa River on the Caribbean coast southeastwardly to the drainage of the Choluteca River and thence across the Nicaraguan lakes to the vicinity of Punta Arenas on the Pacific coast of Costa Rica. Kirchhoff's characterization of Mesoamerica was formulated on the basis of distribution (presence and absence) of cultural traits *ca*. A.D. 1500. He made no attempt to trace its historical development or to emphasize its taxonomic distinctiveness.

Unity of origin and continued cultural interregional exchanges within its component parts also warrant the application of the concept "co-tradition" to Mesoamerica in the sense defined by Bennett with reference to the Central Andes and the Peruvian coast (Bennett 1948). Finally, for the last two thousand years prior to the Spanish Conquest the presence of the functionally interrelated traits diagnostic of civilization characterizes Mesoamerica as a cultural type quite distinct from those represented by the contiguous culture areas to the north and south; its only parallel in the New World developed simultaneously in the Peruvian coast and the central Andean highlands of Peru and adjoining Bolivia (see Steward 1953 for the conceptual distinction between culture area and cultural type). In defining Mesoamerica as a cultural type, distinction should be made between the nuclear zone where the high cultures attained culmination and the marginal regions that seem to have received civilizing impulses from that core without significantly contributing to the development of civilization.

The Isthmus of Tehuantepec conveniently divides Mesoamerica into two sections roughly corresponding to the so-called "Mexican" and "Mayan" areas, and in this summary we are dealing only with the one situated to the west and north of that geographical feature. Nevertheless, in terms of culture history there are many connections across the Isthmus, especially along the axes determined by major ecological zones. One of these is constituted by the Gulf-Caribbean lowlands extending from southern Tamaulipas to northwestern Honduras; the other runs from the central Mexican plateau across Oaxaca and Chiapas into highland Guatemala and beyond over the savanna belt along the Pacific Coast of Central America. Linguistic distribution shows a similar pattern.

ANCIENT FOOD-GATHERERS

Strictly speaking, the early horizons of human occupation known in Mexico north of the Isthmus of Tehuantepec do not belong to the Mesoamerican co-tradition. Mesoamerica does not become distinct as such, perhaps, until the growth of the temple towns during the first millennium B.C. Even after the inception of rudimentary cultivation, the development of farming, and the beginnings of village settlement, the configuration of the culture area might conceivably have been different from what it became in later times. However, these stages constitute the prehistoric foundations for the subsequent developments and as such are included in this summary.

The association of stone artifacts and fossil mammals in Pleistocene sediments at the Mexican plateau was noticed as early as the 1860's by the geologists and paleontologists of the French Scientific Commission active in that area during Maximilian's reign. The reported findings include a hand ax uncovered in an alluvial formation rich in skeletal remains of fossil proboscidians at the Juchipila River valley (state of Zacatecas); stone implements associated with fossil bones—among them a bison molar—at the Cañada de Marfil (state of Guanajuato); and a scraper lying in sediments that also contained proboscidian bones near the town of Tacubaya, now incorporated into Mexico City.

Thus our knowledge of the most ancient inhabitants of Mexico is still very fragmentary. A very old—by American standards—horizon of occupation seems to be represented by the discoveries, recently reported in the press, at Valsequillo, in the Atoyac River Valley a few kilometers south of Puebla City. According to the announcement, lithic artifacts have been found there in some sort of association (specific details have not yet been released) with remains of mastodon. Also, the crude stone and bone industry found in the alluvial deposits of Tequixquiac (on the northwestern watershed of the basin of Mexico), which are rich in faunal fossils and appear to antedate by a long period the Iztapan mammoth killings (see below), may belong to this early epoch (Aveleyra 1955). The Tequixquiac fossil fauna include *Mammuthus (Parelephas) columbi* (Falconer). It is archeologically attested that pachyderms of this species were man's prey elsewhere in North America, and they must have been hunted in the Mexican plateau too, but no evidence of that kind has come to light in this area up to the present time.

A better-defined period is represented by findings at Santa Isabel Iztapan, Tepexpan, and Los Reyes Acozac (all these localities are situated in the basin of Mexico), and again at Valsequillo (San Pedro Zacachimalpa's barranca) in the valley of Puebla. Geologically, this horizon belongs in the Upper Becerra formation (terminal Pleistocene). The associated fossil fauna include proboscidians, equines, and bison. All the identified mammoth skeletons certainly associated with artifacts belong to the species *Mammuthus (Archidiskodon) imperator* (Leidy). Two mammoth kills investigated at the first-named of these places in the 1950's produced considerable information on hunting and butchering techniques (Aveleyra and Maldonado-Koerdell 1952; Aveleyra 1955). The Iztapan mammoths were killed with stone points typologically corresponding to forms dated in the Great Plains in the range 5000–7000

B.C.; the skeleton No. 1 was associated with a point related to the Scottsbluff type, skeleton No. 2 with an Angostura point. At Tepexpan, a short distance to the north of Santa Isabel Iztapan, a human skeleton was found in 1947; it was embedded in the same stratum (Becerra formation) as a mammoth associated with a fragment of obsidian artifact, uncovered at the same locality in 1945 (Arellano 1946; De Terra, Romero, and Stewart 1949). Defective control of the excavation cast some doubt on the precise age of Tepexpan man (Black 1949), for it could be an interment of later age; but the specialists familiar with the site are generally satisfied that the evidence is sufficient to accept him as *bona fide* elephant hunter. The label "mammoth hunters" for the people who killed these pachyderms is convenient but misleading. The fact that they possessed specialized hunting equipment and evidently relished brains (Aveleyra 1955) and choice cuts of proboscidian does not indicate how important the role of these animals, or game in general, may have been in their subsistence. In my opinion, the distinction between hunting and gathering economies in the early stages of human occupation of the New World has been overstressed.

The researches of MacNeish in northeastern Mexico have revealed an outline of the drift from hunting and gathering to increasing reliance on vegetal foodstuffs with incipient cultivation. The combined sequences of the Sierra de Tamaulipas and the escarpment of the Oriental Sierra Madre in the southwestern section of that state can be summarized as follows:

1. Diablo complex (Sierra de Tamaulipas)—Chipped-stone tools, which must be dated 9000 B.C. or before.
2. Lerma phase (Sierra de Tamaulipas)—The artifacts attest to a hunting pattern; the relative importance of wild plants for the subsistence of that people is unknown. A single radiocarbon assay ranges 6300–8300 B.C.
3. Infiernillo phase (Sierra Madre)—Nomadic food-gatherers with considerable hunting; first domesticated plants. Two radiocarbon assays place this phase in the span 5500–7500 B.C.
4. Nogales phase (Sierra de Tamaulipas)—Plant-gathering and hunting with no evidence of cultivation yet. Early Ocampo phase (Sierra Madre)—Same subsistence basis as in the Sierra Madre plus incipient cultivation. The earliest dates for this phase are in the span 2500–4500 B.C.
5. La Perra phase (Sierra de Tamaulipas)—Incipient cultivation (maize) appears, *ca.* 2500 B.C.

Also the material culture (Ajuereado complex) of the earliest horizon of occupation represented in the caves of the region of Tehuacán, in the southeastern corner of the Central Plateau, reveals a subsistence pattern based on gathering of wild plants supplemented by hunting. This horizon is earlier than 6000 B.C., which is the round date for the appearance of the first cultivated plants in the caves' deposits.

The cultural signification of the still poorly defined Chalco complex of lithic artifacts—once believed to represent a food-gathering stage intermediate between the early hunters and the first planters—must be revised in the light of recent discoveries on incipient cultivation. In terrace gravels of the Hondo River (western section of the basin of Mexico) a stratum containing artifacts of the Chalco complex has been dated by a single radiocarbon assay within the range 4000–5000 B.C. It is now proved that in central Mexico experimentation in husbandry began earlier than that date.

INCIPIENT CULTIVATION

Distinction here is made between (*a*) the beginnings of plant domestication, with cultivated plants as a mere addition to an economy still primarily based on gathering of wild plants with supplementary hunting; (*b*) the shift of the economy to established farming as the basis of subsistence and the spread of settled farming communities; (*c*) the development of the high culture or, in Redfield's terms, the growth of the great tradition, as differentiated from the little or folk tradition, which marks the threshold of civilization; and (*d*) the achievement of civilization represented by the rise of urban centers.

On the basis of present archeological evidence, these steps forward in the development of Mesoamerican civilization are distinctly recognizable. Each one is separated from the next by an appreciable interval running from several hundred years for the shortest one to a few millenniums for the longest.

Of course, the development of food production is a prerequisite for the rise of civilization, but the latter is not an inevitable consequence of the first, as attested by the survival of precivilized societies of Neolithic types long after the first urban revolutions took place in both the Old and the New Worlds, notwithstanding the catalyzing effects of expanding civilizations upon peripheral societies. Even within the Mesoamerican sphere, the levels attained, the processes of urbanization, and the sociocultural structures varied in different regions—notwithstanding the fundamental unity of Mesoamerican civilization.

The first of these steps forward can be roughly sketched now on botanical grounds and by the analysis of evidence obtained through the excavation of dry shelters where plant remains are preserved in the trash left by their ancient occupants. On the basis of botanical considerations, the origins of the common bean (*Phaseolus vulgaris*), the lima bean (*P. lunatus*), the scarlet runner bean (*P. coccineus* or *multiflorus*), and perhaps also the squash (*Cucurbita moschata*) are traced to the highlands of central Mexico and Chiapas-Guatemala (Dressler 1953). For the squash, however, the opinion of Cutler and Whitaker (1961) is that this species is of lowland origin and native to Central America. The upland areas mentioned above are the probable hearth of cultivation of two species of amaranth (*Amaranthus leucocarpus* and *A. cruentus*), to judge from the distribution of their relatives (Dressler 1953). Endemic forms of the pumpkin (*Cucurbita pepo*) occur in Mexico and Central America, but the closest related wild species is *C. texana*, found in the southern United States, and archeological evidence—as we shall see later—points to northeastern Mexico as the center of domestication. Another likely progenitor of *C. pepo* is the wild calabazilla or buffalo gourd (*C. foetidissima*), which occurs from central Mexico to southern California to Nebraska; recent Indians of the southwestern United States used it for its seeds and it may well have been dispersed in part by man over its wide area of distribution (Carter 1945). It is worth noting in this respect that archeological evidence in southwestern Tamaulipas reveals gathering of wild calabazilla at the period of incipient cultivation of the pumpkin.

With regard to *Zea mays*, fossil pollen grains of *Maydeae* grasses, some of them identified as maize with high probability, have been found at great depths in the subsoil of Mexico City (Dressler 1953; Barghoorn, Wolfe, and Clisby 1954; Kurtz, Tucker, and Liverman 1960). This is taken to indicate that a wild relative of the cultivated species grew in the highlands of Mexico—and likely to the south, too, in Chiapas and Guatemala—and was available to food-gathering people before the beginnings of cultivation. That the process of domestication of this plant may have begun somewhere in the Mexican uplands northwest of the Isthmus of Tehuantepec is now supported, on morphological and chronological grounds, by evidence unearthed in rock shelters in the neighborhood of Tehuacán in the southeastern corner of the central Mexican plateau.

Significant archeological information on the process of plant domestication has been obtained by MacNeish in dry shelters of two districts in the state of Tamaulipas and those of southeastern Puebla mentioned above. The field work in Tamaulipas was done in the late forties and early fifties; the research at Tehuacán is still in progress at the date of writing (MacNeish 1955, 1958, 1961*a*, 1961*b*). This evidence, together with data from scattered areas elsewhere in the New World (the Southwest and the Middle West in the United States and the Peruvian coast), also permits a tentative assessment—based on the testimony of plant remains—of the role played by the northern section of Mesoamerica in the development of American Indian agriculture.

One of the two districts investigated by MacNeish in the northeast

is the escarpment of the Sierra Madre Oriental in southwestern Tamaulipas. This section is highland environment, about fifteen hundred meters
above sea-level. Evidence of an initial stage of experimentation with plant
cultivation was found in the habitation rubbish fill of caves at the Cañón
del Infiernillo, these deposits being dated by radiocarbon assays within
the range 5000–8000 B.C. The vegetal remains found in the trash included specimens of the following plants: the bottle gourd (*Lagenaria
siceraria*), the pumpkin (*Cucurbita pepo*), and peppers, all apparently
cultivated; a sort of runner bean that may have been cultivated or perhaps was a wild form; and the certainly wild *C. foetidissima*. The rest
of the inventory shows that the people who occupied the caves at that
time were basically dependent on wild plants, with hunting as an important complement of subsistence. Common beans appear in that area
during the fourth or the early third millennium; panic grass, amaranth,
and a primitive pod-pop type of maize about 2000 B.C.; and cotton
and the squash *C. moschata* soon afterward. By 1000 B.C., agriculture
with fully developed maize became established as the basis of the local
economy at the same time that pottery appeared for the first time in
that archeological sequence.

The other district is the Sierra de Tamaulipas, a detached mountain
range rising above the coastal plain in the south-central section of the
state. For that area little is really known about the subsistence basis
during the period about 5000–3000 B.C. (Nogales phase) other than that
it included both vegetal and animal foodstuffs, as attested by the presence of stone mortars, projectile points, and animal bones in the trash
deposits (MacNeish 1958). The earliest cultigens found there appear in
the deposits of the subsequent La Perra phase, roughly dated by radiocarbon within the third millennium; these are maize and *Cucurbita pepo*.
La Perra maize is also of the pod-pop type, but of different race than
the early corn found in the shelters of the Sierra Madre. It seems to be
ancestral to the lowland-adapted (although it also grows at middle altitude) Nal-Tel race still surviving in Yucatán and scattered localities
elsewhere in Mexico. On the other hand, the oldest maize at Infiernillo
Canyon, though superficially like primitive Nal-Tel, is genetically distinct; rather it appears to be related to the earliest corn of Bat Cave,
New Mexico (MacNeish 1955).

The basic data concerning the inception of cultivation, the order of
appearance of cultigens, and the progressive development of farming
economy in the southeastern Puebla area comes from a number of rockshelters—Cozcatlán, Purrón, El Riego, Abejas, and San Marcos—in the
vicinity of Tehuacán.

A sequence of cultural complexes has been established through the
study of the materials unearthed in the rockshelters and in several open

sites. The earlier of these phases are, in order of decreasing antiquity: Ajuereado, El Riego, Cozcatlán, and Abejas. We are not concerned here with later periods. The abundance of plant remains found in the deposits of the earliest horizon of occupation (Ajuereado complex) indicates that gathering of wild plants consituted the major subsistence activity, with hunting—revealed by the presence of projectile points and animal bones in the deposits—as a supplement. At any rate, this is the belief of the excavators (MacNeish 1961*b*). The projectile points belong to the Lerma and Midland types.

In the layers containing artifacts of the El Riego complex (which includes stone mortars and projectile points of Gary, Almagre, Kent, Tortugas, Agate Basin, Abasolo, Kinney, and Plainview types) chili pepper, perhaps a wild form yet, is represented by seeds found in human fecal matter dated around 6000 B.C. on the basis of the stratigraphical location at the Cozcatlán Rockshelter. The refuse overlying this deposit contains specimens of domesticated squash identified as *Cucurbita moschata* and *C. mixta*. Radiocarbon content yielded the range 5500–6000 B.C. for a sample from this stratum. A few tiny maize cobs were also found in the same layer, but disturbed stratigraphic features just above these put their exact age in doubt. Nevertheless, at the San Marcos Rockshelter corncobs from the deepest zone suggest consumption of maize by the people of El Riego culture, although the date of its inception is uncertain because the correlation of levels at the two localities (Cozcatlán and San Marcos) is not precise.

Be this as it may, maize remains are relatively abundant in deposits overlying those just mentioned, both at the Cozcatlán and the San Marcos Rockshelters. According to Mangelsdorf, the corncobs found at San Marcos may be those of a wild plant or perhaps a form of maize in the beginnings of cultivation, but the remains at Cozcatlán certainly represent maize in the early stages of domestication. In both rockshelters the associated artifacts belong to the early phase of the Cozcatlán complex. A radiocarbon assay in the range 4800–5300 B.C. on a sample from Cozcatlán and another about 4100 B.C. on material from San Marcos roughly date these strata in the fifth millennium B.C., perhaps beginning in the sixth. Gourds and, later, beans and amaranth appear in the upper Cozcatlán complex deposits, for which a date near 3000 B.C. seems *terminus ad quem*. Cultivated maize of the Bat Cave type has been found in deposits dating about 3300 B.C. at the San Marcos Rockshelter. Also, the same cucurbits already cultivated during El Riego phase, chili pepper, and agave were consumed by the people of the Cozcatlán culture. However, the pumpkin, so old in Tamaulipas, comes into the Tehuacán sequence not earlier than 3000 B.C.

The succeeding phase is represented by the Abejas complex, primarily found at Abejas, San Marcos, and Purrón rockshelters. From this time on, the role of plant cultivation as the major basis of subsistence is well established.

None of the ancient Mexican village sites known up to the present time seems earlier than 2000 B.C. A time in the span 1600–1100 B.C. for the beginnings of the oldest ones—as represented in the Valley of Mexico by the lowermost layers at Zacatenco—fits the evidence much better. The oldest settlements found in the Huastec area (Pavón phase in the Pánuco sequence) fall approximately at this time. The same sites and levels also produced the earliest ceramics reliably dated so far in the area covered by this summary. Perhaps the research in progress in the Tehuacán area may produce earlier materials attesting to farming settlement and the inception of the potter's craft during the third millennium, but, for the time being, 2000 B.C. appears *terminus a quo* for village life and ceramics in Mexico north of Tehuantepec. The diffusion of the village community pattern and pottery-making (Mesa del Guaje phase in the escarpment of the Sierra Madre Oriental) reached southeastern Tamaulipas about 1000 B.C.

At Zacatenco and El Arbolillo thick deposits of refuse indicate permanent settlements inhabited over long periods; house walls were built of wattle daubed with mud, and the roofs were probably thatched. Little is known of the Pánuco villages of the Pavón phase, but these, as well as the only possibly Mesa del Guaje settlement surveyed so far, seem to have been small (MacNeish 1956; 1958). No temple mounds or other features of communal architecture, or any clear indication of social differentiation, are found in any of these sites of the early sedentary stage.

A few conclusions can be drawn out of this mass of data. First, on the basis of chronology, botanical considerations (wild relatives of the cultivated plants being present in the area), and morphological evidence on the development of cultigens, especially for maize, plus archeological testimony of the progressive integration of domesticated plants in the subsistence complex, we can conclude that the development of cultivation and the spread of farming economy was indigenous in this area. This does not mean that Mesoamerica was the only hearth of agriculture in the New World. Botanical and cultural evidence suggests the operation of a few distinct hearths elsewhere in America. However, on the basis of the dates determined so far, Mesoamerica may well have been the oldest. The testimony of the spade on domestication of cucurbits indicates that at least two separate centers of plant domestication were originally operative in Mesoamerica. One was in central Mexico— perhaps extending into southern Mexico and Guatemala—where *Cucurbita moschata* and *C. mixta* appear early in the sequence, *C. pepo* being comparatively late there. The other was in the northeast, where pumpkin occurs early and squash late. This agrees well with the ideas of the botanists about their possible zones of origin.

Present evidence favors the central Mexican hearth as the center of maize domestication. Also, amaranth does not appear before maize, but the spread of amaranth antedates the development of corn races of "modern" type. This clarifies the role played by corn in the intregation of the seed-planting complex in the area studied in this chapter. It would appear on the basis of archeological evidence that the origins of farming settlements are directly related to the development of improved races of maize (developed by selection under cultivation and repeated hybridization with teosinte and perhaps also with Tripsacum grass [Mangelsdorf 1958]) and the domestication of beans, which, together with the cucurbits, are the triad on which Mesoamerican agricultural economy became established. Also, the development of new races must be related to the spread of maize out of its natural highland habitat into the lowland ecological settings.

Finally, although the story is still sketchy, archeological evidence in this area as well as elsewhere in the New World unmistakably indicates that the achievement of food production was the outcome of a protracted process of haphazardly selective improvement of cultigens. The tentative beginnings in plant culture did not produce a sudden revolutionary change in people's lives. Cultivated plants were at first mere additions to an economy still primarily based on food-gathering. Certainly, in Mesoamerica the shift to economies fully based on agriculture occurred no less than four millenniums after the inception of cultivation. The cultural revolution from savagery to barbarism does not coincide with the beginnings of planting. It is the attainment of a superior level of efficiency in food production, through the propagation of improved high-yield cultigens, that sets the economic basis for the transformation of society. In Mesoamerica the growth of farming village communities seems definitely associated with the spread of "modern" maize.

THE TEMPLE TOWNS

Sociocultural developments above the level of complexity of the simple village communities become conspicuous in central Mexico about the beginning of the first millennium B.C. The earliest manifestations of status distinctions now known for that area were found in a large cemetery excavated in the 1940's at Tlatilco, in the western suburbs of Mexico City. Considerable differences in wealth are indicated by the diversity of grave offerings; some of these include such luxuries as jade and pyrite ornaments. In addition to large numbers of ceramic vessels, the burials contain a multitude of female terra-cotta figurines, possibly representing some fertility cult of the ubiquitous Mother Earth type; others representing warriors, shamans, dancers, and acrobats; and flat and cylindrical clay stamps. Nothing is known of the corresponding settlement—which must have been very large to judge from the extent of the burial grounds—other than a number of domelike excavations, similar to those belonging to the early occupation horizon at Kaminaljuyú, Guatemala, that may have served as granaries. Tlatilco's ceramic art was highly sophisticated and shows the influx of the Olmec style. Jaguar and serpent symbolic motifs of indubitable religious significance were employed to decorate mortuary pottery. The span represented by the cemetery can be roughly dated 1000–500 B.C.

The earliest definitely religious building so far discovered in the Valley of Mexico seems to be the first stage of the construction of Mound 1 at Tlapacoya. It was a modest mud-plastered, stepped platform 26 by 24 meters at the base and 2.6 meters in height. A tomb was found under the top floor. A radiocarbon assay ranges it in the first millennium B.C. A date of about 500 B.C. appears likely on the basis of stylistic comparisons. Shortly afterward, true monumental buildings in the form of truncated conical mounds were erected at Cuicuilco. The largest of these is 120 meters in diameter at the base and 22.5 meters in height. Its earth nucleus is faced with retaining walls of undressed stones. There is some evidence that the Cuicuilco temples were surrounded by a large settlement, but research is impeded by the lava mantle deposited by the eruption of a neighboring volcano about the beginning of the Christian Era. Truncated pyramidal constructions of comparable date (on the basis of ceramic typology) are found at Amaloccan, east from the city of Puebla, but these have never been properly investigated.

Approximately contemporary with the early ceremonial constructions at Tlapacoya and Cuicuilco is the florescence of the Monte Albán I culture. It is primarily represented by the earliest buildings at the type site and by the ruins of Monte Negro in the Mixtec region to the west, but it is also found in many localities all over the state of Oaxaca—at least seventy in the central valley alone (Bernal 1958). It is the earliest horizon of occupation so far identified in that area, although future research should eventually discover phases coeval with the early periods of the Tehuacán sequence and evidence of pre–Monte Albán villages.

The development of ceremonialism in the Monte Albán I culture was quite advanced for the time, as compared with most other areas within Mesoamerica. Stone religious architecture, designs carved in stone (the "danzante" figures), representations of gods of definite identity (although only a few as yet), and hieroglyphic inscriptions, including calendrical symbols, are all present. Monte Albán I art represents the Oaxacan aspect of the widespread Olmec style.

The first ceremonial mounds to appear in the Huastec area of the Tamesí and Pánuco rivers are associated with pottery of the Chila and El Prisco phases of the local sequence (Ekholm 1944; MacNeish 1954), but these sites have been only hurriedly investigated. In age they roughly correspond to the horizon Tlapacoya-Cuicuilco-Monte Albán I.

Influences evidently emanating from the Pánuco River region spread the temple-mound and village pattern to the northeastern periphery. At this point we go back to the sequence at the Sierra de Tamaulipas. In that area Almagre phase follows La Perra. No plant remains, definite evidence for villages, or pottery of this period have yet been identified (MacNeish 1958).

There may be a gap in the known sequence between Almagre and the succeeding Laguna phase. On the basis of typological similarities, that is, distinctive terra-cotta figurines and other ceramic features, trade pottery from the Huastec region (El Prisco black ware), the correlation between the Pánuco-Tampico sequence and sequences of central and southern Mexico, the Laguna phase is roughly dated in the last few centuries before the beginning of the Christian Era. Laguna sites are found not only in the mountains but also in the more level land adjacent to the Sierra on the south and west.

Although wild plants still contributed an appreciable part of the diet, Laguna economy was certainly based on farming. Three new races of maize, all of them showing evidence of teosinte (i.e., teocentli: *Euchlaena mexicana*) introgression, appear in this period; these are the Nal-Tel, Dzit-Bacal, and Breve de Padilla races. All three are lowland adapted; none seems to have been developed locally. They must have been diffused from the Huastec region and perhaps the escarpment of the Sierra Madre, where Breve de Padilla may have originated (MacNeish 1958). The old Primitive Nal-Tel maize was also cultivated. Present-day distribution of the Dzit-Bacal variety is limited to Yucatán and Campeche, where Nal-Tel is also grown. Breve de Padilla is the corn commonly grown in Tamaulipas in historic times.

The Laguna settlements ranged in size from farms with two or three houses to villages numbering up to a few hundred. The larger sites usually had a ceremonial nucleus formed by temple mounds (most often truncated cones, but a few are truncated pyramids) arranged around a plaza. The mounds were revetted with slab masonry, and, in one instance at least, the stone was covered with colored plaster. The walls of the small temples surmounting them were wattle-and-daub construction, the same as common dwellings. The dwelling houses were built on circular earth platforms, many of which were lined with boulders.

Mention has been made of the Olmec style. Primarily, the term applies to the monuments found in a number of sites in the southern section of the Gulf of Mexico lowlands—the zone occupied in historic times by the Olmeca-Uixtotin. [EDITORS' NOTE: See Wauchope, pp. 380 ff.] But the area of distribution of this style is much greater. It certainly includes central Veracruz, the central Mexican plateau, parts of Guerrero, Oaxaca, Chiapas, Guatemala, and western El Salvador; in most places it appears associated with other manifestations of the development of high culture. Indeed, wherever its origin may have been (if any definite center can eventually be determined), its importance as a social phenomenon is more significant than the ethnic identification of the originators of the style.

In its formal qualities the Olmec style is characterized by the absence of the orderly rigidity of the great art of the following period and of the feathery ornamentation of still later times. The artists' will-to-form is expressed in a preference for rounded modeling of volume and the flowing line of the flat designs. The art forms in which this will-to-form is manifested are monumental sculpture, jade-carving, decorated pottery (presumably ceremonial), and terra-cotta figurines. Sculpture in the round, including colossal basalt heads up to 2.85 meters high, carved stelae, monolithic altars, and stone boxes (these including a sarcophagus), are found at the sites in the heartland. Rock carvings in that style are known in central Mexico (Chalcatzingo, state of Morelos) and the Pacific coast of Central America (Las Victorias near Chalchuapa, western El Salvador). In Oaxaca, clay urns from Monte Negro and other sites and the "danzante" carved slabs of the earliest period of Monte Albán show, as noted before, definite features of this style.

Concerning the conceptual contents of the representations, it has been suggested (Stirling 1955) that the colossal heads were individual portraiture of chieftains, and mythical or historical scenes were carved on altars and stelae; but hieratic symbolism revolving around the jaguar and, to a lesser degree, the serpent, constitutes the dominant theme. The esoteric meaning of this symbolism—to judge from what is known of the Mesoamerican religions of latter days—is connected with the gods of rain and fertility. The carved representation on the rock cliff at Chalcatzingo of personages with their faces covered by jaguar masks while performing fertility rites proves that the ideological significance of those symbols was the same at that early date. The religious ideas that crystallized in the complex theology of the subsequent period have their roots in this horizon.

The main centers of Olmec art in its heartland of the Gulf Coast are La Venta, located on an island in the swamps of western Tabasco close to the lower course of the Tonalá River; San Lorenzo and other sites along the Chiquito arm of the Coatzacoalcos River around Tacamichapa

Island; and Tres Zapotes, in the southwestern piedmont of the Tuxtla Mountains in southern Veracruz.

La Venta was a large ceremonial center with temple mounds, sepulchers, stelae, and altars. It may have combined religious and secular functions, for the colossal heads may be chieftains' memorials rather than sacred monuments, but the resident population seems to have been very small (Drucker, Heizer, and Squier 1959). A comparatively large series of radiocarbon assays definitely places La Venta florescence within the first millennium B.C. However, the results are inconclusive in regard to the span of occupation. It would seem that the beginnings can be placed anywhere within 1200–600 B.C., the end somewhere in the range 600 B.C. to the time of Christ. At any rate, the phase of greater splendor belongs in the latter part of the period of occupation.

The archeological record, too briefly sketched in the preceding paragraphs, shows by direct evidence or by inference the growth of social differentiation, the development of specialization in arts and crafts, the roots of the cults that became formalized in the religious systems of the ensuing period, the beginnings of monumental architecture, the birth of high art, and the appearance of hieroglyphic writing and, with it, tangible evidence for the use of the calendric system characteristic of Mesoamerican high culture. This horizon constitutes the threshold of Mesoamerican civilization.

The Achievement of Civilization

As the first millennium B.C. was nearing its end, Teotihuacán and Monte Albán, the earliest urban centers so far identified as such in all Mesoamerica, became the metropolises of the Valley of Mexico and surrounding areas and of central Oaxaca, respectively. The roots of urban development are represented by the ceremonial centers or temple towns of the Formative horizon—Cuicuilco and Tlapacoya in the Valley of Mexico, Monte Negro and early Monte Albán in Oaxaca, La Venta in the Gulf Coast lowlands. There is no doubt that the temple or palace-temple compound constituted the integrative nucleus of city growth. However, the urban center represents a new dimension of society, and its inception marks a profound change in economic relations, the structure of tradition, and the moral order. Since its maintenance requires the concentration of surpluses in much larger scale than the temple town, the existence of cities undoubtedly reflects a higher level of political consolidation, so the beginnings of urbanization at Teotihuacán and Monte Albán indicate a real leap forward in the development of Mesoamerican civilization. Increased religious control alone may have led rather to the reinforcement of the ceremonial center system; indeed, this seems to have been the case in sections of Mesoamerica where true cities did not develop. So the large urban population must reflect other functions besides the service of the gods.

It has been suggested that the growth of the first metropolis of the Valley of Mexico might have been related to the development of control of the hydraulic resources for intensive agriculture—chinampa gardens and/or canal irrigation (Armillas 1948). The location of the ruins in relation to the springs and streams feeding an irrigation system demonstrably pre-Columbian in origin—although its antiquity has not yet been ascertained—and a representation in mural painting at that site (the "Tlalocan" wall at the Tepantitla residence) of apparently irrigated vegetable gardens are the arguments in favor. Direct evidence on the canal layout is still lacking. Sanders' current research on prehistoric rural settlement patterns and land use in that area may eventually provide the answer. Incidentally, application of the soil-conservation technique of terracing on hill slopes seems definitely ascribed to this period (Sanders 1962). If the development of integrated irrigation systems could be proved for that early date, the urban settlement of Teotihuacán might be explained, in part, in connection with the growth of the controlling bureaucracy characteristic of hydraulic societies.

As to Monte Albán, its location on a high hill dominating the surrounding valleys may be taken as indication of a concern for defense; certainly the site is a natural stronghold, which may explain the apparent lack of artificial defensive works. In addition, a number of inscriptions carved in the walls of Monument J contain associations of place glyphs, dates, and what appear to be representations of trophy heads; these have been read as lists of conquests made by the lords of Monte Albán (Caso 1947). That monument dates from period II, coinciding with the growth of the urban center. The combined evidence can be adduced as a token of military forces operating for the creation of an incipient state that will require and support a managerial urban intelligentsia.

Last, but not least, commerce may have been a contributing factor to the development of urban centers from the very beginning. Striking environmental contrasts within short distances characterize many sections of Mesoamerica—compare, for example, the upper Lerma River valley, the basin of Mexico, and the Puebla-Tlaxcala uplands vis-à-vis the deep valleys of the Balsas River tributaries on the southern escarpment of the central Mexican plateau (the state of Morelos and adjoining parts of Mexico, Guerrero, and Puebla). The variety of climates and natural resources favor diversification of regional produce, which creates close, interdependent trading units (Sanders 1956). Regional interchange in luxury goods (jade) and in less valuable materials (cotton) already existed in previous times, this being proved by archeological evidence. Merchant groups must have grown as cities did, for an enormous expansion of long-distance trade is attested for the ensuing period.

Obviously, city-building and the growth of a sophisticated urban elite expanding the market for luxury goods demand the abilities of full-time specialists—masons, painters and sculptors, and artisans in other crafts —who came to constitute an important segment of the urban populace. Whether they occupied separate quarters organized by trades (as did some of the Aztec craftsmen of latter days) or were attached to temples and palaces and dwelt in their dependencies remains to be determined. No systematic research for workshops has been undertaken yet either at Teotihuacán or Monte Albán. However, Millon (1961) reports that one or more of the apartment blocks of the Xolalpan phase in the northwestern section (Oztoyahualco) of Teotihuacán may have been occupied by obsidian knappers.

The beginnings of Teotihuacán (Tzacualli phase) appear to be linked to the Late Formative by a demonstrable transition in ceramic style (Tolstoy 1958). Late Formative (Ticomán) pottery traditions may have persisted elsewhere in the Valley of Mexico until the urban growth of that site was well advanced. If it could be proved, this survival and the subsequent replacement of the Ticomán tradition by the spread of ceramics of Teotihuacán's Miccaotli phase type would constitute evidence of the gradual formation of a peasant culture in the rural areas surrounding a growing urban center. The difference between urban and rural culture seems to have been very sharp in Oaxaca during Monte Albán II times; this situation is explained by the postulated foreign origin of the patriciate of this period (Bernal 1958).

The ruins of Teotihuacán attest that a metropolis, comparable in size and by its mature urban characteristics to the Aztec capital so highly praised by the Spanish conquistadores, flourished in the Valley of Mexico one thousand years before the foundation of Tenochtitlán. The first nucleus of the site (Tzacualli phase) appears to have been located on the sloping ground of the Oztoyohualco section, to the northwest of its later center (Millon 1960, 1961; Millon and Bennyhoff 1961). Very soon the growing city spread over the flatland to the southeast. The period (at the beginnings of the Christian Era) when the urban pattern became established on the lineaments it had during the epoch of greater splendor corresponds with the second (Miccaotli) phase in terms of the sequence of ceramic styles, which in the absence of precise absolute dating, is used as a parameter for relative chronology. By the ensuing Xolalpan phase (probably beginning in the third century of the Christian Era) that capital attained its greater extension.

A compact urban core and a ring of extensive suburbs or satellite communities constituted the city. The center of the nucleus is the major pyramid called the "Sun Temple" by the Aztecs, who, incidentally, seem to have know less about that place than twentieth-century archeologists do. This is a huge stepped mound built to a height of about 65 meters (not counting the temple on top, the size of which is unknown) on a square over 220 meters to the side. The second largest pyramid (the "Moon Temple" in Aztec fancy) stands 42 meters in height to the top platform on a rectangle 150 by 120 meters. Their mud cores were revetted by stone façades plastered with lime mortar; stairways at the center of one of their sides led to the shrines on their tops. These and minor temples, and their dependencies, covered a sizable portion—perhaps 10 per cent of the area—of the urban-core grounds.

Residential quarters in a compact array of city blocks surrounded the sacred buildings. A straight avenue, beginning at the plaza in front of the Moon Temple and traceable southward over three kilometers, constituted the main urban axis; it passed to the front of the Sun Temple and of the palace mentioned below. Side streets intersected that thoroughfare at right angles, and a ravine that crosses the urban zone was channeled to fit in the same pattern. The layout indicates city growth along the lineaments of some regulating plan, not as a result of haphazard congregation. Streets and plazas were paved with hard cement; underground drain conduits, connected to sinks in the pavement of the house courts, ran under these floors.

In the southern section of the nucleus, fronting the avenue mentioned above, stands a large quadrangular compound inclosed by massive stone-faced embankments, 400 meters long on each side. I assume that that edifice was the ruler's palace, by analogy with the *tecpan* of Aztec times. Within the urban ambit, the city blocks are formed by large residences (many of their rooms decorated with mural paintings) and congested clusters of multiroomed apartment-type dwelling units. All houses were one-storied masonry constructions with terrace roofs. Walls and floors were plastered with lime mortar. The aspect of the few dwellings so far investigated in the city's core suggests their habitation by ecclesiastical or secular princes and their retinues, members of the intelligentsia, merchants, and craftsmen. Whether farmers also dwelt within the city limits or only in the suburbs and satellite communities has not been ascertained as yet.

No thorough study of the urban zone has yet been made, but Millon is now ready to undertake this task by aerial mapping and ground survey. According to our present knowledge, Teotihuacán's area of continuous construction—which includes some large open spaces, however —may be figured at 800 hectares (2,000 acres); this estimate does not include the suburbs. On the basis of the extension of the residential zones and studies on urban density in historic sites of the same region (Sanders

1956), the core's population can be figured in the range of 40,000–50,000, and it may have been even higher than that (Sanders 1956, 1962). The suburbs and satellite communities may add perhaps 10,000 persons (my own rough estimate based on Sanders' remarks). At its peak, the total population of the metropolitan area must have been comparable to the figure for Tenochtitlán at the time of the Spanish Conquest, which was over 60,000 by current estimates (Sanders 1956).

Most of the food resources to support that population could have been grown in the immediate vicinity if the valley of the San Juan River had been intensively cultivated with the aid of irrigation (Sanders 1962). Nevertheless, the probability that the rulers of Teotihuacán had control over the surpluses produced in a larger area should not be ignored; otherwise, the stability of its economy would have been rather precarious.

Recent surveys conducted by Sanders throw light on the rural settlement pattern in the immediate area during the period of splendor of the *urbs*. Apparently, the prize agricultural land in the San Juan River Valley below the springs that feed the irrigation system was not used for habitation, which is taken to indicate that these fields were under intensive cultivation. There were extensive suburbs or satellite communities on all sides of the city; these must have been the abode of farmers. One of these neighborhoods covers an area of 100 hectares; its population may be figured in several thousands. Small, clustered village sites were located at the edge of the plain and on the adjacent hill slopes. The largest one, at Maquixco, covers an area of 12 hectares, which indicates a population in the few hundreds; this village had a small pyramid temple. To judge from the evidence obtained through the excavation of one of the ruins at Maquixco (contemporary with the final phase of the city), the farmers' dwellings were of the same plan and construction as the urban apartments, but comprised few rooms. The grouping of the houses suggests lineage units.

Monte Albán's urbanistic pattern is less regular than the layout of Teotihuacán, by reason of its location on top of a large hill, which rises about 400 meters above the surrounding valley. Nevertheless, the main temples and palaces were built in a planned arrangement on the four sides and along the long axis of a large rectangle leveled on the very top of the mountain. The size of the urban area has not been precisely determined but must have been considerable, for, besides the ceremonial core, the residential quarters extended over the slopes on the north side and on ridges of the northeast and to the south of the center.

Mention has been made above of the cleft between the elite and the rural cultures in that area through the Monte Albán II phase. With the passing of time, the spread of the city's influence over the countryside is shown by the growing number of sites where characteristic features of the Monte Albán culture are found in subsequent epochs, sixty-odd sites being found in the central valley of Oaxaca alone by Monte Albán III-a times, with about two hundred in the period III-b (Bernal 1958).

Although archeological evidence on this important subject is still scanty, through lack of researches purposely planned, there are indicia that the interaction between the high culture of the urban elite and the little tradition of the rural communities may have been quite dynamic in the areas surrounding these cities (see, for example, Wicke 1956). A new type of society in which the farming communities became part of larger and compound cultural wholes, a true peasant society, seems to have been steadily developing within spheres of influence of the urban centers since their beginning. Indeed, the foundations for this development had existed since the differentiation of hierarchic culture; its incipient manifestations must have occurred in the earlier temple-town stage. Sociological approach to research on the Olmec style might yield some evidence on this phenomenon.

Definite stylistic relationships link the Xolalpan phase of Teotihuacán with Monte Albán III-a. The spheres of influence of these two centers of cultural irradiance were coterminous in southern Puebla and northwestern Oaxaca (Tehuacán, Yucuñudahui). Direct Monte Albán influence does not seem to have extended far beyond the present time boundaries of the state of Oaxaca, but emanations from Teotihuacán spread in divergent directions out of the heartland formed by the high plateaus of central Mexico. This core includes the Valley of Mexico, sections of Tlaxcala and Puebla (Calpulalpan, Cholula), and the upper Lerma River Valley (Calixtlahuaca). To the west, southwest, and south, distinctive Teotihuacán features appear in pottery and figurines found at Valle de Bravo in the northern drainage of the Balsas River, the middle Balsas River Basin (Tanganhuato, Huetamo), and the Pacific Coast in the vicinity of Acapulco; to the east, Teotihuacán influence reached in force the central Gulf Coast (the early phases at Cerro de las Mesas, the beginnings of Tajín); to the northeast, it fades in the Huastec region (Ekholm's Pánuco III). Far away to the southeast, Kaminaljuyú, in the outskirts of Guatemala City, seems to have constituted at that time (Esperanza phase, in terms of the local sequence) an outpost of the central Mexican metropolis, relaying the influence farther east into Central America to Copán, in Honduras, where it is noticeable in the Early Acropolis phase. Elsewhere in the Guatemalan highlands, Teotihuacán traits appear in the pottery of early date at Zacualpa (Balam phase) and Zaculeu (Aztan phase), and, on the Pacific slope, Teotihuacán vessel forms were produced in the local Tiquisate ware. In the Alta Verapaz, in the northern ranges of the Guatemalan mountains, Teotihuacán features appear in the Chamá 2 phase, and the influx reached the florescent Maya centers of the Petén lowlands (Tzakol phase of Uaxactún) and adjacent British Honduras (San José II).

In the absence of historical information, the extent to which this spread of stylistic influences may reflect political domination is highly speculative, but it is plain, and suggestive, that the directions of expansion are those followed by the Aztec merchants and armies one thousand years later. In highland Guatemala at least, the case for actual colonization of Kaminaljuyú at the hierarchic level—with an aristocracy of Teotihuacán origin superimposed on the native population and keeping ideological ties with the distant metropolis—has verisimilitude on the basis of funeral evidence (Kidder, Jennings, and Shook 1946).

The long-distance relationships between Teotihuacán and the Petén Maya were reciprocal, for imports of Tzakol-style ceramics have been found in excavations at that city (Linné 1942). Also, the diffusion of the Thin Orange ware (a fine pottery apparently manufactured in the district of Ixcaquixtla, in southern Puebla, and certainly spread by commerce) serves as a time-marker linking the golden age of Teotihuacán to Monte Albán III-a, the Esperanza phase of Kaminaljuyú, the Tzakol phase of the Petén, and the Early Acropolis phase of Copán. Through these relationships, this horizon is anchored in the Maya "Long Count" chronology. [EDITORS' NOTE: See Wauchope, Table 1.]

THE "LATE CLASSIC" PERIOD

The concept "Classic" culture, as it was originally formulated with reference to the Lowland Maya historical development reconstructed on the basis of archeological evidence, is fully meaningful primarily in application to the era of splendor in the sequence of El Petén and surrounding regions and by extension to the florescence of a similar culture in Yucatán. [EDITORS' NOTE: See Wauchope, pp. 348 ff.] Transferred to the development of central Mexican civilization, it does not have the same significance. Indeed, the validity of the concept in application to that area is questionable. Nevertheless, the term "Late Classic," as used in the title of this section, could be defined as a horizon-style common to Mesoamerican areas on both sides of the Isthmus of Tehuantepec. Compare, for example, the elaborate effigy-urns of Monte Albán III-b phase with the artistic creations in the "Ornate"-phase style of the central Maya area—and it is also a convenient way of referring to the period *ca.* A.D. 600–900 and, with this chronological connotation, is commonly accepted by archeologists.

About the middle of the millennium (certainly not much later than

A.D. 600) Teotihuacán, the capital city of central Mexico during the preceding centuries, was destroyed. Apparently, the place was put to the torch by a hostile army, for the ruins show widespread evidence of destruction by fire. In any event, it was completely devastated and never rebuilt to its former greatness; the seat of power had shifted elsewhere. After an indefinite pause, people moved into the site, used the debris to form boundary walls, and began tilling the soil accumulated upon the pavements of the ghost city. In the succeeding centuries a sprawling settlement—probably a chain of nearly coterminous villages like those found in the same zone at the present time—grew over the eastern and southern margins of the former urban nucleus (Sanders 1962).

The sudden downfall of a city, seemingly at the peak of its power, has, of course, a dramatic quality. For that reason, its significance in terms of culture history may easily be overstressed. In fact, the event does not imply the end of the great Teotihuacán cultural tradition, for it was kept alive in Azcapotzalco (and probably in other places), and its fundamental features as well as specific traits were transmitted to the successor states of the Olmeca-Xicalanca and the Tolteca. In that light, the destruction of the old metropolis should rather be considered as a historical incident, inasmuch as it did not interrupt the essential continuity of the development of central Mexican civilization.

Roughly coinciding with the destruction of Teotihuacán, Monte Albán—the capital city of central Oaxaca during the previous centuries—entered a period of decadence of indeterminate duration, and finally, it must have lost the reason for its existence, since the monuments were allowed to crumble, although the burial ground, consecrated by tradition, continued to be used long after the buildings fell into ruin.

After the fall of Teotihuacán (before the rise of Tollan and continuing during the Toltec period), Cholollan became a capital city of central Mexico. The "Mixteca-Puebla" style, which afterward pervades all the regional and temporal variants of Mesoamerican art until the time of the Spanish Conquest, seems to have been developing soon after the middle of the millennium in that city of the Pueblan high plateau—and perhaps in other places as well, for there is no reason to assume a unique center of stylistic elaboration. Although the early structures of the huge pyramid temple of Cholollan date from earlier times, the size of the edifice at that stage did not surpass the class of the second largest pyramid of Teotihuacán (the Moon). It appears to have been only after the ruin of the former metropolis and the rise of Cholollan to hegemony that this monument was rebuilt to its final outstanding volume, more than 300 meters to the side at the base and approximately 62 meters high in its present state, exceeding the bulk of the Sun pyramid of Teotihuacán and becoming the largest structure of its kind ever built in America. Un-

fortunately, the great pyramid is the only feature of this key site continuously occupied over a period of two thousand years, up to the
present time, that has been investigated; nothing is yet known of its
urban pattern for this or other periods prior to the early Spanish accounts.

The period of Cholollan predominance may be linked to the accession
to power, at that place, of the dynasty of the Olmeca-Xicalanca, which
is credited by the native historical tradition with five hundred years of
"tyranny," ending in the twelfth or thirteenth century. At their peak,
the Olmeca-Xicalanca appear to have dominated at least the territory
of the modern states of Puebla and Tlaxcala and adjoining sections of the
basin of Mexico and the valley of Morelos. The Mixteca and their
neighbors of the southern Puebla and northwestern Oaxaca zone—the
Chocho-Popoloca, and Mazateca, and the Cuicateca—seem to have
played important roles in the power structure of this political entity
(Lehmann 1922; Kirchhoff 1940; Jiménez Moreno 1942).

The hilltop fortress city of Xochicalco in the valley of Morelos also
dates to the period between the end of Teotihuacán and the rise of
Tollan to capital rank, or roughly from the sixth to the ninth centuries.
Its relative chronological position is fairly well anchored on the basis
of typological evidence (ceramic and architectonic). The decorative
stone carvings on the façades of the elegant temple pyramid of the
Feathered Serpent, which stands on the plaza at the top of the acropolis,
show the flamboyant mannerism characteristic of the styles of this
horizon. The urban nucleus is located on the top and the terraced slopes
of a steep hill. It is surrounded by ramparts and dry moats and further
protected by a citadel (which might have combined the functions of
temple and fortress) built on an adjoining slightly higher elevation. The
urban area has been estimated at 250 hectares. Suburbs extended on the
plain below the two hills mentioned, at least on the north side (Sanders
1956). Xochicalco is the oldest fortified settlement known in central
Mexico up to the present time, but Cacaxtla, another hilltop site, protected by dry moats located on the low range that forms the southern
boundary ot Tlaxcala, might be of comparable age (Armillas 1946).
This fortress overlooks the Puebla plain.

In the lowlands of the Gulf Coast, the florescence of Tajín, near
Papantla, Veracruz, corresponds to the same epoch. The nucleus of that
city was a compact array of temples and palaces that covers about 40
hectares; a suburban zone of scattered habitation sprawls over the surrounding hills, bringing the total extension of the site perhaps up to 200
hectares. On the bases of the area and the density of construction, we
may conclude that its resident population might have been counted in
the thousands but certainly not in the tens of thousands. The art style of

Tajín appears as a development rooted in the regional Veracruz Early Classic tradition and shows aesthetic and ideological affinities with the Puuc of Yucatán (García Payón 1951; Proskouriakoff 1954).

Also, some Tajín architectural features have counterparts in the Maya area rather than in central Mexico. These are two-storied buildings with interior stairways that have parallels at Palenque (Ruz 1952), the corbeled arch, and structural use of poured concrete. Concerning this material, it is well known that the technological development of Mayan engineering led to lime-aggregate monoblock constructions in which the concrete core, not the veneer masonry, takes the load (Roys 1934); at Tajín, poured concrete made of lime mixed with pumice, potsherds, or crushed rock was generally used to form slab roofs and, in one instance, for walls (García Payón 1951). On the other hand, the use of pillars or columns as interior roof supports is a characteristic linking Tajín's architecture to central Mexico and Oaxaca, where the trait is ancient, whereas in the Maya area supports appear only in the period of Mexican influence in Yucatán.

Reference has been made in a previous paragraph to Tajín's art style, which is frequently labeled "Totonac" (after the ethnic name of the historic inhabitants of north-central Veracruz) or, more adequately, "Classic Veracruz." Its salient feature is a type of ornamental design formed by linked or intertwined scrolls. Although the scroll pattern has a wider distribution and appears as early as Early Classic times, its most elaborate manifestations belong to the Late Classic horizon and are localized in central Veracruz. Very characteristic productions of this style are peculiarly shaped stones—yokes, palmate forms, and thin cutaway slabs, with figures represented in profile that are improperly called "axes"—carved with imagery and symbolic or decorative patterns of the interlocking scroll type. What function these stones served is a matter of opinion. I adhere to the view that many of the palmate and profile sculptures may have been set on cornices as pinnacles, but the use of the yokes is even more problematical (Proskouriakoff 1954).

The oldest yokes and profile slabs seem to date from Early Classic times; palmate stones appear to have originated later than the other forms. The greatest variety of shapes and elaboration of design correspond with the Late Classic horizon. The center of distribution of findings of these objects is in central Veracruz—and palmate pinnacles are only rarely found outside that state—but the spread of the other types includes the central Mexican Plateau, Oaxaca, Chiapas, and the Pacific region of Guatemala and western El Salvador.

From an aesthetic viewpoint, with regard to their formal qualities, these stones can be described as abstract creations of volume with low-relief decoration of naturalistic figures and symbolic or decorative designs. Many of them rank among the masterpieces of pre-Columbian sculpture.

To the same (Late Classic) period belong the characteristically central Veracruz terra-cotta "Smiling Face" figurines, whose center of distribution is the area around Tierra Blanca, south of Veracruz City. These small sculptures are remarkable by their expression of individuality and vivaciousness of gesture, which are rather unusual in ancient Mexican art.

Tollan, the Toltecs, and the Northern Frontier of Civilization

It would appear that by the end of the Teotihuacán period the northern marches of civilization were being enlarged over vast stretches of the Mexican Plateau, in the zone of the Bajío (Querétaro and Guanajuato) and northward into San Luis Potosí. To the northwest, a spearhead of this movement followed the inland piedmont (about 2,250–1,800 meters in altitude) of the Western Sierra Madre, along the savanna belt between the mountain forest and the steppe; this pioneer expansion carried an attenuated version of the Mesoamerican cultural pattern to the present Durango-Chihuahua border (Kelly 1956).

The spread of settlement over the northern territories should have brought about some displacement of the center of gravity of highland Mexican civilization. The constitution of a strong political entity north of the Valley of Mexico, and the establishment of its capital, Tollan, in the Teotlalpan district, which is the natural gateway to the Bajío and beyond, to the territories of the new agricultural frontier, can be explained on this basis. Indeed, the epic of Ce Tecpatl Mixcoatl—whose historical validity appears to be confirmed by recent research—reveals that this frontier played an important role in connection with the crystallization of the Toltec state. Mixcoatl steps into historical perspective as a conqueror coming from the northwest (seemingly from the area of northern Jalisco and southern Zacatecas).

Toltec is not an ethnic term, but an appellation derived from the name of the capital. The rulers seem to have been primarily of Nahuatlan extraction. The mass of the Toltec people included Nahua, Otomí, and Nonoalca; the Nonoalcan gens seem to have belonged to the Mazatec and Chocho-Popoloca stock. Multiethnic, large political units have been characteristic of central Mexico since the dawn of history represented by this period, and it seems likely that the same situation may have existed as early as Teotihuacán times.

The ruins of Tollan stand in the outskirts of modern Tula (state of Hidalgo), about eighty kilometers north of Mexico City. Although these are less extensive or impressive than either Teotihuacán or Xochicalco, excavations conducted by Jorge Acosta, since 1940, at the temple-and-palace core of the site, confirm the information on the splendor of the Toltec capital transmitted by historical tradition.

A large plaza about 130 meters to the side is surrounded by pyramid temples, pillared halls, and a ball court. Another yard for the ceremonial game is situated on the far side of a smaller plaza to the north of this nucleus. The pyramid fronting the main square on its east side is badly destroyed. The only carved slab remaining on the railing of its stairway is decorated with the symbol of Tlahuizcalpantecuhtli, the lord of the planet Venus as morning star, one of the numerous manifestations of Quetzalcoatl the god.

The monument facing the plaza on the north side was better preserved, and has been restored to give a fair idea of Toltec pomp. It is a stepped pyramid about 40 meters to the side at the base and 10 meters in height. The profuse ornamentation of its façades consists of friezes of carved slabs representing theriomorphic aspects of the Toltec deities —jaguars, coyotes, eagles feeding on bleeding hearts and panels with the image of the jaguar-quetzal-serpent god. A pillared hall on the south side of the pyramid gives access to the stairway leading to the top. The front of a masonry bench, which runs along the back and side walls of this entrance, is decorated with carved and polychromed figures of spear-carrying warriors. The colors on these reliefs are quite vivid, red, blue-green, yellow, orange ocher, plus white for some details and black to emphasize the outlines. A stone wall, the upper part of which is also carved and painted, forms an inclosure at the back (north side) of the monument. This screen wall is a gem of pre-Columbian art in the harmony of the proportions of its formal composition (alternated bands of curvilinear and angular, geometric and figurative, designs) and the dramatic effect of the ridging crest, which is a lacery of perforated and scalloped stones painted white, silhouetted in strong contrast over the deep-blue sky of the Mexican high plateau.

The lintel and the roof of the temple on top of this pyramid were supported by sculptured segmented stone columns in the form of feathered serpents, carved pillars with figures of warriors and symbolic motives, and colossal telamones—also in warrior guise—4.60 meters in height. The fallen blocks of these architectural elements were found lying in disarray on the pavement of the front hall and at the back of the pyramid; having recently been reset in their original location on the pyramid's top platform, the colossi that once guarded the entrance to the sanctuary now keep their silent watch over the ruins.

Palatial buildings with pillared halls are situated on the east and west sides of the structure described in the preceding paragraphs. These halls are a characteristic feature of Toltec architecture, also common in constructions of this period at faraway Chichén Itzá. Furthermore, all the decorative elements and symbolic representations peculiar to Tollan's art are duplicated on the buildings of this period at that capital of the so-called New Maya Empire (a rather inadequate but popular designation). This corroborates the native historical traditions recording the invasion of Yucatán by foreign people under the leadership of Kukulcán toward the end of the tenth century. "Kukulcán" is the Maya translation of *quetzalcoatl* (Nahuatl for "quetzal-snake," the feathered serpent). By reason of the difference in dates, this personage cannot be the same individual as the Ce Acatl Topiltzin Quetzalcoatl whose sad fortunes are narrated in the saga of the Toltecs' fall. Admittedly, the history of this period is quite tangled for Ce Acatl Topiltzin appears, in another version, as son of Mixcoatl and founder of Tollan. At any rate, it seems that the term "quetzal-snake" was a title of dignity, assumed by different persons in diverse places at various times. What is well established is that these conquerors were the carriers of Toltec ideology.

Kirchhoff's critical analysis of the sagas indicates that Toltec rule was divided between a king and a high priest and reveals the opposition of these powers (Kirchhoff 1955). This is connected with the religious strife between the partisans of the gods Quetzalcoatl and Tezcatlipoca who debilitated the state on the eve of its disintegration. These cults represent theocratic and militaristic tendencies, respectively, in conflict over the control of the sociopolitical structure.

The period of Toltec hegemony over central Mexico must have begun about the ninth century and lasted to the late twelfth. The actual extent of this empire is not certainly known, but it seems to have included the northern territories from Michoacán in the west to the Huastec in the east. On the other hand, although Toltec ideology and style were carried as far as Yucatán and Guatemala, it would seem that this expansion represents the activity of bands of adventurers led by warlords independent of the central authority.

The pressure of barbarians on the frontier, and plague and internal strife at the core of the realm, weakened the Toltec power, and, finally, about A.D. 1200, Tollan fell to vaguely identified plunderers, designated by the historical traditions under the collective name of Chichimecs. This term has diverse connotations, always geographically associated with the north. In latter-day use, it is applied in the strict sense to the hunting-gathering wanderers of the steppes, but it also indicated peoples whose ancestors had lived in the north at some time in the past. Although groups of hunting nomads were certainly involved in these events, their role appears to have been quite secondary; in light of critical appraisals of the data, it would seem that the mass of these invaders, who spread all over the former Toltec domain in central Mexico, was formed by the farming frontier people.

The great wave that engulfed the kingdom was a general movement from the northern territories. In the wake of these peoples, the savages followed to occupy the abandoned lands. The agricultural frontier thus receded southward in central Mexico to the Lerma and the Moctezuma River valleys. There are reasons to suspect that these movements were triggered by environmental deterioration in the sensitive border zone between the savanna and steppe climates. Data from the Southwest of the United States and from the eastern margin of the Great Plains support the ecological hypothesis, for it would seem that the North American arid zone was expanding in all directions between the twelfth and fifteenth centuries (cf. Jennings *et al.* 1956; Wedel 1959).

Little has been definitely ascertained on the confused ethnogeny of the migrant nations. However, it would appear that the lineages of the incomers may have included: the offspring of food-gatherers, partially acculturated by prolonged exposure to the civilizing influence of their sedentary neighbors; tribes of marginal farmers, ancient settlers of the borders of the steppe; and the descendants of the colonists who had pushed the frontier of civilization northward some centuries before. The latter, in fact, would have been returning to the ancestral homeland from where their forefathers had started the conquest of the northern marches.

Although a troubled period followed, and the consequences of political disintegration created a chaotic situation, the collapse of civilization was far from total. Centers of Toltec culture persisted all across central Mexico, from Michoacán to the Gulf Coast. Under their influence, incomers of all cultural shades became rapidly assimilated into the civilized way of life. The outcome of this process of acculturation was that a rejuvenated civilization emerged from the crisis.

One of the migrant nations that settled in the Valley of Mexico during the thirteenth century were the Aztecs, upon whom destiny bestowed in latter times the burden of empire.

Contemporaneously with the florescence of Tollan, Zaachila, Mitla, and other centers succeeded Monte Albán as capitals of central Oaxaca. The ruins of Mitla are famous for the relief decoration (with geometric motifs formed by protruding stone blocks) on the walls of its monuments.

During the Toltec period the "Mixteca-Puebla" style spread all over Mesoamerica, reaching the Huastec region in the northeast, Sinaloa in the northwest, and Central America to the south; beyond the boundaries of Mesoamerica, its influence on the "Mississippian" art of the eastern United States is manifest. Also, this was the time when metallurgy, mostly for ornaments, certainly appeared in Mexico; as yet, no metal objects found in the northern section of Mesoamerica have been positively dated before this epoch.

WESTERN MEXICO

Lack of any unifying great tradition and, indeed, absence, rarity, or scarce development of some of the diagnostic traits of the high culture, set western Mexico apart from the remainder of Mesoamerica.

This region encompasses the states of Michoacán, Jalisco, Colima, Nayarit, and Sinaloa. It is customary to add Guerrero, perhaps for the good (if negative) reason that its antiquities are as little known as are those of the other Pacific states to the north; incidentally, Guerrero geographically belongs to the southern Pacific region of Mexico, its backbone being constituted by the Sierra Madre del Sur, which continues into Oaxaca. However, my own view—based on personal acquaintance with this forgotten area and on archeological reconnaissances by Lister, Weitlaner, Barlow, and others—is that by their general characteristics Guerrero's antiquities are rather related to central Mexico and Oaxaca; here and there specific stylistic features indicate stronger and older cultural connections with the cores of Mexican civilization than are detectable anywhere else in the west.

The insufficiency of archeological research undertaken so far in that extensive zone precludes the application of a functional-developmental approach to the interpretation of its antiquities. Only the historical data on the Tarascans of Michoacán are susceptible of sociological analysis. For the age before history, only a few remarks on stylistic horizons and chronology can be made.

Because of the random scattering of excavations, compounded with the existence of a variety of styles of restricted distribution (which may be the result of inadequate information but also may have historical significance, for its seems to project into the prehistoric past the ethnic fragmentation manifest in the area at the time of the Spanish Conquest), the establishment of correspondences within the different local sequences stratigraphically determined is risky, to say the least. An imaginative attempt at a correlative chronological chart was elaborated at the Fourth Round Table Conference of the Mexican Anthropological Society, which met in Mexico City in 1946 (Sociedad Mexicana de Antropología [1948]). It is noteworthy that none of the sites excavated up to the present time have produced definite evidence of considerable antiquity.

A red-on-brown or red-on-buff ceramic horizon, widespread over the area, corresponds by the general characteristics of the wares to the

Tula-Mazapan horizon style of central Mexico. Furthermore, at Coju-matlán (Michoacán, on the shores of Lake Chapala) it appears to be associated with Mazapan-type clay figurines—also sparsely found else-where in the west—and to Plumbate ware (Lister 1949). Mazapan figurines and Plumbate ware are definite time-markers for the Toltec epoch. Plumbate pottery was made in southwestern Guatemala and widely spread by commerce during that period all over Mesoamerica. Also, the Aztalán style of polychrome ceramics—typically represented by vessels found in a burial mound at Guasave, in northern Sinaloa—shows strong influence, in the design patterns and the symbolism of the motives, of the "Mixteca-Puebla" style. At Cojumatlán, similarly in-fluenced polychrome wares succeed the red-on-brown horizon in the stratigraphic sequence. The vogue of the Aztatlán polychrome style did not last long; rather abruptly, it was replaced by the geometric Culiacán style.

Thus, clearly defined horizon-style links with central Mexico are demonstrable only at the end of the first millennium and for a few cen-turies after. A unique thin-orange pot found in a tomb in Colima con-stitutes evidence of trade in still an earlier period.

The only notable expressions of a prehistoric art peculiar to western Mexico are small terra-cotta sculptures found in Nayarit and Colima. The flourishing of this art seems to precede the red-on-brown ceramic horizon and may perhaps in part overlap it; as yet, its precise relative dating is a matter of opinion (Lister 1955). The Colima statuettes are finished in highly burnished red clay, those of Nayarit are commonly painted. Symbolic content is alien to this art. Its subjects are human and animal beings, and these are depicted with good-natured irony and real feeling for caricature. It is diametrically different from the hieratic styles proper to the hearths of civilization.

The barbarian invasions connected with the fall of Tollan also affected Michoacán. The origin of the Tarascan nation is traditionally traced to that event. The historical nucleus of the Tarascan kingdom was the basin of Lake Pátzcuaro, situated on the western extension of the central plateau. The soils on the lakeshore are suitable for garden agriculture, and there is historical evidence that these were intensively cultivated; abundance of fish and wild fowl add to the economic importance of this basin. The neighboring Tarascan Sierra is a prize rain-farming area, and the tropical products of the Balsas River depression are easily available; copper ores from this southern province and silver from the Tamazula district (now in the state of Jalisco), to the west of the plateau, supplied Tarascan metallurgy. However, there is no archeological evidence that this central Michoacán zone had played any important historical role prior to the rise of the Tarascan power. Even in the latter period, its societal characteristics distinguished the Tarascan nation from the political entities that developed out of city-state nuclei in the post-invasion period of reorganization in central Mexico, a zone (as has been shown in previous sections) of ancient urbanization; notwithstanding high density of population and strong political integration—which explains their military might—the Tarascans were overwhelmingly rural (Stanislawski 1947), and their historic capitals, Tzintzuntzan and Ihuatzio, do not seem to have been towns of consequence.

According to historical tradition, the expansion of the Tarascan dominion began at the end of the fourteenth century, under the rule of Tariácuri, who conquered northwestern Michoacán and adjoining parts of Jalisco, as well as the hot country of the Balsas River Valley to the south of the original core. At his death the realm was divided into three parts, which were reunited again *ca.* A.D. 1460. Between 1460 and 1480, the Tarascans extended their conquests toward the southwest, reaching the Pacific shores of Colima and Michoacán, and defeated an invading Aztec army at Taximaroa, on the eastern boundary of the kingdom. After 1480, they lost control of the coastal provinces on the west, but on the east they again proved successful against the Aztecs, repelling another attempted invasion in the early 1500's and exerting aggressive pressure against the strongholds on the southern sector of their border (Oztuma and other forts in northern Guerrero). On the northern frontier, their military activities remained limited to forays against the nomadic Chichimecs in the Bajío—as punitive expeditions, it would appear—without attempting a permanent conquest of that region.

THE WAY TO EMPIRE

As noted in previous sections of this chapter, political units of considerable size must have existed in Mexico before the dawn of history. Indeed, the splendor of the first cities cannot be explained unless we accept the assumption that these were metropolises with large supporting areas. Nevertheless, whether truly imperial expansion occurred at that early stage is purely conjectural. Extended realms (Toltec, Olmeca-Xicalanca) are certainly recognizable as far back in time as our historical knowledge goes, but the nature of their political structure is obscure in the twilight of confused chronicles. At any rate, these constitute the antecedents of political unification of large territories in the central Mexican area. Consolidation of dominion over the core formed by the valleys of Mexico, Toluca, Puebla, and Morelos, established the basis for the Aztec drive to empire.

The role played by this nucleus in the process of imperial expansion is explained by the conjunction of exceptionally favorable environmental conditions and full exploitation of this advantage. The Valley of Mexico is a great lacustrine basin encircled by ranges. Rich alluvial soils, formed by the deposits left by the torrential streams flowing from the surrounding mountains, and temperate climate permit intensive cultivation if adequate techniques are applied. Moderately wide plains extend in many places between the lakes and the foothills; large sections of these flatlands were irrigated by means of canal networks. It is historically ascertained that, before the rise of the Aztecs to hegemony, the fresh-water lakes of Zumpango, Xaltocan, Xochimilco, and Chalco had been reclaimed for chinampa agriculture. Parts of brackish Lake Tetzcoco were also conquered, undoubtedly those sections that received inflow of fresh water from rivers or springs. How much older than A.D. 1300 the system may be, we do not know, for no archeological investigation of ancient chinampas has been undertaken. The so-called "floating" gardens (chinampas) were artificial islands built in shallow waters by piling up aquatic plants and silt from the lake bottom. The combination of rich organic soil, perpetual moisture at root level, and the use of such techniques as seedbed planting and fertilizing, permitted continuous cultivation of these plots with sustained high yields. Also, terracing, which is a basic conservation measure to prevent soil erosion and to retain moisture by slowing the runoff, made the hillsides available for permanent farming. The growth of crops on many of these terraces seems to have depended on rain, but some were cultivated with irrigation. It is historically and archeologically attested that water was conveyed from the high sierra over a system of canals and aqueducts to irrigate extensively terraced slopes in the piedmont zone east of Tetzcoco, the capital of the Acolhua dominion. The undertaking of this reclamation project is credited to King Nezahualcoyotl; it may be dated about the middle of the fifteenth century (West and Armillas 1950; Palerm 1954, 1955; Wolf and Palerm 1955).

The high productivity of these farming systems sustained exceptionally dense population (see Sanders 1953, comparative data on population density in the Valley of Mexico and central Veracruz, as an example). The capital cities within the valley were urban centers in the tens-of-thousands class—Tenochtitlán in the range of 60,000–70,000, Tetzcoco about half these numbers—and there were many towns counting over 8,000 inhabitants (Sanders 1953). A factor that contributed toward making possible the support of large agglomerations was the facility of transportation presented by the five connected lakes, which were used as waterways to move the rural produce to the urban markets. Owing to it, the entire valley constituted one single economic entity. When politically unified, the ruling power controlled formidable resources to embark on adventures of external conquest. On the base of a total population near the million mark, the conquering Aztec armies could draw from vast reserves of manpower; they moved with support far more substantial than the love of the god Huitzilopochtli.

The produce of the surrounding regions—the valley of Toluca to the west, the Teotlalpan to the north, the Puebla plain to the east, and the valley of Morelos to the south—contributed to the subsistence of the urban centers in the Valley of Mexico (Molíns 1954–55). The nearness of the much lower valley of Morelos made semitropical products easily available; early in the fifteenth century, war was waged to insure a supply of cotton from that direction. The eastern section of this core included a compact irrigation district, the zone to the south of the important commercial center of Cholollan, extending downward to Atlixco and Itzocan; also, in the lower parts of this area the lesser altitude permitted the cultivation of cotton, which does not grow in the high plateau.

The story of the constitution of the Aztec Empire has its beginnings in the events connected with the crumbling of the Toltec state *ca.* A.D. 1200. One of the barbarian nations that entered the Valley of Mexico during the thirteenth century were the Aztecs; the chronicles vaguely locate their former homeland somewhere to the northwest. Out of the confusion brought about by the invasions there emerged, at the end of the thirteenth century and the beginning of the fourteenth, several city-states in mutual competition for hegemony. An Otomí kingdom, whose territories extended as far north as Oxitipan (on the border of the Huastec region), had its capital at Xaltocan, in the north of the valley. Tenayocan, Tetzcoco, Culhuacan, Xicco, and Coatlichan were other leading powers at different times during this period of reorganization.

About the middle of the fourteenth century, the Aztecs settled an island in the marshes to the west of Lake Tetzcoco. The tribe divided into two groups. One faction founded Tenochtitlán, as a protectorate of Culhuacan; the other established Tlatelolco, as a dependency of Azcapotzalco. The protector states gave them princes of their respective dynasties as vassal-kings. Not until 1473 did Tenochtitlán absorb its twin city, a feat requiring the storming of Tlatelolco, during which the last sovereign was killed or committed suicide; thenceforth Tlatelolco became a ward of Tenochtitlán, administered by governors appointed by the crown.

Under the long reign of Tezozomoc (1363–1427), the Tepanecs of Azcapotzalco attained political consolidation of the Valley of Mexico by defeating, one after the other, the competing city-states, reducing them to a position of vassalage. The Tepanec ethnos had originated by the amalgamation of people of Otomí-Matlatzinca-Mazahua stock (who from the upper Lerma River Basin moved into the western section of the Valley of Mexico during the period of the invasions) with the local Toltec population.

The core of Tezozomoc's domain was territories of the Valley of Mexico west of the lakes and, on the other side of the sierra, the upper basin of the Lerma River. As his empire expanded to the east and south, it came to encompass an area of 40,000–50,000 square kilometers, from Itzmiquilpan in the north to Tlachco (today's Taxco) and perhaps to the Balsas River in the south; from Tollocan and Ixtlahuacan in the west to Tollantzinco and Huexotzinco in the east (Carrasco 1950). Thus, the Tepanec conquests unified the key economic area of central Mexico.

After Tezozomoc's death, a rebellion of vassal lords led by Itzcoatl, king of Tenochtitlán, and Nezahualcoyotl, dispossessed heir to the royalty of Tetzcoco, succeeded in overthrowing the Tepanec power. The political vacuum left by the defeat of Azcapotzalco was filled by a Triple Alliance formed by Tenochtitlán, Tetzcoco, and Tlacopan. The last one (modern Tacuba, a suburb of Mexico City) was a Tepanec town that, early in that war, went over to the rebel side. Despite frictions between the three powers, this alliance proved successful in maintaining the political stability of the Valley of Mexico and uniting forces for external conquests. The ninety years' period between the defeat of the Tepanecs and the fall of Tenochtitlán to the Spaniards witnessed the constitution of the Aztec Empire. This development happened in two phases. First, from 1431 to the 1460's, the confederate states under the leadership of the king of Tetzcoco (Nezahualcoyotl) consolidated their rule over the Valley of Mexico and reconstructed the former Tepanecan empire; the conquest of Chalco (1465), last resistant principality in the valley, was the closing episode of this phase. Second, starting with the conquest of Coaixtlahuacan in the northern Mixtec region (1460's), the Tenochtitlán Aztecs gained, *de facto* if not *de jure*, the political hegemony in the confederacy, relegating Tetzcoco and Tlacopan to the position of satellites and extending their dominions to the east coast, south to the Pacific, and southeast as far as the present Mexico-Guatemala border. In the central plateau, only the Tlaxcaltecs, to the east, and the Tarascans, to the west, successfully resisted invasion. Tlaxcala became encircled, was put on the defensive, and was subjected to severe blockade; the Tarascans were able to gain the offensive, menacing the stability of the western boundary of the empire. Systems of fortifications and garrisons were maintained on both sides of the Aztec-Tlaxcaltec and Aztec-Tarascan frontiers.

A popular misconception attributes Aztec bellicosity to demographic pressure at the core of the realm, which would have forced them to acquire territories to accommodate the excess. This *Lebensraum* justification fails to explain the facts. Undoubtedly, the high density of occupation on the central plateau provided stimulus and manpower for aggression. Nevertheless, the purpose of resettling populations is never mentioned as a motive for waging war in the native chronicles, nor did the conquests result in large-scale movements of people, although in some instances military colonists were established in newly conquered marches to defend the frontier. The evidence indicates that the reasons for war were the need to open trade routes, to dominate markets, and to extract tribute from the subjugated states. But men do not fight for reasons, they risk life for motives. Having analyzed function, we must consider ideology. The ideal that inspired the Aztec warriors in their endeavor was the religion of the Sun-God, who feeds on human hearts and blood to sustain his might for the unending fight against the powers of darkness. It was the sacred duty of the People of the Sun to capture enemies to sacrifice on the altars of Huitzilopochtli.

At the time of the arrival of the Spaniards, the extension of the empire, including the core and the tributary provinces, was about 200,000 square kilometers; its total population may be figured in the range of 5,000,000–6,000,000. But the cohesion of this political entity was rather loose. The policy of indirect rule for the peripheral dependencies—with vassal lords only remotely subjected to Tenochtitlán's dictation—and hatred for the tribute exactions made Aztec hold on the conquered territories no stronger than the military might that the oppressors could muster at any time and place to enforce obedience. A comparison of the lists of conquests with the tribute rolls reveals that not all the defeated foes were taxed; it would seem that in some instances the vanquished were only forced to grant free transit to the Aztec armies and merchant caravans (Barlow 1949), perchance to suffer the establishment of garrisons at strategic points (as seems to have been the case on the Chiapas highlands).

Whether the Aztecs, given time, might have consolidated their dominions to constitute a single polity, or whether the empire might have disintegrated before attaining maturity, is an academic question—for then the bearded white men came.

As the Aztec Empire expanded, its capital (Tenochtitlán with annexed Tlatelolco) grew in riches and monuments. The city's size, the urban layout, the temples and palaces, the commercial activity, and the swarm of people frequenting the market places (especially the main one at Tlatelolco, but there were neighborhood markets also) astonished the conquistadores, who were first received in the capital as King Moteczuma's guests in 1519 and saw the city in its full glory. The island where the city stood was linked to the mainland by miles-long causeways and aqueducts built on earth dikes. Its arteries were straight streets and canals, through which canoes moved bringing the produce of the countryside to the market places. Thus, by its location and waterborne traffic the empire's capital resembled Venice, as sixteenth-century descriptions note. In size, it was compared to contemporary Seville or Cordova (Cortés' Second Letter of Relation to His Sacred Majesty Charles Emperor). With due allowance for Iberian hyperbole, the unanimous admiration of different eye-witnesses, coincidence of the descriptions, and archeological evidence—especially the truly monumental sculptures uncovered within the former city's perimeter—indicate that their enthusiasm had basis in reality.

BIBLIOGRAPHY

ARELLANO, A. R. V.
1946 "El Elefante Fósil de Tepexpan y el Hombre Primitivo." *Revista Mexicana de Estudios Antropológicos*, 8:89–94.

ARMILLAS, PEDRO
1946 "Los Olmeca-Xicalanca y los Sitios Arqueológicos del Suroeste de Tlaxcala." *Revista Mexicana de Estudios Antropológicos*, 8:137–45.
1948 "A Sequence of Cultural Development in Mesoamerica." Pp. 105–11 in *A Reappraisal of Peruvian Archaeology*. (Soc. Amer. Arch. Mem. 4.) Menasha.

AVELEYRA A. DE ANDA, LUIS
1955 "El Segundo Mamut Fósil de Santa Isabel Iztapan, México, y Artefactos Asociados." *Dirección de Prehistoria*. (Instituto Nacional de Antropología e Historia Pub. 1.) México, D.F.

AVELEYRA A. DE ANDA, LUIS, and MANUEL MALDONADO-KOERDELL
1952 "Associación de Artefactos con Mamut en el Pleistoceno Superior de la Cuenca de México." *Revista Mexicana de Estudios Antropológicos*, 13:3–30.

BARGHOORN, E. S., M. K. WOLFE, and K. II. CLISBY
1954 "Fossil Maize from the Valley of Mexico." *Bot. Mus. Leaflets*, 16: 229–40. Harvard University.

BARLOW, R. H.
1949 *The Extent of the Empire of the Culhua Mexica*. ("Ibero-Americana," Vol. 28.) Berkeley.

BENNETT, WENDELL C.
1948 "The Peruvian Co-tradition." Pp. 1–7 in *A Reappraisal of Peruvian Archaeology*. (Soc. Amer. Arch. Mem. 4.) Menasha.

BERNAL, IGNACIO
1958 "Monte Albán and the Zapotecs." *Boletín de Estudios Oaxaqueños*, No. 1. Oaxaca.

BLACK, GLENN A.
1949 "Tepexpan Man: A Critique of Method." *Amer. Antiquity*, 4:344–46.

CARRASCO PIZANA, PEDRO
  1950   *Los Otomíes: Cultura e Historia Prehispánicas de los Pueblos Mesoamericanos de Habla Otamiana.* (Instituto de Historia, Universidad Nacional Autónoma de México.) México, D.F.
CARTER, GEORGE F.
  1945   *Plant Geography and Culture History in the American Southwest.* ("Viking Fund Pub. Anthrop.," No. 5.) New York.
CASO, ALFONSO
  1947   "Calendario y Escritura de las Antiguas Culturas de Monte Albán." *Obras Completas de Miguel Othón de Mendizábal I (Homenaje).* México, D.F.
CUTLER, HUGH C., and THOMAS W. WHITAKER
  1961   "History and Distribution of the Cultivated Cucurbits in the Americas." *Amer. Antiquity,* 26:469–85.
DE TERRA, HELMUT, JAVIER ROMERO, and T. D. STEWART
  1949   *Tepexpan Man.* ("Viking Fund Pub. Anthrop.," No. 11.) New York.
DRESSLER, ROBERT L.
  1953   "The Pre-Columbian Cultivated Plants of Mexico." *Bot. Mus. Leaflets,* 16:115–72. Harvard University.
DRUCKER, PHILIP, ROBERT F. HEIZER, and ROBERT J. SQUIER
  1959   *Excavations at La Venta, Tabasco, 1955.* (Bur. Amer. Ethnol. Bull. 170.) Washington, D.C.
EKHOLM, GORDON F.
  1944   "Excavations at Tampico and Panuco in the Huasteca, Mexico." *Amer. Mus. Nat. Hist. Anthrop. Paps.,* Vol. 38, Part 5. New York.
GARCÍA PAYÓN, JOSÉ
  1951   "La ciudad arqueológica del Tajín." *Contribución de la Universidad Veracruzana a la V Reunión de Mesa Redonda de Antropología.* Xalapa.
JENNINGS, JESSE D., *et al.*
  1956   "The American Southwest: A Problem in Cultural Isolation." Pp. 59–127 in *Seminars in Archaeology, 1955.* (Soc. Amer. Arch. Mem. 11.) Menasha, Wis.
JIMÉNEZ MORENO, WIGBERTO
  1942   "El enigma de los Olmecas." *Cuadernos Americanos,* 1:113–45.
KELLEY, J. CHARLES
  1956   "Settlement Patterns in North-Central Mexico." Pp. 128–39 in GORDON R. WILLEY (ed.), *Prehistoric Settlement Patterns in the New World.* ("Viking Fund Pub. Anthrop.," No. 23.) New York.
KIDDER, ALFRED V., JESSE D. JENNINGS, and EDWIN M. SHOOK
  1946   *Excavations at Kaminaljuyu, Guatemala.* (Carnegie Inst. Wash. Pub. 561.) Washington, D.C.
KIRCHHOFF, PAUL
  1940   "Los Pueblos de la Historia Tolteca-Chichimeca: Sus migraciones y parentesco." *Revista Mexicana de Estudios Antropológicos,* 4:77–104.
  1943   "Mesoamérica: Sus límites geográficos, composición étnica y caracteres culturales." *Acta Americana,* 1:92–107.

1952 "Mesoamerica: Its Geographic Limits, Ethnic Composition and Cultural Characteristics." Pp. 17–30 in SOL TAX (ed.), *Heritage of Conquest*. Glencoe, Ill.: Free Press.

1955 "Quetzalcoatl, Huemac y el fin de Tula." *Cuadernos Americanos*, 14: 163–96.

KURTZ, E. B., JR., H. TUCKER, and J. L. LIVERMAN
1960 "Reliability of Identification of Fossil Pollen as Corn." *Amer. Antiquity*, 25:605–6.

LEHMANN, WALTER
1922 *Ein Tolteken-Klagegesang: Festschrift Eduard Seler*. Stuttgart.

LINNÉ, SIGVALD
1942 *Mexican Highland Cultures: Archaeological Researches at Teotihuacán, Calpulalpan and Chalchicomula in 1934/35*. (Ethnog. Mus. Sweden Pub., n.s., No. 7.) Stockholm.

LISTER, ROBERT H.
1949 *Excavations at Cojumatlán, Michoacán, Mexico*. ("Univ. N.M. Pub. Anthrop.," No. 5.) Albuquerque.

1955 *The Present Status of the Archaeology of Western Mexico: A Distributional Study*. (Univ. Colo. Studies, "Ser. Anthrop.," No. 5.) Boulder.

MacNEISH, RICHARD S.
1954 "An Early Archaeological Site near Panuco, Vera Cruz." *Amer. Phil. Soc. Trans.*, n.s., Vol. 44, Part 5. Philadelphia.

1955 "Ancient Maize and Mexico." *Archaeology*, 8:108–15.

1956 "Prehistoric Settlement Patterns on the Northeastern Periphery of Mesoamerica." Pp. 140–47 in GORDON R. WILLEY (ed.), *Prehistoric Settlement Patterns in the New World*. ("Viking Fund Pub. Anthrop.," No. 23.) New York.

1958 "Preliminary Archaeological Investigations in the Sierra de Tamaulipas, Mexico." *Amer. Phil. Soc. Trans.*, n.s., Vol. 48, Part 6. Philadelphia.

1961*a* "Restos Precerámicos de la Cueva de Coxcatlán en el Sur de Puebla." *Dirección de Prehistoria*. (Instituto Nacional de Antropología e Historia Pub. 10.) México, D.F.

1961*b* *First Annual Report of the Tehuacan Archaeological Botanical Project*. (Robert S. Peabody Foundation for Archaeology, Phillips Academy.) Andover, Mass.

MANGELSDORF, P. C.
1958 "Ancestor of Corn." *Science*, 128:1313–20.

MILLON, RENÉ
1960 "The Beginnings of Teotihuacán." *Amer. Antiquity*, 26:1–10.

1961 "The Northwestern Boundary of Teotihuacán: A Major Urban Zone." Pp. 311–18 in *Homenaje a Pablo Martínez del Río en el XXV aniversario de la primera edición de "Los Orígenes Americanos."* México.

MILLON, RENÉ, and JAMES A. BENNYHOFF
1961 "A Long Architectural Sequence at Teotihuacán." *Amer. Antiquity*, 26:516–23.

MOLÍNS FÁBREGA, N.
1954– "El Códice Mendocino y la Economía de Tenochtitlán." *Revista*
55   *Mexicana de Estudios Antropológicos*, 14:303–35.

PALERM, ANGEL
1954   "La Distribución del Regadío en el Area Central de Mesoamérica."
Ciencias Sociales, 5:2–15, 64–74. Washington, D.C.: Pan American
Union.
1955   "The Agricultural Basis of Urban Civilization in Mesoamerica."
Pp. 28–42 in *Irrigation Civilizations: A Comparative Study* (Soc. Sci.
Monog., No. 1.) Washington, D.C.: Pan American Union.

PROSKOURIAKOFF, TATIANA
1954   "Varieties of Classic Central Veracruz Sculpture." *Contribs. Amer.
Anthrop. & Hist.*, 12:61–94. (Carnegie Inst. Wash. Pub. 606.)
Washington, D.C.

ROYS, LAWRENCE
1934   "The Engineering Knowledge of the Maya." *Contrib. Amer. Arch.*,
No. 6, 2:27–105. (Carnegie Inst. Wash. Pub. 436.) Washington, D.C.

RUZ LHUILLIER, ALBERTO
1952   "Exploraciones en Palenque: 1950." *Inst. Nac. de Antropología e
Historia Anales, 1951*, 5:25–45. México, D.F.

SANDERS, WILLIAM T.
1953   "The Anthropogeography of Central Veracruz." Pp. 27–28 in *Huas-
tecos, Totonacos y sus vecinos*. México, D.F.: Sociedad Mexicana de
Antropología.
1956   "The Central Mexican Symbiotic Region: A Study in Prehistoric
Settlement Patterns." Pp. 115–27 in GORDON R. WILLEY (ed.), *Prehistoric Settlement Patterns in the New World*. ("Viking Fund Pub.
Anthrop.," No. 23.) New York.
n.d.   "Teotihuacán Valley Project 1960–1961." Mimeographed.

SOCIEDAD MEXICANA DE ANTROPOLOGÍA
1948   *El Occidente de México: Cuarta Reunión de Mesa Redonda sobre Problemas Antropológicos de México y Centro América*. México, D.F.

STANISLAWSKI, DAN
1947   "Tarascan Political Geography." *Amer. Anthropologist*, 49:46–55.

STEWARD, JULIAN H.
1953   "Evolution and Process." Pp. 313–26 in A. L. KROEBER *et al.*, *Anthropology Today*. Chicago: University of Chicago Press.

STIRLING, MATTHEW W.
1955   "Stone Monuments of the Río Chiquito, Veracruz, Mexico." *Anthrop. Paps.*, No. 43. (Bur. Amer. Ethnol. Bull. 157.) Washington,
D.C.

TOLSTOY, PAUL
1958   "Surface Survey of the Northern Valley of Mexico: The Classic and
Post-Classic Periods." *Amer. Phil. Soc. Trans.*, n.s., Vol. 48, Part
5. Philadelphia.

WEDEL, WALDO R.
1959 *An Introduction to Kansas Archaeology.* (Bur. Amer. Ethnol. Bull. 174).
Washington, D.C.
WEST, ROBERT C., and PEDRO ARMILLAS
1950 "Las chinampas de México: Poecia y realidad de los Jardines Flo-
tantes." *Cuadernos Americanos*, 9:165–82.
WICKE, CHARLES R.
1956 Los murales de Tepantitla y el arte campesino. Pp. 117–22 in *Instituto
Nacional de Antropología e Historia Anales, 1954*, Vol. 8. México. D.F.
WOLF, ERIC R., and ANGEL PALERM
1955 "Irrigation in the Old Acolhua Domain, Mexico." *Southwestern Jour.
Anthrop.*, 11:265–81.

ROBERT WAUCHOPE

Southern Mesoamerica

IN 1948, A. L. Kroeber defined ten major New World culture areas,
six of them in North America and four in South America. The Mexican
or Mesoamerican and the Andean formed a nucleus of high culture for
the Western Hemisphere, the former comprising much of Mexico, all
of Guatemala, and parts of other Central American republics. Kroeber
further distinguished between two subareas of Mesoamerica: a focus of
high culture and a subnuclear region—the former defined by the presence
of a permutating ritual calendar (and associated mathematical concepts,
such as position numerals and zero), hieroglyphic writing, masonry
temples and step pyramids, true stone sculpture and richly symbolic
decorative art, large-scale human sacrifice and bloody rituals, conquest
states imposing tribute, and rulers of high rank and power. To these
might be added a ritual ball game and the importance of markets. Other
traits, such as the corbeled arch in masonry architecture and the stela
cult, are closely identified with the Maya civilization but were not
universal throughout the area covered in this chapter. Here we treat
of southern Mesoamerica, roughly the regions occupied by Maya-
speaking Indians south of the Isthmus of Tehuantepec but including, at
various times through history, enclaves of other linguistic groups with
their distinctive cultural traits.

We begin at a time prior to the classic expression of prehistoric
Maya civilization, in an epoch during which this great culture was
perhaps emerging, but subsequent to the vital discovery of food production. We trace its regional developments in the southern and western
lowlands, northern Yucatan, the Guatemala highlands and Pacific coasts,

ROBERT WAUCHOPE, director of the Middle American Research Institute, and
professor of anthropology, Tulane University, received his doctoral degree from Harvard
University. He has directed research expeditions to Guatemala and Yucatan Peninsula and
conducted excavations at many of the most famous Maya ruins. His archeological interests
also include the southeastern United States. He is the author of many outstanding writings
on these areas. Also well known for his editorial skill, he is presently editing an eleven-volume
encyclopedia on the Indians of Middle America.

and Chiapas. Although this large area shares most of the criteria listed by Kroeber, it can scarcely be considered a homogeneous "culture area," for the identifying traits received greatly varying degrees of emphasis by regions, and the resulting cultural configurations are quite distinct. For example, as Kroeber notes, the highland Maya were somewhat retarded in architecture, sculpture, and science, compared with their lowland neighbors farther north in Peten, Usumacinta, and northern Yucatan.

The remains of early man in this area are scant and are ignored here. As in other parts of the New World and the Old, climatic changes and other factors brought about radically different subsistence patterns, including various incipient forms of agriculture and then the discovery or adoption of true plant cultivation, leading to sedentary ways of life and budding specialization in the farming villages of Early Formative times, at least a thousand years before Christ. At this time maize became the staple crop of the Maya, but their menus included many other cultivated foods: beans, squash, pumpkins, chili, various root and seed products, fruits, and vegetables, including potatoes, manioc, amaranth, sunflower seeds, and cacao (chocolate). These were grown in varying degrees of intensive cultivation ranging from the simple slash-and-burn plots in the lowland jungles to terraced, and perhaps irrigated, farms in the highlands. Other products were agave, maguey, gourds, and cotton, which provided everything from fibers to intoxicating drinks. Many of the ancient planting methods—for example, the use of the digging stick—have persisted in some places to the present. All agricultural practices, the hunting of wild game that supplemented food production, and customs connected with the preparation of food were strictly regulated by religious beliefs.

The sections that follow describe regional variations in settlement patterns, architecture, treatment of the dead, sculpture, pottery, other arts and crafts, and intellectual attainments in calendrics, astronomy, mathematics, and writing.

The Maya domesticated the dog and the turkey but had no draft animals or wheeled vehicles. Travel and transportation were by foot—sometimes in litters—or by canoe. To judge from depictions in their art, cotton and agave textiles were well developed, but the Mesoamerican climate has not permitted their preservation in the quantities found in Peru. Costumes are well known from ancient figurines and Maya art: sandals (except possibly in very early times in the highlands), the simple loincloth worn by the male and huipil tunic by the female, among the ordinary folk, and, among upper classes, elaborate robes, capes, aprons, and headdresses of jaguar skin, textiles, painted bark cloth, and plumage. Upper-class ornaments were elaborate: ropes of large jade beads, elaborate tasseled jade earplugs, turbans and feathered headdresses, heavy bracelets and anklets of jade beads, gorgets, pendants, and other adornments of jade, shell, and gold.

Maya social and political organization underwent changes through time, as we shall see when we look at their changing settlement patterns. But, regardless of how sharply society may have become stratified, or whether political power was vested largely in priests or in secular leaders, the enduring core of Maya society throughout its history was the farmer-peasant class, who lived in villages, in scattered hamlets, or in the environs of the main religious and political centers. From Formative times onward there undoubtedly were also artists, artisans, public servants, priests, traders, and other full- or part-time specialists, forming what one might consider a sort of middle class, especially during the later periods of Maya history, when cities took on a more urban character. Above them were the rulers and aristocracy, during most of Maya history a royal, theocratic, military class, which inherited its roles and prerogatives, sometimes through complicated systems of lineage. Native records like the Quiche *Popol Vuh* and the Cakchiquel *Annals* record generations of kings ruling in sequent sets of four ranks during the last centuries before Spanish conquest, and, long before that Classic period, inscriptions tell the birth or accession dates of rulers and name them and their closest relatives.

As far back as Maya remains have been traced, we find strong evidence of an elaborate pantheon of gods. Some of these go back into Early Formative times, when new deities were probably still appearing as a result of the growth of an agriculturally based sedentary village and town life. In time, as culture became more complex and society more specialized, these deities took on many roles, manifested in different guises, and foreign conquests introduced new gods from Mexico and elsewhere. We shall refer to some of these changes in appropriate places. As Thompson has shown, if one outstanding Maya trait had to be singled out as the most important, it would probably be their complete trust in the gods' control of certain units of time and of all man's activities during those periods and their feeling of security in this divinely supervised and consistent regularity of recurring cycles of time from the beginning of things onward forever into the future.

SOUTHERN AND WESTERN LOWLANDS

The main areas of the southern and western Maya lowlands are the department of Peten in northern Guatemala at the base of the Yucatan peninsula; adjoining parts of British Honduras; the Copan-Quirigua archeological zone of Honduras; the Pasion, Chixoy, and Usumacinta River drainages toward the west; and the adjoining rain forests and Gulf

Coast of southern Campeche, Tabasco, and Chiapas. Although largely a lush tropical jungle, save for its building materials (limestone and lumber) and its abundant wild game, this region was curiously lacking in the natural resources most needed by the Indians who built there one of the greatest civilizations of this hemisphere. The water supply in some parts must have been precarious, the forests difficult to clear for planting, and weeds almost impossible to control with the crude tools then available. There was no metal and, as Thompson has pointed out, little or no salt, jade, obsidian, or quetzal birds—four commodities most highly prized by the ancient Maya. Vanilla, cacao, and rubber grew in appreciable quantities only in the west.

The southern and western Maya lowlands have heavy seasonal rainfall (70–150 inches), supporting great forests of mahogany, sapodilla (zapote), Spanish cedar, ceiba, mamey, rubber, allspice, aguacate, breadnut, and various palms. In northern Peten and southeast Quintana Roo is a central interior drainage basin with surrounding hills, valleys, and lake country. From the hills to the north six rivers flow either west and north to the Gulf of Mexico or northeast to the Caribbean. South of this interior basin and its rim of hills are savanna and clay grasslands, drained by streams flowing south and west. To the east, in southeast Peten and southern British Honduras, the Maya Mountains rise much higher, one peak reaching 3,700 feet. Most of the country, though, is only about 500 feet above the sea, and the underground water-level is deep. Modern efforts to drill for water at the greatest Maya city, Tikal in Peten, were abandoned at a depth of 320 feet! Remains of old reservoirs there attest to the ancients' major concern with the catching and storage of water. There are some sizable rivers—the Hondo, Belize, Motagua, Copan, Dulce, Chixoy, Pasion, Usumacinta, for example— but one can travel overland for days (afoot or on muleback) without seeing a major stream, as one traverses what seem to be endless miles of alternating deeply forested ridges, muddy swamps, and hot, grassy savannas. Ancient trade was widespread, and, to judge from scenes depicted in art, travel—perhaps, for royalty, on a litter—was frequent, so jungle roads (sometimes these were earth and masonry causeways) between cities must have been kept in good condition the year round. Only in parts of Honduras, British Honduras, and Chiapas are there relatively high elevations and mountains. It is still today a magnificently wild and fantastically beautiful region, though paradoxically hostile to human exploitation in ancient Maya terms.

Some Yucatec Maya is spoken in the northern part of this area. In other regions, however, related but different Maya dialects are (and probably were in ancient time) prevalent: Chontal, Chol, Mopan, and, in the west, Chuj, Chaneabal, Tzeltal, and Tzotzil.

PRECLASSIC (FORMATIVE) PERIOD

It is first necessary to explain our terminology. Most archeologists nowadays use an Early, Middle, and Late Preclassic division for the earlier or Formative stages of prehistory in this area; they differ somewhat in what they consider the most appropriate period designations for certain remains. Thus, some assign the earliest known remains in the southern lowland (e.g., the "Mamom" pottery in Peten) to the Early Preclassic and place the subsequent Chicanel remains in Middle Preclassic, leaving the Late Preclassic for certain inferred or hypothesized stages, which have not always actually been found at the major sites so far excavated. Others believe that the earliest Preclassic remains excavated in other parts of Mesoamerica have not yet been found in the southern and western lowland and that the term "Early Preclassic" should be left open for such in case they are found in the future, and also to avoid confusion when referring to these earliest horizons elsewhere. Michael D. Coe has proposed the term "Proto-Formative" for these sparse earliest remains. In 1950 I proposed a tentative tripartite Preclassic sequence for all Middle America (Village Formative, Urban Formative, and Protoclassic), and I assigned Mamom to a transitional stage between the early and middle periods of this sequence. Chicanel fitted ceramically into the middle period. There are conceptual objections to all these terminologies. My developmental scheme has been termed premature, and it has apparently proved confusing to many writers that the smaller or retarded villages of the Urban or "Temple" Formative did not actually have temples. Moreover, major architecture is suspected now for some sites I assigned on ceramic grounds to the Village Formative period. On the other hand, a magic three-stage development of all prehistoric cultures everywhere in the world (Early, Middle, and Late) is highly unlikely, and one suspects that it is a product of the archeologist's habits of analysis and is really often more convenient than real. Nevertheless, in this chapter I shall use the Early, Middle, and Late rubrics at least for the subarea now to be described.

No prehistoric cultural assemblages fitting the criteria of Early Preclassic have yet been identified in the southern and western lowlands, although they do occur not far away in the Huasteca, the Yojoa remains of Honduras, in southern and central Mexico, and probably in the Guatemala highlands. Remains probably transitional to Middle Preclassic are represented chiefly through pottery of the kind known in Peten as Mamom, together with hand-modeled figurines and some artifacts, found stratigraphically earliest at Uaxactun in Peten, and at Benque Viejo, San Jose, Barton Ramie, and other sites on the Belize River.

As yet, Preclassic pottery has not been found in significant quantity in the western lowlands.

Most Mamom slipped or polished pottery has a characteristically waxy texture ("Flores Waxy"). It occurs in red, black, variegated, or orange surface color; usually it is a flat-bottomed plate with flaring sides, a cuspidor-like bowl, or a globular jar with flaring or vertical neck. Decoration, by groove-incising, was simple: triangles, right angles, rectangles, cross-hachure, and so on. There are also an unslipped ware of a finer paste, with orange-colored surface ("Mars-orange"); a red-and-cream pottery; and, among the domestic unslipped types, the many jars daubed with crude red swirls and bands and painted red on the neck ("Palma Daub"). Mamom figurines depicted humans with oversized heads; some of their smaller body features and ornaments were appliquéd, others—such as eyes, breasts, and navel—simply punched in the clay. Hands and feet were either omitted or conventionalized to rudimentary form. Hollow whistles represented humans, animals, or birds. Lowland Maya Preclassic figurines were monotonously uniform compared with the diversity of contemporaneous types in the Valley of Mexico and contrasted with those of the Classic period; as Rands expressed it, action and jauntiness were largely lacking.

MIDDLE AND LATE PRECLASSIC

This seems to have been the stage during which southern lowland Maya culture, or at least that in Peten and adjoining areas, began to attain the strength and vigor of a burgeoning civilization. The two great Peten cities, Uaxactun and Tikal, for example, acquired their first grand scale at this time; the plazas of certain major assemblages of these cities were built on layers yielding massive quantities of Middle Preclassic pottery of types known as Chicanel. So far, little or no Middle Preclassic pottery has been found at the great Usumacinta cities intensively excavated, such as Piedras Negras and Palenque, but current excavations at Altar de Sacrificios are producing some from a ceremonial center dating to about 500 B.C. Pottery of Chicanel type appears at Tiradero.

The first major architecture of the southern lowlands apparently belongs in this period. Pyramid E-VII-sub at Uaxactun is the most famous: a low, squat, stepped pyramid with major and minor stairways on all four sides, big stucco masks with stylistic affinities to the early art of the La Venta region of Mexico, and a perishable superstructure, presumably made of poles and thatch. This terraced pyramid, with its non-rigid, flowing lines and interesting relief and shadow effects, is perhaps unique among New World architectural monuments; it is in no sense the product of wholly unsophisticated builders, although a number of inventions, such as the corbeled vault, were yet to come. Two other small pyramids date to this period at Uaxactun, and others are being found at Tikal and Altar de Sacrificios. A tomb with corbeled vault, the earliest yet found in the Maya area, has been discovered at Altar de Sacrificios.

Burial cists made their first appearance at this time, at least here in the south. The skeletons were usually flexed and often accompanied by jade or shell ornaments. The Maya practice of making cache offerings in or under structures was also known by this time.

Chicanel slipped pottery, like Mamom, tended to feel waxy ("Paso Caballo Waxy"). The slipped wares were red, variegated, black, orange, cream, brown, and buff, or two-color red-on-orange, red-on-buff, black-on-red. There were many new shapes—plates with widely everted and thickened rim (often incised), bowls with recurved sides, and dishes or plates with flaring or outcurved sides. Vessels sometimes had solid cylindrical or nubbin feet, tripod or tetrapod. Groove-incising was again popular, and vessels were further decorated with "crazing," modeled or applied ridges, spikes, bosses, or heads, or were painted in the negative wax-resist or "Usulutan" technique. The domestic wares, chiefly globular jars, were derived from Mamom and were smooth or decorated with striations ("Paila Unslipped"). Unlike Mamom, Chicanel pottery included no figurines or whistles.

Regional variation occurred even on this early horizon. There are some local wares peculiar to British Honduran sites, and Copan Middle Formative pottery displays affiliations with the ceramics of the Ulua and Comayagua valleys of Honduras.

PROTOCLASSIC

Merwin and Vaillant isolated two sealed ossuaries beneath rooms at Holmul, Guatemala, and, noting the singularity of the pottery complex represented here (containing several of the "Q-traits" that Vaillant and Lothrop had proposed as a far-flung early complex of cultural features), called the group Holmul I, the earliest in the sequence there. The close resemblance of some of its ceramic traits to pottery elsewhere—tetrapod mammiform feet, bridged spouts, and other features—was frequently noted. In 1950, in an attempt to form a tentative sequence of Preclassic ceramics for the Middle American area, I assembled the data on Holmul I relationships and proposed the term "Protoclassic" for them, because among them were forerunners of such Classic-period traits as the basal flange in pottery and the corbeled vault in architecture.

Among the curious things about this complex was its sporadic distribution; it seems to have been absent at a number of sites that nevertheless yielded both Late Formative and Classic remains. For example, there appeared to be no identifiable Protoclassic occupation at Uaxactun, which is not far from Holmul; nor was there apparently any at Kaminaljuyu, not far from Zacualpa, which yielded a strong Protoclassic sample. I came to the tentative conclusion that some centers—I could not say areas—apparently went through a Protoclassic stage, whereas others passed directly from a Late Formative culture into the full-blown Classic. It seemed unlikely that these circumstances could be due to incomplete sampling at the sites that lacked the Protoclassic. In several cases, ceramicists nowadays postulate a tentative Protoclassic phase to take account of stray sherds that turn up here and there during excavations, although they cannot pin these together in a stratigraphically demonstrable complex; thus, the Matzanel ceramic phase has been inserted into the Peten sequence between Chicanel and Tzakol, but as yet its features have been found in context at only a few places, such as Holmul, Guatemala, and Mountain Cow, Douglas, and Barton Ramie ("Floral Park" phase), British Honduras.

This widespread situation with regard to the Protoclassic is interesting, for similar phenomena occur in other archeological areas. For example, in the southeastern United States, some places seem to have bypassed the proto-Mississippi (Napier and Woodstock) ceramic expressions and gone straight from Middle Woodland into mature Mississippi culture. One wonders whether it is a sampling error; whether it reflects retarded growth at some centers, which then skipped the transitional stages into later cultural expressions; or whether some other widespread principle of cultural dynamics may be involved.

Protoclassic pottery partook of traits from the preceding periods; among the carry-overs were negative- or resist-painted pottery, punctate-filling of incised designs or the field between them, and basal ridges, which now became more pronounced. Typical new shapes were mammiform tetrapod vessels with outcurving sides and convex base. Several traits indicate that culture was on the threshold of the Classic expression of Maya southern lowland civilization. Polychrome pottery, bridged spouts, basal flanges, rudimentary (perhaps even fully developed) corbeled vaults, carved monuments, and dates inscribed in some sort of Long Count system were all expressions, sometimes in prototypical form, of Early Classic characteristics. I have discussed the Holmul and Uaxactun early vaults in the afore-mentioned paper, and the still earlier vaulted tomb of Altar de Sacrificios has been noted. Thompson believes that the Holmul rooms above the ossuaries had true corbeled vaulting and that the cists were therefore used, if not constructed, after the building of the vaulted rooms; he calls attention also to a vaulted burial chamber with Matzanel pottery at Mountain Cow. Thompson shows that trade, as reflected in pottery, was widespread, and Willey sees evidence of a population explosion at Barton Ramie.

EARLY CLASSIC

By now, lowland Maya civilization had achieved the cultural traits for which it is best known and, to a large extent, by which it is defined: monumental masonry architecture, including the corbeled vault; hieroglyphic writing; and certain mathematical and scientific or pseudo-scientific accomplishments, such as a permutating calendar, place-value notation with arithmetic calculations involving large digits, and an interest in astronomy. In this sense, the southern lowland Maya reached the classic expression of their culture, although this was not necessarily the greatest florescence in all areas occupied by the Maya.

The ceremonial centers, probably organized politically and religiously in something like city-states, with wider allegiances configurating on a theocracy, consisted of masonry buildings assembled around courts and plazas, often on impressive acropolis-like eminences, the latter sometimes connected by causeways. The city plan often depended on the topography, but orientation of the buildings to cardinal points or to astronomically significant directions was widespread.

Ordinary dwellings, probably like those of the preceding period, were thatch-roofed pole, wattle-and-daub, or part-masonry and part-pole houses, erected on low earth and rubble platforms that kept their dirt, marl, or plastered floors dry during the tropical rainy seasons. They were located singly or, more commonly, in small groups arranged around little courts, situated on ridges or other higher terrain around the edges of lakes, swamps, or water holes. Along the Belize River, Willey and associates found them on the alluvial river flats, often so close together that there could have been little room for planting. In northeast Peten, Bullard found small, medium, and large concentrations of these house mounds: "clusters" were little hamlets of five to twelve dwellings in an area perhaps 200 meters square, and spaced 50–150 meters apart. An extended village of several clusters, or 50–100 houses, covered a zone of about 1 square kilometer; each cluster had its minor ceremonial centers, but no stone-slab monuments (stelae), altars, or ball courts. These last occurred, along with temples and "palaces," in districts, dispersed cities averaging about 100 square kilometers of arable or habitable land, presumably the sustaining areas for major ceremonial centers. Density of house mounds ranged from Uaxactun's 78 platforms—about 40 household units—per square kilometer (how many of them were occupied simultaneously is not known) to Barton Ramie's 106 household units in the same-sized tract.

Most major architecture employed the substructure, a pyramid, platform, or terrace with retaining walls supporting earth and rubble fill. On this usually (but not invariably) stood one or more superstructures—temples or "palaces," made of deeply set stone slabs, which not only formed the walls but also supported the corbeled vaults, overlapping slabs that approached each other from the sides of the room until they could be bridged with a single row of capstones. As a result, walls tended to be massive, and rooms quite narrow. The pyramid-temples were sometimes also for mortuary purposes, with a shaft leading from the superstructure down into a burial chamber in the pyramid. Palaces—whether correctly so called is uncertain—usually had more rooms than

A

B

C

D

FIG. 1.—Maya pyramid temples. *A*, Late Formative, Uaxactun, Guatemala. (After Proskouriakoff [1946].) *B*, Late Classic, Palenque, Mexico. (After Holmes [1895].) *C*, Early Classic, Kaminaljuyu, Guatemala. (After Kidder, Jennings, and Shook [1946].) *D*, Classic period, Tikal, Guatemala. (After Proskouriakoff [1946].)

the temples, could have two stories with an interior stairway, and stood on lower substructures.

Buildings were often crowned with huge roof structures (roof combs), either hollow or solid, to make the height more imposing and to increase the area to be decorated. Façades were usually divided into two horizontal zones by a medial molding halfway up the wall and were further decorated with a cornice molding at the roof line. The upper façades and the roof combs were elaborately ornamented with stonework or stucco. There were regional styles of architecture, which we cannot describe here but which render inaccurate any such general description as that given above.

According to Ruz, simple burials in the Early Classic Petén almost disappeared, and there were more cists, graves, and funeral chambers. Burials were both flexed and extended, the former somewhat more popular in important chamber burials at Uaxactun, the latter occurring in rooms at Tikal. There were also some urn burials. Funeral offerings were richer, and there are evidences of human sacrifice. Caches and other offerings of pottery, eccentric flints, incised obsidians, figurines, and ornaments have been found associated with monuments, altars, and structures.

The stelae, carved in relief, which ordinarily stood in the plazas in front of these buildings, or in shrine-like niches of the palace galleries, bear hieroglyphic dates spanning a period of perhaps 256 years. Proskouriakoff has shown that, in addition, there were 70–100 years of the closing Early Classic, when Maya sculptural activity apparently ceased, possibly a period transitional to the Late Classic changes to follow. Both Spinden and Proskouriakoff have painstakingly analyzed Maya sculptural art and can trace in some detail the changes it underwent during Classic times. For example, in the pose and postures of the Maya figures, Early Classic can be distinguished from later trends by the placement of the legs, which never overlap at the level of the knee. One leg is thrust forward and the other is straight, making the angle of the foot and leg a right angle. Both feet point in the same direction. More generally, there was a progression in art from a relatively simple and direct style to one more ornate and elaborate and, later, to less realism and technically less efficient execution. Proskouriakoff notes that the later monuments of the Early Classic do not always compare favorably with earlier productions. Poses became stiff; limbs became simplified and less fluidly outlined.

Tzakol slipped pottery, as described by E. B. Ricketson, Thompson, R. E. Smith, Gifford, and others, characteristically had a gloss finish ("Peten Gloss") and was produced in surface colors of orange, buff, red, brown, black, gray, red-and-black-on-buff, red-and-black-on-orange,

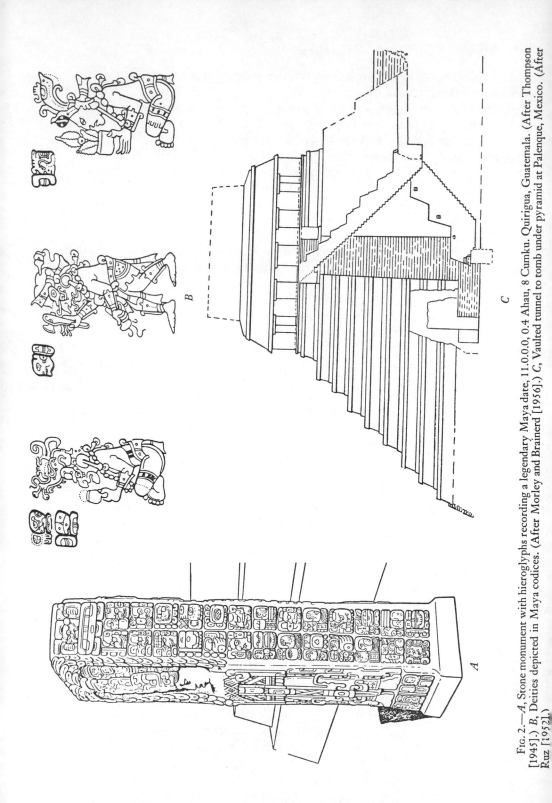

Fig. 2.—A, Stone monument with hieroglyphs recording a legendary Maya date, 11.0.0.0, 0.4 Ahau, 8 Cumku. Quirigua, Guatemala. (After Thompson [1945].) B, Deities depicted in Maya codices. (After Morley and Brainerd [1956].) C, Vaulted tunnel to tomb under pyramid at Palenque, Mexico. (After Ruz [1952].)

and variegated. The prevalent shapes were jars, basal-flange bowls with ring base, tetrapod pedestal-base bowls with flaring sides and accompanying cover, basal ridge or "Z-angle" bowls, and bowls with flaring side. The scutate, flanged cover-handles were cylindrical, zoömorphic, or anthropomorphic. Vessels stood on ring or pedestal supports or on hollow, bulging, or conical feet. Decorative techniques included painting —either direct or resist—and preslip incising, scratching, modeling, and appliqué. The painted designs were usually horizontal stripes encircling the vessels, plus a central wavy line, symbolic and conventionalized animals, and abstract elements, such as triangles, angular scrolls, and reverse angles. Although not a prevalent form, the cylinder tripod vase with slab feet—diagnostic for this period throughout Mesoamerica— was present. Thin orange ware shows cultural contact with highland Guatemala and perhaps also with Mexico.

There were regional ceramic as well as architectural styles. The Rands show that the Tzakol pottery was by no means typical of Palenque, Chiapas, although basal-flange and convex-base low tripod bowls and dishes (including red-and-black-on-orange), ring-base bowls, flat widely everted rims, slab-foot cylinder tripod vases, and other generally early features appear in the lower level of pottery there and link the site at least indirectly with Early Classic Piedras Negras, the Alta Verapaz, and other Maya cities farther east. Palenque was primarily a Late Classic city, however, and its Early Classic pottery is not abundant. Piedras Negras in the Middle Usumacinta, not far from Palenque, had quite different ceramics, distinct, too, from pottery of the Peten–British Honduras and Alta Verapaz regions, although sharing with them certain common denominators of Classic period wares. According to R. E. Smith and Gifford, regional differences were relatively minor, however, and major ceramic types were fairly uniform from Piedras Negras in the west, through central Peten, to Barton Ramie in the east.

Similarly, Copan in western Honduras partook of these widespread ceramic traits—basal-flange polychrome bowls, cylinder tripods, and thin orange ware, for example—but, as Longyear points out, the very universality of these types makes it difficult to determine their place or places of origin. In addition to its Peten–British Honduras ties, Copan shared a number of ceramic connections with highland Guatemala (Kaminaljuyu). In general, however, Copan's ceramic traditions were derived from eastern El Salvador, the Ulua and Comayugua drainages in Honduras—outside the area of masonry buildings, carved stelae, and hieroglyphic writing.

William R. Coe offers the following inventory of artifacts used during Classic times in the Peten–British Honduras region: core, bifaced percussion-flaked flint and limestone implements, probably general utility, chopping and pecking-pounding or agricultural tools; flint and obsidian scrapers and abraders, drills, and perforators and hollow drills used with an abrasive; bone awls and needles; flint and obsidian knives, projectile points, and other blades; milling stones, both the handstone manos and the stationary metates, of which there were at least three types; green and dark stone gouges and celts; and weaving implements, such as spindle whorls. Coe also lists many ceremonial artifacts found in caches or with burials or illustrated in ancient art. These include jade and shell beads and other ornaments, inlaid mosaics, exotically chipped flint and obsidian objects, dental inlays, and pyrite mosaic plaques.

CALENDRICS

One of the diagnostics of classic Maya culture was its system of permutating calendars. The ancient Maya seem to have been fascinated, even obsessed, with recurring cycles of time, some of them ceremonial in origin, having no apparent correspondence to anything in nature; some recording such natural phenomena as the solar year, lunations, eclipses, and other regularities of heavenly bodies as viewed from earth. As Thompson has explained, they thought of time periods as burdens carried on the back of gods, who laid down their burden at the end of the period for another god-number to pick up and proceed on the "journey of time." Since mankind's fortunes depended largely on whether the god-bearer of a given day or year or other period was benevolent or malevolent, calendars were primarily divinatory in purpose. The days on which the completion of two or more cycles coincided were of great ritual and divinatory significance.

One of these cycles was the Sacred Round (tzolkin) of 260 days, consisting of two recurring cycles of different length, the first being of 13 days, recorded as numbers, and the second being of 20 days, recorded as names. A second cycle was the solar year or, more properly, the "vague year" of 365 days, which was divided into 18 divisions of 20 days each (popularly referred to today as "months") plus a 5-day appendix at the end of the year, this last consisdered a dangerous and unlucky period. The completion of these two cycles, the Sacred Round and the Vague Year, coincided every 52 vague years (18,980 days). This larger cycle is called the "Calendar Round." Carved monuments (stelae) were frequently erected at Calendar Round and other intervals.

Among other time cycles running concurrently with the foregoing, and often recorded with them on inscriptions, was a 9-day week, its units named, like our 7-day week, for gods, the nine Maya Lords of the Night. There may also have been a 7-day week of Lords of the Earth. The age of the current moon was recorded for many dates, and, since the Maya corrected for the true length of a lunation by alternating

29-night and 30-night lunar months, they also noted which of these lengths was current.

In addition to indicating the date in a number of these cycles—which, if all of them were recorded, would fix the date accurately within 3,276 years—the Maya stated for the date the amount of elapsed time since the beginning point of their calendar, just as we record the time that has elapsed from the birth of Christ, the beginning point of the Christian calendar.

The calendar underwent changes in later epochs of Maya history. After the Early period in northern Yucatan, they used a Short Count, an abbreviation of the calendar system that has made it difficult to tie the ancient Long Count to the European calendar.

As yet, it is not possible to say with certainty which correlation is correct. Neither of the two most likely satisfies all requirements of all the evidence relevant to the problem. This evidence is of many kinds: historical, archeological, astronomical, and radiocarbon dating. The last, or some more recent or future method of absolute dating, will probably settle the matter, but radiocarbon dating is still imperfect and presents conflicting evidence.

To give an example, the Maya date 8.12.0.0.0, which is the approximate beginning of the Early Classic period, equates with our date A.D. 18 according to one correlation and with A.D. 278 according to another. If we select the Maya date 9.8.0.0.0 as the approximate end of the Early Classic, we have the choice of Christian dates A.D. 333 and A.D. 593.

Various authorities have modified each of the correlations by a few days, and the correlation is often referred to in terms of these scholars. Thus one correlation is known as Spinden's or Makemson's, depending on which slight variation or equation is meant, and the other most favored correlation is known as the Goodman-Martinez-Thompson (GMT) correlation, since each of these epigraphers has modified it by a few days (Table 1).

Another archeological approach to the correlation problem is that of trying to find a reasonably certain contemporaneous Maya tie-up with remains in the southwestern United States, where absolute dating by means of tree-ring studies is available; but, again, such factors as culture lag and the time one must allow for the spread of knowledge from one area to the other have to be taken into account and, so far, have prevented a decision.

ASTRONOMY, HIEROGLYPHIC WRITING, AND OTHER
INTELLECTUAL ACHIEVEMENTS

Most of the glyphic inscriptions to which we have referred so far appear on carved-stone stelae, lintels, stairways, and other monumental remains. In addition, there were once hundreds of sacred books or codices, of which only three are extant: the Dresden, the Madrid, and the Paris, named for the European cities to which they ultimately found their way after the Spanish Conquest. These books, painted on a folding screen of native paper, were divinatory almanacs concerned with agriculture, weather, disease, hunting, beekeeping, astronomy, and other topics.

TABLE 1

CHRONOLOGY*

	Spinden or Makemson	Goodman-Martinez-Thompson
Late Postclassic and Yucatan Decadent (second phase) (postmonumental) (Yaqui)	A.D. 1430–1540	....
Late Postclassic and Yucatan Decadent (first phase) (Mayapan)	1260–1430	A.D. 1200–1540
Yucatan Transition (Black-on-cream pottery)	1150–1260	....
Early Postclassic and Yucatan Modified Florescent ("Mexican" period) (Tohil)	900–1150	975–1200
Interregnum	....	925– 975
Yucatan Pure Florescent	700– 900	800– 925
Late Classic and Yucatan Transition (Tepeu 3)	580– 700	....
Late Classic and Yucatan Early Period (second phase) (Tepeu 1–2) (Pokom)	330– 580	625– 800
Early Classic and Yucatan Early Period (first phase) (Tzakol)	65– 330	325– 625
Protoclassic and Yucatan Transition (Chiapa VI; Matzanel; Aurora)	50 B.C.–A.D. 65	A.D. 210– 325
Late Formative or Preclassic (Crucero; Chiapa V; Chicanel; Miraflores; Dzibilchaltun Formative IV)	300–500 B.C.	210 B.C.–A.D. 210
Middle Formative or Preclassic (Conchas 1–2; Chiapa II–IV; La Venta; Mamom; Dzibilchaltun Formative I–III)	1000– 300 B.C.	
Early Formative or Preclassic (Ocos; Chiapa I)	1400–1000 B.C.	

* This draws on previous charts by Thompson, Wauchope, M. Coe, and Andrews.

The Dresden Codex contains tables noting dates on which solar eclipses would occur over a period of 33 years, whether visible or not in the Maya area. It records with astonishing accuracy the synodical revolutions of the planet Venus in terms of the Maya ceremonial Sacred Round as well as the vague year, even making emendations five times in 301 Venus revolutions to correct for the varying length of those cycles as the planet wobbles relative to the earth, a phenomenon the Maya astronomers could not possibly have been aware of except as it was reflected by Venus' erratic reappearances as morning star.

Although there was no Maya alphabet in the strict sense of this term, and hence there can be no Rosetta stone to act as a key to the translation of Maya hieroglyphic writing, its decipherment has made great strides since some of its fundamental principles were discovered, thanks largely to the scholarship of J. Eric S. Thompson in this field. For a long time epigraphers had noted the attributes of deities and the contexts in which certain recurring glyphs appeared. They learned that certain glyphs represented the sun, moon, eclipse, death, and so on, and then, by applying the sounds of modern Yucatec Maya for the things symbolized, they found that the ancient writing not only was ideographic, the pictures directly representing the words, but also made extensive use of rebus writing, in which the total sound of a term was approximately represented by combining pictures or symbols of things whose spoken names resembled sounds in the term to be recorded. Thompson illustrates with the Maya word for drought, *kintunyaabil* in Yucatec (*kin*, "sun"; *tun*, "intense"; *yaabil*, "for the whole year"), which was written with four glyphic elements, the signs of sun or day (*kin*), stone or 360-day unit of time (*tun*), vague year (*haab*), and the affix *il*. Thompson has published a dictionary of Maya hieroglyphs, and his further studies, along with those of other scholars, are constantly ferreting out additions.

Knorozov and other Russian scholars believe that Maya writing was truly syllabic and hence that it is subject to standard methods of decipherment: matching the most frequent phonemes in modern Maya to the most frequent glyph elements in ancient writing, a method speeded in recent years by electronic aids. Thompson is convinced, on the other hand, that Maya writing was not syllabic, and he presents strong evidence to this effect. We cannot review all of it here, but, as an example, he notes that the majority of glyphic affixes are prefixes only, whereas in syllabic writing most affixes could be both prefixes and suffixes; that many glyphs are confined to the divinatory passages in the codices, while others appear only on the monuments, and that the number of glyphs for a syllabary is usually far smaller than the total number of Maya glyphs known.

The three Maya codices contain a wealth of hieroglyphic writing that lends itself to this fascinating decipherment. The divinatory passages, for example, show pictures of the gods who rule over the days of the Sacred Round, whether they are malevolent or benevolent, what special hazards must be avoided, and for which activities the specified day is propitious. Much of this is written in ideographic and rebus puns, both as symbolic and personified glyphs. Thompson shows how each compartment of four glyphs in a typical codex divination contains an action or verbal glyph, the name of the god ruling the days in question (usually the "subject"), sometimes an object, and the augury resulting from the action or influence of the god (abundance, good times, misery, and so on). Thus, he can translate such passages from the divinatory almanacs as (from the Dresden): "On the days Eb, Kan, Cib, Lamat, and Ahau the death god is the divine punishment the white goddess has in store for us. Much death is the augury."

Thompson, Berlin, Proskouriakoff, and Kelley have shown how

hieroglyphic texts can throw some light on the political and social organization of the Maya during the Classic period. Emblem glyphs, for example, can be identified with single important cities and, in some cases, with groups of cities of minor rank. Thompson suggests that these ceremonial centers possibly formed a politicoreligious unit. He also notes that two important cities of first rank were located within a few miles of each other, possibly reflecting arrangements comparable to those of Tenochtitlan and Tlatelolco in the Valley of Mexico. Proskouriakoff found that the inscriptions on stelae and the groups of figures associated are related, and the names, birth dates or naming dates, and succession of rulers and their families can be recognized. Thompson sees also the possibility of grouped city-states—larger political units—reflected in conformity to or deviation from the use of sets of year-bearers in the calendar.

LATE CLASSIC

This stage is marked by changes in the three categories of archeological remains that we have in most abundance: architecture, sculpture, and ceramics. Inscribed stelae record dates from A.D. 333 or 593 (depending on which correlation one favors) to about A.D. 668 or 928, approximately 335 years.

A marked change in building was to veneer masonry, in which thinner building stones replaced slabs; these were set, but not deeply, into concrete, the latter forming the bulk of the walls and vaults. At Comalcalco, Tabasco, the westernmost major Maya site, baked brick was usual. As the vaults improved, walls became less massive, rooms wider. Multiple doorways, sometimes separated by narrow piers or by columns, became more common, and roof structures became smaller. Again, there were regional variations. Some pyramid-temples at Palenque had a shrine in the innermost chamber, elaborately decorated with panels of bas-relief sculpture. The main Palenque palace is well known for its interior courts, galleries, and four-story square tower. As Pollock says, the Palenque builders were innovators; among their unique or unusual structures were toilets, an aqueduct, and a vaulted bridge. Piedras Negras architecture was less massive. Beam-and-mortar roofs made possible more spacious interiors, well lighted by multiple doors. Perforated roof combs in the Usumacinta added to the "lightness" in architecture. Stucco decoration in many sites there was more popular than it was in the Peten.

Late Classic burials in the southern lowlands occurred in graves, cists, and funeral chambers. Common people were often buried under the floors of dwellings. The funeral chambers of Palenque are famous; they have been found in terraces, mounds, platforms, and mortuary pyramids, and they contained one or more stone sarcophagi. The subterranean tomb under the Temple of the Inscriptions, excavated by Ruz, was connected to the temple sanctuary above by a narrow masonry tunnel. Multiple burials of young men lay at the slab door to the tomb, and a female skeleton was seated in a corner of the funeral chamber. The tomb walls were decorated with stucco and bas-relief sculptures; the sarcophagus was monolithic, with elaborate relief carving on the lid. Ruz says that the Palenque burials were definitely made prior to the construction of the temples. On the coastal plain of Tabasco, Comalcalco tomb walls discovered by Blom were decorated with fine stucco relief figures and glyphs; the skeleton lay on a four-footed platform, possibly in a sarcophagus.

Proskouriakoff has recorded the changes and new trends in Late Classic sculpture. Figures were now depicted with the feet pointing outward in opposite directions when the torso was in front view; in side poses the far leg was almost hidden. During the Late Classic the trend was toward greater complexity of ornament, with emphasis shifting from the subject to the quality of the detail; the artist's attitude appeared to be "more detached from the religious content of his work," more intellectual and analytical. Costume elements changed: for example, the sandal with fringed ankle-guard and cufflike wristlets and anklets became common. Regional styles emerged and, as the period progressed, tended to blend.

Tepeu pottery has been shown by R. E. Smith to have undergone at least three stages of development. Tepeu 1 had several traits in common with late Tzakol pottery, but new features were the vitrified-appearing wares, multicolor-on-orange, -cream, -gray, or -buff; black-on-orange; brown-on-red and brown-on-buff; and red-and-black-on-red. New vessel shapes were the restricted-orifice, incurved-rim bowl; the round-side, incurved-rim bowl; jar with slightly bulging neck; barrel-shaped bowl or vase; fine-ware cylindrical vase; basal- or lateral-ridge tripod plate; and the drum. Feet were hollow and cylindrical or conical. There were also new designs, more naturalistic than those of Tzakol, and some glyph and sky bands. In Tepeu 2, slipped gloss wares predominated as before; others were vitrified in appearance. "Vinaceous Tawny" ware became popular, especially in the Belize Valley. The tripod flaring or outcurving-side plates were new; also slightly flaring or outcurving-side bowls or dishes; notched or stepped tripod basal-flange dishes or plates, and bowls with flaring or outcurving sides, angling to the base. Tripod vessels had flat instead of rounded bases. Geometric designs supplanted the naturalistic trend of Tepeu 1, but there were also naturalistic and glyphic motifs. Polychrome declined in Tepeu 3; new were fine orange, carved ferruginous, fine gray, and Yucatecan slate—most of these trade pottery from elsewhere. Some authorities, such as R. F. Smith and Gifford, consider Tepeu 3 a distinct ceramic stage transitional to the Postclassic. Innovations included incurved-rim tripod dishes; restricted bead-orifice bowls; barrel-shaped, ring-stand vases; tripod dishes with basal angle; grater bowls; double cups ("candeleros"), and other forms. Feet were solid, and handles were more abundant. The unslipped jar and incurved-rim bowl were used throughout the Tepeu ceramic period. Figurines were now mold made.

Tepeu polychrome featured depictions of ceremonies and myths, with hieroglyphic bands around the rim. Thompson has shown that legends of the living Maya are illustrated on several of these prehistoric vessels, as are ceremonies that were practiced long after the Europeans occupied the area.

As in Early Classic times, there were regional styles in pottery. At Copan, for example, Copador polychrome was a specialty; it featured hematite red decoration and distinctive representations of humans and birds. The untempered, highly polished fine orange is more abundant at Altar de Sacrificios on the Pasion. At Palenque, such Tepeu diagnostics as the incurved rim and glyph band were rare. Cylindrical vases of the earlier levels were in part superseded by outflaring or outcurved bowls and beakers, according to the Rands. Bases were flat, and there were some bulbous cascabel tripods. Polychrome tended to be replaced by monochrome wares. Ring-base bowls died out; hanging rims superseded flat, widely everted rims. Basal ridges (Z-angles) were abundant. Unslipped jars now had low, vertical, rather than sloping, necks; shoulders were more nearly squared. There was a pronounced shift from calcite to quartz temper. In the western lowlands, Palenque Late Classic pottery shows little relationship with Tepeu, somewhat more with the Alta Verapaz, and still more with the Tabasco plains, where Berlin isolated three stages in the Late Classic pottery sequence. Tecolpan and Jonuta have Late Classic fine gray, fine black, and polychrome wares. R. E. Smith and Gifford consider these Late Classic regional differences in major types of pottery to be greater than in Early Classic times.

Lowland Maya figurines attained their greatest elaboration and sophistication in the Late Classic period. By now mold-made forms had replaced the Mamom hand-modeled forms; limbs were free of the body, welded to the torso. Many subjects were depicted, human, animal, and grotesque. Rands has noted that, in contrast to the Preclassic figurines, the Late Classic specimens reflected more attention to headdress and clothing than to the body, although the features were more lifelike. He points out regional styles, such as the Palenque hierarchical and the Alta Verapaz dorsoventral flattening with side flanges, and suggests that the more elaborate styles along the western edge of the lowlands from

Campeche to Tabasco and Chiapas, the Usumacinta, and its headwaters in Alta Verapaz may reflect a Mexican source of the Classic-period revitalization of figurine art after its dormancy during Chicanel times.

POSTCLASSIC

One problem of interest is how and why the ancient Maya built such impressive cities in this most forbidding of Middle American environments—the tropical rain forest, with its uncertain water supply, its poor transportation facilities, its most difficult obstacles to agriculture, and its unfavorable share of natural resources. This region, which is practically uninhabited today and has been since the Spanish Conquest, was densely populated in prehistoric times. A second and probably related problem, still not satisfactorily explained, is why the magnificant southern Maya civilization declined at the end of the Late Classic period. Although there is growing evidence that the southern lowlands were by no means completely abandoned and that the decline of the city-states was more gradual than once thought, still, it was a period of dramatic cultural and economic decadence. There are objections that disallow almost every hypothesis that has been proposed so far to explain the phenomenon; on one ground or another, one cannot support as a single explanation crop failure, grass invasion of cornfields, soil exhaustion, plague, loss of water supply, or foreign invasion. The only theory that cannot be completely disproved is that of peasant revolution or some rebellion against established theocratic authority, and there is not a great deal of evidence upholding such an explanation. One can only generalize that in some way the southern lowlands failed to adapt to changing conditions and that their magnificent centers went to ruin as an impoverished population lived under the shadow of their mighty past but did little to build a future. Why, though, was this largely a southern lowland versus highland and northern lowland phenomenon? For the most part, the less impressive highland Maya centers flourished in Postclassic times and, even under the sway of foreign political dynasties, managed to maintain a civilization that was still outstanding in the Western Hemisphere. Northern Yucatan, at least at the great city of Dzibilchaltun, survived this epoch successfully; indeed, as we shall see, its Florescent period followed the Classic period of the south.

The Postclassic periods saw a more intense concentration of dwellings in smaller areas, not only in the heavily populated northern Yucatan cities but also in the southern lowlands. This is especially clear in centers to which the north Yucatecans are known to have moved in late times. At Lake Yaxha, in Peten, Bullard found hundreds of Postclassic mounds and house platfoms crowded on a few small islands, reflecting either Toltec tradition or Maya response to the constant threat of foreign militarism. Topoxte, Tayasal, Santa Rita, and Indian Church in British Honduras and the later remains at Altar de Sacrificios in Guatemala are examples of Postclassic centers showing late and Mexican-derived cultural traits. Topoxte gives evidence of a Late Postclassic (protohistoric) occupation, with Mayapan-type censers among the ceramic remains.

Postclassic materials have been found at other southern lowland sites, including Tikal, Guatemala, and Barton Ramie, British Honduras. In the western lowlands, fine orange pottery occurs at Tecolpan and Jonuta, and other later wares appear. An undecorated fine orange ware of protohistoric date also comes from the western lowlands on what Berlin calls the Cintla horizon there. It appears that there was still a large population in the "Old Empire" region; Thompson suggests that the peasants continued their daily lives there, with little disturbance, under minor headmen. Resetting of stelae fragments in some of the sites suggests to him that these people tried to keep up some sort of stela cult, even though they were so ignorant as not to know when they placed an ancient inscription upside down.

Plumbate and fine orange pottery (two widespread and easily recognized wares of known Postclassic provenience in other parts of Middle America), human-effigy head and "turkish-slipper" feet for tripod vessels, late incense burners, flat stone heads and stone yokes of Mexican derivation, mural art styles, tecali and marble vessels, copper and gold, late (Mexican) architectural features, and figurines and other imports from Postclassic cultures elsewhere are being found in increasing numbers throughout the southern lowlands. Techniques of manufacture were poor, and unslipped wares increased in proportion to the slipped. There was much more monochrome pottery than in Late Classic times.

After their peak of sophistication in Late Classic, lowland Maya figurines declined in number and in excellence of execution. As Rands shows, emphasis turned, instead, to the modeling of elaborate effigy censers. There were some human, bird, and animal whistles, effigies, or figurines. Rands also notes that caryatid-supported platform figurines with a personage on top and strong Mexicanized motifs appeared in Postclassic Tabasco.

NORTHERN YUCATAN PENINSULA

The Northern Yucatan Peninsula is a low, limestone plain, the emergent part of a much larger and still submerged shelf around the deeps of the Gulf of Mexico. Covered in most places with dense thickets of dry, thorny, scrub forest, its surface is flat, its soil shallow or broken with outcrops of the underlying limestone. Although there are sporadically distributed lakes in the interior and extensive lagoons at or near the coast, there are no surface streams; water flows underground and is tapped by the Indians through sinkholes in the limestone crust. These wells range in size from tiny holes scarcely large enough to admit a cylindrical bark bucket up to giant *cenotes* several hundred feet across, with water 60–150 feet deep. Natural resources, other than building stone, wood, and wild game, must have been scarce in prehistoric times.

A low range of hills crosses Yucatan from the Campeche coast at Champoton to central and northern parts of the peninsula in the east. South of these hills are swamps and savannas, surface ponds, and larger rivers; the scrub thickets gradually become taller and finally merge into the great rain forests of the southern Yucatan peninsula.

Reefs, shoals, and the lack of good harbors make navigation difficult on the coasts of the northern peninsula, especially the east coast. Temperatures range from 45 to 105 degrees, the mean falling in the 70's. Rainfall is sparse and seasonal: 30–40 inches in the west, 40–60 inches inland. Cycles of dry years and frequent northers that blow in from the Caribbean are a menace to crops.

A major dialect of the Maya language, Yucatec, is spoken today by Indians in most of this area. It was doubtless the speech of the prehistoric natives as well, except, of course, for their Toltec conquerors relatively late in their history. To judge from depictions in ancient art, the prehistoric Indians were physically like the natives today: relatively short and heavy set, with medium to broad heads, dark straight to wavy hair, swarthy complexions, aquiline noses, full lips and somewhat receding chins, and "almond-shaped" eyes, the last a result of epicanthic fold and heavy-lidded expression.

Because Maya cities were known to have been occupied in northern Yucatan when the Spaniards arrived and because some of the most famous ruins differ so much in architectural styles from the early cities of the southern lowland, it was once thought that northern Yucatan was not occupied when the jungle cities of the south were in their heyday and that it was the second (or what became widely known as the "New Empire") home of the Maya, after they had abandoned the great centers in the south. Although there is still some basis for considering much of ancient northern Yucatan a "New Empire"—its most imposing cities were in general later than those of the Guatemala rain forests—it is now known that the area was occupied, in places at least, fully as long as the southern regions and that, although the "Old Empire" Maya of the south could have moved north, it is by no means certain that many of them did. Instead, northern Yucatan was civilized many centuries before Christ and not only survived the difficult years that spelled decline for the jungle cultures but in some ways achieved the full flowering of its building arts even later.

For example, excavations under the direction of E. W. Andrews at Dzibilchaltun, Yucatan, revealed an uninterrupted occupation from about 1000 B.C. to the present and provided a clear architectural-ceramic stratigraphy for these 3000-odd years, dated at intervals by radiocarbon specimens. This continuous and closely sealed stratigraphy at a single site was unique among the ruins then excavated in the Maya lowlands, providing a continuous sequence to bolster the several floating records of sites occupied for shorter periods, such as Uxmal, Chichen Itza, and Mayapan. Its value from the interpretive and conceptual viewpoint is that it gave the northern Yucatan cultural sequence a mass of data of its own, so that the area's prehistory could be judged on its own terms rather than in those of other areas to which a few trade objects linked it chronologically.

As we have seen, the Maya prehistory of the southern lowlands has led to a period nomenclature of Formative (or "Preclassic"), Early Classic, Late Classic, Early Postclassic, and Late Postclassic. Although the Preclassic remains from that area were scarce, and the Postclassic practically absent, archeologists believed that the earliest layers represented a period during which Maya culture was "formed," and the two succeeding periods (after which it all but died out) were its "classic" expression. Viewed in an unbroken sequence in northern Yucatan, and now documented with tons of pottery and other remains tied to the architectural record, the general character of the periods there appears quite different. Andrews doubts, for example, the wisdom of calling the early sequence "Formative," for he finds it quite foreign to what followed, and he objects even more strongly to labeling the next two periods "Classic," when the full flowering of culture in this area actually came later—after the "Late Classic" cities of the south had gone into decline. He recommends that for the time being we call the first post-Formative periods in northern Yucatan simply "Early" instead of "Classic," that the next period, which saw its full flowering, be called "Florescent," and that the final "Late Postclassic" period be named for what it was, "Decadent."

FORMATIVE PERIOD (PRE-MAYA?)

The last season of major excavation at Dzibilchaltun was devoted exclusively to its earliest occupations. Andrews isolated four stages, the lowest yielding pottery closely resembling Mamom ceramics of the southern lowland Peten area and Chiapa de Corzo III in southern Mexico, the second and third layers corresponding to Peten's Chicanel phase and to Chiapa de Corzo IV–V. A fourth Dzibilchaltun stage, dated by radiocarbon tests at about 300 B.C., reflects local ceramic decadence, and there are indications of a possible fifth stage transitional to the "Early" period that follows; this last may correspond to Peten's Matzanel and Holmul I, the stage known there as Protoclassic.

Andrews believes that this earliest settlement at Dzibilchaltun must have been one of a massive population, with a very long history, and undergoing an evolution of its own. Of its developmental stages, only the fourth and the postulated fifth period of transition to the truly Maya culture that followed seem to have any particular justification for being called "Formative." He writes (1962): "Neither in ceramics nor in architecture do the earlier stages exhibit any germ of the distinctive civilization to follow. Quite to the contrary they seem to have a separate individuality of their own, lost only at the very end." Andrews suggests that they be given a different name, such as "pre-Maya." As a matter of fact, the considerable skeletal material from this earliest sequence, though not yet examined by physical anthropologists, appears quite different from the Maya in a number of ways. Cultural relationships with other areas, as revealed primarily in trade pottery, appear to be very close, especially with the Peten and Chiapa de Corzo, thus contrasting with the locally divergent traditions that developed in the Peten, the Usumacinta, and peninsular Yucatan in the later (Maya) times.

EARLY PERIOD

In general this epoch was characterized by crude architecture of masonry construction (block walls and rough slab vaults), the upper façades of buildings covered with stucco carvings, and quite simple façade profiles, usually broken only by a plain medial molding. Monumental art with hieroglyphic inscriptions was stressed. Early-period pottery consisted largely of gloss wares, monochrome vessels with a waxy surface finish. There was trade with the Peten, evidenced by pottery from the Early Classic Tzakol and subsequent Tepeu ceramic phases there. Toward the end of the Early period, a Transitional period foreshadowed, in some of its developments, the full flowering of Maya culture that was to follow. This period corresponds in time to the latter parts of the Late Classic culture of the southern lowlands and is cross-tied to them by trade pottery of Tepeu 2 and later types. A local style of the potter's art of the Early period, one that because of its appeal to modern art collectors has become famous, developed on the island of Jaina off the Campeche coast, where almost all the graves in an extensive necropolis were provided with figurines of an elegant and refined style, characterized by realistic, free-limbed, heavy-lidded, almond-eyed individuals, usually standing or seated in impassive serenity. Elsewhere, Early-period and Transitional burials were placed in an extended position under the floors of buildings and provided with funeral pottery offerings. In the Puuc, the range of hills crossing Yucatan in the south, burials were frequently made in caves and underground chambers, or chultuns.

FLORESCENT PERIOD

Andrews has stated that in this period the basic techniques and finished products were about as different from those of the Early period as they could be. Block-wall and slab-vault masonry gave way to a pure concrete construction with a thin veneer of beautifully faced and shaped stone blocks. Façade profiles became complex, with multimember moldings. Instead of stucco carvings on the upper façades, we now find elaborate and conventionalized mosaics in carved stone, on both upper and lower zones. Monumental art was less emphasized; hieroglyphic inscriptions were discontinued. In pottery, slate wares became dominant. These have a surface luster with waxy feel and occur in a number of regional styles. Buildings of Pure Florescent style have been found at many sites, including the earliest structures at Chichen Itza, but the best-known concentrations are in the Puuc region, at such ruins as Uxmal, Kabah, and Labna, famous for their steep pyramids, large multistoried "palaces," closed quadrangles, series of ascending courts, and portal vaults, all lending grandeur and grace to the ceremonial centers. The buildings are classics of Pure Florescent architecture, with their carefully prepared veneer masonry, elaborate stone mosaic decoration (latticework, frets, masks, split columns, miniature temple, and serpent motifs), complex façade moldings (up to six members) supporting doorway columns, and perforated roof combs or flying façades, these last the Maya architect's way of providing more height and a sort of crowning feature to his buildings. Among the best-known buildings of this period are the Nunnery (Monjas) at Chichen Itza, the Adivino (Magician) pyramid, Nunnery Quadrangle, Governor's House, and House of the Pigeons at Uxmal, the Portal of Labna, and the elaborately decorated palaces of Kabah and Sayil. The Spaniards named most of these buildings, not because their real function was known but because they reminded the Europeans of things with which they were familiar back home. The House of the Pigeons, for example, has a huge series of triangular perforated roof combs that look like pigeon lofts.

MODIFIED FLORESCENT OR "MEXICAN PERIOD"

Just as Troy and other opulent cities of the ancient world attracted foreign invasion, this prosperous Maya civilization of northern Yucatan, long in apparently close contact with Mexican cultures and strongly influenced by them, now tempted the militaristic Toltecs of continental

Mexico, resulting in an invasion that had perhaps relatively short-lived but nevertheless spectacular effects on the sociopolitical organization, religion, and material culture of the northern plain.

Because of their close resemblance to Mexican cultural traits, particularly those at the Toltec capital at Tula, it has been assumed for a long time that the Yucatecan changes reflect this Mexican Toltec culture moving eastward into the peninsula. A more recent hypothesis advanced by Kubler is that the direction of most of this cultural flow was westward from Yucatan to Mexico. I shall summarize these two theories and the evidence for each.

The first proposes that new Mexican religious cults were introduced, including the worship of the Mexican Kukulcan, to whom many temples were dedicated and whose symbols became favorite architectural ornaments in such things as serpent entrance columns supporting the roof and serpent balustrades (the borders of stairways). New military orders arrived, too—such as the Eagles and Jaguars—and these became the subject of much bas-relief sculpture. Indeed, one entire building, the Temple of the Warriors at Chichen Itza, seems to have been a commemoration to the military conquest, for it features a large colonnaded patio, each of the columns carved and painted on all four sides with depictions of Toltec warriors, and murals in this temple as well as the Temple of the Jaguars depict the Mexicans fighting, leading Maya victims into captivity, or sacrificing them. Tozzer and others have shown how these Mexican soldiers can be distinguished from the Maya in art—by their throwing sticks or atlatls and defensive shields, their mosaic crown headdresses and turbans, mosaic breast ornaments, nose buttons, and conventionalized bird insignia—and also the clear Mexican derivation of the new architectural and art features, which are duplicated at the Toltec capital, Tula. Chac mool figures (reclining men with head turned to one side and knees drawn up, a receptacle or basin in the stomach); bas-relief friezes depicting prowling tigers; new architectural forms, such as the round tower; the gallery patio; the low, truncated and pyramidal sacrificial platform; and such new architectural features as the battered substructure wall and basal superstructure zone and the silhouette stones on the roofs of temples, all were innovations by the Mexicans.

The foreign architects kept some of the old Maya building traditions. They sometimes preferred the corbeled vault to their own flat beam-and-mortar roof, they adopted the Maya façade moldings and masks as ornaments, and they continued to build ball courts, sweat houses, portal vaults, and other Maya-type structures, although modifying them with typically Mexican features.

The Puuc cities were gradually abandoned as Toltec power increased.

FIG. 3.—*A*, Thatch-roofed dwelling by the sea. Canoes carry Toltec warriors. From mural at Chichen Itza, Yucatan (Pure Florescent or "Mexican" period). (After Morris, Charlot, and Morris [1931].) *B*, Noble carried in litter. Late Classic polychrome vase, Alta Verapaz, Guatemala. (After Thompson [1954].) *C*, Toltec warrior in Yucatan. Pure Florescent or "Mexican" period. Sculpture at Chichen Itza. (After Thompson [1954].)

The great center was Chichen Itza, a spacious magnificent capital whose famous buildings—the Castillo, the Great Ball Court, the Temple of the Warriors, and many others—are perhaps the best-known Maya monuments. Chichen Itza's bas reliefs, murals, sacrificial platforms, and Sacred Well (Cenote of Sacrifice), into which offerings of gold, jade, and other valuables, as well as human beings, were cast to the rain god, bear eloquent testimony to the morbid Mexican interest in human sacrifice, an obsession that endured into Aztec times, when it attained a peak of barbarity.

Although expert opinions differ somewhat as to the lasting effects of the Mexican conquest of Yucatan, all agree that the military occupation itself was only temporary and that the final periods of Yucatan prehistory witnessed a revival of Maya traditions. Andrews points out that the Toltec innovations, although strong, were expressed in the old Maya techniques, presumably by the same artisans.

Mexican influences also changed the plan of Maya cities in northern Yucatan. Pollock has pointed out that the Toltec architect's traditions are seen in the spaciousness of the main ceremonial center at Chichen Itza, the axial arrangement of structures, and, as Marquina noted, the orientation of buildings 17 degrees east of north.

The second theory concerning the Chichen Itza and Tula resemblances, advanced by Kubler in 1961, is that most of the traits concerned were evolved or acquired in Yucatan prior to their appearance in Tula and that the Toltecs introduced more ideas than actual material culture when they invaded Yucatan, these ideas, "clothed in Maya forms," later moving back to Tula. In support of this reasoning, Kubler states that prototypical forms of the so-called "Mexican" traits are present in Yucatan in earlier periods but not at Tula and that Maya interpretation of Mexican ideas dates far back into pre-Toltec times, at least to the Early Classic period at Kaminaljuyu in the Guatemala highlands, and certainly to the Late Classic period at Xochicalco in Mexico. For example, Kubler says that the Mexican wind-god concept resulted in the shell-like circular building at Chichen Itza called "El Caracol" but that its architectural features, as with another "Mexican" structure, "El Castillo," were derived from an earlier building underneath and from Early Classic prototypes in the Puuc and Rio Bec areas to the south. Similarly, Kubler derives certain art forms, such as the jaguar sculptured in round, from Classic (Early) period forerunners at Uxmal and in Peten and Usumacinta, and serpent columns from earlier effigy columns at Oxkintok. He considers the atlantean or caryatid forms at Chichen Itza to be prototypes of the colossal caryatids of Tula and traces the local evolution (based on style and on associations with his proposed architectural sequence) and possible derivation of processions and other sculptured themes usually thought to be derived from Tula. He finds precedents for warrior depictions in the Usumacinta and points out that there are more chac mools at Chichen Itza than at Tula. He notes that certain Maya-Toltec objects like the Sacred Cenote gold disks have not been found at Tula at all and that the cardiac sacrifices depicted on these also occur in the Late Classic art of Piedras Negras and Bonampak in the western Maya lowlands. Kubler's thesis, then, is that the invader Toltecs exported more from Chichen Itza than they brought to it.

Arnold and Frost in 1909 and, more recently, Ekholm and Heine-Geldern have assembled a large number of striking parallels between New World cultures and those of ancient India, China, and Mesopotamia. Ekholm (1953) suggests that Asiatic influences in Mexico may focus on the western border of the Maya area in the present states of Chiapas, Tabasco, and Campeche and that they are found in greatest strength in the late Mexican-influenced motifs and styles of Chichen Itza, Yucatan, and the contemporaneous city of Tula in central Mexico, about A.D. 1200. This complex of Asiatic influences may have reached America by A.D. 700. Among these traits are the fire serpent and mythical sea monster, atlantean figures, gods or ceremonial figures standing on crouched humans, stylized or celestial trees with demonic faces in their branches, stairways flanked by serpent balustrades, architectural half-columns, colonnettes, trefoil arches, vaulted galleries, sculptured panels depicting figures grouped around personages on low platform thrones, specific postures of enthroned figures, tiger thrones, lotus thrones, lotus staffs, lotus rhizomes framing reclining human figures and emerging from the mouths of sea monsters or fish, phallic symbols, seated lions or tigers, sun disks, and diving gods. Ferguson (1958) has listed 298 "elements of culture" common to Egypt, Asia Minor, and Mesopotamia, on the one hand, and Middle America, on the other.

These imposing lists of resemblances between Asia and prehistoric Mesoamerica, reinforced by the equally close parallels between Ecuador and Japan reported by Estrada, Meggers, and Evans (1962), keep open to discussion the entire question whether there were accidental, sporadic, or even regular contacts across the Pacific between the peoples of the Old World and the New, a possibility that most American anthropologists have in the past tended to deny. [EDITORS' NOTE: For fuller discussion of this point see Ekholm, pp. 502–4; see also Ekholm's bibliography.]

Modified Florescent-period burials were in tombs and funeral chambers. At Chichen Itza, the High Priest's Grave ("Osario") was a deep pit descending from the temple above into a natural cave beneath. It contained seven burials. Multiple burials of children and of crania have been found at this site.

A   B

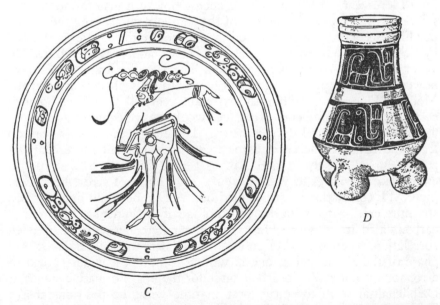

C   D

FIG. 4.—*A*, Formative period pottery, Guatemala highlands. (After Brainerd [1954].) *B*, Classic period jade effigy, Uaxactun, Guatemala. (After Kidder [1947].) *C*, Late Classic polychrome plate, Uaxactun, Guatemala. (After Morley and Brainerd [1956].) *D*, Pure Florescent fine orange pottery, Chichen Itza, Yucatan. (After Morley and Brainerd [1956].)

Slate wares (jars, bowls, and censers, usually with a gray slip and a reddish paste), red wares, and fine orange wares were the favorite pottery types of the Florescent in northern Yucatan. Toward the end of the Mexican period at Dzibilchaltun these suddenly gave way, according to Andrews, to a completely different ceramic complex, black-on-cream wares previously known only as surface material at Chichen Itza and found at the bottom of the brief Mayapan stratigraphy of the subsequent Decadent period. Thus Andrews inserts in the northern Yucatan cultural sequence an additional and transitional period between the Modified Florescent and the Decadent. This is particularly important to the problem of correlating the European calendar with the Maya, for it increases the number of years that must be crowded into the time allowed by a correlation, thus favoring earlier correlations that provide more time room.

Andrews has pointed out that the older archeological sequence for northern Yucatan favored the Goodman-Martinez-Thompson correlation in that the period once thought to include only the last part of the Pure Florescent—believed to have been a northern manifestation considerably overlapping the decline of the southern cities—and the Modified Florescent or "Mexican period" would not fill the 580 years allowed by a Spinden or Makemson correlation but would fit easily into the 320 years allowed by the GMT equation. The Dzibilchaltun excavations, however, added a period of transition at both ends of the Pure and the Modified Florescent, and thus the extra 260 years allowed by an Spinden correlation, far from being excessive, would be welcome to accommodate the extra cultural developments. Two large samples of carbon from the Balankanche cave, associated with Modified Florescent deposits, agreed closely in age: A.D. 870 ± 90 and A.D. 870 ± 100. If either date is correct to within even a large range of error, he thinks, the GMT correlation must be ruled out. A Dzibilchaltun lintel from a structure cross-dated with the Tepeu phase of the Peten has been radiocarbon dated at A.D. 483 ± 140 years, again agreeing with the Spinden correlation, whereas a GMT solution would date the building in Tzakol phase of the Peten, unless one is willing to accept a wider spread of error for the dates. Radiocarbon dates for the final Formative stages at Dzibilchaltun seem to equate best in time with the positions that a Spinden correlation would give them.

DECADENT (OR LATE POSTCLASSIC) PERIOD

A new and important trend in Maya settlement patterns appeared in the final or Decadent period in northern Yucatan and in several other places where remains of this epoch have been found—a trend toward urbanism, the concentration of dense population within walled cities.

The most intensively excavated center of this kind is Mayapan, where mapping and excavations by Jones, A. L. Smith, and Ruppert revealed 2,100 dwelling units or households within the city's defense walls. Another late walled city was Tulum on the east coast, on the edge of a high cliff overlooking the sea.

Willey and Bullard have discussed the sociopolitical implications of these changes. They ask whether the new pattern implies a Maya middle class of artisans, minor priests and officials, and possibly even merchants, living in close quarters—that is, an urban way of life by a more heterogeneous society—and whether this concept was introduced by the Mexican invaders, as Brainerd suggested, or was simply a response to the militarism of the times.

According to Andrews, the Decadent period, in its evolved stages as seen at Mayapan, saw "almost total abandonment of the techniques which characterized Florescent architecture, and a return to those of the Early period." He suggests that this might actually have been a reintroduction into Yucatan of Early Period traits from the Caribbean coastal area, which had somehow escaped the impact of the Florescent tradition. Florescent pottery wares disappeared in favor of gray and, at Mayapan, red pottery. Great emphasis was placed on incense burners representing various deities. After having been largely absent during the Modified Florescent (Mexican) period, pottery figurines reappeared at Mayapan and Santa Rita, but they had degenerated in execution. The Santa Rita specimens, depicting warriors with lances, reflect the continued militarism of the times.

Pollock, who directed the five-year excavation of Mayapan, reports that ceremonial centers of this period were less extensive, civic and religious buildings were smaller, and the quality of workmanship inferior. To hide poorly cut building stones, architects covered the rough masonry with heavy coats of plaster, and decoration returned to the medium of stucco and murals rather than fine mosaic stone carving. The beam-and-mortar roof largely replaced the ancient Maya vault. A new type of structure was the small shrine, a sort of miniature temple. Colonnaded halls, mortuary buildings with mass burials, and round buildings became popular.

Several old Maya traits revived, among them the closed plaza and the stela cult. Some Mexican period features were retained, such as the basal batter on walls, entrance columns and balustrades that simulated serpents, and the general plan of temples.

I have mentioned the mortuary mass burials at Mayapan. There were also simple burials, in vessels, cists, graves, funeral chambers, and chultuns. Some skeletons were cremated. Caches of skulls have been found; in one cave were ten secondary burials; a bottle-shaped pit inside a pyramid contained forty sacrificial victims. Almost all Mayapan burials were flexed. One funerary chamber with an antechamber was reached by a stairway. At Tulum on the east coast there is a cruciform tomb. Bishop Diego de Landa, our main source of information on the Maya of this protohistoric period, wrote of cremation ashes placed in urns, and of skulls split and prepared for preservation. All these factors point toward a form of ancestor worship.

In summary, as Pollock said of Late Postclassic architecture at Mayapan, the culture "incorporated some earlier Maya practices, drew upon the Maya-Toltec architecture of Chichen Itza, and was affected by foreign influences, possibly from the Gulf Coast areas to the west."

Andrews sees in this sequence of three main post-"Formative" periods evidence of ethnic shift, as if new builders were brought in and carried on the artistic heritage of prior cultures, but with a very different set of tools, in one case (the Florescent) outdoing their predecessors, in another (the Decadent), failing miserably even to equal them, possibly as a result of the Toltec political upheavals. On the other hand, he calls attention to the transitional stages between the Early and the Florescent period, and between the latter and the Decadent, for these "point more toward an undisturbed evolution of local culture."

Rio Bec and Chenes Areas

As Pollock has pointed out, if one were to divide all lowland Maya architecture into only two styles, a northern and a southern, the dividing line between these would lie along the border between the Rio Bec and the central areas of the middle Yucatan peninsula; the Rio Bec sites, although sharing traits with both north and south, seem to be more closely allied with the former. They lacked the compact, orderly assemblages, acropolis concept, and lavish hieroglyphic monuments typical of the southern cities, and shared with northern architecture a preference for vertical upper façades and veneer masonry. Typical of Rio Bec buildings were towers with steep, non-functional stairways and false doorways framed in profiled serpent mouths and fanged masks, which, though simulating pyramid temples, did not actually have interior rooms. The lower façades were decorated with split columns, masks, and geometric mosaics; roof combs were perforated, single walls. There were also ball courts and two-story terraced buildings. In terms of northern Yucatan chronology, Rio Bec architecture thus seems to be largely of the Pure Florescent period.

Pollock considers the Chenes sites, such as Hochob, to be closely related to Rio Bec and transitional between the latter and the Puuc, which, as we have seen, was largely abandoned before Toltec influence modified the Pure Florescent culture of the north. Stairways were very steep but functional, and there were false doorways, sometimes framed in serpent-mouth profiles, sometimes not. As in the Rio Bec area, says Pollock, façades were so arranged as to simulate three separate structures. Masonry techniques and flying façades were more northern traits.

GUATEMALA HIGHLANDS

The Guatemala highlands are a spectacular region consisting of plateaus, mountains, and volcanic cones, dissected by deep ravines and pocketed with ash basins of volcanic origin. Inland from the recent volcanoes is an older range, which forms the continental divide and from which arise the streams that flow into the Pacific on the west and the Atlantic on the east. Several rivers also have their source in the Alta Verapaz, whence they drain northward into the Usumacinta, one of the largest waterways in Central America. There are some lakes, one of which, Atitlan, is a giant volcanic crater of great depth, surrounded by more recent cones, their lava terraces dotted with modern Indian villages and prehistoric sites. Except on the highest peaks and mountain passes, the winters are dry and cool, the summers temperate. Rains fall from May to November, and the volcanic soils are fertile. The terrain and its cover range from open grasslands to evergreen and deciduous forests. Fauna consist chiefly of small mammals, but deer and even pumas and jaguars are known here, and the quetzal bird, so prized by the ancient Maya, is still hunted with blowguns in the Cuchumatanes Mountains.

The highlands are—and were in protohistoric times—occupied by Indians speaking various dialects of Maya, among them Quiche, Pokoman, Cakchiquel, Zutuhil, Ixil, Mam, Jacaltec, and Chuj in the northern, central, and western portions; Kekchi and Pokomchi in Alta Verapaz; Cholti and Chorti in the east; and, in the south, Xinca, Pupuluca, Mixe-Zoque, and enclaves of Nahuat Pipil from Mexico.

To facilitate reference to regional differences, I shall use Rands's and R. E. Smith's three-zone terminology for this region: the northern zone, including Alta Verapaz, El Quiche, and Huehuetenango; the western, comprising Solola, Totonicapan, and parts of Quezaltenango and San Marcos; and the central, consisting of Chimaltenango, Sacatepequez, Guatemala, Baja Verapaz, and parts of El Progreso and Jalapa.

PRECLASSIC (FORMATIVE) PERIOD

The earliest materials in the Guatemala highlands come from scattered storage and refuse pits, and their exact chronological position is not yet certain. At or near the great site of Kaminaljuyu outside Guatemala City, in the central zone, a sequence of Preclassic complexes has been recognized. It is not yet certain which of the two earliest phases in this

sequence came first, Arevalo or Las Charcas, although there is apparently growing evidence that they appeared in that order. Authorities differ
in designating them by broad Mesoamerican period names. Here we
shall favor the opinion that it appears wisest to leave as yet unoccupied
(as in the southern and western lowlands) the period called Early Preclassic, for remains comparable to the early Ocos phase of La Victoria
on the Pacific Coast have not yet been found, yet there are resemblances
between Las Charcas and "Conchas" ceramics of slightly later date. We
might tentatively assign the Arevalo phase to the very end of the Early
Preclassic period, and the Las Charcas to the beginnings of the Middle
Preclassic, approximately contemporaneous with Mamom in the southern lowlands. The next Kaminaljuyu phases, called Majadas and Miraflores, or Providencia, can be considered Middle to Late Preclassic,
roughly coeval with Chicanel in the southern lowlands. No chronologically fixed Early or Middle Preclassic pottery is known in the northern
highlands.

To infer from small fragments of burned adobe in these early deposits,
houses were built of poles and thatch, with mud-daubed walls, probably
grouped in small and scattered clusters forming unplanned villages in
the valleys and on the plateaus. Unless some Kaminaljuyu mounds with
Las Charcas pottery on top prove to be of that period, the first major
structures we know of appeared in the Middle Preclassic—what I once,
for this same reason, called the "Urban Formative." These were large
earthen and puddled adobe mounds facing narrow plazas and, in a row,
bisecting the latter lengthwise. They were stepped pyramids, with
roughly modeled terraces and stairways, faced with painted adobe plaster, and supporting perishable superstructures. Some of the huge mounds
(up to 20 meters high) were mortuary. Dwellings remained the same,
but the old scattered rural settlement pattern was radically changed in
that each village or group of villages now had its ceremonial-political
center. At Kaminaljuyu there are over one hundred Preclassic mounds,
a true sacred metropolis.

The tombs of important personages were rectangular, cut into the
mounds above ground and roofed with timbers and mats. The corpse,
painted red, lay on a special wooden platform and was surrounded by
rich funeral offerings and sometimes by sacrificed human retainers.

The earliest highland pottery is quite sophisticated and must have
been either introduced fully developed from some other area or preceded
by as yet undiscovered simpler types. Besides dull and burnished red,
buff, gray-brown, black, and white monochrome wares, there were
painted red-on-white and red-on-buff vessels. Shapes included bowls
with simple rounded or composite silhouettes, incurved and wide everted
rims, large jars, tall tripod cups, three-pronged censers, and shoe-shaped

and effigy vessels. The geometric decoration was incised, fluted, or grooved. Pottery stamps, effigy whistles, and solid figurines were abundant.

By Late Preclassic times (Providencia and Santa Clara or Miraflores phases at Kaminaljuyu) bichrome pottery was more popular, and the painted designs were often outlined by an incised line, a widespread trait that persisted through Protoclassic times elsewhere in Mesoamerica. Black-on-red outlined incised was a popular new ware in the northern zone. Wide-everted lip flanges were decorated, and a common distinctive form of negative painting in multiple-applied wavy lines ("Usulutan ware") shows up here. Small-mouthed jars and vessels with a lateral flange appeared. Feet were solid nubbin or conical, with hollow forms, both tripod and tetrapod, coming in at the end of the period. Tall tripod and three-pronged censers continued to be popular, and the latter evolved into more complex forms. A distinctive new form was the tripod vessel with three heads projecting from the rim. In contrast to middle and later stages of the Preclassic in the southern lowlands, hand-modeled figurines were again abundant, but they disappeared by the Protoclassic, along with stamps and effigy whistles.

Many diagnostic traits of Protoclassic ceramics, such as tetrapod mammiform vessels, bridged spouts, and pedestal bases, have been excavated in the Guatemala highlands, but they occur often if not always in apparently close association with early Classic remains, as in the Balam phase at Zacualpa and in Chama 1 and 1–2 in the Alta Verapaz. Until pure Protoclassic deposits are found, we must assume that the use of these traits did not take place in a cultural context distinct from the Early Classic, although it is not clear just what this implies relative to sites elsewhere with exclusively Protoclassic materials and those with none at all.

The earliest highland non-ceramic artifacts include the usual milling stones, celts and axes, obsidian blades, and spalls or other fragments of flaked- and chipped-stone implements. As the Preclassic cultures evolved, and especially as class distinctions became sharper and opulence more important to the individual, there appeared in increasing numbers luxury items like marble vessels, jade mosaics, and jewelry of many kinds.

Miles points out that most sculptured monuments of the Maya highlands and Pacific Coast are concentrated in a few great sites and heavily inhabited zones: Kaminaljuyu near Guatemala City, Izapa in southern Mexico, the Cotzumalhuapa region of the Pacific slope, and the Quiche area of the central Guatemala highlands. The conditions under which they were found, as well as their subject matter, confirm their primarily religious function, although some may have recorded historical events or individual portraits. They are rich in symbolism and were obviously not intended for what Miles calls "rapid visual understanding." Although few come from controlled excavations with sure ceramic associations, Miles exploits these few to the utmost and combines them with the different styles of execution and the various emphases on subject matter to reconstruct at least a tentative sequence. For example, she shows that a favorite symbolic motif, the dragon head, cannot, in its earliest forms, be surely identified with any particular animal, but that later it took on feline, bird, fish, anthropomorphic, and reptilian features, the serpentine form becoming predominant in Early Classic times. She predicts that eventually we shall be able to trace clearly the history of such emphasis on related forms.

Miles recognizes four "divisions" of the Preclassic sculptures, these corresponding roughly to the known major Preclassic and Protoclassic ceramic phases of the area. The first includes large boulder sculptures of human heads and figures, probably pre-Olmec in date but certainly related to the La Venta and Tres Zapotes colossal heads. The second includes the widely distributed pedestal sculptures of jaguars, pisotes, monkeys, and men carved in round on a square shaft. The third is one of the most brilliant styles developed in Middle America, according to Miles: there are elaborately dressed and masked human figures standing on platforms, with a sky head looking down from above. The fourth, transitional to the Classic period sculptures, has narrative styles, or two facing figures, or single standing figures, and silhouette sculpture.

An interesting form of early highland sculpture is the mushroom-shaped stone, which, as Borhegyi has shown, was of several distinct types, some representing humans, animals, and birds. Borhegyi suggests that these were cult objects connected with the use of "divine mushrooms" to induce hallucinations, a practice of Mixtec, Zapotec, and Mixe divinatory rites in Oaxaca today. A Kaminaljuyu cache of nine miniature mushroom stones, along with nine miniature metates, each with its own mano, further suggests to Borhegyi connection of this cult with the nine Maya Lords of the Night and Underworld.

Borhegyi also proposes that a stela cult not unlike that of Classic times in the southern and western lowlands is reflected in the uncarved but doubtless once-painted basalt columns so common in the Guatemala highlands. Like lowland stelae, they stood in front of platform mounds, often aligned in rows, and Borhegyi believes that they, too, marked the passing of time—probably in terms of the 260-day Sacred Round, a calendar still in operation in highland Indian villages. They disappeared at the end of the Preclassic, probably as the result of Mexican invasions, says Borhegyi.

Borhegyi believes that the stela cult, large boulder sculptures, grotesque jaguar and ophidian symbolism in art, the custom of shaving heads, the use of rubber and cotton, and even the concept of monumental temple and tomb building (along with red-ocher paint in funerary ceremonies) were introduced to the Maya highlanders sometime during Middle Preclassic times from coastal Veracruz and Tabasco, Mexico.

EARLY CLASSIC PERIOD

This was the period of the first full-strength cultural influence and, probably, domination from Teotihuacan, Mexico, perhaps the initial "Pipil" invasion. This Mexican intrusion is clearly reflected in pottery, architecture, and sculpture.

The general settlement pattern remained largely unchanged from the Preclassic, but the ceremonial centers took on different assemblage arrangements and saw radical changes in architecture and building methods. A number of the Preclassic centers were apparently abandoned; many new centers were founded. Borhegyi suggests that certain valleys and plateaus had become overpopulated and that the farmers moved away in search of arable land elsewhere.

Instead of the long, rectangular parallel plazas of Preclassic times, we now find more closely knit groups of smaller mounds surrounding plazas and courts. The builders used much more stone in their constructions, in the mound fill, as masonry facing, in molding and cornices on the pyramids and attached terraces. Bordered stairways led to the doorway of a single-room temple on top, covered with thatch or a beam-and-mortar roof. There were altar platforms and altar shrines. The sloping elements at the base of walls, sloping terraces, and, near the end of the period, sloping summit platform walls were all new to architecture. Most of these features were of Mexican derivation and bolster the strong ceramic and other archeological evidence of a Mexican domination of the Maya highlands during the Early Classic period.

Tombs in the central zone were like their Preclassic predecessors. In the famous Kaminaljuyu Early Classic tombs—rectangular, roofed with timbers, lined with mats—the principal personage was placed in an extended or cross-legged position, surrounded with food and personal treasures and, in some cases, retainer burials. At Nebaj, in Ixil country, richly stocked slab-lined tombs with flat or corbeled-vault roofs were approached by stone-lined tunnels; at Zaculeu, in Mam territory, stairways led to subtemple circular burial chambers, their walls painted red. The common people were buried in stone-lined cists. We find also bundle burials, head deformation, dental and body mutilation. Headless burials and caches of red-painted or otherwise decorated heads attest to the bloody sacrificial or war-trophy rites of the times.

Black and black-brown pottery, smooth to glossy, and often with a soapy surface feel continued into the Early Classic period in the northern zone; other slipped monochrome red, orange, and cream wares were common. Resist-painted decoration in distinct local styles occurred in such typically Early Classic vessel shapes as the cylinder tripod and the basal-flange bowl with ring stand. Polychrome pottery was known but not common; stuccoed pottery with painted decoration, often in pastel colors, was fashionable for tomb offerings. In addition to the cylinder tripods, often with slab feet, and the basal-flange bowls were handled "cream pitchers," tall tripods, censer covers shaped like somewhat comical ducks, double cups or "candeleros," and a number of other forms, most of which are duplicated at Teotihuacan in central Mexico. Vertical fluting, incising, and moldings were other forms of decoration. Incipient vitrification appeared in the Esperanza flesh-color ware at Kaminaljuyu, and there were also some thin orange, fine-paste black and ivory bowls there. In general, Early Classic highland pottery shows affiliations with Teotihuacan in central Mexico, with Puebla, and with the southern lowlands.

Borhegyi has noted that most of these new ceramics were ceremonial and luxury items, and he suggests that they were used exclusively by the invaders and the local upper and priestly classes. He points out that the old Preclassic three-pronged censers, rim-head vessels, almost all figurines, effigy whistles, and mushroom stones disappeared from ceremonial centers, possibly considered "barbaric" by the Mexicans and old fashioned by the native Maya seeking favor in the new regime. The ladle censer, which was to become more common later, appeared, as did mold-made ornaments on pottery.

Borhegyi also notes that, with the exception of a single altar, a few tenoned ball-court jaguar and serpent heads, and a few plain stelae, monumental stone sculpture is lacking in the Early Classic highlands. He thinks that these few stelae may represent lowland Maya influence, with little or no relationship to the Preclassic stela cult of the highlands.

Other artifacts were much the same as in previous epochs. Doughnut-shaped stones, sometimes considered digging-stick weights, and pyrite-incrusted mosaic plaques were new. The latter sometimes carried carved scrolls identical with the style of Tajin Totonac art. A huge jade boulder cache in an Early Classic stairway at Kaminaljuyu emphasizes the value of this stone to the highland Maya. Zacualpa Early Classic deposits yielded many obsidian flake-blades, large obsidian knives with little or no secondary chipping, and greenstone figurines.

Diagnostic Early Classic pottery is lacking from many Guatemala highland sites. Borhegyi suggests the interesting explanation that this Early Classic pottery is all of Teotihuacan derivation and that it will be found only in the larger sites and ceremonial centers actually dominated by the Mexican invaders. He believes that many rural villages were not thus dominated and that their pottery is of the Kaminaljuyu Amatle type, heretofore considered Late Classic. Zacualpa, in the northern zone, was a ceremonial center in Classic times, but we have stratified ceramics from deposits well outside the major mound assemblages, and these have yielded large quantities of what were certainly more domestic wares. The diagnostic Early Classic traits, such as basal flanges, slab feet, ring stands, and black-on-red outlined incised decoration, were present, together with deep flaring-wall bowls, and deep cylindrical and comal-like vessels, frequently with horizontal grooves below the rim exterior, thick-walled spiked censers, and handled jars, the last sometimes decorated with applied chain fillets. Hollow cylindrical and solid feet were present, and some comal and bail handles.

LATE CLASSIC PERIOD

Earthen mounds were again closely grouped around plazas, but the structures were no longer so often big mortuary temple mounds; instead, they tended to be long, low platforms, faced with thickly plastered stones laid in mud mortar. There were regional variations; for example, at some sites the excellent stone masonry required no mortar or plaster. Superstructures were still perishable and approached by stairways; at Zaculeu these were of the split type that was to become so popular later. At Nebaj, stairways were not as steep as before and were painted red.

The ball court, of which there must be several hundred in the highlands, appeared in the Late Classic period, although Borhegyi's classification puts them in the preceding period as well, and he suggests that the Mexican conquerors sponsored the sport as an outlet for native Maya aggression. A. L. Smith made a study of ball-court types and their distribution throughout the Guatemala highlands; he states that these earliest courts were of the open-end type, that is, they had no end zones defined by masonry walls. The bench along the sides had a sloping face and level top. The playing wall was sloping, sometimes with a vertical molding at the top.

In the Department of Quezaltenango, Kidder and Shook excavated a round, subterranean stone sweat house with stone-lined entrance passageway and beehive ceiling. Royal tomb burials continued from the preceding period; an innovation was the urn burial.

Except for the importation of Mexican Gulf Coast thin-stone sculptures ("palmate stones," "yokes," "hachas"), and the reappearance of mushroom stones, stone carving was about the same as it had been during the Early Classic, being limited to ball-court markers, utilitarian objects, pyrite plaques, and jade jewelry; there were few stelae or other monumental sculpture in the Guatemala highlands, save in the north-westernmost corner near Chinkultic, Chiapas.

At Kaminaljuyu, pottery of the Amatle and Pamplona phases has usually been considered of Late Classic date because it was associated with several distinct wares generally thought to be Late Classic on the Pacific Coast and elsewhere: Tiquisate ware, a thin, hard-fired cream-colored to pink-orange pottery; San Juan and, later, Robles Plumbate, hard, lustrous, non-effigy predecessors of the Postclassic Tohil Plumbate; red-on-buff; and certain fine orange types. As mentioned earlier, however, Borhegyi has proposed that Amatle may be an Early Classic ceramic group and that Tiquisate and other supposedly later ceramics may have appeared in that period, too. Among these Late Classic fine thin-walled wares was a group ("Chama Polychrome") that has become famous for its polychrome-painted depictions of gods, animals, and important personages; specimens come mostly from the northern zone and the Verapaz. Resist painting was also popular in these regions. Censers were of many kinds, some of them very elaborately decorated or created in effigy forms, some surviving from earlier styles.

Late Classic highland pottery is best represented in the northern zone from excavations (as yet unpublished) at Zacualpa (Pokom phase), which yielded quantities of domestic, as well as service and ceremonial, specimens, excavated in controlled stratigraphic tests that provided transitional stages from the previous Early Classic (Balam) and into the subsequent Postclassic (Tohil) collections. Here red-on-buff, red-on-orange, red-on-cream, red-on-white, and negative-painted were favorite service wares, along with the thin-walled fine-paste vessels occurring in white, light gray, pinkish or "tea" tones, and even tan, red, and chocolate brown, sometimes carved or incised. Early forms of Plumbate, plus the Tiquisate-like wares, and some polychrome specimens help to fix the foreign relationships of these ceramics. Thick-walled spiked and ornately modeled censer vessels and long-handled "ladle" censers were common. The most common domestic forms, found in great quantities, were deep bowls and "comal" vessels with straight to faintly rounded and slightly flaring walls, and fairly large jars with vertical, flaring, or sharply angled collars, frequently decorated with horizontal bands of chain fillets. Handles were usually oval to round in section, though some strap types were present; the comal handle, a semicircular arch rising vertically from the rim, was the most common type, but there were also bail, ladle, and other forms.

There were many obsidian knife blades in Pokom deposits at Zacualpa and also some obsidian cores from which they were struck, obsidian knives with secondary chipping on one surface only, and obsidian projectile points. The doughnut stone—a club or digging-stick weight—was also present.

EARLY POSTCLASSIC PERIOD

In my Zacualpa report I speculated at some length on whether this was the period when dislodged or expanding post-Teotihuacan Mexican groups reached the Guatemala highlands, bringing the dynasties that had been warring with each other for several generations when the Spaniards arrived in 1524. Few of the fortress sites antedate the Late Postclassic (Protoclassic) period, but native chronicles like the *Popol Vuh* tell of capitals that were moved and place names that were changed from Maya to Mexican, so it seems likely that the new dynasties were there by Early Postclassic times. Indeed, it is likely that many Guatemala highland Maya were never without Mexican rulers from the Early Classic period onward and that the later dynasties were merely new arrivals from (as many of them claimed) Tula, instead of Teotihuacan, or, as Thompson has suggested, were descended from Pipil ruling families of the Classic period, who were later absorbed by the Maya groups they ruled, just as the Yucatec Maya absorbed their Mexican conquerors.

According to A. L. Smith, two principal types of building assemblages were located in valleys or on the slopes of hills close by: (*a*) Late Classic patterns, but with the addition of small platforms (altars or dance platforms) in the centers of courts, and (*b*) compact groups of buildings bordering one or two plazas, with an open-end ball court leading into one of these plazas, which normally had a small platform in the center. Examples of the former type are Chichen in the Alta Verapaz, Chalchitan in Huehuetenango, and San Andres Sajcabaja in Quiche. The latter include sites in the Nebaj-Cotzal-Chajul area, Huitchun and Calchitan near Aguacatan, and Pantzac near San Andres Sajcabaja.

Masonry was the same as in Late Classic times. Temples consisted of a single rectangular room with a large opening in one of the long sides, two square columns creating three entrances; an altar against the opposite wall; and sloping lower zones of exterior walls. A. L. Smith found that ball courts had a vertical bench face, a bench top almost level, and a sloping playing wall with vertical molding. In another type low walls defined the end zones. The courts had drains or water outlets. Markers were stone tenoned heads of animals, sometimes with a human face in the open mouth, set horizontally in the center of the playing walls, near the top.

Important tombs sometimes had a vaulted chamber and anteroom.

Burials were in stone sarcophagi, those of less important people in stone-lined, capped cists.

Among new ceramics was the famous Tohil Plumbate, named for the Postclassic phase at Zacualpa, where its chronological position was stratigraphically demonstrated. This unique ware, widely traded in Middle America, has a lustrous vitrified glazelike surface, produced by its strong iron content fired at very high temperatures; in contrast to the previous ferruginous San Juan and Robles Plumbate, Tohil Plumbate contains no volcanic ash, and it occurs in effigy forms. Shepard's excellent book describes its technological, artistic, commercial, and other cultural characteristics and history. A fine orange ware ("X" Fine Orange) was also popular, as were vessels with mold-made animal-head feet. The Late Classic bichromes continued in use. Perforated, tripod censers, one leg acting as a long handle, were imported or copied from the Mixtec region.

Metallurgy was now practiced, producing objects of gold or copper, and alloys of these with tin, silver, and zinc.

Miles states that Postclassic sculpture lacks artistic merit and shows strong foreign influence, principally Mexican.

PROTOHISTORIC PERIOD

The final stage of Guatemala highland history is fairly well known to us through native chronicles like the *Popol Vuh* and the *Annals of the Cakchiquels*, which record the succession of Indian co-rulers and some of the main events of their reigns. Several sites that have been archeologically investigated are historically documented: for example, Utatlan (the Quiche capital), Iximche (Cakchiquel), and Chuitinamit (Zutuhil). It was a time of constant warfare between the little kingdoms—especially the Quiche, Cakchiquel, and Zutuhil—and this is reflected in the characteristic location of their walled fortress sites on the summits of hills and ridges surrounded by deep ravines. With building area thus limited, the luxury of oriented buildings could not always be afforded, especially when up to eight groups of buildings were crowded on a single tongue of land.

By now Mexican influences on architecture were stronger than ever. This is seen perhaps best in the twin temples on a single substructure. The low substructures had projecting "balustraded" stairways on one to four sides, with a vertical upper zone and often divided by a ramp. Roofs were thatched or of the flat beam-and-mortar type. Long, single-room structures had three or more doorways facing the plaza, and multi-chambered "palaces"—some supported by massive columns—faced paved plazas, with temples and altar platforms at the center. At Utatlan low platforms behind the temple assemblages supported extensive "apartments" consisting of dozens, perhaps scores, of small rectangular rooms, their adobe walls faced with a fine clay veneer and decorated with polychrome murals. These assemblages were crisscrossed with narrow alleys, perhaps the "streets" that Alvarado spoke of when he reported his conquest of the city in 1524. A. L. Smith states that ball courts were inclosed, that is, they had high walls with stairs leading out of each end and steeply sloping playing walls bordering the narrow playing alley. A long, single-room building sometimes stood on top of these ranges, which were terraced at the back. End zones expanded, giving the court the shape of an **I**.

Borhegyi believes that the bulk of the population continued to live in nearby hamlets or satellite farming villages. As in the final period of northern Yucatan, Guatemala highland society by now had surely taken on such things as merchant guilds and other marks of a more urban culture.

Cremation, the ashes placed in tall-necked polychrome or orange jars, tended to displace inhumation of the dead. The bow and arrow was increasingly used instead of the spear-thrower.

Protohistoric pottery was quite different from its predecessors in this area: Plumbate disappeared completely. The new favorite ware was a hard, thin, dark-red pottery, often decorated crudely with carelessly applied white paint. Polychromes were also different, consisting of dark, flat colors (usually red, black, and white), and there were new bichromes. A distinctive innovation was pottery with large amounts of mica mixed in the paste. Effigy feet of the previous period became more stylized. Censers also took on new shapes, but the ladle type persisted. There were regional differences in pottery; except for mutually traded wares, the ceramics of Utatlan and Iximche, although not very far apart geographically, were quite different.

Chiapas and the Pacific Coast of Guatemala

The Pacific coastal plain is a relatively narrow strip of lowland, with trees scattered, except along the streams, and with many savannas. It has fertile volcanic alluvial soils. Along the shores are silted-up sand bars separated from the mainland by lagoons, mud flats, and mangrove swamps. This lowland climbs into a piedmont country forming the warm, wet lower slopes of the highland volcanic ranges and is heavily covered with rain forest. Seasonal rainfall is heavy in the piedmont— over 180 inches annually reported in places—and decreases toward the coast, where M. D. Coe reports that Champerico, Guatemala, has only about 38 inches. The climate is hot the year round. Wild game and fish, mollusks, shrimp, and other seafood are plentiful, and Coe estimates that in aboriginal times there was a ratio at the coast of one fisher-man to ten farmers.

Before the Mexican invasions, the principal language spoken on the Guatemala coast may have been Mixe-Zoque, according to Coe. The first Mexican domination, possibly "Pipil," is reflected, as in the high-lands, in the Early Classic period with its Teotihuacan affiliations, in the later Mexican elements in Cotzumalhuapa art, and in many cultural traits from then on until the Spanish Conquest, when wars and alliances between the Pipil and the Guatemala highland kingdoms are a matter of record.

PRECLASSIC (FORMATIVE) PERIOD

Except for Shook's explorations and extensive surface collec-tions, our knowledge of the early stages of prehistory on the Pa-cific Coast comes almost exclusively from Coe's excavations at La Victoria, a site near the coast, just south of the Chiapas-Guatemala frontier. Here he found remains of four archeological phases, three of them Formative, followed by a Late Classic occupation. The Ocos phase is among the earliest cultures yet discovered in Middle America, preceded, according to Coe, only by Pavon farther north, Yojoa Monochrome pottery, and the earliest Yarumela remains in Hon-duras. Ocos is thus "Early Formative" in age; Coe equates it tem-porally with Chiapa I, which we shall describe later, and Ulua Bichrome pottery in Honduras, estimating this period at about 1500–1000 B.C. The Indians lived in wattle-and-daub houses. Plants were doubtless impor-tant food sources—prepared with milling stones, mortars, and pestles— and the brackish estuary provided abundant oysters, mussels, strombus, and other seafoods. Fresh water was probably obtained from wells. The natives made cloth, cordage, and pottery and traded with distant regions, most of their communication taking place by sea, according to Coe. He sees resemblances with cultural traits of the Formative Chorrera phase in coastal Ecuador.

The next two phases, Conchas 1 and 2, equate temporally with Ma-mom and Chicanel in the Peten, Las Charcas in the Guatemala high-lands, and Chiapa III–V. The cane- or pole-thatched houses were mud daubed and had rounded corners; they were arranged at random in compact little communities of ten or so houses. Hunting and fishing were still important, though milling stones suggest that plants were also eaten, maize probably being the most important. The Indians made basketry, pottery, stone axes, and celts. Trade with the Gulf Coast and perhaps the Guatemala highlands and Chiapas probably utilized the lagoon sys-tems. According to Coe, Conchas 1 shows resemblances with the Chorrera phase in Ecuador, and Conchas 2 with the Tejar phase there. Burials were extended, with no offerings.

Crucero phase is Late Formative, equating with the "latter part of Chicanel," Chiapa V, Miraflores in the highlands, and the Usulutan pottery horizon.

We have referred earlier to Miles's four divisions of Preclassic development of Pacific coast and Maya highland sculpture. The first of these, which featured the large boulder figures and heads, may have been Pre- or Proto-Olmec; the second division, characterized by pedestal sculptures, suggests to Miles sporadic Olmec influences along the Pacific Coast at this time. There are Olmec-style stelae, for example, at Tonala, on the coastal plain of Chiapas. Lowe and Mason think that these monuments may have been brought in from nearby Tzutzuculi.

Miles's third division, we remember, saw the peak of Preclassic sculptural achievement; during this period there was apparently contact between Kaminaljuyu, in the Guatemala highlands, and Izapa, in the Soconusco district of Chiapas. The Izapa monuments are sculptured in a style related to Olmec art farther north and to early Maya art in the south, as Stirling has shown. Pottery types also indicate a Preclassic occupation there. The famous narrative style of Izapa sculpture belongs to Miles's Division 4, the final Preclassic stage. Stela 5 at Izapa, for example, depicts an involved visual myth.

Chiapa de Corzo, in the Central Depression or Upper Grijalva Basin of Chiapas, is the most thoroughly investigated site in this area. The New World Archaeological Foundation exposed here or in neighboring sites a full sequence of remains extending in time from the Early Preclassic, about 1300 B.C., through the colonial period. The earliest, Chiapa I, appears to be what Lowe and Mason call a less-sophisticated or provincial expression of the Ocos phase of La Victoria farther south in Guatemala. Hand-modeled figurines, three-pronged incense burners, and stone-faced terrace and foundation platforms appeared in Chiapa II, with connections chiefly in the Guatemala highlands. Cross-ties with Peten and the south brought in "waxy"-slipped wares (like those of Mamom) in Chiapa III, and platforms became stepped and higher. According to Lowe and Mason, cultural interchange with the west and north widened in Chiapa IV, reaching Monte Alban and the Los Tuxtlas region; the plumed serpent appeared in art, together with the earliest stucco-painted vessels, shell-backed pyrite mirrors, and cache offerings. The final Late Preclassic period, Chiapa V, saw greatly modified ceramics (medial and labial flanges, numerous composite silhouette forms, tetrapod nubbin, and hollow feet, for example), as figurines disappeared. Adobe bricks became popular, although major building seems to have stopped temporarily.

Protoclassic Chiapa VI–VII witnessed a trend away from Maya low-land to highland connections, as cut-stone architecture—still without the corbeled vault—and mammiform tetrapod vessels appeared. Lowland Maya influence was still weak in the Early Classic Chiapa VIII, but incised black ware with basal frieze or raised zone and Maya polychrome tie the period to Tzakol in the Peten. Lowe and Mason believe that western Chiapas, with its first real stone-faced pyramids, was a major cultural center during this period just preceding the arrival of classic Teotihuacan traits from the north.

EARLY CLASSIC PERIOD

Chiapa de Corzo was apparently abandoned at the end of the Protoclassic, but it yielded isolated later archeological specimens. Elsewhere in the Central Depression, sites with hillside terracing, open-end ball courts, and corbeled vaulted tombs with stone-lined passage entrances, show close relations with highland Guatemala and the Classic-period Pacific Coast.

Tonala, on the Pacific coastal plain of Chiapas, is best known for its massive architecture of dressed-stone masonry, its stone-paved ramps and causeways, and the three wall-inclosed religious precincts, each with a central temple. There are some Olmec-style stelae; the main occupation was in the Classic period.

The Early Classic is not well represented on the Pacific Coast of Guatemala. Shook's surveys showed that, although the coast in the vicinity of Puerto San Jose had a long Preclassic occupation, there was little evidence of Early Classic activity. There is a scarcity of Early Classic sites between the Melendrez-Naranjo and Suchiate rivers. We thus have little to study of the period that presumably saw the first "Pipil" or Teotihuacan-derived culture in this area.

LATE CLASSIC PERIOD

On the Pacific slopes are clusters of sites, as in the Cotzumalhuapa district, sharing a sculptural style and associated, at El Baul, with San Juan Plumbate pottery, as Thompson demonstrated. Ball players, death manikins, and eagle- and jaguar-society warriors depicted in the art point to close Mexican connections. Tiquisate ware was popular, but polychrome, in contrast to the Alta Verapaz and the souther lowlands, was rare. Copador ware, a horizon-marker in El Salvador and Honduras, turns up in the Tiquisate region. Distinctive stone sculpture included mushroom stones, thin stone heads, and yokes. Shook's surveys indicate a heavy Late Classic occupation of the coastal plain, especially along the Rio Los Esclavos and from the beach to the highlands.

La Victoria was apparently not occupied during Early Classic times, but Coe has isolated a Late Classic phase there that he calls "Marcos," which yielded San Juan Plumbate pottery, coarse bowls with incurved rims, and red-slipped pottery decorated with white-slipped and incised zones.

Fine orange and Tepeu 3–related ceramics are known in western Chiapas, and Izapa—in the Soconusco district—also had San Juan Plumbate pottery like that of Cotzumalhuapa. According to Lowe, large ceremonial centers in parts of the Grijalva Basin appeared in the Late Classic and survived into subsequent periods. Moxviquil is a Late Classic ruin investigated by Blom and Weiant on a mountain top above San Cristobal Las Casas. Adams' survey of over forty sites in the central highlands of Chiapas showed that, although there were earlier sites there, the most widespread occupation was during the Late Classic; Cerro Chavin is one of the fortified centers of this period. The Comitan Plain in the high Chiapas lake district is the location of many Late Classic ruins: Chinkultic on the Guatemala frontier, nearby Tenam, and Santa Elena Poco Uinic have fine masonry construction. There are dated monuments at Chinkultic and Tenam, and the former site produced a ball-court marker and several stelae in Late Classic style, according to Proskouriakoff.

EARLY POSTCLASSIC PERIOD

This period is identified in the region under discussion chiefly through the presence of Tohil Plumbate pottery and associated wares and a style of stone sculpture, rather than through intensive or stratigraphically controlled excavations. It is perhaps best represented in Chiapas at the Sumidero site and the Ruiz site. At the former, Berlin found stucco-surfaced earthen mounds, floorpainting, circular interior altars, and gallery-like entrances with rubble pillars. At San Pedro Buenvista he found a stone-faced platform with stairways on three sides.

Shook reports that cultural material and sites of the Postclassic are virtually unknown in the Puerto San Jose–Escuintla region of the Guatemala Pacific coast. Intensive investigations in this region are needed to clarify problems centering on the known Pipil occupation of the Escuintla area at the time of the Spanish entry. A southern tradition was also involved in the late sculpture of the Pacific slopes: short, round pedestal sculptures of human and anthropomorphic figures, with legs in low relief on the side of the pedestal (a Nicaraguan trait) and phallic depictions.

As in the Guatemala highlands, according to Miles, Postclassic sculpture was crude and showed strong foreign influence, primarily Mexican.

LATE POSTCLASSIC (PROTOHISTORIC) PERIOD

At the time of the European entry, the Chiapas highlands figured in trade and conquest routes between Mexico and the Guatemala highlands and the Pacific slopes. Amber, feathers, and salt were important; control of the last commodity stimulated the Zotzlem-Chiapaneca wars, just as cacao control spurred rivalries in Guatemala. The Chiapaneca-Colonia stratigraphy has been defined by Navarrete. There were Mixtec connections, and, as with many other late sites of Mesoamerica, these centers shared certain traits with Nahuatl-occupied Naco in Honduras. According to Lowe, the Late Classic ceremonial centers in parts of the Grijalva Basin survived into Postclassic periods. Soconusco sites, whose foreign relations had been mainly southern in earlier periods, now shifted to or added Mixtec or Mexican-related connections.

SOUTHERN VERACRUZ–TABASCO

The southern Veracruz–Tabasco strip is 100 kilometers wide, lies along the fertile Gulf Coast, and has a volcanic history. In spite of their proximity to the wet and densely forested coast and savannas, some of the most important Indian sites lie in upland plateau or plains country, for the mountains on the Isthmus of Tehuantepec and in the region to the south reach almost to the Gulf. In places the land is so low that Gulf tides flood and ebb in the meandering rivers emptying into mangrove swamps and lagoons. From major volcanic peaks like Tuxtla and San Martin, mountain streams rush coastward, eroding the sedimentary peneplain and resulting in sandy ridges and plateaus that look down on the river bottoms and swamps along the Gulf.

This area was heavily populated in ancient times, to judge from the numerous clusters of mounds and the rich remains that have been uncovered in the few sites so far tested. It was apparently the home of the now famous La Venta or "Olmec" culture, which produced a striking and easily recognized art style of early date and played an important role in the development of the earliest Mesoamerican civilizations. Only three sites here have been adequately excavated, and the relationships and chronological correlations between their sequences of remains have been difficult to establish; they are La Venta, Tres Zapotes, and Cerro de las Mesas.

PRECLASSIC

La Venta is famed for its carved-basalt monuments, colossal stone heads, fences of stone columns, serpentine-paved areas with lavish offerings of carved celts, figurines, and jewelry. The sculpture is in "Olmec" style, featuring conventionalized jaguar faces (sometimes called "baby faces" because of their infantile features) and helmeted human heads with flat noses, chubby cheeks, and full lips. Pottery, including flat-bottomed dishes with flaring sides incised near the rim, gadrooned bottles, rocker-stamped vessels, and solid handmade figurines, suggests an early date for La Venta; M. Coe assigns it to the Middle Preclassic, approximately contemporaneous with Tlatilco in the Valley of Mexico, Chiapa II and Conchas to the south, and Mamom in the Peten. La Venta was destroyed before the end of the Formative period.

The origin of La Venta is lost in the past. So far, we have no prototypes, but it must be admitted that we know very little of earlier Meso-american culture in this region or anywhere else.

Tres Zapotes, at the base of the Tuxtla Mountains, has produced important but confusing data. The chronological position of its phases is uncertain, for the pottery recorded from them includes traits inconsistent with generally held beliefs regarding the order in which these traits appeared. "Lower Tres Zapotes," the earliest layers, produced simple cursive incising and figurines comparable to Middle Zacatenco to the north in Mexico, according to Drucker. It lacked incised red ware, negative-painted pottery, outline incised painted areas, basal or medial ridges, and other features of the later Formative period. On the basis of selecting typologically early ceramic features from various strata, linking them with closely associated cache and burial materials, and ignoring some recorded stratigraphy, M. Coe assigns the earliest Tres Zapotes occupation to the Late Preclassic, roughly contemporaneous with Chicanel in the Peten, Chiapa IV and V, to the south. The ceramic features thus selected include, for example, wide everted and grooved rims and composite silhouette bowls; the absence of rocker stamping was also taken into account. Coe interprets the many associated earlier traits as of Middle Preclassic heritage. These "early" traits are so numerous, however, as to make one wonder whether the heritage did not all but smother the new features. One finds, for example, white-rimmed and tan-rimmed black vessels—products of a somewhat complex firing technique—as well as bowls with flat bases and flaring sides, jars with unsupported spouts, and solid handmade figurines (which disappeared in Chicanel), many of them of Olmec-like or La Venta–like style; furthermore, some monumental sculpture here is in Olmec style. It is to be hoped that this situation will be clarified by further excavations in the area, for a new style of sculpture, the Izapan—the "visual myth" style, which we have already described—appears at Tres Zapotes, and also what appear to be the earliest bar-and-dot numerals and Long Count dates yet known in Middle America.

PROTOCLASSIC

This period is best represented in a burial and its funeral offerings at Cerro de las Mesas. Besides the usual Protoclassic pottery and jewelry were a turtle shell engraved in Izapan style and a polished-stone yoke, the latter known hitherto only in much later (Classic period) contexts. This and most other burials of the period were flexed. Rich graves were by now frequent; one excavated by Medellin Zenil at Nopiloa contained 140 offerings of pottery, jewelry, stone and bone figurines, and large anthropomorphic whistles.

Middle Tres Zapotes B produced some Protoclassic pottery, such as bridged spouts, mammiform feet, and polychrome pottery (red and black on the base color).

EARLY CLASSIC

Upper Tres Zapotes and the remains originally called Cerro de las Mesas Upper II yielded many Early Classic traits, among them concave-walled cylinder tripods with slab legs and ornaments around the base, stucco-painted ware, candeleros (small double cups), and carved monuments. As in the Guatemala highlands and Pacific Coast region, the pottery resembled that of classic Teotihuacan and probably reflects its influence or domination. There were large mounds and richly stocked caches; two stelae bear Long Count dates; carving is in Izapa style. Teotihuacan influences are also strong in the architecture.

LATE CLASSIC

This period is represented at Tres Zapotes, Los Cerros, Nopiloa, and elsewhere. Polychrome pottery, Jaina- and Jonuta-style figurines (which we described for northern Yucatan), and the famous smiling-face figures are hallmarks of the epoch, the first three reflecting closer ties with the Maya Yucatan peninsula. Thin stone heads, yokes, and "palma" stones are reported from apparently Late Classic deposits at Tres Zapotes and sites near Santiago Tuxtla.

POSTCLASSIC

The nature of this period in southern Veracruz and Tabasco is not well known because of lack of intensive excavations. That there was a Postclassic occupation is known, however, from reports of copper artifacts, marble vessels, and pottery resembling late wares in other areas. The direction of closest cultural relationships is as yet unknown, though it may be suspected that, as in many parts of the Maya area we have discussed, they were northward with Toltec Mexico.

PROTOHISTORIC

We know little of the actual culture of this terminal period. The sparse remains—including late polychrome pottery and clay figurines—again show affiliations with the north, often Cholula, but Aztec artifacts have not been found.

BIBLIOGRAPHY

ANDREWS, E. WYLLYS
  1960 "Excavations at Dzibilchaltun, Northwestern Yucatan, Mexico." *Amer. Phil. Soc. Proc.*, 104:254–65. Philadelphia.
  1962 "Excavaciones en Dzibilchaltun, Yucatan, 1956–1962." *Estudios de Cultura Maya*, 2:149–83. Mexico.
BERLIN, HEINRICH
  1956 "Late Pottery Horizons of Tabasco, Mexico." (Carnegie Inst. Wash. Pub. 606, pp. 95–153.) Washington, D.C.
BORHEGYI, STEPHAN F.
  1956 "Settlement Patterns in the Guatemalan Highlands, Past and Present." Pp. 101–6 in GORDON R. WILLEY (ed.), *Prehistoric Settlement Patterns in the New World*. ("Viking Fund Pub. Anthrop.," No. 23.) New York.
  n.d. "Synthesis of Guatemala Highland Archaeology." Manuscript to be published in the forthcoming *Handbook of Middle American Indians*. Austin: University of Texas Press.
BRAINERD, GEORGE W.
  1954 *The Maya Civilization*. Los Angeles: Southwest Museum.
  1958 "The Archaeological Ceramics of Yucatan." *Univ. Calif. Anthrop. Records*, Vol. 19. Berkeley.
COE, MICHAEL D.
  1961 *La Victoria: An Early Site on the Pacific Coast of Guatemala*. ("Peabody Mus. Amer. Arch. & Ethnol. Paps.," Vol. 53.) Cambridge, Mass.
DIXON, KEITH A.
  1959 *Ceramics from Two Preclassic Periods at Chiapa de Corzo, Chiapas, Mexico*. ("New World Arch. Foundation Paps.," No. 5.) Orinda.
EKHOLM, GORDON F.
  1953 "A Possible Focus of Asiatic Influence in the Late Classic Cultures of Mesoamerica." Pp. 72–89 in *Asia and North America Transpacific Contacts*. (Soc. Amer. Arch. Mem. 9.) Salt Lake City.
ESTRADA, EMILIO, BETTY J. MEGGERS, and CLIFFORD EVANS, JR.
  1962 "Possible Transpacific Contact on the Coast of Ecuador." *Science*, 135:371–72.
FERGUSON, THOMAS STUART
  1958 *One Fold and One Shepherd*. San Francisco: Books of California.
HOLMES, WILLIAM H.
  1895 *Archaeological Studies among the Ancient Cities of Mexico*. (Field
  –97 Columbian Mus. Pub., Vols. 8, 16; "Anthrop. Ser.," No. 1.) Chicago.

KELLEY, DAVID H.
   1962 "Glyphic Evidence for a Dynastic Sequence at Quirigua, Guatemala."
         Amer. Antiquity, 27:325–35.
KIDDER, ALFRED V.
   1947 *The Artifacts of Uaxactun, Guatemala.* (Carnegie Inst. Wash. Pub.
         576.) Washington, D.C.
KIDDER, ALFRED V., JESSE D. JENNINGS, and EDWIN M. SHOOK
   1946 *Excavations at Kaminaljuyu, Guatemala.* (Carnegie Inst. Wash. Pub.
         561.) Washington, D.C.
KUBLER, GEORGE
   1961 "Chichén-Itzá y Tula." *Estudios de Cultura Maya*, 1:47–80. Mexico.
LONGYEAR, JOHN M., III
   1952 *Copan Ceramics: A Study of Southeastern Maya Pottery.* (Carnegie Inst.
         Wash. Pub. 597.) Washington, D.C.
LOTHROP, SAMUEL K.
   1924 *Tulum: An Archaeological Study of the East Coast of Yucatan.* (Carnegie
         Inst. Wash. Pub. 335.) Washington, D.C.
MAUDSLAY, ANNE CARY, and ALFRED PERCIVAL MAUDSLAY
   1899 *A Glimpse at Guatemala and Some Notes on the Ancient Monuments of
         Central America.* London: John Murray.
MORLEY, SYLVANUS G.
   1915 *An Introduction to the Study of Maya Hieroglyphs.* (Bur. Amer. Ethnol.
         Bull. 57.) Washington, D.C.
   1938 *The Inscriptions of Peten.* 5 vols. (Carnegie Inst. Wash. Pub. 437.)
         Washington, D.C.
MORLEY, SYLVANUS G., and GEORGE W. BRAINERD
   1956 *The Ancient Maya.* Stanford, Calif.: Stanford University Press.
POLLOCK, H. E. D., RALPH L. ROYS, TATIANA PROSKOURIAKOFF, and A.
      LEDYARD SMITH
   1962 *Mayapan, Yucatan, Mexico.* (Carnegie Inst. Wash. Pub. 619.) Wash-
         ington, D.C.
PROSKOURIAKOFF, TATIANA
   1946 *An Album of Maya Architecture.* (Carnegie Inst. Wash. Pub. 558.)
         Washington, D.C.
   1950 *A Study of Classic Maya Sculpture.* (Carnegie Inst. Wash. Pub. 593.)
         Washington, D.C.
RANDS, ROBERT L., and BARBARA C. RANDS
   1957 "The Ceramic Position of Palenque, Chiapas." *Amer. Antiquity*, 23:
         140–50.
ROYS, RALPH L.
   1943 *The Indian Background of Colonial Yucatan.* (Carnegie Inst. Wash. Pub.
         548.) Washington, D.C.
RUZ, ALBERTO
   1959 In CARMEN COOK DE LEONARD (ed.), *El Esplendor de México Antiguo*,
         Vol. X. Mexico, D.F.: Centro de Investigaciones Antropológicas de
         México.

SATTERTHWAITE, LINTON, and ELIZABETH K. RALPH
  1960 "New Radiocarbon Dates and the Maya Correlation Problem."
        Amer. Antiquity, 26:165–84.
SHOOK, EDWIN M., and TATIANA PROSKOURIAKOFF
  1956 "Settlement Patterns in Meso-America and the Sequence in the Gua-
        temalan Highlands." Pp. 93–100 in GORDON R. WILLEY (ed.), *Pre-
        historic Settlement Patterns in the New World*. ("Viking Fund Pub.
        Anthrop.," No. 23.) New York.
SMITH, A. LEDYARD
  1950 *Uaxactun, Guatemala: Excavations of 1931–1937*. (Carnegie Inst. Wash.
        Pub. 588.) Washington, D.C.
  1955 *Archaeological Reconnaissance in Central Guatemala*. (Carnegie Inst.
        Wash. Pub. 608.) Washington, D.C.
SMITH, A. LEDYARD, and ALFRED V. KIDDER
  1951 *Excavations at Nebaj, Guatemala*. (Carnegie Inst. Wash. Pub. 594.)
        Washington, D.C.
SMITH, ROBERT E.
  1955 *Ceramic Sequence at Uaxactun, Guatemala*. 2 vols. (Middle Amer. Res.
        Inst. Pub. 20.) New Orleans.
SORENSON, JOHN L.
  1955 "A Chronological Ordering of the Mesoamerican Pre-Classic." Pp.
        41–68 in *Middle American Research Records*, Vol. 2, Nos. 1–8. (Middle
        Amer. Res. Inst. Pub. 18.) New Orleans.
SPINDEN, HERBERT J.
  1913 *A Study of Maya Art*. (Peabody Mus. Amer. Arch. & Ethnol. Mem.,
        Vol. 6.) Cambridge, Mass.
  1924 *The Reduction of Mayan Dates*. ("Peabody Mus. Amer. Arch. &
        Ethnol. Paps.," Vol. 6, No. 4.) Cambridge, Mass.
STEPHENS, JOHN L.
  1841 *Incidents of Travel in Central America, Chiapas, and Yucatan*. 2 vols.
        New York: Harper & Bros.
  1843 *Incidents of Travel in Yucatan*. 2 vols. New York: Harper & Bros.
THOMPSON, J. ERIC S.
  1948 *An Archaeological Reconnaissance in the Cotzumalhuapa Region, Escuin-
        tla, Guatemala*. ("Contribs. Amer. Anthrop. & Hist.," Vol. 9, No. 44;
        Carnegie Inst. Wash. Pub. 574.) Washington, D.C.
  1950 *Maya Hieroglyphic Writing: An Introduction*. (Carnegie Inst. Wash.
        Pub. 589.) Washington, D.C.
  1954 *The Rise and Fall of Maya Civilization*. Norman: University of Okla-
        homa Press.
  1958 "Symbols, Glyphs, and Divinatory Almanacs for Disease in the Maya
        Dresden and Madrid Codices." *Amer. Antiquity*, 23:297–308.
  1959 "Systems of Hieroglyphic Writing in Middle America and Methods
        of Deciphering Them." *Amer. Antiquity*, 24:349–64.
TOZZER, ALFRED M.
  1941 *Landa's Relación de las Cosas de Yucatan* ("Peabody Mus. Amer. Arch.
        & Ethnol. Paps.," Vol. 18.) Cambridge, Mass.

TOZZER, ALFRED M.
  1957   Chichen Itza and Its Cenote of Sacrifice. (Peabody Mus. Amer.
         Arch. & Ethnol. Mems. 11–12.) Cambridge, Mass.
WAUCHOPE, ROBERT
  1948   "Excavations at Zacualpa, Guatemala." In *Middle American Research
         Records*, Vol. 1, Nos. 1–16. (Middle Amer. Res. Inst. Pub. 14.) New
         Orleans.
  1950   "A Tentative Sequence of Preclassic Ceramics in Middle America."
         Pp. 211–50 in *Middle American Research Records*, Vol. 1, No. 14.
         (Middle Amer. Res. Inst. Pub. 15.) New Orleans.
  1954   "Implications of Radiocarbon Dates from Middle and South Ameri-
         ca." Pp. 17–40 in *Middle American Research Records*, Vol. II, Nos.
         1–8. (Middle Amer. Res. Inst. Pub. 18.) New Orleans.
WILLEY, GORDON R.
  1955   "The Interrelated Rise of the Native Cultures of Middle and South
         America." In *New Interpretations of Aboriginal American Culture His-
         tory*. (75th Anniv. Vol. Anthrop. Soc. Wash.) Washington, D.C.
  1956   "Problems Concerning Prehistoric Settlement Patterns in the Maya
         Lowlands." Pp. 107–14 in GORDON R. WILLEY (ed.), *Prehistoric Set-
         tlement Patterns in the New World*. ("Viking Fund Pub. Anthrop.,"
         No. 23.) New York.
WOODBURY, RICHARD B., and AUBREY S. TRIK
  1953   *The Ruins of Zaculeu, Guatemala*. 2 vols. Richmond, Va.: William
         Byrd Press.

NOTE: The reader's attention is called to the forthcoming *Handbook of Middle American Indians*, one volume of which will be devoted to the archeology of the area covered in this chapter. The *Handbook* is being edited at Tulane University's Middle American Research Institute and will be published by the University of Texas Press.

South America

IRVING ROUSE

The Caribbean Area

THREE CULTURE AREAS impinge upon the Caribbean Sea. Meso-america borders it on the northwest, in Yucatan, Guatemala, British Honduras, and a part of Spanish Honduras. To the southwest, extending through the rest of Central America and Colombia into western Venezuela, is the Intermediate area, so-called because it lies between the civilizations of Mesoamerica and Peru. The rest of northern Venezuela, the northern part of the Guianas, and the West Indies comprise the Caribbean area proper (Fig. 1).

It is with this Caribbean area that the present paper is concerned. Mesoamerica and the Intermediate area will be brought into the discussion only insofar as they seem to have contributed to cultural developments within the Caribbean area.

GEOGRAPHY

The area is shaped like the letter *J* lying on its left side. The left upright of the *J* is formed by the mainland of Venezuela and the adjacent parts of the Guianas; its base, by the series of small islands known as the Lesser Antilles, which curve northward from the mainland in a great arc; and its other upright, by the larger islands of the Greater Antilles, extending westward from Puerto Rico through Hispaniola—the present countries of Santo Domingo and Haiti—to Cuba (Fig. 1). The Intermediate area lies atop the left upright and Mesoamerica atop the right upright, providing the opportunity for east-west diffusion south and north of the Caribbean Sea, respectively.

IRVING ROUSE received his Ph.D. degree from Yale University, where he is at present professor of anthropology and chairman of the Department of Anthropology. His major field of interest has been the Caribbean area, where he has conducted extensive field research. His many articles and monographs have provided much new data on the Caribbean and include outstanding writings on theory and systems of classification. He has held many administrative posts in learned societies and institutions and was the recipient of the Viking Fund Medal in Anthropology in 1959.

Both the mainland and the islands consist of coastal plains, which are often quite narrow, backed by extensive mountain ranges. Behind the Venezuelan coastal ranges is a vast, low-lying plain known as the Llanos, and behind the Llanos are the Guiana highlands. Two drainage features have played an important role in the prehistory and history of these regions: Lake Valencia, situated in an intermontane basin of central Venezuela, and the Orinoco River, which flows between the Llanos and the Guiana highlands, draining both of them and emptying into the sea in front of the island of Trinidad, at the beginning of the Lesser Antillean arc (Fig. 1).

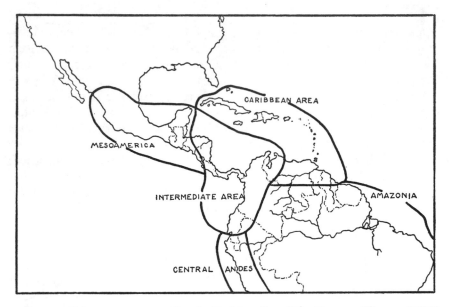

Fɪɢ. 1.—Culture areas surrounding the Caribbean Sea. (After Rouse and Cruxent [1953*b*, Fig. 1].)

At sea level, the climate is tropical, but it becomes temperate as one moves up into the mountains. The coasts that face the northeastern trade winds—among them the delta of the Orinoco River—receive heavy rainfall, permitting the growth of dense forests. Most lee coasts, on the other hand, have arid vegetation because they lie in the shadows of the mountains. The Llanos consist largely of grasslands. Swamps or marshes are also common in poorly drained areas along the coast, in the Valencia Basin, and on the Llanos. It is important to note these contrasting kinds of environment because they have provided the opportunity for distinct cultural traditions to become established in separate ecological niches.

ARCHEOLOGICAL RESEARCH

After the United States obtained Puerto Rico as a result of the Spanish-American War, J. Walter Fewkes (1907) was assigned by the Bureau of American Ethnology in Washington to investigate the archeological resources of our new possession. Subsequently, the Museum of the American Indian, Heye Foundation, in New York City engaged him to make a survey of the entire Antilles (Fewkes 1922). That Museum also sponsored the work of a number of other American archeologists in the period immediately before and after World War I, notably de Booy (1916) on Margarita Island in Venezuela and Harrington (1921) in Cuba. European archeologists who worked in their colonial possessions of the period include Hatt (1924) in the Virgin Islands and De Josselin de Jong on the Dutch islands (De Josselin de Jong 1947; Du Ry and Heekeren 1960).

In the late 1920's, Dr. Rafael Requena, private secretary to Juan Vicente Gomez, then dictator of Venezuela, became interested in the mounds around Lake Valencia. He not only sponsored much local work (reported in Requena 1932) but also arranged for the mounds to be dug by three American archeologists, Bennett (1937), Osgood (1943), and Kidder (1944). Osgood subsequently developed a program at Yale University for research in the Caribbean area that has resulted in major excavations by Rainey (1935) in Puerto Rico, Rainey (1941) and Rouse (1939, 1941) in Haiti, Osgood (1942) and Rouse (1942) in Cuba, G. D. Howard (1943) at Ronquín on the middle Orinoco River in Venezuela, Rouse (1953) and Goggin in Trinidad, R. R. Howard (1956) in Jamaica, McKusick (1960) on St. Lucia, Hahn (1961) in Cuba, and Gallagher (1962) at La Pitía in western Venezuela. In addition, Osgood and Howard (1943) undertook an archeological survey of Venezuela, Osgood (1946) made one of British Guiana, and Rouse (1952) made a series of more than fifty strata tests in Puerto Rico. Osgood's British Guianan survey has recently been followed up by Evans and Meggers (1960).

In 1945 J. M. Cruxent, Walter Dupouy, and Antonio Requena, of the Museo de Ciencias Naturales in Caracas, dug intensively at El Palito on the central coast of Venezuela, using the stratigraphic techniques that had been introduced by Bennett, Osgood, and Kidder in the time of Rafael Requena. In the 1950's Cruxent joined forces with Rouse for large excavations at Saladero on the lower Orinoco River, Manicuare, La Aduana, and Punta Gorda, off the east coast of Venezuela, and Tocuyano, in the foothills of the Andes. Rouse and Cruxent also undertook a more intensive survey of Venezuela, designed to bring Osgood and Howard's previous survey up to date, and Cruxent and his students from the Universidad Central de Caracas investigated a number of additional sites in various parts of northern Venezuela. We have published a detailed compendium of this work (Cruxent and Rouse 1958–59) and have prepared an interpretive book based on it (Rouse and Cruxent, 1963*b*).

Among the current projects in the area are Cruxent's (1961, 1962) study of Paleo-Indian remains; Rouse and Cruxent's (1963) excavations at Rancho Peludo in the Maracaibo Basin; Evans, Meggers, and Cruxent's (1959) work in Venezuelan Guiana; R. P. Bullen and F. W. Sleight's excavations in the Virgin Islands; and William G. Haag's field work on St. Lucia and Martinique. When one adds to these the very considerable research that has been done by such local archeologists as Cosculluela (1951) in Cuba, Alegría in Puerto Rico (Alegría, Nicholson, and Willey, 1955), and Bullbrook (1953) in Trinidad, it will be apparent that there is a relatively broad factual basis for the following historical reconstruction.

CHRONOLOGY

Introduction of stratigraphic research during the 1930's made it possible to develop a relative time scale consisting of five periods, which were arbitrarily numbered from I to V. Subsequently, these five periods were grouped into four epochs, as shown on the left side of Figure 2.

The first epoch has no corresponding period because, unfortunately, its remains had not yet been discovered at the time the system of periods was set up. The first three epochs correspond, respectively, to the Early Lithic, Archaic, and Formative of Willey and Phillips (1958), but, unlike the latter, they refer primarily to time rather than to degree of cultural evolution. The final epoch is beyond the scope of the present paper but is included in Figure 2 for the sake of completeness.

With the development of radiocarbon analysis in the 1950's, the opportunity arose to determine the ages of the epochs and periods. A series of fifty-eight radiocarbon dates has been obtained for the Caribbean area, and another fourteen are now in process, thanks to a grant from the National Science Foundation. (For the dates obtained through 1960 see Rouse 1962, Tables 1–4; the entire list for Venezuela has been published as an appendix to Rouse and Cruxent 1963*b*). The results to date are summarized on the right side of Figure 2.

As is to be expected, our sample of dates is poorest for the earliest periods; we possess only three valid dates for the Paleo-Indian epoch and seven for the Meso-Indian epoch. There are also relatively few dates for the islands as compared with the mainland. These biases will be largely corrected by the analyses now in process; meanwhile, the tabulation must be considered tentative.

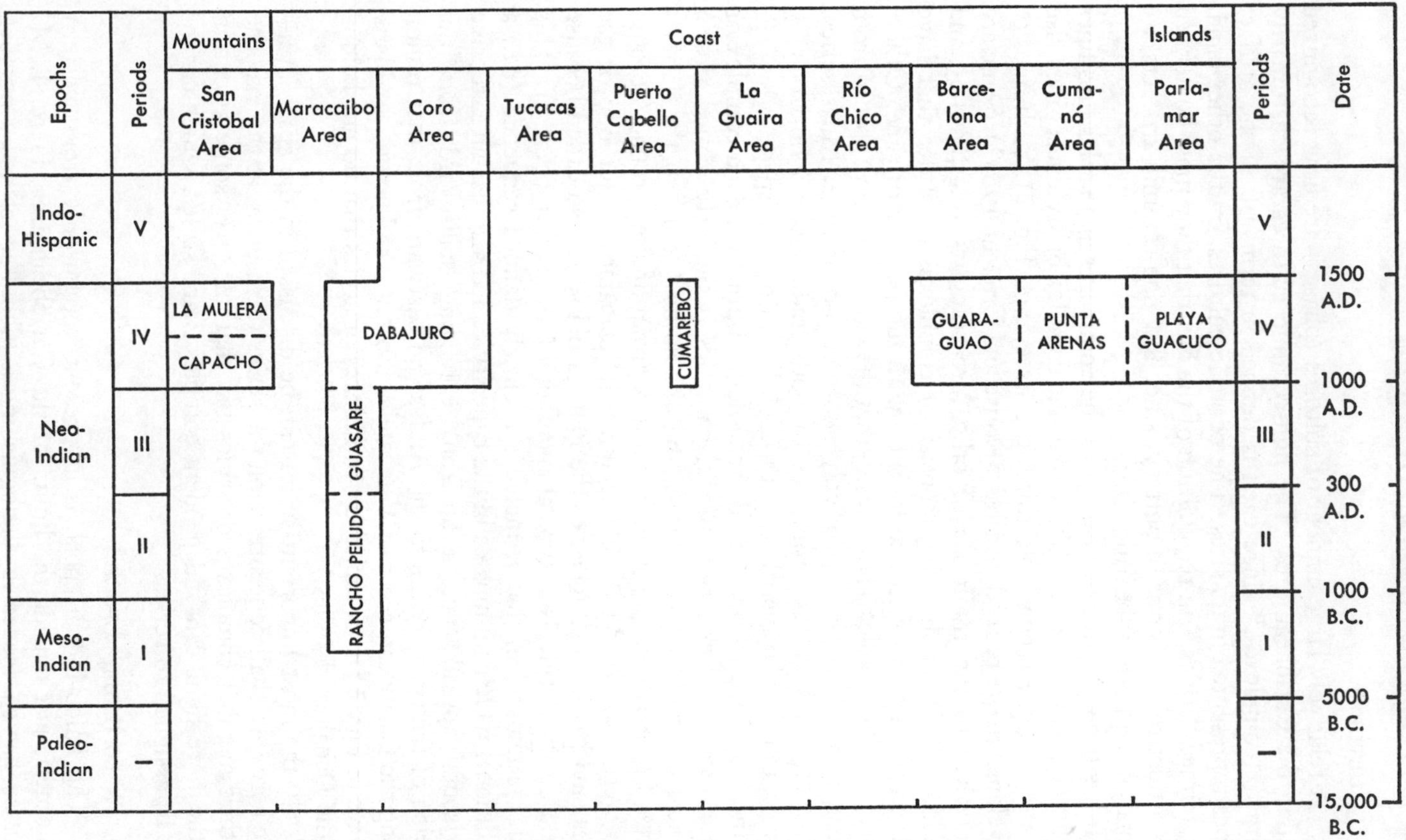

Date	Periods	Islands: Parla-mar Area	Coast: Cumaná Area	Coast: Barce-lona Area	Coast: Río Chico Area	Coast: La Guaira Area	Coast: Puerto Cabello Area	Coast: Tucacas Area	Coast: Coro Area	Coast: Maracaibo Area	Mountains: San Cristobal Area	Periods	Epochs
1500 A.D.	V											V	Indo-Hispanic
1000 A.D.	IV	PLAYA GUACUCO	PUNTA ARENAS	GUARA-GUAO		CUMAREBO	CUMAREBO		DABAJURO	DABAJURO / LA MULERA	LA MULERA / CAPACHO	IV	Neo-Indian
300 A.D.	III									RANCHO PELUDO / GUASARE		III	Neo-Indian
1000 B.C.	II											II	Neo-Indian
5000 B.C.	I											I	Meso-Indian
15,000 B.C.													Paleo-Indian

FIG. 2.—Chronology of the Dabajuroid series. (After Rouse and Cruxent [1963b, Fig. 9].)

CULTURES

A relatively large number of cultures (phases) are now recognized within the Caribbean area. The non-ceramic cultures are customarily termed "complexes," since each is defined in terms of all the artifact types represented in its sites. The ceramic cultures, on the other hand, are termed "styles," in recognition of the fact that they must be defined almost entirely in terms of pottery, since few non-ceramic artifacts are found in the pottery-bearing sites.

It has been possible to fit most of the complexes and styles into lines of development, that is, to show that one complex or style has given rise to a second, the second to a third, etc. (see, e.g., Fig. 2). Such lines of development are termed "series" (Rouse and Cruxent 1963*b*). Some are equivalent to the traditions of other archeologists (e.g., Willey and Phillips 1958), in that they consist of complexes or styles that have succeeded each other in one locality with the passage of time. Others are more comparable to horizons in that they appear to have spread from place to place within a relatively short period of time. Most series, however, combine the properties of both traditions and horizons by having an irregular distribution through both time and space.

In accordance with standard archeological practice, each complex or style is named after a type site. Each series is similarly named after a typical complex or style by adding the suffix "-oid" to the latter's name. For example, the style found in a group of sites around Coro on the west coast of Venezuela is termed "Dabajuro" after one of the sites, and has been assigned to the Dabajuroid series, so-called because the Dabajuro style is a typical member of the series (Fig. 2). This series is unusual in that it includes a clearly defined sequence (i.e., a tradition), which culminates in the type style, and also has an extensive horizontal spread (i.e., a horizon) extending southward from the region of the type style into the Andes and eastward from that region along the Caribbean coast of Venezuela. (So far as is known, the blank spaces in Fig. 2 are occupied by complexes or styles that do not belong to the Dabajuroid series.)

Only the most important series can be discussed in the space available here. We shall concentrate on the series themselves, at the expense of their member complexes or styles but shall also pay some attention to the more significant independent complexes and styles, which cannot yet be assigned to series.

PALEO-INDIAN EPOCH

The Paleo-Indian epoch is at present known only from western Venezuela, just outside the limits of the Caribbean area. Here, J. M. Cruxent has succeeded in distinguishing a Joboid series and a number

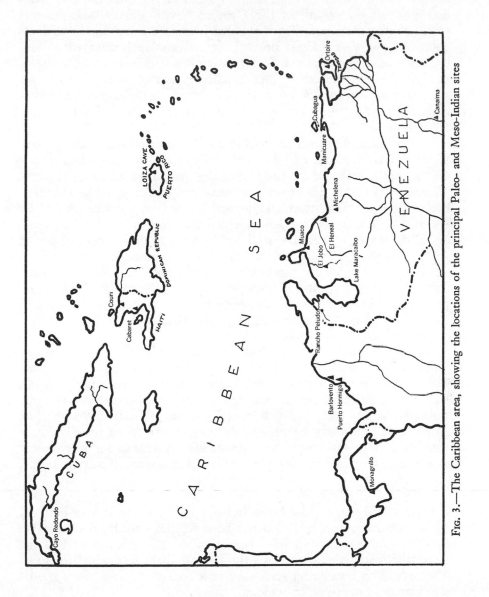

FIG. 3.—The Caribbean area, showing the locations of the principal Paleo- and Meso-Indian sites

of independent complexes (Rouse and Cruxent 1963*b*). Similar remains should eventually turn up in eastern Venezuela, the Guianas, and Trinidad, just off the mouth of the Orinoco River, since the latter was joined to the mainland, but the Paleo-Indians are not likely to have colonized the West Indies, since those Indians were oriented toward the land rather than the sea. So far as we know, they lacked the ability to travel by sea. Moreover, they apparently had no incentive to do so, since they did not eat sea food and the large, presently extinct land mammals, such as the mastodon, on which they concentrated, were lacking in the islands.

According to Cruxent, the Joboid series consists of four complexes, Camare, Las Lagunas, El Jobo, and Las Casitas, which succeeded one another in the valley of the Río Pedernales, inland from Coro in western Venezuela (Fig. 3). These are associated, respectively, with the uppermost, upper middle, lower middle, and lowermost terraces formed by the river. The Camare sites have yielded only crude choppers and scrapers of quartzite, which may well have served to make wooden spears for use in hunting the mammals. The Las Lagunas sites contained, in addition, large bifacially worked blades, which could have been hafted in heavy thrusting spears. In the subsequent El Jobo complex, lanceolate projectile points were made; these are small enough to have been used to tip darts. The final complex, Las Casitas, also has a few stemmed points with triangular blades.

Three radiocarbon dates of *ca.* 13,000–11,000 B.C. have been obtained, two from Muaco on the coast near the mouth of the Río Pedernales and one from Rancho Peludo, in the Maracaibo Basin farther west, where a presumed Paleo-Indian deposit underlies successive occupations by Meso- and Neo-Indians (Rouse and Cruxent 1963*a*). The Muaco site apparently belongs to the Joboid series, but the deposit at Rancho Peludo represents the Manzanillo complex, an independent culture characterized by chopping tools of fossil wood (Cruxent 1962).

Meso-Indian Epoch

As already noted, the Meso-Indian epoch is equivalent to Period I of the relative chronology and has been radiocarbon dated from 5000 to 1000 B.C. It may well have been touched off by extinction of the large land mammals upon which the Paleo-Indians had relied for food. This would have caused a search for new sources of food, with results that varied from region to region.

GUIANA HIGHLANDS

If we may judge by the recently discovered site of Canaima in Venezuelan Guiana (Fig. 3), the Indians of that region continued to rely primarily upon game, turning to the smaller animals that still survived. They specialized in the triangular, stemmed points of stone that had begun to be made in Las Casitas, the latest Joboid complex (Rouse and Cruxent 1963*b*). Similar points have also been found in British Guiana (Evans and Meggers 1960), suggesting that a hunting population was widespread through the Guiana highlands at this time.

COAST AND NEARBY ISLANDS

The Meso-Indians of the coast turned instead to products of the sea, as evidenced by a series of non-ceramic shell heaps along the shores of Venezuela and British Guiana and on the nearby islands. We have been able to distinguish a single Manicuaroid series, which is limited to eastern Venezuela, being best represented at the great shell heap of Punta Gorda on Cubagua Island (Fig. 3). Here our main trench, 15 deep feet, yielded a succession of three complexes. The Cubagua complex, in the lowermost levels, is characterized by bone points, which are thought to have been hafted in fishing harpoons or hooks, by bipointed stones for use in slings or bolas, and by shell cups and hammers. To these are added shell gouges, beads, and pendants in the Manicuare complex of the intermediate levels and shell points and celts in the Punta Gorda complex of the uppermost levels. The invention of the gouge may have been particularly significant, since it would have made possible the manufacture of dugout canoes.

Radiocarbon analyses of samples from Punta Gorda and other sites date the Cubagua complex in the third millennium B.C. and the Manicuare complex in the second millennium B.C., confirming their position in Period I. The Punta Gorda complex is not radiocarbon dated but may be placed in Period II because of its association with trade pottery of the Saladoid series. It would seem, therefore, that the series survived beyond the end of the Meso-Indian epoch, overlapping the Neo-Indian developments in other parts of Venezuela.

Several coastal shell heaps in the vicinity of Tucacas, on the border between the Caribbean and Intermediate areas, are grouped together as the El Heneal complex (Fig. 3). These lack the bone and shell artifacts of the Manicuaroid series; their most distinctive type of artifact is a stone with grinding facets on its edges rather than its sides. Radiocarbon analyses place the El Heneal complex in the fourth to second millenniums B.C., well within the Meso-Indian epoch. Both this complex and the two earliest complexes of the Manicuaroid series are associated with a sea-level at least 50 centimeters lower than the present one.

WEST INDIES

The coastal Indians' reliance upon seafood must have caused them to develop some interest in navigation, and this may have been furthered, as already noted, by invention of the gouge and celt for use in making dugout canoes. Some sea-faring ability is demonstrated by the colonization of islands, such as Cubaga. From there, the Manicuaroid Indians might be expected to have continued out into the West Indies proper. However, we possess no evidence of them—or of any other Meso-Indians—in the Lesser Antilles. Trinidad, which had now become separate from the mainland, is the exception; it has yielded an Ortoire complex, but this cannot be assigned to the Manicuaroid series because it lacks bipointed stones and shell artifacts (Rouse 1960).

The distribution of Meso-Indian remains in the Greater Antilles does not favor the theory of Manicuaroid migration either. On Puerto Rico, the easternmost island, Alegría, Nicholson, and Willey (1955) have distinguished a Loiza Cave complex, which has none of the artifact types of the Manicuaroid series but does share the edge-grinder with the El Heneal complex of western Venezuela (Fig. 3). The two complexes known from Hispaniola, Couri and Cabaret, also lack the Manicuaroid types; they are characterized by large lamellar flakes trimmed only on the edges in Central American fashion (Coe 1957). Only in Cuba, the island farthest removed from eastern Venezuela, do we find remains comparable to those of the Manicuaroid series. Cayo Redondo and Guayabo Blanco, the two complexes recognized here, both have shell gouges and hammers, bone points, and several other Manicuaroid traits (Rouse 1960).

To account for these distributions and for the absence of Meso-Indian remains in the Lesser Antilles, we have suggested that various groups of Meso-Indians may have accidentally been blown out to the Greater Antilles from different parts of the Caribbean mainland, including Central America and possibly even Florida, since shell gouges and bone points occur there in preceramic sites. The times of arrival are uncertain. Although there is evidence that the Meso-Indians reached Cuba before the ground sloth became extinct there, this means nothing, since the Indians are likely to have caused the extinction. Radiocarbon dates of about the time of Christ have recently been obtained for the Krum Bay site in the Virgin Islands and Loiza Cave in Puerto Rico (personal communications from Ripley P. Bullen and Minze Stuiver), but these do not necessarily refer to the earliest Meso-Indian inhabitants.

Isolated groups of Meso-Indians survived the coming of Neo-Indians in the more remote parts of Haiti and Cuba and were still there in the time of Columbus. One radiocarbon date from Cuba documents their survival; it refers to Period III of the relative chronology.

VALENCIA BASIN AND THE LLANOS

A large area in the interior of Venezuela remains to be discussed, including the mountain valleys, such as Valencia Basin, and the Llanos. What kind of adjustment did the inhabitants of these regions made to the changes in fauna at the beginning of the Meso-Indian epoch? Fewer fish and shellfish were available to them, game may not have been so plentiful, but in compensation they probably had larger supplies of wild fruits and vegetables. Under such circumstances in other parts of the world (e.g., in Tehuacan Valley, Mexico, which is now being investigated by MacNeish [1962]) man came to rely more and more upon wild vegetable foods and eventually began to cultivate the plants. Did this happen in Venezuela?

We are only beginning to obtain the answers to these questions. Recent excavation for the foundation of a new factory at Michelena in the Valencia Basin has uncovered a series of stone pestles, axes, and a milling stone that might have been used by a gathering people, but this find is unique (Cruxent and Rouse 1958–59). Better evidence is supplied by our excavations during the last two years at Rancho Peludo in the interior of the Maracaibo Basin, western Venezuela (Rouse and Cruxent 1963*b*).

As already noted, Rancho Peludo may have originally been inhabited by Paleo-Indians of the Manzanillo complex. The main part of the deposit, with which we are here concerned, consists of urn burials, potsherds, and a few hammers and grinders of stone that are eroding out of the bank of the Río Guasare at a depth of 1–2 meters. We encountered no hunting or fishing tools, and bones and shells were so rare as to indicate that meat and fish were not important in the diet. We assume, therefore, that the inhabitants relied primarily upon vegetable foods. Presumably, they gathered most of them wild, though the presence of two fragments of clay griddles, like those which the agricultural Indians of the Caribbean area still use to bake cassava cakes, suggests that some cultivation may have been carried on.

The Rancho Peludo pottery and burial urns consist of simple bowls and jars, some provided with annular bases. They are coarse, thick, and grit tempered and are crudely decorated by means of fabric impression, appliqué work, and punctation. The pottery looks old, and its antiquity is confirmed by a series of five radiocarbon dates ranging between 2700 and 300 B.C.

The pottery is comparable in its degree of development—though not in its stylistic details—to three other ceramic finds in the Intermediate area, at Barlovento and Puerto Hormiga near Cartagena, Colombia, and at Monagrillo in Panama. All three of these finds have radiocarbon dates of the same order as Rancho Peludo's—between 3000 and 2000 B.C. Willey (1960) has attributed the beginnings of agriculture to these sites, as we do to Rancho Peludo. If we are correct, they mark the beginning of a trend that was to culminate in the fully developed agriculture of the Neo-Indian epoch.

Eventually, it should be possible to find similar sites in the Caribbean area proper, especially in the Valencia Basin and on the Llanos, for the earliest Neo-Indian sites of those two regions have such advanced pottery and, inferentially, so effective agriculture that they must be the product of an extended development during the Meso-Indian Epoch. Documentation of this development is the most pressing problem in Caribbean archeology at the present time.

Neo-Indian Epoch: Introduction

The Neo-Indian epoch is divided into Periods II, III, and IV, lasting from 1000 B.C. to A.D. 300, A.D. 300 to 1000, and A.D. 1000 to 1500, respectively. It is begun at the culmination of the development just discussed, that is, at the point at which crops and the techniques of agriculture had improved to such an extent that they could become the basic source of food. At this point, hunting, fishing, and gathering, which had been the main economic pursuits of the previous epoch, could be relegated to a secondary position.

It is of interest to inquire whether the change was a matter of local development or was due to diffusion of new crops and new techniques of agriculture from Mesoamerica and the Intermediate area. We shall have to await further information about the previous (Meso-Indian) development before a definitive answer to this question can be supplied, but we may obtain some idea about it by projecting the situation during the Indo-Hispanic epoch back into Neo-Indian time. In the former epoch, bitter manioc was the most important crop in the Caribbean area. There were complicated techniques to squeeze the poisonous juice out of its roots, make flour from them, and bake the flour into cakes. Unfortunately, most of the implements and utensils used were composed of perishable materials, so have not been preserved in the sites, but clay griddles for baking the cakes have survived. Fragments of griddles are found not only in the Indo-Hispanic but also in the Neo-Indian sites, and therefore it is probable that the cultivation of manioc goes back to the Neo-Indian epoch. Since griddle fragments have likewise been found at the Meso-Indian site of Rancho Peludo, as already noted, it may be concluded that the cultivation of manioc was an indigenous development.

By contrast, the principal Indo-Hispanic crop of Mesoamerica and the Intermediate area—including western Venezuela—was maize. Metates and manos, used to prepare it, are common in the sites, and griddles are lacking. Since this also holds true for the earlier, Neo-Indian sites, we may infer that maize, rather than manioc, was the principal crop of both Mesoamerica and the Intermediate area during

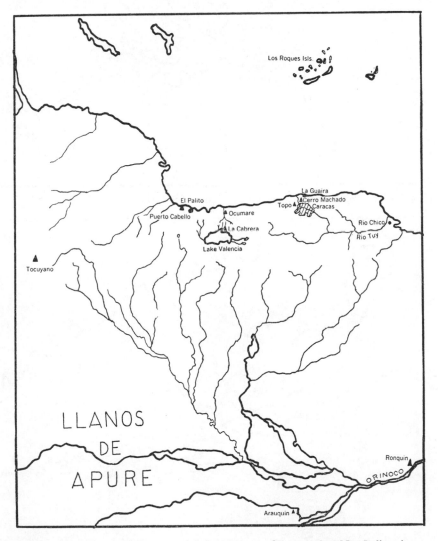

FIG. 4.—Central Venezuela, showing the locations of the principal Neo-Indian sites

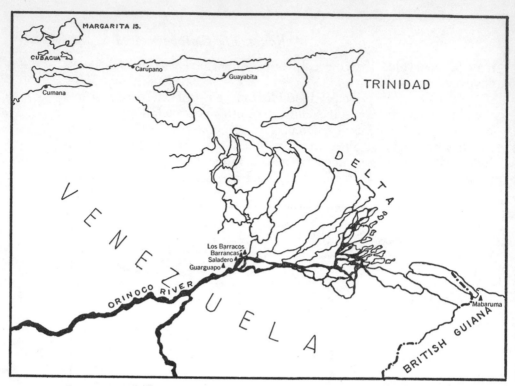

FIG. 5.—The Delta region, showing the locations of the principal Neo-Indian sites

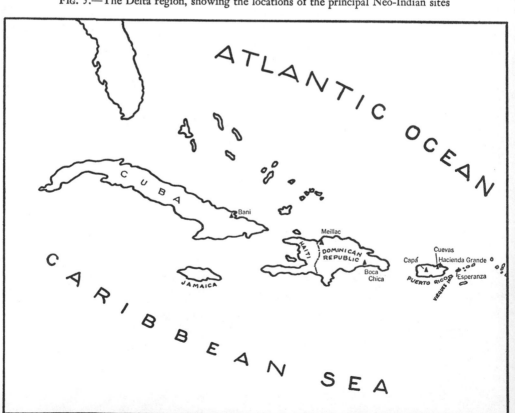

FIG. 6.—The Central Antilles, showing the locations of the principal Neo-Indian sites

the Neo-Indian epoch. Presumably, its effective use as the major crop developed in Mexico at the beginning of the Neo-Indian epoch and spread from there into South America, including western Venezuela (Collier 1962).

These archeological hypotheses agree with the conclusions reached by Sauer (1952) on botanical grounds. He postulates independent development of "root agriculture," based on manioc, and of "seed agriculture," based on maize, and suggests that domestication of these plants may have taken place in "the Venezuelan savannas" and Meso-america, respectively.

We tentatively conclude, then, that the typical Neo-Indian culture of the Caribbean area was a local development based on the domestication and gradual improvement of manioc during the Meso-Indian epoch. But there is also evidence (to be discussed below) that the Mesoamerican–Intermediate-area type of agriculture, based on maize, intruded into a part of the Caribbean area during the Neo-Indian epoch.

Three major focuses of Neo-Indian culture can be distinguished within the area (Figs. 4–6).

1. *Central Venezuela:* the Valencia Basin and the adjacent parts of the mountains and the coast.

2. *Delta region:* the land around the Orinoco Delta, including the Barrancas region, just above the delta; the Paria Peninsula, to the northeast; the island of Trinidad, to the north; and the northwest district of British Guiana, to the southeast.

3. *Central West Indies:* the Virgin Islands, at the northern end of the Lesser Antillean arc, and Puerto Rico, Hispaniola, and Cuba in the Greater Antilles.

Insofar as can be told from present evidence, the archeology of the regions around and among the foregoing focuses is simpler and less significant, so it need not be considered in this summary paper. However, we should note that future exploration may reveal additional focuses of higher development, for example, in the Llanos de Apure at the big bend in the Orinoco River, where, as we shall see, several ceramic series may have originated.

Neo-Indian Epoch: Central Venezuela

Some knowledge of the geography of central Venezuela is essential for an understanding of its culture history. The fertile Valencia Basin, in the middle of the mountains, seems to have been a center of population during Neo-Indian time, as it is today (Fig. 4). From this basin a route of travel and of possible diffusion extends eastward through the mountains to the Caracas area and on to the coast at Río Chico. Another route runs from south to north across the mountains, beginning in the Llanos and passing through the Valencia Basin onto the coastal plain in the vicinity of the present city of Puerto Cabello. The coastal plain, in turn, lies at the juncture of two lines of diffusion, one east and west along the Caribbean shore line and the other northeastward down the Yaracuy Valley from the Venezuelan Andes. The convergence and crossing of these various lines of diffusion has produced a culture history of great complexity, only the major outlines of which can be presented here.

We know nothing about the beginning of this culture history during the first half of Period II. When we pick up the archeological record, at about the time of Christ, there were already two distinct ceramic series in the region, Barrancoid and Tocuyanoid. We shall consider the Barrancoid series first because, even though its radiocarbon dates are not quite so old, it probably had a longer history in central Venezuela.

BARRANCOID SERIES

The series consists of two groups of styles, one in central Venezuela and the other in the Delta region. The series is clearly intrusive in the latter region, as will be noted below, but it need not have originated in central Venezuela. It would not be surprising if it ultimately proves to have arisen in the Llanos de Apure and to have moved from there in two directions, down the Orinoco River into the Delta region and up across the Llanos into central Venezuela. Willey (1958) has suggested that it may originally have been derived from the Meso-Indian styles of Barlevento in Colombia and Monagrillo in Panama, to which reference has already been made.

Three Barrancoid styles have been distinguished in central Venezuela: La Cabrera in the Valencia Basin and El Palito and Taborda in the Puerto Cabello area (Fig. 4). La Cabrera and El Palito are placed in Periods II and III, and this is confirmed by radiocarbon dates of A.D. 321 and 346 for La Cabrera. Taborda dates from Period IV; it appears to be a degeneration from El Palito, affected by influences from along several of the lines of diffusion outlined above (Cruxent and Rouse 1963*b*).

The two earlier styles, La Cabrera and El Palito, are very much alike. Both have a considerable variety of shapes, including bowls, jars, and bottles. Annular bases are common; solid legs, rare. The rims are characteristically flanged, and the flanges sometimes bear simple, curvilinear incised designs. More complex modeled-incised lugs, often in the form of human heads, are the most prominent feature of the decoration. Strap handles also characterize the two styles; most are situated vertically on the vessel wall, but a few extend horizontally between two spouts.

One might expect the Barrancoid potters to have used their skill in modeling and incision for the production of figurines, but they did not. However, they did use these techniques to decorate the bowls of clay pipes, which are either elbow or platform shaped. Clay griddles occur in all sites, indicating the Caribbean type of agriculture. Only village sites have been found; there are no ceremonial structures or complex burials.

TOCUYANOID SERIES

In central Venezuela, the Tocuyanoid series is represented by a single style, Cerro Machado, at the site of the same name in the vicinity of La Guaira, the port for Caracas (Fig. 4). This is a shell heap, again without any ceremonial or burial structures. The pottery consists of bowls and ollas, the former characteristically provided with long, hollow legs that extend up the sides of the vessels almost to the rims. There are no flanges. Decoration includes crude punctations and rectilinear incised designs on the vessel wall, simply modeled serpents, and complex curvilinear designs painted in red and black on a white slip. The absence of griddles provides the inference that agriculture was of the western, Intermediate-area type.

Indeed, the Tocuyanoid series seems to have originated in western Venezuela, its center being the modern city of Barquisimeto at the base of the Andes, whence it apparently diffused down the Yaracuy valley to the vicinity of Puerto Cabello on the coast and thence eastward to the La Guaira area. There is a radiocarbon date of 225 B.C. for the Tocuyano style in the west and of A.D. 27 for Cerro Machado, which suggest that it intruded into the coastal part of central Venezuela during the middle of Period II, possibly about the time that the Barrancoid series was making its appearance inland in the Valencia Basin. Ultimately, the origin of the Tocuyanoid series may go back to the northeastern coast of Colombia, where similar polychrome pottery is widespread (Rouse and Cruxent 1963*b*).

OCUMAROID SERIES

Along the coast of central Venezuela, the Tocuyanoid series seems to have given rise to a new series, called Ocumaroid, at the close of Period II. This new series continued the shapes of the Tocuyanoid series and its polychrome tradition of decoration, though its designs were rectilinear rather than curvilinear, in conformity with the trend at the time in the Intermediate area farther west. On the other hand, the series also has some modeling and incision, presumably as the result of contact with the Barrancoid series, with which it coexisted on the central coast throughout Periods III and IV, if our chronology is correct. All its sites have yielded griddles, which again suggest Barrancoid influence. Traces of ceremonial development continue to be lacking; the sites consist simply of shell middens.

VALENCIOID SERIES

The final series of central Venezuela is named after the style and basin of Valencia, where it occurs in its most elaborate form (Fig. 4). Related styles are distributed through the mountains, down to the coast in the La Guaira and Rio Chico areas, and out into the Los Roques Islands off La Guaira. Everywhere, these styles seem to date from Period IV.

The Valencia style is the best known in Venezuela, thanks especially to the work of Requena (1932), Bennett (1937), Osgood (1943), and Kidder (1944). Kidder was able to demonstrate a stratigraphic sequence of the La Cabrera (Barrancoid) and Valencia styles and to correlate them respectively with periods of rising and falling water-level in Lake Valencia. His findings provide the basis for placement of La Cabrera in Periods II–III and of Valencia in Period IV; they are supported by radiocarbon dates of A.D. 931, 961, and 1000 for the Valencia style (Rouse and Cruxent 1963b).

Like La Cabrera, the Valencia style is monochrome. Its shapes are unchanged, except that Valencia pottery lacks legs and flanges and has convex collars, some of which are decorated with human faces in appliqué work. Incised designs occur only on the vessel wall and are limited to straight lines. This shift from the curvilinear designs of the La Cabrera style parallels the development of rectilinear painting in the Ocumare style and in the polychrome pottery of western Venezuela and eastern Colombia. Horizontal rod handles are another diagnostic of the Valencia style. Lugs consist of minute geometric and animal-shaped figures done in appliqué work. These contrast markedly with the modeled lugs of the Barrancoid series; for example, they have coffee-bean eyes, whereas the Barrancoid eyes are doughnut shaped.

There is some holdover from the La Cabrera style in the custom of making clay pipes. Figurines of clay are common, their features being delineated by the technique of appliqué work rather than modeling. Urn burial makes its appearance in the Valencia Basin for the first time, and so also does the custom of building artificial mounds. Traces of pile dwellings have been found; there is reason to believe that such dwellings were also constructed during the previous La Cabrera period.

The Valencia style may best be regarded as a local development out of the La Cabrera style, by a process of degeneration in the latter's modeling and incision and by the addition of new traits from the Llanos to the south, that is, from a series known as Arauquinoid, which centers in the Llanos de Apure. Foremost among the traits that may be said to have diffused from this source are appliqué work, the face-and-collar design, rectilinear incision, and figurines, though many of them may ultimately be derived from western Venezuela, where they are likewise common during Period IV. Mound-building and urn burial also appear to have diffused from the Arauquinoid series; the former must have been equally useful in the Valencia Basin and on the Llanos for raising dwellings above the floods of the rainy seasons.

As one moves out of the Valencia Basin, the styles belonging to the Valencioid series become simpler and simpler, and such traits as pipes, figurines, and mound-building disappear. These facts indicate that the spread of the series was probably due not to a mass migration but to diffusion of individual ceramic traits. In the Topo style, around La Guaira, on the coast, we even find an occasional painted sherd, which is probably due to contact with the Ocumaroid series, centering on Puerto Cabello farther west along the coast (Fig. 4).

NEO-INDIAN EPOCH: DELTA REGION

The culture history of the Delta region is less complex than that of central Venezuela. For one thing, the region is more remote, so that it was not subjected to so many influences from the Intermediate area; for another, it does not lie athwart so many lines of diffusion. So far as present evidence indicates, culture could spread only up and down the Orinoco River and from east to west along the coast. As a result, series did not coexist in the Delta region to the same extent as in central Venezuela; nor, indeed, are there so many of them.

The swamp lands of the delta extend southeastward into British Guiana and northwestward along the coast of the Gulf of Paria to the base of the mountain range that forms the Paria Peninsula (Fig. 5). This range is relatively difficult to cross to reach the Caribbean Coast. Together, therefore, the swamps and the mountain range form a great barrier that cuts off the Llanos and the Orinoco Valley from the Paria and Caribbean coasts and from the adjacent islands, including Cubagua, Margarita, and Trinidad.

At the beginning of the Neo-Indian epoch, that is, during the first half of Period II, very different cultures existed south and north of the barrier. South of the barrier were Neo-Indians, who had presumably descended from the gathering peoples of the previous Meso-Indian epoch. North of the barrier, the fishing people of Meso-Indian time still survived in the form of Manicuaroid series, in the vicinity of Cubagua Island, and of the Ortoire complex in Trinidad. During the latter part of Period II the Neo-Indians finally broke through the barrier and seized the coast and islands. Meso-Indians continued in the swamps of the delta, however, and one group of them, the Warrau Indians, has survived until modern time (Rouse and Cruxent 1963*b*).

SALADOID SERIES

The earliest-known pottery in eastern Venezuela is that of the Saladoid series, named after a site near Barrancas on the Orinoco River, just above the delta (Fig. 5). The pottery at the bottom of the site of Ronquin on the middle Orinoco is very similar, suggesting that the series may have been widespread through the middle and lower Orinoco Valley at the beginning of the Neo-Indian epoch. Its origin is a mystery.

The Saladero site has yielded radiocarbon dates of 915, 745, and 615 B.C. Technologically, its pottery is thin, fine, and so hard that it rings when struck. Shapes are simple, consisting predominantly of bowls with flat bases, gracefully flaring sides, and plain or beveled rims. There are vertical strap handles, some bearing simple, knobbed lugs, without the modeling-incision of Barrancoid lugs. Incision occurs on vessel walls in the form of arched parallel lines. Painting is most distinctive; it includes crosshatching done in red on a plain background and curvilinear designs in white on a red background. Frequently, areas of white and red paint are juxtaposed to form designs; in such cases a thin white line is placed on the red bordering the edge of the white area. Red paint, however, is never placed on a white background, as in the polychrome styles of western Venezuela.

Clay griddles are common, testifying to the importance of manioc in the diet. There are very few objects of other kinds; cylindrical pot rests of clay are perhaps the most typical. Evidences of ceremonial activity have not been found.

Toward the middle of the first millennium B.C., the Barrancoid series intruded into Saladoid territory. We have already suggested that this intrusion may have come from farther up the Orinoco River, on the Llanos de Apure. If so, the Barrancoid people must have bypassed the Saladoid settlements along the middle Orinoco, for these settlements continued in existence and we find Barrancoid sites only in the lower part of the Orinoco Valley. The Saladoid and Barrancoid series may have coexisted on the lower Orinoco for a while, since the latter's earliest dates of 895, 865, and 845 B.C. overlap the former's, but soon the Barrancoid people seem to have pushed the Saladoid population out through the delta onto the Paria Peninsula and Trinidad.

The Barrancoid intrusion, then, split the Saladoid series into two parts, one on the middle Orinoco and the other below the delta. These were in existence during the latter half of Period II and all of Period III, that is, throughout the first millennium A.D. Above the Barrancoid intrusion, the series expanded as far as Cotua on the upper Orinoco. Below the intrusion, it spread westward along the Caribbean Coast to Carúpano and Margarita Island (Fig. 5) and northward through the Antilles to Puerto Rico (Fig. 6). Whether it likewise diffused southeastward into British Guiana remains to be determined. Everywhere, it came in contact with the Meso-Indian fishing populations, as evidenced, for example, by the trade pottery found in the latest complex of the Manicuaroid series, the Punta Gorda. It is entirely possible that many of the Meso-Indians eventually adopted pottery and agriculture from the Saladoid people, thereby raising themselves to Neo-Indian status. Conversely, the Saladoid people may have acquired from the Meso-Indians the seafaring skills they needed to reach Cubagua and Margarita islands and to colonize the Antilles.

The Saladoid pottery existed in a pure state only before the Barrancoid intrusion. The subsequent styles, both above and below the intrusion, show Barrancoid influence in the presence, for example, of annular bases, flanges, modeled-incised lugs, and greater emphasis on incision (e.g., Howard 1943). Zoned crosshatching died out above the intrusion; below, it came to be done in incision rather than in red paint. Other painted designs were also done in incision or a combination of incision with painting. Pure white-on-red painting persisted, too, and remained the most diagnostic feature of the series. Indeed, the combination of zoned, incised crosshatching and white-on-red painting provides a distinctive time-marker for the spread of the series from the mainland into the Antilles; a set of thirteen radiocarbon dates fix this event between A.D. 1 and A.D. 300.

Above the Barrancoid intrusion, the Saladoid series eventually gave way to another series, the Arauquinoid, which began to spread down the Orinoco River at the close of Period III. Below the intrusion, the Saladoid series was likewise replaced at the end of Period III by two new series, Guayabitoid on the mainland and Chicoid in the Greater Antilles.

BARRANCOID SERIES

The Barrancoid people produced two successive styles on the lower Orinoco River—Barrancas and Los Barrancos—before they, too, came under the influence of the Arauquinoid diffusion during Period IV. Barrancoid pottery also spread in period III to Trinidad and British Guiana, crossing the barrier of swamps as the Saladoid series had previously done. Erin, the Barrancoid style in Trinidad, remained in existence only a short time before giving way to the Guayabitoid pottery of Period IV, but in the northwest district of British Guiana the Mabaruma "phase" apparently lasted until the coming of the Europeans (Evans and Meggers 1960).

The Barrancoid pottery of the Delta region is thicker and heavier than that in central Venezuela; some of its vessels must have been enormous. It is also more elaborately decorated. Both lugs and incised designs are exceedingly complex, and there are intricate modeled-incised figures on the vessel walls, including human faces, spirals, and other curvilinear motifs. Some of the earlier Barrancas-style pottery of Period II has white-on-red painting, apparently as a result of Saladoid influence. The later Los Barrancos style of Period III is more purely Barrancoid and may be regarded as the classic pottery of the series (Osgood and Howard 1943).

During Period IV, Los Barrancos was succeeded on the lower Orinoco by the Guarguapo style, which is difficult to classify because it shows a blend of Barrancoid and Arauquinoid traits. The modeled-incised decoration of the Barrancoid series is still present, though in a rather degenerate form, but to it are added typically Arauquinoid designs consisting, for example, of appliqué faces with coffee-bean eyes, simple geometric lugs, and rectilinear incision. About half the pottery is grit tempered, as in both the Barrancoid and Saladoid series, while the rest is tempered with sponge spicules in Arauquinoid fashion.

There is a striking parallel between the spread of Arauquinoid traits downstream to the Barrancoid people of the lower Orinoco and the diffusion of comparable traits across the Llanos to the Barancoid settlements of the Valencia Basin, that is, between the Los Barrancos–Guarguapo sequence on the lower Orinoco and the La Cabrera–Valencia sequence in the Valencia Basin. It is important to note, however, that this parallel is limited to ceramics. The Barrancoid people of the lower Orinoco did not adopt mound-building, figurines, urn burial, or other Arauquinoid ceremonial traits, as happened in the Valencia Basin; nor did they ever make clay pipes.

GUAYABITOID SERIES

On the Orinoco, the Arauquinoid diffusion was halted by the swamps of the delta. Beyond them, on Trinidad, the Paria Peninsula, and the adjacent Caribbean Coast, a new series developed known as Guayabitoid (Fig. 5), which, essentially, may be regarded as a degeneration from the previous Saladoid series: the vessel shapes were simplified into ollas without flanges or handles, the painted decoration disappeared, zoömorphic lugs died out, and incision became limited to simple parallel lines. Indeed, this pottery bears very little decoration of any kind. Traces of ceremonial development are likewise absent. The whole impression is one of a cultural backwater, developing in relative isolation behind the barrier of the swamps and the coastal range.

We possess three radiocarbon dates, A.D. 1240, 1271, and 1665, for the Guayabitoid series, indicating that it persisted from Period IV into the Indo-Hispanic epoch, as was also true of the Guarguapo style on the other side of the delta. Apparently, it was the Guayabitoid people whom Columbus encountered when he explored the Delta region.

NEO-INDIAN EPOCH: CENTRAL ANTILLES

We have seen that agricultural, pottery-making Indians of the Saladoid series moved out into the West Indies during the first centuries A.D. When they reached Puerto Rico, they again came in contact with non-ceramic, Meso-Indian fishermen, as they had on the Venezuelan coast. The subsequent prehistory of the Greater Antilles is one of gradual encroachment of the Neo-Indians upon the territories of the Meso-Indians. The latter succeeded in retaining their own cultural identity (they never adopted pottery, for example) but by the time of Columbus they had been pushed back onto the southwestern peninsula of Haiti and into the swamps and islands of southern and western Cuba (Fig. 6)[1]

SALADOID SERIES

The Saladoid Indians reached the Central Antilles toward the close of Period II, seizing the Virgin Islands and Puerto Rico from the Meso-Indians but leaving the islands farther west in the latters' hands (Rouse 1951). The earliest remains of the intruders are strikingly similar to the earliest Saladoid remains in the Lesser Antilles and on the coast of Venezuela, as is to be expected in the case of a migration from the mainland. For example, the earliest sites everywhere contain more crab remains and fewer shells than do the later sites (cf. Rainey 1935), they all have griddles and lack ceremonial paraphernalia, and the earliest pottery is everywhere characterized by D-shaped handles, zoned crosshatched-incised designs, minute-featured zoömorphic lugs, and the ubiquitous white-on-red painted designs.

In Puerto Rico the pottery with these features is known as the Hacienda Grande style. It was succeeded by the Cuevas style, in which the features gradually died out so that, when the Cuevas style came to an end at the beginning of Period III, there was little decoration left (Rouse 1952).

INTERMEDIATE STYLES

The resultant pottery, known as the Ostiones style, gave rise to a series of as yet undefined styles in the Dominican Republic, Haiti, and Jamaica, all of which are similarly characterized by loop handles, tabular lugs, and red paint. They indicate further encroachment of the Neo-Indians upon the Meso-Indian aborigines of the Central Antilles.

In Haiti and in Jamaica, the Ostiones-like pottery developed into two new styles (the one in Haiti is named Meillac [Rouse 1939]), which have face lugs with appliqué features and rectilinear parallel-line incision. The incision may well have resulted from contact with the Meso-Indians, who customarily decorated their shell- and stonework with similar designs.

Meillac-like pottery spread in turn to Cuba and the Bahamas, marking a further stage in the expansion of the Neo-Indians at the expense of the Meso-Indians. This pottery survived in Jamaica, central Cuba, and parts of the Bahamas until historic time—the Baní style of central Cuba was still being made when Columbus arrived and for some time thereafter (Rouse 1942).

CHICOID SERIES

In the central Antilles, a new series arose during the latter part of Period III. This series appears to have had its origin in the Dominican Republic, presumably out of the Ostiones-like style that had originally become established there. From the Dominican Republic it spread westward into Haiti and eastern Cuba and eastward into Puerto Rico and the Virgin Islands at the beginning of Period IV, giving rise to a series of similar styles. There is enough variation in these styles to indicate that the spread was largely a matter of diffusion of ceramic traits rather than one of migration, though we know that some lesser movements of people were involved. For example, we have evidence that a group of Dominican Indians with the original Boca Chica style settled on the south coast of Puerto Rico and influenced the local Indians to produce two new Chicoid styles, Capá in western Puerto Rico and Esperanza in eastern Puerto Rico (Rouse 1952).

Chicoid pottery retains the basic bowl shape of the previous Ostiones-like pottery, but the loop handles of the latter give way to, or else are dwarfed by, large modeled-incised head lugs. Painting disappears, and its place is taken by curvilinear incised designs situated on bevels inside the rims of open bowls—a favorite place for painting in the previous Ostiones-like styles—or on the shoulders of bowls with inturned sides. Both the lugs and the incised designs look quite Barrancoid, but the Chicoid and Barrancoid series are not likely to have been directly connected. Instead, the Chicoid potters probably obtained their tradition of modeling and incision via Barrancoid influences on the Saladoid series.

The Chicoid series is accompanied by the greatest artistic and ceremonial development within the Caribbean area, a development that began during the latter part of Period III and reached its climax at the end of Period IV, when Columbus first encountered the Chicoid Indians. Archeological evidences of this development include ball courts and dance plazas, lined with upright stone slabs; stone idols, some large enough to be set up in the plazas; carved-stone collars and "elbow stones"; and three-pointed stones, which are likewise carved with elaborate designs. From the accounts of Columbus and his contemporaries, we know that these carvings were meant to represent deities called "zemis," some of which were human, and others animal. We are told that the Indians were also accustomed to portray the zemis on their household equipment, and this is borne out by the presence of carvings on stone celts, pestles, and other artifacts. Indeed, the modeled-incised lugs of the Chicoid pottery itself may have been meant to represent zemis (Rouse 1948).

The sources state further that the Indians built temples to house the figures of zemis, but none has survived, since they were made of perishable material. The zemis were also worshiped in caves, in which have been preserved a number of wooden statues and stools, carved like the stone-, bone-, and shellwork found in the open sites. Finally, the petroglyphs that abound in the Central Antilles may have depicted zemis, for they occur frequently on slabs lining ball courts and dance plazas, where the worship of zemis took place (Lovén 1935).

The cult of zemis probably had a multiple origin. Some traits apparently developed *in situ;* for example, we have seen that the modeled-incised pottery lugs can be derived from the earliest Saladoid pottery of Period II. Similarly, the carved, three-pointed stones undoubtedly go back to smaller, largely undecorated three-pointed stones, which were distributed throughout the West Indies from Trinidad to Cuba during Period III (Rouse 1961). Other traits, such as stone collars, may have originated in Mesoamerica, where there are similar artifacts. Ekholm (1961) has suggested that, in the Central Antilles as well as in Mesoamerica, these artifacts were worn as belts by ball players; and, indeed, the whole ball-game complex may be derived from Mexico. Other Mexican-like traits include the application of plaster and paint to stone carvings and the inlaying of shell and gold in the wood-carvings of the Central Antilles (Lothrop 1927).

Neo-Indian Epoch: Conclusions

In 1947 Julian H. Steward proposed a theory that runs counter to the foregoing reconstruction. He included the entire cult of the zemis within a Circum-Caribbean complex, which, according to him, originated in the Andes of Colombia, spread from there down to the coast, and then passed around the southern and eastern sides of the Caribbean Sea into the Greater Antilles. This theory was reasonable at the time but has not been supported by the subsequent archeological discoveries. As we have seen, central Venezuela does seem to have come under influences from the Intermediate area—though these apparently originated in the lowlands rather than in the Andes, as Steward supposed—but the Delta region did not. Specifically, the Barrancoid people of the Valencia Basin adopted such western traits as moundbuilding, urn burial, and clay figurines, but the Barrancoid people of the Delta region rejected these traits.

We conclude, therefore, that the Delta region was a cultural backwater during the latter part of the Neo-Indian epoch. It lay between two centers of higher development, one in central Venezuela, which was subjected to influences from the Intermediate area, and the other in the Central Antilles, which shows the effects of possible contacts with Mesoamerica. There appear to have been few, if any, contacts between these two centers via the Delta region.

Steward also suggested in his 1947 paper that the Central Antillean center may have contributed to the rise of ceremonialism in the southeastern United States. This suggestion, too, has failed to meet the test of further research. Not only does Southeastern ceremonialism seem to have begun earlier than the comparable development in the Central Antilles, but also the similarities between the two are more apparent than real (Sturtevant 1960). It now seems better to regard the Central Antilles and the Southeast as end points in separate lines of diffusion from Mesoamerica, which did not directly influence each other to any great extent, possibly because they were separated by areas where Meso-Indians survived, in western Cuba and southern Florida.

BIBLIOGRAPHY

ALEGRÍA, RICARDO, H. B. NICHOLSON, and GORDON R. WILLEY
   1955   "The Archaic Tradition in Puerto Rico." *Amer. Antiquity*, 21:113–21.
BENNETT, WENDELL C.
   1937   "Excavations at La Mata, Maracay, Venezuela." *Amer. Mus. Nat. Hist. Anthrop. Paps.*, Vol. 36, No. 2. New York.
BOOY, THEODOOR DE
   1916   *Notes on the Archeology of Margarita Island, Venezuela.* ("Contribs. Mus. Amer. Indian, Heye Foundation," Vol. 2, No. 5.) New York.
BULLBROOK, J. A.
   1953   *On the Excavation of a Shell Mound at Palo Seco, Trinidad, B.W.I.* ("Yale Univ. Pub. Anthrop.," No. 50.) New Haven, Conn.
COE, WILLIAM R., II
   1957   "A Distinctive Artifact Common to Haiti and Central America." *Amer. Antiquity*, 22:280–82.
COLLIER, DONALD
   1962   "The Central Andes." Pp. 165–76 in ROBERT J. BRAIDWOOD and GORDON R. WILLEY (eds.), *Courses toward Urban Life.* ("Viking Fund Pub. Anthrop.," No. 32.) New York.

Cosculluela, J. A.
1951 "Cuatro años en la Cienaga de Zapata." *Revista de Arqueología y Etnología*, secunda época, 6:31–168. La Habaña.
Cruxent, J. M.
1961 "Huesos quemados en el yacimiento prehistórico Muaco, Edo. Falcón." *Instituto Venezolano de Investigaciones Científicas, Departmento de Antropología, Boletín Informativo*, No. 2, pp. 20–21. Caracas.
1962 "Artifacts of Paleo-Indian Type, Maracaibo, Zulia, Venezuela." *Amer. Antiquity*, 27:576–79.
Cruxent, J. M., and Irving Rouse
1958 *An Archeological Chronology of Venezuela*. 2 vols. (Pan American
–59 Union Soc. Sci. Monog., No. 6.) Washington.
Du Ry, C. J., and H. R. van Heekeren
1960 *Studies in the Archaeology of the Netherlands Antilles: I–II*. (Uitgaven van de "Natuurwetenschappelijke Werkgroep Nederlandse Antillen," No. 10.) Curacao.
Ekholm, Gordon F.
1961 "Puerto Rican Stone 'Collars' as Ball-Game Belts." Pp. 356–71 in Samuel K. Lothrop et al., *Essays in Pre-Columbian Art and Archaeology*. Cambridge, Mass.: Harvard University Press.
Evans, Clifford, and Betty J. Meggers
1960 *Archeological Investigations in British Guiana*. (Bur. Amer. Ethnol. Bull. 177.) Washington, D.C.
Evans, Clifford, Betty J. Meggers, and J. M. Cruxent
1959 "Preliminary Results of Archeological Investigations along the Orinoco and Ventuari Rivers, Venezuela." Pp. 359–69 in *Actas del 33ra Cong. Internac. de Americanistas, San José, 20–27 Julio 1958*, Vol. 2. San José.
Fewkes, Jesse Walter
1907 "The Aborigines of Porto Rico and Neighboring Islands." Pp. 3–220 in *Bur. Amer. Ethnol. 25th Ann. Rpt., 1903–4*. Washington, D.C.
1922 "A Prehistoric Island Culture Area of America." Pp. 35–281 in *Bur. Amer. Ethnol. 34th Ann. Rpt., 1912–13*. Washington, D.C.
Gallagher, Patrick
1962 "La Pitía." *El Farol*, 24:6–14. Caracas.
Hahn, Paul G.
n.d. "A Relative Chronology of the Cuban Non-Ceramic Tradition." Ph.D. diss., Yale University, 1961.
Harrington, M. R.
1921 *Cuba before Columbus*. 2 vols. (Mus. Amer. Indian, Heye Foundation, "Indian Notes and Monographs," Vol. 17.) New York.
Hatt, Gudmund
1924 "Archaeology of the Virgin Islands." Pp. 29–42 in *Proc. 21st Internat. Cong. Americanists*, Part 1. The Hague.
Howard, George D.
1943 *Excavations at Ronquín, Venezuela*. ("Yale Univ. Pub. Anthrop.," No. 28.) New Haven, Conn.

HOWARD, ROBERT R.
1956   "The Archeology of Jamaica: A Preliminary Survey." *Amer. Antiquity*, 22:45–59.
JOSSELIN DE JONG, J. P. B. DE
1947   *Archeological Material from Saba and St. Eustatius, Lesser Antilles.* (Meddelingen van het Rijksmuseum voor Volkenkunde, Leiden, No. 1.) Leiden.
KIDDER, ALFRED, II
1944   *Archaeology of Northwestern Venezuela.* ("Peabody Mus. Amer. Arch. & Ethnol. Paps.," Vol. 26, No. 1.) Cambridge, Mass.
LOTHROP, R. W. and S. K.
1927   "The Use of Plaster on Porto Rican Stone Carvings." *Amer. Anthropologist*, 29:728–30.
LOVÉN, SVEN
1935   *Origins of the Tainan Culture, West Indies.* Göteborg.
McKUSICK, MARSHALL B.
n.d.   "Distribution of Ceramic Styles in the Lesser Antilles, West Indies." Ph.D. diss., Yale University, 1960.
MacNEISH, RICHARD STOCKTON
1962   *Second Annual Report of the Tehuacán Archaeological-Botanical Project.* Andover, Mass.
OSGOOD, CORNELIUS
1942   *The Ciboney Culture of Cayo Redondo, Cuba.* ("Yale Univ. Pub. Anthrop.," No. 25.) New Haven, Conn.
1943   *Excavations at Tocorón, Venezuela.* ("Yale Univ. Pub. Anthrop.," No. 29.) New Haven, Conn.
1946   British Guiana Archeology to 1945. ("Yale Univ. Pub. Anthrop.," No. 36.) New Haven, Conn.
OSGOOD, CORNELIUS, and GEORGE D. HOWARD
1943   *An Archeological Survey of Venezuela.* ("Yale Univ. Pub. Anthrop.," No. 27.) New Haven, Conn.
RAINEY, FROELICH G.
1935   *Porto Rican Archaeology.* (N.Y. Acad. Sci., Scient. Surv. Porto Rico and the Virgin Islands, Vol. 18, No. 1.) New York.
1941   *Excavations in the Ft. Liberté Region, Haiti.* ("Yale Univ. Pub. Anthrop.," No. 23.) New Haven, Conn.
REQUENA, RAFAEL
1932   *Vestigios de la Atlántida.* Caracas.
ROUSE, IRVING
1939   *Prehistory in Haiti: A Study in Method.* ("Yale Univ. Pub. Anthrop.," No. 21.) New Haven, Conn.
1941   *Culture of the Ft. Liberté Region, Haiti.* ("Yale Univ. Pub. Anthrop.," No. 24.) New Haven, Conn.
1942   *Archeology of the Maniabón Hills, Cuba.* ("Yale Univ. Pub. Anthrop.," No. 26.)
1948   "The Arawak." Pp. 507–39 in JULIAN H. STEWARD (ed.), *Handbook*

of South American Indians, Vol. 4. (Bur. Amer. Ethnol. Bull. 143.) Washington, D.C.

1951 "Areas and Periods of Culture in the Greater Antilles." *Southwestern Jour. Anthrop.,* 7:248–65.

1952 *Porto Rican Prehistory.* (N.Y. Acad. Sci., Scient. Surv. Porto Rico and the Virgin Islands, Vol. 18, Nos. 3–4.) New York.

1953 *Indian Sites in Trinidad.* Pp. 94–111, Appendix B: "On the Excavation of a Shell Mound at Palo Seco, Trinidad, B.W.I." by J. A. BULL-BROOK. ("Yale Univ. Pub. Anthrop.," No. 50.) New Haven.

1960 *The Entry of Man into the West Indies.* ("Yale Univ. Pub. Anthrop.," No. 61.) New Haven.

1961 "The Bailey Collection of Stone Artifacts from Puerto Rico." Pp. 342–55 in SAMUEL K. LOTHROP *et al., Essays in Pre-Columbian Art and Archaeology.* Cambridge, Mass.: Harvard University Press.

1962 "The Intermediate Area, Amazonia and the Caribbean Area." Pp. 34–59 in ROBERT J. BRAIDWOOD and GORDON R. WILLEY (eds.), *Courses toward Urban Life.* ("Viking Fund Pub. Anthrop.," No. 32.) New York.

ROUSE, IRVING, and JOSÉ M. CRUXENT

1963a "Some Recent Radiocarbon Dates for Western Venezuela." *Amer. Antiquity,* 28:537–40.

1963b *Venezuelan Archeology.* New Haven, Conn.: Yale University Press.

SAUER, CARL O.

1952 *Agricultural Origins and Dispersals.* New York: American Geographical Society.

STEWARD, JULIAN H.

1947 "American Culture History in the Light of South America." *Southwestern Jour. Anthrop.,* 3:85–107.

STURTEVANT, WILLIAM C.

1960 *The Significance of Ethnological Similarities between Southeastern North America and the Antilles.* ("Yale Univ. Pub. Anthrop.," No. 64.) New Haven, Conn.

WILLEY, GORDON R.

1958 "Estimated Correlations and Dating of South and Central American Culture Sequences." *Amer. Antiquity,* 23:353–78.

1960 "New World Prehistory." *Science,* 131:73–86.

WILLEY, GORDON R., and PHILIP PHILLIPS

1958 *Method and Theory in American Archaeology.* Chicago: University of Chicago Press.

CLIFFORD EVANS

Lowland South America

LOWLAND South America (Fig. 1) will encompass, for the purposes of this paper, the Amazon and all its major tributaries, including the major rivers of eastern Peru, lowland Bolivia, and eastern Ecuador that eventually flow into the Amazon; that portion of the interior of British Guiana that shows definite relationships with adjoining Brazilian and Venezuelan tropical forest and savanna; the upper and middle Orinoco and its major tributaries, especially those rivers that drain out of eastern Colombia; and the Casiquiare River, which links the Orinoco drainage to the Amazon drainage. The coastal portions of the northern Guianas, Venezuela, and Colombia, although lowland in elevation, will not be considered because they more properly belong to the preceding chapter on the Caribbean. The other segment of lowland South America to be discussed will be those portions of southern Brazil, Paraguay, Uruguay, and northern Argentina that are drained by the Rio Paraná and its many tributaries.

To organize a discussion of the development of prehistoric man in the lowland areas of South America, several different approaches could be made: a purely regional one, area by area; a chronological or a stage-of-development one; or a combination of the two. Whichever one is utilized, the reader must understand that the amount of data based on sound scientific archeological reconnaissance and controlled excavations is so limited in comparison to other areas in the symposium that attempts to generalize might seem premature to those accustomed to the quantity of information available for such regions as the American Southwest. Lacking an abundance of information, the relationships or interpretations may seem tenuous at times; but to continue talking about lowland South America in terms of sites only or complexes of artifacts (usually

CLIFFORD EVANS, curator, Division of Archeology, United States National Museum, Smithsonian Institution, received the Ph.D. degree from Columbia University. He and his wife, Betty J. Meggers, were joint recipients of the Washington Academy of Sciences Award for Scientific Achievement in 1956. His extensive field research and publications have centered upon and made major contributions to the archeology of lowland South America.

Fig. 1

pottery, owing to problems of preservation) from a series of independent sites, or the sequence in one area only, is not very fruitful in trying to reconstruct the total picture of man's development in the New World and to understand why one stage of development was reached in the lowlands and another in the Andean highlands.

Several recent summaries of South American archeology (Willey 1958; Rouse 1961, 1962) have painted the picture in the lowlands as even bleaker than it actually is because they have ignored reports of recent field work published in *American Antiquity* and have failed to include publications in Spanish, Portuguese, and German (e.g., Hilbert 1955a, 1955b, 1957, 1958, 1959a, 1959b; Hanke 1959; Becker-Donner 1956, 1958). This summary will not attempt to catalogue or comment on all the publications on lowland South American archeology because there are good sources in bibliographic compendiums (see *Handbook of Latin American Studies*, Vols. 1–24, published annually by the Hispanic Foundation of the Library of Congress and the University of Florida Press) and the "References Cited" sections of several monographs (Meggers 1948; Meggers and Evans 1957; Evans and Meggers 1960; Cruxent and Rouse 1958). It is of historical interest to note, however, that considerable bad literature has been written on the lost civilizations of El Dorado, proof of Old World connections with the Phoenicians based on pictographs in the Amazon, mysterious civilizations so vividly described in the legends and mythology of the Indian tribes of the tropical forest, and the "great unknown" to be discovered as explorers penetrate the "Green Hell of the Amazon." All this tends to befog the true history of man's development in the area. With a few exceptions, references on the area that are older than twenty years are based on such poor excavation techniques that they are of limited usefulness without up-to-date chronology.

This paper will offer a tentative reconstruction of man's prehistory from the early hunters to the arrival of the Europeans, dividing the lowlands into two natural areas: the Amazon-Orinoco Basin and the southern plains. Since the cultural sequences of southern Brazil, Paraguay, and northern Argentina, scattered around the Rio Paraná, are not directly related to those of the Amazon and Orinoco drainages to the north, it is more logical to discuss the stages or levels of cultural development within each region separately. Beginning with the Amazon-Orinoco drainage, the archeology of each area will be discussed in a framework of four levels or stages of development: the hunting-and-gathering stage, sometimes called Paleo-Indian or Archaic; the Incipient Agricultural; the Tropical Forest slash-and-burn agricultural; and the Sub-Andean, more intensely agricultural.

AMAZON-ORINOCO DRAINAGES

HUNTING-AND-GATHERING STAGE

Subsistence in the hunting-and-gathering stage is based exclusively on hunting game, gathering wild seeds, roots, and plants, and obtaining food from the sea and rivers by fishing or gathering molluscs. The pattern of supplying food limits the size of groups so that family bands or extended family bands usually form economic, as well as sociopolitical, units. The type of habitation site varies from a simple windbreak structure on shell middens to rockshelters to simple thatch-covered huts. Technology is not well advanced except in the careful manufacture of shell or bone fishhooks and chipped-stone artifacts for hunting. The tools include points for spears, hand held or thrown by the atlatl, and knives, scrapers, choppers, and hammerstones. An extensive use of hard tropical woods for a variety of artifacts probably fills out the tool complex. There is no distinct burial pattern or differential treatment of the dead. The permanency of the habitation site is dependent upon availability of food supply, whether it is a simple camp site of short seasonal duration or a more permanently located living place near a constant and good food supply.

In another paper in this volume, Krieger has dealt with the hunting-and-gathering stage of development in South America as a whole, but it is worthwhile at this point to indicate the presence of this level in the history of man's development in lowland South America and to comment on the field problems of discovering evidence of the stage. The heavy growth of the tropical forest, the general absence of good rock shelters or caves, the scattered type of camp sites and chipping stations associated with the Paleo-Indian and Archaic hunting-and-gathering stage, and the limited occurrence of raw materials are factors that explain the rarity of known sites of this culture complex in the Amazon-Orinoco drainages. Evidence, so far limited to sporadic finds mostly from the savanna country adjoining the network of rivers in eastern Venezuela and the Guianas, consists of large points, blades, and choppers. Since these are similar to artifacts found in association with extinct Pleistocene fauna in stratified positions in Mesoamerica, caves in Argentina, and various sites in the United States, they have been considered to represent the Paleo-Indian hunting horizon in this area as well.

In British Guiana, the non-ceramic lithic remains from the savanna lands of Rupununi District are limited to sporadic accidental finds. One small chipping station with crude choppers, scrapers, and flakes of chert, felsite, and quartz was found near the Tabatinga River, Rupununi District. From four other localities, all in the Essequibo Province, on the Barima, Cuyuni, Ireng, and Palikúa rivers, seven large, well-chipped points of chert, quartz, jasper, or chalcedony have been accidentally found during the washing of gravels in search of diamonds. These specimens are long, delicately tapered, triangular in shape, with a parallel-sided, stemmed base or a contracting rounded base, except for one broad, leaf-shaped artifact, sometimes categorized as a blade. The chipping in all cases is very well executed, with fine retouch.

Objects of the same general types come from the adjacent savanna in Venezuela, and the two regions together form a distinct lithic complex, undoubtedly related in time. From three localities on the Rio Paragua in the state of Bolivar, where smaller tributaries of the Rio Asá and Rio Chiguano join the Rio Paragua, and on the banks of the Rio Paragua itself (Dupuoy 1958), three separate finds of large projectile points have been accidentally made. Chipped from quartz, jasper, and chalcedony, they are trianguloid with contracting stemmed bases. In the adjoining Gran Sabana of Venezuela, identical in environmental features with the Rupununi Savanna of British Guiana, two large plano-convex scrapers of jasper with fine retouch on the edges have been recovered from the banks of the Rio Icabaru and Rio Kukenán.

This evidence, although meager, scattered, and poorly documented, permits the inference that the lowlands of the Amazon-Orinoco drainage were not devoid of peoples in Paleo-Indian times. When the Incipient Agricultural stage began, it probably resulted from the adoption of simple agricultural techniques by the existing hunting peoples, producing a type of cultural pattern similar to that practiced by the wandering Sirionó Indians of lowland Bolivia (Holmberg 1948, 1950), who return to planted fields when crops are ready to harvest, the rest of the time wandering around in small bands following game. There is also the possibility that the peoples bringing in agriculture migrated into the region and the two groups continued to live their own way of life side by side, without either basically influencing the cultural pattern of the other.

INCIPIENT AGRICULTURAL STAGE

Food supply is mainly from hunting, fishing, and gathering, but, in addition, some dependence is on consciously planted crops, allowing a permanency of the living site not otherwise possible. Probably both root and seed crops were planted. Villages are still very small, and the sociopolitical unit is still no more than several extended families now banded together where their joint communal effort would make the agricultural exploitation of the tropical forest more feasible. The technology now includes pottery, and there is a decline in the variety and abundance of chipped-stone artifacts. There is no distinct burial pattern or no differential treatment of the dead, suggesting a simple, unstratified society without distinct class differences.

In contrast to the situation in dry-climate areas, where the first appearance of plant remains and the botanical changes that occur as a result of domestication can be documented by actual specimens that botanists can study in great detail, the wet tropical forest of lowland South America leaves the archeologists with nothing except pottery and stone. Hence, the postulation of an incipient agricultural stage must be based on inference from settlement patterns. The earliest pottery-producing sites in the Amazon drainage show characteristics of village refuse accumulation that differ from sites typical of the Tropical Forest slash-and-burn culture complex, suggesting a slightly different subsistence base. If this conclusion is acceptable, the Incipient Agricultural stage is represented by sites of the Zoned Hachure Horizon Style of pottery decoration, such as Ananatuba on Marajó, Jauarí on the lower Amazon, Yasuní on the Rio Napo in eastern Ecuador, and Tutishcainyo on the Ucayali in eastern Peru (Meggers and Evans 1961).

A detailed description of the total cultural complex of the Ananatuba Phase on Marajó, Brazil, will give the details upon which the reconstructed picture of this stage is based.

The peoples of the Ananatuba Phase lived in isolated villages on the north-central part of Marajó Island. A single communal dwelling, large enough to house between one hundred and one hundred and fifty individuals, formed the village, which was located in a forested area at the edge of a small natural savanna near a small river as a source of water. Streams large enough for dugout navigation were as much as 1 kilometer away. The village refuse marking the extent of the former village covers an area of 300–700 square meters and is circular or oval in outline; the deposit is typically 0.60–1.00 meter in depth, with abundant sherds. The houses were probably raised on piles, and clay lumps bearing twig and cane impressions suggest that the walls may have been of wattle-and-daub construction. No cemeteries have been found, and there is no evidence to suggest the manner of disposal of the dead.

Ceramically, the phase is identified by two undecorated plain wares tempered with ground potsherds. The most common decorated types are principally two: brushed and incised. The incised designs are simple but are tastefully and carefully executed, with a variety of motifs, including wavy, scalloped lines below the rim, zoned areas filled with fine or large crosshatch, circles, parallel incised lines, and single incised lines. Although there are some percentage changes in popularity of the pottery types through the duration of the phase, on the whole the designs, quality, and texture of the pottery and the vessel shapes remain fairly stable. Thus, all the evidence, whether derived from village location, ceramic quality and stability, or village duration of typically one hundred years (Meggers and Evans 1957), points to a quiet, peaceful existence, uninterrupted by exhaustion of food supply or by raids from neighboring tribes. The stratigraphic position in the sequence of occupation of the lower Amazon places the Ananatuba complex as the initial pottery-using occupant of the area, followed by five other complexes. The estimated beginning of this culture is around 500 B.C., although at present this is a guess not verified by absolute dating techniques. The long village duration is the principal reason for inferring primary dependence on the abundant supply of fish and game on Marajó Island, supplemented by agriculture, since it has been frequently demonstrated that primary dependence on agriculture in this region results in frequently moved villages, expressed archeologically in shallow refuse deposits.

The site of Jauarí, on the Lago Grande do Curuá west of Alenquer on the lower Amazon (Hilbert 1959*a*), is located in a swampy area, where two slight elevations with shell-midden refuse mark the location of old habitation sites. Excellent water holes and fishing are near by. The sherds from this site were classified into a shell-tempered ware representing the Castalia Phase, and a *cauixi* (sponge spicule)-tempered ware with brushing, incising, and zoned hachure, and a few modeled sherds, called the Jauarí Phase. The incised-zoned-hachure design of motifs and the method of execution are in many aspects identical with those of the Ananatuba Phase. Hilbert (1959*a*) interprets the relationship of the two phases as follows: (1) the Castalia Phase, with shell-tempered pottery, is the earlier, probably an intermediate stage between a marginal form of culture with a sambaquí (shell-midden) aspect and the Tropical Forest type of culture, and (2) the Jauarí Phase with *cauixi*-tempered ware is later. Sherds containing both tempering materials suggest the interpretation that the sequence represents a development from the Castalia Phase to the Jauarí Phase under the stimulation of outside influence.

On the Rio Napo in eastern Ecuador, the Puerto Miranda site near Tiputini is the type site for the Yasuní complex, the earliest of three pottery complexes in this area. The site is on a natural hill that is above the flood plains of the Rio Napo, with the sherds found to a depth of 20–30 centimeters. The pottery is decorated with incised designs and zoned hachure, thus placing this complex in the Zoned Hachure Horizon Style.

Near Pucallpa on the Rio Ucayali, there is a large lake with a modern Shipibo village known as San Francisco de Yarinacocha (Lathrap 1958). An archeological site of some extent and depth located here has four phases, the earliest of which is called Early Tutishcainyo. The pottery is usually tempered with shell, sand, or *cariapé* (burned siliceous bark) and decorated with zoned incision and hachure, punctation, and, occasionally, red paint in the zoned areas. No absolute dates are available for this culture, but both Lathrap (1958) and Willey (1958) suggest that it is as early as 1000 B.C.

Summarizing the Incipient Agricultural stage, we have a good example of the scattered nature of archeological evidence in the lowland tropical forest regions of South America. The Zoned Hachure Horizon Style, represented at sites from the Rio Ucayali, Rio Napo, and lower Amazon, is a culturally related complex representing the movement into the lowland area of ideas and/or peoples, bringing pottery and probably agriculture. The exact origin is unknown, for no single culture in the Andean area appears to be the parent stock. Meggers and Evans (1957) first suggested a remote relationship to the Chavín horizon in the Andes, postulating that by the time the elements diffused into the lowlands there was much dilution as a result of time and space. Later, Willey (1958) and Lathrap (1958) share a similar point of view and extend the argument even further to suggest remote relationships with other Formative Period cultures of Colombia, Ecuador, and Middle America, such as Monagrillo of Panama, Barlovento and Momíl of Colombia, Valdivia of Ecuador (Meggers and Evans do not agree), and pre-Cupisnique of Peru. With the recent work in Mexico in the Valley of Tehuacán there seems to be no argument about the Mesoamerican origin of plant domestication in the New World at an early period and its diffusion southward to the Andean area. With evidence of earlier hunting, fishing, and gathering in the South American lowlands, even though skimpy, there is a base on which to transplant new ideas that would develop into the Tropical Forest slash-and-burn agricultural stage. If Tropical Forest lowland South American archeology receives more attention in the future, the Incipient Agricultural stage will be represented by more than its present handful of sites and the sloping horizon of diffusion from the Andean area to the Tropical Forest lowland will not have such vast gaps between our steppingstones of knowledge across the wet lowlands.

TROPICAL FOREST SLASH-AND-BURN AGRICULTURAL STAGE

The main source of food supply is from the agriculture of both root and seed crops, including manioc and maize, with a more secondary use of hunting and fishing to supplement the diet. The agriculture is limited in the tropical forest to a type known as slash-and-burn, in which the virgin forest is cut down, allowed to dry, and burned, and then—without removal of large trunks, branches, and stumps—the crops are planted in between. The ash from burning and the rotting materials add to the fertility of the field, but heavy rainfall, high humidity, and high temperature cause leaching and rapid decomposition, resulting in a weak soil that cannot support agriculture for more than four to six years. This factor limits village size and permanency so that fields and villages move frequently. A variety of house types ranges from several single-family thatch houses arranged around a plaza to large communal houses up to 100 feet in diameter. Although some social stratification begins to develop, no elaborate class structure or sociopolitical systems exist. Technology includes pottery, basketry, feather work, textiles, and stone axes. Although the work is clearly distinguished into men's and women's work, and often reaches a high degree of technological and artistic competence, the arts and crafts are still individually executed, without mass production and standardization. Burial pattern is often secondary, sometimes in large burial urns.

Sufficient archeology has been conducted in the Amazon and Orinoco drainages to define the Tropical Forest slash-and-burn stage very well and even to show with some degree of assurance the direction of the spread of influences and the movements of peoples. For clarity in discussion, this section will be divided into three subsections: two sections based on horizon styles defined on cultures with related pottery traditions and one section dealing with those various cultural complexes that do not fit into these two styles because of local variations or derivation from other antecedents.

The Incised Rim Horizon Style. Three pottery complexes on the lower Amazon and three on the middle and upper Orinoco share certain distinctive characteristics that appear to qualify the complexes as a horizon style. The stratigraphic position of the complexes and the difference in settlement pattern from the previous Incipient Agricultural stage and the following Sub-Andean stage provide enough additional information to warrant the establishment of this horizon style. The most distinctive trait of the pottery is a broad, flat-topped rim produced by interior thickening, giving a heavy trianguloid cross-section. The surface of this rim is usually decorated with broad, incised lines and the exterior and/or interior surfaces of many vessels are covered with a red paint or red slip. Modeling is typically lacking except for an occasional adorno.

In the lower Amazon, the Mangueiras Phase representing this horizon style is clearly defined by work on Marajó and Caviana islands (Meggers and Evans 1957). Sites are located in the forest, where the land is not subjected to annual flooding from the rainy season yet is accessible to a navigable stream, with little or none of the concern about proximity to the savanna that was typical of the sites of the earlier Incipient Agricultural Phase. The sites are not directly on the shore of the river but are within 250 meters of a stream navigable in dugouts and are no closer than 3 kilometers to the ocean. The village refuse is from 0.05 to 1.00 meters deep, scattered over 2,000–4,000 square meters, suggesting that the village consisted of several large communal houses. No cemeteries were found. The estimated duration of the villages is from 10 to 118 years (according to the village refuse accumulation formulae), with more sites toward the middle bracket of this range (Meggers and Evans 1957). It is important to note that there are a number of villages that show simultaneous occupation, indicative of a flourishing and expanding culture. There is clear-cut evidence on Marajó Island that the Ananatuba Phase peoples were dominated and assimilated by the Mangueiras upon their arrival in the lower Amazon, but the process included adoption of many of the Ananatuba Phase traits into the culture. The vessel shapes and decorated motifs of the incised and zoned hachure pottery of the earlier Ananatuba Phase were immediately copied in the local pottery types of the Mangueiras Phase. The pottery of the phase was well made, durable, with a variety of artifacts, such as tubular pipes, labrets, and figurines. The entire ceramic history of the Mangueiras Phase, the different settlement pattern, the clear introduction of an expanding group that dominated and assimilated the existing Ananatuba culture on Marajó Island, caused Meggers and Evans to depict this culture as fully developed Tropical Forest slash-and-burn agricultural in contrast to the Incipient Agricultural stage of the earlier Ananatuba Phase. This is in contrast to Willey's (1958) summary of the Amazon Delta sequence, in which he lumps the Mangueiras with the Ananatuba Phase and declares them both to be representative of "small hunting fishing and marginal agricultural communities of an Archaic type. . . ."

Other cultures in the Incised Rim Horizon Style along the Amazon are found at Boim on the Rio Tapajos and Manacapurú on the Amazon above the mouth of the Rio Negro (Meggers and Evans 1961). In the Orinoco drainage Nericagua, Cotua, and Los Caros are ceramic complexes all related to the Incised Rim Horizon Style and, in other respects, good examples of the Tropical Forest slash-and-burn agricultural stage (Meggers and Evans 1961). The Nericagua Phase (Evans, Meggers, and Cruxent 1959) is the best defined. It is based on the study of fifteen village and two ceremonial sites on the banks of the upper Orinoco, the lower part of the Ventuari, and the Atabapo, both tributaries of the upper Orinoco. The environment is gallery forest, with extensive tree-dotted savanna and tree-covered hills adjacent. The amount of the land that escapes total flooding with each rainy season along the river banks and is suitable for habitation and slash-and-burn agriculture is relatively limited, and the unusually poor quality of the lateritic soil definitely restricts the length of time that an area can be used for productive agriculture.

All the Nericagua Phase habitation sites are found on high banks along the river, with the refuse distributed over an area 50–400 meters in maximum diameter. With one exception, the refuse is scattered over the entire area; one site showed a distinct plan of a series of refuse mounds arranged around an oval central plaza, measuring 110–125 meters, completely devoid of refuse. The contours of a path were visible leading from the plaza to the water's edge. The refuse mounds adjacent to the water's edge were generally oval, measuring 40–80 meters long and 8–10 meters wide, with those in the rear blending into one another, producing an irregular ridge 235 meters long and 8–15 meters wide. Stratigraphic excavations indicated that the refuse extended from the surface of the habitation middens to the level of the plaza, representing an accumulation of 1.25–3.00 meters of living refuse. No cemeteries or other evidence indicating the manner of disposal of the dead were found. Two roughly shaped granite pillars within the zone of Nericagua Phase occupation, and the sparsity of sherds around them, suggest that these sites are ceremonial and part of the aboriginal stone alignment tradition characteristic of the Tropical Forest cultures and widespread in the Guianas (Meggers and Evans 1957).

The pottery has some very interesting features, relating it to both the Amazon and the Orinoco drainage. The most common ware is tempered with large quantities of *cariapé*, obtained by burning the bark of a tree that has silica deposited in the cells (cf. Meggers and Evans 1957). Other pottery types include one tempered with spicules of fresh-water sponge (*cauixi*), and another tempered only with water-worn sand. The most popular form of decoration is incision, with most of the motifs rectilinear. Incision declines in popularity in the upper part of the sequence and is replaced by modeling, negative (resist) painting, and red-slipped ware. Cylindrical pottery stamps also appear.

For the Nericagua Phase, there are nine radiocarbon dates from five different sites, based on charcoal samples of charred palm nuts. More recently, the University of Pennsylvania laboratory dated *cariapé*-tempered sherds by grinding up large quantities of sherds to extract the organic matter (Evans and Meggers 1962). The Nericagua Phase sequence dates range from A.D. 1339 ± 103 (P-162) in the upper part to A.D. 761 ± 93 (P-160) and A.D. 791 ± 122 (P-161) in the lower part. These dates fit into the sequence seriated on pottery and allow the many innovations and changes in the Nericagua Phase to be pinpointed with considerable exactness. *Cauixi* temper makes its appearance on this part of the Orinoco at about A.D. 800, undoubtedly coming from the Amazon Basin, the area of its greatest abundance and widest distribution. Negative (resist) painting and cylindrical stamps are undoubtedly of western origin, where they are common in the highlands of Colombia. Although negative painting appeared early in the sequence, it is characteristic only during the time that the cylindrical stamps were in use in the Nericagua Phase sequence, or after A.D. 1107 ± 96 (P-166). When the Colombian highland sequence is better known, it may be possible to relate this strong influence in the Nericagua Phase of the Orinoco to a similar development in the Colombian highlands and the eastward expansion into the lowlands at the same time. Traits present at the beginning of the Nericagua Phase, such as traits belonging to the Incised Rim Horizon Style and tempering with *cariapé*, must be given a minimum antiquity of A.D. 500.

A site on Cotua Island (Cruxent 1950), on the Orinoco down river from the Nericagua Phase sites, reveals a complex of pottery that is comparable in most respects to the Nericagua Phase. The same is true of Los Caros style (Cruxent and Rouse 1958), defined from artifacts coming from Los Caros mound in the vicinity of Cazorla in the San Fernando de Apure area of Guarico State, Venezuela. Incision is the most prominent kind of decoration. Cruxent and Rouse (1958) place both Cotua and Los Caros in Period III of their chronological sequence, which corresponds to A.D. 350–1150, and Meggers and Evans (1961) place both styles in the Incised Rim Horizon Style, which they give a time span of A.D. 100–800.

The Incised and Punctate Horizon Style.   A group of sites along the Amazon, Orinoco, and in both Brazilian and British Guiana have in common a series of pottery decorations combining incision, punctation, and modeling in several consistent ways. They have been grouped in the Incised and Punctate Horizon Style, dated A.D. 1000–1500 (Meggers and Evans 1961). For convenience, the style was named for the most universal traits: a combination of incision and punctation as alternating bands occupying the interior of bowl rims or the exterior of jar necks. However, equally diagnostic are the filling of areas with finely drawn, evenly parallel, and closely spaced incised lines and the combination of incision and punctation with modeling, especially in the form of anthropomorphic, zoömorphic, and geometric forms. Red slipping is another important element common to the horizon style, and the pottery griddle, equated with bitter manioc preparation, is generally associated with the horizon.

Although the settlement pattern, types of sites, etc., generally fit the detailed description given for Tropical Forest sites of the preceding horizon style on the Amazon-Orinoco drainage, there are a few minor differences for the various areas worth mentioning. This horizon style is represented by sites belonging to the Mazagão Phase in the southern part of the territory of Amapá (Brazilian Guiana); sites of the Santarem culture along the Amazon and at the mouth of the Rio Tapajós; sites at Itacoatiara on the middle Amazon; various sites near Konduri on the Rio Trombetas, a northern tributary of the lower Amazon, by the Mabaruma Phase in the Northwest District of British Guiana in the Barima River region; and at sites around Arauquín on the middle Orinoco.

Sites of the Mazagão Phase in Amapá Territory are typical of the Tropical Forest pattern mentioned for the Mangueiras Phase, with a few additional innovations. The sites are all located on naturally high land near a constant water supply, above the flooded lowlands. The refuse varies in thickness from the surface to only 45 centimeters in depth and is scattered over areas ranging from 10 meters to 75–83 meters in diameter. Cemeteries are associated with a series of habitation sites. Interment is secondary, in burial urns, accompanied by offerings of small bowls, beads, and an occasional stone and typically covered with a lid. The arrangement of the urns in the cemetery appears to be haphazard, with little concern for a previous burial. Often the vessels were placed upon the surface of the ground or only partially buried. Some changes are evident in the popularity of some of the pottery types throughout the Mazagão Phase, with the most noticeable change in the plain wares. The earlier wares are tempered with quartz, while those most popular in the latter part of the phase are tempered with *cariapé*. Decorated vessels are more common in the cemeteries than in the village refuse, suggesting a deliberate manufacture of certain wares for burial and others for domestic use. The effect of strong outside influences on this group is evidenced in certain vessel shapes, such as anthropomorphic burial urns found on the Rio Maracá that have definite affiliations with the Andean area of Colombia. The presence of griddles in the Mazagão Phase indicates that bitter manioc was cultivated.

Around the lower Tapajós River, along the main stream of the Amazon, and on all the small tributaries and larger ones from the lower Xingú upriver almost to Manaus is the culture complex known as Santarem style. Hundreds of sites are located in areas where the refuse accumulation has made the soil unusually black in comparison to the sterile soil near by, hence, to the non-specialist the term "terras pretas" has become synonymous with the Santarem culture. Actually, the culture has one of the widest distributions in the Amazon. Most of the work is based on summaries prepared from study of museum collections (Palmatary 1939, 1960; Barata 1950, 1951, 1953), and only recently have stratigraphic excavations begun to unravel the problems of sequence (Hilbert 1955*b*). In spite of abundant pottery, coming from numerous sites, and concentrated efforts to search for cemeteries, no burials of any sort have been uncovered. The explanation is probably related to the method of disposal of the dead described by early travelers —the body was left exposed until all the flesh had decayed, then the bones were pulverized and the powder mixed with *chicha* (beer) and drunk. This Tropical Forest trait might explain the absence of cemeteries in other cultures of the lowlands. The pottery from the Santarem culture is distinguished by its highly ornate modeling of birds, animals, and some human figures, combined with incision and punctate, all affixed to the vessels in a variety of ways. Much of the pottery is tempered with *cauixi* and, although the surfaces are often badly eroded, traces of red and yellow paints are not uncommon. In spite of some minor local variations owing to regional development, the Santarem complex is an excellent representation of the Incised and Punctate Horizon Style.

Up the Amazon River in the region around Oriximiná on the Trombetas and Jamundá rivers, Hilbert (1955a, b) has conducted archeological excavations that uncovered a pottery complex related to Santarem but in many respects different. The modeled tradition and the use of *cauixi* for temper relate the materials to the Santarem modeling tradition. For this discussion, the most significant item is the occurrence of tripods. Evidence of the attachment of supports to the bottoms of bowls was known on Santarem pottery, but this was usually attributed to the caryatid supports rather than to tripod feet. In the Oriximiná region conical supports, mostly plain but sometimes with modeling on the upper part, were attached to the underside of bowls as tripod or polypod feet. They are common, and caryatid vessel supports are not found. The identification of the tripod vessel in the lower Amazon is of considerable importance to lowland South American archeology, for it adds one more trait to the list of Amazonian archeological traits whose origin is outside the region of the Andes or northwestern South America.

The chronological position of these pottery complexes belonging to the Incised and Punctate Horizon Style is uniformly late throughout both the Amazon and Orinoco drainages. The Santarem complex is generally accepted as protohistoric. Arauquín is dated by Cruxent and Rouse as Late Period III and Period IV, corresponding to about A.D. 1000–1500. The influence of this horizon style appears in the latter part of the Mabaruma Phase in British Guiana, dated as subsequent to A.D. 1000, and the Itacoatiara Phase follows the earlier Guarita Phase, which gives it a late relative position on the Amazon. European trade items are found with the Mazagão Phase. This horizon style is apparently the result of influences coming out of the highlands of Colombia, spreading down the Orinoco to its mouth and down the numerous tributaries that drain into the Orinoco as well as up the Orinoco, across the Casiquiare River into the Amazon and down that river to its mouth (Meggers and Evans 1961).

Other Tropical Forest complexes. Before leaving the Tropical Forest slash-and-burn agricultural stage of the Amazon-Orinoco drainages, some mention must be made of the cultural complexes that do not fit into one of the various horizon styles just described.

In the headwaters of the Ventuari River, a tributary of the upper Orinoco, and along the Manipiare River, a tributary of the Ventuari, there are twelve habitation sites that produced pottery representing the Corobal Phase (Evans, Meggers, and Cruxent 1959). These sites had shallow refuse, with only one site with a deposit deeper than 40 centimeters, and each site area ranges from 20 meters in diameter to 300 meters in length. One site had the sherd refuse highly concentrated in four mound areas, suggesting that it was of some special significance. No stone alignments or cemeteries were identified, but stone walls, meandering for several kilometers in the forest without any apparent pattern, are constructed of irregularly shaped rocks. The existing height is 50–75 centimeters. Their purpose is unknown. No sherds came from near by.

The pottery of this phase is distinct from that of the Nericagua Phase in paste, temper, and decoration. The principal tempering material is sand. The ovoid vessel shapes, with a lobe protruding like the prow of a boat and a small vertical loop handle attached to the exterior of this lobe, are suggestive of lobes, handles, and vessel shapes of the Antilles rather than those from other parts of the Amazon-Orinoco drainage or the nearby Andean regions to the west. The pottery is decorated principally by appliqué in the form of small bumps or nubbins, incised, finger-pressed, or punctate fillets and highly elaborate adornos, usually anthropomorphic or zoömorphic. These adornos are very intricate and complex, many representing headdresses with animals, birds, feather, and basketry. Pottery artifacts include large griddles for the preparation of bitter manioc, diamond-shaped pottery spindle whorls, and flat, circular stamps with a short, conical handle, a trait also related to the Antilles.

The duration of the Corobal Phase and its position in an absolute time scale are unknown. But, in the reconstruction of the prehistoric movements of peoples and cultures in the northern part of South America, it is important to note that in addition to the clear-cut movements and diffusion of ideas out of the Andean area into the lowland tropical forests there is also evidence of relationships with the prehistoric cultures of the Antilles. Detailed comparative studies and additional field work in northern South America and the neglected islands of the Lesser Antilles should clarify some of these connections.

In the interior of British Guiana there are several cultural complexes that show late movements—just preceding and at the time of European contact—from the Amazon tributaries of the Rio Mapuera and the Rio Branco. Whereas the region was once postulated to be a fountainhead of indigenous Tropical Forest cultural development by Steward (see Meggers and Evans [1957] for a detailed discussion of the literature on this subject), the cultural sequence for British Guiana substantiates the hypothesis that the Guianas functioned as a late refuge area rather than a point of developmental origin of Tropical Forest culture. In fact, there is a strong possibility that the Rupununi savanna of central British Guiana and the region of the upper Essequibo would not yet have been invaded and settled by Tropical Forest cultures if the arrival of the Europeans had not upset the aboriginal balance and exerted external pressures on various groups, causing them to retreat farther inland. A brief reconstruction of the Rupununi, Taruma, and Wai Wai complexes will illustrate the point.

The Rupununi is a large savanna in central British Guiana, broken up into several sections by small, low rolling hills and separated by the Takutu River from the Brazilian savanna that extends into the territory of Rio Branco. Twenty-nine habitation sites in the savanna represent Rupununi Phase villages, with refuse scattered over a circular or ovoid area of 1,000–5,000 square meters but never extending more than 3 centimeters below the surface, indicating a very short period of occupation. Slash-and-burn agriculture must have been practiced on the slopes of the nearby hills. The fact that the villages were not necessarily near large streams or rivers implies that the watercourses were not the main avenue of transportation. The pottery is extremely crude and very rarely decorated. Large burial jars were placed in rock shelters with secondary burial, accompanied by glass beads and plates with food offerings. The most distinctive stone tools are a stubby, rectanguloid hoe and a partially grooved ax. Pottery griddles indicate the use of bitter manioc. Comparison of the archeological and ethnographic data for the Rupununi Phase indicates that all the Rupununi sites belong to the Macushi Indians, who occupied the area from 1780 to 1850. Apparently, the movement to the savannas so long a time after European contact can be correlated with the introduction of cattle-raising and the desire to live near the European settlements in order to obtain work. Ethnohistorical information speaks of peoples moving from the Rio Branco area of Brazil. It was once proposed that the Macushi came from the Orinoco because of certain language relationships, but the ethnohistorical data are not specific enough to pinpoint the area; only future archeological work in adjoining Brazil and Venezuela will solve the riddle.

Another example of the late movements of peoples into the Guianas is documented by archeological and ethnohistorical records on the Taruma and Wai Wai Indians, who lived in the headwaters of the Essequibo. The Taruma are reported to have originally lived near the mouth of the Rio Negro, from which area they disappeared in the seventeenth century. The present-day inhabitants of the area, the Wai Wai, came into the region from the headwaters of the Mapuera in Brazil around the beginning of the twentieth century and have survived today as a living example of Tropical Forest slash-and-burn agricultural peoples.

Description of the Taruma Phase is based on the investigation of twenty-four village sites and eleven former field clearings in the head-waters area of the Essequibo River (Evans and Meggers 1960). The village sites vary considerably in area, and the field clearings are cor-related in size with the amount of nearly level, elevated land, ranging from 50 by 70 meters to 200 by 500 meters. It is probable that the larger fields represent successive increases in the size of the clearings as the earlier portions become less productive after a few years of plantings. Temporary shelters of palm leaves were often built in the fields, around which a few sherds are usually found. The pottery is quite distinctive, with incised, stamped, and painted red-on-white the most common type of decoration. Griddles attest to the use of bitter manioc. Diagnostic pottery artifacts include clay pot rests, pottery whis-tles, and disk-shaped spindle whorls. No burial urns were found, and this correlates with the ethnographic information that the Taruma prac-ticed cremation. Other ethnographic information on the Taruma also confirms the interpretations derived from the archeological evidence that this group is typical of the Guiana variety of the level of develop-ment termed the Tropical Forest slash-and-burn agricultural.

In recent years the former Taruma Phase territory has been occupied by the Wai Wai Indians, with approximately as many in British Guiana as over the mountains at the headwaters of the Mapuera in Brazil. This Carib-speaking tribe gradually moved into the void left by the disap-pearance of the Taruma in the 1920's. In 1952–53, when the field study was made, they had been in the area too short a time to leave many archeological remains, but two old village sites were studied and com-pared with notes made on the living Wai Wai (Evans and Meggers 1960). Archeological documentation for the Wai Wai is slight, but this opportunity of applying ethnological observations of a group only re-cently in extensive contact with European trade goods but basically unacculturated provided excellent information on the reliability of mak-ing a reconstruction of the Tropical Forest way of life from a minimum of archeological evidence.

In the lower Amazon there is another group very prominent in the ethnohistorical literature of the area: the Aruã (Meggers and Evans 1957). This phase is defined from archeological evidence in Brazilian Guiana, the islands of Marajó, Mexiana, and Caviana and from written records. The last group of 279 survivors lived on Caviana Island as late as 1816. This Tropical Forest culture did not arrive in the area via a down-river movement as did the other phases but, instead, appears to be related to the Arawak culture from the Antilles, suggesting a spread southward at approximately the same time that the Arawaks spread out from the mainland to the Lesser Antilles and into the Greater Antilles. The Aruã Phase is defined by habitation sites, on both the mainland and the islands, located on the bank of a navigable stream in the forest generally not far inland from the coast. The sherd refuse is thinly scattered in a small circular or oval area, rarely covering more than 300 square meters and usually from the surface to a depth of only a few centimeters. Cemeteries are also located in the forest, but farther inland and away from the streams. Secondary urn burial was practiced, with the urns set directly on the surface or in a shallow hole. Although associated materials are not typical, various burials contained polished-stone axes, small pottery bowls, pottery and nephrite beads and pendants, and objects of European manufacture. Stone alignments are characteristic of the Aruã sites on the mainland but have not been reported on the islands, probably because of the rarity of natural stone. The stones were set on end in a linear, circular, or triangular arrangement on an elevated spot without sherd refuse or cemeteries near by. Ceramically, the phase is identified principally by one sherd-tempered plain ware, without any well-defined tradition of ceramic decoration, except an occasional use of appliqué, impressed circles, or simple brushing. The phase, which began only a short time before the European entry, appears first on the mainland of Brazilian Guiana and then moves to the islands of Caviana, Mexiana, and Marajó. The downfall of the Aruã Phase began when the Europeans conquered the area and colonized the islands, but for several centuries after A.D. 1500 the Aruã fought a losing battle with the Portuguese. They finally disappeared from sight through mass removal, depopulation, acculturation, and racial intermixture by the early part of the nineteenth century. The termination of the Aruã Phase brings to an end the archeological sequence of Tropical Forest cultures in the lower Amazon.

At the opposite end of the continent, mention should be made of the various phases not mentioned in the horizon-style discussion and defined by the stratigraphic work of Lathrap (1958) at the sites of Tutishcainyo and Hupa-iya near Yarinacocha on the Rio Ucayali, eastern Peru. Lathrap, lacking comparative materials because of the pioneer nature of his work in this lowland area, found it difficult to establish relationships beyond the site. During the current year he is continuing archeological field work in this region. In the meantime, it is pertinent to mention that, in addition to the earlier phase and stratigraphically lowest complex, the Tutishcainyo, he has defined the Shakimu, Hupa-iya, and Modern Shipibo complexes. The Shakimu is defined by the presence of distinctive pottery with excised decorations in highly complex scroll and step motifs, associated with a highly polished plain ware. Lathrap (1958) believes that the comparison of the excised series from Shakimu is closer to Marajoara pottery than to the Napo and would even go so far as to point out the similarity and possible relationship with the excised pottery of the early Formative Valdivia culture on the coast of Ecuador. Without the published descriptions of the Yarinacocha, it is difficult to evaluate these comparisons, but one wonders whether, when the final analysis is made, the entire excised tradition of highland Colombia, the Napo, Marajoara, and Shakimu may not be more closely related as examples of diffusion in sloping horizons than is now thought to be the case.

Underneath the modern Shipibo village Lathrap defined the Hupa-iya complex. This has the thickest and most widespread refuse and suggests a density of population and intensity of occupation not equaled before or after the period. Hupa-iya is an incised-ware complex with vertical strap handles, adornos, horizontal lugs, and appliqué pellets with a punctate dot in the center. Lathrap compares this complex with the Los Barrancos style of the Barrancoid Pottery Series of the lower Orinoco. Whether this is a direct relationship, with one being the parent of the other and gradually spreading, or whether both derive from some point of common origin, only future field work in the lowlands can determine. The important point is that stratigraphic archeology in the Ucayali has shown that the modern Shipibo did not develop in this region but are a relatively late introduction into this part of the lowlands.

SUB-ANDEAN AGRICULTURAL STAGE

The subsistence pattern depends on more intense agriculture than can be practiced in Tropical Forest slash-and-burn conditions. The greater yield per output of manpower and the less frequent moving of fields and villages allowed a population concentration and permanency to develop into a socio-political structure with a stratified society. Occupational division of labor permitted elaboration in technology, especially in pottery, with the perfection of extremely complex decorative techniques. Large cemeteries and villages, often on artificial mounds, required planning and leadership capable of manipulating large-scale manpower. Differential treatment of the dead, construction of special burial mounds separate from habitation village sites, and the use of special burial urns and grave furniture are other indications of social stratification. Developed in an environmental situation that would permit intense agriculture, the cultures began to decline when reduced to dependence on slash-and-burn or shifting cultivation.

Third in the sequence of horizon styles proposed for the Amazon-Orinoco drainages is the Polychrome Painting Style (Meggers and Evans 1961). Not only do various sites share certain outstanding ceramic characteristics—such as the diagnostic trait of a thick white slip with polychrome painting, usually red-and-black-on-white—but other relatively complex decorative techniques are also typically associated. They include excision; excision of a double-slipped surface so that removal of one layer reveals the contrasting color of the second slip below; incision and excision retouched with a red or white paint before firing; grooving; anthropomorphic modeling; and incision or excision on a red or white slipped surface as well as on plain surfaces. Some vessel and rim forms are variable from area to area, but the cambered rim, an exteriorly thickened rim with a squarish or rhomboidal cross-section, and complex vessel shapes are also important diagnostic traits of the horizon style.

All the pottery complexes in the Amazon drainage identified with the Polychrome Horizon Style have a similar chronological position relatively late in the sequence, or about A.D. 600–1300. The absence of any real continuity with the earlier horizon styles supports the inference that the Polychrome Horizon Style represents a clear-cut introduction of a new complex rather than a local development. There is also sufficient evidence to indicate that the pottery represents a level of technology associated with arts and crafts conducted by special craftsmen and with a more advanced sociopolitical organization. Hence it has been assigned to the Sub-Andean (or Circum-Caribbean) stage of cultural development.

The Polychrome Horizon Style is represented by sites along the Rios Napo and Aguarico in eastern Ecuador (Meggers and Evans 1958), at Araçá, Coari, and Guarita on the middle Amazon (Hilbert 1955a, 1959b), by a multitude of sites of the Marajoara Phase on Marajó Island at the mouth of the Amazon, and by the Aristé Phase in the northern part of the territory of Amapá (Brazilian Guiana).

For the purposes of describing a typical complex of this horizon style and of the Sub-Andean level of development, the most dramatic and scientifically accurate story, based on extensive archeological excavations, is that of the Marajoara Phase on Marajó Island. Known for decades before scientific excavations identified its correct sequential position, this culture has provoked much speculation. The mounds had been looted for years, so Marajoara pottery is scattered in museums throughout the world. Although the fancy painted urns and elaborate excised pottery art had whetted the imaginations of romantic writers, travelers, serious scholars, scientists, and "odd-ball authors," no serious excavations were made utilizing stratigraphic methods and applying the type concepts of classification to the specimens until 1948–49. Sites of the Marajoara Phase are distributed over the northeast portion of Marajó Island. Using the site of Pacoval by Lago Ararí as the center of a circumscribed circle whose radius measures from the lake to the north coast of the island, this circle includes all the recorded sites, numbering into hundreds. The sites consist of artificial mounds on the boundaries of the savanna and forest. The largest concentration is east of Lago Ararí, where the savanna is most unbroken by trees. Habitation mounds are typically on the shores of streams or lakes and are circular, oval, or long and narrow.

The extensive excavations of 1948–49 (Meggers and Evans 1957) did not support the early interpretations that the same mound was used both for habitation and for burial. Instead, separate mounds were constructed for each purpose and are easily distinguishable by their contents and by their size. The habitation mounds are comparatively small and low. The largest in the Camutins group is 51 meters long, 35 meters wide, and 6.25 meters high; the largest in the Fortaleza group measures 91 meters long and 2 meters high. Sherds are sparse, and 92–100 per cent of the pottery represents undecorated, utilitarian vessels.

The Marajoara used a dirt-floored house instead of a pile dwelling, and occasional sterile layers of white mud and fire-burned orange clay suggest a periodic renewal of the house floor. The sherds and other refuse were dumped out over the edge of the mound. The customary use of the same dump explains the greater accumulation of sherds on one slope. The relatively small area available suggests a communal rather than an individual family house on the summit of each mound. Each group of house mounds has associated at least one cemetery mound, with a ratio of habitation mounds to cemeteries of 13:1 at Fortaleza and 18:2 for Camutins. Often this burial mound stands out because of its size. The largest one so far recorded is in the Camutins group, measuring 255 meters long, 30 meters wide, and 10 meters high above the highest water level. The history of the burial practices of the Marajoara is incomplete, and there appears to have been a chronological change, in addition to variations that can be explained by differential treatment of the dead. The oldest secondary burials in Guajará cemetery of the Camutins group of mounds are in large plain, painted, or excised jars covered with a plain or excised, basin-shaped, or carinated bowl inverted or set upright in the jar neck as a lid. A pottery pubic covering (tanga) was placed inside with the bones, which sometimes had been painted red, along with bowls and miscellaneous animal, bird, and crocodilian bones. Cremation displaces secondary burial as the dominant practice in the upper part of the mounds, jars become smaller and less ornate, and tangas are never associated. Some burials contained a grouping of several urns, as if a person of some outstanding importance was involved, while other bodies are buried directly in the earth, but often with an associated tanga. These differences undoubtedly reflect differential treatment of the dead in recognition of distinction in class or rank. A few skeletal scraps indicate that frontal deformation of the skull was practiced, and anthropomorphic urns show the ear lobe and lip pierced for ornaments. The quantity of sherds from vessels of all types, both decorated and plain, the great number of broken tangas and pottery stools, and the presence of fire-burned clay suggest that the cemeteries were the scene of some sort of elaborate ceremonial.

The pottery of the Marajoara Phase was divided into two plain wares and seven major types of decoration. Contrary to the impression received from museum collections and publications on art styles of the pottery (Palmatary 1950), the two plain wares comprise a majority of all the pottery at both habitation and cemetery sites. The plain wares showed a decrease in popularity of a partially oxidized, gray-cored ware and an increase in frequency of a completely oxidized orange ware from the earliest to the latest levels in the stratigraphic excavations. The decorated pottery was classified according to the primary categories of surface treatment—excision, three distinctive types of incised design, scraping, painting, and red slipping—and then subdivided into types based on a combination of these with alternative types of slipping, such as red, white, red-over-white, and none. All these complex types, for which Marajoara pottery is so well known, were discovered by these stratigraphic studies to be the most abundant and best made in the early part of the phase. As time passed, they were gradually replaced by simpler types. There is no evidence that any of the alternations in the Marajoara culture were the result of outside interference, but rather they seem to reflect an internal change.

The mound-building, a burial pattern with differential treatment of the dead, elaborate pottery with standardized forms made during the first half of the Marajoara Phase, and other kinds of evidence imply a level of sociopolitical development attained by this phase that makes it stand out, in contrast to the other cultures of the Amazon-Orinoco drainages and relates it to the Sub-Andean or Circum-Caribbean cultures. With the decline of all these elements during the history of the Marajoara Phase on Marajó Island, we can conclude only that the Marajoara arrived with an advanced culture, which could not be maintained in the environmental situation offered by the island. At the time of the initial field study in 1949 (Meggers and Evans 1957), the duration of the Marajoara Phase could not be estimated accurately because of the absence of cross-dating by radiocarbon. It was postulated that the culture arrived at the mouth of the Amazon around A.D. 1200 and had become extinct by the time of the arrival of the Europeans in A.D. 1500. It was also proposed at the time that the origin of the Marajoara was not the South American tropical forest but that this phase was intrusive, probably coming from the northwestern part of the continent.

Subsequent field work on the Rio Napo in eastern Ecuador (Meggers and Evans 1958) and on the middle Amazon (Hilbert 1959b) not only has confirmed the proposed migration route and origin of the Marajoara Phase but has added interesting data to substantiate the formation of a Polychrome Painted Horizon Style spreading out of the Andean foothills into the tropical forest. In fact, a few of the steppingstones in the upper and middle Amazon are now clearly defined, and the Rio Napo in eastern Ecuador has produced pottery comparable in all respects to that of the early part of the Marajoara Phase on Marajó.

In the lowlands of Bolivia, along the Bení, Guaporé, and Mamoré rivers, there are artificial mounds containing urn burials and polychrome pottery reminiscent in both technique and motif of the Polychrome Horizon Style (Nordenskiöld 1913, 1930). Undoubtedly, this material is related to the Polychrome Horizon Style as a whole, but whether the artifacts described are from one cultural complex or several is at the moment uncertain. Moreover, other features in the lowland Bolivian material, such as tripods, adornos, corrugated collars on large burial urns, etc., are more closely related to materials from other parts of the continent, so it is difficult to discuss with any degree of understanding the chronological sequence of lowland Bolivia without extensive stratigraphic excavations.

It should be noted that the introduction of urn burial into the Tropical Forest area appears to accompany the spread of the Polychrome Horizon Style. At least, at the present time there is no evidence of this form of burial in any of the earlier complexes identified with the Zoned Hachure and the Incised Rim Horizon Styles. All occurrences of urn burial, whether primary, secondary, or cremation, in the tropical forest of the Amazon-Orinoco drainage not associated with the Polychrome Horizon Style appear to be later and are probably derived from this complex. Pottery griddles associated with the preparation of bitter manioc are present in the Napo and Araçá complexes in the west but are not reported from other sites of this horizon style, farther down the Amazon drainage.

The Polychrome Painted Horizon Style was estimated to extend from A.D. 600 to 1300, although radiocarbon dates were unavailable at the time this was proposed (Meggers and Evans 1961, 1957). In the meantime, some experimental work has been done on dating sherds tempered with charcoal (Evans and Meggers, 1962), and two samples from the Rio Napo have given dates of A.D. 1181 $\pm$ 51 (P-269) and A.D. 1168 $\pm$ 53 (P-347).

Meggers and Evans (1957, 1958) explain the elaborate polychrome pottery manifestations along the Amazon and the associated mound complex, urn burial, etc., as indicative of a highly developed sociopolitical organization reminiscent of the Sub-Andean stage of cultural development that moved rapidly and at a late time out of the northern Andes into the Amazon drainage. A general collapse and decline of this level of cultural development occurred because of inability to maintain the way of life under Tropical Forest environmental conditions, in which intense agriculture will not produce large yields in one area over long periods of time. Collier (1958) has suggested instead that there was a long ceramic development in the Montaña that was influenced not only from the northern Andes but also from Peru and that the migrations into the Amazon drainage started from the Montaña. Until the southern highlands and intermontane valleys of Colombia are more thoroughly explored from an archeological standpoint, a good case can be made for the headwaters of the Rio Putumayo-Aguarico as being a likely point of origin. Only future work will determine the correct answer. Rouse has argued against the long-range migration theory of Meggers and Evans (1958), preferring the trait-unit-diffusion idea. However, recent work by Hilbert (1959*a*) in the middle Amazon has produced several "steppingstones" for the movement of the Polychrome Painted Horizon Style. The radiocarbon dates from the Rio Napo add weight to the long-range migration theory, since they imply that the time involved in the spread was relatively short.

More recently, Rouse appears to have accepted the long-range migration theory but believes that the explanation of the Marajoara culture's decline as a result of being poorly adapted to the tropical forest conditions at the mouth of the Amazon is not valid. He states (Rouse 1962) that

the Circum-Caribbean cultures of the Greater Antilles and central Venezuela flourished in the same kind of environment. We would suggest that a difference in agriculture may have been the determining factor. Both the Greater Antillean and central Venezuelan cultures were built upon vegetative agriculture, which was well adapted to tropical forest conditions, whereas Marajoara culture, if it did come from Colombia, was probably based upon seed agriculture, which could not be efficiently carried on in the jungles of Amazonia.

Space does not permit extensive discussion of these differences of interpretation here, but it is worthwhile to note that Rouse stands alone in his point, and no geographer, soil expert, or authority on tropical forest agriculture will concede that the agricultural potentials of the Antilles and the Amazon-Orinoco drainages are equivalent. There is considerable difference in the environmental factors of the Antilles that places them in a much more potentially favorable position for more intense agriculture than the lowlands of the Amazon Basin (cf. Meggers 1954). Whether one culture exploited maize and another only manioc will always remain a debatable question in areas where preservation of the actual remains is impossible.

PARANÁ DRAINAGE

The lowlands of the Paraná drainage constitute an area of lowlands and plains intermixed with forest and grasslands that was the focus of a series of rather uniform cultural complexes. In terms of modern political boundaries, the region covers part of southern Brazil, Paraguay, Uruguay, and northeastern Argentina, drained by the Rios Paraná, Uruguay, and their tributaries. This area appears to be outside the Andean influences that so strongly affected the northwestern part of Argentina and remained a peripheral area where preceramic hunters, fishers, and gatherers survived with the marginal way of life for millenniums. In fact, the first European contact still found many of the Indians living principally by hunting and fishing. Pottery is introduced very late. Lacking the actual plant remains, one can never prove the point absolutely, but there appears to be some change in the way of life with the introduction of pottery. Perhaps we can infer the Incipient Agricultural stage, in which pottery shows up sporadically on the upper levels of shell middens, and the fully developed stage of Tropical Forest agriculture at those inland sites where the pottery refuse is abundant. Most of the field research in this area has been conducted in the last decade, but there is considerable literature as a result of a century of speculation on the problems of the antiquity of man in the area, including the "early" finds of the Lagoa Santa region, the age and chronology of the sambaquis (shell middens), and, more recently, the pottery-producing sites of Tupiguaraní origin.

HUNTING, FISHING, AND GATHERING STAGE

Krieger's chapter on Paleo-Indian and Archaic cultures has mentioned the problem of these early cultures in this part of South America, so it is only necessary to refresh our memory on several points. The contemporaneity of man and extinct mammalian species in the Lagoa Santa area is still being disputed, although now well defined in Patagonia and central and northern Argentina. The same problem of unproved antiquity hampers interpretation of the large quantities of chipped-stone artifacts from the Paraná drainage and along the Argentine coast. The situation is complicated by the fact that the people discovered by the Europeans in the Greater Pampa area in the sixteenth and seventeenth centuries were still living a hunting, fishing, and gathering life and utilizing a chipped-stone technology. Undoubtedly there is considerable time depth to some of these cultures, and a new outlook and classificatory approach will undoubtedly permit the breakdown of the artifact types into several distinct stages.

The same problem characterizes the shell middens that occur on the east coast of South America, especially concentrated on the coast from Rio de Janeiro to Buenos Aires. Recent work by Hurt and Blasi (1960), Laming and Emperaire (1959), Bigarella, Tiburtius, *et al.* (1954), Bigarella (1950–51, 1959), Orssich (1956), and Rohr (1959) has subdivided the shell-midden culture into several phases. A little more excavation using up-to-date techniques and analysis of the materials will add considerably to our understanding of the archeology of this zone. It is beyond the scope of this paper to carry the preceramic discussion any further; it was merely important to note that, just as in the Amazon-Orinoco drainage, the base of the cultural sequences along the coast and inland along the river drainages of lowland Paraná is a fairly widespread, simple hunting, fishing, and gathering way of life.

INCIPIENT AGRICULTURAL STAGE

The top levels of certain of the shell middens around the Paraná drainage have pottery (Krone 1914; Bigarella *et al.* 1954). In many cases the pottery is clearly Tupi-guaraní; in others it is pre–Tupi-guaraní. It may never be possible to determine whether fully developed agriculture was accepted by the sambaqui-dwellers or whether there was a transitional period corresponding to Incipient Agricultural. However, since the Tupi-guaraní pottery-bearing sites are so distinct from those having a little pottery on top of the shell middens, it is reasonable to assume the existence of this stage in the Paraná drainage. Willey (1958) also postulates an initial phase of pottery in southern South America by placing the Salto Grande pottery and the Brazo Largo incised, punctate, and plain pottery of Uruguay into an early pottery stage.

TROPICAL FOREST SLASH-AND-BURN AGRICULTURAL STAGE

Pottery-bearing sites in the area can be divided into at least two complexes. One is clearly related to the historic Tupi-guaraní, who have been estimated to have arrived in southern Brazil around A.D. 800. Recent work by Schmitz (1957, 1958, 1959), Rohr (1959), Blasi (1961), Silva (1958, 1962), Silva and Blasi (1955), Pereira (1957), Laming and Emperaire (1959), and a few others makes it possible to define the Tupi-guaraní complex from an archeological as well as an ethnohistorical standpoint.

The Tupi-guaraní lived in small villages along the fertile lowlands of the Paraná drainage, cultivating maize and squash but still depending heavily on fish, occasionally supplementing their diet with human flesh. Burial was usually in large pottery urns, with a lid or inverted vessel covering the mouth, grouped together in a sort of mound or cemetery. The pottery decoration is characterized by corrugation on necks of large jars, fingernail imbricated designs, and polychrome painting in geometric designs of red (brown) and black-on-white slipped surfaces or red on plain. The geometric designs and polychrome painting are reminiscent of those from the lowlands of Guaporé, just as are some of the corrugated techniques. Insufficient stratigraphic evidence exists in both areas to reconstruct a point of origin and direction of spread, but the Tupi-guaraní pottery complex has many features that link it more close-ly to the lowland Guaporé area than to any other part of South America. The Tupi-guaraní material of the Paraná drainage could be the final result of a movement down into the Paraná to its delta and then south-ward and northward along the coast. Such a movement is in keeping with historical information about the Tupi-guaraní and with archeologi-cal evidence in Argentina, where painted-pottery and burial-urn com-plexes of the Tupi-guaraní tradition are reported from Arroyo Sarandí and Arroyo Malo in the Paraná Delta (Lothrop 1932) and from sites in southeastern Paraguay (Schmidt 1934). Up the Brazilian coast as far north as the state of Bahia (Ott 1945, 1958) there is evidence of large Tupi-guaraní occupations, with more of them post-European the farther one gets away from the São Paulo area.

Another pottery tradition in the region, believed by all scholars who have studied the sequence to be pre–Tupi-guaraní, emphasizes punctate and incised techniques of decoration. These sites totally lack the poly-chrome types. They are reported from Santa Catarina State in south Brazil, on the São Paulo coast (Schmitz 1959; Tiburtius *et al.* 1951), and on the pampas of Argentina. Willey postulates that this punctate and incised tradition is one of the oldest in the area. In a more recent sum-mary, Silva and Meggers (1963) estimate this tradition, which, for want of a better name at the moment, is called an older Tupi-guaraní, to have appeared some twelve hundred years ago in southern Brazil.

In spite of a great number of publications on the southern part of South America, very few of them deal with interpretations based on sound archeological field work. It is hoped that this region will be attacked on a systematic scale by South American scholars located at universities and museums bordering the region so that, the next time a summary of New World archeology is proposed, the southern part of South America can receive its own chapter and not be treated as a sort of appendage to the Amazon and Orinoco drainages.

Summary or Conclusions

The over-all understanding of lowland South American archeology in 1962 cannot be compared with that of archeology in other parts of the New World. It is better to compare the area within itself as to what has happened in the last several decades. Twenty years ago this summary would have been a pure descriptive listing of miscellaneous artifacts scattered throughout museums of the world. All the conclusions, efforts to interpret, theorize, establish chronology or sequences, and explain environmental factors and their effect on cultural development would have been pure conjecture and armchair anthropology. In fact, the famous compilation about South American anthropology edited by Julian H. Steward and published as the six volumes of the *Handbook of South American Indians* from 1948 to 1950 was the first major theoretical step forward in viewing the pre-Columbian cultures in terms of the stages and levels of cultural development in South America and the Caribbean. Based on the available knowledge at the time and the total absence of stratigraphic archeology in lowland South America, the theories were the best that could be proposed. This stimulated field work to prove or disprove some of the ideas. Now archeological excavations in the Guianas, the lower and middle Amazon, the Rio Napo of eastern Ecuador, the Ucayali of the Peruvian lowlands, the headwaters of the Rio Orinoco and its major tributaries, and the south coast and interior of the southern states of Brazil have uncovered data that modify much of the theoretical framework (Meggers and Evans 1956, 1957, 1963; Evans and Meggers 1960). The tragedy of these past twenty years in lowland South American archeology is that most of the work is still being done by the same few professionals and their faithful protégées.

BIBLIOGRAPHY

BARATA, FREDERICO
    1950   *A arte oleira dos Tapajó.* I. *Considerações sobre a cerâmica e dois tipos de vasos característicos.* (Inst. Antrop. e Etnol. do Pará. Pub. 2.) Belém.
    1951   *A arte oleira dos Tapajó.* II. *Os cachimbos de Santarém.* (Revista do Museu Paulista, n.s., Vol. 5.) São Paulo.
    1953   *A arte oleira dos Tapajó.* III. *Elementos novos para tipologia de Santarém.* (Inst. Antrop. e Etnol. do Pará Pub. 6.) Belém.

BECKER-DONNER, ETTA
    1956   "Archäologische Funde am mittleren Guaporé (Brasilien)." *Archiv für Völkerkunde* (Vienna), 11:202–49.
    1958   "Archäeologische Funde vom mittleren Guaporé, Brasilien." Pp. 306–14 in *Proc. 32d Internat. Cong. Americanists*, Copenhagen.

BIGARELLA, JOÃO JOSÉ
    1950   "Contribuição ao estudo dos sambaquis no Estada do Paraná. I.
    –51   Regiões adjacentes às baías de Paranaguáe Antonina." *Arquivos de Biologia e Tecnologia*, 5–6: 231–92; "II. Regiões adjacentes à Baía de Guaratuba," *ibid.*, pp. 293–314. Curitiba: Instituto de Biologia e Pesquisas Tecnologicas.
    1959   "O sambaqui da Ilha dos Ratos." *Anhembi*, 33:483–90. São Paulo.

BIGARELLA, JOÃO JOSÉ, G. TIBURTIUS, and A. SOBANSKI
1954 "Contribução ao estudo dos sambaquis do litoral norte de Santa Catarina." *Arquivos de Biologia e Tecnologia*, 9:99–140.
BLASI, OLDEMAR
1961 "Algumas notas sôbre a jazida arqueológica de 3 Morrinhos, Querência do Norte, Rio Paraná." *Boletim Paranaense de Geografia*, Nos. 2–3, pp. 49–78.
COLLIER, DONALD
1958 *Comments on* "Archaeological Evidence of a Prehistoric Migration from the Rio Napo to the Mouth of the Amazon." Pp. 17–19 in RAYMOND H. THOMPSON (ed.), *Migrations in New World Culture History*. (Univ. Ariz. Soc. Sci. Bull. 27.) Tucson.
CRUXENT, JOSÉ M.
1950 "Archaeology of Cotua Island, Amazonas Territory, Venezuela." *Amer. Antiquity*, 16:10–16.
CRUXENT, JOSÉ M., and IRVING ROUSE
1958 *An Archeological Chronology of Venezuela*. (Pan American Union Soc. Sci. Monog. No. 6.) Washington, D.C.
DUPOUY, WALTER
1958 "Dos piezas de tipo Paleolítico de la Gran Sabana, Venezuela." *Boletin de Museo de Ciencias Naturales*, 2–3: 95–102. Caracas.
EVANS, CLIFFORD, and BETTY J. MEGGERS
1960 *Archeological Investigations in British Guiana*. (Bur. Amer. Ethnol. Bull. 177.) Washington, D.C.
1962 "Use of Organic Temper for Carbon 14 Dating in Lowland South America." *Amer. Antiquity*, 28:243–45.
EVANS, CLIFFORD, BETTY J. MEGGERS, and JOSÉ M. CRUXENT
1959 "Preliminary Results of Archeological Investigations along the Orinoco and Ventuari Rivers, Venezuela." Pp. 359–69 in *Actas del 33ra Cong. Internac. de Americanistas, San José, Costa Rica, 1958*. San José.
HANKE, WANDA
1959 "Archäologische Funde im oberen Amazonagebiet." *Archiv für Völkerkunde* (Vienna), 14:31–66.
HILBERT, PETER PAUL
1955a "Tripods in the Lower Amazon." Pp. 825–28 in *Anais do 31 Cong. Internac. de Americanistas, 1954*, Vol. 2. São Paulo.
1955b *A cerâmica arqueológica da região de Oriximiná*. (Inst. Antrop. e Etnol. do Pará Pub. 9.) Belém.
1957 "Contribução a arqueologia do Amapá." *Boletim do Museu Paraense Emilio Goeldi*, n.s., "Antropologia," No. 1, pp. 1–37.
1958 "Urnas funerárias do Rio Cururú, Alto Tapajós." *Boletim do Museu Paraense Emilio Goeldi*, n.s., "Antropologia," No. 6, pp. 1–13.
1959a *Achados arqueológicos num sambaqui do baixo amazonas*. (Inst. Antrop. e Etnol. do Pará Pub. 10.) Belém.
1959b "Preliminary Results of Archeological Investigations in the Vicinity of the Mouth of the Rio Negro, Amazonas." Pp. 370–77 in *Proc. 33d Internat. Cong. Americanists, San José, Costa Rica, 1959*.

HOLMBERG, ALLAN R.
  1948   "The Sirionó." Pp. 455–62 in JULIAN H. STEWARD (ed.), *Handbook of South American Indians*, Vol. 3. (Bur. Amer. Ethnof. Bull. 143.)
  1950   *Nomads of the Long Bow: The Sirionó of Eastern Bolivia.* (Smithsonian Inst., Institute Soc. Anthrop. Pub. 10.) Washington, D.C.
HURT, WESLEY R., and OLDEMAR BLASI
  1960   *O sambaquí do Macedo, A.52.B—Paraná, Brasil.* (Universidade do Paraná, Departamento de Antropologia, Arqueologia, No. 2.) Curitiba, Brazil.
KRONE, R.
  1914   "Informações etnográficos do Valle do Rio Ribeiro de Iguape." *Exploração deo Rio Ribeiro de Iguape, Comissão Geográfica e Geológica do Estado de São Paulo,* 2d ed.
LAMING, ANNETTE, and JOSÉ EMPERAIRE
  1959   *A jazida José Vieira, um sitio Guarani e pre-ceramico do interior do Paraná.* (Universidade do Paraná, Departamento de Antropologia, Arqueologia, No. 1.) Curitiba, Brazil.
LATHRAP, DONALD W.
  1958   "The Cultural Sequence at Yarinacocha, Eastern Peru." *Amer. Antiquity,* 23:379–88.
LOTHROP, SAMUEL K.
  1932   "Indians of the Paraná Delta, Argentina." *N.Y. Acad. Sci. Ann.,* 33: 77–232. New York.
MEGGERS, BETTY J.
  1948   "The Archeology of the Amazon Basin." Pp. 149–66 in JULIAN H. STEWARD (ed.), *The Handbook of South American Indians,* Vol. 3. (Bur. Amer. Ethnol. Bull. 143.) Washington, D.C.
  1954   "Environmental Limitation on the Development of Culture." *Amer. Anthropologist,* 56:801–24.
MEGGERS, BETTY J., and CLIFFORD EVANS
  1956   "The Reconstruction of Settlement Patterns in the South American Tropical Forest." Pp. 156–64 in GORDON R. WILLEY (ed.), *Prehistoric Settlement Patterns in the New World.* ("Viking Fund Pub. Anthrop.," No. 23.) New York.
  1957   *Archeological Investigations at the Mouth of the Amazon.* (Bur. Amer. Ethnol. Bull. 167.) Washington, D.C.
  1958   "Archaeological Evidence of a Prehistoric Migration from the Rio Napo to the Mouth of the Amazon." Pp. 9–16 in *Migrations in New World Culture History.* (Univ. Ariz. Soc. Sci. Bull. 27.) Tucson.
  1961   "An Experimental Formulation of Horizon Styles in the Tropical Forest Area of South America." Pp. 372–88 in SAMUEL K. LOTHROP *et al.,* *Essays in Pre-Columbian Art and Archaeology.* Cambridge, Mass.: Harvard University Press.
MEGGERS, BETTY J., and CLIFFORD EVANS (eds.)
  1963   *Aboriginal Cultural Development in Latin America: An Interpretative Review.* ("Smithsonian Misc. Coll.," Vol. 146, No. 1.) Washington, D.C.

NORDENSKIÖLD, ERLAND
1913 "Urnengräber und Mounds im bolivianischen Flachlands." *Baessler-Archiv.*, 3:205–56.
1930 "L'Archéologie du Bassin de l'Amazone." *Ars Americana*, No. 1. Paris.

ORSSICH, ADAM, and ELFIEDE STADLER ORSSICH
1956 "Stratigraphic Excavations in the Sambaquí of Araujó II, Paraná, Brazil." *Amer. Antiquity*, 21:357–69.

OTT, CARLOS F.
1945 *Vestígios de cultura indígena no sertão da Bahia*. (Publicações do Museu da Bahia, No. 5.) Bahia.
1958 *Pré-história da Bahia*. (Publicações da Universidade da Bahia, No. 7.) Bahia.

PALMATARY, HELEN CONSTANCE
1939 "Tapajó Pottery." *Etnologiska Studier*, 8:1–136. Göteborg.
1950 "The Pottery of Marajó Island, Brazil." *Amer. Phil. Soc. Trans.*, n.s., Vol. 39, Part 3. Philadelphia.
1960 "The Archaeology of the Lower Tapajós Valley, Brazil." *Ibid.*, Vol. 50, Part 3. Philadelphia.

PEREIRA JUNIOR, JOSÉ ANTHERO
1957 "Contribuição para o estudo da arqueologia do extremo norte paulista." *Revista do Instituto Historico e Geográfico de São Paulo*, 54:313–57.

ROHR, ALFREDO
1959 "Pesquisas páleo-etnográficas na Ilha de Santa Catarina." *Pesquisas*, No. 3, pp. 119–266.

ROUSE, IRVING
1961 "Archaeology in Lowland South America and the Caribbean, 1935–60." *Amer. Antiquity*, 27:56–62.
1962 "The Intermediate Area, Amazonia, and the Caribbean Area." Pp. 34–59 in ROBERT J. BRAIDWOOD and GORDON R. WILLEY (eds.), *Courses toward Urban Life*. ("Viking Fund Pub. Anthrop.," No. 32.) New York.

SCHMIDT, MAX
1934 "Nuevos hallazgos prehistóricos del Paraguay." *Revista de la Sociedad Científica del Paraguay*, 3:132–36. Asunción.

SCHMITZ, IGNACIO
1957 "Um paradeiro guaraní do alto Uruguai." *Pesquisas*, No. 1, pp. 122–42.
1958 "Paradeiros guaranis em Osorio (Rio Grande do Sul)." *Ibid.*, No. 2, pp. 113–43.
1959 "A cerâmica guaraní da Ilha de Santa Catarina." *Ibid.*, No. 3, pp. 267–324.

SERRANO, ANTONIO
1958 *Manual de la ceramica indigena*. Córdoba. Editorial Assandri.

SILVA, F. ALTENFELDER
1958   "Considerações sôbre a jazida de Estirão Comprido." 3a. *Reunião Brasileira de Antropologia, Recife.*
1962   "Considerações sôbre alguns sítios Tupi-guaranis no Sul do Brasil." *Revista do Museu Paulista.* São Paulo, n.s., Vol. 12.
SILVA, F. ALTENFELDER, and OLDEMAR BLASI
1955   "Escavações preliminares em Estirão Comprido." *Anais do 31 Cong. Internac. de Americanistas,* 2:829–45. São Paulo.
SILVA, F. ALTENFELDER, and BETTY J. MEGGERS
1963   "Cultural Development in Brazil." Pp. 119–29 in *Aboriginal Cultural Development in Latin America: An Interpretative Review.* ("Smithsonian Misc. Coll.," Vol. 146, No. 1.) Washington, D.C.
TIBURTIUS, G., I. K. BIGARELLA, and J. J. BIGARELLA
1951   "Nota prévia sôbre a jazida paleo-etnográfica de Itacoara (Joinville, Estado de Santa Catarina)." *Arquivos de Biologia e Tecnologia,* Vols. 5–6, Art. 19.
WILLEY, GORDON R.
1958   "Estimated Correlations and Dating of South and Central American Culture Sequences." *Amer. Antiquity,* 23:353–78.

ALFRED KIDDER II

South American High Cultures

THE MOST widely used classification of the native cultures of the South American Indians, based on their relative technological and social complexity, is that of Steward upon which the organization of the seven-volume *Handbook of South American Indians* was based. Therein the Indians are described as Marginal (mainly living in the far south of the continent), Tropical Forest, Circum-Caribbean, and Andean. All the high cultures, civilizations, or what are termed Classic cultures in several schemes based on regional development from simpler ways of life, existed in the greater Andean area. Most of it, with the exception of Colombia, was controlled by the Inca Empire at the time of the Spanish Conquest. At the core, in Peru and parts of Ecuador it represents the southern peak of New World civilization, to be compared with that of Mesoamerica to the north.

This vast area is still relatively little known archeologically, but, as in Mesoamerica and the rest of South America, a great deal of new information has been amassed since 1945. Most of the new data applies to whole cultures that were completely unknown prior to 1940; many of them are stratigraphically earlier than those that had come to light before that date. Since a number of radiocarbon dates have been obtained from the newly excavated sites and from a number of cultures that were known before 1940, the over-all effect has been, as elsewhere in American archeology, to lengthen the time scale, especially at the lower end, taking us back in time to dates for early agricultural and other technological developments that would have been truly astonishing as late

ALFRED KIDDER II, who received his doctoral degree from Harvard University, where he taught for a number of years, is presently associate director of the University Museum and professor of anthropology at the University of Pennsylvania. He has engaged in extensive archeological research in Guatemala, Bolivia, Peru, Venezuela, and the American Southwest and is the author of many writings on the ancient art and archeology of these areas. He has held many offices in learned societies and organizations and was decorated by the governments of China, France, and Brazil for his work in training foreign air force personnel during World War II.

as 1945. Examples of these developments, which make possible comparative studies of a long history of cultural growth in the area with those of other civilizations and their backgrounds in other parts of the world, will be given in their appropriate geographical contexts. It must be understood, however, that in a short appraisal of this kind it is not possible to present the detailed, technical evidence (mostly ceramic, but in the early periods lithic and even perishable remains) upon which this emerging prehistory is based. My approach, then, is frankly quite highly selective, with emphasis on the core of the area in Peru-Bolivia and coastal Ecuador.

In the development of all civilizations there is an intricate relationship between geographical environment, the exploitation of that environment by means of simple technologies known to the earliest inhabitants, and the effects upon technology brought about by diffusion of ideas from other areas. In the Andean area, especially in the Central Andes (Peru and highland Bolivia), the physical environment offered the Indians one of the best potential settings for eventual cultural growth of a high order to be found anywhere in the world. In the Central Andes the high mountains rise steeply from the deep, cold waters of the Peru Current, leaving only a narrow coastal plain. This is a relatively cool desert, conditioned by the relationship of westerly winds, cold water, and steep high mountains. Lack of rainfall is compensated for by the short rivers that created oases at their mouths periodically along the coast and later provided water for elaborate systems of canal irrigation. The cold water, upwelling from the deeps, combined with river-borne minerals eroded from the hills, is one of the world's richest sources of plankton and hence one of the world's richest fisheries, which, under dry conditions, has made the coastal islands and headlands the world's greatest source of guano. North of Peru, where the Peru Current bears westerly, the coastal fishing is less abundant, but shellfishing on the coast of Ecuador was very important before agriculture was well established. North of Ecuador the coast is less well suited for large populations; it is heavily forested and with high annual rainfall.

The Andean highlands of Peru and Bolivia are often regarded as an inhospitable area. In fact, although they offer relatively little arable land on account of both terrain and altitude, the highland basins, such as those of Lake Titicaca, Cuzco, the Mantaro and Cajamarca, are the home of a large number of indigenous root crops, notably the white potato, and of quinoa, a hardy grain of the pigweed family. They also provide pasture for large herds of llamas and alpacas, the domesticated members of the camel family that were so important as sources of wool and meat for a very long but as yet unknown length of time. Once adapted to living at altitudes of between 8,000 and 14,000 feet, the Indian populations of the large highland basins grew to considerable size. Today these basins in Peru, Bolivia, and Ecuador contain the largest Indian populations of the New World.

The highlands were also the source of metals—gold, copper, silver, and tin—which made possible an early and highly developed metallurgy. Two distinctively Andean cultural elements—true metallurgy and heavy use of wool—thus depended directly on highland resources, one of which, wool, was unique in America and the other, metals, was present in greater abundance and variety than in Mesoamerica.

On the wooded, eastern slopes of the Andean chain the transition to a necessarily Tropical Forest way of life was abrupt. This area, however, cannot be overlooked in a consideration of the over-all geographical basis of Andean culture. From the tropical forest a number of plants successfully cultivated on the coast were introduced—the sweet potato, sweet manioc, and the peanut were important crops, as was coca, a leaf chewed with lime to produce a narcotic effect. During at least two thousand years of Peruvian history prior to A.D. 1500, the coast, highlands, and eastern slopes were bound together in trade involving tropical products, such as woods, feathers, and jaguar skins, and plant products, highland metals, wool, minerals, and coastal fish and produce.

In Ecuador, as well as in northwestern Argentina and Chili, the highland basins are not as large or as productive as are those in Peru.

Colombia is characterized geographically by great diversity of altitude and climate. The rugged western third of the country was, and is, occupied by most of the population; the plains of the eastern two-thirds are outside the area of high culture. Adaptation to the complex topography of the mountain slopes and high plateaus in Colombia seems to have begun, and continued, as a result of the introduction of maize agriculture, following a period of occupation of lowland "littoral, riparian and lagoonal environment" (Reichel-Dolmatoff 1961).

In assessing the relationship of environment and cultural growth in South America as a whole, it is clear that the Andes offered far more advantages for early development than did the tropical forest, in which high culture was never achieved. It is also clear that, although the grasslands of the east had great agricultural potential, they could not be exploited by hunting Indians with a simple technology, as was also the case on the North American plains and prairies. It was no accident, therefore, that Andean developments were in such contrast to the simple cultures of the east. Within the Andean area there is again a clear correlation between the natural environment and cultural growth. It was only in Peru and part of adjacent Bolivia and coastal Ecuador that truly Classic or Florescent stages were obtained. This is precisely the region that combines good soil on both coast and highland, easily worked with simple tools; high potential for coastal irrigation; domesticable animals able to bear burdens and produce wool; abundant and various metals; extraordinarily rich maritime resources; and easy access to the products of the tropical forest. Elsewhere, some of these advantages either were lacking or, as in the case of highland basins, were smaller and poorer both to the north and to the south of Peru and Bolivia.

Krieger has discussed the evidence for the presence of early hunters and food-gatherers in the New World as a whole. In assessing our knowledge of the Andean area at this level, one is impressed by the paucity of remains from this period. This is largely attributable to the enormous wealth of remains of much later cultures and to the consequent lack of any real interest in searching for sites of the hunting stage. It has been demonstrated, however, that adaptation to high altitudes took place sufficiently early to allow several thousands of years for the domestication both of the llama and of the distinctive highland crops. As will be apparent below, a great deal more must be learned about this transition from dependence on hunting and wild plants to the beginnings of food production in the highlands. Any systematic search for such evidence of incipient agriculture will surely turn up much more evidence of earlier occupation; and recent finds, such as that at Lauricocha, will certainly stimulate further interest in the earliest inhabitants of the high Andes. For the area as a whole there still appears to be a long interval, perhaps as much as 3,000 years, between the early lithic remains now known and the preceramic horticultural sites on the coast and the as yet undiscovered early highland horticulturists. (The long interval referred to has just been filled by field work on the foothills just north of Lima [Lanning 1963].)

Peru—Horticultural Villages
(*Ca.* 4500 b.c.–*Ca.* 800 b.c.)

Prior to 1946 nothing whatever was known of the beginnings of Andean agriculture, although there had been much speculation on the possible Andean origin of maize, and a number of other plants (especially the potato and other tubers) had been determined as indigenous to the Andes.

In a planned search for an early fishing village on the coast, Bird (1948) excavated a large mound (125 meters long, 50 meters wide, and 12 meters high) called Huaca Prieta, near the mouth of the Chicama River in northern Peru. It had always been supposed that this was a wind-eroded structure of the great Mochica culture, but Bird soon proved it to be not a structure but an accumulation of domestic refuse, filled with rough retaining walls and, in the upper levels, subterranean houses lined with cobbles and roofed with poles and whale bones (probably from beached whales). The refuse, consisting largely of ash, firestones, sea-urchin spines, and some shell, contained no pottery. This was the first preceramic site to be excavated in the Andes. Radiocarbon dates show that the occupation of the village and the accumulation of refuse on which it rose lasted from about 2500 B.C. to about 1200 B.C. During this time there was no discernible change in material culture and no evidence of any exploitation of the upper valley away from the beach and lagoons at the mouth of the Chicama River.

The people of Huaca Prieta made their living by net fishing close to the shore, by gathering sea urchins, shellfish, and wild plant food and by simple horticulture. Several kinds of fruits, tubers of rushes, and cattails were truly wild. Cotton, bottle gourds, one species of squash, lima beans, peppers, jack beans, and perhaps achira (*Canna edulis*) were probably cultivated, although some of these may have been wild or semiwild. Cotton was used to make fish nets, which were floated by stoppered gourds and weighted by stones with holes pecked through them. It was also used to make small textiles, largely twined, but with some true over-and-under weaving in patterns. Such textiles were not sewed into clothing and could hardly have been used as anything but pubic coverings or small shawls. Matting and basketry of reeds were also much used; gourds provided containers for water. Bark cloth, used by the Indians of the Tropical Forest, was also made, but the source of the bark is unknown.

Stone tools were the simplest kind of hammerstones and pebble cores, from which flakes were struck. They show no retouching of edges; there is no pressure flaking, nor do projectile points occur. The only weapons were a few toy slings, a form of weapon that has remained typically Peruvian until the present day. The lack of effective hunting weapons and the complete lack of bones of land mammals, combined with the seashore location and emphasis on fishing and sea-urchin gathering, all attest a strong "beach orientation," with complete lack of communication with the interior. The static quality of the material culture for well over one thousand years further strengthens the impression of isolation from any sources of ideas or new food plants that might have affected and changed the technology of the Huaca Prieta people. They were not, as further investigation was to show, unique along the coast of Peru. Since 1946 a large number of sites with no pottery but with a variety of cultivated plants other than maize have been found (Engel 1957a, b, c, 1958).

On the south coast many such sites do contain simple projectile points, some of which are of the roughly lanceolate forms associated with the preagricultural hunters of the interior. Throwing sticks (atlatls) for hurling darts, and some land-mammal bones show that land hunting was practiced to some extent and that Huaca Prieta cannot be taken as typical of all preceramic sites on the coast. Additional classes of artifacts not found at Huaca Prieta include occasional shell fish-hooks, simple bone tools, and simple, flat grinding stones and hand stones. Villages were small groupings of simple above-ground houses.

Until very recently, all preceramic sites sufficiently well situated to allow their preservation have produced cotton. Engel (1960, n.d.) has reported earlier sites from three localities on the south coast (Paracas, Chilca, and Nazca) in which no cotton occurs, although there are the usual matting and netting of other plant fibers. Bone tools, a bone fish-hook, vicuña hides, darts and projectile points, the grindstone, and gourd containers all occur at one or more of these sites. Lima beans were found at both Chilca and Nazca. The absence of cotton with these finds appears to be correlated with greater age than that of those having cotton. Radiocarbon dates range from about 4700 B.C. to about 3000 B.C. This places incipient agriculture in Peru on a chronological level roughly equivalent with that of Mexico. It is also possible, if similar early sites lacking cotton are discovered along the coast, that archeological evidence may emerge in support of the hypothetical introduction of Asiatic cotton bearing thirteen chromosomes, hybridized with native, lintless cotton to produce distinctive Peruvian cotton at about 3000 B.C.

The origins of the very long, relatively static way of life on the Peruvian coast, from about 4700 B.C. to the first appearance of outside influence in the form of maize at a few sites at about 1400 B.C., is a puzzling problem. The differences between, for example, the use of throwing sticks and projectile points in the south and their lack at Huaca Prieta, as well as differences in houses, suggests differences in origins. One might speculate on the possibility that people living on different parts of the coast may have reached these districts on foot along the coast or from different parts of the highlands, bringing with them somewhat varied inventories of tools, techniques, and ideas. The other alternative is that some of these people, all of whom are without known antecedents, arrived by means of boats; lack of evidence for developed sea-mammal hunting and off-shore fishing on a large scale makes this unlikely, if not impossible. Regardless of origin, the people of the coast, by 1500 B.C., were reaching the end of a period of isolation from culturally meaningful contact with other regions. They had achieved a stable economic balance between sea and shore line, particularly river mouths, but it was an equilibrium that obviously did not permit any major population increase without utilizing up-valley lands. This eventually did take place, but only after a considerable length of time and the reception of new cultivable plants, notably maize. A few cobs of a primitive variety have been found in the upper levels of four sites on the central Peruvian coast (Collier 1961, 1962). This is earlier than its appearance at Huaca Prieta, suggesting a possible water-borne arrival in Peru, but, as Collier (1961) has noted, there is still too little evidence to negate the evidence for a north-to-south diffusion of maize on the coast. Whatever course it may have taken in its early spread locally in western South America, it is now quite certainly of Meso-american origin.

For several centuries the new and potentially tremendously produc-tive crop made no real difference in the subsistence economy of the coastal Peruvians, nor did the advent of pottery at about 1200 B.C. in the form of simple, competently made plain ware, showing no resem-blance in form or style to any specific area to the north. The highlands are again a purely speculative region of origin. At about the same time as the introduction of pottery, the peanut, a trans-Andean plant, also appears on the coast (Engel 1957c). Whether there is any connection between the two is unknown.

Cultist Temple Centers (800 b.c.–300 b.c.)

Often referred to as the Chavín horizon, the Cultist Temple Centers stage marks the first of three peaks or climaxes, in Kroeber's (1939) sense of that term, in Peruvian history. The second and third were the great Florescent cultures, typified by Mochica and Nazca, and the Inca Empire.

The transition from the simple, static life of Horticultural Villages was slow. No specific date can be said to mark the change, for about four centuries passed before the advent of the Chavín climax. In con-trast to Mesoamerica, the shift from a basically Archaic existence to one foreshadowing fully developed civilization was more rapid in Peru, at least on the coast. This was probably because arable lands were so much more limited than they were in Mesoamerica that populations were necessarily more tightly concentrated, forcing more rapid develop-ment of agricultural resources.

The evidence for change is basically that which indicates release from major dependence on the seashore. I have elsewhere characterized the culture of the Horticultural Villages at the end of the stage as representing a state of "river-mouth efficiency," using Caldwell's (1958) concept of the term "efficiency." In order to break away from this beach-oriented condition, it was necessary for people to move up the valleys, where maize could begin to bring about a much greater dependence on agriculture. The archeological evidence shows that such a move did take place, with more sites well up the valley as time went on, although seashore sites were still occupied throughout the stage. A fair inference from this evidence is that some form of irrigation was being applied, although there is as yet no physical evidence of canals. Large sites occupied at the height of this stage in Casma Valley, for example, could hardly have been supported without irrigation on a fairly large scale. There is evidence for a further stimulus of agriculture toward the beginning of the stage in the form of an improved form of maize at about 900–800 B.C. and the introduction of warty squash, sweet manioc, and avocados at about the same time (Collier 1962).

Specialized structures, presumed to be temples, appear to antedate the full development of the Chavinoid style in pottery and stone carving. The oldest known may well be that of Las Aldas, near Casma on the central coast. Here a very long platform and associated mounds are thought, on ceramic grounds, to be pre-Chavín (Engel 1957c; Lanning 1959; Collier 1962), and there are other small platforms or temple substructures at some sites of the same transitional period. Later, by about 500 B.C., temples show considerable variation, some being small platforms of stone or adobe and others much more elaborate stepped pyramids of the same materials, decorated with painted clay relief and some carved stone in the coastal version of the great Chavín style.

The most elaborate of all such structures is the Castillo at Chavín de Huantar, in the northern highlands. It is built of stone masonry, decorated with carving in low relief and tenoned heads, and it contains many interior stone-lined passages. A great deal of low-relief sculpture in the form of both free-standing stelae and carved slabs for architectural use has also been found at Chavín. The site is still undated by radiocarbon and may be somewhat later than many of the coastal sites.

Temples like that of Chavín and those of the coastal valleys were built to serve the needs of what were relatively small communities by later standards. These were "scattered-house" villages, supported by agriculture, with maize presumably the most important crop, but as yet a long way from the full potential of the valleys. Presumably, highland agriculture, based on the potato, other tubers, quinoa, and the domesticated llama (for which there is evidence on the coast at perhaps as early as about 1000 B.C.), had reached a comparable stage of development.

Other aspects of technology follow a course of development similar to that of agriculture. True weaving took the place of twining in textiles. Some gold jewelry was made, probably late in the stage, decorated in Chavín-style designs by répoussé. Small stone bowls, bone work, and earplugs were carved in the same style. By about 700 B.C., pottery, still largely unpainted, was being decorated by polishing, incising, and modeling. Some of the specific traits of pottery decoration and shape now suggest influences from the north, perhaps from as far away as southern Mexico. These included zoned incision, the flat-bottomed, gently flaring-sided bowl, stirrup spouts, and rocker stamping. The latter form of decoration is characteristic of the Olmec culture of southern Mexico. Recently, Smith (1962) has discerned what he considers to be Olmec influence not only in the traits listed above but also in the figures carved on the stone slabs at Cerro Sechin, in the Casma Valley, and in some small stone specimens, mainly of turquoise, from the far northern coast of Peru. He also has noted Olmec elements in some of the pottery from pre-Chavín levels at the site of Kotosh in the central highlands. Coe (1962) has independently made similar observations based on another specimen from the same period at Kotosh. In Smith's view (personal communication),

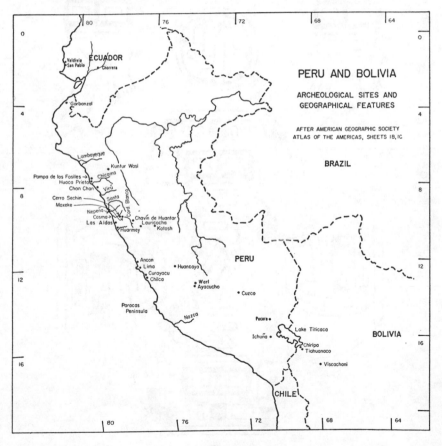

FIG. 1

we see the real possibility that Olmec may have directly or indirectly influenced the northern coast of Peru at a time prior to the full development of Classic Chavín art as known at Chavín de Huantar . . . and at such places as Cerro Blanco in Nepeña Valley and at Moxeke in Casma Valley. At any rate, after a thousand years of settled agriculture something sets off a florescence of art and the first indications that the communities of a region are united in common economic, religious, artistic and architectural endeavors.

Whether or not this condition of unity is to be attributed altogether to diffusion from the Olmec is still controversial and will be further commented upon. It is, however, a fair statement of the general social condition of the times. A temple cult with strong emphasis on representation of the jaguar (or perhaps the puma), raptorial birds, and the serpent was in vogue over northern and much of central Peru. Internally,

Fig. 2.—Carved design on a gourd from Huaca Prieta, about 2000 b.c. (After Bird, 1962)

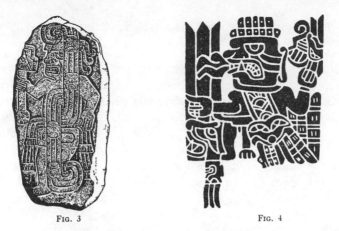

FIG. 3   FIG. 4

FIG. 3.—Carved stone slab, Cerro Sechin
FIG. 4.—Design carved on a small stone vessel, northern Peru

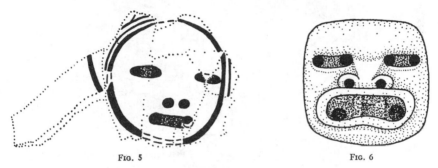

FIG. 5   FIG. 6

FIG. 5.—Boss on a pottery vessel from pre-Chavín level at Kotosh
FIG. 6.—Small head carved in turquoise, northern Peru, probably pre-Chavín

FIG. 7.—Two-faced pottery vessel, northern Peru. Cultist Temple Centers

there appears to have been no major warfare, for there are as yet no fortified sites and no evidence of conquest, so usual in later stages. Sufficient economic growth had been achieved to allow at least some specialization in crafts and to support a priestly class to recruit and direct labor and conduct ceremonies on a considerable scale. By the end of this stage the foundations of Peruvian civilization had been firmly laid.

As to the question of diffusion from the north, there are several points that deserve further comment. First, it cannot safely be assumed that an emphasis on large felines, raptorial birds, and serpents must be

Fig. 8.—Combination of feline and bird carved in stone. Chavín

attributed to an outside source. Bird (1962) has shown that condors and snakes were depicted on textiles dating from the stage of Horticultural Villages. Bird's (1962) illustrations of faces carved on gourds may not represent full-face felines, but they certainly resemble some later representations, although they lack fangs. These very early designs are, in the case of the condor, remarkably similar to those of the Chavín style. This is not to deny that certain elements of Olmec style may be present but simply to point out that, basically, these creatures were important to the Indians long before the Olmec culture existed.

Second, the stirrup-spouted vessel cannot be attributed out of hand to southern Mexico. This very specific and spatially restricted type of spout is present in the Machalilla Phase and later Chorrera Phase of the

Ecuadorian coast (Estrada 1958; Evans and Estrada, personal communication), the former dated between 2000 B.C. and 1500 B.C. It is thus quite possible that this trait, and perhaps others, may have originated in Ecuador and reached southern Mexico and Peru at about the same time. If this hypothesis should eventually be upheld, some explanation for the long time lag between the early ceramics of Ecuador and those of northern Peru should be found. As a speculation, bearing in mind the lack of a close similarity between the wares of the two regions at the time of the earliest Peruvian pottery, it might be possible in the future to demonstrate a slow diffusion from coastal Ecuador through the highlands to the Peruvian coast. Geographically, the wide desert of the far-northern coast of Peru is a formidable barrier to land travel. During the course of a long, roundabout overland diffusion through the highlands, the wares of ultimate Ecuadorian origin could, perhaps, have so changed that by the time they reached the coast of Peru they would no longer resemble their ceramic ancestors. These speculations point up the desirability of more work in the far-northern highlands of Peru, where almost no archeological work has been done.

The foregoing has been concerned only with northern Peru. Until quite recently the Chavín style was known only from this area. Recent work in the central highlands (Flores Espinosa 1960; Casafranca 1960) indicates that Chavín pottery and, presumably, Chavín religious ideas (although apparently not expressed in stone carving) reached as far south as the Ayacucho region. Chavín symbolism is also clearly present on the south coast in Early Paracas, where it appears on the painted pottery of the succeeding stage. Further south in the highlands early local ceramic traditions were developing that are best discussed as background to later manifestations in that area.

REGIONAL STATES—FORMATIVE (300 B.C.–A.D. 200)

The Formative stage is one of transition to full Peruvian civilization. It is marked by many technological advances and expanding irrigation in the coastal valleys. On the north coast in the Virú and Chicama valleys, the best-documented region of Peru at this stage, there was a further expansion of population up the valleys. This must surely have been accompanied by canal irrigation, although the physical evidence for it has been much obscured by later developments. The kidney bean became an important additional source of protein for the increasing population, and settlement patterns in the Virú Valley (Willey 1953) reflect this growth. The older "scattered-house" villages change to more concentrated arrangements of conjoined rooms or house units. These are still small in comparison with later towns but clearly foreshadow them. Large pyramid-platform mounds must have supported temples, but there is, on the north and central coasts, a marked lack of religious symbolism in architecture and pottery decoration in contrast to the preceding stage. Defensive fortification indicates that warfare was beginning to become a part of Peruvian life.

Technological developments, in addition to agricultural advances, include the use of copper and a gold-copper alloy. On the north and central coasts the older, predominantly monochrome pottery, often beautifully finished, was replaced by rather sloppily painted white-on-red wares. On the north coast the earlier tradition of modeling continues. On the south coast, in the Nazca-Paracas region, the southern polychrome tradition began earlier than the use of paint farther north. Chavinoid designs are not uncommon on Early Paracas vessels in the late phase of that culture.

The highlands are very little known at this stage. As has been noted, Chavín influences are found as far south as Ayacucho. Farther south, in the Cuzco and Titicaca basins, the earliest ceramics include some simple painted wares that on the basis of technique and radiocarbon dates fall within the stage, but there are still earlier indications of a ceramic tradition that shows no stylistic affiliation with the Chavín styles of the north. Perhaps the oldest wares of the south, provisionally dated by radiocarbon at about 900 B.C.–700 B.C., are from Qaluyu in the northern Titicaca Basin. Decorated Qaluyu pottery is of two types: a ware painted in simple geometric designs in dark brown on a white slip and a plain ware decorated with broad, curvilinear incision or "trailing."

At Chiripa, on the Bolivian shore of Lake Titicaca, a roughly circular village of fifteen contiguous houses dates from about 300 B.C. Simple white-on-red pottery may be related to the early white-on-red wares of the coast. In the lower levels of the site, perhaps as early as 900 B.C., simple plain wares predominate. Chiripa and Qaluyu, as well as the early phases at Tiahuanaco (recently explored by the Bolivian government's excavations under the direction of Carlos Ponce Sanguines) all point to the existence of non-Chavinoid local ceramic traditions in the south highlands that began well before the Regional States–Formative. In the Cuzco region a similar situation seems to have obtained, although no radiocarbon dates have been secured from there.

These early cultures of the south highlands must still be far from the beginnings of settled agricultural life. At Chiripa, where the village of about 300 B.C. was destroyed by fire, charred remains of tubers, quinoa grain, and fish bones, as well as numerous llama bones, point to a mixed agricultural, fishing, and herding economy. Unless other related sites can be found, it will be practically impossible to tell how far advanced they were agriculturally, and it will probably never be possible to distinguish, from their bones, the difference between domesticated llamas and their wild ancestors.

Thus far, no specialized religious structures have been found at this stage in the south highlands. So little work has been done there, however, that their absence cannot be certain. It is quite possible that the influences of the Chavín cult had not reached the region and that it was not until the succeeding stage that organized cults and associated structures existed in the Titicaca and Cuzco basins.

REGIONAL STATES—FLORESCENT (A.D. 200–A.D. 600)

The second great cultural climax in Peru and, at least to our eyes, artistically the most brilliant is the Florescent. Accurate dating is still difficult because no really adequate series of radiocarbon determinations has been made for the coast. Somewhat arbitrarily, A.D. 200 is chosen for the approximate beginning, but some phases, as at Pucara in the Titicaca Basin, date to about 50 B.C. By A.D. 200, however, the full agricultural potential of the coast had been reached and, in the Titicaca Basin, Classic Tiahuanaco was probably at its peak. As for earlier times, there is still a serious imbalance between knowledge of the coast and knowledge of the highlands, for little is known of the northern and central highlands other than local pottery styles. In the southern highlands large sites like Tiahuanaco and Pucara indicate a great increase in population after Chiripa times. The exact nature of the great site of Tiahuanaco itself is still uncertain, but its size and the extent of domestic refuse make it appear as a large town rather than a periodically occupied ceremonial center.

Collier (1962) has noted that for this stage the full utilization of the technologies developed earlier "emphasized the geographical differences of size and fertility of regions, and these differences played a part in the development of marked regional specialization." The stage has been called Regional Classic (Willey 1948) in a discussion of ceramic stylistic history in Peru. Regionalism is particularly evident in art styles, especially in pottery and textiles. Basic technology seems to differ to a much smaller degree. On the coast the climactic styles of Mochica and Nazca—the former a product of a ceramic tradition emphasizing modeling, the stirrup spout, and two-color painting, the latter representing the height of the southern polychrome tradition—are the most familiar to non-specialists. Craft specialization on a large scale is evident in ceramics, textiles, and minor arts. Metallurgy became increasingly important, especially on the northern coast. Casting was developed, and tools and weapons of copper were in common use. Silver appeared for the first time, and alloys of gold, copper, and silver were manufactured. Trade from distant regions was well developed.

All these evidences of richness and productivity reflect the full utilization of the land, with large and well-controlled irrigation and the use of fertilizer. Populations increased markedly, living in large villages and agglutinated towns of a thousand or more dwellings. Great adobe stepped platforms and round temple substructures with encircling ramps were built. Those of the northern coast were never exceeded in size. From all this it could be inferred that there was strong social control,

FIG. 9.—Mochica fishing scene, painted on pottery, north coast of Peru

FIG. 10.—Mochica deity catching a fish demon, painted on pottery, north coast of Peru

probably theocratic. This is proved by the famous scenes of Mochica life painted on pottery and, in some cases, on walls. Here are seen great rulers, apparently often in the guise of dieties; common people at work; ceremonial scenes; and, most strikingly, many scenes of battle. The Mochica culture, in its later days, has been characterized as an expanding war state (Willey 1948). This is in strong contrast to the Early Classic of Mesoamerica, where militarism is considerably later. It is to be expected, however, in an area where arable land is strictly limited and cannot be expanded by cutting and burning more forest. In coastal Peru growing populations had to live in concentrations near limited sources of water, which could be brought, through limitations

Fig. 11.—Mochica deity subduing a demon while a lizard-man looks on. Painted on pottery, north coast of Peru.

Fig. 12.—Mochica warrior defeating an enemy with a stabbing club. The enemy is armed with a throwing stick, darts, and shield. Painted on pottery, north coast of Peru.

of volume and terrain, only so far. These limits, once reached, became barriers to further power and influence of the ruling class that only conquest could overcome. It is, therefore, no surprise that the art of Nazca, and even more so that of the Mochica, shows so much belligerent activity. In the north this lead to the expansion of the Mochica state south to the central coast, a conquest that has been well documented archeologically in the intervening Virú Valley (Collier 1955; Willey 1953).

FIG. 13.—Mochica warrior with the clothes and weapons he has stripped from his naked prisoner. Painted on pottery, north coast of Peru.

Warfare, evident to some extent earlier, by this stage had led to conquest. This condition remained a fact of Peruvian life for the rest of its prehistory, which is marked for the next millennium by continuing struggle for political control of arable land, whether on the coast or in the highland basins.

CITY BUILDERS (A.D. 600–A.D. 1000)

The penultimate stage of Peruvian history seems in retrospect a logical consequence of the foregoing period of regionalism and interregional rivalry. It is a time during which for a while a single powerful force, perhaps that of a religious cult backed by militant leaders, greatly affected most of Peru. This force appears ultimately to stem from Tiahuanaco, but, archeologically, the course of events is not entirely clear. There is still much to be learned as to the social and political nature of the spread of ideas and religious symbolism from Tiahuanaco and Wari, near Ayacucho, to the northern coast and south into northern

Chile and northwestern Argentina. Several interpretations have been offered; that of Lumberas (1960*b*) seems the most acceptable at present, but fuller archeological evidence is still needed before certain alternatives can be discarded. In this view, it is felt that a complex series of stylistic influences, probably combined with military action, brought about the establishment of a strong center at the large walled site of Wari, inland in the highlands northeast of the Nazca region. Lumbreras believes that here in the Ayacucho region influences from late Nazca were, in turn, strongly affected by Classic Tiahuanaco, producing the characteristic pottery styles of Wari (often referred to as Coast Tiahuanaco). These influences are all expressed in style, with no evidence for accompanying political or military expansion from Tiahuanaco itself. There is no doubt as to the presence of many Tiahuanaco elements in Wari pottery, but they are not necessarily derived from Tiahuanaco pottery. Bennett (1934) noted that the coastal manifestations of Tiahuanaco design much more closely resembled those on the stone sculpture at Tiahuanaco and suggested that such designs may have been carried by easily transportable textiles. This idea is strengthened by the fact that direct Classic Tiahuanaco influence is not to be found north of the type site (except at Wari), even in the Titicaca Basin, and is certainly not present in Cuzco, posing the problem of how Wari received undoubted Tiahuanaco design elements. Wari undoubtedly was a center of further dispersion of its own version of Tiahuanaco symbolism, presumably inspired by a vigorous cult with which it was associated. This certainly affected the Cuzco region, Nazca, and eventually the coast and, to a lesser degree, the highlands as far north as perhaps Lambayeque. In contrast, the influence of the pure style of Bolivian Tiahuanaco was limited to the far south of Peru, eastern Bolivia, northern Chile, and, to some degree, northwestern Argentina.

The major problem of the enormous stylistic dispersion of Wari ceramic and textile motifs is that of the extent of its military backing. Lumbreras sees it as direct conquest from Wari itself and states (personal communication 1962) that there is evidence of pre-Inca roads, presumably of military importance, to strengthen his view.

Alternative speculations are that a cult, symbolized by Wari versions of Tiahuanaco designs, was spread to the coast and there pushed farther to the north by coastal militarists. Whatever the case may eventually prove to be, local styles along the coast, most dramatically in the Mochica kingdom, were completely wiped out. This must have been by conquest, which, from whatever source, was not long enduring or comparable in its effects to that of the Inca. There is no evidence for the kind of garrison occupation that is archeologically (as well as historically) typical of Inca conquest. Although Wari influence was relatively short lived, it was intensive, not only in ceramic and textile style, but in all handicrafts.

The association of urban living with the Wari expansion was of more basic and lasting importance to coastal populations. Coincidentally with the replacement of local styles by those of Wari, great high-walled compounds containing hundreds of dwelling units were built near Cuzco and on the central and northern coasts. Much of the population was thus urbanized, and it remained so until the Spanish Conquest. This apparently enforced concentration of people in cities was surely undertaken in part for defensive purposes and also, perhaps, in order to make more land available for cultivation or for more easy control of labor. Schaedel (1951) has discerned two types of these large, concentrated centers, an "urban elite" form, with religious structures and palaces for the upper classes, and an "urban lay" type, lacking such buildings. The effect of coastal urbanization eventually was to reduce the active farming population. It has been tentatively estimated that this reduction was on the order of 8–10 per cent, with non-farming populations as high as 50 per cent in large towns.

As has been stated, the Wari styles were in vogue for a relatively short time. There are very few reliable dates against which to measure the breakdown of the original Tiahuanaco stylistic conventions into geometric and often very carelessly rendered designs. By about A.D. 1000 all traces of the distinctive elements of Tiahuanaco symbolism had disappeared, foreshadowing a return to artistic regionalism in the first part of the final stage.

New Kingdoms and Empire (a.d. 1000–a.d. 1532)

The ultimate stage of native Peruvian history is known about as much from the chronicles of the Spaniards as from archeology (see Rowe 1944, 1946). Technologically there was little change; intervalley irrigation reflected the control of adjacent valleys by powerful rulers of what can properly be termed "kingdoms," and bronze, an alloy of copper and tin excellently suited for casting, was widely used, especially during the Inca Empire, both for tools and for ornaments. The great urban centers of the coast (such as Chanchan, the capital of the Chimu Kingdom on the northern coast and the largest of these cities) grew to great size. Chanchan covered about six square miles and had an estimated population of 50,000 (Collier 1962). Many of its walls were richly decorated by low-relief arabesques in adobe and were elaborately painted.

The Chimu Kingdom was the largest on the coast, extending south to Paramonga. Lesser kingdoms consolidated the valleys of the central and southern coasts.

In the highlands regional alliances were being formed, as in the Titicaca Basin, where, after the decline of Tiahuanaco, a marked degeneration of pottery style seems to reflect much internal strife. In other highland basins, such as Cuzco, local chiefdoms were formed that do not appear as rich or highly organized as the kingdoms of the coast.

This regrowth of regional political groupings, sharing a basic technology and with strong emphasis on organization and control of labor, is linked with artistic regionalism, mainly reflected in ceramics and, to a much less degree, in textiles. Chimu pottery, almost altogether polished black ware, was, with the exception of large storage jars, made in molds in great quantities (Collier 1955). Mochica themes and forms, notably the stirrup spout, are again used, probably as a result of the retention of old traditions in the far north beyond the reach of Wari influence in the preceding stage. Other regional styles include the black and white of the central coast and the polychromes of the southern coast. Under the Inca Empire these styles were maintained, sometimes showing Inca influence, as in the Chimu black-ware copies of typical Inca vessel shapes.

Mass production of pottery, textiles, and metal objects indicates industrial specialization and the production of rather stereotyped goods for the population at large. For the upper classes, including members of the Inca royal family and the imperial court, highly specialized craftsmen turned out quantities of luxury goods, reflecting the highly stratified and highly organized condition of society, especially coastal society.

The emergence of the Inca Empire as the final climax in Peruvian history, and as a unifying force far more powerful than any preceding it, represents a tremendous achievement. That it was by the Quechua Indians of the Cuzco region, rather than by a larger and richer kingdom (the Chimu, for example) seems to have been chiefly due to the great military and political ability of three successive Incas, Pachacuti Inca Yupanqui, Topa Inca Yupanqui, and Huayna Capac, from 1438, when Pachacuti took control during bitter fighting with the Chanca, to the death of Huayna Capac in 1527. Prior to 1438 the Inca dynasty seems to have ruled over a small area and to have been no more powerful than any of the other highland chiefdoms. As Rowe (1946) has pointed out, none of the raiding states, including those of the Titicaca basin and the Chanca of the Andahuaylas region northwest of Cuzco (who were eventually to give the Inca their strongest opposition), had thought of consolidating their enemies' territories politically. Rowe attributes the idea of such political expansion to two generals who served with Pachacuti's father and with Pachacuti himself. By 1470 under Pachacuti and Topa Inca (commanding the army from 1463), the Quechua were in control of the territory from Lake Titicaca to beyond Quito, in

Ecuador. It was not until Topa Inca succeeded to the throne in 1471 that he directed the great expansion to central Chile. Huayna Capac, succeeding Topa Inca in 1493, added some much smaller territories in the north, pushing the boundary of the empire to the border of present-day Colombia. He successfully held the empire together, putting down revolts and improving organization. Shortly before his death, in 1527, he was told of the arrival of Pizarro's preliminary expedition on the far-northern coast. This late and explosively rapid version of the history of Inca expansion may come as a surprise to those whose knowledge of it is based on the work of authors (e.g., Means 1931) who derived their historical views from chronicles now generally thought to have been mistaken (Rowe 1946). Archeology has also confirmed Rowe's insistence on a late expansion of the empire.

It seems apparent in reading his history of rapid conquest that the need for organization and control—political and administrative consolidation of territories—was of fundamental importance to the formation of such an empire. Rowe credits Pachacuti with the organizational brilliance needed to gain the political stability essential to maintain the military momentum that made the Inca increasingly difficult to oppose. Obviously, any weakening of centralized government could have been disastrous under the hierarchical system of Inca government, with the Inca himself in supreme command. In the struggle for succession following Huayna Capac's death, the empire was found in a badly disorganized position for the first time in its history. The Spaniards took full advantage of this vulnerability, but it is doubtful that the Indians could have resisted them in the long run even if they had been ruled by a man of Pachacuti's or Topa Inca's great ability.

Much has been written of the details of Inca administration, and space forbids even a short summary. As Rowe (1946) has stated, they had achieved very much greater unity than had ever previously existed, spreading the Quechua language over large areas as a common tongue, imposing a unifying state religion, and leveling differences in wealth and institutions. This was achieved by skilful incorporation of local leadership into the central bureaucracy, shifting of dissident populations, and maintenance of garrisons where needed. It was facilitated by an excellent communications system over a network of roads linking administrative centers, over which armies and messengers in relays could move rapidly. Its efficiency was greatly enhanced by the keeping of accurate numerical records of troops, supplies and other inventories by means of knotted and colored strings called "quipus." All these achievements of government have been described in general works and in Rowe's (1946) excellent summary, but less emphasis has been placed on the archeological evidence for empire. In earlier times there is stylistic evidence for the spread of the Chavín cult and the later, probably more militarily inspired, spread of Tiahuanaco-Wari symbolism. For the Inca period there is a wealth of evidence of direct connection with Cuzco; garrison quarters built in Cuzco-style masonry, associated with pottery of Cuzco manufacture, often locally imitated, are common. Inca architecture in the typical Cuzco tight-fitting courses of stone is found in a number of places on the coast, associated with adobe construction incorporating the equally typical Inca trapezoidal niches and wall openings. The spread of bronze over the whole area was certainly accelerated by Inca forces, and quipus are found all along the coast. In short, even without the Spanish chronicles, it would have been possible to infer quite clearly the existence of an empire and to locate its capital at Cuzco.

Ecuador*

Some of the most significant discoveries in all American archeology have been made very recently in Ecuador. For many years Ecuadorian prehistory has been based primarily on a scanty knowledge of rather late sites and has lacked chronological depth. The coast has been only superficially known. This has been changed, primarily on the southern coast, through the work of the late Emilio Estrada, a gifted amateur archeologist, collaborating with Clifford Evans and Betty J. Meggers.

At this writing, since comparable advances in highland archeology are lacking, it appears that the coast was of greater significance than the highlands in cultural development and diffusion. In what follows, the new, well-documented knowledge of the coast is therefore emphasized.

Estrada and Evans (personal communication) have divided Ecuadorian prehistory into four long periods, each based on major cultural change. The first, called the "Preceramic" era, is still little known, and Krieger (p. 67 above) has discussed its highland manifestations. On the Guayas coast some heavily eroded shell middens contain no artifacts or other proof of human occupation. Evidence for a long period of preceramic life, with or without incipient agriculture, is therefore lacking, but Estrada and Evans are confident that the southern coast, at least, was occupied by preceramic hunters, fishermen, gatherers of wild-plant foods and shellfish. This seems entirely reasonable in view of the presence of the Horticultural Village people on the Peruvian coast. In Ecuador the evidence for a comparable situation would be difficult to prove, since no perishable materials survive.

* The generosity shown by Evans, Estrada, and Meggers in allowing me access to much new material is gratefully acknowledged.

FORMATIVE PERIOD

The Formative period is defined as beginning with the first use of pottery, which appears at 2500 B.C., over a thousand years earlier than in Peru. The earliest phase of this culture, called Valdivia (Evans, Meggers, and Estrada 1959), is confined to the northern shore of Guayas Province. It represents one of the most intriguing situations in American archeology. The pottery is associated with an apparently non-agricultural population, subsisting mainly on shellfish. It is extraordinary because its forms and decoration share so many detailed similarities with the wares of the early Middle Jomon culture of southern Japan, dating between approximately 3000 B.C. and 2000 B.C. The

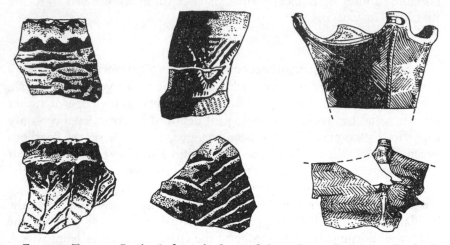

FIG. 14.—*Top row*, Potsherds from the Jomon Culture, Japan. *Bottom row*, Potsherds from the Valdivia site, Guayas, Ecuador. (After Estrada, Meggers, and Evans, 1962.)

comparative similarities between the early Valdivia and Jomon wares are very striking (Estrada, Meggers, and Evans 1962). They include castellated rims, folded over; finger-pressed rims; and small tetrapod feet. None of those elements of shape is to be found in any other early American pottery. Decorative similarities, including many similarities in design as well as execution, are finger grooving, fingernail impressions, corrugation, shell stamping, shell scraping, incision, and polished red slip. There are differences between the Valdivia and Jomon ceramics, and early Valdivia is also characterized by distinctive, small stone figurines, which do not relate to Jomon. Nevertheless, the similarities between the two pottery complexes are so striking and the datings are so fitly in agreement that a transpacific introduction of pottery at about 2500 B.C. seems to be the only logical explanation of the facts.

The Valdivia culture underwent many changes in the course of its thousand-year history. Stone figurines were superseded by female figurines of clay, and pottery techniques were improved, especially in combinations of polishing and incision or excision.

Between 2000 B.C. and 1500 B.C. a completely different kind of pottery appears on the Guayas coast, still apparently without agriculture. The new wares, characterizing the Machalilla culture, arc of very high quality, with thin walls and polished surfaces decorated by fine incision, red-painted bands, streaked by pcbble polishing, and punctation. Shapes include bowls with compositc silhouette and stirrup-spouted jars. The origin of this complex is as yet unknown. As stated above, the stirrup spout is earlier here than anywhere else so far known in America.

The people of the Machalilla culture co-existed with those of late Valdivia for some time prior to a third incursion of outsiders or at least a strong outside influence, in this case from Mesoamerica. At about 1500 B.C. the Valdivia culture disappears for reasons not yet apparent and the Machalilla culture, combined with new elements from the north, becomes the Chorrera culture. At the same time, there was a rapid expansion away from the seashore to the fertile lands of the Guayas basin and into the province of Manabí. This is explicable only by postulating the introduction of maize, long in use in Mesoamerica and, it will be recalled, first used on the Peruvian coast at what seems to have been only slightly later.

The Mesoamerican traits reaching Ecuador at this time are mainly those of ceramic form and painting and also include the typical ear spools of napkin-ring shape and small obsidian blades so characteristically Mesoamerican and non-Andean. Many traits of Machalilla stylc held over; some new forms, such as whistling jars, may be local products of the amalgamation. The total ceramic complex was of the highest quality. Estrada and Evans (personal communication) state that the thin walls and mirror-like polished surfaces produced by the Chorrera potters were never equaled, much less surpassed, in later cultures. Very little else is known of Chorrera. Sites were small and without identifiable buildings, which were probably of perishable material. Specialized religious buildings are likely to have been in use, for the level of development attested by ceramic excellence indicates craft specialization and a probable concomitant social and religious development. Chorrera spread over much of the Ecuadorian coast, save for the far northern and southern extremes, and into the southern highlands. Estrada and Evans have noted similarities between Chorrera and Chavín pottery that suggest to them a further diffusion into Peru.

REGIONAL DEVELOPMENTAL PERIOD

Chorrera culture was diffused over a large area of widely differing altitudinal and climatic regions. Estrada and Evans (personal communication) note a strong correlation between such environmental zones and the regionally characteristic cultures of the regional developmental period, dating from about 500 B.C. to A.D. 500. A number of local cultures have been described, mainly on the basis of ceramics, both on the coast and in the highlands. This regionalism equates in time with that of Peru during the Regional States Formative and Florescent stages, but in Ecuador there seem to have been more extreme differences between regions both in material culture and in over-all social complexity. Unifying elements in ceramics are the common heritage of Chorrera styles and two new types of decoration that mark the beginning of the period on the coast. These are white-on-red painting and resist dyeing or negative painting, widely spread over the area.

Space forbids a summary of the ceramic similarities and differences between the numerous local cultures, some of which developed very distinctive local styles. Such regional differences may be illustrated by comparing the rather simple culture of the Jambelí Phase, located in the mangrove swamps of the southern coast, and the brilliantly florescent Bahía Phase on the coast of Manabí Province between Manta and Bahía de Caráquez. The Jambelí Phase was still based largely on the early subsistence pattern of shellfishing and gathering, perhaps with limited agriculture. Although it was not isolated from the richer cultures to the north, its much simpler and less varied ceramic decoration reflects its unfavorable agricultural situation.

The Bahía Phase represents a highly developed culture comparable in technology and in social and religious development to the Classic civilizations of Mesoamerica and the Florescent cultures of Peru. Good-sized towns are inferred from large sites with mounds and reservoirs for water storage. Stone-faced platforms are interpreted as ceremonial structures, and the island of La Plata is thought to have been a specialized religious sanctuary. This small island, lying about twenty miles off the southern Manabí coast, lacks domestic refuse but has produced thousands of pottery figurines of a number of types and other objects thought to be of ceremonial nature. Apparently the Bahía people were skilful navigators and active traders. Their goods are found all along the Ecuadorian coast, and there are indications of possible contacts as far south as southern Peru. A long maritime relationship with Mesoamerica also seems to have been established. Evidence for this is the presence of figurines, pottery masks, and stamps of Mexican style on the Manabí coast at this time. Estrada and Evans (personal communication) state that the lack of such objects between Ecuador and Mexico strongly indicates direct voyages between the two areas.

During this period the coast of Ecuador seems again to have been visited by voyagers from Asia. At about 200 B.C. a complex of unique and non-American objects appears in the Bahía area and on the Esmeraldas coast farther north (Estrada and Meggers 1961). The evidence consists of pottery neck rests; pottery models of houses with columns and deep, saddle roofs; figurines with legs folded one above the other;

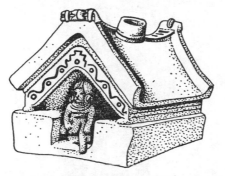

Fig. 15.—Pottery house model from coastal Ecuador. (After Estrada and Meggers, 1961)

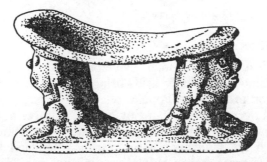

Fig. 16.—Pottery neck rest from Manabí, Ecuador. (After Estrada and Meggers, 1961)

pottery earplugs that resemble golf tees; pottery net weights; and stone and pottery pendants in the form of tusks. This Complex, appearing generally to be eastern Asiatic in origin, may also include the coolie yoke, depicted on a spindle whorl from Manabí and, less certainly, symmetrically graduated pan pipes, which were also widely used in Peru at about the same time. Most of these elements have a very restricted distribution in Ecuador (none of them appear, for example, in the regional culture immediately south of the Bahía region). There is no evidence for continuing contacts with Asia, and, as noted by Estrada and Evans (personal communication), it is not likely that the arrival of an Asiatic vessel fundamentally changed the culture of the Ecuado-

rian Indians, already much exposed to foreign influence from Mesoamerica.

In contrast to regionalism on the Peruvian coast, that of coastal
Ecuador seems to have been unaccompanied by warfare and conquests.
There are no remains of defensive works, nor are there any indications
of conflict leading to political control of neighboring peoples. This
would seem to reflect the sharp geographical contrast between the
two areas.

Fig. 17.—Pottery figurine, from Manabí, Ecuador. (After Estrada and Meggers, 1961)

Integration Period

At the close of the Regional Developmental period the climate of
the coast became increasingly arid, bringing about changes in agricultural adaptation to the land. Populations grew larger and were concentrated in urban centers. Three major coastal cultures have been distinguished, and in the highlands the major basins were dominated by local
tribes in much the same way as in pre-Inca highland Peru. In some
areas there was great mound-building activity to provide building platforms and burial. Agricultural terracing was also practiced in suitable
locations. Most of the archeological information from the period is from
graves and burials, which indicate by their comparative richness both
craft specialization and strong social stratification. Metallurgy, which
was limited to a little gold work in the preceding period, was rich and
varied. Many copper tools as well as ornaments were used. Silver and
gold jewelry was produced for the elite, including golden nose ornaments and earrings that are said to rank among the most beautiful metal
work of native America. The working of platinum, which occurs in
Esmeraldas Province on the north coast, is unique in the New World.
Apparently it was used more as a substitute for silver than for its own
properties. In Esmeraldas both gold and platinum were fashioned into

miniature jewelry; the tiny ornaments of minute platinum beads fused together represent one of the highest metallurgical achievements of the American Indians.

Although conditions for preservation of perishable materials are poor, there is evidence, from an urn burial late in the period, for fine wood-carving, basketry, and elaborate textiles. Both pattern weaving and ikat decoration (tie-dyeing yarns before weaving) have been noted. Beaded fabrics, shirts decorated with gold and silver bangles, and plumed headdresses occurred in the same burial, providing physical evidence for the richness and variety of perishable regalia that could otherwise have been only inferred.

As in Peru, pottery in the late period shows the effects of mass production. While still of high quality, especially in resist-dye decoration, it is standardized and less varied than that of earlier times.

The Inca conquest of Ecuador began with the march of Topa Inca through the highlands north to Quito shortly after his succession in 1471. This expedition was extended to the Manabí coast but did not reach the Guayas estuary. That region and the far-northern highlands were not taken over by the Inca until Huayna Capac's reign, at about the turn of the sixteenth century. Archeological evidence of Inca domination is fairly abundant in the highlands but is very sparse on the coast. It is interesting that direct Cuzco control can be inferred archeologically only from the islands of La Plata and Puná, the latter strategically commanding the entrance to the Guayas estuary. This is a further indication of the importance of sea routes all along the Ecuadorian coast in prehistoric times.

The Sub-Andean Cultures

Both to the north and to the south of the Central Andes the Indians approached, but never equaled, the high civilizations of the core area. Willey and Phillips (1958) do not accord Classic status in their hemispheric classification of American archeological cultures to any South American areas except Peru and adjacent highland Bolivia. Much of coastal Ecuador may now be added, but beyond these limits we are dealing with what have been termed "Sub-Andean" and "Circum-Caribbean" cultures, classified by Willey and Phillips as Formative. This means that the cultures of highland Ecuador, Colombia, northern Chile, and northwestern Argentina did not reach a stage of technological or social complexity comparable to that either of the Central Andes or of Mesoamerica. It does not mean that in these areas, especially in Colombia, there were not fairly large populations, practicing agriculture and often displaying skills, especially in metallurgy, quite on a par with those of the Central Andeans.

In northern and central Chile and northwestern Argentina, with a lower agricultural potential than is to be found farther north, basic Andean crops were grown and the llama was domesticated. Settlements were small, and, although stone architecture is present at many sites, buildings were small and masonry rough. Ceremonial structures were also small and simple. Fortification of villages indicates conflict, probably suppressed after Inca occupation. In the late history of this area influences from Tiahuanaco resulted in painted pottery and metallurgy. During Inca times in northwestern Argentina, bronze was produced in considerable quantity. Nowhere in the area, however, were there urban centers or political developments that warrant the inclusion of these cultures within the range of Central Andean civilization.

In Colombia the situation was similar, but in several respects the achievement of a truly Classic level was more nearly reached than in Chile and Argentina. Until quite recently, knowledge of Colombian archeology was based almost entirely on pottery and metal objects looted from graves and surface observations of sites. Much excavation since World War II has produced a long and impressive sequence of cultures in northern Colombia and expanded information in other regions. These developments have recently been well summarized by Angulo Valdes (n.d.), mainly on the basis of ceramic changes.

The earliest-known pottery-bearing sites in Colombia are in the lowlands. They appear, as do those of early coastal Ecuador, to have been without maize agriculture, and shell middens are associated with several of them. Reichel-Dolmatoff (1961) has noted that these early settlements are "limited to a littoral, riparian, and lagoonal environment." He sees the possibility that a primitive type of maize may have been cultivated on the mountain slopes at the same or even an earlier time but is convinced that the cultivation of productive types of maize, possible only in favorable higher country, brought about the expansion of the population into highland regions. Some of these early cultures, without agriculture or relying in part on root crops, relate ceramically to the Formative stage of Mesoamerica in specific stylistic ways. In Angulo Valdes' chronological scheme they date perhaps as early as 3000 B.C. (although this date is not fully confirmed) to about A.D. 500. One of the most interesting sites of this period, in contrast to the small villages of the lowlands, is that at San Agustín in the highlands of southern Colombia. Temples, burial mounds with stone-covered tombs, subterranean galleries, as well as monumental stone sculpture and architecture in stone, all indicate an important religious center. It dates at about 545 B.C. The sculptural style has often been compared to that of Chavín de Huantar; the two do share some themes, notably figures that depict felines or semifeline beings with protruding fangs, but the detailed treatment is as much Central American as Peruvian. Nevertheless, the site as a whole does suggest a cultist temple center not unlike that of the Peruvian northern highlands at about the same time.

The later cultures of upland and northern coastal Colombia have been described by Reichel-Dolmatoff (1961) as "chiefdoms." Including even the most impressive, he describes them as "small, class-structured village federations, politically organized under territorial chiefs." Some of these were more powerful than others, with chiefs striving to gain leadership of small states. Everywhere there is evidence of priest-temple-idol cults, but nowhere were there monumental religious structures of stone or settlements that can be considered more than large towns. Warfare has been correlated by Reichel-Dolmatoff to a considerable degree with the desire to enhance power and prestige by the acquisition of better farm land by military means. An important additional motive for war was the capture of prisoners either for sacrifice, for slavery, or for victims of cannibalism, which was widespread. The over-all picture of late prehistoric Colombian life in the highland and northern coastal region is that of intense regionalism, constant conflict, and a sense of comparatively greater barbarism than is evoked either by the Peruvians, as harsh as they certainly were on many occasions, or by the people of Mesoamerica, notwithstanding the sacrificial excesses of the Aztec. This was coupled with great technical skill, especially in the casting of gold and the use of gold-copper alloys. The most famous center of gold-working was among the Quimbaya of the Magdalena Valley, whose castings were nowhere exceeded in size and quality.

APPRAISAL

The preceding rather sketchy summaries of Andean and Sub-Andean culture and civilization are based on both archeological and early historical sources. They reflect a vast amount of detailed work by specialists, whose careful stratigraphic excavations and detailed studies of artifacts (largely ceramic) have produced many long, cultural sequences completely unknown twenty years ago. It is a tribute to them that so much can be said beyond mere description of pottery types and that something can be stated for much of the area concerning social, political, and religious life. Andean archeology has made great progress since 1940, but there are still many gaps in our knowledge. In the Central Andes there is still a serious imbalance between knowledge of coastal and of highland culture, markedly in the north, where highland cultural remains are almost untouched. The central and southern highlands have received relatively more attention, but there are still large areas that should be investigated before meaningful comparisons with coastal regions can be made. The lack of information on the early development of highland food plants has already been stressed. Coupled with lack of information from specific regions is the lack of sufficient information, beyond the establishment of ceramic sequences, needed to understand whole cultures. With striking exceptions, notably the contributions of participants in the Virú Valley Project, archeological reports seldom go beyond the presentation of pottery sequences and the descriptions of artifacts and such buildings as can be seen on the surface or may have been excavated. We need more extensive excavation of sites in order to produce "site ethnographies"—over-all views of the lives of their inhabitants embracing everything that can be archeologically inferred. This, of course, applies to most areas of the hemisphere, but the problem is more difficult in Peru and other areas of high and relatively high culture where sites are large. It is still true, however, that no large site in Peru has been adequately sampled, not to say fully excavated, from the point of view expressed above. For the Andean area generally, the existing gaps will surely be attacked and will produce regional sequences within a relatively short time. I am not so optimistic about the full exploitation of large sites.

From the chronological point of view, the periods from which more information is needed include those of earliest occupation, in which increasing interest is now manifest, and that of early transition to agriculture, especially in the highlands. So much recent work at this stage has been accomplished that it may seem to be carping to emphasize its importance. Engel's (n.d.) most recent contribution, however, does demonstrate that there is still a great deal to be learned about the transition and that there are still surprises awaiting us.

For later periods there is little to add that has not already been implied in previous discussion. The origins and growth of cultist temple centers, especially those of the highlands, and their relationship with Mesoamerica and Ecuador need to be further explored. We have a great deal of information on the nature of the great Florescent cultures that follow but relatively little save ceramic sequence on the preceding Formative stage. Even for the Florescent or Classic stages there is much to be done. The internal artistic sequence of the great Mochica culture has been demonstrated but remains unpublished. More importantly, a full, systematic study of the vast collections of our richest source of pre-Columbian ethnographic detail—the Mochica peoples' pottery depictions of their own way of life—has yet to be undertaken. It is a formidable task, but would be most worthwhile, especially if it were to be correlated with large-scale excavation.

One of the least understood phenomena of Andean history is that of the sociopolitical nature of the Tiahuanaco-Wari expansion. This can be determined only by larger-scale excavation than has yet been undertaken and must necessarily involve further highland archeology in key spots, such as Wari, Cuzco, and north of Wari.

Finally, although the final stage is well known in many respects,we are confronted with numerous enormous sites whose cemeteries have been looted for centuries but of which we do not even have plans, in most cases. These sites must contain all sorts of revealing information on the location and relationships of rulers, craft specialists, bureaucrats, and the military. This applies to Inca establishments with equal force. It is curious that it was not until 1942 that any controlled, stratigraphic archeology was undertaken in Cuzco, the capital of the only true empire established in the New World (Rowe 1944). Since then a long sequence has been worked out in the Cuzco region but is still not published in detail.

To conclude, Andean archeology, relatively neglected until quite recently, is now in such condition that wise choices of sites for excavation and the means for full exploitation of such sites can make possible interpretations on a far more satisfactory level of cultural and historical insight and understanding than is now possible.

BIBLIOGRAPHY

GENERAL WORKS

BENNETT, WENDELL C., and JUNIUS B. BIRD
  1949   *Andean Culture History.* (Amer. Mus. Nat. Hist. Handbook, No.15.) New York.
BUSHNELL, G. H. S.
  1957   *Peru.* ("Ancient People and Places Series," GLYN DAVID [ed.].) New York: Frederick A. Praeger.
MASON, JOHN ALDEN
  1957   *The Ancient Civilizations of Peru.* (Penguin Books, No. A395.) Harmondsworth, England.

LITERATURE CITED

ANGULO VALDES, CARLOS
  n.d.   "Colombia—Periods and Sequences of Cultural Development." Paper read at 35th Internat. Cong. Americanists, August 19–25, 1962, Mexico City.
BENNETT, WENDELL C.
  1934   "Excavations at Tiahuanaco." *Amer. Mus. Nat. Hist. Anthrop. Paps.*, 34 (Part 3):359–494. New York.
  1936   "Excavations in Bolivia." *Amer. Mus. Nat. Hist. Anthrop. Paps.*, 35 (Part 4):329–507. New York.
BENNETT, WENDELL C., and JUNIUS B. BIRD
  1949   *Andean Culture History.* (Amer. Mus. Nat. Hist. Handbook, No. 15.) New York.

BIRD, JUNIUS B.
  1948   "Preceramic Cultures in Chicama and Viru." Pp. 21–28 in WENDELL
         C. BENNETT (assemb.), *A Reappraisal of Peruvian Archaeology*. (Soc.
         Amer. Arch. Mem. 4.)
  1962   "Art and Life in Old Peru: An Exhibition." *Curator*, 5:147–209. New
         York.

CALDWELL, JOSEPH R.
  1958   *Trend and Tradition in the Prehistory of the Eastern United States.*
         (Amer. Anthrop. Assoc. Mem. 88.) Springfield, Ill.

CARDICH, AUGUSTO
  1960   "Investigaciones Prehistoricas en los Andes Peruanos." Pp. 89–118
         in *Antiguo Peru: Tiempo y Espacio, Trabajos Presentados a la Semana de
         Arqueologia Peruana*. Lima.

CASAFRANCA, JOSÉ
  1960   "Los Nuevos Sitios Arquelogicos Chavinoides en el Departmento de
         Ayacucho." Pp. 325–33 in *Antiguo Peru: Tiempo y Espacio, Trabajos
         Presentados a la Semana de Arqueologia Peruana*. Lima.

COE, MICHAEL D.
  1962   "An Olmec Design on an Early Peruvian Vessel." *Amer. Antiquity*,
         27:579–80.

COLLIER, DONALD
  1955   "Cultural Chronology and Change as Reflected in the Ceramics of
         the Viru Valley, Peru." *Fieldiana: Anthropology*, Vol. 43. Chicago.
  1961   "Agriculture and Civilization on the Coast of Peru." Pp. 101–9 in
         JOHANNES WILBERT (ed.), *The Evolution of Horticultural Systems in
         Native South America—Causes and Consequences: A Symposium*. Cara-
         cas: Sociedad de Ciencias Naturalles, La Salle.
  1962   "The Central Andes." Pp. 165–76 in ROBERT J. BRAIDWOOD and
         GORDON R. WILLEY (eds.), *Courses toward Urban Life: Archaeological
         Considerations of Some Cultural Alternates*. ("Viking Fund Pub. An-
         throp.," No. 32.) New York.

ENGEL, FREDERIC
  1956   "Curayacu, a Chavinoid Site." *Archaeology*, 9:98–105.
  1957a "Early Sites on the Peruvian Coast." *Southwestern Jour. Anthrop.*,
         13:54–68.
  1957b "Early Sites in the Pisco Valley of Peru: Tambo Colorado." *Amer.
         Antiquity*, 23:34–45.
  1957c "Sites et Établissements sans Ceramique dans le Côte Péruvienne."
         Jour. Société des Américanistes de Paris, 46:67–155.
  1958   "Algunos Datos con Referencia a las Sitios Precerámicos de la
         Costa Peruana." *Arquelógicas*, Vol. 1, No. 3. (Museo Nacional de
         Antropologia y Arqueologia, Lima.)
  1960   "Un groupe humain datant de 5000 ans a Paracas, Pérou." *Jour. So-
         ciété des Américanistes de Paris*, 49:7–35.
  n.d.   "El Preceramico sin Algodon en la Costa del Peru." Read at 35th
         Internat. Cong. Americanists, August 19–25, 1962, Mexico City.

ESTRADA, EMILIO
1958 *Las Culturas Pre-Clasicas, Formativos e Arcaicas del Ecuador.* (Museo Victor Emilio Estrada Pub. 5.) Guayaquil.
ESTRADA, EMILIO, and BETTY J. MEGGERS
1961 "A Complex of Traits of Probably Transpacific Origin on the Coast of Ecuador." *Amer. Anthropologist,* 63:913–39.
ESTRADA, EMILIO, BETTY J. MEGGERS, and CLIFFORD EVANS
1962 "Possible Transpacific Contact on the Coast of Ecuador." *Science,* 135:371–72.
EVANS, CLIFFORD, BETTY J. MEGGERS, and EMILIO ESTRADA
1959 *Cultura Valdivia.* (Museo Victor Emilio Estrada Pub. 6.) Guayaquil.
FLORES ESPINOZA, ISABEL
1960 "Wichqana: Sitio Temprano en Ayacucho." Pp. 335–44 in *Antiguo Peru: Tiempo y Espacio, Trabajos Presentadas a la Semana de Arqueologia Peruana.* Lima.
ISHIDA, EICHIRO, TAIJI YAZAWA, HISASHI SATO, IWAO KOBORI, MANUEL CHAVEZ BALLON, *et al.*
1960 *Andes: The Report of the University of Tokyo Scientific Expedition to the Andes in 1958.* Tokyo: Andean Institute, University of Tokyo.
KIDDER, ALFRED, II
1942 Speculations on Andean Origins. *Proc. 8th Pan-Amer. Sci. Cong.,* 2:161. Washington, D.C.
1943 *Some Early Sites in the Northern Lake Titicaca Basin.* ("Peabody Mus. Amer. Arch. & Ethnol. Paps.," Vol. 27, No. 1.) Cambridge, Mass.
1956 "Settlement Patterns, Peru." Pp. 148–55 in GORDON R. WILLEY (ed.), *Prehistoric Settlement Patterns in the New World.*("Viking Fund Pub. Anthrop.," No. 23.) New York.
KIDDER, ALFRED, II, LUIS G. LUMBREAS S., and DAVID B. SMITH
1963 "Cultural Development in the Central Andes: Peru and Bolivia." In *Aboriginal Cultural Development in Latin America: An Interpretative Review.* ("Smithsonian Misc. Coll.," Vol. 146, No. 1.) (In press.) Washington, D.C.
KROEBER, ALFRED LOUIS
1939 "Cultural and Natural Areas of Native North America." *Univ. Calif. Pub. Amer. Arch. & Ethnol.,*" Vol. 38. Berkeley.
LANNING, EDWARD P.
1959 "Early Ceramic Chronologies of the Peruvian Coast." Mimeographed. Berkeley.
1962 *Review of* EICHIRO ISHIDA, TAIKI YAZAWA, HISAHI SATO, IWAO KOBORI, MANUEL CHAVEZ BALLON, *et al., Andes: The Report of the University of Tokyo Scientific Expedition to the Andes in 1958. Amer. Antiquity,* 27:594.
1963 "Pre-agricultural Occupation on the Central Coast of Peru." *Amer. Antiquity,* 28:360–71.
LANNING, EDWARD P., and EUGENE A. HAMMEL
1961 "Early Lithic Industries of Western South America." *Amer. Antiquity,* 27:139–54.

LARCO HOYLE, RAFAEL
1941   *Los Cupisniques.* Lima.
LUMBRERAS S., LUIS G.
1960a   "Espacio y Cultura en los Andes." *Revista del Museo Nacional,* 29:
222–39.
1960b   "Algunos Problemas de Arquelogia Peruana." Pp. 129–48 in *Antiguo
Peru: Tiempo y Espacio, Trabajos Presentados a la Semana de Arqueologia
Peruana.* Lima.
MEANS, PHILIP A.
1931   *Ancient Civilizations of the Andes.* New York: Charles Scribner's Sons.
REICHEL-DOLMATOFF, GERARDO
1961   "The Agricultural Basis of the Sub-Andean Chiefdoms of Colombia."
Pp. 83–100 in JOHANNES WILBERT (ed.), *The Evolution of Horticul-
tural Systems in Native South America—Causes and Consequences: A
Symposium.* Caracas: Sociedad de Ciencias Naturales, La Salle.
ROWE, JOHN H.
1944   *An Introduction to the Archaeology of Cuzco.* ("Peabody Mus. Amer.
Arch. & Ethnol. Paps.," Vol. 27, No. 2.) Cambridge, Mass.
1946   "Inca Culture at the Time of the Spanish Conquest." Pp. 183–330 in
JULIAN H. STEWARD (ed.), *Handbook of South American Indians.* Vol.
2. (Bur. Amer. Ethnol. Bull. 143.) Washington, D.C.
SCHAEDEL, RICHARD P.
1951   "Major Ceremonial and Population Centers in Northern Peru." Pp.
232–43 in SOL TAX (ed.), *The Civilization of Ancient America.* ("Sel.
Paps. 29th Internat. Cong. Americanists.") Chicago: University of
Chicago Press.
SMITH, DAVID B.
n.d.   "Chavín and Its Antecedents." M.A. thesis, University of Pennsylvania, 1962.
STRONG, WILLIAM DUNCAN, and CLIFFORD EVANS, JR.
1952   *Cultural Stratigraphy in the Viru Valley, Peru: The Formative and Florescent Epochs.* ("Columbia Studies in Arch. & Ethnol.," Vol. 4.) New
York.
WILLEY, GORDON R.
1948   "A Functional Analysis of 'Horizon Styles' in Peruvian Archaeology." Pp. 8–15 in WENDELL C. BENNETT (assemb.), *A Reappraisal
of Peruvian Archaeology.* (Soc. Amer. Arch. Mem. 4.)
1953   *Prehistoric Settlement Patterns in the Viru Valley, Peru.* (Bur. Amer.
Ethnol. Bull. 155.) Washington, D.C.
WILLEY, GORDON R., and PHILIP PHILLIPS
1958   *Method and Theory in American Archaeology.* Chicago: University of
Chicago Press.

Special Studies

GORDON F. EKHOLM

Transpacific Contacts

THE QUESTION of transpacific contacts in Precolumbian times, whether or not the civilizations of the Old World significantly influenced the
origin and development of those in the New World, is one of the most
challenging and important problems of American archeology. The question has obvious bearing on the American archeologist's primary target
—the reconstruction as far as is possible of the history of the American
Indian. Perhaps even more significant, however, are the implications
that this question has on certain theoretical considerations of the culture
process—of the factors involved in the growth of civilizations—of the
over-all great burst in the cultural progress of mankind that has occurred
during the last eight or ten millenniums.

It becomes more and more apparent that the several growth centers
of early civilization in the Old World—Egypt, the Near East, India,
and China—were variously interrelated. Each of these civilizations is
distinctive in many ways, and, to certain degrees, they obviously developed independently and created their own distinctive styles, not only
in art, but in their ways of thought, religion, and societal structure.
Without question, however, they underwent extensive cross-fertilization by the passage of ideas from one to the other. It might even be
suggested that this situation could in fact be a necessary condition for
the emergence of civilization. One may think of those regions in Europe,
Asia, and Africa as being a large reservoir of population composed of
several nuclear cultural centers established in varying environments and
reacting to problems of existence in different ways. Ideas born in one
center might become fully realized only when they became transferred

GORDON F. EKHOLM, curator of Mexican archeology, American Museum of Natural
History, received the doctoral degree from Harvard University. He has conducted field
research in Mexico and Central America, which served as the basis for various of his publications, and is a specialist in the Precolumbian art of this area. He is past-president of the
Society for American Archeology. In addition to his museum post, he holds appointments
as lecturer in anthropology at Columbia University and consultant to the Museum of
Primitive Art in New York.

to another and fell on what, for either simple or subtly complex reasons, was more fertile ground.

This partial unity of the early civilizations of Eurasia gives the early civilizations of the Americas an outstanding importance for the theorist, especially if, as is commonly held, there was no transoceanic contact. It would, indeed, be good fortune for the anthropologist if it could be proved, or if he could continue to assume, that the civilizations of Eurasia and those of America were separate, unrelated developments. In that case we have two examples of a most important phenomenon in the culture history of man, and, although two examples hardly provide a statistically significant sample, it would be far better than having only one.

This is the ultimate value of the problem we are considering, and it is of such importance that we must give very serious attention to the basic question of whether contacts did occur. Did people or ideas from China, India, or elsewhere reach the Americas, and, if so, did they influence in any appreciable way the American Indian cultures—particularly the higher cultures or civilizations of Nuclear America that extended from northern Mexico to the southern Andes and in turn influenced the cultures of other portions of the continents? If such contacts did occur, were the influences that were received sufficiently strong to have caused the growth of those civilizations—or to have modified or determined in any way their content or form?

It must be made clear that the problem we are concerned with here is not that of the origin of the American Indian. Studies in physical anthropology, paleontology, and the archeology of early man have shown that the aboriginal population of the New World is basically Mongoloid in a racial sense and that it came out of Asia across the Bering Straits. The migration began at a still unknown date, but certainly long before the beginning of agricultural life in either hemisphere. Although these migrations may have continued until recent times, they were movements of people who were necessarily adapted to a subarctic environment and culturally not unlike the Siberians and Eskimos now living in the area. These migrational movements along this route cannot be entirely separated from what we are referring to as transpacific contacts, but in the main they are distinct. We are interested here in possible contacts between the high cultures or the possibility that influences from the high cultures of Asia have stimulated the growth of those in the New World.

The history of thought on the subject of transpacific contacts is of interest to our inquiry. Ever since the European discovery and conquest of the Americas, beginning in the late fifteenth century, it has excited great interest and controversy. In early times there were those who correctly thought that the American Indian had his origin in Asia, but there were others who supposedly felt it necessary to adhere to the then overwhelming belief in biblical history and identified the Indians with one or another of the lost tribes of Israel. This has continued to our day. Another theme that has consumed vast quantities of paper and ink has been the fanciful land bridges, the lost continents in the Atlantic and the Pacific that have been considered the means by which the Indian himself and the civilizations of the Old World found their way to the New. Robert Wauchope (1962) reviews the long history of this often fanciful historical groping.

Without entering into the details of this many-faceted controversy, it is important to point out that during the period of the growth of scientific archeology—from the time of Thomas Jefferson, perhaps, and John Lloyd Stephens—the general trend among the more thoughtful students of the subject of American origins has been toward considering the American Indian civilizations to have been completely independent developments. This gradual trend toward a strong belief in the independence of the New World cultures has not been, it seems to me, the result of completely dispassionate judgment on the now rapidly accumulating body of knowledge that is American archeology. I may be guilty of overemphasis in order to make a point, but I wonder whether there are not several non-reasoned factors that have been involved in this trend of which we have not been fully aware. One of these has been the mere necessity for concerted opposition to the admittedly wild speculations on lost tribes and sunken continents that have so captured popular interest, as well as such over-all diffusional schemes as that of the *Kulturkreis* school. We have argued against these for so long that perhaps it has become a habit.

Other reasons for the isolationist trend can undoubtedly be found in the history of the anthropological theory that has been most influential in American archeology since the turn of the century. Whatever this has been, it might be said in simple terms that it has resulted in a great emphasis on the "scientific" approach to archeology. I mean by this, not science as a body of integrated theory and knowledge, but the "practice of science," which seems to involve a primary concern with the inductive approach and a disinclination to speculate beyond the concrete evidence that happens to be available at the moment. The data of archeology come very slowly and with great labor, and their complexities require most archeologists to become specialists in one region or another. This, in turn, has had the effect of suppressing interests in certain larger problems, such as those of interregional relationships.

Along with this emphasis on scientific proof and on regional specialization, archeologists have not always been innocent of overemphasizing the historical importance of their own areas. It is something that might be called "archeocentrism" that impels one to claim that the Valley of Mexico or Veracruz or some other region where he has happened to work is probably the center of things. Fortunately, this archeocentric tendency is now disappearing rapidly, but it does apply to some extent, I am certain, to the American archeologist's thinking about the New World as a whole. He naturally wants his work to be important, and I suggest that there is something of an emotional factor involved in his objection to ideas of transpacific contact, which could relegate "his cultures" to peripheral status.

In opposition to this widely held conviction that the American civilizations were completely or almost completely independent developments, a counter-current of doubt and questioning has arisen in the last few years. This has of necessity taken the same form as that of the earlier and generally discredited attempts to show a cultural dependence on Asia—that of pointing to various cultural similarities in the two areas and suggesting that these are evidence of historical contact. There is the difference, though—or I like to think there is—that these more recent studies have been somewhat more cautious and reasoned than the earlier ones and therefore less liable to immediate and total rejection. As might be expected, however, they have elicited quite varied reactions. Many have accepted the idea of transpacific contact avidly. For others it has signaled the need to consolidate their position and to attack and oppose every suggestion that is made. Among a great many, however, we find a "wait and see" attitude and a growing interest in the subject, and it is becoming more and more respectable to think and talk about transpacific contacts.

When I was first planning for this symposium, my intention was to present a discussion, as unbiased as possible, of the present status of thought on the subject of transpacific contacts. I soon discovered, however, that this would not result in a very meaningful presentation. We all know that the diffusionist position is exploratory and tentative and that no very solid body of evidence, and none incontrovertible, has as yet been discovered. We are all much interested, nevertheless, in knowing more fully what can be offered in support of the contention that transpacific contacts did occur, and this course of inquiry, it seemed to me, was indicated. In effect, how good a case can be made for transpacific contacts?

I have chosen to look at the problem by examining some of the reasoning behind my concern with the problem of transpacific contacts. This could be of value because the case for Asiatic influences in America rests heavily at the moment on the manner in which we look at archeological evidence generally and the scattered but special evidence that pertains to the problem. The discussion of the question of transpacific contacts leads one into a number of difficult byways of anthropological theory and practice. All are closely intertwined, and it is difficult to separate the various themes. For the sake of emphasis, however, these will be discussed under separate headings.

The Diffusionist Approach

One of the consequences of becoming interested in the problems of transpacific contacts is to be branded as a diffusionist. One is placed on that side of the confrontation of diffusionism versus independent invention—a controversy that has long been famous in anthropology. This involves the burden that one is identified in many minds with extremists like Elliot Smith, who brought all civilization from Egypt, or even like Le Plongeon, who with a kind of airy magic had culture traits passing from one part of the world to another.

While I completely disavow any such extremism, I do believe that diffusion is a far more potent factor in the process of the formation and change of cultures than most American archeologists have credited it with being. More than most, I tend to emphasize diffusion when the choice between it and independent invention must be made to explain the origin of certain specific cultural similarities, but, as I shall indicate later, I do not believe that it is an explanation of all similarities. A greater emphasis on diffusion, nevertheless, does become a particular approach or way of looking at problems in American archeology. There is a difference between thinking as a diffusionist and thinking as an independent inventionist that might best be understood by looking at a concrete example.

Nearly twenty years ago, before I became interested in the subject of extra-American relationships, there was discovered at the site of Panuco in the Huasteca, where I had just completed a season of excavation, a small, hollow clay animal equipped with clay wheels. At about the same time Matthew Stirling and his party found similar objects at Tres Zapotes. These finds directed attention to several other examples that were in the literature or in museum collections. This struck me as something of extraordinary interest—something that was in need of explanation and worthy of a special paper on the subject (Ekholm 1946). I looked into what was known of the history of the wheel in the Old World and all available theories as to its origin. I also searched widely for other similar occurrences wherein a toy or miniature object involved some important mechanical principle not put to practical use in the culture. Nothing was very helpful, and I concluded that, despite the unexpectedness of finding wheeled toys in Mexico, I could only suggest

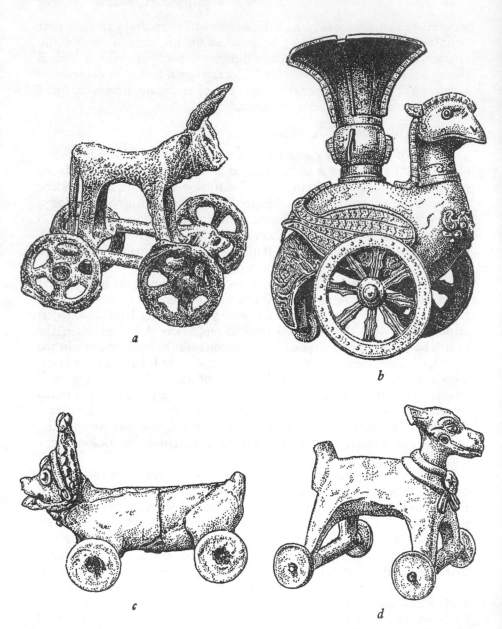

Fig. 1.—Miniature wheeled vehicles from Asia and America. *a*, Phoenician, Syria; *b*, China, a type attributable to the Han dynasty; *c*, Panuco, the Huasteca, Mexico; *d*, Tres Zapotes, Veracruz, Mexico.

that it was probably an example of a purely New World invention—the grasping of an idea and the making of a model. At about the same time, Caso brought together and published with apparent excitement the comments of several specialists on this discovery of wheeled toys in Mexico (Caso *et al.*, 1946). In soliciting the papers for this symposium, Caso probably expected some controversial discussion of Old World–New World relationships. He had undoubtedly heard many times the statement that the American civilizations could not have been influenced by the Old World because, among other things, they had not learned the principle of the wheel. No one rose to the bait, although one commentator discoursed generally on the improbability of extra-American relationships.

At the time, my reaction to this discovery of wheeled toys was consonant with my training and with current, accepted opinion. It was only after I became interested in the question of Asiatic influences in the New World and became what is commonly called a "diffusionist" that my opinion on the origin of Mexican wheeled toys was reversed. It now seems to me that by far the most logical and economical explanation is that the idea for these wheeled toys came out of Asia. This cannot be proved in any decisive way, but it is, to my way of thinking, a sound hypothesis. In bringing together materials for a thorough study of the subject, I find, for instance, that miniature wheeled vehicles, the so-called "cult chariots," were widely used in Europe and the Near Eastern regions in the Bronze Age and later. The practice spread into China in Han times—where they were usually in the form of birds, with a wheel on either side—and has continued in use up to the present. Miniature wheeled animals also have a long history in India and are found ethnographically in Japan and Siberia. There is some difference of opinion among those who have studied the Chinese bird chariots as to whether they were originally made for ceremonial use or were always merely toys. My impression at the moment is that they probably had ceremonial uses, which would account for their being cast in bronze as well as for their wide distribution. I suspect, too, that we have mistakenly referred to the Mexican wheeled animals as toys, since they appear to be found in graves or ceremonial caches, and toys are not usually found in such contexts.

Being of a diffusionist turn of mind, I find it difficult to avoid anything but a similar explanation for a number of other cultural items that turn up in the New World. The art or craft of pottery-making is one of these. It has long been assumed that pottery-making was a New World invention or even that it was invented here in a number of places. It is, however, a complex technical process that, in my view of the inventive potentialities of early cultures, is not likely to be invented more than once. Actually, there is evidence suggesting that some of the oldest-known ceramic complexes—the cord-marked Woodland-type pottery of northeastern North America and the early Valdivia pottery of Ecuador —are transplants from Asia. [EDITORS' NOTE: See Griffin, p. 236, and Sears, p. 261.] These are problems that are actively being worked on, and it is probable that we will eventually get the whole history. Until this history is known, however, I shall be inclined to think that diffusion of the potter's art from Asia to America is a far better explanation of its occurrence here than is the hypothesis that it was an independent invention.

There are many other things of an archeological nature that for various reasons excite my suspicion that they might have been brought from the Old World. The clay stamps that are found with some of the earliest of the high cultures in Mexico and Peru are an example of these. They seem somehow out of place in these early Preclassic cultures, where they had no apparent specific function as did the stamps or seals that occur in early periods in the Near East or India. In these latter cultures stamps played a role as identification marks in connection with a writing system. Still another parallel that I cannot discard as being accidental is the complex of iron pyrite mirrors in Mesoamerica. Mirrors are not a "necessary" development in any sense, and their parallels with the bronze mirrors of China make them look somehow related to them. For the same reason, the thin copper axes that were used as currency in Aztec-period Mexico and that occur also in Ecuador must have had some connection with the knife and ax money of China.

In the non-archeological realm there are also, of course, a number of items to attract the diffusionist. The blowgun, bark-cloth making, pan pipes, and coca-chewing may be mentioned as but examples of a great many things that show various arbitrary features and similarities to things in the Old World and that point to historical connections. But I do not make definite claims that these or the archeologically known traits I have mentioned as examples are necessarily Old World in origin. They are of interest as things that could have been imported and need careful study on a world-wide basis before their history can be known. At the same time, they are the kinds of things that at this stage prevent me from concurring with the doctrine of complete independence for the New World civilizations.

NOT EVERYTHING IN AMERICA IS DIFFUSED FROM THE OLD WORLD

Those who have refused to admit any intrusions from Asia have often dismissed the diffusionists' claims completely by saying that the diffusionists want to ascribe *everything* to outside sources and that this demonstrates the absurdity of their views. While it is true that exorbitant claims have been made for the wholesale diffusion of culture traits from Asia, they should not be allowed to hinder the considerations of the more modest and reasonable efforts to find historical connections between the two areas.

It is obvious that the civilizations of the New World, as with cultures everywhere, were subject to whatever regularities may govern culture growth and change. The New World cultures evolved just as did all others. They adapted themselves to their particular physical and cultural environments, and undoubtedly many innovations were made that can be described as discoveries or inventions.

To be more specific, there are a number of cultural items or traits in the New World that do not occur elsewhere, and we can therefore be certain that they had their origins here. The use of rubber is one of these. The value of its properties was discovered, and it was applied to several special uses—for waterproofing, for making balls and syringes. This was completely a New World development. Smoking, the direct inhalation of fumes from burning materials by means of pipes, cigarettes, or cigars, is also entirely of the New World. It is even beginning to appear from the recent important discoveries in Mexico that the beginning stages of agriculture underwent development independently in America. Going back, as they do, to 5000 or 6000 B.C., there is little possibility that outside influence is responsible, for the practice of agriculture is not that early in eastern Asia. And, as has often been pointed out, the recognition of the usefulness of a number of specific food plants and of their cultivability is a discovery that was made here in America— because the plants are exclusively American. There are also many special developments of particular forms and motifs that are clearly and completely of New World origin. For example, the whistling jar is a specific New World modification or invention, since, as far as I know, it occurs nowhere in the Old World. There are no non-American examples of the stepped grecque, a design motif that for some unknown reason has a wide distribution and long history in Mesoamerica and in the Andes. Many other examples of the kind could be listed.

It is, furthermore, certain that developments closely paralleling those that occurred in other parts of the world also took place here. These are inevitable because of the limitation of cultural possibilities that always exists. There are, for instance, a limited number of basic forms that pottery vessels can have, and the same applies to the forms of houses, clubs, bark buckets, and various stepped designs in basketry or textiles, to name but a few. Thus we see that, in attempts to discern the role of diffusion from the Old World, the selection of traits, to be meaningful, must be made on the basis of their probability of being the kinds of things that in the course of normal cultural evolution would not easily have been developed repeatedly.

CHRONOLOGY

In any attempt to show the existence of transpacific contacts, it is essential, of course, that strict attention be given to chronology. The diffusion of any element or complex from one area or culture to another can hardly be postulated unless it can be shown that it was in existence at the proper time, or there is some chance that it was. In fact, the perfection of accurate chronologies for the American cultures and for those of Asia may be of crucial importance to the eventual outcome of all studies of contacts between the two areas. If it can be shown that culture forms have a regular pattern of appearing slightly earlier in the Old World than in the New, we have presumptive evidence that the two sequences are related and, if the opposite is true, that they are not.

In trying to fit together the scattered bits of evidence for transpacific contacts, one is, of course, continually beset with complex questions of chronology, and adjustments and speculative assumptions of varying degrees of probable validity must be made. In attempting to develop the concept of what I called Complex A—which consists of a series of art motifs occurring in the Late Classic period Maya cultures of about A.D. 700 that bear resemblances to things in the Hindu-Buddhist art of Southeast Asia—I grappled, aided by Robert Heine-Geldern, with many of these problems. An element of possibly great importance is the cross motif seen in the Temples of the Cross and the Foliated Cross at Palenque. A good comparable example from Southeast Asia could not be found, so we had to be content with a modern shadow-play figure from Bali and an incomplete archeological example from Cambodia. This was probably justifiable, however, because we know that the whole complex of ideas that is Hindu-Buddhist art has a long history in that area. Even though we could not find a good comparable example of the motif that was of the right date, we felt justified in thinking that the motif was probably in use at that time.

Such problems would be much simplified, of course, if we had complete histories for both areas of every element we use for such comparisons. We must contend not only with uneven preservation but also with incomplete archeological knowledge and incomplete publication, plus the difficulty of finding the materials that are published.

A somewhat different problem is that of having comparable elements that appear to be too early in the supposed donor culture. We find, for instance, that there are remarkable similarities between the fully developed Tajín or Classic Veracruz decorative style of A.D. 500–1000 and the Late Chou style of China of 700–200 B.C. Must we disregard such similarities because of the chronological difference? I think not; for there are various possible explanations. Contacts could have occurred closer to the time of the full development of the style in Asia, and it could have been maintained in wood-carving for hundreds of years before it appeared in stone in Veracruz. Or, as we know to be partly true, elements of Late Chou style continued into later dynastic periods and may have diffused at that time. Furthermore, the effective contacts could have been with a peripheral style in China that retained the full Late Chou pattern much longer than was the case in central China, where our known Chinese sequence obtains. Many complex problems arise, of course, in the attempt to equate ethnographically known traits that leave little or no archeological traces. Relative time depths must then be inferred from often meager evidence.

ARCHEOLOGICAL EVIDENCE AND CULTURE HISTORY

In our speculations on the possible role of transpacific contacts and their effect on the American Indian cultures, it would seem to be especially important to be aware of the great discrepancy that almost always exists between archeological evidence and culture-historical events. In other words, the nature of archeological evidence is such that only a small fraction of the history of any culture can be reconstructed from the remains of that culture. This becomes apparent when we look at the history of certain early civilizations, such as those of the Mediterranean and Near Eastern areas, where we have written records. From them we learn that the Egyptians had close trading relationships with other centers, but there is relatively little precise archeological evidence of those relationships. Without the written accounts, we would have no realization of the many specific events wherein interchanges of ideas must have taken place.

Returning to our wheeled toys for an illustration of what the implications of this principle might be, let us suppose that through a careful study we can make a good case for the Mexican wheeled toys as being a trait that was somehow transferred from Asia to America. This would be of great interest to all of us, but in some quarters it would be considered of merely esoteric value. Wheeled toys, it might be said, are of no real cultural importance; it would be different if the idea of the wheel had been introduced, along with the techniques of putting it to practical use, as a means of transport. As it is, the introduction of wheeled toys had no importance in materially affecting the growth and nature of Mexican civilization. All this might, perhaps, be true, but there is a further interpretation. If contacts did occur that were strong enough to have introduced the idea of wheeled toys, it is most probable that other ideas were also introduced for which we cannot expect to find concrete archeological evidence. Conceivably through the same contacts, which would have been at about the beginning of the Classic period (*ca.* A.D. 1), Mesoamerica may have received a set of ideas about the serpent cult that appears to have replaced in over-all popularity the role of the jaguar in the earlier Preclassic art. Perhaps significant ideas concerning the practice of irrigation, or of astronomy, or of the calendar may have been introduced. Certain ideas about divine kingship might also have been introduced, but these would be mainly lost to us except as they might be apparent in associated elements, such as the use of the umbrella or the litter as insignia of rank.

If we insist on being completely objective in our interpretation of archeological remains, we cannot go beyond the concrete evidence of a particular introduced trait, such as the wheeled toys. If we do, we enter into a realm of speculation that may easily carry us to extremes. We must agree, however, that some degree of this kind of speculation is a necessary part of a scientific attitude toward archeological evidence. The traits mentioned are examples of those great segments of any culture that can never be completely documented through archeology. It becomes evident that it is far from frivolous and unimportant to talk about wheeled toys as possible indications of transpacific contacts.

Under this heading we must also consider the matter of trade objects as indicators of culture contact. Critics of the idea that transpacific contacts could have occurred are prone to point to the fact that no Asiatic objects have been found in the New World. This is indeed true, but merely on the basis of the laws of probability we could not expect to find them, and, if we do, it would be an extraordinary stroke of good luck. One could point to the fact that despite the abundant evidence that is now accumulating that contacts between Peru and Mesoamerica were of fairly common occurrence, no trade objects from either have been found in the opposite area. The same is true in the case of the United States Southeast, where there is abundant evidence of influence from Mexico but where no single object of clearly Mexican manufacture has ever appeared as a documented find. [EDITORS' NOTE: Cf. Sears, pp. 274 ff. re "Long-Nosed Gods."]

Finally, it must be mentioned that in any culture area that is poorly known archeologically it is easy enough to believe that the cultural developments in that area are local developments. Thus in the past we have thought that southwestern United States culture was a largely independent growth, and Mesoamerica and the Andes, except for the holding in common of certain cultivated plants, were thought to be largely separate. With greater knowledge, however, and the more accurate adjustment of chronologies, we have come to see that many transfers between these areas did occur. With this in mind, we should be careful to beware of what seem to be independent developments; for certain traits that appear to result from evolutionary trends may indeed be the result of the intrusion of ideas from outside.

THE QUESTION OF ABSENCES

Another of the criticisms that is often heard and probably would be considered as one of the major arguments against the possibility that transpacific contacts might have occurred is that concerning certain *notable absences* of outstanding Old World traits in the cultures of the New World. There is the absence of the use of the wheel, of the true arch, of metallurgy in Mesoamerica at an early period, and of iron at any time, as well as a number of other special items. There is also the problem of the lack of the introduction of any of the more important Asiatic food plants or of domesticated animals.

These absences are undoubtedly significant, but in my opinion they have been greatly overemphasized. They do signifiy that no massive migration from Asia occurred and that there could have been no long and continuous and overpowering contact, but they fail to prove that *no* contacts occurred.

In a consideration of these absences it is most important to remember that the process of diffusion is primarily a process of one culture's making selections from such portions of another culture as are made available to it by contact. For this process to be complete, the items selected must be absorbed into, and adapted to, the purposes of the receiving culture. What is selected from a foreign culture is dependent on a multitude of factors that combine in innumerable ways, so general rules of how it can be expected to work in any given situation are almost impossible to make. It is certain, however, that the selection that is made from a foreign culture will be especially restricted if the donor and receiving cultures are distant from each other and if the contacts are intermittent. A very important factor is, of course, the one of the relative complexity or degree of general development of the two interacting cultures. Also, in this case of transpacific influence, there are the very practical problems of the mere transportation of such things as viable plant seeds or of domestic animals and, if some of those did arrive, of their establishment in the New World.

Because of the difficulty of establishing rules to apply to what might have happened in a process of long-distance diffusion to the New World, it seems to me absurd to point to the absence of such things as have been mentioned as proof that America was not influenced from afar. Again we might best look to specific examples for clarification. Certainly the true arch would have been known to the Khmer peoples of Cambodia through their connections with India and westward, if not through the brick tombs of the Han period. Even so, they chose to use the corbeled arch in their temples at Angkor, as did the Maya in Mesoamerica. We know that very close contacts existed between the Classic Maya and Teotihuacán, as well as with many other centers in the highlands and lowlands of Mexico. But the corbeled vault of the Maya was rejected in Mexico, as was in most places the erecting of hieroglyphic stelae. Relationships between Mexico and the southwestern United States were close enough, but the use of pyramid-temples did not diffuse in that direction to any degree. These are simple examples, but they point up the fact that the absences cited as proving the independence of the American civilizations must themselves be examined as carefully as the suggestions that they were influenced from Asia.

In discussions of what might be expected in diffusion situations it is often claimed that traits having obvious practical or economic uses are more readily accepted than are elements in the field of religion or in the arts that are religious expressions. This might be true in most cases, but there are probably many exceptions, and the New World civilizations may have been especially prone to the latter direction. It is amazing to me, for example, how the introduction of metallurgical techniques within the Old World led everywhere to the use of metal tools and weapons and caused a kind of economic revolution, but how in the New World metals continued for hundreds of years to be used almost exclusively for ornaments. In a very strange way these civilizations were remarkably conservative when it came to adapting or developing mechanical principles. It therefore seems perfectly in character that they did not take over the use of the wheel even if they knew its principle or were at one time exposed to the full idea of its use in transport.

Trait Complexes as Evidence for Transpacific Contacts

Long a basic argument against suggestions of transpacific influence in America has been the contention that the various cultural similarities that do exist are not only scattered in time and place but do not seem to form the complexes or patterns that should be expected if contacts did occur. We should expect, for instance, that if a particular landing place for transpacific voyages was established at some point, we would find there a concentration of Asiatic traits ascribable to a particular horizon, and this, it is claimed, would be adequate proof that contacts did occur. This we must agree is one of the best means of showing the existence of contacts, and it would be well to search out and see whether such complexes can be located.

While this is good procedure, we cannot hope that such precise localizations can often be found; for, unless contacts were far more intense and longer lasting than those now visualized, it is unlikely that actual colonies of Asiatics were ever formed in America. It is far more likely that small groups of persons (boatloads, if you will) landed at different places and moved inland to some of the major cultural centers. Whatever influences they may have had on the local cultures would have diffused out in various ways from those centers. If we assume, as I think we must, that there was fairly close and regular contact between most of the major centers, it is possible that certain of the introduced ideas or traits might have taken root more readily in some centers rather distant from where the primary contact occurred. It is easily conceivable, therefore, that there might have resulted a far more diffuse record of transpacific contacts than we have been expecting or hoping to find.

Once more we must employ an example to illustrate the point. We know from historical accounts from Europe and China that from about the time of Christ until the eighteenth century travelers went back and forth with increasing regularity between those areas and that transfers of many cultural ideas were made. Needham (1954) points to a number of mechanical and other techniques, including the compass, paper, printing blocks, and the crossbow, that found their way to the West, and there were probably many items of other kinds that took a similar path. We know of these historically, but, if there were no historical accounts, it would be very unlikely that we would ever be able to work out a history of this diffusion by archeological reconstruction. This example applies as well to our previous discussion of archeological evidence and culture history, but here I would make the particular point that it would be extremely difficult, perhaps impossible, to localize any one center or complex in the Western world that would help to prove the Chinese origin of these various traits.

Thus, while we cannot expect to find precise comparable complexes in the New and the Old World that will quickly prove that transpacific contacts did occur, we may be fortunate enough to find something of the kind. The pottery type found by Estrada, Meggers, and Evans (1962) at Valdivia in Ecuador, which closely resembles the Jomon pottery of Japan, is, in effect, composed of a complex of elements including form, decorative features, and surface finish that might prove contact. Also, the complex of Asiatic-appearing traits that Estrada and Meggers have reported from coastal Manabí in Ecuador (1961) is chronologically localized in the Bahía and Jama-Coaque phases of about the time of Christ and gives promise of pin-pointing a particular contact.

For Mesoamerica nothing of quite the same nature has as yet come to light, although a number of individual traits, motifs, and technical processes having varying degrees of resemblance to things Asiatic and appearing at different times have been pointed out. There can be seen in these, however, a certain patterning as regards their times of first appearance that suggests a sequence of relationships with Asia.

As yet no one has very seriously suggested an Asiatic origin for some of the major elements in the Olmec complex, but this is a likely prospect and should be studied in detail. It is of special interest because the Olmec culture appears at the present stage of knowledge to be the earliest of the high cultures of Mesoamerica and presents some extraordinarily sophisticated features for which no previous developmental sequence has yet been found. In a general way the Olmec culture would seem to have possible relationships to early bronze-age China, specifically, the cultures of the Shang dynasty dating from the sixteenth century B.C. to 1027 B.C. Not many trait resemblances are found, but one must look with suspicion at the great emphasis on the tiger motif in both Shang and Olmec art. It is of interest, as Heine-Geldern has shown in detail (1959b), that some of the most specific parallels to the mode of representing the tiger in Shang art are seen at Chavín in South America and that Olmec art and Chavín art are also undoubtedly related. There are, furthermore, the great interest and technical proficiency in jade-working among the Olmec and in Shang China that one can suspect of showing relationships, even though there are not much more than general similarities in the objects produced, except, perhaps, a few ceremonial implement forms.

The second vague complex of association with China that I tend to see in Mesoamerica is one that appears at the beginning of the Classic period, at about the time of Christ. I have compared in some detail the cylindrical tripod pottery form of Teotihuacán and related sites with the bronze and pottery vessels of similar form characteristic of the contemporary Han Period of China. The resemblance in form, including a conical lid with occasionally a bird ornament at the apex, the arrangement of the designs, and the use of mold-made ornaments are, in my opinion, highly suggestive of relationships. I postulate that this was the occasion of the introduction of the technique of the ceramic mold that was later extensively used in the manufacture of figurines.

Another element that might have come with the Teotihuacán pottery form is the so-called Classic Veracruz or Tajín interlace design that seemingly first appears, as Heine-Geldern (1959a) has shown, at Teotihuacán in the Teotihuacán II period. This is one of the most convincingly Asiatic traits in Mesoamerica. I also suggest that the fresco technique used in the decoration of walls, pottery, and probably a multitude of perishable items might have been derived from the lacquer technique that was so extensively used in Han China. Finally, I would add the wheeled toys that seem to have made their first appearance in Mexico at about this time.

The third Mesoamerican complex of possibly Asiatic affiliation is that which I have described as Complex A (1953). It consists of a number of motifs and elements in sculpture and architecture that appear in the Late Classic period at Palenque and other northern Maya sites and continue in the Postclassic at Chichén Itzá and in central Mexico. Included in this complex are such things as lotus panels, tiger thrones, the "tree of life" motif, phallic sculptures, and a number of others. None of these appear to have any relationship with things in China. The

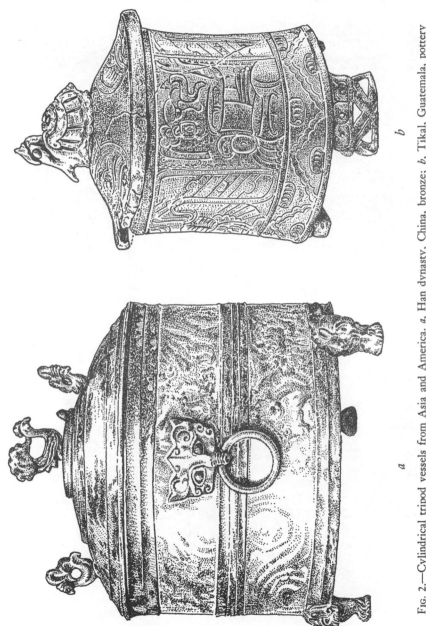

Fig. 2.—Cylindrical tripod vessels from Asia and America. *a*, Han dynasty, China, bronze; *b*, Tikal, Guatemala, pottery

b

a

Fig. 3.—Hierarchic figures from Asia and America, showing similar postures and holding a lotus plant. *a*, India; *b*, Palenque, Mexico.

direction of relationships has changed to focus on the Hindu-Buddhist civilization of India and Southeast Asia.

What we can see, therefore, *is* a kind of patterning within Mesoamerica of the various traits that seem to be Asiatically related. In the Preclassic and early Classic the influences would be from China, while in the late Classic and Postclassic they would come from the Hindu-Buddhist areas farther south. This is tentative in the extreme and is to be considered as a suggestion that can be validated only by many more comparative studies than have as yet been attempted.

How Could Transpacific Contacts Have Occurred?

A well-established rule in anthropology that applies to the question of diffusion versus independent invention is that diffusion can be inferred when the cultural similarities are complex and convincing and when there is an apparent opportunity for contact to have occurred. This last part of the rule is, of course, the great stumbling block to theories of transpacific influence. The Pacific Ocean is indeed a great barrier to human travel and the spread of cultures. If our cultural comparisons appear to be of significance, how did the civilizations of Asia come in contact with those of the Americas?

There are three possibilities: (1) direct transpacific sailings, (2) coastal navigation around the north Pacific, and (3) land travel through the Bering Straits region and down through North America.

Little direct evidence can be adduced for transpacific sailings. I can only observe, as Heine-Geldern and I have previously, that Chinese literary accounts refer on several occasions to rather extensive shipping in large boats in the Southeast Asia area at about A.D. 400. There was also considerable merchant shipping between Roman ports and India in the centuries immediately preceding and just after the time of Christ, but there is apparently no literary evidence of any extensive Chinese shipping until considerably later times.

In this matter of transpacific sailings one can only point to very tangential evidence and project a reasoned speculation that it might have occurred in early times. The magnetic compass was invented in China, but just how early it was applied to navigation is a matter of conjecture. There is the well-known ability of oceanic peoples, particularly the Polynesians, to make extraordinary voyages to landfalls on tiny islands, and this could reflect an origin in a more complex navigation tradition somewhere on the coasts of Asia. Also, the recent postulation of Edwards (1960) that the fore-and-aft sailing rig was in use on the rafts of Peru and Ecuador in Precolumbian times is a matter of great significance. The fore-and-aft rig is a special and complex device that in itself is impressive evidence of transpacific contact, to say nothing of its possibly providing a mechanism for transpacific sailings. The similarities of South American rafts to those of Formosa, as pointed out by Estrada and Meggers (1961), is also of special interest. Finally, if we can agree with Michael Coe that sea voyages between Guatemala and Ecuador are the best explanation of the cultural connections between those two regions, we might assume that sailing, in parts of America, was somewhat more advanced in ancient times than it was later in the sixteenth century. This last is a dangerous statement to make, however, for it will be claimed that we are relying on the disappearance of navigational skills as a prop for our argument that transpacific sailings did occur. I think, nevertheless, that navigation skills may very well have been something that for economic or historic reasons did decline before the Spanish Conquest.

In speculation on the possibility or impossibility of direct transoceanic voyages, it is often thought that such sailings must necessarily have been in the form of island-hopping and that we must expect to find archeological evidence of it on the islands, or memories of such voyages in the mythologies of oceanic peoples. However, if such voyages were single events—the sailings of individual ships from Asia to the Americas—it is quite possible that no islands would have been touched. The history of the Manila Galleon is most instructive in this regard (Schurz 1959) From 1565 until 1815, for a period of 250 years, one ship sailed in either direction each year between Acapulco and the Philippines. These ships were sailing under rigid instructions to go directly to their destinations, but it is a remarkable fact that they did not touch upon any of the Polynesian islands. They knew certain of the islands farther to the west, the Carolines and the Marianas, but had little to do with them.

The route of the Manila Galleon seldom varied. The westward voyage from Acapulco to the Philippines was southwestward from Acapulco to about the tenth or eleventh parallel and then directly westward. When a start was made at the proper time of the year, the voyage lasted about three months and was relatively easy because of the steady but mild trade winds. The eastward voyage was more difficult. The route was invariably to the northeast to about 30 degrees of north latitude and then eastward with the prevailing westerlies to make a landfall on the coast of California or Lower California. The eastward voyage was most easily accomplished in those northern latitudes, despite the difficulties that they entailed, and this is also evident from the fact that the winds and currents have caused many a disabled Japanese junk to be driven onto our Pacific shore. Such involuntary drift voyages may have been the means by which oriental peoples could have first learned of the New World. It is conceivable that survivors from such driftings might have found their way back to the Far East and instigated subsequent travel in that direction.

Coastal travel around the northern Pacific is a distinct possibility, but I know little of the practical difficulties that such a route would entail. Obviously, it would best be done in ships of sizable capacity so that there would be no need to land at frequent intervals. Once the route was known and landmarks established, it could be done without the more advanced navigational skills that would seem to be more necessary for direct crossings of the Pacific. Coastwise shipping was well established in early times in Asia and was engaged in by the Romans, the Indians, and, later, the Arabs, and it seems in some ways a more probable route from Asia to the Americas than direct ocean crossings.

As with transpacific crossings, coastal navigation would probably leave little archeological evidence of its having occurred, or at least so little evidence that we could not expect it to have been found up to the present time. Presumably, coastal navigators would have stopped at certain favored spots, but those landings would probably have been in the nature of forays for water or food. Touching a shore line so lightly and for such short duration of time would scarcely leave a discernible archeological record, and not having found any evidence of their passing is no proof whatsoever that such travels did not occur.

In a previous paper (1955) I pointed out that overland travel across the Bering Straits and down through North America is not as impossible as it may sound and could account for contacts between China and Middle America. It seems, however, that such travel by land is considerably less likely than travel by the sea routes, either coastwise or directly across the Pacific.

The comments I would make in countering a particular argument that has been directed against the idea of transpacific contacts will serve to bring this discussion to a close. If transpacific contacts did occur, it is held, one would expect that the proof would present itself more quickly than it has; with all the work that has been done in American archeology, it would seem that the evidence for such contacts would be more obvious and would fall into place far more readily; and we still do not have any sound proof that any transpacific contacts ever did occur.

Actually, the substance of this paper has been an attempt to counter this view. It is my contention that evidence for transpacific contacts is not likely to appear by itself. It will have to be assiduously sought out in a great many ways and in many places, and this will require the attention of numerous researchers over a considerable period of time. Such research, however, will be undertaken only when we begin to examine more fully than we have the premises on which we base our assumptions that the New World civilizations are independent. This, I believe, will lead to more thorough examination of the processes of long-distance diffusion and of the hints already at hand that transpacific contacts did occur.

BIBLIOGRAPHY

CASO, ALFONSO, M. W. STIRLING, S. K. LOTHROP, J. E. S. THOMPSON, J. GARCIA PAYON, and GORDON F. EKHOLM
    1946   "Conocieron La Rueda Los Indigenas Mesoamericanos?" *Cuadernos Americanos*, Año 5, 1:193–207.

EDWARDS, CLINTON R.
    1960   "Sailing Rafts of Sechura: History and Problems of Origin." *Southwestern Jour. Anthrop.*, 16:368–91.

EKHOLM, GORDON F.
    1946   "Wheeled Toys in Mexico." *Amer. Antiquity*, 11:222–28.
    1953   "A Possible Focus of Asiatic Influence in the Late Classic Cultures of Mesoamerica." Pp. 72–97 in MARION W. SMITH (ed.), *Asia and North America: Transpacific Contacts*. (Soc. Amer. Arch. Mem. 9.) Menasha.
    1955   "The New Orientation toward Problems of Asiatic-American Relationships." Pp. 55–109 in *New Interpretations of Aboriginal American Culture History*. (Anthrop. Soc. Wash. 75th Anniv. Vol.) Washington, D.C.

ESTRADA, EMILIO, and BETTY J. MEGGERS
    1961   "A Complex of Traits of Probable Transpacific Origin on the Coast of Ecuador." *Amer. Anthropologist*, 63:913–39.

ESTRADA, EMILIO, BETTY J. MEGGERS, and CLIFFORD EVANS, JR.
    1962   "Possible Transpacific Contact on the Coast of Ecuador." *Science*, 135:371–72.

HEINE-GELDERN, ROBERT
    1959a   "Chinese Influences in Mexico and Central America: The Tajin Style of Mexico and the Marble Vases from Honduras." Pp. 195–206 in *Actas del 33ra Cong. Internac. de Americanistas, San José, Costa Rica, 1958*. San José.
    1959b   "Representation of the Asiatic Tiger in the Art of the Chavín Culture: A Proof of Early Contacts between China and Peru." Pp. 321–26 in *Actas del 33ra Cong. Internac. de Americanistas, San José, Costa Rica, 1958*. San José.

NEEDHAM, JOSEPH
    1954   *Science and Civilization in China*. Vol. 1. Cambridge (England): Cambridge University Press.

SCHURZ, WILLIAM LYTLE
    1959   *The Manila Galleon*. New York: E. P. Dutton Co.

WAUCHOPE, ROBERT
    1962   *Lost Tribes and Sunken Continents*. Chicago: University of Chicago Press.

BETTY J. MEGGERS

North and South American Cultural Connections and Convergences

I N THE SUMMER of 1958 a small group of archeologists gathered
around a table in San José, Costa Rica, where a handful of potsherds
had been laid for comparison. The sherds were small and not particularly
colorful but bore decoration in faint bands of finger width that glittered
with an iridescent sheen. Some were from the coast of Ecuador;
others from the coast of Guatemala. Their similarity led the archeologists to conclude that direct contact had occurred between the
inhabitants of these two areas a millennium or more before the beginning
of the Christian Era. Analysis of associated elements in both areas
brought to light other parallels that served to verify and strengthen the
conclusion (Coe 1960). Although inexactness of dating permits experts
to disagree about the direction in which the influence traveled, few
would contest the fact that contact existed.

Not all comparative analyses result in such pleasing unanimity. Laymen—and even on occasion other anthropologists—are often confused
as to what kinds of similarities may be interpreted as indicative of
connections, since the theoretical premises on which the evaluation is
based are not made explicit. Furthermore, extraneous factors sometimes
influence a decision that should be based on the evidence alone, as is
the case in the opposition to recognition of transpacific contact because
of the assumed barrier represented by the Pacific Ocean. Arbitrary as
a conclusion may sometimes appear, comparative analysis is based on

BETTY J. MEGGERS, research associate, Smithsonian Institution, holds a Ph.D. in
anthropology from Columbia University. Her anthropological interests are broad, and she
is the author of numerous publications in both archeology and ethnology, especially with
reference to South America and the subject of cultural evolution. She has also contributed
to the field of anthropology through generous efforts in various administrative positions in
professional societies. She and her husband, Clifford Evans, have done extensive field research
in archeology in South America. They were jointly given the Washington Academy of Sciences Award for Scientific Achievement in 1956.

a body of theoretical information and a series of unspoken premises, which an anthropologist employs in arriving at his decision. It will be appropriate to summarize the most important of these as an introduction to discussion of some of the cultural connections and convergences that may be observed between North and South America in pre-European times.

Let us examine in more detail the question of the iridescent painting mentioned above. This was discovered first on the coast of Ecuador, where it appears suddenly in the archeological sequence, without apparent antecedents, in association with ceramic elements widely distributed in Mesoamerica and Peru on the Formative horizon. The possibility that it was locally invented has been discounted on the basis of the peculiarity of the technique and the excellence of execution, which do not seem congruent with experimental efforts. Since this type of decoration was unknown in neighboring Peru, where potters of great skill experimented with a variety of methods of decoration, the conclusion seems warranted that it is not something so appropriate to the working of clay that it would be readily discovered in the practice of the ceramic art. Incision, punctation, and painting with red, by contrast, seem to have been repeatedly and independently resorted to by primitive potters to embellish their wares.

Three criteria—uniqueness of the trait, absence of local antecedents, and absence of functional causality—constitute three of the principal considerations on which a judgment of connection between two or more occurrences is based. A fourth criterion was fulfilled after the discovery of the existence of pottery with the same decoration on the coast of Guatemala, and this is the presence of other elements held in common. In other words, there was duplication of a complex of traits including not only pottery decoration but also unusual vessel shapes and other kinds of artifacts. Although it is sometimes held that duplication of single traits in widely separated areas may result from independent invention, the coincidence of a complex of similar traits generally tips the balance in favor of assuming some connection on the ground that independent invention, in two or more places, of several unique traits without functional association is beyond the limits of reasonable probability.

While rare and complicated techniques of pottery decoration, such as painting after firing, with a variety of colors or cutting out portions of the surface and filling them with red or white pigment, are readily categorized as elements whose presence in two regions is probably indicative of diffusion, other traits are less easily evaluated. When we consider types of decoration like punctation, incision, and corrugation, our tendency is to discount their value for showing connection on the ground that they are simple and widely distributed, which we interpret as indicative of repeated independent invention. In this we may be correct; on the other hand, we may be too conservative, and the techniques may not be as obvious as we tend to believe.

The functional objection to inference of cultural connection is most readily observed in non-material culture. Sociopolitical organization, for example, is a function of population density, reliability of food supply, and various other factors, and it cannot be diffused directly. Similar kinds of social structure, such as slavery, monarchy, or military organizations, develop independently and apparently inevitably (other things being equal) when the cultural context is appropriate. Other traits represent adaptations to similar environmental settings, such as the pit houses of northwestern Argentina and the southwestern United States or the bark canoes of the Amazon Basin and the eastern Woodlands of North America. People living in similar kinds of environments, having similar needs for protection from the elements and possessing comparable degrees of technological skill, are likely to stumble upon similar methods of solving problems of survival, resulting in parallels possibly as specific as those considered indicative of diffusion but failing in the criterion of absence of functional causality.

With this introduction, let us proceed to the examination of some of the cultural similarities that exist between North and South America. Among these are the clues used by archeologists to reconstruct the prehistory of the New World from the first peopling, marked by the distribution of lithic industries from North America to Tierra del Fuego, to the introduction of metallurgy from the west coast of South America in late pre-European times. The criteria are purely archeological, and the conclusions derive from geographical distribution and from relative temporal position of the various traits in local sequences. In most cases the areas under investigation are adjacent, and gaps in trait distributions are easily accounted for by inequalities of preservation or insufficient field work.

Two other kinds of parallelism may be distinguished: duplication of constellations of traits among primitive groups living at opposite ends of the New World and duplication of elements in the cultural development of areas far removed from each other. These two forms of parallelism share the characteristic that they occur in the interior of continents rather than on the seacoasts, being rare or absent in the intervening area, so that they seem not to fit the usual kinds of explanation resorted to by anthropologists. The traits are too unusual to be the result of independent invention and too widely separated to seem the result of diffusion from one center to the other. Yet they must be accounted for in any consistent theory of cultural development.

The first type of parallelism—that involving the presence of a number of unique traits among surviving primitive groups in northern North America and southern South America—was the subject of considerable investigation a few decades ago (Cooper 1941; Ehrenreich 1905; Nordenskiöld 1910, 1912, 1931). Nordenskiöld, in particular, devoted much effort to the identification of traits prevalent among the marginal or non-agricultural groups of the Gran Chaco, Patagonia, and Tierra del Fuego in southern South America and also among North American wandering tribes but rare or absent in the intervening area. The majority of the traits in question are not essential to survival and hence not explainable as independent adaptations to similar subsistence exigencies or community patterns. Among the sixty-four traits tabulated by Nordenskiöld (1931) are such items as the sweat house; embroidery on leather; three-feathered arrows; fish glue; fire-making with pyrite and flint; sewed bark vessels; smoke signaling; taking of scalps; several types of games, such as a form of hockey, ring-and-pin, and games of chance using dice. Other investigators have pointed to striking correspondences in puberty rites (Loeb 1931), in religious concepts (Schmidt 1929), in musical style (von Hornbostel 1936), and in folklore (Métraux 1939), the latter including adventures of a trickster.

The conclusion to which these researchers have come has been well expressed by Cooper (1941):

> These numerous and specific cultural resemblances between the marginals of the far north and far south of America appear to be satisfactorily accounted for on no other hypothesis than that of tarriance from early pre-horticultural days with partial retention of pattern. On this hypothesis, in very early—not necessarily the very earliest—human time on the continent, an archaic pre-gardening culture with a considerable common inheritance and a considerable measure of uniformity would have prevailed very widely or perhaps universally or well-nigh universally over both North and South America. Later, a good 2500 years ago and probably earlier, [there] rose in the more central regions of the continent horticulture and other more advanced arts, and spread outward, far and wide, replacing, overlaying, and swamping out the earlier archaic culture, but not diffusing over the total continental area. The far northern and far southern regions lay beyond the limits of these diffusions, as did also a number of more remote and isolated enclaves within the broad central area. Here, relatively undisturbed, have persisted the externally and internally marginal cultures these twenty-five or more centuries, retaining in part their ancient pattern.

If we grant the reasonableness of this conclusion, we can project these elements of non-material culture backward to the preagricultural complexes found archeologically throughout the Americas. This possibility not only enormously increases our understanding of the kind of life led by these early people but gives us some insight into the stability that seemingly inconsequential cultural traits may possess and leads to questions about why this should be the case. Relatively little work has been done in this field, but certain explanatory factors seem likely (cf. Swadesh 1951). The surviving traits concentrate in non-material aspects of the culture, which nourished the mind but did not encumber the body under the exigencies of wandering life. It has been demonstrated that traditional forms of behavior provide a feeling of security in time of crisis, and such psychological factors would favor retention of ritual elements. Games are well-known outlets for aggressions provoked by close living but not permitted direct expression. Other elements may have persisted because they were well suited to the general cultural organism of which they form part or because of little-understood mechanisms of learning (Bruner 1956). This whole problem is intriguing and significant and deserves far more attention than it has thus far received.

Turning to adjacent regions in both North and South America brings us to another problem in cultural connections and convergences. Portions of the southwestern United States are so similar environmentally to portions of northwestern Argentina that photographs cannot be distinguished. The buttes and plateaus, rocky cliffs, talus slopes, dry washes, semidesert climate, and even the appearance of the vegetation are almost identical. It has been pointed out that some of the cacti and sagebrush are closely related botanically. What is remarkable, however, is not the environmental similarity but the cultural resemblances. The following quotation, for example, is applicable to parts of the United States Southwest (Gonzalez n.d.):

> At the beginning of this period . . . communal pit houses were used extensively, without stone walls or floors. . . . Later, there develops a form of habitation consisting of smaller rectangular houses with stone floors or walls built on the surface of the ground. The final stage is characterized by the appearance of towns of up to 250 or more rooms situated on more or less protected hills or mesas, with or without defense walls. The rooms have stone walls and are arranged in a variable plan but typically in irregularly agglutinated complexes.

It nevertheless describes, not the Southwest, but rather the region of Valliserrana, northwestern Argentina, during the Belén-Santamaria period. Resemblances between these two areas also occur in artifact inventory: stone mortars and metates, grooved stone axes, sandstone abraders, small stemmed projectile points, bone awls and gouges, copper bells, coiled and checker-woven basketry, knotted netting, and crudely modeled pottery figurines with punctate decoration on the forehead. These items are not merely similar; they are practically identical in form and construction (Figs. 1–2). Additional striking resemblances

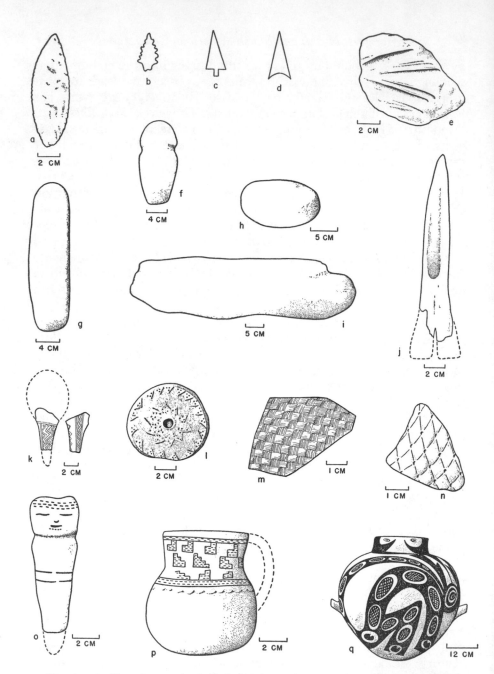

Fig. 1.—Artifacts from archeological sites in northwestern Argentina. *a*, Stone blade (after Palavecino 1948, Fig. 39-12); *b–d*, Projectile-point types (*op. cit.*, Fig. 39-7); *e*, Awl polisher (*op. cit.*, Fig. 39-10); *f*, Grooved stone ax (*op. cit.*, Fig. 39-1); *g*, Sandstone polisher (*op. cit.*, Fig. 39-11); *h–i*, Grinding or rubbing stones (*op. cit.*, Fig. 39-14); *j*, Bone punch (*op. cit.*, Fig. 39-3); *k*, Pottery ladle (*op. cit.*, Fig. 38-2); *l*, Pottery spindle whorl (*op. cit.*, Fig. 38-4); *m*, Checker-work mat impression on pottery (*op. cit.*, Fig. 38-6); *n*, Net impression on pottery (*op. cit.*, Fig. 38-6); *o*, Pottery figurine (*op. cit.*, Fig. 38-5); *p*, Pottery pitcher (*op. cit.*, Fig. 38-1); *q*, Pottery jar with horizontal strap handles (after Serrano 1958, Pl. 25-1).

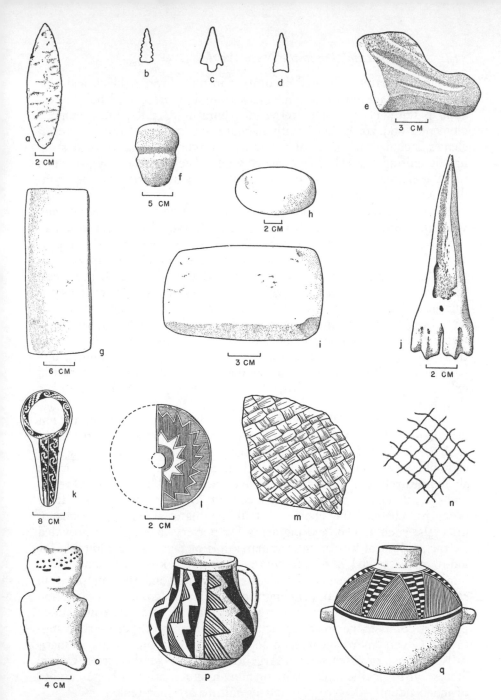

Fig. 2.—Artifacts from archeological sites in the southwestern United States. *a*, Stone blade (after Judd 1954, Pl. 28-j); *b–d*, Projectile-point types (*op. cit.*, Pl. 73B-f, k, j); *e*, Sandstone awl-sharpener (*op. cit.*, Fig. 32); *f*, Grooved stone ax (*op. cit.*, Pl. 70-d); *g*, Sandstone tablet (*op. cit.*, Pl. 27-c); *h–i*, Rubbing or grinding stones (*op. cit.*, Pl. 25-f, i); *j*, Bone punch (after Kidder 1932, Fig. 172-a); *k*, Pottery ladle (after Judd 1954, Pl. 61-e); *l*, Wooden spindle whorl (*op. cit.*, Fig. 42-b′); *m*, Checker-work matting (after Mera 1938, Pl. 15A); *n*, Netting (*op. cit.*, Pl. 19B); *o*, Pottery figurine (after Kidder 1932, Fig. 84-i); *p*, Pottery pitcher (after Hough 1914, Pl. 9-2); *q*, Pottery jar with horizontal strap handles (after Gladwin 1957, p. 244, *lower left*).

exist in the pottery. Painted decoration in polychrome (black-and-red-on-white), black-on-white, and black-on-red is present in both areas, and, in both, geometric patterns incorporating parallel lines, stepped elements, and zones filled with hachure are typical. Common vessel shapes include such unusual forms as a pitcher with a vertical strap handle uniting a tall slightly concave walled neck with a short, rounded body, a canteen-like globular jar with two low-set horizontal loop handles, and a spoon or dipper.

In view of recent arguments for contact between Mesoamerica and western South America, or between the New World and Asia, one may wonder why this remarkable parallelism has not been similarly emphasized. The traits involved are as unique and complex as those used to make other interareal comparisons, and most have at best a scattered distribution in the intervening area. Whatever the reasons for this lack of attention, the result is that the case is not one on which sides have been taken. It can therefore be discussed somewhat more objectively than some other cases of parallelism, and the various considerations involved in the analysis of such instances can be examined dispassionately. No attempt will be made to deal with the material exhaustively; probable or possible explanations will be noted rather than thoroughly explored.

Let us begin with the environment. Although environments do not determine cultural traits, they offer a series of possibilities that men with similar needs and capacities may exploit in similar ways. For example, extremes of heat and cold in the semidesert climate make shelter desirable, as well as some form of clothing. The scarcity of trees, and the abundance of rocks of convenient form and size spalled from outcrops, channel the choice of building material. Certain kinds of minerals, such as clay and pigments for pottery-making, are provided by the geological formations. Similar kinds of fauna are exploitable for hides to be sewed into garments with similar kinds of bone awls. Similar kinds of grain and wild seeds are available, and their preparation requires similar forms of grinding tools. The problem of transportation and conservation of water is best solved with globular, narrow-necked jars that combine maximum capacity with minimum exposure to evaporation. Given environments as much alike topographically and climatically as those of northwestern Argentina and the southwestern United States, with specific limitations for human exploitation, a large number of independently derived parallels in culture are inevitable.

There remain, however, a considerable number of items that seem to have no environmental adaptation and for which other explanations must be supplied. Since non-adaptive traits as specific as black-on-red painting, for example, are generally presumed until proved otherwise to be linked by diffusion, this avenue must be explored. Two general categories of diffusion may be distinguished: that deriving from the spread of preagricultural peoples throughout the continents, mentioned earlier, and that emanating from the centers of higher civilization in Nuclear America. Some of the basic technologies shared by northwestern Argentina and the southwestern United States, such as chipped-stone projectile points, grooved axes, techniques of basketry and netting, are undoubtedly traceable to a common ancient heritage, since these are also widely distributed in other parts of the Americas and are archeologically documented as having considerable antiquity.

An argument can be made for mutual derivation of certain other traits from Nuclear America. The technique of pottery-making is the most obvious member of this category, since, although its exact place of origin is still a matter of uncertainty, it has been shown that pottery-making reached the southwestern United States from Mesoamerica and moved into Argentina from Bolivia and Peru. In the nuclear area, interchange of ceramic information began in the Formative period prior to the first millennium B.C., and techniques of red and white slipping and painting in one or more colors are widely employed at an earlier time than their appearance at either extreme. Thus, the similarities in ceramic style, as far as technique and motif in decoration are concerned, can without difficulty be traced to parallel influence from the adjacent centers of higher culture.

A similar origin can be attributed to the small copper bells. It has been shown that copper objects came into the southwestern United States from Mexico, apparently principally the product of interareal trade (Pendergast 1962). In all Mesoamerica, metalworking is late, and appears at places and in contexts that imply an introduction from the south. The appearance of metallurgy in northwestern Argentina has been traced to Peru and Bolivia (Gonzalez 1963). Thus, both the technique of working copper and the form of the artifact are traceable ultimately to a common source. This diffusional pattern is later than, and independent of, that distributing the ceramic similarities, and the reconvergence of the two distributions is therefore a product to some extent of chance.

A few common characteristics that cannot be explained either by environmental influences or by diffusion are the product of the developmental process in culture. Into this category falls the similar pattern of increase in settlement size, as evidenced by the development from small stone houses to large multiroom structures. In both areas, experience brought more efficient agricultural techniques, increased harvests, and a more reliable and more abundant food supply. These, in turn, permitted larger population concentrations and made possible the improvement of arts and crafts and the amassing of forms of wealth. As these luxuries caught the eye of less favored and more nomadic neighboring groups, people in both areas found it necessary to take defensive measures, reflected in hilltop locations and inclosing walls. Added to the likeness in building materials, these factors resulted in constructions of remarkably similar appearance.

The identification of parallels resulting from environmental adaptation, diffusion, and trends inherent in the process of cultural evolution leaves very little unaccounted for. Two exceptions that come to mind are the small pottery figurines and the pitcher vessel shape. Close examination shows both these to have a range of variation in which few specimens incorporate all the mutually held characteristics. Given the relative cultural complexity of the two areas involved, it is not stretching probability too far to suggest that these two items may have been independently invented. This conclusion is strengthened by the fact that neither appears to occur in the intervening area, as well as by the complete absence of any other indication that direct contact ever existed between northwestern Argentina and the southwestern United States in the pre-European period.

By way of introducing the subject of connections between Mesoamerica and northwestern South America, it might be well to mention one other aspect of the United States–Argentina case that could be used to discount the existence of direct connections. This is the fact that the traits exhibiting close resemblances do not in general occur together; on the contrary, they are present at different times and in different local archeological complexes. This factor was suppressed in the preceding analysis because, although it has been widely cited as an argument against the existence of contact, it is not necessarily relevant as examination of the evidence for prehistoric Mesoamerica-Ecuador connections will show.

The first indications of direct contact between Mesoamerica and Ecuador occur during the early Formative period (Coe 1960; Evans and Meggers 1957; Meggers and Evans 1962), when the effective cultivation of maize appears to have been introduced from the north. Following this interval, during which a number of types of pottery decoration and vessel shapes were exchanged, there appears to have been a relatively long period of isolation. At the present time, at least, there is no clear-cut evidence on the coast of Ecuador of any Mesoamerican introductions between about 1200 and 500 B.C. This was a period during which maize agriculture spread over the coast and into the highlands, bringing in its wake sedentary village life. The foundation was gradually laid for regional variation and cultural elaboration, both characteristic of the period that followed.

By about 500 B.C. in coastal Ecuador, local complexes had become clearly differentiated both in material culture and in inferred level of sociopolitical development. The most advanced occupied the central and northern coast, corresponding to Manabí and Esmeraldas provinces, where, at about this same time, Mesoamerican traits again begin to appear. In Mexico the counterpart of this contact is observable in the form of new elements of South American appearance (Borhegyi 1959–60; Evans and Meggers n.d.). How intensive this intercommunication was, and how extensive were its effects, are questions yet unsatisfactorily answered—not only because of the incompleteness of our knowledge of local complexes and sequences in both areas but also because of the transformations wrought on exchanged elements by receiving cultures, producing a result sometimes subject to interpretation as convergence or independent invention.

Another problem confronting evaluation of the evidence is the lack of coincidence in distribution of many of the traits. For example, shaft and chamber tombs, copper "ax money," figurine molds, and elbow pipes are earlier in Ecuador than in Mexico, but in neither area are they all represented in a single archeological complex. Conversely, ornamental inlaying of the incisor teeth, stamps or seals of pottery, and construction of burial mounds appear centuries earlier in Mexico than in Ecuador, but once again they seem independently distributed in both time and place. Numerous other similarities have been noted between the two areas, such as the presence of pottery figurines with movable limbs; figures tied to beds; post-fired painting in green, yellow, black, and white; three-pronged incensarios; mirrors of pyrite and obsidian; realistic and fantastic masks of pottery; warrior figures with feather costumes and headdresses provided with a diamond-shaped opening for the face.

None of these elements can be explained as adaptation to similar environmental possibilities, nor does their particular form satisfy a universal human need. Diffusion from a common source in the intervening area is ruled out by the fact that few of the traits occur in Central America or Colombia and, when they do, are apparently later than in either Mexico or Ecuador. While one or two striking resemblances might be explained as convergence or independent invention, several dozen cannot be so construed without destroying the entire theoretical framework within which anthropologists operate. The conclusion suggested by these similarities is consequently that direct contact between the two areas must have existed, that this contact lasted over a long period of time, that the points of origin and destination fluctuated, and that the possibilities for cultural diffusion varied with the tastes of the individuals who made the trips (cf. Willey 1955; Porter 1953).

Other traits widely distributed over both North and South America tell other stories about contact, diffusion, and the possibilities for convergence and divergence in cultural development. The rubber-ball game is one that has been studied (Stern 1948). Others, such as the manufacture of bark cloth and the use of the blowgun (Riley 1952), deserve more thorough investigation than they have received. Attention has been called to similarities in complexes with non-continuous distributions, such as those between Olmec and Chavín art (Kidder II, Lumbreras, and Smith 1963), between ceramic styles from the middle Amazon and the lower Mississippi (Palmatary 1939, 1960), or between the general cultural configuration prevalent in late pre-European times in the southeastern United States and the Caribbean Coast of South America (Steward 1947). The significance of these parallels is not yet clear, nor is that of the duplication of such traits as the cog stones of Archaic coastal shell middens of southern California and Chile (Iribarren 1962); castellated rim-form pottery vessels from the northeastern United States (Holmes 1903; MacNeish 1952) and the Valdivia culture of coastal Ecuador (Estrada 1961); or the corrugated surface-finish on jars of the Tupi-guaraní culture of southern Brazil and the Anasazi culture of the United States Southwest. Whether these represent convergent developments, influence from a common source, or direct contact, the conclusion is significant for a complete understanding of cultural development in the New World (cf. Goggin 1949).

The evaluation of cultural similarities is a difficult task, one that depends upon the differential weighing of a variety of factors. Judgments have too often been made on irrelevant bases, as, for example, the objection that investigators of transpacific contact are weary of hearing: "How can it be explained that in all pre-Columbian America there was no such thing as a wheeled vehicle?" (Means 1916). Or the comment too often heard even from anthropologists: "Being an optimist and humanist, I prefer to believe that genius can arise, through the infinite genetic variability of man, in any setting . . ." (Coon 1962). Proof does not consist in finding a series of sites linking one occurrence with the other or of identifying actual objects traded, although such evidence is useful in reconstructing the manner in which contact was achieved and maintained. Comparative analysis is founded on a set of theoretical principles that must be objectively applied to each case. It is an unusual ability to seize upon significant evidence that makes it possible for certain individuals to suggest connections overlooked by their co-workers, and not simple accident or luck, as it so often appears to the layman. Since it looks so easy, the literature is flooded with pseudo-scientific attempts to show connections, making anthropologists more wary than they need be about engaging in such analysis themselves (cf. Wauchope 1962).

Nevertheless, to penetrate into the lives of our predecessors is one of the most fascinating challenges that confronts us. We are less interested in the details of how they shaped their tools and built their houses than in knowing something about the horizons that confined their world. How did they feel, what did they believe, where did they go, and what did they find? Our imaginations are attracted by the idea that people from Asia may have landed on the shores of the New World several millenniums before Christ (Estrada 1961) or that colonists moved from the highlands of the northern Andes down the Amazon to face the same problems that confront European colonists there today (Meggers and Evans 1958), or that seafaring Ecuadorians engaged in long-range trading expeditions not unlike the Phoenicians of the ancient Middle East. Whether our interest stems from a need to forget the overwhelming complexities of today's world, or from a desire to rescue from oblivion people like ourselves who contributed to the culture we inherit, or from a wish to know that people of whatever time or place, whatever culture or race, are motivated by similar needs and aspirations is not really important. Solving the mystery of man's past is among the most exciting problems that confronts us, and the opportunity to assist in its solution is among the most rewarding aspects of being an anthropologist.

BIBLIOGRAPHY

BORHEGYI, STEPHAN F. DE
1959   *Pre-Columbian Cultural Connections between Mesoamerica and Ecua-*
-60   *dor.* (Middle Amer. Res. Inst. Pub. 18; Middle Amer. Res. Records, Vol. 2, Nos. 6 and 7.) New Orleans.
BRUNER, EDWARD M.
1956   "Cultural Transmission and Cultural Change." *Southwestern Jour. Anthrop.*, 12:191–99.
COE, MICHAEL D.
1960   "Archeological Linkages with North and South America at La Victoria, Guatemala." *Amer. Anthropologist*, 62:363–93.
COON, CARLETON S.
1962   *The Story of Man: From the First Human to Primitive Culture and Beyond.* 2d ed. rev. New York: Alfred A. Knopf.
COOPER, JOHN M.
1941   *Temporal Sequence and the Marginal Cultures.* ("Catholic Univ. America Anthrop. Ser.," No. 10.) Washington, D.C.
EHRENREICH, P.
1905   "Die Mythen und Legenden der südamerikanischen Urvölker und ihre Beziehungen zu denen Nordamerikas und der Alten Welt." *Zeitschrift für Ethnologie*, Vol. 37, Supplement.

ESTRADA, EMILIO
  1961   *Nuevos elementos en la cultura Valdivia*. (Publicación del Sub-Comite
         Ecuatoriano de Antropología, Instituto Panamericano de Geografía
         e Historia.) Guayaquil.
EVANS, CLIFFORD, and BETTY J. MEGGERS
  1957   "Formative Period Cultures in the Guayas Basin, Coastal Ecuador."
         Amer. Antiquity, 22:235–47.
  n.d.   "Relationships between Mesoamerica and Ecuador." In ROBERT
         WAUCHOPE (ed.), *Handbook of Middle American Indians*, Vol. 5. In
         preparation by Middle American Res. Inst., Tulane Univ.
GLADWIN, HAROLD S.
  1957   *A History of the Ancient Southwest*. Portland, Me.: Bond Wheelwright
         & Co.
GOGGIN, JOHN M.
  1949   "Plaited Basketry in the New World." *Southwestern Jour. Anthrop.*,
         5:165–68.
GONZALEZ, ALBERTO REX
  1963   "Cultural Development in Northwestern Argentina." In *Aboriginal
         Cultural Development in Latin America: An Interpretative Review*.
         ("Smithsonian Misc. Coll.," Vol. 146, No. 1, pp. 103–29.)
  n.d.   "Las etapas de desarrollo cultural en el N. O. Argentino y sus posi-
         bles vinculaciones con las areas arqueológicas vecinas de Chile y
         Bolivia." Manuscript.
HOLMES, W. H.
  1903   "Aboriginal Pottery of the Eastern United States." *Bur. Amer. Ethn.*,
         20th Ann. Rpt., 1898–99. Washington, D.C.
HOUGH, WALTER
  1914   *Culture of the Ancient Pueblos of the Upper Gila River Region, New
         Mexico and Arizona*. (U.S. Natl. Mus. Bull. 87.) Washington, D.C.
IRIBARREN CH., JORGE
  1962   "Correlations between Archaic Cultures of Southern California and
         Coquimbo, Chile." *Amer. Antiquity*, 27:424–25.
JUDD, NEIL M.
  1954   *The Material Culture of Pueblo Bonito*. ("Smithsonian Misc. Coll.,"
         Vol. 124.) Washington, D.C.
KIDDER, ALFRED V.
  1932   "The Artifacts of Pecos." *Phillips Academy Expedition Paps.*, No. 6.
         New Haven, Conn.
KIDDER, ALFRED II, LUIS G. LUMBRERAS S., and DAVID B. SMITH
  1963   "Cultural Development in the Central Andes—Peru and Bolivia." In
         *Aboriginal Cultural Development in Latin America: An Interpretative
         Review*. ("Smithsonian Misc. Coll.," Vol. 146, No. 1, pp. 89–101.)
LOEB, E. M.
  1931   "The Religious Organizations of North Central California and Tierra
         del Fuego." *Amer. Anthropologist*, 33:517–56.

MacNeish, Richard S.
1952 *Iroquois Pottery Types: A Technique for the Study of Iroquois Prehistory.* (Natl. Mus. Canada Bull. 124; "Anthrop. Ser.," No. 31.) Ottawa.

Means, Philip A.
1916 "Some Objections to Mr. Elliot Smith's Theory." *Science*, 44:533–34.

Meggers, Betty J., and Clifford Evans
1958 "Archaeological Evidence of a Prehistoric Migration from the Rio Napo to the Mouth of the Amazon." Pp. 9–19 in Raymond H. Thompson (ed.), *Migrations in New World Culture History.* (Univ. Ariz. Soc. Sci. Bull. 27.) Tucson.
1962 "The Machalilla Culture: An Early Formative Complex on the Ecuadorian Coast." *Amer. Antiquity*, 28:186–92.

Mera, H. P.
1938 *Reconnaissance and Excavation in Southeastern New Mexico.* (Amer. Anthrop. Assoc. Mem. 51.) Menasha, Wis.

Métraux, Alfred
1939 "Myths and Tales of the Matako Indians (The Gran Chaco, Argentina)." *Ethnologiska Studier*, 9:1–127. Göteborg.

Nordenskiöld, Erland
1910 "Spiele und Spielsachen im Gran Chaco und in Nordamerika." *Zeitschrift für Ethnologie*, 42:427–33.
1912 "Une contribution à la connaissance de l'anthropogéographie de l'Amérique." *Jour. Société des Américanistes de Paris*, n.s., 9:19–25.
1931 "Origin of the Indian Civilizations in South America." *Comp. Ethnog. Studies*, No. 9. Göteborg.

Palavecino, Enrique
1948 "Areas y capas culturales en el territorio argentino." *Gaea, Anales de la Sociedad Argentina de Estudios Geográficas*, 8:447–523. Buenos Aires.

Palmatary, Helen C.
1939 "Tapajó Pottery." *Ethnologiska Studier*, 8:1–136. Göteborg.
1960 "The Archaeology of the Lower Tapajós Valley, Brazil." *Amer. Phil. Soc. Trans.*, n.s., Vol. 50, Part 3. Philadelphia.

Pendergast, David M.
1962 "Metal Artifacts in Prehispanic Mesoamerica." *Amer. Antiquity* 27: 520–45.

Porter, Muriel Noé
1953 *Tlatilco and the Pre-Classic Cultures of the New World.* (Viking Fund Pub. Anthrop., No. 19.) New York.

Riley, Carroll L.
1952 "The Blowgun in the New World." *Southwestern Jour. Anthrop.*, 8:297–319.

Schmidt, W.
1929 *Der Ursprung der Gottesidee*, Vol. 2, Part 2. Münster.

Serrano, Antonio
1958 *Manual de la cerámica indígena.* Editorial Assandri, Córdoba.

STERN, THEODORE
    1948   *The Rubber-Ball Games of the Americas.* (Amer. Ethnol. Soc. Monog.,
          No. 17.) New York.
STEWARD, JULIAN H.
    1947   "American Culture History in the Light of South America." *South-
          western Jour. Anthrop.,* 3:85–107.
SWADESH, MORRIS
    1951   "Diffusional Cumulation and Archaic Residue as Historical Explana-
          tions." *Southwestern Jour. Anthrop.,* 7:1–19.
VON HORNBOSTEL, E. M.
    1936   "Fuegian Songs." *Amer. Anthropologist,* 38:357–67.
WAUCHOPE, ROBERT
    1962   *Lost Tribes and Sunken Continents: Myth and Method in the Study of
          the American Indians.* Chicago: University of Chicago Press.
WILLEY, GORDON R.
    1955   "The Interrelated Rise of the Native Cultures of Middle and South
          America." Pp. 28–45 in *New Interpretations of Aboriginal American
          Culture History.* (Anthrop. Soc. Wash. 75th Anniv. Vol.) Washing-
          ton, D.C.

MORRIS SWADESH

Linguistic Overview

C HANGES in language are on the whole so slow that relationships
are often obvious even when related languages are mutually unintel-
ligible. Anyone who comes to know two or more languages that have
diverged from a common form within a period of about two thousand
years can recognize their similarity and realize that they are in some
sense kin. For example, if anyone endowed with ordinary human judgment knows some English, German, Italian, and Spanish, he certainly
can detect that the first two and the last two go together. But, unless he
is a skilled comparative linguist, he will not see the ancient similarities
that bind all four together and are traceable to a common origin about
six or seven thousand years back. The fact that scientists have discovered this unquestionable truth is partly due to the fact that they have
been able to use in the comparison such ancient forms of the common
Indo-European language phylum as Latin, Greek, and Sanskrit and that
some of the languages have closer ties with each other because of contacts after the group began to separate. For instance, present-day
English and Spanish, when tested with a quantitative index of their
vocabularies, show the equivalent of only about four thousand years of
divergence. Otherwise, it is doubtful whether early techniques of
linguistic science would have discovered relationships going back as
much as sixty centuries.

When one applies these ideas to America, it is clear why many
linguistic relationships in America were detected by the first explorers,
missionaries, and traders and why others were discovered in the nineteenth and early twentieth centuries by pioneer scholars. The great

MORRIS SWADESH, research professor in the Instituto de Historia of the Universidad
Nacional, Mexico City, received the Doctorate of Philosophy in Linguistics from Yale
University. He has carried out extensive linguistic field research on Vancouver Island, in
Louisiana, and among various peoples of Mexico. His writings have made important contributions to the theory and method of linguistics. Of special interest to archeologists are his
writings on techniques of linguistic analysis useful in reconstructing history and on the
subject of languages of the American Indians.

effort along these lines came at the turn of the century, when Major Powell and his associates achieved an over-all classification of the languages of North America that has stood up in large part down to our own day. However, the students who continued to work in American languages, including some who took part in the Powell survey, subsequently discovered, besides a few simple corrections at certain points in the total picture, many new hints of deeper relationships. Since then, American comparative linguistics has continued to advance, often by bold leaps, followed later by lingering doubts, which even led at times to efforts to deny the new insights altogether.

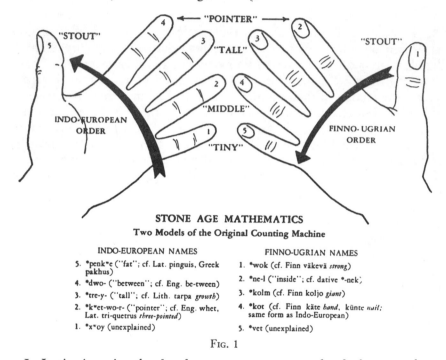

STONE AGE MATHEMATICS
Two Models of the Original Counting Machine

INDO-EUROPEAN NAMES

5. *penkʷe ("fat"; cf. Lat. pinguis, Greek pakhus)
4. *dwo- ("between"; cf. Eng. be-tween)
3. *tre-y- ("tall"; cf. Lith. tarpa *growth*)
2. *kʷet-wo-r- ("pointer"; cf. Eng. whet, Lat. tri-quetrus *three-pointed*)
1. *xʷoy (unexplained)

FINNO-UGRIAN NAMES

1. *wok (cf. Finn väkevä *strong*)
2. *ne-l ("inside"; cf. dative *-nek)
3. *kolm (cf. Finn koljo *giant*)
4. *kot (cf. Finn käte *hand*, künte *nail*; same form as Indo-European)
5. *vet (unexplained)

Fig. 1

In Latin America the developments came more slowly because there never was any single bold survey, like that of Powell, but in its essentials the history of study was similar. Many relationships were recognized early by the first soldiers, priests, and settlers; others came later through the work of scholars. The model of the Powell classification and some of the later syntheses often served as the basis for guiding the theories of those who worked in the southern part of this hemisphere, and this led, even more than in North America, to bold leaps and later uncertainties.

The hesitations and pessimism of some modern scholars stand in sharp contrast to the vision and hopes of some of the earlier scholars who, like Thomas Jefferson, gave as the great reason for studying American languages that this would lead, by comparison with the languages of the Old World, to knowledge of the origin of the men of the New World. Were these men unduly optimistic? Did they expect more of science than it can give? Before we make any affirmative answer, let us note that not a few scholars today show a new confidence in the possibilities of relating the languages of America among themselves and with those of the Old World. This confidence comes in part from encouraging experiences of those who have worked long and hard on difficult problems of relationship to eventually find solutions for many seemingly unyielding points of detail. It comes also in part from experimentation with new methods of dealing with large masses of data, such as the use of indices obtained with selected samples of evidence and the employment of data-processing systems. Perhaps the hopes of the early scholars will yet be richly fulfilled.

Whether large or small, the capabilities of comparative linguistics for solving the most difficult problems of prehistory are nonetheless important because they add a dimension to archeological research. That is, even aside from the possibility of solving the difficult problems of deep time-level research, at least its capacities for the more recent periods ought to be utilized. Its possible functions, as amply proved in Europe but so far only to a limited extent in America, include establishing prehistoric links between different peoples and indicating the approximate time and place in which they once were located. Many specific features of the culture of the common period can also be determined from linguistic study. When this information is linked with the evidence of dirt archeology, new clarity can be gained. It is our purpose to indicate some of the ways in which linguistic prehistory sheds light on the past, both distant and recent.

THE ORIGIN OF AMERICAN LANGUAGES

The archeological date of man's first appearance in the New World has been pushed back, possibly to something over 30,000 years ago. Linguistic differentiation in America is great, but it probably is not great enough to require more than half the time given by the foregoing archeological date. That is, it is conceivable that the forerunners of the American Indians could have been speaking nearly identical dialects of a single language fifteen to twenty thousand years ago and yet, by the slow process of language change, have come by now to speak the approximately twenty-two hundred different languages known in historical times. Yet we do not assume that they spoke only one language at the time mentioned. On the contrary, some groups were already in the country and others were living in different portions of

Eurasia. If all the variations that could have developed in this time had actually been preserved, there probably would be more profound differences in the languages of the New World than we now find in all the continents. The inference, then, is that many languages have disappeared, including, presumably, all those belonging to the earliest waves of immigrants.

There is every reason to believe that man has had the use of language for hundreds of thousands of years, even though the earliest phases of it must have been much closer to animal communication than were the languages known in historical times. By 35,000 years ago, language had already developed to something very similar to present-day tongues. It must have already acquired that great characteristic that belongs only to human language, namely, local differences. Primitive food-gathering communities range over large territories, and language may consequently be the same over large regions. Perhaps such areas were not as great as some of the modern nations, but surely they embraced more than the small areas commonly found in those parts of America where subsistence agriculture developed. If we use the linguistic map of the New World at the time of contact as our base and exclude both the large areas of a few empires and the small enclaves just mentioned, we can get some idea of the amount of space that must have been occupied by languages of long ago. We may guess that there were only about eight hundred languages in all the world 35,000 years ago. These were probably all ultimately related but fell into about sixty different stocks. The mesh principle, by which geographically close groups tend to show closer linguistic affinity, must have applied in those days as today.

In the ancient times of which we are speaking, cultures must have been relatively uniform, but there were already some differences. Probably the highest development of production techniques and social organization was found somewhere around Asia Minor, while the peripheral areas were considerably behind. The first settlers to seep into the New World must have been far behind the most advanced groups of their day. In consequence, when later migratory waves followed, these had strong advantages over the first. Hence, it was possible for the first groups to be overwhelmed and absorbed by the later ones. With this absorption, there was a tendency to lose the earlier languages in favor of the later ones. This process could have gone on for a long time, and this could account for the reduced variation in the languages of America and, indeed, of the whole world.

After thousands of years there came a time when America had a relatively numerous and stable population, whose culture could maintain itself in the face of new groups. It was possible to receive technological improvements and absorb, at times, the new immigrants who brought them. From this time forward the disappearance of earlier languages slowed down, and new languages did not necessarily take root. The last extant language to enter the New World was apparently the forerunner of Eskimo-Aleutian. This shows about thirty-five minimum centuries of internal divergence and a separation from Chukchian of Siberia in the neighborhood of fifty centuries.

We thus see the history of American languages as a long process, in which hundreds or thousands of dialects came in at different times. Sometimes the new groups found relatives already here. One way or another they interacted, often being absorbed by or absorbing their antecedents. Some time around 15,000 years ago languages that were already here began to be strong enough to resist amalgamation with those arriving later. About 5,000 years ago they had definitely reached the point of absorbing newcomers.

There is no reason to believe that everything about the first groups was lost. Leaving languages for the moment, we can mention a hereditary biological trait, the Diego blood factor, now mainly present in Carib. Indians, which was probably brought in by some of the first settlers. The Carib-speaking population today constitutes a secondary area for this trait. The suggestion is that the original Diego-bearing population was not Carib-speaking at all but was later absorbed by various groups, the trait remaining most concentrated in regions later dominated by Carib. In similar fashion, New World variants of some very old cultural traits may have passed down from the first settlers to later groups. It is likely also that words of the first languages are still used today. It is conceivable, though by no means a simple matter, that such words will eventually be identified by their pattern of occurrence in the later languages.

It would be interesting to suggest which of the present-day languages of America may have been the earliest of those still preserved, but the answer can come only from a well-constructed classification of all the languages; this task will require a great deal of systematic work. In terms of my tentative classification, one might guess that the oldest of the languages still extant might be three relatively isolated groups of South America, the Tinigua, the Omurano, and the Nambicuara. The next arrivals (first in North and later in South America) may have been the group we have called Macro-Carib, including the Gê Indians. The next great group was Macro-Arawakan, then Macro-Quechuan, then Macro-Mayan, which still occupies most of North America, and, finally, a portion of the Bask-Dennean group, which includes four American stocks, Kutenay, Wakashan, Nadennean, and Eskaleutian, but which is otherwise distributed throughout Eurasia.

What is important to understand about the movement of languages

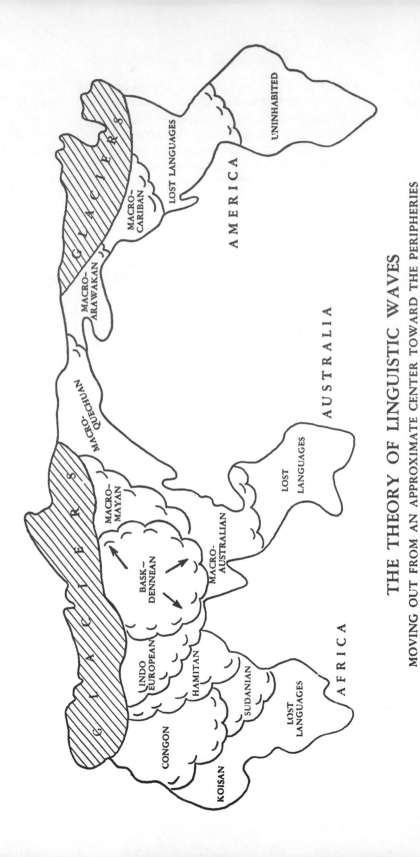

THE THEORY OF LINGUISTIC WAVES

MOVING OUT FROM AN APPROXIMATE CENTER TOWARD THE PERIPHERIES
HYPOTHETICAL SCHEME ABOUT 25,000 B.C.

Fig. 2

into the New World is that many separate groups must have entered and that all were in a constant state of slow change before, during, and after their entrance. Many new languages have come into being by the splitting-up of older units, and, at the same time, many dialects and languages have been lost, particularly by absorption, whether by relatives or strangers. The total result of constant movement, of differentiation and absorption, is such as to present at all times a great network of interrelationship, sometimes with small and sometimes with large breaks as one passes from point to point. Moreover, the linguistic network that spreads through America is merely a continuation, linking up across Bering Strait, of that which spreads through the entire world.

The Nature of the Evidence

Some may imagine that the large over-all picture presented of language prehistory for many thousand years back is a matter of pure speculation, lacking proof. In point of fact, a part of it is based on already achieved scientific demonstrations of extremely high confidence levels. The rest represents a theory that attempts to fill in the gaps and to provide a framework for future research.

The bedrock of comparative linguistics is found in the laws of language change demonstrated over a hundred years ago. One of the key principles is that of the regularity of phonetic change. If a phoneme of a language is modified in a certain way in any given word, it tends to change in exactly the same way in every other word that has the sound in a similar phonetic environment. This means that it is possible to set up phonological equations, satisfied by large numbers of words. Wherever and whenever a language community has separated, so that the speakers in each part have lost contact with those in the other, phonetic changes could have gone different ways in each. In one an old sound may have remained as it was, while it underwent one or more changes in the other; or there might have been different changes in each of them. Because of the principle of regularity, it is possible to trace common words in such related languages, and so to find out, thousands of years after the separation, that they had a common history.

As everyone knows, truth in science is not considered to be absolute but is a matter of varying degrees of probability. If one calculates, for example, the chances that English *horn* may be similar to Latin *cornus* by sheer accident, the odds against chance prove to be about 1 to 4,000. If one then asks for the chance factor involved in some hundreds of old words (aside from all the borrowings) that agree between English and Latin, it is one in many millions, and it is millions of times more improbable if one takes into account all the other languages that make up the group called Indo-European: Celtic, Germanic, Baltic, Slavic,

Greek, Armenian, Iranian, Indic, Hittite, etc. In sum, then, without speaking of absolute truth, we can be extremely sure that languages like English and Latin, along with scores of other languages of Eurasia, were once a single language. By quantitative indices in linguistics and through archeology, we know that their common period must go back at least about seven thousand years.

The kind of inference about original identity made regarding the Indo-European languages has also been made, on the basis of similar evidence, with many other linguistic families or stocks throughout the world. Our problem, then, is the interrelationship of these known groups.

A procedure used in the last several years with interesting results is that of exploratory sampling with a diagnostic word list. It operates with one hundred selected items of basic meaning, the kind of expressions that everyone acquires, regardless of specialty and education, and that include body parts, simple objects of nature, bodily actions and movements, some simple qualitative and quantitative notions, etc. We know that such closely related languages as English and German have about 70 per cent of common items in the test list and that such distantly related tongues as English and Latin agree in about 30 per cent. We can say that any two languages that show 25 per cent or more of common vocabulary may be considered as promising subjects for a linguistic comparison. If several languages show such agreement of each to each, the case is particularly favorable, since it gives the possibility of multiple focus.

When this exploratory test was applied to different cases, many previously unsuspected sets were found that offered possibilities for deeper study. One of them was at the point of geographic contact between America and Asia, namely, between the Eskaleutian languages on this side and the Chukchian languages on the other. Having blocked out the area, we proceeded by standard linguistic comparative procedures, except that we used punch cards in a special data-processing system intended to make the work more rapid and more thorough. In the course of this work, we discovered the kind of phonological equations already referred to and large numbers of examples confirming them. To illustrate the results, we present several examples of words satisfying the equations (Table 1). It will be seen in the examples that the meanings, though similar, are not always identical. This also agrees with established linguistic principle, to the effect that meanings are subject to gradual change by extension and transfer of semantic associations. To illustrate this with a parallel in Indo-European, one may cite English *thumb*, related to Latin *tumor*.

To complete the study, an examination of inflections and word formations was made with respect to the two language families. A large number of general and specific agreements in these matters confirmed the indications of relationship shown by the cognate words. Favorable percentages of agreement were found to connect many of the established families and stocks, and it is on this basis that we feel some confidence in speaking of the interrelationship of all the languages. The follow-up research has varied with each case, but it is to be hoped that the next several years will see the definitive solutions that are required.

TABLE 1

PROOF OF COMMON ORIGIN BY STRICT PHONOLOGICAL EQUATIONS
(Illustrated with Chukchian-Eskaleutian Examples)

a) Kamchadal *p* = Chukchi *p* ═══ Aleut *h* = Eskimo *p*

Ch. **palqat**- *old*	E. **palaq** *bad, miserable*
Ch. **pang-at**- *feels tired*	A. **hangi-na**- *difficult*, **hang-u-ga**- *pilies*
Ka. **ple-z**- *scrapes*	E. **pilaa**- *cuts with knife*
Ch. **pue**- *soot*	A. **hwa**- *soot*
Ka-Ch. **pamya**- *stockings*	A. **hamga**- *stockings*
Ch. **pir-i**- *carries*	A. **hid-u-sa**- *carries away*
Ch. **pic̷k-ew**- *gets accustomed*	E. **pitq-u-siq** *custom*
Ka. **p'ag-cuc** *boy*	E. **pag-niq** *buck*

b) Kamchadal *m* = Chukchi *m* ═══ Aleut *h* = Eskimo *m*

Ch. **maglal**- *rider*	A. **hagu**- *load*
Ka. **manzin** *palm*, Ch. **maneg**- *cloth*	E. **manig**- is *smooth*, A. **hani**- *lake*
Ka. **mazamaz** *summery*	E. **masa**- *sun*
Ch. **mayo**- *hill*	E. **mayuq**- *climbs slope*

There is another important scientific principle that seems to be abundantly demonstrated in the explorations. It is one that was known in the last century as the "wave principle" but that is probably better described as the "mesh principle." It refers to the fact that languages that are spread out over extensive areas tend to develop local varieties, which normally show greater similarity between close than between distant points. This is obviously due to differences in the amount of contact, so groups that are in communication to some extent tend to retain the same old expressions or to adopt the same new ones. There is no sharp difference between speech forms in contact and not in contact, but there are degrees of intercommunication everywhere, varying from indirect and slight to direct and saturated. When local dialects move apart and develop more and more profound differences in the course of time, they still tend to reflect the old network of relationships that characterized them when they were subdivisions of the same speech community. The effect of this principle on comparative linguistic research is that we may expect to make successful studies of language A with language B, then B with C, and so on, where it would be extremely difficult to compare A with N directly. An example is seen in

TABLE 2

EURASIAN-AMERICAN LINGUISTIC RELATIONS SHOWN BY FINN-KWAKIUTL COMPARISONS

Eurasian Parallels	Finn	Meaning	Kwakiutl	American Parallels
Mongol kelen Gilyak hilx Greek glōtta English call	kiele	*tongue*	k'l-m	Yuk Eskimo ulu Haida khiłqa (*language*) Kutenai kłee- (*to name*)
Magyar ki Turk kim Latin quis English who	kuka	*who*	ʔn-kwa	Hailtsuk ʔa-kwi Eskimo kina Nutka qui- (*what*) Zuni kwaʔ-pi
Turk gez Ainu ahkas Korean kạạr English go	kä-vellä	*walk*	qhas	Kutenai -qqaatsee- Takelma k'iyak Wintun q'aya Navaho -kaał
Vogul wit English water	vesi, vet-	*water*	'wa-p	Sahaptin watam (*lake*) Santa Cruz weto (*drink*)
Cheremiss kᵫc Tavgi katu English cat	kᵫnsi	*nails*	qets'-m	Navaho -kheš-kaan Quechua kicka (*barb*) Tarasco katsali- (*bite*)
Cheremiss tyestye Nanai tava (*fire*) English twinkle	tähti	*star*	t'ut'u	Nutka t'at'uus Chipewyan tθen Santa Cruz tawa (*hot*)
Vogul law	san-no-	*say*	nik'	Navaho ni Nutka nu- (*sing*)
Yurak soo (*gullet*) Latin sonāre (*sound*)	suu	*mouth*	sms(*swms)	Nutka -aq-suł Navaho -zeeʔ Haida su (*say*)
Magyar tool Magyar sør (*hair*) Turk sᵫy	sulka	*feather*	ts'lk	Eskimo suluk Navaho ts'os Nahua tolli (*rushes*)
Mordvin korga Gilyak qhos English gullet	kaula	*neck*	q'uq'un'a	Eskimo quŋga-siq Kutenai -kookaak Navaho -k'os
Yurak tøhøri	tie	*path*	t'x-	Aleut taka-luq Tlingit te Totonaco tɨhiʔ
Ostyak tyety- Japanese tatta- English stick	seiso-	*stand*	tlaxw-	Chinuk -txw Nisenan diki Quechua chaki (*foot*)
Nanai ulikse German leich (*corpse*)	liha	*flesh*	ʔls	Aleut uluq Kutenai -ułaks Yokuts lak'in (*belly*)

discovering the link between Eurasian and American languages. Here we have been able to compare Wakashan (Kwakiutl and Nutka) with Eskaleutian, the latter with Chukchian, this latter with Uralic and Altaic, and both these with Indo-European.

As a further illustration of the possibilities of comparison, we present thirteen words out of the hundred-word diagnostic list that evidently show agreement between Kwakiutl, of British Columbia (Canada), and Finn, of northern Europe. That these are no mere accidental agreements is suggested by the fact that parallels are found for each item, both in Eurasia and in America (Table 2).

THE TRANSPACIFIC QUESTION

A few decades ago, Rivet astonished students of American prehistory by presenting evidence for linguistic relationship first between Malayo-Polynesian languages of the Pacific and the Hokan languages of North America and later between those of Australia and the Chonan group of South America. In both cases, he supported his stand with sets of similar words on either side of the Pacific in sufficiently large quantities that it was difficult to explain it all away as pure chance. Various scholars tried their hands at attacking the evidence, but the only serious charge was that Rivet may have searched too many languages to bring together his examples and that they perhaps did not represent greater than chance expectancy after all. But the arguments did not ring entirely true. The same may be said of Dixon's suggestion that the similarities were too close to represent the end product of long periods of divergent development. The strongest argument set against Rivet was indifference, since the bulk of United States linguists merely shrugged and said among themselves that it could not be; thus they broke off communication with those who were persuaded by the evidence.

A few years ago, we undertook to set up objective measures that might test once and for all whether the Rivet materials were to be taken seriously. The hundred-word test list mentioned earlier seemed to be an appropriate device for this. Lists were obtained in four Australian languages from different parts of the subcontinent and were lined up not only with Ona (chosen to represent the Chonan group) but also with scattered other languages in America, including Quechua, Tarasco, Zuni, and Wintun—a spread from southern Chile to central California. Percentages of agreement from about 8 per cent to about 12 per cent were found. In such lists of words, the chance factor may be calculated mathematically and tested experimentally, say by taking a hundred words of two languages at random and giving them pretended meanings belonging to the hundred-word diagnostic list but selected by some chance procedure. If one uses a criterion of similarity more or less appropriate in real language comparison, it turns out that about 2 or 3 per cent of agreements might result from the play of chance. Adding a margin for safety, if in a test one finds more than 5 per cent, this should represent some factor other than accident. This test was met by all the Australian-American pairs that were matched.

Do we then confirm Rivet's theory that Australians came across the sea about five thousand years ago and were the ancestors of the Chonan Indians? No, because the percentage of agreement in that case should be somewhere close to 30 per cent. Furthermore, for the theory to be correct, the test should have come out positive with Chonan but not with Quechua, Zuni, and Wintun. Our conclusion, then, has to be that the concordance is due to a common prehistory for all Australian languages and all Indian languages. This may go back to the time when both were located in Eurasia and need not represent anything closer than the relationship of either American or Australian languages with Eurasian languages. These matters have yet to be studied in proper detail.

Though it turns out that neither Australian nor any other language of the Old World that might have come across the Pacific has lived on in the Americas, this does not prove that there were no transpacific contacts. A number of archeological traits, several common agricultural plants, and certain features of calendars represent parallels that could hardly have come about either by pure chance or by migration across Bering Strait. If there has been diffusion of any sort, there is every reason to suppose that some loan words must also exist. A number of concrete similarities can be mentioned, like the following:

TABLE 3

Aymara **kumar** *sweet potato* (also N. Quechua)	Maori **kumara** *sweet potato*
Muchik **op** *sweet potato* (also S. Quechua apichu)	Oceanian **kape, ape,** etc. *taro*
Antilles **mahu** *hibiscus*	Oceanian **mau** *hibiscus*
Mapuche **toki** *stone ax, chief*	Maori, etc. **toki** *ax, strike*
Quechua **Tupak-Yupanki** *an Inca*	Mangareva **Tupa** *legendary captain from the east*
Nahua **teo-tl** *god*	Greek **theo-s** *god*
Maya **lamat** *calendrical sign: Venus*	Hebrew **lamed** *alphabetic sign*

The first five examples are cited by Rivet; the last two come from other sources. Each is a separate problem. The best case for borrowing, of course, is that in which we have knowledge of the specific contact of the peoples concerned, with specific information of the first use, as is true, for example, of many Latin and French borrowings into English. We can, however, infer borrowing between unrelated languages by certain types of evidence, such as similar form and meaning; absence of similar forms in related languages on one side of the comparison, presumed to be the receiver; phonetics at odds with what is usual in the borrowing language. Some of the examples cited (Table 3) seem to meet these criteria. One of them even has some aspects of historical support in the story of Tupak-Yupanki, who, in Quechua tradition, led an expedition of hundreds of balsa rafts over the sea, returning in nine months. The Mangarevans, on their part, also have a legend about a visit by a large party on rafts led by a chief called Tupa. The fit is so complete as to give strong confirmation both of the historical event and of the preservation of the name on the far side.

The word for *sweet potato* in Aymara and Maori meets several criteria of evidence for borrowing: the full agreement in meaning and the essential agreement in form; the fact that the word is widespread in Oceania but is found only in a few geographically close dialects on the American side; the fact that words with three consonants, the last of which is not a formative suffix, are not typical of Quechua and Aymara.

Maya **lamat** is also fairly convincing. The meanings are not identical, but they have a strong point of contact in the fact that the Semitic alphabetical names, *ox*, *house*, *camel*, etc., appear to be derived from zodiacal names. Also, the Hebrew word fits the triconsonantic pattern of the language, while the Mayan word falls somewhat outside the usual. Still, the comparison can by no means be considered proved. Perhaps future studies on both sides will sufficiently clarify the issues to indicate whether borrowing is or is not tenable.

The word given for *hibiscus* appears to be a reasonably good comparison, but the detailed information given is insufficient for judgment. There is a suspicion that two sets of varying forms covering a variety of plants on each side may have happened to coincide at some point. This suspicion can be resolved or confirmed by detailed information and careful study.

The case of Nahua **teo-tl** *god* is also strongly suggestive, although it leaves one to wonder how Greeks in particular might have reached America. Perhaps the transfer took place indirectly. The main point in favor of the connection is that languages related to Nahua do not generally have an abstract word for *god*. Nahua itself often uses another expression, **tekw-tli** *lord*, evidently related to Yaqui **tepwa** *to cut*, and represents the frequent transfer from the idea of *weapon* to the person who wields the weapon or who carries it as a sign of authority. However, before definitely accepting **teo-tl** as a loan from the Old World, it is necessary to note that the chief god of all the Utonahua peoples is the sun, called **toonal-li** in Nahua, **tau** in Huichol, **tahaneri** in Guarojío, etc. Evidently the Nahua word is a compound from *taho-na'a-l-li*, meaning originally perhaps *sun-warmth*; the first stem is related to Yaqui **tahi** *fire* and may be distantly related to Gothic **dags** *day*. It is quite possible,

A THEORY OF THE PEOPLING OF MEXICO

BASED ON LINGUISTIC DIVERGENCES

Legend:
- Oldest Agriculturists in central Mexico
- Earliest ex-nomads from north of Mexico
- Latest ex-nomads from north of Mexico
- Old groups of northern Mexico

MAYAN

MAYAN

TOTONACO

OTO PAMIAN

TARASCO

OAXACAN

MIXEAN

UTO AZTECAN

Fig. 3

or even probable, that the Nahuas formerly also had a shorter word for *sun*, which must have been ***too-tl** or ***too-t**. If, then, they came into contact with outsiders from whom they obtained their present word for *god*, necessarily they would have associated it with a similar ancient word for *sun*. There is also a possibility that **teo-t** itself might be ancient, representing a variant form for *sun*.

The case of Muchic **op** and Quechua **apichu** for *sweet potato* is difficult to defend. The similarity of the form cannot be denied, but the meaning is not the same. Moreover, the root has the earmarks of a well-known ancient one, primarily ***kap,** as in Latin **caput** *head* and Greek **kapros** *goat*, but also with variants of the two first consonants, as English *gable;* one of the developments is loss of the first consonant, as in Latin **aper** *boar* and English *apple*. The general meaning is evidently *head*, *head-shaped fruit*, or *big-headed animal*. A thorough study would probably turn up hundreds of variants in many languages referring to different fruits, bulbs, etc.

A somewhat similar situation may be involved in Mapuche **toki** *ax*. Several authors have been struck by this case and, on investigation, have found similar words for *ax*, *weapon*, *cut*, and *poke* in many parts of the world. But such roots refer not only to weapons but also to trees, sticks and fingers, arms, erect position, and the act of placing or working, etc. Examples are English *stick, stake, tack, take, toe* (from ***doki**), *thatch*, Latin **tacere** *to touch*, Greek **tak-** (as in English *syntax*) *to put*, Nutka **tlaqa** *tree*, Nahua **tlaka-tl** *man*, Mayan **te'** *tree*, etc. The underlying forms and the general meanings of the American and Old World roots are so widespread that reconvergence of original common elements is possible in Mapuche and Polynesian.

It is evident that every specific problem of possible transpacific diffusion presents its own problems of proof. Up to now, the study has depended largely on chance observations. For the future, something much more systematic is to be desired. The best would be to make the search for loan words a normal part of a thorough system of linguistic comparison. In the course of a total study of the words in each American linguistic group, some items will be found that are relatively isolated. Among these one may seek elements that have strayed in from outside.

Languages of Long Ago

One of the products of linguistic comparison is the reconstruction of old languages dating back before the separation of the derived tongues. To do so for very ancient languages, going back so far that the descendents have often changed into very different forms, requires patient observation of signs of vestigial features in each group of languages that tie up with features of other groups. On this basis, we may draw some inferences about what languages may have been like fifteen or twenty thousand years ago.

Two types of roots existed, demonstrative and representative. The first type consisted of a single consonant followed by a vowel; the second, of two consonants, each with its vowel. The principal type of inflection was internal, made by reduplication (repetition of part or all of a root) and by internal changes of the component consonants and vowels. Reduplication, common in the ancient languages, has been narrowed down in English to several types of somewhat playful intensives and sound imitatives, like *goody-goody, tick-tock, swish-swash.* In ancient Greek and Sanskrit, it was used in certain tense formations. In many American languages, reduplication is a very important device, expressing the intensive, the repetitive, and the distributive, that is, the ideas of "very much," "again and again," and "here and there." Sound-imitative reduplication is found almost everywhere. Probably all the functions of reduplication that have been mentioned are old features.

There are traces of internal sound change also in English. Vocalic variation is reflected in the demonstratives *this* and *that,* differentiating near and distant location; in verbal stems, like *sing/ sang/ sung/ song,* the difference between present and past and non-verbal is shown. Of functioning consonant change, all that is left is the formation of pet names with the use of *l* in place of *r,* as in *Sally* from *Sara, Molly* from *Mary, Hal* from *Harold.* These examples give a small idea of the things that can be accomplished expressively by alternations of vowels and consonants and thereby may serve to clarify what language was like long ago. There is every reason to believe that the alternations were much more far-reaching. Besides indicating near and far, in space and time, apparently vowel change once represented physical form, as follows: the vowel sound *i,* more or less as in *stick,* expressed what was thin or pointed; the vowel *u,* as in *Lulu,* expressed cylindrical or round shape; vowel *a,* pronounced not as in *flat* but as in *father,* expressed what was flat or extended. One can give some examples of such words in English, but the old use must have applied to all words, so that, for instance, **piki* was a *pointed bone* or a *feather,* **puku* a *cylindrical or round bone,* **paka* a *flat bone.* However, there was no strong division between the names of things and actions, so that **piki* might also refer to thrusting with a point, **puku* with a round thing, **paka* with the flat. It is possible that this system does not exist anywhere today in the form in which we have reconstructed it, but ample evidence of its existence in the past has been found, for example, in Altaic, of Asia, and Wakashan, of North America.

In some languages there has been a change in function, as in Huave, where a front vowel represents a small thing or a brief action, and a back vowel, a large thing or abundant action. In some Altaic languages the difference between *i* and *a* marks a difference of sex, except that different languages of the group show opposite sex interpretations—for example, some think of the man as broad-shouldered and the woman as slender, others of the woman as broad in the hip and the man as thin.

As for consonantal alternation, it must be explained that many consonants had front, back, and central variants, and all consonants distinguished between simple, glottalized, aspirated, and doubled. Front and back variation, which we may call horizontal, referred to small *vs.* large, to bright *vs.* dull, to happy *vs.* sad. The other variations, which may be called vertical for contrast, had the following values: glottalized for lively, quick, bouncy, and active; aspirated for slow and steady, strong, heavy, or stationary; doubled for intensity. Now, intensive doubling still lives on in Semitic languages, and traces of all the other uses are to be found in various Eurasian languages, but the best examples are found in American languages. Chinuk expresses "small" by front consonants, presumably an archaic usage, but has also put glottalization to work in the same sense, evidently a natural extension of the idea of "lively." Glottalization is found for aorist or instantaneous, that is, for quick action, in Takelma and in Southern Paiute. The change of *n* to *l*, generally with intensive reduplication, is found in Sahaptin, where we can cite the name of the city Walla Walla, Washington, based on walawala *creek* as against wana *river.* Evidently *l* represents the front variant of *n* in many languages. These few examples will give some idea of the living indications of what must have been a main feature of human language. Traces live on in hundreds of languages of the world but have not yet been systematically studied.

The fact that many consonants were in horizontal and vertical alternation, means that there were only a few basically separate consonants, or archiphonemes. There were just ten, including *h* (which was used only in demonstratives) and nine others: *p, t, k, kw, s, m, n, y, w.* Since all vowels alternated with each other, there was only one vocalic archiphoneme, which may for convenience be spelled *e.* With nine consonants, used two to each root, the maximum total number of root forms was 9×9, or 81. Each of these could have several meanings, but even so, the number of independent roots was very limited as compared to languages of our time, even those belonging to the most primitive tribes. That this was evidently the basis of expression some thirty thousand years ago is consistent with the fact that the culture of those times was more elemental than that of any historic group. The gradual development of culture must indeed have placed a strain upon the old system, which was then extended in various ways. The simplest procedure was the use of compounds and derivatives, consisting of a pair of roots or of a root and a demonstrative, which more than squared the available number of operating units. Another device consisted in sacrificing all or part of the old inflexional alternations, giving separate meanings to the variants. These processes post date the period of unity of existing languages. The fact that different developments occurred in different areas is what accounts for the great structural variation in the languages of the world.

In efforts to compare widely divergent languages in the past, one of the great obstacles was the difficulty of getting the phonemes to match according to strict equations in the way that the comparative linguist requires in order to prove relationships. The clue to the problem is now before us. It is due to the old phoneme alternation, liquidated in different fashions in different regions in the process of stretching out the root inventory of the old-type languages. Having this key in our hands, we know that we may expect to find different old variants for the same or similar meanings, like English *stick*, Nutka **tlaqa-pt** *tree*, and Mayan **te'** *tree*, all based on the old archiform *teke but with three different variants: the English on *t'ek'o with an old *s* demonstrative as prefix, the Nutka on *taqa, the Mayan on *taq'i. The recognition of old alternations does not eliminate the possibility of finding exact variants but only warns us that they may show changed meanings. To give but one example, Nutka **tlaqa-pt** *tree* compares with Nahua **tlaka-tl** *man*, so called evidently because of his erect stance.

Old Concepts

One of the expectations in the reconstruction of a prehistoric language is to obtain hints about the environment and culture of the common period. This is a task for the future, which can be best accomplished by working back step by step, but it may be interesting to mention a few points. In mathematics, it is certain that Mesolithic man did not have fixed number words but may have already invented the system of using his fingers and of calling them by nicknames, perhaps like *tiny, inbetweeny, tallboy, pointer, fatty*. However, there were two directions used in counting, beginning with the pinky and going to the thumb or vice versa; and the nicknames varied a great deal from region to region. Perhaps side by side with this system, there was still in use an older and cruder one based on the arms instead of the fingers. The count was *this* and *these*, or *separate* and *both*, expressing the ideas of "one" and "two." There are still a few languages in the world whose counting is based on *two*, which express *three* as one and two, and *four* as *two* and *two*. It would take us too far afield to give all the detailed evidence for these reconstructions, but a little of it has already been published and more will be forthcoming when it has been more fully worked out.

In the area of religion, it seems possible that in earliest times there was no special word for *soul* or *spirit* but that these were identified with individual beings and objects of nature. The property of life was called *breath* or *warmth* or *movement*, and such terms sometimes came to represent the soul. The notion of *god* did not exist until social organization had advanced to the point of recognizing the authority of the elder or, still later, that of the owner or master. All these layers of conceptualization are found reflected in the languages of the world, and some of the specific references go back a long way. For example, the modern English word *soul* corresponds to an older **sawol**. It is evidently cognate with the Greek **hēlios** and Latin **sol** *sun*. The relationship is exactly like that of the Nahua **toonalli**, which means *sun*, *warmth*, and *personal spirit*, although built up with other roots. However, the Indo-European form we have mentioned is analyzable. The initial *s* is a prefix, probably of ancient demonstrative origin. What remains goes back to a form **hawe-lo,** evidently related to Latin **avus** *grandfather* or *ancestor*. It is evidently also present in the Nutka and the Maya words for *chief*, **haw'ilh** and **ahaw,** respectively. Variant forms of the underlying root included ***kewe**, ***khewe** (Indo-European ***ghewe**), ***k'ewe** (IE ***gewe**). Each of these can be illustrated in Eurasian and American languages: the first in Russian **svatóy** *holy* (from ***kwa-to-y**) and in Huave **kawish** *up*, the second in Gothic **guθs** *God*, the third in Maya **k'u** *god, holy*

PROBLEMS OF CLASSIFICATION

At the time of first contact with Europeans, there were about twenty-two hundred languages in the New World, many of them with more or less marked regional variations. Some, like Zuni, Yuchi, or Huave, are apparently isolated, but scientific study has discovered deep-lying similarities with other languages of the kind that show they were once, long ago, the same. Hence, they are lacking, not in relationships, but only in close relationships. In most cases, we find that each language has a whole gamut of kin, from very close to very distant. For the prehistorian, it is vital to know what languages are related in each degree. In fact, in the modern stage of archeology, equipped with many devices for dating the past, there is a need for a corresponding time scale in linguistic relations. This is satisfied to some extent by glottochronology, a technique already mentioned, which uses the percentage of common vocabulary in a diagnostic word list to obtain an index of divergence related to the time and degree of separation of two dialects or languages. In addition, various methods of quantifying or analyzing lexical, grammatical, and phonetic similarities help indicate relative degrees of relationship.

Despite all the old and new linguistic techniques available today, it is impossible to say with any assurance at this moment that our twenty-two hundred languages fall into just so many language families. There are two reasons for this state of affairs, one connected with the difficulty of agreeing on a scale of relationship within which we are to operate, and the other related to the amount of research needed to determine with accuracy the linguistic position of so many individual tongues.

It is noteworthy that Powell and his collaborators, who achieved a general classification of the languages north of Mexico into fifty-odd families at the turn of the century, were hardly aware of the problem of scale. For them, all the languages that could be shown to be related at all were considered to form a family. Later on, in the researches of Kroeber, Dixon, and Sapir, it turned out that many of the supposedly independent groups were related to one another. This eventually led to Sapir's classification of the languages of North America into six super-stocks, but this scheme in turn suffered the same fate. Sapir himself in his later years recognized the possibilities of certain intercrossings, and recently one linguist after another has become convinced that the old lines of division do not hold. In Central and South America, some eighty groups have been recognized more or less on the Powell scale, and there have been various suggestions of reductions reminiscent of the developments in North America.

Once it is granted that no firm classification is possible without a definite scale of relationship, there is still the problem of choosing between or reconciling the family-tree and the mesh forms of kinship. In the past, the majority of classifications followed the model of generational genealogies. Scientific linguists did not maintain that languages split neatly at well-spaced intervals, but it was considered by many that this was a sufficiently satisfactory model, so that one could overlook its inaccuracy. However, the attempt to reduce relationships to the tree form on a large scale often led to serious contradictions, for example, when a language can be classed equally well with two or more groups or when it is definitely closer to one particular language of a set than to the rest.

The mesh principle gives a more satisfactory explanation of all such contradictions. Instead of drawing family-tree diagrams, we show a two-dimensional scheme of points connected by different lengths of lines or one of boxes with different kinds of common boundaries. It can be objected that any such scheme suggests that the rate of differentiation of two languages is approximately the same through time, while in fact it sometimes happens that for a long time they remain in close contact and are later separated more fully, or vice versa. The upshot is that no kind of simplified classification or diagram is completely satisfactory. Any of them gives important help to the prehistorian if he will but bear in mind the limitations of the scheme as he proceeds in his patient effort to reconstruct the past.

It is of course possible to adopt a scale of relationship and work out the number of groups of languages in America according to it. Thus, Lamb deduces that, based on a time depth of six thousand years, there are twenty-six linguistic "orders" in North America and Mexico. Greenberg, evidently attempting to operate on a scale similar to, or perhaps greater than, that of Sapir, finds three phyla in South America. I have attempted several times, each time with a little more assurance, to arrive at a scaled mesh of relationships, but it will still be some years before it can be made with adequate reliability. As it stands at present, the languages of the Americas fall into 110 groups or isolated languages such that any part of one of them is separated by at least 41 "minimum centuries" from the closest language of the next group. If 41 m.c. is taken as the criterion, there are five extensive "phyla": "Bask-Dennean," which covers many Eurasian languages, plus Eskaleutian, Wakashan, Kutenai, and Nadennean, of North America; "Macro-Mayan," including the bulk of the linguistic groups of North and Central America, along with Chibchan and Tucanoan in South America; "Macro-Quechuan," which includes Zuni in North America, Tarasco in Mexico, and a number of groups in western South America; "Macro-Arawackan," which includes Timucuan of North America and many languages of the Antilles and South America; and "Macro-Cariban," which extends from the Antilles south. Besides, there are four isolated languages or groups that stand apart at the phylum level: Beothuk, in North America, and Tinigua, Omurano, and Nambicuara, in South America.

Several comments need to be added to the figures just given. First, most of the calculations on which they are based are highly tentative. Second, these calculations give us an index, not a direct measure; the index is of minimum divergence time and not of the full time since first separation. Third, it is likely that certain systematic errors are involved, including the factor of linguistic drift (pointed out by Shiro Hattori), which implies that all calculations fall short of the supposed time by up to about 50 per cent for periods around a thousand years, and less for longer times. There is also the distortion caused by the concentration of the more stable diagnostic items with the passage of time. Fourth, it must be remembered that the lexicostatistic method emphasizes the network pattern of linguistic differentiation; hence, its effect is not so much to count individual languages for past periods as to help reconstruct the network of relationships that existed formerly.

TABLE 4

EVIDENCE FOR TIMUQUA AFFILIATIONS WITH ARAWACKAN

Meaning	Timuqua	Arawackan
I, me	-ni-	Proto-Ar. *nu
this	ka-ki	Campa oka
	ora	Campa ora (*that*), Wapisana ulir, Achagua ruane, Lokono rihi
that	oka	Campa oka (*this*)
who	chita	Paraujano sheeta, Machiguenga tiana, Ipurina kata
what	tako	Machiguenga tata, Campa pai-ta
not	te	Campa -te, Machiguenga tera
woman	nia	Baniva neyawa
man	wiro	Proto-Ar. *hi-winari: Manao irinari, Siriana waychali
fish	kuyu	Bare ko-bati, Achagua ku-bai
blood	isi	Catapolitani iti
bone	yabi	Proto-Ar. *yahpuna: Achagua yahe, Wapisana bone, Galifuna abu
feather	me-tele	Paraujana ntina
head	chito	Machiguenga yito, Campa -ito, Catapolitani tuti
ear	tik	Lokono diki, Manao teki, Wapisana tai-n
drink	naku	Baniva nakurua, Proto-Ar. *nika (*eat*)
see	ene	Machiguenga nea, Campa neri
know	nakia	Bare nukakesa
come	pono	Machiguenga poka
sun	ela	Achagua eri
rain	uki	Proto-Ar. *wun-kia: Catapolitani uko, Lokono onia-kia
stone	yobo	Proto-Ar. *yipa: Manao ipa, Achagua iba, Bare d-iba
fire	taka	Wapisana tiker, Guapichana tikere, Piro chichi
night	ilake	Lokono orika-hu
kill	ikino	Campa -ākiri

MIGRATIONS

One of the strongest contributions of comparative linguistics to the study of prehistoric man consists in providing hints of movements and areas of dispersion of peoples. Studying the geographical location of the languages belonging to single group and the degrees of relationship between each pair among them makes it possible to infer their approximate center of dispersal and the movements by which the dialects spread. This can best be shown with an example, for which let us consider the Utonahuan (or Utoaztecan) languages.

This group consists of about thirty distinct languages, extending from the Comanche in Oklahoma and Texas to the Pacific Ocean and from the Monachi (or Northern Paiute) in Oregon and Idaho to the far outliers of the Aztec Empire in Central America. The distribution is almost continuous except that (1) the Comanche apparently moved away from traditional territory alongside their close relatives, the Shoshoni, after acquiring horses, which means in very recent times, (2) the Nahua language is found in scattered parts of Mexico and Central

America separated at a number of points from the main area of this tongue, apparently representing old garrisons or colonies of the Aztec Empire, and (3) there is a break in the north-to-south continuity of Utonahua in the southwestern United States, where Navahos and Apaches, on one side, and Yumas, to the west, form a large corridor across the territory.

Since there is adequate evidence of a historical nature on the first two points given above, our main problem is that of the break in the Southwest. To help solve this question, we have excellent linguistic informa-

SOME OLD UTO–AZTECAN
CULTURE TRAITS REVEALED BY
COMMON VOCABULARY

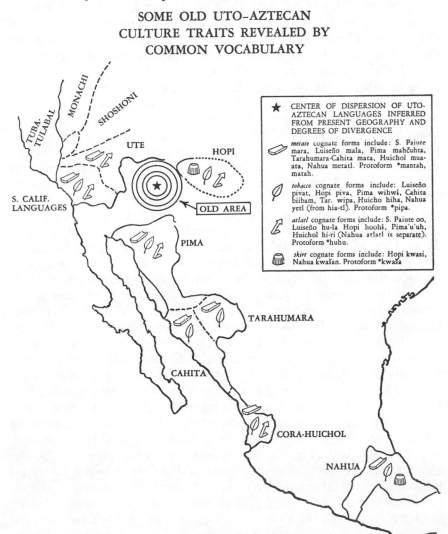

★ CENTER OF DISPERSION OF UTO-AZTECAN LANGUAGES INFERRED FROM PRESENT GEOGRAPHY AND DEGREES OF DIVERGENCE

metate cognate forms include: S. Paiute mara, Luiseño mala, Pima mahčuhta, Tarahumara-Cahita mata, Huichol mua-ata, Nahua metatl. Protoform *mantah, matah.

tobacco cognate forms include: Luiseño pivat, Hopi piva, Pima wihwí, Cahita biibam, Tar. wipa, Huicho hiha, Nahua yetl (from hia-tl). Protoform *pipa.

atlatl cognate forms include: S. Paiute oo, Luiseño hu-la Hopi hoohí, Pima'u'uh, Huichol hi-ri (Nahua atlatl is separate). Protoform *huhu.

skirt cognate forms include: Hopi kwasi, Nahua kwašan. Protoform *kwaša.

Fig. 4

tion, including complete tables of lexicostatistic divergence for most of the languages of the Utonahua complex (e.g., see Table 5), and we also have such information regarding Navaho-Apache and Yuma. One of the striking things seen in these figures is that Hopi, a Utonahuan island in the middle of Navaho-Apache, is geographically close to the Ute dialects but is linguistically a little closer to Serrano of California and to Opata and Tarahumara in Mexico. Navaho-Apache is a close-knit set of mutually intelligible dialects, forming essentially a single language. The Yuma dialects, which interrupt the continuity of Utonahuan, are also closely related, while the closest Utonahuan languages across this area are separated by about thirty minimum centuries of divergence. The implication of these figures, seen in relation to the location of the languages on the map, is that Navaho-Apache must have moved in and cut apart the Utonahuan continuum. The position of Yuma could be explained in two ways. Either it also expanded into its present territory or the Utonahuan languages, pushed by the Navaho-Apache, by-passed them to the north and south. The great divergence of the Utonahuan languages of California, and their respective divergences from the language north and south, suggests that they may represent refugees from the area of displacement. However, in addition, it seems likely that some Utonahuan languages were lost in the push, the people being either assimilated by the invader or cast together with brother tribes. We greatly miss in these calculations the data regarding several languages of northern Mexico, supposed to be Utonahuan, such as Suma, Jumano, Concho, Toboso, and Jova. One might guess that these may have been closer to Hopi than are any of the other languages of Mexico and that the exact figures would greatly clarify the picture.

We can turn now to further questions about the dispersion of the Utonahuas. First, in the north, the great spread of Monachi, Shoshoni-Comanche, and the Ute dialects is evidently something recent, belonging to the last eight centuries, more or less. Before that, this group may have concentrated around Nevada and Utah. To the south, the spread is evidently less recent but belongs within the last two or three thousand years. This is evident from the magnitudes of divergence, which are in fact less for all Mexico than for southern California. All this points to the fact that a thousand years before Christ the antecedents of modern Utonahua languages must have clustered around the Southwest of the present United States. Somewhere within this area must be the center of earlier spread. Since the greatest divergences of the family go back almost five thousand years or, allowing for systematic errors, perhaps six or seven thousand, there is still much to be ascertained if we are concerned about the very earliest times. Getting back thus far, the perspective merges with that of the Kiowa-Tanoan languages of New

TABLE 5

INTERRELATIONS OF THE UTONAHUAN AND TANOAN LANGUAGES

(With Divergences in "Minimum Centuries")

Legend:

- ° Calculated on 51–75 word pairs
- * Calculated on 26–50 word pairs
- ** Calculated on 1–25 word pairs
- x Insignificant per cent of agreement

```
CAI
28  TEG
28  18  TOG
33  19  18  TAO
64  49  46  50  MON
50  49  45  45  11  SHO
49  41  42  42  10  14  COM
49  40  38  46  12  13  28  PAY
49  47  53  50  33  30  34  28  TBT
66  51  51  46  41  42  30  34  34  FER°
55  54  55  46  42  40  39  39  32  10  GAB°
66  52  52  50  42  41  41  30  30  26  26  CAU°
64  47  46  46  36  34  31  30  28  24  25  24  SRR
76  60  57  57  39  36  31  35  35  40  31  28  27  LUI
71  64  64  64  52  52  44  40  40  48  33  32  40  31  HOP
60  47  49  49  40  34  36  29  26  24  40  33  40  31  29  TAR
64  49  60  60  42  36  38  31  30  36  24  20  18  24  27  16  GUA
71  64  60  60  36  34  37  31  31  20  21  21  21  19  21  17  13  OPA
60  50  57  57  39  37  32  27  27  17  19  22  24  19  24  21  11  11  CAH
68  80  64  43  52  48  44  30  40  28  28  17  24  29  28  20  36  23  19  TBR*
76  71  61  57  49  34  36  36  29  36  35  30  37  30  30  24  21  19  25  38  PAP
57  74  60  60  52  36  38  47  31  39  39  40  41  32  32  32  22  22  32  36   6  PIM
67  61  60  60  50  39  40  37  34  40  34  37  38  30  27  29  20  21  19  40   5   5  TPW
57  60  50  50  49  34  35  30  27  36  30  45  34  31  21  21  18  19  28   5   6   5  TPC
49  50  57  57  39  39  38  35  30  35  52  33  40  31  24  20  19  17  28  20   5  22  22  HUI
53  54  50  50  40  38  38  31  31  35  35  30  28  28  24  22  23  21  25  26  27  11
59  49  59  59  52  51  47  37  37  35  39  40  32  33  32  27  22  22  32  39  39  25  29  22  12  MEX
66  54  63  63  50  47  40  34  34  34  34  34  37  31  30  29  24  21  19  29  29  28  30  26  20  23  12  PCH
60  53  53  53  49  47  43  36  36  39  39  42  45  34  30  29  23  24  36  30  30  30  30  25  27  27  12  36  MEC
47  47  47  59  47  47  59  24  48  48  52  80  59  38  91  31  47  55   x  91  91 140  91  80  38  59  26  13  24  MAR**
```

Mexico and Texas, and still further back the problems touch upon those of the Maya, Cuitlatec, Lenca, and Chibchan, in Mexico, and southward as far as upper South America.

The example of Utonahuan is something of a model of what can be done with comparative linguistics in prehistory. So far, there are few other such examples, except for Mayan, Salishan, Athapascan, and Hokan. However, it is only a matter of time before detailed comparative data, including index quantification, will be available for all groups.

LINGUISTIC RECONSTRUCTION OF PREHISTORIC CULTURES

Cultural reconstruction by linguistic comparison, known as linguistic paleontology, has been a valuable adjunct of prehistory in Europe for some time. In America it is just beginning to be employed, having been used so far mainly in central Mexico and to a slight extent in the Utonahuan family. Its procedure consists of comparing the words used for different artifacts, techniques, and social concepts, along with features of the physical environment, in all the languages of a set based on common origin. Where cognate expressions are used, it can be inferred, with certain cautions and reservations, that we are dealing with artifacts or concepts known to the peoples in some earlier common period of their history. It need not be identical with the beginning of their separation but could go back to a period when they were still in close contact. If a clear pattern of areal distribution can be shown, the inference is that the item referred to came in when the dialects were already separate and without complete contact among them.

By these means it is possible to trace the agricultural complex back at least six thousand years in central Mexico. Corn, chile, and squash appear to be the oldest plants, followed on different levels by beans, cotton, tomato, and maguey. Very interestingly, there are definite words for *town* and *barter* that seem to go back perhaps four thousand years.

In Utonahua there is a notable difference in the indications of linguistic paleontology. While limited agriculture and the milling of seeds was known, there are evidently no cognates that suggest the existence of village life or barter. This shows quite clearly that agriculture had advanced little in common Utonahuan times. In fact, if we combine this evidence with that of divergence and geography, we must infer that the first concepts of agriculture came up from the south to the early Utonahua territory when the group was already scattered in a number of divergent dialects. Agriculture was first taken up by the subtribes living on the southern periphery of the area and caused great changes among them. One of these was probably an increase in population, which may have been the first cause of their expansion southward, which brought them eventually into central Mexico itself.

To make these comments more concrete, it may be well to cite a specific case. Utonahuan words for *metate* or *hand millstone* include: Nahua **metla-tl** or **meta-t**, Huichol and Tarahumara **matá**, Yaqui **mata**, Paiute **mata-tti** (pronounced "madach"), Luiseño **mala-l**, Papago **mahchuhti**. From these varying forms, on the basis of the theory of development of Utonahuan phonemes, the comparative linguist reconstructs **matah** and **mahtah** as the earlier common forms. It is probable that the word is an old compound, perhaps made up of **maha** *hand* and **taha** *flat stone*. In any event, since cognate forms are found in many scattered languages of the family, it has to be inferred that the instrument was already known in the common period. Because of its excellent distribution north and south, we can even deduce that it was one of the earliest diffused instruments among the old Yutonahuans. Perhaps the northern tribes used it for the milling of wild seeds at a time when the southerners were already using it for cultivated corn. [EDITORS' NOTE: Compare the passage above with Armillas, pp. 297 ff., and Jennings, p. 159.]

LINGUISTIC IDENTIFICATIONS OF ARCHEOLOGICAL SITES

It is always highly desirable in archeological work to identify the people responsible for each site. In recent time levels it is often possible to do so on the basis of characteristic cultural features, coinciding with those of some contemporary people. For older periods the problem is more difficult. Yet it is evident that, if it can be solved, it will be with the help of glottochronology and linguistic paleontology. Thus, in the case of Utonahua, the first line of evidence tells us to look perhaps in Arizona and New Mexico around 5,000–7,000 years ago for the early home. The second one, paleontological word comparisons, gives us a series of cultural items, including the metate, as already explained, and also tobacco, the dart-thrower, some kind of skirt, etc., for a period, perhaps not at the earliest mentioned date but well within the time when the people formed a close-knit group, say 4,000–5,000 years ago. Thus, we have an area, a time level and some specific traits, with which it is not very hard to find archeological sites that fit. One must not be either hasty or dogmatic in identifying a language with a set of archeological finds because, even when there is a reasonably good fit, some other people may also have a claim for consideration. One can only hope to make some probable identifications and wait for evidence to accumulate that will either give a still greater probability or destroy the case.

To present an additional example with historic interrelations with the previous one, we may note that the Utonahuan area is flanked by Hokan languages showing affinity with each other at a time level somewhat greater than the Utonahuan expansion. It seems reasonable to suppose that these are the remnants of an older far-flung network of dialects, which was cut through by the Utonahuans. If we look for a center of dispersion for these people, it must be somewhere within present-day Utonahuan territory. If the proper linguistic study of these south Hokan groups is made, it may be possible to identify old sites connected with once-existing groups linguistically related to them.

It is one thing to study a large group of related languages and to make some inferences about the area they may have occupied in the period when they first began to diverge. It is another matter to identify the people connected with a given archeological site, unless it happens to coincide in time, place, and culture with one of the dispersion centers. This can be shown with the example of the ruins of Teotihuacán, *City of Gods*, in the language of the Nahuas, but built a thousand years before their time. There have been many suggestions about who might have been the builders, but each offers problems. It could not be the Aztecs, because they found it already in ruins in the twelfth century. Could it have been some earlier band of Nahuas? What we have already seen about the Utonahuan dispersal suggests that they must still have been far to the north. Some say it was the Olmecs, which is understood to mean those non-Nahua peoples who preceded the Aztecs in the Valley of Mexico and who can be approximately identified with historical Otopameans and Oaxacans, since these peoples coexisted with the Nahuas in the Valley of Mexico in historic times. Yet the Otopame-Oaxacan dispersal has a time depth of about six thousand years, too long for Teotihuacán to coincide with their first separation. It is perfectly possible that some tribe among them occupied the Valley of Mexico in the time period that concerns us, but there is nothing that forces the inference that they were the only group in the area or that they had to be the founders of the city. Several other groups have linguistic relations and geographic spread that make it possible that they may have passed through the area in question about the appropriate time. Thus, the Mixeans, with distant linguistic ties to Penutian of California and to Mayan, and at present occupying a territory that cuts between the two Mayan areas, could well have moved through the Valley of Mexico. Then there is a tradition of the Totonacs, known historically in northern Veracruz, that they were the builders of the Temple of the Sun and the Temple of the Moon. The legend gains some support from the fact that Cerro de la Mesa, in Veracruz, shows great similarity to Teotihuacán. This may be the strongest case, but so far it depends principally upon a legend. A final possibility is that the builders of the legendary city spoke some language that had no close relationship to any of those we have mentioned and that has now either gone out of use or has passed on to places now distant from central Mexico. Thus, there are a number of reasonable possibilities, but none that logic and evidence thus far force us to accept.

If this problem has no sure solution today, it does not mean that it need always remain a mystery. Future archeology is sure to turn up a few more clues about the direction in which the humbler aspects of Teotihuacán culture moved; and comparative linguistics must some day make paleontological reconstructions of earlier cultures for a number of peoples, some one of which may dovetail with the known facts about Teotihuacán in such a way as to permit the identification of its builders.

In linguistic reconstruction, as we have already shown, the work has barely begun. This means that there are many, many facts of prehistory that can be known but that have not yet been studied.

Are there things that can never be known? Presumably yes, but it is too early to start writing off the books any single problem or set of problems. Sydney Lamb has called attention to the fact that many more languages must have disappeared in American prehistory than have actually been preserved. However, many of them were lost before they were born, so to speak, or, in other words, dialects were lost before they had become separate languages and were replaced, probably in the majority of cases, by some other dialect of the same language. In these cases a language in process of formation was lost but its essence was not, because a closely similar dialect lived on. In other instances, like that of the Hokan languages presumably crowded out by the on-pushing Utonahuans, we have the means to infer something about them from their surviving relatives. In still other cases it may be possible to deduce that a people had some kind of affiliation with other known groups. Therefore, we continue work, on the assumption and with the hope that many problems of prehistory can be solved, certainly not 100 per cent, but a great deal better than none. In linguistics, as in archeology itself, there is a conception of a full picture that can be patiently and systematically filled in with reasonable hypotheses and theories, covering all the points of the map and all the periods of time as long as man has existed.

BIBLIOGRAPHY

GREENBERG, JOSEPH H.
  1960 "The General Classification of Central and South American Languages." *Sel. Paps. 5th Internat. Cong. Anthrop. & Ethnol. Sci.*, pp. 791–94.
HAAS, MARY R.
  1959 "Some Genetic Affiliations of Algonkian." Pp. 977–92 in STANLEY DIAMOND (ed.), *Culture in History: Essays in Honor of Paul Radin.* New York: Columbia University Press.

LAMB, SYDNEY
  1959   "Some Proposals for Linguistic Taxonomy." *Anthrop. Linguistics*, 1:
          33–49.
LONGACRE, ROBERT E., and RENE MILLON
  1961   "Proto-Mixtecan and Proto-Amuzgo-Mixtecan Vocabularies: A Pre-
          liminary Cultural Analysis." *Anthrop. Linguistics*, 3 (No. 4):1–44.
SAPIR, EDWARD
  1916   *Time Perspective in Aboriginal American Culture: A Study in Method.*
          (Canada Geol. Surv. Mem. 90; "Anthrop. Ser.," No. 13.) Ottawa.
SWADESH, M.
  1959   "Linguistics as an Instrument of Prehistory." *Southwestern Jour.
          Anthrop.*, 15:20–35.
  1962   "Linguistic Relations across Bering Strait." *Amer. Anthropologist*,
          64:262–91.
  1962   "Nuevo Ensayo de Glotocronologia Yutonahua." *Anales del Instituto
          Nacional de Antropologia e Historia*, 15:263–302.
TAYLOR, WALTER W.
  1961   "Archaeology and Language in Western North America," *Amer.
          Antiquity*, 27:71–81.

Closing Address

IGNACIO BERNAL

Concluding Remarks

THE PRECEDING papers organize coherently a tremendous amount of material, both published and unpublished, and give us a general picture of the prehistory of the New World. I shall not attempt to repeat in a still more abbreviated way what each of the authors has done. Like my colleagues, I specialize in a part of the whole. For knowledge of other specialties, most of us must rely on our colleagues' information and remain in the position of interested bystanders. There is truth in the statement that, when dealing with areas other than our own, we specialists become the general public. I shall make it my role here to make some remarks on the state of progress of the archeology of the New World and the problems it faces.

Since we are here celebrating the fiftieth anniversary of Rice University, it seems fitting to look briefly at the circumstances of fifty years ago and compare them with those of today as revealed by the papers of this symposium. Two of the major contributions toward an understanding of the archeology of the Americas as a whole were published just fifty years ago: Beuchat's *Manuel d'Archéologie Américaine* (Paris, 1912) and Joyce's *South American Archaeology* (London, 1912). To these may be added Joyce's *Mexican Archaeology* (London, 1914). I have been unable to find a general book on North American archeology published at the same approximate time, but it seems unlikely that any such book would alter the circumstances I shall describe.

We find that neither of these authors says much about what we would today call archeology. It must be remembered that in 1912 stratigraphic

IGNACIO BERNAL, subdirector of Technical Investigations, Instituto Nacional de Antropologiá e Historia, Mexico, and Professor of Archeology, Escuela Nacional de Antropologiá, received his Doctor of Letters specializing in Archeology from the Universidad Nacional Autónoma de México. The recipient of many honors in his field, he is also well known in the field of diplomacy, having served as the permanent delegate from Mexico to UNESCO and as cultural adviser of the Mexican Embassy in France. He is also President of Sociedad Mexicana de Antropologiá. He has participated in field research in Middle America and is the author of various writings on this subject. One of his major interests is the protection and preservation of Mexican antiquities.

excavation was new. A little had been done in Peru, but it was only about to begin in Mexico and the Southwest. Thirty years of study encompass the whole archeology of the Great Plains, as Dr. Wedel has pointed out. Most of the useful work in lowland South America began even more recently. Similar circumstances apply to other areas, and the New World may be described as an archeological *terra incognita* fifty years ago. Of course, many objects were known and some monuments had been explored here and there from the end of the eighteenth century, but the sum of knowledge gave no clear idea of the prehistory of the two continents. The books of Joyce and Beuchat are principally ethnographies of ancient America, which combine and fail to distinguish between archeology and ethnology. They do not attempt to see sequences of cultures but simply discuss the latest ones and those leaving written data. Lack of stratigraphies and typologies simplified the work of Joyce and Beuchat.

We can hardly compare the present symposium with these books of fifty years ago because it is precisely during these fifty years that American archeology has developed. These five decades have produced nearly all the field research done with scientifically valid techniques. Most of the early works are, however, foundations upon which later scholars have built. Knowledge of placement in time is essential to archeology. No possible perspective, developmental scheme, culture, or process can be understood if the element of time is omitted. Although the early archeological studies were deficient in this way, certain pioneer researches, some of them done even before 1912, nevertheless represented sensational advances in knowledge. We have only to recall such works as Forstemann's and Goodman's studies of Maya hieroglyphs, which aided later scholars to understand placements in time.

There is no doubt that during the last fifty years tremendous technical advances have been made in archeology and that immense quantities of data have been gathered. We are also now well aware of the value of knowledge of the archeology of the Western Hemisphere as a whole and of the entire world. We also see clearly the need for knowing interrelationships between the various culture areas. Many gaps in our knowledge nevertheless remain, and, of course, no region may be described as fully known archeologically.

Let us now move on from the subject of the collection of data to the far more complex matter of our conceptual thinking. A brief discussion of two recent books in archeology will help clarify the points I wish to discuss. I refer to Armillas' *Cronologia y periodificacion de la historia de America precolombina* (1956) and Willey and Phillip's *Method and Theory in American Archaeology* (1958). Both are modern endeavors to study the same subject that interested Beuchat and Joyce.

Armillas mentions two great problems in trying to establish a sequence of cultural development valid for the whole of the Americas. These are lack of information on many aspects and areas and great differences in the degree of development of the various cultures. The first problem will, of course, become smaller as more research is done. The second problem will doubtless long remain serious. In an attempt to cover all areas, Armillas is forced to reduce the whole story to three great periods: preagricultural to 3000 B.C.; protoagricultural to 500 B.C.; and, finally, where they appear, civilizations enduring until the arrival of Europeans. Of course, we are made to understand that many groups never attained the last level, some not even the second, and some peoples are culturally marginal. Armillas' scheme is a useful mode of exposition, but it also has the weakness, inherent in the use of widely embracive categories, of including so much that a sharply defined picture does not emerge. This is particularly true of Armillas' last period, which includes the whole history of civilized America. Thus the various shorter phases of the process of civilization are lost. The first two long periods are differentiated by one main factor, agriculture. Outstanding features of the last phase are described, but little attention is given to their causes. The question of what produces civilization is hardly touched.

The book by Willey and Phillips is similar. It divides the past into five cultural periods. This finer division defines the cultural phases more sharply and gives a better idea of process and change. But the book does not handle the whole of American archeology. It is rather an essay establishing certain main developmental stages of American cultures, a historical-developmental classification that in some measure combines history with cultural evolution. The book may also be described as a testing of predetermined cultural stages.

Lumping all cultures of the New World into only a few categories has an additional weakness. Comparison with each other of these few highly generalized cultural types, which represent markedly different degrees of development, is for many purposes unrewarding. Comparison of cultures of similar levels, a procedure that is fruitful in various ways, becomes impossible.

The purpose of these comments is not to criticize these useful books but to show how difficult it is to formulate a comprehensive synthesis. These books and numerous others have, in fact, done much for our conceptual thinking. A considerable degree of sophistication is apparent now, and we have seen in these lectures much evidence of it. The pendulum is moving today from the simple descriptive statement of past decades toward the hypothesis. We archeologists are, however, still not strongly inclined toward broad approaches, such as those used by historians and philosophers of history. We are aware of the importance of these approaches but rather afraid of what appear to be their unscientific leanings.

An example to the point is the poor view most archeologists take of the ideas expressed in Arnold Toynbee's *A Study of History*. I once attempted to explore the usefulness of applying Toynbee's ideas on the birth, growth, and death of civilizations to the known facts of Meso-american archeology. It became evident that nearly all his factual data are inaccurate, incomplete, or badly outdated. I tried to show that his ideas could nevertheless be applied usefully to Mesoamerican develop-ments and that they constitute at least one mode of interpretation offer-ing a plausible explanation of the "why" of civilization as well as the "how." I believe that my efforts were received with a sad smile, which seemed to say we live in a free world and every man is entitled to a little foolishness.

I mention this, not as defense of Toynbee's ideas or of my own, but as an illustration of a more important matter, our considerable distrust of history as a scholarly study. If we look at history not as a chronicle of unique events but as a social science that tries to formulate generali-zations about human society and culture, I think we find it little different from what archeologists are trying to do. We say that we are archeolo-gists and therefore prehistorians rather than historians; thus we tend to forget that in a real sense there are no such things as prehistory or prehistorians. Prehistory is simply a division of history. It is the history of those peoples who left no written records. The presence or lack of written documents seems hardly to consitute the dividing point between the two fields of scholarship; it seems more appropriate to think of them as dividing two parts of the same book.

We are all very conscious of the considerable difference between simple facts as recovered by the field archeologist and their interpreta-tion into a coherent narrative. Whether our work of interpretation is called anthropology or history, however, the result is the same. It has been said that Darwin was the greatest of historians. Some of the arche-ologists who followed Joyce and Beuchat viewed ancient objects in a way that I shall call "archeolographic." The objects were classified into types but were given no further interpretation; thus, in the words of Hamlet, they "lose the name of action" and become meaningless. Thanks to data provided by field research, we are now able to trace history to much greater depth than formerly, but our knowledge has depended upon interpretation of these data. It seems reasonable to say that we know more about the ancient history of the New World than its Precolumbian inhabitants ever did. Prehistory has been aptly called the *last* chapter of the history of history. I believe that our role as archeologists most properly identifies us as historians of ancient America.

New World prehistory often has another meaning to English-speaking archeologists of North America. It is the history of those who formerly lived in the same geographical area as the archeologists but who are not their ancestors. For the speaker of English, the events of prehistory are not part of his own tradition, and they are usually regarded as entirely dead. The view of the Spanish-speaking archeologist often differs. To him, the events of the ancient past of the Americas tend to be looked upon as part of his cultural heritage and even of his living culture. It is not that he forgets that he is also of European descent. But he is in constant contact with Indian life and language and feels a continuum that may evoke an emotional response. Thus, the motivations of archeologists of these differing backgrounds also may differ.

And now let us turn directly to this symposium and interpretations that may be inferred from it. The contents of the areal papers give us a list of cultures and their time spans that may be placed in chronological order. In the remarks that follow concerning this succession of cultures, I have not drawn from Krieger's paper, which covers both continents, presents views conflicting with those appearing in other papers, and is organized in a way that differs from the areal accounts. No other paper, for example, presents the fourfold division that Krieger proposes. Because of strongly conflicting points of view regarding the dating of early man, I shall omit reference to most of the earlier evidences of culture. I shall also omit cultures of the Arctic and Northwest Coast. Although the earlier periods there follow the general pattern fairly well, both areas, and especially the Arctic, fall out of line as soon as the Eskimo appears. The Eskimo and peoples of the Northwest Coast seem to be culturally un-American and to have a strong Asiatic flavor. They seem to have had virtually no part in shaping Precolumbian historical developments over the hemisphere.

Let us consider the North American continent first. Around 6000 B.C. there seems to have been a general dividing line between the Big Game Hunters (Intermontane Tradition of Jennings or Paleo-Indian tradition of Sears) and the Archaic. In the Desert West, Jennings places this dividing line earlier, around 6500 B.C. Reed's view of the Southwest and Armillas' view of Mesoamerica place the dividing line another thousand years earlier. This is noteworthy, since it seems that Mesoamerica started its climb toward more advanced stages before any other area in North America. It was soon followed by the Southwest, with which it is closely linked. Thus a similar level of culture (the Lithic of Willey and Phillips) appears to have existed over the whole continent at one time. Then one area, Mesoamerica, begins to move onward and is followed first by the Southwest.

A second general stage appears to have existed from about 5000 to 2000 B.C., the Archaic of all areas of the United States (Desert Archaic, Hunter and Gatherer epoch, or the Early period in California). This corresponds fairly well with a phase in northern Mesoamerica, where plants are now being domesticated, although they do not as yet form the basis of the economy. Many subareas remain at the Lithic stage, and this lag continues. Differences in developmental stages become greater as time passes, especially after civilization arises in Mesoamerica.

After 2000 B.C. the early maritime cultures of the Northwest Coast and the "bone" or Middle period in California appear. Various regional patterns develop in the Desert West. Pottery appears in the Southeast, and maize (soon to be followed by other domesticated plants) in the Southwest. In Mesoamerica there are already permanent settlements economically based on established practices of farming.

No other major temporal divisions of North America seem even moderately clear. We note, however, events that occurred a few centuries before the beginning of the Christian Era: the influence of Woodland-Hopewell in the Great Plains; the transition to Burial Mound I in the Southeast; and, a little later, the transition to civilization (Armillas' "Urban Revolution") in northern Mesoamerica. The Maya civilization in southern Mesoamerica appears still later; its early classic emerges after the equivalent in northern Mesoamerica. It is interesting to note that this sequence in Mesoamerica is the reverse of earlier thinking.

The role Mesoamerica plays as a center of the diffusion of important cultural traits stands out prominently in the papers of this symposium. It is a continual subject of Reed's paper on southwestern North America. He speaks of people of the Cochise culture receiving, more than four thousand years ago, maize from central or southern Mexico; of a series of Mexican traits at Snaketown, and even of the arrival in southern Arizona of an actual group of colonists (or conquerors?) from farther south in the Pioneer Hohokam stage. He finds, after A.D. 1050, Mexican architectural features and suggestions of the cult of Quetzalcoatl. Reed states that the Pueblo, Anasazi, and Mogollon cultures represent the northern frontier provinces, outlying rural offshoots, of Mesoamerican civilization, although they have many local developments and special modifications. He refers also to final glimmerings of these reflections of Mexico in more distant areas.

Sears, who has managed to present an understandable picture of the southeastern United States, also thinks that the great developments in ceramics in that area a few centuries before the beginning of the Christian Era, the temple mounds, and perhaps the Southern Cult indicate Mesoamerican influences. Griffin refers to a stimulus to cultural development in northeastern North America as a result of the introduction of agriculture from Mesoamerica.

It is possible to regard the whole North American continent, except the Northwest Coast and Alaska, as one great culture area, an area that differs regionally in stages of development but has a common basis (the Lithic or early Lithic period) and a related history. The cultural peak is Mesoamerica, principally northern Mesoamerica, from which influences spread in ever wider and ever weaker circles. This view seems useful in attempting to understand the general current of North American culture and processes of diffusion and culture change. We need to note at the same time that Mesoamerica itself is influenced by incoming northern ideas.

The papers dealing with South America and the Caribbean area show the tremendous advances in knowledge that have been made for this area, on which no illuminating summary could heretofore have been attempted. No general pattern emerges yet, but here again we have continuous mention of the influences that spread from the areas of civilization. Discussing the Caribbean area, Rouse does not mention evidence of direct connection, but he speaks frequently of Mesoamerica and the Intermediate area, suggesting that they were the source of new crops and new techniques of agriculture. Much later, a rather important list of Mexican-like traits is present in the Chicoid series, at the end of Rouse's Period IV. Evans, referring to the incipient agricultural stage in the Amazon-Orinoco drainage area, states that no single culture in the Andean area appears to be the parent stock of the Zoned Hachure Horizon style. In the later Nericagua Phase, however, an origin in the highlands of Colombia seems certain, and Andean influences are obvious in the very late Corobal Phase. As may be inferred from its title, the whole Sub-Andean stage is clearly associated with the Andean civilization. This trend does not, however, seem to be obvious in the Paraná drainage.

If we now turn to Kidder's paper on Sub-Andean cultures (highland Ecuador, Colombia, northern Chile, and northwestern Argentina), we see that they occupy a position with respect to the Andean civilization that is roughly comparable with those of the North American Southwest and Southeast in their relation to Mesoamerica. Still one gets the impression that the Andean civilization did not directly or indirectly influence its eastern neighbors as much as Mesoamerica did those to its north. Perhaps this impression results from incomplete knowledge. Perhaps it reflects varying geographical situations or different expansion possibilities of the Andean and Mesoamerican civilizations. These are problems that need examination.

These remarks lead to the problem discussed by Meggers of the relations between the two continents. What I wish to say is well expressed by Meggers in an address delivered this year at the International Congress of Americanists:

> One conclusion is so overwhelmingly documented that future research can only add to its support, namely, that a tremendous amount of contact existed aboriginally between widely separated geographical areas, not only by diffusion from group to group, but in the form of long range commerce and migration by land and sea. From the early Formative, if not before, there is evidence of direct communication between Mesoamerica and the west coast of South America, and from these primary centers influences passed in all directions.

North and South American cultural connections and convergences are still difficult to understand. It is possible, however, to see the Mesoamerican and Andean civilizations as one unit with two focuses linked by the Intermediate Area. The unit may be seen as surrounded by cultures of diminishing complexity. Part of the similarities between the two continents probably derives from the common culture that they shared in ancient times. Swadesh's paper on native languages of the New World presents important evidence of formerly unsuspected linguistic connections and also illustrates the value of lines of investigation outside archeology proper. The subject of cultural influences upon the New World stemming from Asia and the Pacific is most complex. Ekholm's paper on this subject shows once again the considerable degree of sophistication that American archeology is attaining. The trend today is toward seeing many relationships among civilizations of the Old World. We have mentioned a similar trend in connecting the New World civilizations. It is possible that we may one day think civilizations arose only once in the Old World and only once in the New World. Should important contacts be proved between the two worlds, we may arrive at the conclusion that civilization was invented only once and that the various individual civilizations are only local manifestations of a single phenomenon. Whether these ideas and others expressed by participants in this symposium will prove to be sound and useful, only research in future years can reveal.

Index

Abalone shell; *see* Shells

Abbott Farm culture, 253

Abejas complex (phase), 298; rockshelter, 297, 299

Abraders, 164; flint, 344; grooved, 198; obsidian, 344; sandstone, 515

Acapulco, Guerrero, 309, 408

Acasta Lake site, 60, 62

Acculturation, 189, 317, 436; absence of, 435

Acegua site, 49, 50

Acolhua dominion, 321; Tetzcoco, capital of, 321

Acoma, 188

Acorns, 162; economies based on, 129, 267; preparation of, 125

Acosta, Jorge, 315

Acropolis: concept, 364; -like eminences, 339; at Xochichalco, 312

Adams, 379

Adena, 421; burials, 234; culture, 7, 236–40, 254; development and demise, 236; Ohio Valley, 235, 238; physical type, 237; populations, 238; sites, 237, 241; traits, 238

Adena-Hopewell, 241–43

Adobe: bricks, 377; burned, 366; compounds, 188; construction, 473; floors, 182; mounds, puddled, 366; plaster, 366; pyramids, 358; walls, 375, 470

Adzes, 96, 133, 166, 231; basalt, 164; beveled, 230, 231; blades, 103, 104, 134; chipped, 229, 231; ground, 230, 231; heads, 103; hematite, 229; splitting, 135

Agate Basin, 60, 62, 197

Agave, 298, 332

Agogino, George A., 52, 54, 55, 61, 62, 68, 69, 72, 73, 199, 215

Agriculture (agricultural), 10, 34, 35, 129, 181, 203, 207, 223, 237, 243, 245, 247, 251, 254, 256, 263, 265, 274, 283, 294–96, 302, 334, 346, 351, 400, 409, 423, 426, 442, 452, 457, 458, 479, 482, 290, 552, 561, 565; Andean, 454, 458; beginnings of, 296, 299, 400, 497, 552; bottomland, 207; Caribbean, 403, 405; centers, 273; complexes, 248, 552; development, 35, 61, 464; diffusion, 400; eastern Asian, 497; economy, 251, 283, 300; fertilizer, use of in, 466; frontier, 317; fully developed, 274, 400, 444, 455, 515; garden (horticulture), 305, 319, 321, 454; hoe, 207, 211; Hopewellian, 243; incipient, 195, 205, 292, 294, 295, 332, 454, 456, 473, 476, 565; infiltration into eastern United States, est. date of, 237; intensive, 209, 305, 308, 437, 442; Intermediate area type, 403, 405; maize, 205, 213, 214, 251, 297, 453, 480, 520; marginal, 428; Mesoamerican-Intermediate, 403; Mississippian, 243; peoples, 34, 158, 176, 251, 254, 399, 411, 540; plants, 237, 538; potential, 442, 465, 480; preceramic, 178; root, 403, 426; seed, 403, 426, 442; semiagricultural (semihorticultural) peoples, 176, 178, 207, 213, 214; settled, 460, 464; slash-and-burn, 332, 426–37; stages, 421; subsistence, 530; supplementary, 425; surpluses, 209; techniques, 248, 332, 400, 423, 519, 565; tools, 343; tropical forest, 442, 443

Aguacatan, Guatemala, 373

Ajuereado complex (phase), 294, 298

Alabama, 63, 259, 266, 267, 271, 278, 279, 281; northern, 234, 267; southern, 266, 271, 283

Alaska, 37, 39, 55, 59, 62, 85, 88, 89, 91, 95, 99, 100, 106, 117, 565; Arctic Coast of, 87–89, 91, 97, 103, 108, 135; central, 62; culture stages of, 106; cultures of, southern, 102; northern, 87, 91, 98–100, 103; southern, 91, 101, 102, 105, 132; traditions of, 90, 101; western, 62; *see also* individual cultures, sites, and geographical places by name

Albee culture, 253
Alberta, 212, 215, 244
Albritton, Claude C., 81
Alegria, Ricardo, 392, 398, 414
Alenquer, Brazil, 425
Aleutian cultures, 102, 240
Aleutian Islands, 86, 91, 102; early inhabitants of, 105
Algonkian; see Algonquin
Algonquin Indians, 241–42, 245, 247, 248, 254, 255
Alkali Ridge, 181
Allanson, A. A., 124, 147
Allen site, 60, 61; radiocarbon date, 62
Alluvium (alluvial), 40, 46; formations, 293; plain, Mississippi, 249; river flats, 339; terraces and soils, 243, 321
Almagre phase, 302; points, 298
Alta Verapaz, Guatemala, 309, 343, 351, 358, 365, 372, 373, 378; ceramics, 350; Chama phases, 310, 367; figurines, 350; region, 343
Altar de Sacrificios, 336; ceremonial center, est. date for, 336; fine orange ware, 350; late remains at, 352; pyramids at, 337; tomb with corbeled vault at, 337, 338
Altars, 304, 339, 341, 370, 373; carving on, 303; circular interior, 379; monolithic, 303; platform, 369, 373, 374; as shrines, 369
Altithermal period, 150, 151, 196, 200, 214; est. dates for, 150
Alto focus, 246, 273, 282; ceramics, 274; period, 274
Altoparanense complex, 49, 50
Alvarado, Pedro de, 375
Amaloccan, Puebla, 301
Amapa (Brazilian Guiana), territory of, 420, 430, 431; northern part of, 483
Amaranth; see Plants
Amargosa site, 158
Amatle ceramic phase, Kaminaljuyú, 371, 372
Amazon Delta sequence, 428
Amazon-Orinoco drainage area, 421, 422 ff., 430, 432, 433, 437, 440–42, 444, 445, 565; lowlands of, 423
Amazon River, 419, 420, 421, 428, 430–32, 441, 523; Basin, 429, 442, 513; drainage, 419, 421, 424, 427, 429, 432, 438, 441, 442; lower, 424–28, 430, 432, 435, 436, 446; middle, 430, 438, 440–42, 446, 522; mouth of, 438, 440, 442; tributaries of, 419, 420, 430, 431, 433; upper, 441
Amazonia(n), 390; archeological traits, 432; jungles, 442

American Bottoms, 249, 278
American Falls site, 43, 44; radiocarbon date from, 44
American Indian languages, 527–48; est. dates for absorption of new and resistance to amalgamation of, 531; extant, 531; history of, 531; number of, 529, 545, 547; origin of, 529–32, present-day, 531
American Indians; see individual tribes and groups by name
American language(s), 528–48; groups 541; origins of, 529–32; roots of, 541
Ampajango complex, 49, 50, 51
Amsden, Charles, 122, 136
Anaktuvuk Pass (Brooks Range, Alaska), 87
Ananiuliak (Anangula) Island, 102
Anasazi, 6, 169, 175, 178, 181–87, 246, 522, 564; early period of, 179; Great Kiva of, 186; pottery of, 187; San Juan, 180, 181, 183, 184, 186; site plans, 183; see also Basketmaker, Pueblo
Anathermal period, 150, 157, 158; est. dates for, 150
Anatuba phase (complex), 424–25, 428; ceramics, 424; est. beginning date for, 425; houses, 424; peoples, 424, 428; site, 420, 424; traits, 428
Ancon, Peru, 459
Andahuaylas region, Peru, 471
Anderson focus, 196, 206, 233, 240
Andes (Andean), 331, 394, 414, 426, 451–54, 481–83, 497, 500; agriculture, 454; central, 292, 390, 452, 479–81, 565–66; Colombian, 413, 431; culture elements, 453; earliest inhabitants of, 454; foothills, 391, 405, 441; highlands, 292, 421, 452–54; influences elsewhere, 443, 565; Montaña, the, 442; northern, 441, 442, 523; plants indigenous to, 454; regions of, 432, 433, 453, 454, 482; southern, 490; Venezuelan, 391, 404
Andover conference, 31, 42, 51
Andrews, E. Wyllys, 346, 354–56, 359, 362–64, 383
Andrews culture, 252
Angel: culture, 253; site, 251
Angostura: complex, 197, 199; points, 67, 85, 87, 88, 89, 294; site, 153, 196
Angulo Valdes, Carlos, 480, 483
Animal(s): alpaca, 452; beaver, 224, 233, 244; big game, 199, 224; bones (see Skeletal remains); caribou, 105, 107, 224; carvings of, ivory, 103; clay, 493; communication among, 530; coyotes, 47, 156, 315; designs, 343; domesticated, absence of and transportation of, 501; dogs, 105, 107, 176, 198, 332;

draft, 332; effigy (*see* Effigy, Zoömorphism); elk, 224, 228; foods, 224, 297; fox, 107; game, 178, 182, 208, 260, 332, hare, 107; -head feet, on pottery, 372, 374; heads, as ball-court markers, 370, 373; llamas, 396, 452, 454, 458, 465, 480; moose, 224; musk-ox, 224; peccary, 47; -shaped mushroom stone cultures, 368; skin, 186 (*see also* Skins); small, 224, 397; wheeled, miniature, 495; wolf, 47, 228; zemis, 413; *see* also Fauna, extinct; Bison; Felines; Game; Jaguars; Sea mammals

Annals of the Cakchiquels; see Cakchiquel, *Annals*

Antelope Creek focus, 196, 206

Antevs, Ernst, 61, 62, 79, 150, 151, 156, 158, 170, 173

Anthropomorphic: cover handles, 343; fillets (ceramic), 433; modeling, 432, 438; motifs, 368, 430; mounds, 247; pedestal sculptures, 379; urns, 431, 439; whistles, 382; *see also* Human figures

Antilles, 409, 433, 435, 442; archeological survey of, 391; central, 402, 411–14; colonization of, 398, 409; Greater, 389, 398, 403, 409, 411, 413, 436, 442; languages of, 538, 547; Lesser, 389, 390, 398, 403, 411, 433, 436; Netherlands, 391; prehistoric cultures of, 433; *see also* West Indies

Antler(s): arrowheads, 103, 106; artifacts, 103, 106, 163, 198, 204; bow guards, 212; camas-digging-stick handles, drilled, 133, 166; carving, 165; elk, dagger, 228; harpoons, 134, 245; knife handles, 155; ornaments and/or gaming pieces, 198; projectile points, 127, 244; tools, 155, 179; wedges, 133, 134, 166; worked, 229; wrenches, 155

Antofagasta, Chile, 50, 57

Apache, 189, 196, 213, 549; language, 550; Plains, 213

Apalachicola River, Florida, 283

Appalachian (Mountain) cultures, 261; ceramic tradition, 269

Aprons; *see* Clothing

Aquaducts, 321, 324, 348

Aquaplano culture, 34, 60, 63

Araca: complex, 441; site, 438

Arauquin: ceramic complex, est. dates for, 432; sites, 401, 420, 431

Arauquinoid series, 406–7, 409, 410; designs, 410; diffusion of, 409, 410

Arawak: culture, 435; languages, 548

Archaic stage (period, horizon), 29, 30, 68, 136, 152, 153, 176, 178, 200, 231, 255, 256, 259, 260, 263, 269, 292, 421, 422, 457, 563, 564; artifacts, 260, 522; Boreal (New England), 164, 233; Boreal, Early and Late, 230; Boreal, Maine, 231; Coastal (Gulf Coast), Late, 240; Coastal (New England), 235; complexes, 225, 229–32; cultural development, 225, 229; culture(s), 27, 85, 129, 199, 225, 227, 228, 243, 252, 255, 259, 260, 261, 263, 275, 428, 443, 514; definition of, 225; Desert (*see* Desert Archaic); Early, 33, 34, 59, 227–29, 252; Eastern, 164, 199, 214, 232; end of, in Southeast, 261; Full, 33, 38, 59, 68; Great Lakes–New England area, 227, 231; hunters (hunting), 240, 252, 263; Late (*see* Late Archaic); Middle, 252; Ohio Valley, 230; Plains, 199; shell middens, 522; sites, 227, 229, 260; traditions, 200; traits, 162; types, 88

Archeology (archeological): areas, 118, 338; complexes, 210, 254, 285, 520, 521; excavations, 438; field methods in, 25, 117; hypotheses, 403; investigations in, 132; knowledge, 498; reconstruction, 503; record(s), 208, 404, 434; research in, 23, 135, 318, 391, 419, 529; sequences, 228, 362, 512; synthesis, 225; terminology, 26; traits, 133, 432, 538

Arches; *see* Architectural features

Architectural features
  Arches (vaults), corbeled, 313, 331, 336–40, 357, 360, 369, 378, 501, 502
  Balustrades, serpent, 357, 360, 363
  Bastions, vaulted, 348
  Colonnettes, 360
  Columns, 313, 348, 374, 476; basalt, painted, 368; carved and painted, 357; doorway (entrance), 356, 363; effigy, 359; fences of, 380; sculptured stone, 315; serpent (entrance), 357, 359
  Compounds, quadrangular, 307
  Doorways: false, 364, 365; multiple, 348, 374; serpent-mouth and fanged mask, 364; slab, 349; triple, 373
  Drain conduits, 307, 373
  Entranceways, 206; gallery-like, 379; stone-lined, 371, 378, 379
  Façade(s), 312, 315, 341; arranged to simulate three separate structures, 365; flying, 356, 365; lower, 364; lower, stone mosaics on, 356; moldings, 341, 356, 357; profiles, 355, 356; upper, 341; upper, stone mosaics on, 356; stucco carving on, 355, 356; vertical, 364
  Floors; *see* Houses
  Frets, stone, 356
  Friezes, 315; bas-relief, 357

Architectural features—*Continued*
Galleries, 348; palace, 341; patio, 357; subterranean, 480; vaulted, 360
Halls: colonnaded, 363; pillared, 315–16, 363
Latticework, stone, 356
Lintels, 315, 345; *see also* Dzibilchaltun
Moldings, 369; cornice, 341; façade, 341, 356, 357; medial, 341, 355; multimember, 356; vertical (ball-court walls), 371, 373
Niches, trapezoidal, 473
Passages, interior; *see* Tunnels (*below*)
Patios, colonnaded, 357; gallery, 357
Pillars, 313; carved, 315; granite, 429; halls with, 315; rubble of, 379
Pinnacles, on cornices, 313
Quadrangles, closed, 356
Ramps, stone-paved, 378
Roof(s) (ceilings), 315, 357; beam-and-mortar, 348, 357, 363, 369, 374; beehive, 371; combs, 341; combs, perforated, 348, 356, 364; corbeled-vault, on tombs, 369; flat, on tombs, 369; pole and whalebone, 455; saddle, 477; slab, 313; supports, interior, 180, 184, 206, 208, 313, 357; terrace, 307; thatched, 125, 299, 339, 358, 369, 374; timber and mat, on tombs, 366, 369
Rooms, 340, 348, 374; burials in, 341; interior, absence of, 364; rectangular, 374; vaulted, 338
Stairways, 307, 315, 345, 364, 366, 369, 379; balustraded, divided by ramp, 374; bordered, 369; Early Classic, Kaminaljuyú, 370; interior, 313, 340; major, 336; minor, 336; red-painted, 371; with serpent balustrades, 357, 360; split type, 371; steep, functional, 364–65; steep, non-functional, 364
Streets, cement-paved, 307
Substructure(s), 340, 341, 374; temple, 374, 358, 466; walls, battered, 357
Telamones, colossal, 315
Toilets, 348
Towers: Rio Bec, 364; round, 357; square, 348; triple-walled, 186
Tunnels: masonry, 349; stone-lined, 369, 458; vaulted, in tombs, 342
Veneer: clay, 374; masonry, 313, 348, 356, 364; stone, 358
See also Caryatids, Courts, Masonry, Platforms, Stelae, Terraces, Tombs, Walls
Architectural materials: concrete, 313, 348, 356; lime, 313, 371; mortar, 307, 317, 371; mud, 307, 366, 371; plaster, 302, 363, 366, 371, 413; rubble, 339, 340

Architectural styles, 353, 356, 364
Architecture, 186, 207, 332, 335, 337, 340, 348, 355, 369, 382, 464; communal, 229; cut-stone, 378; Cuzco, 473; Early, northern Yucatan, 355, 363; Florescent, northern Yucatan, 363; highland Maya, Mexican influences on, 374; Inca, 373; Late Classic, Maya lowlands, 340, 348; Late Postclassic, Mayapan, 364; lightness in, 348; Lowland Maya, 336, 364; masonry, 331, 339; Maya-Toltec, Chichén-Itzá, 364; monumental, 304, 339; Palenque, 313, 348; Piedras Negras, 348; regional styles in, 341; religious, 301 (*see also* Ceremonial structures); residential, 187; Rio Bec, 364; stone, 380; Tajin, 313; Tollan, 315; Toltec, 315, 316; *see also* Monuments, Sculpture, Structures, Temples
Arctic, 6, 85, 88, 91, 101, 150, 224; American, 85, 108, 245, 90; Canadian, 91, 98–101; central, 99, 106, 107; coastal, 87, 88, 246; cultures of, 39, 563; eastern, 90, 106, 107; materials of, 88; regions of, 39, 86; retardation in, 89; Small Tool tradition, 87, 90, 107, 108, 232; Woodland hunters, 240, 246
Arellano, A. R. V., 294, 325
Arevalo phase, Kaminaljuyú, 366
Argentina, 36, 51, 67, 420, 422, 445; central, 34, 58, 65, 443, 519; coast of, 443; northeastern, 443; northern, 419, 421, 443; northwestern, 50, 58, 443, 453, 469, 479, 480, 513, 515–20, 565; pampas of, 420, 445; *see also* individual cultures, sites, and geographical places by name
Ariste: phase, 438; site, 420
Arizona, 52, 54, 57, 62, 123, 125, 151, 156, 553; central, 159, 176, 186, 188; eastern, 176, 181, 189; northeastern, 31, 44, 62, 181, 184, 186, 187; northern, 176, 177; southeastern, 36, 54, 60, 62, 156, 188; southern, 37, 63, 117, 176, 177, 180, 182, 186, 188, 189, 197, 564; southwestern, 64; western, 44, 176, 180, 189; *see also* individual cultures, sites, and geographical places by name
Arkansas, 269; River, 208, 209, 213
Armenta Camacho, Juan, 44, 47
Armies: Aztec, 310, 320, 322, 324; Inca, 472
Armillas, Pedro, 2, 8, 183, 291, 305, 312, 321, 325, 229, 553, 560, 561, 563, 564
Armlets; *see* Ornaments
Arms, Bernard C., 172
Arnold, 360
Arnold, Brigham A., 44, 69

Arnold, J. R., 90, 108
Arrow(s): compound, 155; with end and side blades, 104; foreshafts, wooden, 160; points, 121, 212; three-feathered, 514
Arrowheads, 103, 104; antler, 106; barbed, 106; bone, 89–90, 96, 107; inset side blades, 104; ivory, 96; non-functional antler, 103; slotted, 98, 106; tanged, 106; *see also* Projectile points
Arroyo Malo, Argentina, 420, 445
Arroyo Sarandi, Argentina, 420, 445
Art(s), 96, 101, 332, 344, 427, 514, 520; fluorescence of, 460; forms, 359; as religious expressions, 502; symbolic, 331; types, 92; *see also* Ceramics, Designs, Painting, Sculpture
Art styles: Chavín, 458, 460, 462, 463, 480, 504, 522; high, 304; Hopewellian, 238; La Venta, 336; Mexican, 314, 357; Mississippian, 317; Mixteca-Puebla, 311, 317, 319; Mochica, 465; Nazca, 465; Olmec, 301–3, 309, 377, 380, 459–62, 504, 522; "Ornate" phase, 310; peripheral, Chinese, 499; Puuc, 313; Tajin, 312, 313, 370, 498; Tollan, 316; Totonac (Classic Veracruz), 313, 370
Artigas, Uruguay, 50
Artisans; *see* Social stratification
Aruã, 435–36
Arzberger site, 196, 209
Aschmann, Homer H., 126, 136, 151, 169
Ash: falls, 155; Pleistocene, 18; pumice, 155; refuse, 455; volcanic, 374
Ash Cave, 53; lowest level of, 54
Ash Hollow Cave, 153, 196; B-E, 212
Asia(tic), 9, 10, 55, 102, 245, 256, 360, 489, 490, 492, 496, 498, 499, 503, 505, 506, 508, 509, 518, 523, 534, 542, 563; civilizations, 507; coastal shipping, 507, 509; colonies, 502; connections with Ecuadorean coast, est. dates for, 474, 477; cotton, 456; cultures, 498; diffusion from, 496, 497; eastern, 477, 497; food plants, absence of, 501; influences in Americas, 360, 492–507; migration from, 490, 501, 503, 530; northeastern, 224; northern, 236; Southeast, 9, 498, 507; trade objects, 550
Asiatic origin: of American Indian, 97, 490, 491; of clay stamps, 496; of early American ceramics, 496; of iron pyrite mirrors, 496; of Mexican wheeled toys, 495
Aspects, 7; *see also* individual aspects by name
Assimilation, 428, 550

Astronomy, 14, 18, 332, 339, 345, 346, 500; lunations, 344; solar eclipses, 346; solar year (vague year), 344; Venus (planet), 315, 346
Atabapo River, Venezuela, 420, 428
Atlantean figures; *see* Caryatids
Atlantic Ocean, 365, 402; Coast, 244; lost continent in, 491
Atlatl, 126, 127, 154, 155, 156, 158, 161, 176, 178, 179, 181, 260, 261, 263, 357, 422, 456, 553; absence of, 456; darts, 155; weights, 131, 164, 260, 549 (*see also* Bannerstones); *see also* Spear-thrower
Atlatongo (Teotihuacán), 308
Atlixco, 322
Atoyac River Valley, Puebla, 293
Atrisco culture, 240
Aurora phase, 346
Australia(n)(s), 532, 538; languages, 537, 538
Aveleyra Arroyo de Anda, Luis, 39, 44, 47, 53, 54, 69, 76, 293, 294, 325
Awatovi, 188
Awl(s), 156; bone, 32, 123, 126, 127, 155, 160, 198, 225, 343, 515, 518; copper, 233, 234; horn, 160; polishers, 516; rib-edge, 208; scapula, L-shaped, 155, 161; sharpeners, sandstone, 517
Axe(s): copper, as currency, 496; diorite, ¾ grooved, 182; hand, 50, 293; money, Chinese, 496; monolithic, 264; polished, 436; stone, 178, 179, 181, 367, 376, 399, 427; stone, ceremonial, 275, 278, 279; stone, grooved, 202, 229, 230, 231, 237, 260, 434, 515, 516, 517, 519; stone, ¾ grooved, 182, 184, 187; stone, full-grooved, 184, 229
Ayacucho, Peru, 459, 464, 468; region; 463
Ayampitin: complex, 65, 66; radiocarbon date for, 65; points, 36, 58, 65
Azcapotzalco, 311, 322–23
Aztalan, 246, 250, 252
Aztan phase, 309
Aztec(s), 307, 317, 320, 322–24, 359, 554; armies, 310, 320, 322, 324; artifacts, 383; capital, 306; copper axe currency, 496; craftsmen, 306; empire, 320, 322, 323, 324, 548, 549; fortresses, 320, 321; merchants, 310, 324; population, 324; sacrifices, 481; *tecpan*, 307

Bache, Charles, 62, 73
Badin culture, 240
Baerreis, David A., 202, 206, 207, 209, 215
Baggerly, Carmen, 44, 69

Bags: medicine, 154, 155; twined, 154, 160, 178, 179; woven, 178
Bahamas, 412
Bahía, Brazil, 420, 445
Bahía de Caráquez, Ecuador, 476; area, 477
Bahía phase, 476, 503; est. date of, 503
Baja California, 43, 44, 176, 177; archeology of, 126; central, 44; coast of, 508; demography of, 126; ecology of, 126; northern, 126, 136; southern, 175
Baja Verapaz, Guatemala, 365
Bajio, the (Mexico), 291, 314, 320
Balam phase, 309, 367, 372
Balankanche cave, radiocarbon dates from, 362
Balcones phase (culture), 37, 60
Baleen: artifacts, 100; fragments, 92; implements, 104
Ball courts, 182, 186, 315, 339, 357, 364, 371, 373, 378, 412, 413; distribution of, 371; Great, Chichén Itzá, 359; heads, jaguar and serpent, in, 370; Hohokam, 182, 186; inclosed, 375; I-shaped, 375; low walls defining end zones of, 373; markers, 372, 373, 379; playing alleys in, 375; playing walls of, sloping, 371, 373; slab lining of, 413; types of, 371; worship of zemis in, 413
Ball game(s), 522; complex, 413; ritual, 331
Ball players, 378; stone belts for, 413
Balls: clay, baked, 126; clay, grooved, 132; rubber, game, 522; stone, grooved, 163
Balsas River, 309, 319, 320, 323
Balustrades; see Architectural features
Bands; see Social organization
Bani: site, 402; style, 412
Bank, Theodore P., II, 102, 108
Bannerstones, 96, 233; birdstones, 233–35; bipennate, 231; boatstones, 131; fragments, 229; see also Atlatl, weights
Barata, Frederico, 431, 446
Barbarism, 300, 322, 481
Barbour, E. H., 62, 69
Barbs; see Tools
Barcelona (Venezuela) area, 393
Bare Island culture, 253
Barfield, Lawrence, 51, 69
Barghoorn, E. S., 296, 325
Barima River, British Guiana, 420, 422; region, 431
Bark: beds, 154; birch, containers, 204; buckets, 353, 497; burned, tempering (cariape), 425, 429, 430, 431; canoes, 513; cloth, 332, 455, 496, 522; -covered houses, 212; trowels, 158; vessels, 176, 514
Barlovento site, 395, 400, 404, 426; radiocarbon dates for, 400

Barlow, R. H., 318, 324, 325
Barnes culture, 252
Barquisimeto, Venezuela, 405
Barracão site, 49, 50
Barrancas, Venezuela, 402–3, 408, 420; style, 409, 410
Barrancoid series, 404, 405, 406, 408–10, 412, 437; absence of figurines in, 405; central Venezuelan, 404, 406; Delta region, 404, 408–9; influence of, 406, 409, 412; origin of, 404; people, 408–10, 414; in Trinidad, 409
Barrow Strait, 86, 100
Barter; see Trade
Bartlett, Katherine, 31, 44, 69
Barton, Ramie, British Honduras, 335, 338–39, 343, 352; "Floral Park" phase, 338
Basalt, 48, 51, 130; adzes, 164; black, 48, 58; brown, 48; columns, 368; flaked, 129; heads, 303; knives, 165–66; monuments, 380; points, 131
Basin-and-Range province, 117
Basin Plateau province, 149
Basketmaker, 176, 179, 240; I, 177; II, 178, 179; III, 180; est. dates for, 181; San Juan, 179; storage cists, 183; traits, 181
Basketry, 126, 132, 155, 156, 161, 178, 186, 248, 376, 427, 479; Catlow Twined, 155; checker-woven, 515; coiled, 126, 127, 154, 160, 178, 179, 213, 515; containers (utensils), 176, 181; est. age of in Southwest, 176; hoppers, 124, 128; reed, 455; representations in ceramic adornos, 433; stepped designs in, 497; techniques, 156, 161, 519; twined, 126, 154, 155, 160, 161
Bastions; see Architectural features
Bat Cave, 297; -type maize, 297, 298
Battle Rock phase, 105, 106
Battles; see Warfare
Baumhoff, M. A., 119, 126, 131, 132, 135, 136, 137, 141, 170, 171
Baytown cultures, 269; ceramics, 274; late, 246, 277; mounds, 269, 274, 277
Beach(es), 455; Algonquin-stage, Lake Michigan, 228; fossil, 159; Krusenstern, 106; lines, 15, 88, 92, 120, 150, 228; -ridge sequence, Kotzebue Sound, 104; orientation, 455
Beads, 179, 431; bone, 94, 155, 163, 165, 179, 225; copper, 234, 237; on fabrics, 479; glass, 204, 434; hematite, 178; jade, 332, 333, 344; jet, 164; lignite, 178; nephrite, 436; pearl, 238, 245; platinum, 479; pottery, 436; seed, 178; serpentine, 164; shell, 125–28, 132, 161, 162, 166, 178, 209, 213, 234, 271, 344,

397; steatite, 164; stone, 125, 164, 166; turquoise, 178; wooden, 178

Beals, R. L., 125, 137

Beans, 178, 179, 182, 186, 202, 207, 248, 298, 332, 552; common, 295, 297; domestication of, 300; jack, 455; kidney, 463; lima, 295, 455, 456; in Plains, earliest appearance of, 202; scarlet (runner), 295, 297; in Sierra Madre Oriental, beginning date of, 297; in Southwest, beginning date of, 178

Beardsley, Richard K., 29, 69, 126, 129, 137

Becerra formation, 294; radiocarbon dates from, 47

Becker-Donner, Etta, 421, 446

Beds, bark, 154; grass, 154; skin bedding, 225

Beekeeping, 346

Belcher focus, 282

Belém, Brazil, 420

Belen-Santamaria period, 515

Belize River, 334, 339; sites on, 335; Valley, 349

Bell, Robert E., 16, 65, 67, 69, 76, 202, 206, 207, 209, 215, 257

Bell culture, 252

Bells; see Ornaments

Belous, Russell E., 126, 137

Beni River, Bolivia, 420, 441

Bennett, John, 257

Bennett, Wendell C., 292, 325, 391, 406, 414, 469, 483

Bennett focus, 196, 208, 210

Bennyhoff, James A., 126, 127, 131, 132, 135, 137, 167, 170, 306, 327

Benque Viejo site, 335

Benson, Richard H., 18, 19

Bentzen, Raymond, 201, 215

Beregovaia, N. A., 100, 108

Bering Sea: Coast, 105; Eskimos, 98, 101; region, 103, 105; see also Old Bering Sea, Okvik–Old Bering Sea

Bering Strait, 86, 91, 92, 100, 102, 105, 107, 490, 509, 533, 538; Cape Prince of Wales, 91, 98, 99; culture, 102

Berlin, Heinrich, 347, 350, 352, 379, 383

Bernal, Ignacio, 2, 5, 301, 306, 309, 325, 559

Berreman, J. V., 132, 137

Berthold, Sarah M., 67, 78

Beuchat, Henri, 560, 562

Beveling; see Techniques

Bichrome pottery; see Ceramic wares

Bierman, A., 123, 147

Big game, 158, 168, 177, 199, 244; Early Hunters, 51, 195, 196, 197–99; hunters, 88, 152, 159, 167, 177, 200, 214, 563; hunting (stage), 29, 38, 151, 152, 159; Pleistocene, 32; tradition, 151

Big Leap site, 164

Big Sandy River, Kentucky, 238, 254

Bigarella, I. K., 450

Bigarella, João José, 444, 446, 447, 450

Biota, 149, 150, 151, 159

Bird(s), 94, 107, 224; bolas, 94; bone(s), 94, 163, bone beads, 165; condors, 462; cult chariots, Chinese, 495; darts, 96; designs, 265, 368; effigy figurines, 352; effigy mounds, 247; effigy whistles, 336, 352; and feline combination, 462; hunting, 94; insignia, conventionalized, 357; macaws, 186; ornaments, 504, 505; parrots, 186; quetzal, 334, 365; raptorial, 460, 462; representations of, modeled, 432; representations of, on pottery, 350, 433; -shaped mushroom stone sculptures, 368

Bird, Junius B., 34, 38, 51, 57, 58, 64, 65, 67, 69, 120, 137, 454, 460, 462, 483, 484

Birdshead Cave, 153, 200, 212

Birnirk culture (stage), 90, 91, 98, 99, 100; harpoon heads, 98, 99–100; Kurigitavik site, radiocarbon dates on, 99; potsherds, 100; -to-Thule sequence, 99

Bison, 32, 38, 54, 59, 64, 87, 156, 198, 201, 202, 203, 214, 251; *B. antiquus*, 177; *B. bison*, 196; *B. latifrons*, 44; *B. occidentalis*, 196, 199; bone, 200, 201; fossil, 293; frontal scoops, 293; molar, 293; scapula hoes, 205, 211; skulls and/or skeletons in burial mounds, 204

Bison hunters, 197, 200; mounted, 211, 214; nomadic, 196; pedestrian, 213

Bitter manioc; see Manioc, bitter

Bitterroot culture, 168

Black, Glenn A., 251, 257, 294, 325

Black Rock Cave, 60, 62

Black (black-on-white, etc.) wares; see Ceramic wares

Black's Fork complex, 43, 44

Blackduck focus, 204; I, II, 252; ceramics, 251

Blackwater Draw (Clovis) site, 53, 54, 197; diatomite stratum, 54; gray sand stratum, 54; Portales complex at, 60, 62

Blades, 90, 198, 422, 516, 517; adze, 103, 104, 134; backed, 90, 108; bifacially worked, 396; bipointed, 122; bladelets, 125; cache, leaf-shaped, 237; end, 88, 104, 106, 107; flint, 244, 344; horn, 178; industries, 30; knife, 103; lozenge-shaped, 87, 423; micro-, 88, 90, 102, 107, 108; missile, 104; obsidian, 133, 344, 367, 370, 373, 475; side, 88, 90, 104–6, 107; slate, 102, 103, 134, 135; Solutrean-like, 88; techniques, 30

Blancagrandian complex, 49, 50

Blanchard River sites, 60, 63
Blankets, 178; feather (cloth), 161, 179, 181; fur (cloth), 155, 161, 178, 179, 181; twisted fur, 154; as wrappings for dead, 178;
Blasi, Oldemar, 444, 447, 448, 450
Bliss, Wesley L., 200, 215
Blom, Frans, 349, 379
Blowguns; see Weapons
Bloxsom, Mr. and Mrs. Dan E., vii
Blue Earth culture, 252
Bluhm, Elaine, 172, 191
Boat(s), 124, 456; Chinese, 507; fore-and-aft sailing rig on, 507; -loads of persons, 502; ships, 509; skin-covered, 134, 225; types, 117; umiak, 135; -using groups, 117; see also Canoes
Boca Chica: site, 402; style, 412
Boim culture and site, 428
Bolas; see Weapons
Bolivar, Venezuela, state of, 423
Bolivia(n), 51, 65, 292, 420, 451, 452, 453, 454, 459, 519; eastern, 469; government, 464; highlands, 452, 453, 479; Lake Titicaca basin, 452, 464, 465, 469, 471; lowlands of, 419, 423, 441; Potosi, department of, 50; southern, 50; Tiahuanaco, 469
Bonampak, 360
Bone(s), 156, 211; animal (see Animals); arrowheads, 89–90, 96, 107; artifacts, 37, 38, 45, 46, 52, 59, 88, 100, 103, 125, 163, 202, 204, 205, 208, 213, 397; awls, 32, 123, 126, 127, 155, 160, 198, 225, 344, 515, 518; beads, 155, 165, 179, 225; beamers, 202; bear teeth, 202; bolas weights, 94; bow guards, 212; bracelets, 212; burned, 46, 67; carving, 163; dice, 154; discs, 225; figurines, 382; fishhooks, 118, 132, 207, 260, 422, 456; flageolets, 213; fleshers, serrated metapodial, 212; flint-chipping bars, 155; fossil, 52, 127; fragments, 48, 92, 119, 165; grass-cutters, 160; gorgets, 245, 247; gouges, 515; "green," 45; handles for rattles, 154; harpoon heads, 210; harpoon points, 51; harpoons, 132; hoes, 205; hooks, 260; ice creepers, 104; knife-handles, edge-slotted, 212; implements, 42, 67, 107, 176, 178, 179, 181, 230; industries, 26, 119, 129, 133, 293; lances, 89–90; loon metatarsal, 228; musical rasps, 208; needles, 32, 198, 344; objects, 47, 198; ornaments and/or gaming pieces, 198; paint applicators, wedge-shaped, 208; period (California), 564; Potter

Creek, 119; proboscidean, 47; projectile points, 87, 88, 127, 225, 233, 263, 297, 398; prototypes for copper tools, 234; punches, 123, 127, 516, 517; rattle handles, 154; refuse, 201; scraps, 155; sickles, 160; skin-working tools, 210; spear heads, unilaterally barbed, 210, 213; splinters, 42, 47, 165; split, 46; sweat-scrapers, 127; tools, 133, 186, 456; tubes, 42, 48, 127, 128; whistles, 127, 155, 212; worked, 168, 458; worked, carved, 46, 413
Boone focus, 248, 252
Booy, Theodoor de, 391, 414
Borax Lake: complex, 130; site, 36, 130, 152, 158
Borden, Charles E., 54, 69, 134, 137
Boreal: Archaic (see Archaic, Boreal); forests, 223; traits, est. date of arrival in Columbia Plateau, 164–65; zone, North America, 230
Borhegyi, Stephan F., 368, 369, 370, 371, 372, 375, 383, 521, 523
Bormida, Marcelo, 50, 70, 76
Botanical evidence (botany), 17, 295, 299, 300, 403; paleobotany, 242
Bottles; see Ceramic forms
Bourdier, F., 119, 138
Bow and arrow; see Weapons
Bowls, ceramic (see Ceramic forms); steatite, 236; stone, 134, 166, 182, 231, 458
Box(es): handles, 96; wooden, 178, 179
Boylston Street Fishweir, 230; culture, 253; radiocarbon dates for, 230–31
Bracelets; see Ornaments
Brainerd, George W., viii, 342, 361, 363, 383, 384
Branco River; see Rio Branco
Brazil(ian), 58, 420, 434, 459; coast of, 445; eastern, 57; government of, 451; southern, 419, 420, 421, 443–45, 446, 522; see also individual cultures, sites, and geographical places by name
Breast ornaments; see Ornaments
Breeden site, 206
Brew, J. Otis, 188, 189
Brewster site, 55, 60, 62; Folsom level, radiocarbon date from, 55
Bridges; see Architectural features
Bristol Bay, Alaska, 86, 91, 98, 103
British Columbia, 36, 54, 133–35, 167, 168, 537
British Guiana: archeological survey of, 391; central, 434; coast of, 397; cultural sequence, 433; Essequibo Province, 422; interior of, 419, 433; northwestern, 403, 409, 431

British Honduras, 291, 310, 333, 334, 337, 352, 389
British Mountain, 87, 226
Broeker, Wallace S., 131, 138
Brohm: culture, 253; site, est. date for, 228
Bronze, 470, 473, 480, 495; Age, 495; mirrors, Chinese, 496; ornaments, 470; tools, 470; vessels, Chinese, 504, 505
Brooks culture, 252
Brooks Range, Alaska, 62, 86, 87; Anaktuwuk Pass, 87
Brown County, Wisconsin, 228
Brown (brown-on-white, etc.) wares; *see* Ceramic wares
Browns Valley: culture, 252; points, 32, 85, 88
Bruner, Edward M., 523
Bryan, Alan L., 170, 173, 174
Bryan, Kirk, 44, 62, 70, 150
Buena Vista Lake, California, 127
Buenos Aires, Argentina: city of, 420, 444; province of, 50
Buick focus, 203
Building(s); *see* Architecture, Houses, Palaces, Pueblos, Pyramids, Structures, Temples
Bull Brook: culture, 253; site, 226
Bullard, William R., Jr., 339, 351, 363
Bullbrook, J. A., 392, 414
Bullen, Ripley P., 392, 398
Burgh, Robert F., 178, 179, 191
Burgl, Hans, 50, 70
Burial(s), 42, 178, 184, 186, 228, 231, 263, 332, 344, 375, 422, 423, 478; ceremonies, 235, 245, 271, 431; cults, 262; earliest North American, 32
Burial mound(s), 202, 203, 204, 235–37, 244, 247, 256, 262, 263, 265–67, 269–71, 273–75, 282, 283, 319, 437, 439, 478, 480, 521; cultures, 262–70, 564
Burial places: caves, 178, 356, 360, 363; cemeteries, 38, 249, 300, 311, 355, 431, 436, 437, 439, 440, 444, 483; chambers, 282, 338, 340, 341, 348, 349, 356, 360, 363, 369, 374; cists, 337, 338, 341, 348, 363, 369, 374; crypts, stone slab, 247; graves, 52, 59, 249, 271, 337, 341, 348, 355, 363, 382; house floors (rooms), 249, 337; pits, 204, 271, 363; refuse pits, 249; sarcophagi, 303, 348, 349, 374; tombs, 301, 319, 337, 338, 342, 348, 349, 360, 364, 366, 369, 374; vessels, 363, 434, 439
Burial types: bundle, 247, 369; cremated, 164, 228, 363, 435, 438 (*see also* Cremation); cross-legged, 369; extended, 127, 132, 187, 188, 341, 355, 369, 377;

flexed, 123, 125, 127, 133, 178, 187, 234, 248, 337, 341, 363, 382; half-seated, 179; headless, 369; intrusive, 204, 282; multiple, 106, 204, 236, 245, 247, 348, 360, 363; primary, 125, 127, 132, 204, 271; prone, 123, 126; reburials, 123; retainer, 271, 366, 369; secondary, 203, 204, 245, 271, 363, 427, 431, 434, 436; simple, 237, 241, 363; urn(s): 341, 371, 399, 406, 407, 410, 414, 427, 431, 436, 437, 439, 441, 444, 479; wrapped, 178, 179
Burin(s), 38, 39, 47, 88, 90, 108, 125, 163, 164; Dorset Eskimos, use by, 90; -making, 105; spalls, 90, 108; tradition, 90
Burnett, E. K., 286
Bushnell, G. H. S., 483
Busk (Green Corn) ceremonialism, 279; non-Muskhogean practice of, 281
Butler, B. Robert, 36, 44, 54, 62, 70, 73, 134, 138, 164, 165, 170
Buttons; *see* Ornaments
Byers, Douglas S., 44, 54, 70, 231, 257

C. W. Harris site; *see* Harris site
Cabaret: complex, 398; site, 395
Cacao (chocolate); *see* Plants
Cacaxtla site, 312
Cache(s), 344, 382; blades, 237; in caves, 155; ceremonial, 273, 495; of jade boulders, 370; materials, 381; of miniature mushroom stones, metates, and manos, 368; offerings, 337, 377; pits, 63, 211; of pottery, 271, 341; of red-painted or decorated heads, 269; sites, 161; of skulls, 363; of trianguloid points, 235; *see also* Pits, storage
Cactus; *see* Plants
Caddoan: area, 269, 273, 274, 277, 278, 279, 282, 283, 284, 286; artifacts, 276; ceramics, 269, 274, 276, 280, 282; ceremonial centers, 274; culture(s), 269, 274, 275, 278, 279, 280, 282, 285; earth lodges, 277; ideas, 274; influence, 278, 279, 281, 282; –Middle Mississippi axis, 285; prehistory, 282; projectile points, 269; sites, 269, 273; Village tribes, 195
Cahokia: Old Village complex, est. dates for, 250; site, 250, 278; Trappist phase, 251, 252
Cairo, Illinois, 244
Cajamarca, Peru, basin, 452
Cakchiquel: *Annals*, 333, 374; dialect, 365; kingdom, 374; Iximche, capital of, 374
Calchitan, Guatemala, 373
Caldwell, Joseph R., 257, 286, 457, 484

Caldwell, Warren W., 145, 173
Calendar(s) (calendrics, calendrical), 332, 538; Christian, 345, 346, 362; correlation(s) of, Maya and Christian, Goodman-Martinez-Thompson (GMT), Spinden's or Makemson's, 345, 346, 362; idea of, 500; lunations, 344; Maya, 338, 344, 345, 348, 368 (*see also* Chronology, Maya calendar); permutating ritual, 331, 339, 344; symbols, 301; systems, 303
California, 54, 59, 62, 117, 119, 124, 129, 131, 160, 564; *see also* individual cultures, sites, and geographical places by name
Calixtlahuaca, Mexico, 309
Calpulalpan, Tlaxcala, 309
Camare: complex, 49, 50, 51, 396; sites, 396
Cambodia: Angkor, 501; archeological example of cross motif from, 498; Khmer peoples of, 501
Cambria culture, 246, 252
Campbell, Elizabeth W. Crozer, 54, 70, 121, 138
Campbell, John M., 62, 70, 87, 108
Campbell, Thomas N., vii
Campbell, William H., 54, 70, 121, 138
Campeche, 44, 302, 333–34, 351, 353, 355, 360
Campus site, 60, 62, 232
Camutins mound group, 439; Guaraja cemetery, 439
Canada, 6, 37, 59, 62, 85, 89, 107, 155, 213, 223, 357; central, 100; eastern, 107; interior, 88; northern, 39, 91; Northwest Territories, 36, 62; northwestern, 236; Prairie Provinces, 195; southern, 201; Yukon Territory, 36, 54; *see also* individual provinces by name
Cañada de Marfil, 293
Canaima site, 395, 396
Canaliño cultures: Early, 240; Late, 246
Canalas, 305, 321, 324
Canals Frau, Salvador, 28, 70
Canoes, 324, 332, 358; bark, 513; drift, 124; dugout, 38, 135, 225, 397, 398, 424, 427; plank, 118; *see also* Boats
Cañon del Infiernillo; *see* Infiernillo Canyon
Capa: site, 402; style, 412
Capacho site, 393
Capdeville, Augusto, 51, 70
Cape Denbigh, Norton Sound: 90, 104; Iyatayet site, 104
Cape Dorset, 86, 107
Cape Krusenstern, Kotzebue Sound, 87, 88, 89, 105, 106
Cape Mendocino, California, 132, 135

Cape Prince of Wales, Bering Strait, 86, 91, 98, 99
Caracas, Venezuela, 401; area, 403; Museo de Ciencias Naturales, 391; port for, 405; Universidad Central de, 391
Carbon-14 dating; *see* Radiocarbon dating
Carcarañense complex, 49, 50
Cardich, Augusto, 57, 65, 71, 484
Caribbean, 9, 292, 334, 353, 419, 565; agriculture, type of, 403, 405; archeological research in, 391; archeology of, 400; area, 389, 390–95, 397, 399, 400, 412; chronology of, 392; climate of, 390; geography of, 389–90; levels of development in, 446; radiocarbon dates for, 392
Caribbean Sea, 389, 390, 395, 402, 413
Caribou; *see* Animals
Carlson, Roy L., 134, 138
Carrasco Pizana, Pedro, 323, 326
Carson culture, 232
Cartagena, Colombia, 400
Carter, George F., 31, 44, 46, 71, 119, 121, 138, 296, 326
Cartier, Jacques, 254
Carupano, Venezuela, 402, 409
Carving(s) (carved): antler, 165; bone, 163, 413; ceramics, 266, 372; columns, 357; fetishes, 166; gourds, 460; ivory, 103; rock, 303; shell, 182, 413; stone, 161, 166, 182, 315, 371, 413, 458, 459, 461, 462, 463; stucco, 355, 356; turquoise, 461; wood, 134, 135, 163, 165, 413
Caryatid(s), 360; at Chichén Itzá, 359; colossal, at Tula, 359; -supported figurines, 352; supports for vessels, 432
Casa Grande (Arizona), 188
Casafranca, José, 463, 484
Casamiquela, Rodolfo M., 50, 71
Casapadrense complex, 39, 65, 66, 67; est. date for, 67
Casas Grandes (Chihuahua) culture, 185, 188
Casiquiare River, 419, 420, 432
Casma, Peru, 458
Casma Valley, Peru, 457, 459, 460
Caso, Alfonso, 305, 326, 495, 510
Cassava; *see* Manioc
Castalia phase, 425
Castillo: at Chavín de Huantar, 458; at Chichén Itzá, 359
Catalan Chico site, 49, 50
Catalan Grande site, 49, 50
Catamarca, Argentina, 50
Causeways, 339; earth, 324, 334; masonry, 334; stone-paved, 378
Caves (caverns), 14, 32, 33, 36, 41, 52, 63, 153, 154, 155, 168, 179, 422; of Argen-

tina, 422; burials in, 178, 356, 360, 363; deposits in, 212, 213, 294, 295; of eastern Colorado, 203; in Great Basin, 35, 55; in Oregon, 169; Sierran limestone, 131; sites of, 126, 160; in Utah, 154, 156; worship of zemis in, 413; *see also* individual cave sites by name

Caviana, Brazil, island of, 420, 427, 435, 436

Cayo Redondo: complex, 398; site, 395

Cazador complex (stage), 61; radiocarbon dates for, 61, 63

Cazorla, Venezuela, 430

Ce Acatl Topiltzin, 316

Ce Tecpatl Mixcoatl, epic of, 314, 316

Celts, 135, 367, 376; carved, 380, 412; ceremonial, 276; copper, 234; green and dark stone, 343; ground-stone, 230; 234; invention of, 398; nephrite, 164; polished stone, 183; shell, 397

Cemeteries, 38, 249, 431, 436, 437, 440, 444, 483; absence of, 424, 428, 429, 431, 433; Jaina, island of, 355; Monte Alban, 311; mounds in, 439; *see also* Burials and Burial places

Cenotes; *see* Wells

Central Algonkian groups; *see* Algonquin Indians

Central America(n), 37, 39, 53, 291, 296, 309, 317, 365, 389, 398, 481, 489, 521, 548; lamellar flakes, 398; languages, 546, 547; Pacific Coast of, 292, 303; preceramic sites in, 398; republics, 331; *see also* Mesoamerica

Central Antilles; *see* Antilles

Central Depression (Upper Grijalva Basin), Chiapas, 377; Late Classic ceremonial centers, 379, 380; sites, 378

Central Plains tradition (phase), 194, 196, 202, 203, 206–9

Central (Mississippi) Valley cultures, 269, 283

Centro de Investigaciones Antropologicas de Mexico, viii

Ceramic(s), 348, 355, 410, 465, 471, 481, 565; art, 181, 186, 512; associations, 245, 343; complexes, 248, 267, 281, 283, 285, 362, 419–20, 427, 428, 432, 438, 475, 496; decadence (degeneration), 354, 406, 410, 471; early, 463, 474; horizons, 180, 201, 284, 318, 319, 377; -making peoples (*see* Pottery-making peoples); mass production of, 471; molds, 504; phases, 180; sequences, 306, 482; series, 393, 403, 403 ff.; similarities, 519; stability, 424; stylistic history, 465; surface finish, 236; *see also* Vessels

Ceramic decorative styles and techniques, 188, 236, 247, 248, 261, 313, 336, 337, 349, 350, 366, 370, 375, 399, 404, 405, 410, 437, 438, 440, 464, 476, 512, 519, 520; absence of, 410, 411

Appliqué, 343, 371, 399, 406, 407, 410–12, 433, 436, 437

Brushed, 267, 282, 284, 286, 424, 425, 436

Carved, 266, 372

Cord-marked (impressed, roughened), 202, 203, 206, 208, 244, 267, 275, 281, 495; single cord, 203, 208, 247; exterior and interior, 235, 236

Cord-wrapped, 248

Corrugated, 184, 187, 441, 445, 474, 512, 522

Crazed, 337

Crosshatched: incised, 336, 409; painted, 408; zoned, 411, 424, 425, 518

Engraved, 273, 274, 278, 281, 282

Excised, 436–40, 475, 512

Fabric-impressed (marked), 236, 261, 267, 269–71, 280, 399

Finger grooved (pressed), 433, 474

Fingernail impressed (imbricated), 445, 474

Fluted, 366, 370

Fresco, 512

Grooved, 366, 438

Impressed, 436

Incised, 96, 106, 127, 204, 243, 247, 261, 265, 266, 268, 269, 271, 273, 337, 343, 366, 370, 372, 378, 379, 404–13, 427–31, 433, 435, 437, 440, 444, 445, 458, 474, 475, 512; carinated bowls, 273, 282, 284; complex, 410; crosshachured; 366, 409, 411, 424, 425; four arches, 278, 281; groove, 336, 337; horizontal, below rim, 270; modeled, 405–13, 433; outlined, 367, 371, 381; parallel lines, 408, 410, 412, 424, 430; punctate-filled, 338; retouched, 438; simple cursive, 381; single lines, 424; trailed, 208, 211; zoned, 270, 425, 459; zoned, crosshatching, 409, 411, 424, 425

Mat-marked, 261

Modeled, 278, 337, 343, 425, 429, 430, 458, 465; absence of, 427; anthropomorphic, 432, 438; birds and animals, 432; bosses, heads, ridges, spikes, 337; -incised, 405, 406, 408–10, 412, 413; -incised tradition, 412, 464; serpents 405

Mold-made, 370, 471; animal-head feet, 374; ornaments, 370, 504, 505

Moldings, vertical, 370

Ceramic decorative styles and techniques—
Continued
Painting, 181, 184, 265, 271, 237, 370, 407, 409, 412, 439, 440, 463, 464, 480, 519; absence of, 412; bands, 349, 475; direct, 343; glaze-, 188, 209; iridescent, 511, 512; Mochica, 466–68; negative (wax-resist), 265, 338, 343, 370, 372, 381, 429, 476, 479; negative, bottles, 281; negative, Usulutan ware, 337, 367; post-firing, 512, 521; -pottery complexes, 445; stucco, 370, 377, 382; yellow, 432; *see also* Ceramic wares
Plain surface, 247
Polished, 180, 182, 186, 187, 336, 350, 436, 458, 471, 474, 475
Punctated, 247, 278, 399, 405, 430, 431, 444, 445; dots, 437; fillets, 433; filling of incised designs, 338; on foreheads of figurines, 515; incised tradition, 445; linear, 261
Scraped, 440; shell, 474
Scratched, 343
Stamped, 261, 265, 271, 435; check-, 238, 261, 263, 267, 273, 275; check-, est. date for, in peninsular Florida, 274; complicated-, 244, 266–69, 271, 273, 275, 279; complicated-, angular, 271; complicated-, overstamped, 284; dentate, 243, 244, 245; rocker, 202, 263, 381; rocker, absence of, 381; rocker, zoned, 266; shell, 474; simple, 206, 208, 238, 263
Striated, 337
Stuccoid, 370, 377, 382
Trailed, 208, 211, 464
Unpainted, 458
Unpolished, 182
Zone-decorated, 202, 265, 269, 270, 518
Ceramic designs: animal figures, 206; anthropomorphic, 430; Arauquinoid, 410; Chavinoid, 464; curvilinear, 404–6, 408, 410, 412, 464; dentate stamp, 244; face-and-collar, 407; geometric, 349, 366, 430, 445, 470, 518; glyphic, 349, 350; interlace, 405; naturalistic, 349; parallel lines, 518; rectilinear, 336, 405–7, 410, 429; scroll(s), interlocking, 313, 370; scroll and guilloche, 283; scroll and meander, 273; scroll and step, 436; spiral, 204, 410; stepped elements, 518; straight lines, 406; Tajin, 313; Tiahuanaco, 469; Tollan, 315; triangles, 336; Tzakol, 343; zoömorphic, 430
Ceramic forms (shapes), 236, 424, 475, 497
Adornos, 427, 433, 437, 441
Bases, annular, 399, 404, 409; conoidal,

247; convex, 338, 343; flat, 236, 266, 349, 350, 408; ornaments around, 382; pedestal, 343, 367; ring, 343, 350, 370, 371; rounded, 247, 349
Beakers, outflaring or outcurved, 350
Bosses, 461
Bottles, 278, 404; engraved, 273, 274; gadrooned, 381; lobed, 281; negative painted, 281; plain, 281
Bowls, 277, 278, 281, 283, 284, 336, 337, 343, 349, 350, 362, 366, 370, 371, 372, 379, 381, 399, 404, 405, 408, 412, 430, 431, 436, 439, 459, 475; barrel-shaped, 349; basal-flange, polychrome, 343; basal-flange, ring-base, 343; basal-ridge (Z-angle), 343; basin-shaped, 439; carinated, 283, 284, 286, 439; carinated, engraved, 273, 282; carinated, incised, 273, 282, 284; composite silhouette, 366, 377, 381, 475; cuspidor-like, 336; deep, 372; effigy-head, 281; flaring sides, 349; flat-bottomed, 459; greater, 350; incurved-rim, 349, 350, 379; inturned sides, 412; long, hollow legs, 405; outflaring or outcurved, 350; restricted orifice, 349, 350; ring-base, 350, 370; round-side, incurved rim, 349; simple rounded, 366, 399; tetrapod, pedestal-base, 343; tripod, basal-flange, 370; tripod, convex-base, 343
Candeleros, 350, 370, 382
Censers, 352, 363, 371, 375; covers, duck-shaped, 370; effigy, 352, 372; elaborately decorated, 372; ladle, 370, 375; ladle, long-handled, 372; Mayapan-type, 352; spiked, thick-walled, 371, 372; tall perforated, 374; tall tripod, 367; three-pronged, 366, 367, 370, 377, 521
Collars: convex, 406; corrugated, 441; flaring, 372; sharply angled, 372; vertical, 372
Comal: handles, 371, 372; -like vessels, 372
"Cream pitchers," handled, 370
Cups, double (candeleros), 350, 370, 382; tall tripod, 366
Dippers, 518
Dishes, 337; basal angle, 350; flaring or outcurving sides, flat-bottomed, 381; tripod, 343; tripod, incurved rim, 350; tripod, notched or stepped basal-flange, 349
Effigy, 268, 273, 374; censers, 353, 372; -head bowls, 281
Feet, 266; animal-head, mold-made, 374; bulging, 343; conical, 343, 349, 367; effigy, 375; hollow, 343, 349, 367, 371,

377; human-effigy head, tripod, 352; mammiform, 337, 382; nubbin, 337, 367; nubbin, tetrapod, 377; polypod, 432; slab, 343, 370, 371; solid, 350, 371; solid, cylindrical, 337, 349, 371; tetrapod, 261, 263, 337, 367, 474; tripod, 337, 367, 432; "turkish-slipper," tripod, 352

Flanges, 409; absence of, 405, 406; basal, 337, 338, 343, 370, 371; basal, notched or stepped, 349; on cover handles, 343; labial, 377; lateral, 367; medial, 377; on rims, incised, 404; wide-everted, 367

Handles, 282, 350, 433; bail, 371, 372; comal, 371, 372; cover-, flanged scutate (anthropomorphic, cylindrical, zoömorphic), 343; cylindrical lug, 236; D-shaped, 411; drum-, 104; ladle, leg of tripod acting as, 372, 374; loop, 277, 411, 412, 433; loop, horizontal, 518; oval to round, 372; rod, horizontal, 406; strap, 278, 281, 372; strap, horizontal, 404, 516, 517; strap, vertical, 404, 408, 437, 518

Jars, 236, 247, 284, 285, 343, 349, 372, 373, 399, 404, 430, 444, 445, 516, 517, 522; brushed-surface, 282; bulging neck, 349; burial, 434, 439; corrugated neck, 444; globular, 336, 337; globular, canteen-like, 518; globular, narrow-necked, 518; handled, 371; large, 284, 366; plain, 278; round-bottomed, 278; small-mouthed, 367; stirrup-spouted, 475; storage, 471; strap-handled, 281; tall-necked mortuary, 375; tetrapod, 263; unslipped, 350; unsupported spout, 382; whistling, 475, 497

Ladles, 516, 517

Legs: absence of, 406; long, hollow, 405; slab, 382; solid, 404; tetrapod, tripod (*see below*)

Lids: conical, 504, 505; bowls used as, on burial jars, 439; on burial urns, 431

Lips, 247

Lobes, 433

Lugs: appliqué, 406, 410, 411, 412; Barrancoid, 406, 408; complex, 410; head, large, modeled-incised, 412, 413; horizontal, 437; modeled-incised, 404, 406, 409; simple geometric, 410; simple knobbed, 408; tabular, 411

Necks: bulging, 349; corrugated, 444; flaring, 336; incised and punctated, alternating bands, 430; low, 350; low vertical, 336; sloping, 350; walled, concave, 518

Ollas, 121, 405; without flanges or handles, 410; ovoid, 433

Pitchers, 516, 517, 518, 520

Plates, 434; flat-bottomed, flaring sides, 336, 337; incised, 337; polychrome, 361; thickened, everted rim, 337; tripod, 349

Pots, globular, 275

Ridges: basal (Z-angle), 338, 343, 349, 350, 381; lateral, 349; medial, 381

Rims: beveled, 408; beveled, incised, 412; broad, flat-topped, 427; cambered, 438; cambered, cross-hatched, 265; castellated, 522; castellated, folded over, 474; cord-impressed, 203, 248; cord-wrapped decorated, 248; effigies on, 277; finger-pressed, 474; flanged, 404; flat, widely everted, 337, 343, 350; forms of, 438; hanging, 350; heads on, 370; hieroglyphic bands on, 350; horizontal grooves below, 371; incised, 247; incised bands, alternating with punctated, 430; incised below, 381, 424; incised horizontally, 270; incurved, 349, 350, 366, 379; notched, 284; pinched, 284; plain, 408; punctated, 247; widely everted, 366; widely everted, grooved, 381

Shoe-shaped, 366

Shoulders: incised or trailed, 208, 412; squared, 350

Sides: flaring, 337, 343, 381, 408; outcurving, 337, 338; recurved, 337

Spoons, 518

Spouts: bridged, 337, 338, 367, 382; four, 265; stirrup, 278, 459, 462, 465, 471, 475; two, 404; unsupported, 381

Tetrapod: bowls, pedestal-base, 343; feet, 377, 474; jars, 263; platforms, 349; vessels, 261, 337, 367; vessels, mammiform, 338, 367, 378

Tripod(s), 432, 441; bowls, 343, 370; bulbous cascabel, 350; censers, perforated, 374; censers, tall, 367; conical, 432; cups, tall, 366; cylinder, 343, 370, 504, 505; cylinder, concave-walled, 382; dishes, 343, 350; metates, 183; plates, 349; tall, 370; with three heads on rim, 367; vases, 343; vessels, 278, 337, 352, 367, 432; vessels, with flat and rounded bases, 349

Urn(s): anthropomorphic, 431, 439; burial(s), 341, 371, 399, 406, 407, 414, 427, 431, 436, 437, 439, 447, 479; burials, absence of, 410, 414, 435, 444; clay, 303, 444; cremation ashes in, 364; Monte Alban IIIb, 310; painted, 438

Ceramic forms (shapes)—*Continued*
Vases: barrel-shaped, 349; barrel-shaped ring-stand, 350; cylindrical, 350; cylindrical fine-ware, 349; cylindrical slab-footed tripod, 343; polychrome, 358
Walls: incised, 408; modeled-incised figures on, 410; rounded, slightly flaring, 372; thin, 475
Ceramic horizon styles
Incised and punctate, 430–32; est. dates for, 430; influence, 432; sites, 430
Incised rim, 427–30, 441; est. dates for, 430
Polychrome (painted), 437–42; est. dates for, 430, 441; radiocarbon dates from Rio Napa, 441, 442
Zoned hachure, 425, 426, 428, 441, 565; origin of, 426; sites, 424
Ceramic techniques: firing, 181, 381; paddling (paddle-and-anvil), 182, 187, 278; stamping, 278; Usulutan negative painting, 337, 367; *see also* Ceramic decorative styles and techniques
Ceramic tempering: calcite, 203, 350; *cariape* (burned siliceous bark), 425, 429, 430, 431; *cauixi* (sponge Spicule), 410, 425, 429, 432; charcoal, 441; clay, 244, 250, 269; fiber, 126, 236, 261, 263, 267; grit, 206, 250, 399, 410; limestone, 250; mica, 375; quartz, 350, 431; sand, 104, 425, 429, 433; shell, 206, 211, 277, 278, 280–82, 285, 425; sherds, ground, 424, 436; steatite, 238; temperless, 274, 350
Ceramic traditions, 8, 262, 265, 306, 343, 427, 445, 463, 464, 465; excised, 437; local, 464; Lower Mississippi Valley, 265, 269, 270, 280; modeling-incising, 412; punctate and incised, 445
Ceramic types (phases, styles), named: Adeena Plain, 237; Alto focus, 274; Arua, 436; Aztalan (Sinaloa), 319; Baytown, 274; Blackduck, 251; Brazo Largo, 444; Caddoan, 269, 274, 276, 280, 282; Canteen Cord-marked, 250; Canteen Plain, 250; Castalia phase, 425; Chama Polychrome, 372; Cherokee, 268, 284; Chiapa de Corzo, 354; Chila phase, 302; Chimu, 471; Chorrera, 475; Classic, 343; Coles Creek (incised), 270, 273; Conchas phases, 346, 366, 376, 377, 381; Copador polychrome, 350, 378; Copan, 337, 343, 350; Culiacan, 319; Cuzco, 473; Deptford, 261, 263, 265–69; Early Classic, 338, 343, 370–72, 382; Early Paracas, 463, 464; Early (Yucatan), 355; El Prisco, 302; Erin, 409; Etowah, 268, 280, 284; Fayette

Thick, 237; Flores Waxy, 336; Florescent, 356, 362, 363; Formative (Guatemala highlands), 361; French Fork Incised, 270; Gibson aspect, 276, 282; Gila Polychrome, 188; Gulf (Coastal Plain), 265, 266, 271, 273, 281; Havana complex, 239, 243; Holmul I, 337, 355; Hopewell Zone Stamped, 244; Hupaiya, 437; Huron-Petun, 251; Inca, 471; intermediate styles (Central Antilles), 411, 412; Iroquois, 254, 255; Izapa, 377, 379; Jomon, 474, 503; Kolomoki, 268; Las Charcas, 366, 376; Late Classic, 348, 350, 358; Laurel complex, 240, 244, 251; Los Caros, 428, 430; Loseke Creek, 203; Lower Mississippi Valley, 272, 273; Machalilla, 475; Madison Cord-impressed, 247; Marajoara, 437, 438–44; Marcey Creek, 238; Marksville, 266, 269; Mars-orange, 336; Matzanel phase, 338, 346, 355; Meillac, 412; Miccaotli phase, 306; Michigan, 243; Middle Preclassic, 336; Mississippian, 249, 250, 264, 274, 278, 281; Mixteca-Puebla, 319; Montgomery Incised, 237; Moundville, 281–83; Napo, 437, 441; Natchez, 272; Nericagua, 429–30, 433; Ornate phase, 310; Ostiones, 411, 412; Owens Valley Brown, 131, 162; Paila Unslipped, 337; Palma Daub, 336; Paso Caballo Waxy, 337; Pavon, 299, 376; Petén Gloss, 341; Plaquemine, 272; Point Peninsula, 244, 245, 251; Porter complex, 267; Postclassic, 350, 352, 372, 374, 382; pre-Chavín, 459; pre-Tupi-Guarani, 444; Preclassic, 336, 366, 368, 370; Protoclassic, 338, 367, 368, 373, 382; Protohistoric, 375; Qualuyu, 464; Rancho Peludo, 399; Robles Plumbate, 372, 374; Rupununi, 434; Salto Grande, 444; San Juan Plumbate, 372, 374, 378, 379; Shakimu excised, 436–37; Sikyatki Polychrome, 188; South Appalachian, 265–68, 271, 280; Swift Creek, 244, 266–69; Taruma, 435; Tchefuncte, 261, 263, 265, 269, 272; Tiahuanaco, 469; Thin Orange, 310, 319, 343, 370; Ticoman, 306; Tohil Plumbate, 372, 374, 379; Troyville, 266, 267, 269, 271; Tula-Mazapan, 319; Tupi-Guarani, 444; Ulua (Bichrome), 337, 343, 376; Valdivia (excised), 437, 474–75, 496, 503, 522; Vinaceous Tawny, 349; Vinette I, 236, 238; Wari (Coast Tiahuanaco), 469, 470; Weeden Island, 262, 268, 271, 273, 274; Woodland, 131, 201, 496;

Woodland, Early, 235, 236, 238, 239; Woodland, Late, 247, 250; "X" Fine Orange, 374; Yojoa Monochrome, 376; *see also* Art styles, Chicanel, Kaminaljuyú, Mamom, Teotihuacán, Tepeu; Tzakol

Ceramic typology, 301

Ceramic wares

Bichrome, 367, 374, 375; black-on-cream, 346, 362; black-on-orange, 349; black-on-red, 184, 337, 367, 371, 518; black-on-white, 184, 187, 445, 518; brown-on-buff, 349; brown-on-red, 349; brown-on-white, 464; red-on-brown, 181, 184, 318, 319; red-on-buff, 182, 188, 318, 337, 366, 372; red-and-cream, 336; red-on-cream, 336, 372; red-on-orange, 337, 372; red-on-white, 184, 366, 372, 435; white-on-red, 409, 410, 411, 464, 476; Ulua, 376

Ceremonial and luxury, 372, 431

Ferruginous, 374; carved, 349

Fine (paste) (thin-walled), 349, 372, 408; black, 350; carved, 372; chocolate brown, 372; gray, 349, 350, 372; incised, 372; orange, 349, 352, 361, 362, 372, 379; orange, untempered and polished, 350; orange "X", 374; pinkish or "tea," 372; red, 372; tan, 372; white, 372

Gloss, 341, 349, 355

Monochrome, 350, 352, 355, 366, 370, 406, 464; black, 302, 366, 337, 341, 366, 369, 471; black, fine paste, 350, 370; black, incised, 378; black, tan- and white-rimmed, 381; black-brown, 369; brown, 184, 337, 341; brown, northern and southern, 180; brown, polished, 180, 182, 184, 187; buff, 182, 337, 341, 366; cream, 337, 370; cream, Tiquisate, 372; flesh-color, 370; gray, 341, 363; gray, indented corrugated, 184, 187; gray, plain, 180; gray, unpolished, 182, 187; gray-brown, 336; gray-cored, 440; ivory, 370; orange, 336, 337, 341, 370, 374, 379, 440; orange, fine, 349, 350, 352, 361, 362, 372, 374; pastel, 187, 370; pink or "tea," 372; pink-orange, Tiquisate, 372; red, 336, 337, 341, 362, 363, 366, 370, 512, 581; red, fine, 372, 375; red, incised, 381; red, Mogollon, 181; red, polished, 186, 187, 366; tan, fine, 372; white, 366, 471; white, thin, 372; Yojoa, 376

Plain, 100, 180, 181, 202, 206, 236, 269, 274, 275, 424, 431, 436, 438, 439, 440,

444, 457; bottles, 281; gray, 180; Mogollon, 181

Plumbate, 319, 352, 372, 357; effigy, Tohil, 372, 374, 379; non-effigy, ferruginous, 372, 374, 378, 379

Polychrome, 184, 188, 338, 350, 358, 361, 370, 375, 378, 382, 383, 405, 406, 408, 437, 441, 445, 471, 518; absence of, 445; Aztalan, 319; black-and-red-on-white, 518; bowls, 343; Casas Grandes, 188; Chama, 372; Cojumatlan, 319; Copador, 350, 378; funeral jars, 375; Gila Pueblo, 188; Maya, 378; multicolor-on-buff, -cream, -gray, -orange, 349; murals, 374; Protohistoric highland, 375; red-and-black-on-buff, 341; red-and-black-on-orange, 341, 343; red-and-black-on-red, 349; red-and-black-on-white, 405, 437; Sityatki, 188; Tepeu, 349, 350; tradition, 464, 465

Slatewares: bowls, 362; censers, 362; Florescent, Yucatan, 356, 362; jars, 362; Yucatecan, 349

Slipped, 336, 337, 341, 349, 352, 370; double-, 438, 440; red-, 379, 427, 429, 430, 438, 440, 445, 474, 519; "waxy," 355, 356, 377; white, 379, 437, 438, 440, 519

Tiquisate, 309, 372, 378

Unslipped, 336, 350, 352, 440

Utility (culinary, domestic, utilitarian), 184, 236, 269, 270, 281, 336, 337, 371, 372, 431, 439; corrugated gray, 184, 187; polished, paddle and anvil, 184, 187

Variegated, 336, 337, 342

Vitrified, 349, 374; incipient, 370

Ceremonial(s), 249, 350, 440, 462; artifacts, 166, 256, 265, 275–80, 344, 476, 504; ball games, 315, 331, 522; bird chariots, Chinese, 495; caches, 273, 495; celts, 276; council houses, semi-subterranean, 277, 278; cycles of time, 344; figures, 360; mounds, 302; patterns, 242; pottery, 273, 303, 370, 372, 431; scenes, 465; sites, 428, 429; structures, 184, 186, 187, 231, 238, 263, 278, 280, 281, 282, 284, 301, 348, 363, 369, 405, 406, 408, 410, 476, 480 (*see also* Ball courts, Kivas, Mounds, Temples); wares (luxury), ceramic (*see* Ceramic wares)

Ceremonial centers, 249, 266, 271, 274, 275, 285, 286, 304, 339, 465; Altar de Sacrificios, 336; Caddoan, 274; Chichén Itzá, 359; Davis site, 273, 274; Deptford, 263; Early Classic, 369; Fort Walton,

Ceremonial centers—*Continued*
283; fortified, 277; Harlan site, 274; isolated, 282; Kolomoki, 271; La Venta, 304; large, 282; Late Classic, Grijalva Basin, 379, 380; Lower Mississippi Valley, 270; major, 270, 279, 281, 339; Marksville, 265; Maya (Guatemala), 339, 348, 351, 356, 360, 366, 370, 379, 380; Mississippian, 278; Monte Alban, 308; Preclassic, 369; Postclassic, 352; Southern Cult, 278; system, 304; Teotihuacán, 307; Troyville, 266; Yucatan Decadent, 363; Zacualpa, 371
Ceremonialism, 101, 207, 267, 275, 279, 283, 284; Adena-Hopewell, 242; burial, 234, 245, 271; Busk (Green Corn), 279, 281; Central Antilles, 413–14; Deptford, 263; Mexican, 248; Monte Alban, 301; Ohio Hopewell, 271; religious, 271; rise of, in southeastern United States, 414
Cerro Blanco site, 459, 460
Cerro Chavín site, 379
Cerro Largo, Uruguay, 50
Cerro Machado: ceramic style, 405; radiocarbon date for, 405; site, 401, 405
Cerro de las Mesas site, 380, 382, 554; early phases, 309; Protoclassic burial at, 382; Upper II, 382
Cerro de Montevideo site, 49, 50
Cerro Sechin site, 459, 461
Chac mools, 357, 360
Chaco Canyon, New Mexico, 185
Chains; *see* Ornaments
Chalcatzingo rock carvings, 303
Chalcedony: artifacts, 51; Dakota, 242; projectile points, 242, 422, 423; spears, 242
Chalchitan, Huehuetenango, Guatemala, 373
Chalchuapa, El Salvador, 303
Chalchuites culture, 183
Chalco complex (culture), 60, 63, 295; radiocarbon dates for, Hondo River, 295
Chalcolithic stage, 29
Chaluka site, 90; radiocarbon date for, 90, 102
Chama phases, 309, 367
Chama River, 188
Champe, John L., 202, 206, 212, 213, 216
Champerico, Guatemala, 375
Champoton, Campeche, 353
Chanchan, 459, 470; population of, 470; walls of, 470
Channel Islands, California, 118
Chapman, Carl H., 212, 215
Charcoal, 14, 46, 48, 52, 55, 63, 64, 67, 127, 239, 245, 429; tempering, 441
Chard, Chester S., 98, 100, 108

Charles V of Spain, 325
Charlot, Jean, 358
Chattahoochee River, 266, 284; lower, 263; valley of, 2-3
Chavez Ballon, Manuel, 485
Chavín: ceramics, 459, 461, 463, 475; cult, 465, 473; horizon, 426, 457; de Huantar site, 458, 459, 460, 480; influences, 464; pre-, 458, 459, 461; religious ideas, 463; styles, decorative. 458, 460, 462, 463, 464, 504, 522; symbolism, 463
Chenes area, 364; Hochob, 364
Cherokee: culture, 281; pipes, 268; pottery, 268, 284; tribe, 281
Chert; *see* Minerals
Chesapeake Bay, 238
Chetco, Oregon, 132
Cheyenne River, 206, 208
Chiapa de Corzo sequence, 355, 377, 378; est. dates for, 377; I (Early Preclassic), 377; I, est. dates for, 346, 376; II, 377, 381; II, est. dates for, 346; III, 354, 377; III, est. dates for, 346; IV, 354, 376, 377, 381; IV, est. dates for, 346; V (Late Preclassic), 346, 354, 377, 381; VI–VII (Protoclassic), 346, 378; VIII (Early Classic), 378
Chiapas, 63, 292, 303, 313, 332, 334, 351, 360, 375, 376; Central Depression, 377; -Guatemala frontier, 376, 379; highlands, 296, 324, 379, 380; Pacific coastal plain of, 377, 378; southern, 333, 334; western, 378, 379
Chicama River, Peru, 459; mouth of, 454, 455; Valley, 459, 463
Chicanel ceramic period (ceramics), 335, 336, 338, 346, 351, 354, 366, 376, 377, 381
Chichén, Alta Verapaz, Guatemala, 373
Chichén Itzá, 316, 354, 356, 358, 359, 360, 362, 504; atlantean or caryatid forms, 359; ceramics, 361; ceremonial center, 359; El Caracol, 359; El Castillo, 359; Great Ball Court, 359; High Priest's Grave (Osario), 360; Maya-Toltec architecture of, 364; Nunnery (Monjas), 356; Sacred Well, 359; Temple of the Jaguars, 357; Temple of the Warriors, 357, 359; Tula resemblances and est. date for, 359, 360
Chickinising Creek site, 231
Chicoid: ceramics, 412, 413; Indians, 412, 413; series, 409, 565; styles, 412
Chiefdoms: Colombian highland, 481; Peruvian highland, 471
Chieftains (chiefs), 539; memorials to, 304; portraiture of, 303; territorial, 481; war, 481

Chihuahua, 175, 180, 314; great houses of, 188; northern, 177; northwestern, 176, 188

Chilca locality, 456, 459; radiocarbon dates for, 456

Childe, V. Gordon, 121, 138

Chile, 34, 50, 51, 57, 67, 120, 459, 522; central, 471, 480; coast of, 49, 51; northern, 58, 469, 479, 480, 565; Patagonian part of, 58, 64; southern, 537

Chili peppers; *see* Plants

Chillicothe, Ohio, 241

Chilocco Historic sites, 209

Chimaltenango, Guatemala, department of, 365

Chimu kingdom, 470, 471; ceramics, 471; ceramics, Inca influence on, 471

China (Chinese), 489, 490, 502, 504, 507, 509; ancient, 360; art styles, 498, 499; bird chariots, 495; bronze mirrors, 496; bronze vessels, 504, 505; central, 499; culture sequence, 499; early bronze age of, 504; government of, 451; Han dynasty (period), 494–96, 503–7; parallels with New World, 360, 504, 505; Shang dynasty, 504, 507

Chinampas, 321; fossil, 321; gardens, 305, 321

Chinkultic, Chiapas, 372; ball-court marker, 379; dated monuments at, 379; Late Classic stelae at, 372

Chinook–Coast Salish area, 118, 132

Chipped stone, 168; adzes, 229, 231; artifacts (implements, tools), 37, 38, 51, 52, 85, 96, 102, 104, 122, 156, 158, 163, 176, 197–98, 231, 294, 367, 422, 423, 443; bifacially, 51; choppers, 229; drills, 178, 179; flints, 45; knives, 104, 161, 178, 179, 204; points, 164, 179, 422, 519; scrapers, 178, 179; slate, 102; spear heads, 204

Chiricahua complex (stage), 60–63, 169; radiocarbon dates for, 61, 63

Chiripa, 465; site, 459, 464; site, est. date for lower levels of, 464; village, est. date for, 464

Chixoy River, Guatemala, 333, 334

Choco, Colombia, department of, 49, 50

Cholollan, 311, 322; Olmeca-Xicalanca dynasty, 312; period, 312; pyramid-temple at, 311; rise of, 311

Cholula, Puebla, 309, 383

Choluteca River, Honduras, 292

Chopper-scraper stage, 159; in Desert West, 151

Choppers, 36, 50, 87, 122, 123–52, 154, 155, 156, 197, 198, 229, 422; chipped, 166; 229; cobble, 164; flint, 225, 344; fossil wood, 50, 396; limestone, 344; pebble, 164, 165; quartzite, 396

Choris culture, 88, 91, 105; Kotzebue Sound, 90, 104, 105; late Choris phase, 89; pre-Choris phase, 89; radiocarbon date for, Cape Krusenstern, 89; site, 89; site, radiocarbon date for, 89, 104

Choris-Norton: ceramic complex, 236; –Near Ipiutak tradition, 91, 101, 102, 106

Chorrera phase (culture), 376, 377, 462, 475, 476; est. date for, 475

Chronicles, 472; native, 320, 322, 324, 333, 373, 374; Spanish, 213, 311, 470, 473

Chronology (chronologies), 7, 8, 15, 16, 18, 64, 68, 91, 92, 131, 135, 159, 169, 296, 299, 318, 346, 354, 365, 406, 421, 446, 451, 482, 498–99, 500, 560; American and Asiatic, need for, 498; Caribbean area, relative, 392, 396, 399, 430; Dabajuroid series, 393; dendrochronology, 16, 17, 206, 215, 345; geochronology, 16, 17; glottochronology, 119, 534, 545; Maya Long Count, 310; Maya Short Count, 345; of Northeast Woodlands area, 252, 253; of northern Yucatan, 354, 364; Plateau, 116; regional, 94; relative, 94, 306; of sambaquis, 434; *see also* Dating, Radiocarbon dates

Chubut, Argentina (Patonia), 67

Chuitinamit (Zutuhil), Guatemala, 374

Cienega Creek, Arizona, 156

Cienega sequence (Point of Pines, Arizona), 158

Cienegas complex (Frightful Cave, Coahuila), 60, 62

Cigliano, Eduardo Mario, 71

Cincinnati, Ohio, 241

Cintla horizon, 352

Circum-Caribbean: complex, 413; cultures, 440, 442, 451, 479; stage, 438; theory, 413

Circumboreal complex, 230

Cists: burial, 337, 338, 341, 348, 363, 369, 374; storage, 178; *see also* Pits

Cities, 304, 305, 307, 320, 333, 336, 339; building of, 306; groups of, emblem glyphs for, 348; growth of, regulated, 374; jungle, 353; Maya, 334, 343, 348, 351, 353, 354, 359, 364, 373 (*see also* individual cities by name); Puuc, 356, 357; -states, 320, 322, 339, 348, 351; walled, 362, 363, 470; *see also* Urban centers

City Builders stage, 468–70; est. dates for, 468

Civilization(s), 48, 176, 292, 295, 355, 452, 457, 479, 564, 566; American (Indian), 490, 491, 492, 502, 507; American, Nuclear, 490; Andean, 451, 481, 565, 566; Andean Peruvian, 389, 462, 463, 480; Asian, 507; collapse of, 317; diagnostic traits of, 292; emergence of, 489; Eurasian, early, 490; growth of, 489, 490; hearths of, 319; high, centers of, 519; Hindu-Buddhist, 507; Maya(n), 291, 331 ff., 564; Mayan highland, 351; Mayan southern lowland, 338, 350; Mayan Yucatan, 356; Mediterranean, 499; Mesoamerican, 175, 295, 304, 380, 389, 451, 476, 564, 566; Mexican, 291, 310, 311, 314, 318, 499; Near Eastern, 499; New World, 451, 591, 496, 497, 502, 510, 566; northern frontier of, 314, 317; Old World, 489, 491, 566; process of, 561; rejuvenated, 317

Clark, J. D., 119, 138

Clarks Pond culture, 253

Classic stage (period), 310, 333, 340, 341, 348, 351, 354, 359, 361, 368, 371, 373, 382, 476, 482; Andean, 453; artifacts, 310, 338, 351; beginning of, est. date for, 499, 504; ceramics, 343; culture(s), 451, 479, 480; figurines, 336, 351; Pacific coast, 378; remains, 338; sculpture, 368; Tiahuanaco, 465, 469; traits, 337; Willey and Phillips, 30, 479

"Classic Veracruz" art style; *see* Art styles, Tajin

Clay, 518; animals, with clay wheels, 493; balls, baked, fiber-tempered, 126; balls, grooved, 132; basketry impressions in, 126; burnished red, 319; conical or mammiform objects of, 202; figurines, 165, 182, 319, 383, 406, 414, 475; fireburned, 440; griddles, 399, 400, 405, 408, 430, 431; pipes, 245, 405, 406, 410; pot rests, 408, 435; relief, painted, 458; stamps, 301, 496; tempering, 244, 250, 269; urns, 303; veneer, 374; vessels, unfired, 178, 179; working of, 512

Claypool site, 60, 62

Claws (*see* Ornaments)

Clemsons Island culture, 253

Cliff complex, 240

Climate (climatic), 169, 193, 198, 207, 209, 255, 305, 375, 390, 453; barriers, 255; Caribbean, 390; changes, 27, 35, 150, 151, 225, 227, 332, 478; climatology, 150; conditions, 223; cyclic variations in, 150, 151; deterioration, 245; factors, 167; Mesoamerican, 332; oscillation, 227; periods. 150, 157, 251; recent

Western, 150; regions, 476; savanna, 291, 317; semidesert, 515, 518; shifts, 256; steppe, 291, 317; temperate, 321; *see also* Aridity, Rainfall, Temperature, etc.

Clisby, K. H., 296, 325

Cloth, 376; bark, 332, 455, 496, 522; feather, 179, 181; fur, 154; weaves, 238

Clothing (costumes), 332, 349, 350, 455, 468, 518; aprons, 154, 161, 178, 332; capes, 332; decoration of, 102; Eskimo, 100; huipils, 332; loincloths, 332; robes, 332; robes, deerskin shoulder, 178; robes, feather, 160, 280; robes, fur and feather, 161; sashes, woven, 178; shawls, 455; skin, 225, 518; snow goggles, 103; tumplines, 154; turbans, 333, 357; *see also* Headdresses, Sandals

Clovis: hunters, 223; points, 31, 35, 36, 37, 39, 45, 51, 52, 55, 57, 59, 68, 88, 130 (*see also* Projectile points); site, 88, 96 (*see also* Blackwater Draw site)

Clovis-Folsom fluted point tradition, 199

Clubs: forms of, 497; grooved, 156; grooved, curved, 158, 179; grooved "rabbit" or "fending stick," 178; rabbit, 154; "slavekiller," 132, 165; stabbing, 467; stone, 134, 164, 166; whalebone, 133, 165; wooden, 154

Coahuila, 37, 62, 63, 156, 176, 179

Coahuila culture, 240

Coalescent tradition, 209

Coari site, 420, 438

Coast Range(s), 126, 129; archeology, 130; northern, 130; northern, Late Horizon sites in, 130; section (Sacramento Valley), 130; valleys, 130

Coast Salish–Chinook: area, 118, 133; tribes, 134

Coatlichan, 322

Coats Island, Hudson Bay, 86, 107

Coatzacoalcos River, Chiquito arm of, 303

Cobbles; *see* Pebbles

Coca; *see* Plants

Cochise culture, 61, 123, 156, 177, 185, 564; appearance of maize in, 177; horizons, 178; late, preceramic, 179; -like materials, 156, 158; (lithic) sequence, 156, 177, 178; sequence, est. beginning date for, 63

Cochise culture stages: Cazador, 61; Chiricahua, 60, 61, 156, 158; San Pedro, 61, 156; Sulphur Spring, 60, 61, 152, 156; radiocarbon date for, 156

Cochumatanes Mountains, Guatemala, 365

Codices, Maya (Dresden, Madrid, Paris), 342, 346, 347

Cody complex, 60, 72
Coe, Michael D., 335, 346, 375, 376, 379, 381, 383, 459, 484, 508, 511, 520, 523
Coe, William R., II, 343, 398, 414
Cohen, Mrs. Mimi, vii
Cojumatlan, Michoacan, 319
Cold Creek site, 166
Cold Springs site, 165
Cole, Fay-Cooper, 15, 16, 251, 257
Coles Creek: ceramics, 273, 274, 276; culture, 246, 277, 280; period, 270, 273, 274; sites, 273
Colima, 318, 319; figurines, burnished, 319; Pacific coast of, 320
Collier, Donald, 403, 414, 442, 447, 457, 458, 465, 468, 470, 471, 484
Collins, Henry B., 1, 6, 39, 71, 85, 89, 91, 92, 93, 94, 99, 100, 101, 105, 106, 107, 108–9
Colombia(n), 49, 50, 389, 400, 404, 420, 426, 442, 451, 472, 479–81, 521, 565; Andes of, 413, 431; archeology, 480; coastal, 419; coastal northeastern, 405; early cultures of, est. dates for, 480; eastern, 406, 419; geography of, 453; highland chiefdoms, 481; highlands of, 429, 430, 432, 437, 442, 480, 481, 565; intermontane valleys of, 442; life, late prehistoric, 481; lowlands, 480; northern, 480, 481; southern, 480
Colonies (colonial, colonists), 182, 317, 523, 564; Asiatic, 502; Aztec, 549; European, 223, 254, 523; Hohokam, 183; military, 324; period, 377
Colonization: of Caribbean islands, 398, 409; of Kaminaljuyú, 310
Colonnettes; see Architectural features
Colorado, 52, 55, 62, 175, 178, 197, 201, 207; eastern, 177, 203; eastern slopes of mountains of, est. dates for early agriculture on, 237; mountains of, 201, 213; northeastern, 54; southeastern, 213; southwestern, 176, 181, 184
Colorado Plateau, 149, 152; central, 177; southern, 177
Colorado River, 125, 185, 187; lower, 175, 180, 189; region, 128
Columbia Plateau, 149, 150, 152
Columbia River, 133, 134, 165; drainage, 163, 164; Lower valley, prehistory of, 134
Columbus, Christopher, 399, 411, 412, 413; encounter with Chicoid people, 412; encounter with Guayabitoid people, 411
Columns; see Architectural features
Comalcalco, Tabasco, 348, 349
Comayagua Valley, Honduras, 337, 343

Comb Ridge, 177
Combs, 104, 245; see also Roofs
Comitan Plain, Chiapas, 379
Commerce, 305, 310, 319, 322, 324, 566; see also Trade
Compounds; see Architectural features
Conchas phases, 346, 366, 376, 377, 381
Concho, Arizona, 156; complex, 60, 62; site, 153, 158
Concrete; see Architectural materials
Congdon: complexes, 62, 164; complexes, est. dates for, 164; site, 60, 62, 164
Conquests, 182, 241, 314, 317, 321, 323, 324, 333, 462, 464, 468, 469; absence of, 478; Alvarado's, of Utatlan, 375; Aztec, 324; Aztec, of Chalco, 323; Aztec, of Coaixtlahuacan, 323; Inca, 469–72; Mochica, 468; routes, 380; states, 331; Tarascan, 320; Tepanec, 323; Toltec, of Yucatan, 356, 357, 359; Wari, 469; see also Militarism
Consonant(s)(al), 541, 543; alternation of, horizontal and vertical, 543; alternation of, with vowels, 542, 543, 544; change, 542; simple, glottalized, aspirated, doubled, 543; single, followed by vowel, 542; two, each with vowel, 542; variants, front, back, and center, 543, 544; words with three, 539
Contacts, cultural, 238, 262, 263, 265, 273, 499, 500, 520, 522, 552, 566; between Asia and New World, 360, 489–510, 518, 534; direct, 511, 520, 521, 522, 538; historical, 492; intermittent, 501; linguistic, 547; between Mesoamerica and Intermediate area via delta region, 414; between Mesoamerica and western South America, 518, 521; opportunity for, 507; between Peru and Mesoamerica, 500; transoceanic, 490; transpacific, 360, 489–510, 511, 522, 535, 538
Cook, S. F., 127, 128, 138, 141
Cook de Leonard, Carmen, viii
Cook Inlet, 86, 90, 101, 102
Cooking: direct-fire, 125; by stone-boiling, 126; techniques, 154; vessels, 101, 125
Coon, Carleton S., 522, 523
Cooper, John N., 514, 523
Cooper, Paul, 206, 216
Cooperton, Oklahoma, 197
Copacabaña (Viscanchani I) complex, 49, 50, 51
Copan, 343; archeological zone, 333; ceramics, 337, 343, 350; Early Acropolis phase, 309, 310
Copan River, Honduras, 334

Copena: artifacts, copper and stone, 267; burial mound complex, 267; culture, 240

Copper, 244, 279, 352, 453, 464, 470; alloys, 374, 465, 481; artifacts (objects), 202, 204, 244, 267, 374, 382, 519; awls, 233, 234; axes as currency, 496, 521; beads, 234, 237; bells, 182, 515, 519; bracelets, 237; celts, 234; -covered rattles, 280; -covered stone ear spools, 278; earl spools, 239, 242, 262, 265, 267, 278; embossed, 249; glaze paint, 188; gorgets, 234, 237; gouges, 234; industries, 234; knives, 233; masks, Long-Nosed God, 274–76; ores, 319; ornaments, 271, 478; panpipes, 268; répoussé plate, 234; rings, 237; sheet, eagle and head, 264; tools (implements), 233–35, 465, 478; weapons, 465; -working techniques, 519

Coquille River, Oregon, 132

Corbeled arches (vaults); *see* Architectural features

Corbett, John M., 286

Cordage, 126, 155, 156, 160, 376; human hair, 178, 179; snares, 160; wefts in matting, 161

Cordilleran tradition, 87

Cord-marked pottery; *see* Ceramic decorative styles and techniques

Córdoba, Argentina, province of, 65

Core(s), 38, 102, 343; and flake stage, 30; hammerstones, 122; industries, 30; pebble, 455; prepared, 38, 39, 90, 108, 224; scrapers, 231; tools, 42

Corn, cornfields; *see* Maize

Cornices; *see* Architectural features

Cornwallis Island, 100

Coro area, Venezuela, 393, 394, 396

Corobal phase, 433, 565; ceramics, 433; sites, 433

Coronado, Francisco Vasquez de, 213

Corrugated pottery; *see* Ceramic decorative styles and techniques

Cortes, Hernando, 325

Cosculluela, J. A., 392, 415

Cosgrove, C. B., 179, 190

Costa Rica: northwestern, 291; Pacific coast of, Punta Arenas, 292; San José, 511

Costumes; *see* Clothing

Cosumnes Valley, California, 127

Coteau du Missouri, 204

Cotter, John L., 88, 109, 286

Cotton, 181, 182, 186, 305, 322, 332, 369, 455, 456, 552; absence of, 456; Asiatic, 456; cloth, 184, 186, 332 (*see also* Textiles); native lintless, 456; Peruvian, est. date for, 456; in Sierra Madre Oriental, est. date for, 297

Cotua: complex, 428, 430; site, 409, 420, 430

Cotua Island, Venezuela, 409, 420

Cotzumalhuapa region, Guatemala, 367; art, 376; ceramics, 379; sites, 378

Cougar Mountain Cave, 53, 60, 62; lowest level, 54; upper levels, 62

Counting systems (on fingers and arms), 544; Finno-Ugrian and Indo-European, 528

Couri: complex, 398; site, 395

Courts, 339, 369; ball (*see* Ball courts); central platforms in, 373; house, 307; interior, 348; series of ascending, 356

Cowdin, Karren, vii

Cowles, John, 54, 62, 71

Coxcatlan complex, 60, 63

Coyote Gulch sites (locality), 44, 121

Coyotes; *see* Animals

Cozcatlan rockshelter, 297, 298; maize at, 297; radiocarbon dates for, 298

Crab Orchard culture, 252

Crabtree, Robert H., 145, 173

Cradle(s): -boards, 184; hoop, 154

Craft(s), 332, 427, 520; -men, 186, 306, 307, 471; specialization, 129, 306, 438, 462, 465, 475, 478, 483

Crane Creek sites, 53, 54

Crane, H. R., 52, 71, 228, 230, 257

Cranial deformation; *see* Deformation, cranial

Cremation, 123, 125, 127, 128, 163, 164, 182, 188, 231, 235, 245, 247, 363, 435, 438; with ashes in jars, 375; with ashes in urns, 364, 441; burial complex, 228; in Northeast, est. beginning date, 235

Cressman, L. S., 54, 62, 71, 119, 132, 133, 138, 154, 155, 163, 164, 165, 170

Crevenna, Theo, 23

Croneis, Carey, vii, 1, 5, 13, 14, 19

Cronin, Constance, 191

Crook, Wilson W., Jr., 44, 45, 71

Crop(s), 209, 353, 400, 401, 423; Andean, basic, 480; Andean, highland, domestication of, 454; failure, 351; Indo-Hispanic, 401; native American, 223; new, 400, 565; root, 423, 452, 480; seed, 156, 423

Crucero phase, 346, 377

Cruxent, José M., viii, 48, 50, 51, 57, 71, 78, 390, 391, 392, 393, 394, 396, 397, 399, 404, 405, 406, 408, 415, 417, 421, 428, 430, 432, 433, 447

Cuba, 389, 391, 392, 395, 402, 403, 413; central, 412; eastern, 412; ground sloths in, 38; Manicuaroid series remains, 395, 398; Meillac-like pottery of, 412; Meso-Indians in, 398–99, 411; Period III, radiocarbon date from, 399; southern, 411; western, 411, 414

Cubagua Island, Venezuela, 395, 402, 407, 409; complex and radiocarbon date for, 397, 398

Cuchumatanes Mountains, Guatemala, 365

Cucurbits; 179, 182, 186; domestication of, 299; *see also* Pumpkins, Squash

Cuevas: site, 402; style, 411

Cuicuilco, 301, 302, 304; possible settlement of, 301; temples, 301

Culhuacan, 322

Cult(s), 304, 365, 469; bear, 248; burial, 262; chariots, 495; Chavín, 465, 473; clay figurine, 165; fertility, 301, 303; mushroom, 368; objects, 368; priest-temple-idol, 481; of Quetzalcoatl and Tezcatlipoca, 316, 564; religious, Mexican, 357; religious, Peruvian, 468; religious, Quetzalcoatl, 186; serpent, 500; Southern (*see* Southern Cult); stela, 331, 352, 363, 368, 370; temple, 460; zemis, 413

Cultigens; *see* Plants, cultivated

Cultist Temple Centers stage, 457–63; ceramics, 461; ceramics, decorated, est. date for, 458; est. dates for stage, 457; improved variety of maize, est. date for, 458; temples, variations in, est. date for, 458

Cultivation, 399; continuous, 321; inception of, 297; intensive, 319, 321, 332; of manioc, 400, 401; plant, 332, 399; shifting, 437; stage, 29; *see also* Agriculture

Culture (cultural), 544, 560, 561; adaptation, 125, 133, 162, 237, 497, 501; anthropology, viii, 4; areas, 132, 259, 262, 291, 292, 293, 331, 332, 389, 390, 498, 500, 565; assemblages, 335; backwaters, 410, 414; centers, 378, 489, 502, 503; change, 26, 37, 41, 51, 52, 67, 91, 92, 94–95, 102, 132, 151, 153, 162, 168, 169, 178, 211, 225, 228, 248, 251, 254, 259, 261, 262, 282, 285, 440, 473, 493, 497, 561, 565; chasms, 291; climaxes, 239, 457, 465, 471; comparisons, interareal, 256, 262, 263, 518; complexes, 5, 117, 227, 241, 297, 422, 424, 427, 432, 433, 443, 498, 502, 503 (*see also* names of individual cultures); configurations, 105, 106, 332, 522; connections, 318, 508, 511–22; 566; contacts (*see* Contacts, cultural); continuum (continuities), 39, 88, 91, 92,

161, 238, 241, 244, 261, 280 563; convergence(s), 9, 511–22, 566; cross-fertilization, 489; decadence (decline, deterioration), 211, 251, 256, 351, 437, 442; differences, 456; diffusion (*see* Diffusion); divergence, 522; drift, 88; dynamics, 10; elements, 183, 188, 242, 360, 475, 498, 512, 513, 521; evolution, 8, 10, 121, 183, 364, 392, 497, 511, 520, 561; fractionation, 119; growth, 212, 237, 249, 256, 451, 453, 490, 497; history, 4, 7, 37, 176, 259, 260, 292, 311, 403, 404, 407, 490, 499, 503; isolation, 455; interchange, 377; intensity, 238, 247; lag, 89, 345, 564; material, 42, 43, 52, 55, 58, 64, 103, 182, 206, 213, 294, 357, 359, 455, 476, 521; non-material, 513, 514, 515; origins, 28; parallels (*see* Parallels); patterns (*see* Patterns, cultural); peak, 565; periods, 561; process, 489, 493, 519, 560, 561; progress, 489; provinces, 132; regional, 37; relationships, 233, 355, 382, 507, 529, 566; resistance, 129, 414; retention, 89, 514; revolution, 300; selection, 501; sequences (*see* individual cultural sequences by name); similarities, 492, 493, 502, 507, 511, 513–22; stability, 515, 530; stages (*see* individual cultural stages by name); stimulus, 153; sub-areas, 132, 135; survivals, 514; synthesis, 274; traits, 89, 331, 339, 352, 376, 518, 531, 549, 564; traditions (*see* Traditions); transmission, 244; trends, 223; types, 262, 292; variants (variations), 206, 224, 281; local, 260; units, 61, 259; zones, 40

Cultures, 121, 284, 497, 498; ceramic, 394; donor, 498, 501; hierarchic, 309; high (*see* High cultures); living, 563; local, 476, 502; non-ceramic, 394; primitive, 543; prior, 364; receiving, 501, 521; *see also* names of individual cultures

Cumana area, Venezuela, 393, 402

Cumarebo site, 393

Cumberland points, 31, 52

Curayacu, Peru, 459

Curl, Rani L., 18, 19

Currency: Chinese knife and axe, 496; thin copper axe, 496

Custer focus, 196, 206, 246

Cutler, Hugh C., 172, 191, 296, 326

Cutting tools, 52, 197, 198, 201, 260

Cuyuni River, British Guiana, 420, 422

Cuzco, Peru, 459, 464, 469, 470, 471, 473, 479, 483; basin, 452, 464, 465, 471; pottery, 473; sequence, 483; -style architecture, 473

Dabajuro: site, 393, style, 394
Dabajuroid series, 394; chronology of, 393
Daifuku, Hiroshi, 180, 190
Dakota Mounds, 196
Dallas: ceramics, 281; culture, 281; site, 281; stage, 279
Dallas, Texas, 45
Dalles, the; *see* The Dalles
Dalton: culture, 252; points, 228; site, 60, 63
Damon, Paul E., 63, 64, 71
Danger Cave, 53, 60, 61, 62, 153, 156, 158, 166–67, 176, 177, 226, 232; Level I, 54, 61, 152, 167, 169; Level II, 156, 169; Level V, 153; radiocarbon dates for, 61, 156
"Danzante" figures; *see* Figures
Dart(s), 155, 156, 158, 161, 396, 456, 467; -arrows, 154; atlatl, 155, 263; bird, 96; compound, 155; detachable barbed, 102; foreshafts, 160; game, 155; heads, sealing, 105; pointed hardwood shafts for, 154; points, 176, 178, 181
Darwin, Charles, 562
Dates, estimated; *see* Radiocarbon dates, Dating, and names of individual cultures and cultural elements
Dating, 42, 454; absolute, 345; cross-, 160, 362; of early man, 563; by linguistic paleontology, 552; morphological, 42; potassium-argon, 18; by rate of refuse accumulation, 428; relative, 319; *see also* Dendrochronology, Glottochronology, Radiocarbon dates, Radiocarbon dating
Daugherty, Richard D., 28, 62, 72, 134, 138, 160, 167, 168, 169, 170
Davis, E. Mott, 61, 62, 71, 72, 216
Davis, James T., 125, 128, 138, 139
Davis site, 273, 274, 282
De Laguna, Frederica, 90, 91, 101, 102, 111, 135, 143
De Terra, Helmut, 44, 54, 63, 72, 294, 326
Deadman Cave, 60, 62
Death Valley, California, 158; northern end of, 121; Shoshoni, 121
Death Valley complexes (phases, cultures, sequence), 123, 158; I, 53, 54, 122, 158, 159; II, 60, 62, 158; III, 158; IV, 158
Debetz, G., 105, 109
Decadent (Late Postclassic) stage (period, horizon), northern Yucatan, 354, 362, 363, 364, 375; settlement patterns of, 362–63
Deer, 186, 202, 203, 224, 260, 365; bone beaming tools, 202; bones, 165; -hoof, objects made from, 155, 161; -hunting, 211; metapodial, objects made from, 210, 212; -skin shoulder robes, 178

Deer Creek site, 196
Defensive (works), 208, 210, 305, 464, 470, 520; ditches, 205, 206, 280, 312; earthworks, 204, 237, 238, 241, 260, 265, 307, 478; fortifications, 323; location, Monte Alban, 305; palisades, 249, 254, 280; stockades, 205, 206, 208, 211; walls, 515; walls at Mayapan and Tulum, 363; at Xochichalco, 312
Deformation, cranial, 369; frontal, 439; occipital, cradleboard, 178–79, 181; occipital, "lambdoid," 181, 184, 187; occipital, vertical, 181, 187
Deities; *see* Gods
Delaware Valley, lower, 238
Delta region, Venezuela, 402, 403, 404, 407–11, 413; Barrancoid series in, 409–10; culture history of, 411; Saladoid series in, 409; swamps of, 407, 409, 410
Denbigh: art style, 106; Flint complex, 60, 62, 88, 89, 90, 104, 106, 107, 232
Dendrochronological dates: Dismal River materials, 213; Kincaid site, 16; Thomas Riggs focus, 206
Dendrochronology, 16, 17, 206, 215, 345
Dent site, 196, 197; radiocarbon date for mammoth from, 55
Denver, Colorado, 201
Deptford: burial mounds, 263, 265; ceramic complex, 261, 263, 265–69; ceremonialism, 263; culture, 263, 266, 267, 269, 271, 280; sites, 263, 265
Desert(s), 64, 149, 150, 177, 178, 452, 463; environment, 51; Sonoran, 117; southern California, 121
Desert Archaic, 153, 160, 162, 163, 165, 167, 176, 177, 187; core traits, 153–55; eastward extension of, est. dates for, 153; foragers, 178; stable period, est. dates for, 153, 176; stage, 151, 162, 163; tradition, 151; *see also* Desert Culture
Desert Area Tradition, 157
Desert Culture(s), 6, 35, 36, 37, 59–62, 64, 122, 126, 152, 153, 155, 157–59, 160, 166, 167, 168, 181, 200, 201, 232, 240; archeological, 152; area, 226; artifact complex, 152; beginning of, est. date for, 35; concept, 166; datings on, 61; duration of, est., 167; generalized base of, 153; industries, 159; Late, 246; late prehistoric phases of, 160; local variations of and est. date for, 153, 160, 167; materials, 35; sites, 59, 156, 159; traits, 159; Western, 159
Desert Culture tradition, 122, 159, 169; Historic, 35; Horticulture and est. dates

for, 35; Peripheral Big-Game Hunting and est. dates for, 35

Desert West, 149, 150, 151, 152, 153, 155, 162, 167, 563, 564; age of cultural remains from, 154; cultures of, 169; duration of stable environment in, 151; prehistory of, 150

Design(s): bird, 265, 368; ceramic (*see* Ceramic decorative styles); Denbigh, 106; Old Bering Sea, 91, 92, 96; patterns, 319; Punuk, 96; Scytho-Siberian motif, 103; stepped grecque motif, 497

Detering, Lenora, vii

Developmental period (Intermontane tradition), 157, 167, 169

Devils Lake district (focus), 204

Diablo complex, est. date for, 294

Dialects, 119, 241, 529, 531, 545; distribution, patterns of, 552; divergent, 552; geographically close, 539; local, 535; lost, 533, 555; Maya, 334, 365; Navajo-Apache, 550; networks of, 554; spread of, 548; Ute, 550; Yuma, 550

Dice, 179; bone, 154; games of chance using, 514; stick, 154, 164

Dick, Herbert, 62, 72

Diego blood factor, 531

Diffusion(al) (ism) (ist), 9, 10, 39, 68, 124, 131, 177, 210, 230, 249, 255, 263, 302, 310, 389, 407, 410, 412, 426, 433, 437, 452, 460–63, 473, 475, 476, 493, 495–99, 502, 503, 512–14, 519–22, 538, 564, 566; agricultural, into Caribbean area, 400; of Arauquinoid series, 407, 409, 410; categories of, 519; of Chicoid series, 412; of Folsom points, 36; of ideas, 227, 255, 269, 285, 426, 433, 452; *vs.* independent invention, 507, 593; *Kulturkreis* school, 491; lines (routes) of, 403, 404, 407, 414; long-distance, 501, 510; of maize into South America, 403; of metate in Utonahuan area, 553; of milling stones and manos, 34; position (approach), 492, 493–96; of pottery and village life into Sierra Madre Oriental, 299; of pottery-making from Asia to America, 496; process of, 501, 565; of Saladoid series, 409; situations, 502; of technicuqes, 255; of Tocuyanoid series, 405; trait unit, 442; transpacific, 118, 541; of Wari design elements, 469

Digging stick(s), 154, 155, 158, 178, 179, 332; antler handles for, 133, 166; metapodial tip, smooth-bladed, 210; weights, 370, 372

Diomede Islands, Alaska, 86, 91, 92, 98

DiPeso, Charles C., 188, 189, 190

Dishes; *see* Ceramic forms

Dismal I culture, 232

Dismal River culture, 196, 213; complex, 213; materials, dendrochronological dates for, 213; western sites of, 213

Divinatory: almanacs, 346, 347; calendars, 344; passages in codices, 347; rites, of augury, 347; rites, of Mixtec, Zapotec, and Mixe, 368; rites, of scapulimancy, 105

Dixon, Keith A., 119, 383

Dixon, Ronald B., 139, 537, 546

Dobbelaar culture, 252

Documents (documentary sources), 189, 211, 435; Spanish, 213

Dogs; *see* Animals

Domestic wares; *see* Ceramic wares, utility

Dominican Indians, 412

Dominican Republic, 395, 402; Boca Chica and Meillac sites, 402; Chicoid series, origin of, 412; intermediate styles, 411; Ostiones-like pottery, 412

Doorways; *see* Architectural features

Dorset: culture, 90, 91, 106–8, 240, 246; Eskimos, 90, 106, 107; Greenland, 240; pre-, sites, radiocarbon dates for, 107; sites, 107; T1 site, radiocarbon dates for, 90–91; tradition, 106

Double Adobe site, 61; dates from, 61

Douglas, British Honduras, 338

Dragoo, Don W., 230, 238, 257, 258

Drain conduits; *see* Architectural features

Dresden Codex; *see* Codices, Maya

Dressler, Robert L., 296, 326

Drill(s), 32, 131, 212, 344; bits, 104; bow, 103–4, 107; chipped stone, 178, 179; expanded base, 233; hollow, 344; side-notched base, 233

Drink(s): *chicha*, drinking of ashes of dead in, 431; intoxicating, 332

Drucker, Phillip, 132, 134, 135, 139, 304, 326, 381

DuBois culture, 253

Duck decoys, 160, 161

Duff, Wilson, 134, 139

Dugout; *see* Canoes

Dulce River, Guatemala, 334

Dune Dweller culture, radiocarbon date for, 123

Dunlevy, M. L., 208, 216

Dupouy, Walter, 391, 423, 447

Durango, 175, 177, 180, 183, 314

Durham, Bill, 117, 139

Durst culture, 252

DuRy, C. J., 391, 415

Dustin culture, 232, 252

Dwellings; *see* Houses

Dynasties; *see* Rulers

Dzibilchaltun, 354, 355; earliest occupations, 354; est. dates for, 346, 354; excavations, 362; Formative I–IV, 354, 355; fourth stage, radiocarbon dates for, 354, 362; lintel, radiocarbon date on, 362; Mexican period, 362

Eagle(s): -being, 279; feeding on hearts, 315; military order of, 357; from Rose Mound, 282; sheet copper, 264; warriors, 378
Ear spools (ear plugs); 279, 458; copper, 239, 242, 262, 265, 267, 278, 280; copper-covered stone, 278; jade, 333; napkin-ring, 475; pottery golf-tee, 477
Early Acropolis phase (Copan), 309, 310
Early American (Big Game) Hunters, 51, 195–200, 214; est. date for end of, in Plains, 214; sites, 198
Early Archaic stage; *see* Archaic stage
Early Besant culture, 240
Early Boreal Archaic, 230, 232, 253; artifacts of, 231; est. dates for, 231
Early Classic stage (period, horizon), 313, 339, 341, 350; Chiapas and Guatemala coast, 376, 378, 379; Guatemala highlands, 359, 367, 368, 369, 370, 371, 372, 373; Mesoamerica, 466; Petén, 341; Puuc and Rio Bec architectural prototypes, 359; southern and western lowlands, 338, 339, 340, 341, 343, 345, 346, 354, 355, 507, 564; southern Veracruz-Tabasco, 382
Early Formative stage (period, horizon), 566; Northern Mesoamerica, 300; Southern Mesoamerica, and est. dates for, 332, 333, 346, 376, 437, 520
Early Historic period (southeastern United States), 283
Early Hopewell; *see* Hopewell
Early Horizon period (California and Northwest Coast), 126–30; radiocarbon dates for, 126–27; sites, 127
Early Lithic stage; *see* Lithic
Early Man, 28, 38, 41, 59, 119, 120, 177, 332; archeology of, 490; dating of, 563; in New World, 23, 27, 68, 120; in North America, 28, 38; sites, 177; in South America, 28
Early Maritime cultures, 134, 564; est. date for, 564
Early Milling Stone culture, 64
Early (Middle) Mississippi, 246, 250, 275, 277, 281; beginning of, 282; ceramic complex, 277; cultures, 277; est. date for beginning of expansion of, 275, 277; *see also* Mississippian

Early Paracas period, 463, 464
Early Postclassic stage (period, horizon): Chiapas and Guatemala coast, 379; Guatemala highlands, 373; southern and western lowlands and est. dates for, 346, 354
Early Preclassic stage (period, horizon), 335; Guatemala coast, 377; Guatemala highlands, 366; Honduras, 335; Huasteca, 335; southern and central Mexico, 355; southern and western lowlands, 335, 346, 366
Early Woodland: complexes, 238; culture, 228, 233, 235, 237, 238, 243, 252, 256; New England, est. date for, 238; northern, 235; Ohio Valley, 235; pottery, 235, 236, 238, 239; pottery, distribution of, 236
Earth(en): causeways, 324, 334; fill (for substructures), 340; lodge(s), 165, 206, 207, 208, 211, 277; lodge-dwelling peoples, 208, 211; middens, 260; mounds, 182, 249, 301, 366, 371, 379 (*see also* Mounds); ovens, 154; platforms, 302, 339; pyramids, truncated, 266
Earthworks (embankments), 204, 260, 265; circular, 237, 238, 241; Ohio Hopewell, 241; stone-faced, 307
East Cape, Siberia, 106
Eastern Archaic; *see* Archaic
Eastern Village farmers, 240
Eastern Woodland culture area, 223
Eberhart, Hal, 54, 64, 72, 123, 139
Ecology (ecological): adjustments, 129, 390; definition, 291; habitat, 277, 279; human, 193, 215; hypotheses, 317; life zones, 149, 176; locale, tidal shore and valley riverine, 129; prehistoric, of western United States, 150; situations, 169, 260; units, 259; zones, 125, 149, 163, 225, 292, 300
Economy (economic) (economies), 123, 165, 214, 262, 266, 280, 283, 564; acorn, 267; Adena-Hopewell, 242; agricultural (farming), 251, 274, 283, 297, 299; agricultural-fishing-herding, 464; agricultural, Mesoamerican, 300; areas, 323; bases, 225, 226, 278; bison-hunting, 201; change, 265, 285; complex, acorn, 129; components, 270; decadence, 351; diversified, 168; exploitation, 133; food-gathering, 294, 300; food-grinding, 63; food-producing, 214; growth, 462; hunting, 214, 255, 294; hunting-gathering, 150, 203, 214, 260, 263, 295; hunting, mammal, 124,

134; lacustrine-based, 163; Laguna, 302; level, 31; nut, 267; patterns, 32, 427; Poverty Point, 260; pursuits, 400; relations, 304; revolution, 33, 502; riverine-based, 163; seed-gathering, 123, 131; shellfish, 260, 261; subsistence, 195, 198, 199, 203, 205, 211, 424, 457, 514; systems, 262, 271, 273, 277, 285; at Teotihuacán, 308; traits, 502; transformation, 281; units, 321, 323, 422, 460; *see also* Agriculture, Farming, Fishing, Gathering, Hunting, Subsistence

Ecuador(ean)(s), 67, 420, 426, 451, 453, 459, 463, 472, 473–79, 482, 496, 503, 508, 520, 521; coast(al), 376, 377, 437, 452, 453, 463, 473, 475–80, 511, 512, 520, 521, 522; copper axe currency of, 496; differentiation of local complexes, est. date for, 521; early ceramics of, 463; eastern, 419, 424, 425, 438, 440, 441, 446; highland(s), 453, 463, 473, 475, 476, 479, 520, 565, 578; Inca conquest of, 479; Indians, 477–78; parallels with Asia, 360, 474, 477; parallels with Mesoamerica, 520; prehistory, 473; rafts, 507; seafaring, 523; *see also* individual cultures, sites, and geographical places by name

Eden-Scottsbluff tradition, 32, 38

Eden site, 60, 62, 196; complex, 198, 199

Edwards, Clinton R., 507, 510

Edwards Plateau aspect, 196; "burnt-rock middens," est. dates for, 201

Effigy (effigies): censers (ceramic), 352, 353, 372; columns, 359; cover handles, 343; feet, ceramic, 352, 375; figurines, 319, 350, 352; -head bowls, 281; jade, 361; lugs, ceramic, 404, 406, 410–12; mounds, 247; non-Plumbate wares, 372, 374; pipes, 206, 237, 239, 267; Plumbate, Tohil, 374; rim, 277; vessels, 268, 271, 367; whistles, 336, 352, 366, 370

Effigy Mound culture, 246, 247, 252

Eggan, Fred R., 189, 190

Egypt(ian), 489, 493; parallels with Middle America, 360; trade, 499

Ehrenreich, P., 514, 523

Eiseley, L. C., 62, 79

Ekholm, Gordon F., 2, 9, 10, 302, 309, 326, 360, 383, 413, 415, 489, 493, 507, 510, 566

El Arbolillo site, 299

El Baul, Guatemala, 378

El Dorado, 421

El Heneal: complex, 397, 398; complex, radiocarbon date for, 397; site, 395

El Inga: complex, est. date for, 68; site, 65, 66, 67

El Jobo: area, 57; complex, 48, 50, 51, 56, 57, 396; district, Venezuela, 49, 50, 51; points, 36, 57; scrapers, 57; site, 395

El Palito: ceramic style, 404; site, 391, 401

El Petén; *see* Petén

El Prisco phase, ceramics, 302

El Progreso, Guatemala, department of, 364

El Quiché, Guatemala; *see* Quiché

El Riego: complex (phase), 60, 63, 298; culture, 298; rockshelter, 297

El Salvador, 291, 378; Chalchuapa, 303; eastern, 343; western, 303, 313

El Totoral complex, 56, 57, 58

Elephant(s): kills, 177; late glacial forms of, 244; *see also* Mammoth, Mastodon

Elliot Smith, Sir Grafton, 493

Elsasser, Albert B., 130, 131, 135, 137, 139, 141, 170

Embossing; *see* Techniques

Emerson, Norman, 257

Emperaire, José, 50, 75, 444, 448

Empires (imperial): Aztec, 317, 320, 322, 323, 324, 548, 549; Inca, 451, 457, 470, 471, 472; Tepanec, 323; Toltec, 316

Engel, Frederic, 455, 456, 457, 458, 482, 484

Engigstciak site, British Mountain (lowest) level, 87

Engraving (engraved), 104, 249; bottles, 273, 274; carinated bowls, 273, 282; ceramics, 273, 274, 278, 281, 282; shell, 249, 264; style, 106; tablets, 237; technique, 103, 104, 106, 249, 278; tools, 103

Entranceways; *see* Architectural features

Environment(al)(s), 152, 198, 213, 215, 224, 227, 234, 239, 290, 437, 442, 452, 453, 489, 518, 544; adaptations, 64, 260, 513, 518, 520, 521; Arctic, 224; changes, 27; conditions, 214, 320, 440; cultural, 497; desert, 35, 150; deterioration, 317; exploitation of, 210, 207, 225, 518; factors, 89, 167, 225, 442, 446; forest, 165, 234; Great Basin, 150; highland, 297; influences, 519; lake, 165; "littoral, riparian and lagoonal," 453, 480; lowland, 296; phonetic, 533; physical, 497; Plains, 193; regional, 225, 255; resources, 29; semidesert, 198; short-grass, 198; similarity, 513, 515; stable, in Desert West, 151, 153; subarctic, 490; tropical forest, 351; words for features of, 552; zones, 476

Eolithic stage, 120

Epimiolithic stage, 29

Epiprotolithic stage, 29

Epochs, 392, 393; Caribbean area, 393; Hunter and Gatherer, 564; Indo-Hispanic, 400, 401; Meso-Indian, 392, 396, 400, 403, 407, Neo-Indian, 397, 400, 414; Paleo-Indian, 392, 394, 396

Escuintla area (region), Guatemala, 379

Eskimo(s), 85, 89, 91, 92, 94, 99, 490, 563; Aleuts, 91; ancestors of, 85; Angmassalik (Greenland), 107; areas, 180; Bering Sea, 91, 98, 101, 105; clothing, 100; culture(s), 85–108; Dorset, 90, 106, 107; eastern, 101; Eskimoid cultures, 134; houses, modern, 94; influence, 135; Ipiutak, 105; Kodiak Island, 91; language, 101, 535, 536; material, 94; northern, 105; physical type(s), 101, 105; Point Barrow, 101; pre-Eskimo cultures, 85–89; Prince William Sound, 91; Punuk, 96; St. Lawrence Island, 94, 98; territory, southern periphery of, 101; traits, modern, 107; western, 102; Yuit (Siberia), 98

Esmeraldas, Ecuador, 477, 479, 521

Esperanza (Puerto Rico): site, 402; style, 412

Esperanza phase (Kaminaljuyú), 309, 310, 370

Essequibo, British Guiana: province of, 422; River, 420, 434, 435

Estrada, Emilio, 360, 383, 463, 473, 474, 475, 476, 477, 478, 485, 503, 508, 510, 522, 523, 524

Etching, 182

Ethnography (ethnographies) (ethnographic), 126, 135, 166, 241, 495, 553, 560; evidence (data), 128, 434, 435; investigations, 132; people, 133; practices, 132; pre-Columbia, 482; site, 482; times, 119, 122; traits, 134, 499

Ethnohistory, 434, 435, 444

Ethnology (ethnological), 162, 254, 511; observation, 435; research, 3; of the West, 166

Etna Cave, 60, 62, 153

Etowah: ceramics, 268, 280, 284; communities, 280; culture, 281; site, 279, 280, 281; variant of South Appalachian culture, 279, 285

Eurasia(n), 10, 88, 530, 531, 537, 538; -American linguistic relations, 536, 537; early civilizations of, 490; languages, 534, 538, 543, 545, 547; Mesolithic, 90; northern, 103, 223, 230; pit houses, 180

Eureka Valley, California, 121

Europe(an)(s), 90, 207–8, 211, 350, 356, 421, 443, 489, 495, 502, 529, 552; Caucasus, 230; colonists (colonies), 223, 254, 523; contact, 204, 206, 211, 255, 284, 433, 434, 443, 530, 545; control, 189; descent, 563; discovery and conquest of Americas, 490; entry, 380, 409, 434, 436, 440; epidemics, origin of, 283; explorations, 223; explorers, missionaries, and traders, 527; missionary efforts, 189; northern, 537; northern, Mesolithic of, 90; northwestern, 230; settlements, 434; soldiers, priests, and settlers, 528; trade goods, 166, 205, 432, 435, 436; traits, 189

Evans, Clifford, 2, 8, 9, 360, 383, 391, 392, 397, 409, 415, 419, 421, 424, 426–30, 432, 433, 435, 437, 438, 440–42, 446–48, 463, 473, 474–76, 484, 486, 503, 510, 511, 520–25, 565

Evans, Glen L., 44, 45, 72, 79, 197, 119

Evans culture, 246

Evansville, Indiana, 251

Evolution(ary): cultural, 8, 10, 121, 183, 364, 392, 497, 520, 561; local, 282, 359, 364; stages, 8; trends, 500

Excavation(s), 40, 61, 88, 91, 92, 99, 101, 102, 107, 128, 132–35, 154, 156, 236, 247, 266, 267, 273, 291, 294, 308, 315, 318, 331, 338, 362, 363, 372, 376, 380, 392, 399, 432, 444, 454, 464, 480, 482, 483, 493; archeological, 438, 446; controlled, 25, 368, 379, 419; data, 228; dome-like, 301; large-scale, 482; stratigraphic, 429, 431, 440, 441, 481, 560; techniques, 421

Excising; *see* Ceramic techniques

Ezell, Paul H., 189, 190

Fabrics; *see* Textiles

Façades; *see* Architectural features

Fairbanks, Alaska, 87, 88

Fairbanks, Charles H., 286

Falcon, Venezuela, 48, 50, 57

Falcon culture, 232

Fanning site, 211, 212

Farmer, Malcolm F., 34, 72

Farmer(s), 186, 307, 308, 317, 369, 376; houses of, 308; marginal, 317; -peasant class, 333; Southwestern, early, 240; Southwestern, late, 246; *see also* Agriculture

Farm(ing)(s), 564; individual, 285; rain, 319, 321; -steads, 302; villages, 300, 332, 375; *see also* Agriculture

Farmington: complex, 31, 43, 44; site, radiocarbon dates for gravels at, 130

Faulkner culture, 232, 252

Fauna(l): changes in, 399; extinct, 27, 32, 38, 44, 45, 46, 47, 50, 52, 54, 57, 58, 61, 63, 64, 67, 87, 154, 156, 197, 396, 398,

422, 443, 518; extinct, radiocarbon dates on dung of, 58, 61, 155; fossil, 45; material(s), 229, 233; modern, 156, 365; Wisconsin-age, 45; *see also* Bison; Mammoth; Mastodon; Pleistocene, fauna

Fay, Mr. and Mrs. Albert, vii

Feather(s)(ed), 332, 380, 453; boxes, 179; bunches of, 154; -cloth blankets, 161, 179, 181; costumes, 521; headdresses, 333, 521; headdresses, on pottery, 433; robes, 160, 161, 280; serpent(s), 312, 315, 316, 377; turkey, 187; wands, 154; work, 427

Feeheley culture, 252

Feline(s), 480; and bird combination, 462; features, 368; large, 462; lions, seated, 360; pumas, 365, 460; semifeline beings, 480; *see also* Jaguars, Tigers

Fell's Cave, 58, 65, 66, 67; Magellan Periods I, II, III, 65; radiocarbon date for, 67

Fenenga, Franklin, 126, 141, 143

Ferguson, Thomas Stuart, 360, 383

Ferndon, Edwin N., Jr., 186, 188, 190

Ferry culture, 253

Fewkes, Jesse Walter, 391, 415

Fiber(s), 332; agave, 332; apron-skirt, 154, 161; sandals, 155; -tempering (*see* Ceramics, tempering); vegetable, 160

Figures: boulder, 368, 377; carved, 458; ceremonial, standing on crouched human, 360; "danzante," 301, 303; geometric and zoömorphic appliqué lugs, ceramic, 406; grouped or enthroned on panels, 360; human, 360, 368, 379; and postures in sculpture, 341, 349, 360, 506; in profile, 313; single standing, 368; "smiling face," 382; stucco relief, 349; tied to beds, 521; two facing, 368; warrior, 521; warrior, carved and polychromed, 315; of zemis, 413

Figurine(s), 134, 301, 309, 332, 341, 352, 370, 380, 381, 407, 428; absence of, 405, 410, 414; Alta Verapaz, 350; appliquéd features, 336, 406; art, 351; bone, 382; caryatid-supported platform, 352; Classic period, 336, 351; clay (pottery), 132, 165, 182, 319, 363, 383, 414, 474, 476, 478, 515, 516, 517, 520; death manikins, 378; effigy, 352; folded legs, 477; greenstone, 370; hand-modeled, 335, 366, 367, 377, 381; Jaina style, 355, 382; Jonuta style, 382; Lowland Maya, Late Classic, 350, 352; Lowland Maya, Preclassic, 336, 350; Mamom, 336, 337, 350; Mayapan, 319; mold-made, 350, 504; molds, 521; mov-

able limbs, 521; Palenque, 350; punched features, 336; Santa Rita, 363; stone, 382, 474, 475; terra cotta, 300, 302, 303, 314, 319; *see also* Ceramics

Finger Lakes site, 226

Finley site, 196

Fire: areas, 160; drills, 154, 155, 156, 160; -making, with pyrites and flint, 231, 514; pits, 63, 67, 182, 206 (*see also* Hearth pits); -places, 206; -production technique, 225; serpents, 360; stones, 455; tongs, 156; -wood depletion, 254

Firth River, Alaska, 87

Fish(ing), 94, 107, 127, 128, 131, 134, 135, 165, 207, 211, 224, 225, 245, 319, 375, 376, 399, 400, 422, 423, 425, 426, 428, 443, 444, 452, 453, 473; bones, 163, 464; cod, 94; demon, Mochica, 466; equipment (tools), 103, 230, 397, 399; glue, 514; gorges, 164; live, as carriers of artifacts, 124; in Maya sculpture, 360; motifs, 368; nets, 455; off-shore, 456; scene, Mochica, 466; shell, 452; villages, 454

Fishbone Cave, 153

Fisher focus, 252; est. date for, 254

Fishhooks, 103, 160, 397; bone, 118, 132, 207, 260, 422, 456; composite, 102; shell, 51, 118, 123, 124, 125, 128, 422, 456

Fisk, H. N., 18, 19

Five-Mile Rapids site, 53, 226; lowest level, 54

Flagstaff, Arizona, 183, 184, 186, 187

Flake(s)(d), 46, 225, 260, 367, 422, 455; -blades, obsidian, 370, choppers, 165; flint, 121; industries, 30; knives, 104, 125, 231; large lamellar, edge-trimmed, 398; points, 125; prismatic, 38, 39, 50; scrapers, 87, 122, 123, 125, 130, 165; tools (implements), 38, 42, 51, 125, 129, 130; triangular-sectioned, 107

Flaking: bifacial, 121; diagonal, 104; parallel, 32, 59; percussion, 30, 42, 51; pressure, 51, 58, 59, 455; ripple, 227

Flint(s), 121, 130; abraders, 344; artifacts, 45, 46, 51, 58, 237, 260; bladelike sections of, 224; blades, 104, 243, 344; chipped, 45, 161; choppers, heavy, 225; cores, prepared, 224; disks, conical, 202; eccentric, 341, 344; firemaking with, 231, 514; flakers, 103; flakes, 121; Flint Ridge, 242; fractured pieces, 119; hoes, 248, 250; knives, 344; plano-convex, 46; projectile points, 344; scrapers, 225, 344; specimens, 156; tools, percussion-flaked, 343

Flint, Richard Foster, 17, 19

Flint Creek complex (tradition), 53, 54
Floor(s): adobe, 182; deeply excavated, 206; dirt, 339, 439; house, 231; house, burials under, 249, 337, 341, 348, 355; lime, 307; lime-plastered, 339; marl, 339; painted, 379; prepared, 160; renewal of, 439; shallowly excavated, 206; stone, 515; tombs, 301
Floral Park phase, 338
Flores Espinosa, Isabel, 463, 485
Florescent stage (period, horizon): northern Yucatan, 351, 354, 356, 362, 363, 364; Peru and Andean area, 453, 457, 476, 482
Florida, 88, 259, 261, 263, 275, 398; northwestern, 242, 266, 271, 282, 283; peninsular, 263, 271, 273, 274, 275, 283; preceramic sites in, 398; southern, remnants of Meso-Indians in, 414; west coast, 282
Fluted Blade Hunters, 223, 224, 227, 228, 229, 252, 255; cultures, 225; Eastern, 226; est. dates for, 224, 255; lifeway, 224
Fluted point(s) (blades), 30, 31, 32, 33, 34, 36, 37, 57, 59, 61, 85, 197, 224, 227, 228; channel, 177; cultures, 35, 37, 65; est. date of disappearance of, in North America, 33; sites, 53, 54, 177; stage, 51; style, 224; tradition, 26, 151, 199; *see also* Projectile points
Flutes (flageolets), 248; cane, 155; reed, 179
Fluting: ceramic, 366, 370; projectile points, 36, 55, 67, 224
Focus(es), 7, 16, 41, 203; *see also* individual focuses by name
Förstemann, E. W., 560
Folsom: -Clovis fluted point tradition, 199; complex, 54, 196, 197; culture, 34, 35, 226; hunters, 223; points, 31, 36, 38, 39, 51, 55, 57, 59, 64 (*see also* Projectile points); points, est. and radiocarbon dates for, 55; pre-Folsom, 34, 36
Food(s), 225, 229, 396; -collecting, 177, 179, 203; cultivated, 332; gatherers, 292, 296, 317, 454, 530 (*see also* Gatherers); -gathering, 38, 300; -gathering stage, 28, 295; -grinding, 32–37, 52, 55, 57–59, 61, 63–65, 214 (*see also* Grinding); insects, edible, 121; new, 455; nuts, 33, 58, 176, 224, 267, 429; offerings (*see* Grave goods); plants, 178, 179, 260, 455, 482, 497, 501; -producing (production), 179, 203, 204, 214, 295, 300, 331, 332, 454; -producing stage, 28; resources, 209, 255, 308; scrap (debris), 155, 156, 163; speciali-

zation, 165; -storage, 237; -storage pits, 198 (*see also* Pits, storage); -stuffs, animal and vegetal, 294, 297; supply, 245, 256, 422, 423, 424, 426, 513, 519; surpluses, 209; vegetal (vegetable), 33, 201, 399
Forager(s) (foraging), 150, 165, 201; Desert Archaic, 178; lifeway, 212; Plains, 195, 214; Wyoming Basin, 196; *see also* Gathering
Forbis, Richard G., 62, 72
Ford, James A., 98, 100, 109, 136, 139, 279, 286, 287
Forest(s), 176, 334, 380, 390, 439, 443, 452, 466; American arctic, 236; boreal, 223, 234, 236, 245; composition, 224; deciduous, 200, 224, 230; evergreen and deciduous, 365; gallery, 428; mixed, 227, 234, 245; rain, 333, 353, 375; rain, tropical, 351, 424, 433; scrub, 352; sites, 260, 427; spruce-fir, 224, 230, 256; tropical, 419, 421, 422, 423, 426, 440, 441; zones, northern, 248
Forestdale Valley, Arizona, 181
Formative stage (period, horizon), 304, 333, 381, 426, 512, 519; Andean area, 482; Ecuador, 474–75; Ecuador, Chorrera phase, 376; Ecuador, Machalilla phase, 462, 475; Ecuador, Valdivia phase, 426, 474–75; Guatemala highlands, ceramics, 361; incipient, 129; Middle, Copan ceramics, 337, 346; southern Mesoamerica, 381, 480; southern and western lowlands, 335, 354, 355; Willey and Phillips, 30, 129, 392, 479; Yucatan, northern, 354, 355
Fort Ancient: culture, 246, 253, 254; est. date of Mississippian dominance of, 254; people, 242, 254
Fort Liard complex, 53, 54
Fort Rock Cave, 53, 155, 226; lowest level, 54; Levels II, III, IV, 153
Fort Walton: ceramics, 283; culture, 283, 284; est. date for, 283; sites, coastal and inland, 283
Fortaleza mound group, 439
Fortifications; *see* Defensive works
Fortresses: Aztec, 320; Cacaxtla, 312; Cerro Chavín, 379; Guatemala highlands, 373, 374; Monte Alban, 305, 308; Xochichalco, 312
Fossil(s), 14; beaches, 159; cinampas, 321; fauna (*see* Fauna); human and animal bone, 127, 293; lakes, 150; pollens, *Maydeae* grasses, 296; proboscideans, 293; terraces, 159; watercourses, 150, 159; wood, 50, 396

Fowler, Melvin L., 63, 72, 229, 257
Frankforter, W. D., 61, 62, 69, 72, 79, 199, 215
Fraser River, British Columbia, 54; delta of, 134
Freeman, Leslie G., Jr., 191
Fremont culture, 246
French Scientific Commission, 293
Fresco, 504
Frets; *see* Architectural features
Friesenhahn Cave, 43, 44, 45; zones 2, 3, and 4, 46
Friezes; *see* Architectural features
Frightful Cave, 37, 62, 156; bottom level, 63; radiocarbon dates for bottom level of, 63, 156
Frontier complex, 60; at Allen site, 62; at Lime Creek site, 199
Fruits; *see* Plants
Frye, John C., 18, 19
Full Archaic stage; *see* Archaic
Full Historic period (Southeastern United States), 284–85
Fulton aspect, 282
Fur: blankets, 154, 161; cloth, 154; -cloth blankets, 178, 179, 181; robes, 161; strips (blanket?), 155

Gadsden purchase, 175
Gainesville, Florida, 259
Galena; *see* Minerals
Gallagher, Patrick, 391, 415
Galleries; *see* Architectural features
Gallina River, New Mexico, 184
Gambell (Sevuokok): mountain, 92; old section of, 93, 94; sites, 92–95, 98, 99; sites, harpoon heads from, 96; village of, 92, 93
Game, 178, 182, 208, 260, 332, 397, 399, 422, 423, 425; depletion of, 227; large, 198, 200, 201; small, 201, 203; wild, 332, 334, 353, 375
Games, 514, 515; ball (*see* Ball Game, Balls); hockey, 514; of chance, with dice, 514
Garbanzai, Peru, 459
Garcia Payon, José, 313, 326, 510
Garments; *see* Clothing
Garrison(s), 323, 324, 469, 472; Aztec, 549; quarters, 473
Garzon site, 49, 50
Gathering (gatherers), 33, 124, 180, 150, 225, 261, 269, 400, 423, 426, 443, 473, 476; advanced, 39; -collecting-hunting, 150; -collecting stage, 29; cultures, 158; economies, 294; food, 38, 292,

294; nomadic, 291; people(s), 35, 399, 407; plant, 294; seasonal, 154; seed, 123; shellfish, 123, 125, 128; wild plants, 294, 298; *see also* Hunters and Gatherers
Geist, Otto W., 91, 93, 94, 109
Geoanthropology, 13, 17
Geographic(al): contact, 534; differences, 465, 478; distribution, 513; divisions, 176, 193, 259; features, 459; location of languages, 548; spread, 554
Geology (geological) (geologists), 13, 14, 15, 17, 24, 45, 151, 166, 293; data, 160; delineation, 15; epochs, 17 (*see also* Pleistocene); formations, 24, 27, 293, 294, 518; glacial, 17; stream deposits, correlation of, 156; units, 259
George Lake: culture, 253; site, 228, 231
Georgetown phase, 181
Georgia, 259, 284; central, 263, 277; coast of, 261, 275; northern, 265, 271, 279, 284; southern, 259, 263, 266, 271, 275, 283, 284
Ghatchi complexes: I, 49, 50, 51; II, 56, 57, 58
Ghost Cave, 196, 212
Gibson aspect, 282; Alto focus levels of, 282; ceramics, 282; Early, 276; later components and focuses, est. date for, 282
Giddings, J. L., Jr., 62, 72, 85, 87, 88–91, 93, 98, 103–7, 109, 110, 113
Gifford, E. W., 125, 128, 139, 341, 343, 350
Gila Butte phase, 181
Gila River, 175, 185; Lower, 180; Upper, 179, 187
Glacial: advances, 150; elephant forms, 224; features, 16, 18, 234; post-, age, 24, 35, 46, 68, 130; stages, 24, 36, 46, 224; Wisconsin, 27, 45, 68
Glacial Kame: burial complex, 234, 236; culture, 228, 234, 235, 252; est. dates for, 234; sites, 234
Gladwin, Harold S., 180, 190, 517, 524
Gladwin, Nora, 190
Glass, H. D., 18, 19
Glottochronology, 119, 534, 545, 553; *see also* Lexicostatistics
Glyph(s) (hieroglyphs), 347, 560; action or verb, 347; affixes, 347; augury, 347; bands on pottery, 349; date, 305; decipherment of, 346, 347; dictionary of, 347; elements, 347; emblem, 348; personified, 347; place, 305; stucco relief, 349; subject or object, 347; symbolic, 347

God(s) (deities), 301, 342, 347, 363, 466, 538, 539; attributes of, 346; control of time by, 333, 344; death, 347; demons, Mochica, 466, 467; diving, 360; fertility, 303; Huitzilopochtli, 322, 324; jaguar-quetzal-serpent, 315; Maya, 333, 344, 368; Mochica, 466, 467; new, 333; notion of, 545; polychrome painted, Chama ware, 372; Quetzalcoatl, 315, 316; rain, 303, 359; service of, 305; standing on crouched human figures, 360; sun (solar), 273, 324, 538; Tezcatlipoca, 316; Tlahuizcalpantecuhtli, lord of Venus as morning star, 315; Toltec, 315; white goddess, 347; wind, concept of, Mexican, 359; zemis, 413
Godwin, H., 16, 19
Goggin, John M., 275, 286, 391, 522, 524
Gold(en), 352, 453; alloys of, 374, 464, 465, 481; bangles on shirts, 479; casting of, 481; dishes, 360; earrings, 478; inlays, in wood carvings, 413; jewelry, 458, 478, 479; nose ornaments, 478; offerings, 359; ornaments, 333, 374
Gold Hill, Oregon, 133
Gomez, Juan Vicente, 391
Gonzalez, Dr. and Mrs. Richard J., vii
Goodman, J. T., 345, 560
Goodman-Martinez-Thompson   (GMT) correlation, 345, 356, 362
Gorden's Intermediate period, 134
Gorgets; see Ornaments
Gouges, 231; bone, 515; copper, 234; invention of, 397, 398; shell, 397, 398; stone, green and dark, 344
Gourds, 237, 298, 332; containers, 455, 456; faces carved on, 460, 462; of squashes and pumpkins, 178; stoppered, 455; see also Plants
Graham Cave, 60, 61, 63, 226, 228; lowest levels, 63, 228, 229, 252; middle level, 229; radiocarbon dates from, 61, 228; upper levels, 228
Grain; see Plants
Gran Chaco, 514
Gran Sabana, Venezuela, 420, 423
Grand Canyon of the Colorado, 180
Grand River, 210; culture, 252
Grand Valley, Michigan, 243
Grange, Roger T., Jr., 172, 191, 208, 219
Grant, Campbell, 125, 139
Grant Lake culture, 232
Grant mound, 275
Grass: beds, 154; cutters, 155, 160; invasion of cornfields, 351; lodge, 208; lodge-dwelling peoples, 209, 211; panic, ap-

pearance of in Sierra Madre Oriental, 297; seeds, 162; *Tripsacum*, 300
Grasslands, 200, 214, 215, 365, 390, 443, 453; clay, 334; depletion of, 227; Plains, 193, 224
Grave goods, 103, 127, 131, 178, 235, 236, 238, 245, 248, 249, 265, 281, 282, 300, 341, 355–56, 366, 369, 370, 380, 382, 431, 434, 437; absence of, 377; burned, 128, 132
Gravel(s), 47, 423; auriferous, 87; est. dates for artifacts from auriferous, in Sierra Nevada, 130; Farmington site, 131; Farmington site, radiocarbon dates from, 130; lake, 62; spit, 92; terrace, Hondo River, 295; Trenton, New Jersey, 44
Gravers, 103, 163, 198, 225; beaver-teeth, 244
Graves, 59, 63, 233, 274, 279, 284, 341, 355, 382, 478, 480, 495; see also Burials
Great Basin, 6, 35, 36, 125, 126, 131, 149, 152, 153, 157–62, 167–69, 176, 201, 214, 215; caves, 35, 55; cultural continuum in, 161; cultures, 154; environment, 150; history, 160; Humboldt area of, 160; peoples, 118, 153, 158; regional variations in, est. date, 161; southern, 158; traits, 162; western fringe of, 132
Great Bear River culture, 232
Great Bend aspect, 196, 208, 209, 210
Great Lakes, 244, 248, 251, 255; drainage basin, 233, 238
Great Lakes region (area), 54, 63, 224, 230, 231, 235, 254; first appearance of Archaic in, est. date, 227; lower, 230, 254; Upper, 34, 228, 233, 234, 236
Great Plains, 6, 32, 35, 36, 37, 38, 52, 54, 55, 57, 59, 62, 67, 149, 177, 193, 564; archeology, 6, 193, 214, 215, 560; eastern margin of, 317; environment, 1, 193, 195; geographic subdivisions of, short-grass (steppes), tall-grass (prairies), 193; high (*see* High Plains); manos in, 34; region, 34, 38, 193, 195, 199
Great Salt Lake, 175
Greater Antilles; see Antilles
Greater Pampa area, Argentina, 420, 443
Greenberg, Joseph H., 547, 555
Greengo, Robert E., 129, 139
Greenland, 85, 89, 91, 99, 100, 105, 106, 107; culture, 102; dialects, 101; Dorset culture, 240; eastern, Angmassalik Eskimos of, 107; harpoons, 96; northwestern, 100; western, 100
Greenlandic Norse culture, 100, 246

Greenman, Emerson F., 120, 139
Griddles, clay (pottery), 400, 405, 408, 411, 430, 431, 433, 434, 435, 441; absence of, in Indo-Hispanic sites, 401; absence of, in Tocuyanoid series, 405; comales, 371, 372; fragments of, 399, 400; in Neo-Indian and Meso-Indian sites, 400; in Ocumaroid series, 406
Griffin, James B., viii, 2, 7, 8, 15, 16, 19, 33, 34, 59, 72, 85, 204, 216, 223, 230, 233, 241, 247, 251, 254, 257, 279, 286, 287, 496, 565
Grijalva Basin, Chiapas, Upper; *see* Central Depression
Grinding, 33, 59, 68, 134, 135; acorn, 125; food (*see* Food); seed, 122, 125, 127; slabs, 164; stones, 61, 176, 225, 399, 456, 516, 517; -stone edge, 397, 398; tools (implements), 122, 518 (*see also* Manos, Metates, Milling stones, Mortars, Mullers, Pestles)
Grosscup, Gordon L., 161, 171
Ground stone, 233; adzes, 230, 231; artifacts, 204, 231, 234; celts, 230; mortars, 229; projectile points, 55; tools, 197, 225, 231, 260; woodworking tools, 230
Grove culture, 232
Gruhn, Ruth, 62, 72, 131, 139, 166, 171
Gruta de Wabeto, 49, 50
Guanajuato, 293, 314
Guaporé, Brazil, lowland, 445
Guaporé River, 420, 441
Guaraguao site, 393
Guarguapo: site, 402; style, Indo-Hispanic epoch, 411; style, Period IV, 410, 411
Guarico, Venezuela, 430
Guarita: phase, 432; site, 438
Guasare site, 393
Guasave, Sinaloa, 319
Guatemala(n), 43, 44, 149, 291, 299, 303, 316, 323, 331, 380, 389, 451, 508; Altar de Sacrificios, 336, 337, 338, 350, 352; coast of, 511, 512; department of, 365; Pacific coast (slope of), 236, 309, 313, 331, 367, 372, 375, 376, 377, 378, 379, 380, 382; *see also* individual cultures, sites, and geographical places by name
Guatemala highlands, 292, 296, 310, 331, 333, 335, 343, 359–82; earliest materials in, 365; history of, 374; pottery of, 366, 372; society of, 375
Guaviare River, Venezuela, 420
Guayabita site, 402
Guayabitoid people, 411; Columbus' encounter with, 411
Guayabitoid series, 409–11; radiocarbon dates for, 411
Guayabo Blanco complex, 398
Guayas, Ecuador: basin, 475; coast, 473, 475; estuary, 479; northern shore of, 474
Guerrero, 303, 305, 318; antiquities of, 318; northern, 320
Guiana(s), 389, 396, 422, 429, 433, 434, 446; Brazilian, 430–38; British, 397, 402, 407, 409, 420, 422, 430, 432, 435 (*see also* British Guiana); French, 420; highlands, 390, 397; highlands, Meso-Indian epoch in, 396–97; northern, 389, 397, 419; slash-and-burn agriculture in, 435; Venezuelan, 392, 395, 396; *see also* individual cultures, sites, and geographical places by name
Gulf Coast(al), 265, 364, 371, 376, 380; conch shells, 265; cultures, 277; Plain, 265, 267, 271, 273, 281; Plain, pottery of, 266
Gulf of Georgia, British Columbia, 133, 134
Gulf of Mexico, 291, 303, 317, 334, 352, 380; lowlands, 303, 304, 312
Gulf of Paria, 407
Gulf tradition, 262, 265, 267, 269, 270, 271, 275, 280, 281, 283, 284; cultures, 273; pottery, 271, 273
Gunnerson, Delores A., 213, 216
Gunnerson, J. H., 213, 216
Gunther Island site: lower levels of, 132; radiocarbon date for base of, 132
Gutentag, Edwin, 18, 19
Gypsum Cave, 38, 60, 61, 62, 151, 153, 155, 177; earliest levels, 167; points, 155, 229; radiocarbon dates from, 61; upper levels, 153

Haag, William G., 392
Hass, Mary R., 555
Habitat; *see* Ecology
Habitation(s), 428; middens, 429; mounds, 439; sites, 422, 425, 428, 431, 433, 434, 436, 437
Hacienda Grande: site, 402; style, 411
Hackman, Robert J., 85, 113
Haekel, Josef, 128, 140
Hagen site, 196
Hahn, Paul G., 391, 415
Haiti(an), 389, 391, 395, 402, 412; intermediate styles in, 411; isolated remnants of Meso-Indians in, 398–99, 411; Meillac style, 412; Ostiones-like pottery of, 412; southwestern peninsula of, 411
Hakataya culture; *see* Patayan culture
Haley focus, 282

Halifax culture, 232
Halls; *see* Architectural features
Hamilton, Henry W., 286
Hamlets, 207, 333, 339, 375
Hammel, E. A., 28, 58, 65, 66, 68, 75, 485
Hammers; *see* Tools
Hammerstones; *see* Tools
Han dynasty; *see* China
Hand stones; *see* Manos
Handles: on boxes, 96; digging-stick, antler, 133, 166; drum, 104; horn-core, 210; on knives, 96, 98, 155, 160, 212; on pottery (*see* Ceramic forms); on pottery stamps, 433; on rattles, 154
Hanke, Wanda, 421, 447
Harding, M., 124, 140
Hardy, Mrs. W. C., vii
Harlan site, 274, 282; ceramics, 274; mounds, 274
Harmons Creek culture, 246
Harner, M. J., 119, 125, 140
Harp, Elmer, Jr., 87, 107, 110
Harpers Ferry culture, 252
Harpoon(s), 94, 96, 98, 104; antler, 134, 245; barbed, 127, 134, 135; bone, 132; butt end of, 96; composite, 96, 133; finger rests, 96, 103, 107; fishing, 397; foreshafts, 96, 103; Greenland, 96; lances, 90; points, bone, 51; socket pieces, 96, 103, 107; "winged objects," 96, 97
Harpoon heads, 90, 91, 94, 95, 96, 98, 104; Birnirk, 98, 99; bone, 210; Dorset, 107; early Punuk, 94; Ipiutak, 103; ivory, 91; modern, 95, 96; one- and two-piece, 134; toggle-, 96, 102, 104, 105; whaling, 94, 104
Harrington, Mark Raymond, 36, 44, 46, 62, 72, 73, 130, 140, 155, 160, 171, 172, 391, 415
Harris, Mary Frances, vii
Harris, R. K., 44, 45, 71
Harris site (C. W. Harris site), 121, 122, 159; radiocarbon dates for, 159; San Dieguito level, radiocarbon dates for, 123
Hat Creek site, 165
Hatt, Gudmund, 391, 415
Hattori, Shiro, 547
Haury, Emil W., 52, 54, 62, 63, 64, 73, 119, 122, 140, 156, 171, 181, 183, 190
Havana: ceramic complex, 239, 243; Mound, 6, 239; phase, 237
Haynes, Vance, 52, 54, 55, 73
Head(s): animal, 370, 373, 374 (*see also* Animals); deformation (*see* Deformation, cranial); human (*see* Human

heads); lance, 282; sheet copper, 264; sky, 368; tenoned, 458; thin stone, 352, 378, 382; trophy, 305
Headdresses, 332; adornos on pottery, 433; feathered, 333, 521; on figurines, 350; mosaic, 357; plumed, 479
Heart River focus, 208, 210
Hearth(s), 37, 45, 46, 156, 198, 208; basin-shaped, 42, 44; fire drill, 154, 158; pits, 52; wooden, 155, 160
Hecker, Thad C., 208, 220
Heekeren, H. R., van, 391, 415
Heicksen, M. H., 130, 147
Heine-Geldern, Robert, 360, 498, 504, 507, 510
Heizer, Robert F., 1, 6, 31, 44, 62, 73, 80, 102, 110, 117, 118, 119, 120, 123, 124, 125–35, 137, 138, 140–41, 143, 147, 154, 161, 168, 171, 304, 326
Hell Gap, 197; points, radiocarbon date for, 55
Hematite: adzes, 229; beads, 178; decoration on polychrome wares, 350
Henrietta focus, 196, 209
Hester, Jim J., 45, 73
Hester, Joseph A., Jr., 28, 75, 125, 137
Hewes, G. W., 127, 141
Heye, G. G., 125, 142
Hibben, Frank C., 15, 19, 54, 73
Hidalgo (state of), Tula, 314
Hidden Valley culture, 252
Hides; *see* Skins
Hierarchic figures: American 506; Asian, 506; at Palenque, 350
Hieroglyphs (hieroglyphic): bands on vessel rims, 350; dates, 341; inscriptions, 301, 342, 355, 356; monuments, 364; stelae, 502; texts, 348; writing, 304, 331, 339, 343, 345, 346, 347; *see also* Glyphs
High cultures, 303, 309, 318, 331, 453, 479; of Asia, 490; centers of, 519; Meso-american, 292, 295, 304, 503; of Mexico, 496; of Nuclear America, 490; of Peru, 482, 496; South American, 451 ff.; *see also* Civilizations
High Plains, 32, 153, 155, 189, 200, 205, 213; *see also* Great Plains
High priests; *see* Priests, high
Highland County, Ohio, 241
Highland culture: Plains, 246; Santa Rosa Island, radiocarbon dates for, 123
Hilbert, Peter Paul, 421, 425, 431, 432, 438, 440, 442, 447
Hilburn, James A., vii
Hill, A. T., 202, 206, 211, 216, 217
Hillside site, 92, 93, 94, 96, 106; harpoon heads from, 96; *see also* Gambell, sites

Hi-lo culture, 252
Hindes, M. G., 131, 142
Hindu-Buddhist: areas, 507; art motifs, 498; civilization, 507
Hispaniola, 389, 398, 403; *see also* Dominican Republic, Haiti
History, 15, 17, 39, 40, 561, 562, 565; of American languages, 531; Andean, 482; of Caribbean area, 390; of culture, 176, 259, 260, 403, 404, 407, 490, 499, 503; of Guatemala highland, 374; of Maya, 333, 345; Peruvian, 453
Hiwassee Island: culture, 246, 277; Dallas stage, 279; Hiwassee Island stage, 281
Hoe(s): agriculture, 207, 211; bone, bison scapula, 205, 211; flint, 248, 250; iron, 205; stone, rectanguloid, 434
Hohokam: area, 176, 180, 183, 188; ball courts, 182, 186; Classic stage, 188; colonies, 183; culture, 6, 169, 175, 182, 183, 185, 240, 246; Gila Butte phase, 181; influence, 183; Pioneer period, 182, 564; Sacaton (Sedentary) period, 182; Santa Cruz (Colonial) period, 182; sequence, 181; Snaketown phase, 181; textiles, 183; transitional stage, est. dates for, 186; Vahki phase, 180; villages, 182
Holcombe culture, 252
Holder, Preston, 62, 73, 197, 217, 278, 279, 287
Hole, Frank, vii
Holmberg, Allan R., 423, 448
Holmes, W. H., 24, 130, 142, 340, 383, 522, 524
Holmul, Guatemala, 338; corbeled vault at, 338; Holmul I ceramic complex, 337, 355; ossuaries at, 337
Holtved, Erik, 100, 107, 110
Hondo River, Mexico, 295, 334
Honduras (Spanish), 333, 334, 378, 389; Early Preclassic of, 335; northwesern, 292; Ulua Bichrome pottery of, 376; western, 291, 343
Hopewell(ian), 214, 239, 241, 243, 244, 247, 248, 249, 253, 256, 267, 270, 271; agriculture, 243; artifacts, 241, 263, 265; Baehr, 252; bases, 278; burials, 234, 236, 267; communities, 239, 242; conch shells, 265; craftsmen, 244; cultural level, 242; culture(s), 7, 243, 244, 245, 262, 265, 284, 285; culture climax, northern, 239; development, 245; disappearance of, 245; Early, 237; eastern, 202; elements, 239, 274; Illinois, 239, 240, 241, 243; Illinois, ceramic complex, est. beginning date for, 237; influence, 242, 244, 245, 263, 266, 269, 564; Kansas City, 196, 252; late, 247; Middle, 243; midwestern, 262, 263, 265; Norton, 252; occupation of Plains, probable dates for, 202; Ohio, 239, 240, 241, 242; Ohio, Mound, 25; Ohio, radiocarbon dates for, 239; political organization, 241; projectile points, 244; sites, 202, 203; sites, diversity of materials from, 241; social organization, 241; stimulus, 245; styles (art), 238, 243; system, 266; tradition, 265, 269; Trempealeau, 252; Western, 240
Hopi: district, 187, 188; language, 549, 550; villages, 185, 188
Hopkins, M. L., 44, 73
Horizon(s), 8, 32, 292, 304, 310, 312, 335, 337, 394, 502; Archaic, 260; ceramic, 180, 202, 318, 319; Chavín, 426, 457; Cintla, 352; Cochise, 178; culture, 32; Early Classic, 313; Formative, 304, 512; Lamar, est. date for, 284; Late Classic, 313; lower Sacramento Valley, 126, 127; markers, 9, 203, 208, 378; Milling Stone, 123; Oak Grove–Topanga–La Jolla–Milling Stone, 127; occupation, 293, 294, 298, 301; Paleo-Indian hunting, 422; sloping, 437; style(s), 9, 310, 318, 319, 424–32, 438–42, 565 (*see also* Ceramic horizon styles); time, 206; Tlapacoya-Cuicuilco–Monte Alban 1, 302; transitional, 259; Tula-Mazapan, 183; Usutulan ceramic, 377
Horn: artifacts, 205; awls, 160; blades, 178; -core handles, 210; grass-cutters, 160; pendants, 161; wrenches, 154, 155, 178; *see also* Antler
Hornbostel, E. M. von, 514, 526
Horner site, 60, 62, 196; radiocarbon dates for, 198
Horse, 195; adoption of, by Comanche, 213, 548; culture (Plains), 168; extinct (native American), 32, 38, 46, 47, 63, 64, 67, 87, 156, 293; introduction of, 209, 214; -using tribes, 193
Horticultural Villages stage (Peru), 454–57, 462, 473; est. dates for, 454
Hough, Walter, 184, 190, 517, 524
House(s), 94, 98, 273; concentration of, 351; construction, 94; courts, 307; differences in, 456; floors, 231; models, pottery, 477; platforms, 302, 308, 339, 351, 407; posts, 237, 238; ruins, 92, 93; sweat, 357

House forms, 497; circular, 208, 231, 237, 238, 247; dome-shaped, 94; entranceways, 182, 206, 231; four roof supports, 180, 184, 206, 208; long, 204, 206, 207, 208; long, Iroquois, 254; oblong, 182; oval, 166, 182, 247; rectangular, 165, 206, 238, 247, 250, 254, 515; rounded (elliptical), 160, 206, 376; shallow excavations, 166, 182; square, 103, 104, 206, 208

House materials: bark-covered, 212; driftwood, 103; earth lodge, 165, 206, 207, 212, 277; grass lodge, 208, 209, 211; jacales, 182, 188, 254, 299, 339, 376, 424; mat, 163; mat-covered, 166, 212; mat siding, 165; mud-daubed, 376; part masonry, part pole, 339; plank, 163, 166; plank-walled, 133; skin-covered, 94; stone, 519; stone and turf, 107; thatch(ed) (roofs), 125, 299, 339, 358, 422, 427; thatched, cane, 376; thatch and pole, 339, 366, 376; wood, 166

House types, 94, 101, 206, 211, 213, 250, 427; above-ground, 456; apartment, 306, 307, 375; communal, 424, 427, 439; contiguous (conjoined), 463, 464; council, 249, (ceremonial) 277, 278; dirt-floored, 439; great (Chihuahua), 188; huts, 422; multiroom, large, 307, 519; permanent multifamily, 205; pile dwellings, 406, 424, 439; pit, 178–84, 187, 188, 513, 515; semi-subterranean, 250, 455; single family, 427; subterranean (underground), 92, 107, 455; wigwams, 248, 254

Howard, Edgar B., 62, 73
Howard, George D., 391, 409, 410, 415, 416
Howard, Robert R., 391, 416
Howard Lake culture, 252
Hrdlička, Aleš, 24, 25, 44, 58, 73, 91, 102, 105, 110
Huaca Prieta site, 454–57, 459; carved gourd from, est. date for, 460; people of, 455, 456; radiocarbon dates from, 455
Huancayo Rockshelters, 65, 459
Huanuco, Peru, 57, 65
Huarmey, Peru, 459
Huastec(a)(n), 316, 493, 494; early Preclassic, 335; Panuco sequence, 299, 302; region (area), 299, 302, 309, 317, 322
Huayna Capac, Inca, 471, 479; death of, 471, 472; succession to throne, 472
Hubbs, C. L., 123, 146
Hudson Bay, 86, 90, 100

Hudson Strait, 86, 107
Huehuetenango, Guatemala, 373
Huetamo site, 309
Huexotzinco, Mexico, 323
Huff; focus, 196, 210; site, 207, 209
Hughes, Jack T., 217
Huila, Colombia, department of, 50
Huitchun, Guatemala, 373
Human bones, 58, 336, 349, 355, 363
Human effigies; see Effigy
Human figure(s), 319, 350, 352, 360, 368; crouched, with gods or ceremonial figures standing on, 360; faces of, in appliqué, 406; faces of, in mouths of animal ball-court markers, 373; faces of, on vessel walls, 410; and heads, boulder sculptures of, 47, 368, 377; mushroom-shaped stone sculptures of, 368; pedestal sculptures of, 368, 379; representations of, on pottery, 350, 432; see also Anthropomorphic
Human flesh, eating of, 444
Human heads: boulder sculptures of, 47, 368, 377; colossal, 303, 304, 368, 380; helmeted, 381; lugs, ceramic, 404, 412; of turquoise, 461
Human sacrifice, 324, 331, 341, 357, 359
Humboldt Bay, Oregon, 132
Humboldt Cave, 153, 161
Hunt, Alice B., 54, 62, 74, 158, 171
Hunt, Charles B., 172
Hunters, 33, 122, 130, 224, 295, 443, 473; Archaic, 240; Arctic, 240, 246; Big Game, 88, 152, 167, 177, 200; bison, 197, 200 (see also Bison hunters); caribou, 88, 89; Clovis and Folsom, 223; early, 421, 454; Fluted Blade, 223, 224, 226, 227–29, 252, 255; and gatherers 205, 214, 252; Lagoa Santa, 58; mammoth, 197, 294; nomadic, 291; Northern Woodland, 240; pedestrian, 213; Plains, 196, 199, 246; preagricultural, 456; sea mammal, 88; T-1, 240
Hunters and Gatherers (Foragers), 195, 199, 205; epoch, 564
Hunting, 122, 123, 125–27, 131, 150, 176, 177, 186, 207, 214, 225, 245, 251, 255, 261, 294, 295, 297, 298, 332, 346, 376, 400, 422, 426, 428, 443, 454; Archaic, 263; bands, 223; big game, 38, 152; bird, 94; bison, 211; cultures, 122, 123, 130, 224, 225; deer-, 211; economies, 214, 255, 294; -fishing grounds, northern, 232; -gathering (collecting) cultures (complexes), 130, 202, 203, 260, 263, 269, 294, 316; -gathering-fishing cultures, 199, 231, 255, 423, 443; In-

dians, 453; land-mammal, 456; patterns, 294; peoples (groups, tribes), 32, 35, 39, 107, 159, 210, 215, 223, 316, 423; sea (mammal), 134, 456; turkey, 187; weapons (tools), 399, 455

Hunting (fishing)-and-gathering stage (South America), 65–68; Andean area, est. duration of, 454; lowlands, 421–23; Paraná drainage, 443–44

Hupa-iya: ceramics, 437; complex, 436, 437; site, 436

Hurt, Wesley R., Jr., 28, 57, 58, 74, 119, 142, 202, 206, 217, 444, 448

Husbandry; *see* Agriculture

Huscher, Betty H., 213, 217

Huscher, Harold A., 213, 217

Hymes, D. H., 119, 142

Ice advances; *see* Glacial advances

Ichuna rockshelter, 65, 66, 459

Idaho, 54, 162, 166, 548; southern, 36, 44, 62; western, 54

Idol(s): -priest-temple cults, 481; stone, 413

Ievoghiyog site, 92, 93, 94 (*see also* Gambell, sites); radiocarbon dates for, 99

Igloolik III culture, 240

Ihuatzio, 320

Illinois, 61, 63, 199, 228, 233, 234, 237, 239, 242, 243, 244, 247, 248, 250, 252, 262, 265, 275, 280; central, 237, 251; northern, 228, 233, 234; River, 249, 250, 254, 277; River Valley, 242, 243; sites, 242; southern, 16, 229, 237, 251; western, 243

Imlay Channel sites (complex), 43, 44

Inca, 471, 472, 483; architecture, 473; capital cities of, 473, 483; ceramics, 471; conquests, 469; dynasty, 471; Empire, 451, 457, 470, 471, 472; government, 472; imperial court, 471; influence, 471; occupation, 479, 480; period, 473; royal family, 471

Incensarios; *see* Ceramic forms

Incense burners; *see* Ceramic forms

Incipient Agricultural(ists) (stage): lowland South America, Amazon-Orinoco drainages, 421, 423–28, 443, 565; Paraná drainage, 444; Plains, 195, 205

Incised decoration, ceramic; *see* Ceramic decorative styles and techniques

India(n), 489, 490, 496, 501, 506, 507; ancient, 360; coastal shipping, 509; hierarchical figure from, 506; Hindu-Buddhist civilization of, 507; Indic language, 534; miniature wheeled animals in, 495

Indian Church, British Honduras, 352

Indian Knoll culture, 232

Indian Well site, 53, 54, 164

Indiana, 234, 236, 251, 253; eastern, 242; southeastern, 254; southwestern, 244

Indians (American); *see* individual tribes and groups by name

Indo-Hispanic epoch: Caribbean area, 393, 400, 411; importance of maize in, 401; sites, 400; sites, absence of griddles in, 401

Industries, 26, 41, 121, 129; basalt, chipped, 51; blade, 30; bone, 26, 119, 129, 133, 293; chopper-chopping tool, 121; copper, 234; core, 30; Desert Culture, 159; flake, 30; San Juan (Valley of Mexico), 54; shell, 26, 129; stone (lithic), 26, 89, 104, 121, 129, 293; weaving, 183

Infiernillo: Canyon, 297; phase, 294; radiocarbon dates for, 294, 297; vegetal remains in, 297

Inflection(s)(al), 535; alternations, 543, 544; internal, 542

Inglefield Land, Greenland, 100

Inhumation; *see* Burials

Inscriptions, 305, 333, 344, 348, 352; glyphic, 345; hieroglyphic, 301, 342, 355, 356; Long Count dates, 338

Integration period (Ecuador), 478–79; coastal cultures, 478; metallurgy in, 478

Intermediate area, 389, 390, 397, 400, 401, 405, 565, 566; agriculture, type of, 403, 405; ceramic finds in, 400; influences, 407, 414

Intermediate cultures, 124, 125; estimated dates for, 124

Intermontane (Western) tradition, 157, 160, 167, 168, 563; Developmental, Late, Historic periods, 157, 167, 169; Early, Transitional, 168, 212; est. beginning dates for, 167

Interregional (interareal): relationships, 215, 292, 491; rivalries, 468; trade, 519

Interregnum (Mesoamerica), est. dates for, 346

Intihuasi Cave, 65, 66; radiocarbon dates for, 34, 65; points, 58

Intrusive Mound culture, 253

Inugsuk culture (stage), 91, 100, 101

Invention(s), 497; bifacial flaking, 121; celt, 398; fluting technique, 55; gouge, 397, 398; independent, 512, 513, 520, 521; local, 188, 512; New World, 495, 497

Iowa, 228, 242, 247, 250, 252; eastern, 243; northwestern, 243, 251; western, 61

Ipiutak culture, 88, 89, 90, 98, 102–6; radiocarbon date for, 89, 103

Ireng River, British Guiana, 420, 422

Iribarren Ch., Jorge, 522, 524
Iron, 204, 211; absence of, in New World, 501; chains, 103; hoes, 205; point on engraving tool, 103; pyrite mirrors, 496; pyrites, 231, 233
Iroquois (Iroquoian), 253–55
Irrigation, 308, 321, 322, 454, 457, 463, 466, 500; canals (ditches), 182, 305, 321, 452, 463; intervalley, 470; systems, 305, 308; terrace, 332
Irving, William N., 85, 107, 110
Irwin, Carol, 59, 76, 228, 258
Irwin, Cynthia, 47, 201, 217
Irwin, H. J., 201, 217
Ishida, Eichiro, 485
Isle Royale, Michigan, 244
Israel, lost tribes of, 491
Issaquena sites, 240
Isthmus of Tehuantepec; *see* Tehuantepec, Isthmus of
Itacoatiara: phase, 432; sites, 420, 430
Itzmiquilpan, 323
Itzocan, 322
Ivory: arrowheads, 96; artifacts, 100; artifacts, Dorset, 107; artifacts, Ipiutak, 103; bolas weights, 94; carvings, animal and openwork, 103; chains, 103; etched, 105; fragments, 92; harpoon heads, 91; hooks, 103; incised, 92; objects, decorated, 92, 93, 94; scrapers, cup-shaped, 103; sled runners, 96, 104; "winged objects," 96, 97
Ixcaquixtla district, Puebla, 310
Iximche (Cakchiquel), Guatemala, 374; ceramics, 375
Ixtlahuacan, 323
Iyatayet site, 104; radiocarbon date for, 104
Izapa(n) site, 367, 377, 379; ceramics, 377, 379; monuments and sculpture, 377, 381, 382
Iztapan; *see* Santa Isabel Iztapan

Jacales; *see* House(s)
Jacobaccense complex, 49, 50
Jade, 305, 334; beads, 332, 333, 343; boulder cache, 370; -carving, 303; earplugs, 333; effigies, 361; jewelry, 372; mosaics, 367; offerings, 359; ornaments, 300, 333, 337, 344; -working, 504
Jaguar(s), 315, 365, 460, 500; extinct, 64; faces, 381; heads, ball-court, 370; hieratic symbolism of, 303; masks, 303; military order of (warriors), 357, 378, 382; motifs, 301; pedestal sculptures of, 368; prowling, 357; -quetzal-serpent god, 315; sculpture, 359; -skin(s), 332, 453; symbolism, grotesque, 369; Temple of, 357

Jaina, Campeche, island of, 355, 382
Jalapa, Guatemala, 365
Jalisco, 318–20; northern, 314
Jama-Coaque phase, est. date for, 503
Jamaica, 391, 402, 412; intermediate styles of, 411, 412; Ostiones-like pottery in, 412
Jambeli phase, 476
Jamunda River, Brazil, 432
Japan(ese), 102, 124; junks, 508; language, 536; Middle Jomon culture of, 474; miniature wheeled animals in, 495; parallels with Ecuador, 360, 474, 503
Jars; *see* Ceramic forms
Jasper: artifacts, 51; projectile points, 422, 423; scrapers, 423
Jauari: phase, 425; site, 420, 424, 425
Jeddito, Arizona, 181, 264
Jefferson, Thomas, 491, 529
Jefferson Barracks bridge, St. Louis, 249
Jelks, Edward B., 29, 51, 67, 80, 201, 219
Jemez River, New Mexico, 188
Jenks, Albert E., 59, 74
Jenness, Diamond, 91, 101, 107, 110, 195, 217
Jennings, Jesse D., vii, viii, 1, 6, 8, 10, 15, 16, 19, 34, 35, 54, 62, 74, 126, 142, 149, 150, 152, 154, 155, 167, 168, 172, 176, 179, 183, 190, 191, 200, 217, 227, 257, 287, 310, 317, 326, 340, 384, 553, 563
Jepsen, Glenn L., 62, 74
Jersey Bluff complex, 248, 252
Jewelry; *see* Ornaments
Jillson, P., 146
Jimenez-Moreno, Wigberto, 312, 326
Joboid series, 394, 395; Camare, El Jobo, Las Lagunas complexes, 396; Las Casitas complex, 397; Muaco site, 396
Jochelson, Waldemar, 102, 110
Johnson, Frederick, 31, 63, 74, 85, 111, 119, 142, 230, 257
Johnson, Dr. and Mrs. Gaylord, vii
Joinville, Brazil, 420
Jomon culture (Japan): ceramics, 474, 503; est. dates for, 474
Jones, Mr. and Mrs. John T., Jr., vii
Jones, Morris R., 363
Jonuta stage, 350, 352; -style figurines, 382
Jornada culture, 246
Jose Vieira site, lower levels, 49, 50
Josselin de Jong, J. P. B. de, 391, 416
Joyce, T. A., 559, 560, 562
Juchipila River Valley, Zacatecas, 293
Judd, Neil M., 517, 524
Juke Box Cave, 156
Jungle(s): cities, 353; cultures, 353; roads, 334; tropical, 334

Kabah, 346
Kachemak Bay cultures (stage), 102, 240, 246; I, radiocarbon date for, 90
Kamchatka, 102; eighteenth-century, 180
Kaminaljuyú, Guatemala, 301, 309, 338, 340, 343, 359, 365, 372, 377; ceramic phases, 309, 310, 366, 367, 370–72; colonization of, 310; cult stones, cache of, 368; Early Classic stairway at, 370; Preclassic mounds, 366; Preclassic sequence, 365; tombs, 366, 369
Kanawha River, West Virginia, 238, 254
Kankakee River, Illinois, 243
Kansas City, Missouri, 202, 206, 243, 247
Kansas, 43, 206, 210; central, 208, 209; eastern, 203; northeastern, 200; northern, 202, 203; River, 202; southern, 208; western, 213
Karlo site, 153
Kawumpkan Springs culture, 240
Kayenta: culture, est. dates for, 186; district, 187
Kays culture, 232
Kayuk complexes, 60, 62, 232, 240
Kehoe, Alice B., 203
Kehoe, Thomas F., 217
Keim, Charles H., 85, 113
Keith focus, 196, 202, 203
Keithahn, E. L., 135, 142
Kelley, David H., 347, 384
Kelley, H., 125, 141
Kelley, J. Charles, 35, 36, 74, 183, 314, 326
Kelley complex (phase), 43, 44, 253
Kelly phase, est. date for, 231
Kennerly, T. E., 44, 45, 74
Kentucky, 230, 236, 237; north-central, 241; northern, 242, 254; shell heaps, 228; western, 251
Keyhole Reservoir, 196
Kidder, Alfred V., viii, 310, 326, 340, 361, 371, 384, 385, 517, 524
Kidder, Alfred V., II, 2, 8, 9, 391, 406, 415, 451, 485, 522, 524, 565
Kill sites, 26, 32, 38, 52, 59, 197, 199, 203
Killarney Bay culture, 240, 252
Kincaid: culture, 252; site, 16, 251
King, Arden R., 134, 142
Kingdoms (dominions): Acolhua, 321; Cakchiquel, 374; Chimu, 470, 471; Guatemala highland, 374, 376; Otomi, 322; Peruvian (coast), 470, 471; Peruvian Mochica, 469; Quiche, 374; Tarascan, 320; Toltec, 317; Zutuhil, 374
Kings; see Rulers
Kings Beach complex, 131
Kingsley Cave complex, 131
Kirchhoff, Paul, 291, 292, 312, 316, 326, 327

Kivas, 183–84, 186–87
Kivett, Marvin F., 202, 216, 218
Klamath Lake: area, prehistory of, 165; sites, 169; sites, est. age of, 165
Klamath River, Oregon, 132, 133; radiocarbon date for late site on, 133
Kneberg, Madeline, 287
Knight site, Mound 8, radiocarbon date for, 239
Knives, 50, 51, 52, 68, 96, 176, 198, 208, 212, 224, 422; basalt, lanceolate, 165–66; bifacial, 42, 51, 58, 65, 231; bipointed, 122, 231; blades, 103; chipped-stone, 104, 125, 156, 161, 164, 178, 179, 204, 212, 344; copper, 233; as currency (China), 496; end-bladed, 103; hafted, 154, 155; handles, 96, 98, 155, 160; obsidian, 370, 373; semilunar (ulus), 107, 231, 233; side-bladed, 103; slate, ground, 134, 135; triangular-sectioned, 90
Knorozov, J. B., 347
Knuth, Eigil, 107, 111
Kobori, Iwao, 485
Koby, F. E., 119, 142
Kodiak Island, 86, 91, 102, 135; Eskimos, 91
Koens-Crispin culture, 253
Kogruk site (complex), 43, 44; British Mountain level, 87
Kolenda, Mrs. Konstantin, vii
Kolomoki, 259, 268, 271
Konduri sites, 420, 430
Kotosh site, 459, 461
Kotzebue Sound, Alaska, 86, 88, 91, 98, 104; Choris culture, est. date for, 90
Kowta, M., 125, 142
Krieger, Alex D., 1, 5, 6, 8, 23, 28, 29, 31, 42, 44, 45 51, 54, 55, 61, 67, 74, 79, 80, 81, 85, 119, 132, 142, 143, 151, 152, 153, 154, 155, 161, 162, 170, 171, 199, 201, 207, 209, 218, 219, 259, 273, 287, 422, 443, 454, 473, 563
Kroeber, A. L., 117, 118, 119, 122, 125, 128, 129, 132, 133, 135, 136, 142–43, 149, 153, 172, 195, 212, 218, 331, 332, 457, 485, 546
Krone, R., 444, 448
Krum Bay site, radiocarbon date for, 398
Kubler, George, 357, 359, 360, 384
Kukenan, Venezuela, 420
Kukulcan; see Quetzalcoatl
Kukulik site, 94
Kuntur Wasi, Peru, 459
Kurigitavik site, 99; est. date of occupation of, 99; radiocarbon dates for, 99
Kurtz, E. B., Jr., 296, 327
Kuskokwim River, Alaska, 98

La Aduana site, 391
La Cabrera: ceramic style, 404, 406; dwellings, 406; radiocarbon dates for, 404; site, 401; -Valencia sequence, 406, 410
La Guaira, Venezuela, 401, 405, 406; area, 393; Topo style, 407
La Jolla, California, 124, 127
La Jolla complex (cultures), 60, 62, 64, 122, 123, 126; II phase, 124
La Motte culture, 253
La Mulera site, 393
La Perra phase, 294, 297, 302
La Pitia site, 391
La Piata, Ecuador, island of, 476
La Rioja, Argentina, 57
La Roche: focus, 210; site, 196, 208
La Vela de Coro site; see Muaco site
La Venta: art style, 336; ceramic phase, est. dates for, 346; ceramics, 381; colossal heads, 368, 380; culture, 380; est. dates for, 304, 381; -like figurines, 381; monuments, 380; origin of, 381; region, 336; sculpture, 380–81
La Victoria site, 346, 366, 376, 377, 379
Labna, 356; Portal of, 356
Labrador, 233
Labrets; see Ornaments
Lacquer, 504
Lago Arari, Marajo Island, Brazil, 420, 438, 439
Lago Grande do Curua, Brazil, 425
Lagoa Santa Caves, 56, 57, 58, 420; radiocarbon dates from, 58; region, 443
Laguna phase, 302; est. date for, 302
Lake(s), (lacustrine), 321, 339, 352, 365; basins, 120, 122, 321; beds, dry, 149 (see also Playas); extinct, 35, 40, 125; fossil strand lines on, 150; gravels, 62; mounds, 439; specialization, 163, 167
Lake(s): Atitlan, 365; Chalco, 321; Chapala, 319; Erie, 224, 242; Huron, 224, 228, 238, 244, 251; Michigan, 228, 248, 251; Mohave, 120–23, 125; Patzcuaro, 319; Superior, 228, 233, 235, 244, 248, 251; Tahoe, region, 131; Tetzcoco, 321, 322; Titicaca, 452, 459, 464, 465, 469, 471; Valencia, 390, 391, 401, 406; Xaltocan, 321; Xochimilco, 321; Yaxha, 351; Zumpango, 321
Lake Chapala Basin sites, 43, 44
Lake County, California, 130
Lake George site, 250
Lake Manix: complex, 43, 44, 120, 125; tufa, 120, 121; radiocarbon date for, 120
Lake Mohave complex, 53, 54, 64, 122, 158;

est. date for, 121; radiocarbon date for, 120
Lake Winnebago culture, 252
Lamar horizon; see Horizons
Lamb, Sydney, 162, 172, 547, 555, 556
Lambeyeque, Peru, 459, 469
Laming, Annette, 50, 75, 444, 448
Lamoille culture, 252
Lamoka: culture, 229, 230, 232, 253; est. date for, 230; points, 229; site, 225
Lamps, 101, 103; oil, 135; stone, 102, 104
Lance(s): bone, 88–89; harpoon, 90; heads, 282; points, 231; poisoned, 102; with side blades, 104, 107
Lanceolate (leaf-shaped): blades, 237, 423; knives, basalt, 165–66; projectile points, 30, 31, 37, 52, 57, 58, 59, 65, 67, 122, 227, 228, 396, 455
Land: agricultural adaptation to, 478; arable, 208, 339, 369, 452, 457, 466, 468; travel, 507; use, patterns of, 291, 305
Landa, Bishop Diego de, 364
Language(s), 376, 529, 530, 533, 535, 537, 546, 552, 553, 555; American Indian (see American Indian languages); of Antilles, 538, 547; Australian, 537, 538; borrowing, 539; California, 118; Central American, 546, 547; changes in, 527, 529, 533; communities, 533; development of, 543–44; differentiation, rate of, 546–47; disappearance of, 530, 531, 533, 555; dispersion, centers of, 554; earlier, 530, 531; elements, 541; emergence of, est. date for, 530; Eurasian, 534, 538, 543, 547; families (groups, stocks), 119, 241, 531, 534, 535, 546, 547, 552; geographical location of, 548; isolated, 547; local differences in, 530; lost, 532, 533; Mexican, 547, 550; movement of into New World, 531–33; new, 531, 533; New World, 530, 566; North American, classifications of, 528, 546, 547; number of, American Indian, 529; number of, in early world, 530; number of, in New World at time of European contact, 545; Oceanian, 538, 539; old, 541–44; Old World, 529, 538; receiver, 539; related, 533, 534, 538, 554; relationship(s), 434, 527, 535, 546; semantic associations, 534; South American, 546, 547; structural variations of, 544; superstocks, 546; unrelated, 538; variants, 541; variation in local, 535; variation, reduced, 530; vestigial features of, 541; widely divergent, 544; see also Dialects, Linguistics, and individual

languages, language families, and societies by name
Lanning, Edward P., 28, 58, 65, 66, 68, 75, 132, 143, 458, 485
Laramie Cave, 153
Larco Hoyle, Rafael, 486
Largo phase, 184
Larsen, Helge, 62, 75, 103, 104, 105, 106, 107, 111
Larter: focus, 196; tanged points, 233
Las Aeldas site, 458, 459
Las Casitas complex, 396, 397
Las Charcas phase, 366, 376
Las Lagunas: complex, 396; sites, 396
Las Victorias rock carvings, 303
Late Archaic stage (complexes, period), 38, 225, 228, 229, 231, 234, 235, 236, 244, 252
Late Boreal Archaic, 230, 233, 235, 240, 246, 253; est. dates for, 231
Late Classic stage (period, horizon), 310, 313, 314, 372; Chiapas and Guatemala coast, 372, 376, 378, 379; Guatemala highlands, 371, 372, 373, 374; northern Mesoamerica, 310, 359; regional differences, 350; southern Veracruz-Tabasco, 382; southern and western lowlands, 340–41, 343, 346–51, 352, 354, 355, 361, 498, 504, 507
Late Formative stage (period, horizon), 338; Guatemala coast, 377; northern Mesoamerica, 306; southern and western lowlands, 306, 340, 346 (*see also* Late Preclassic stage)
Late horizon (period) (California–Northwest Coast), 127–29, 131; est. dates for, 127; sites, 130–31, 134
Late Mississippi(an), 281, 282; complexes, 251; period, 278, 279, 281, 283; period, est. beginning date, 282
Late period (Intermontane tradition), 157, 167, 169
Late Postclassic (Protoclassic, Protohistoric) stage (period, horizon): architecture, Mayapan, 364; Chiapas and Guatemala coast, 380; Guatemala highlands, 373; northern Yucatan (*see* Decadent stage); southern and western lowlands, 346, 352, 354
Late Preclassic stage (period, horizon), 335, 336; Guatemala coast, 377; Guatemala highlands, 366, 367, 377; southern and western lowlands, est. dates for, 346; Veracruz and Tabasco, 381
Late Prehistoric period (Plains), est. date for, 212

Late Woodland, 249, 250, 252, 254; ceramics, 247, 250, 251; complexes, 245, 248, 254; cultures, 245, 246, 248, 251, 254, 256; early, 247, 248, 251; est. dates for, 247
Lathrap, Donald W., 131, 143, 148, 172, 425, 426, 436, 437, 448
Latin America; *see* America, Latin
Latticework; *see* Architectural features
Lauderdale culture, 232
Laughlin, William S., 90, 102, 111, 133, 143
Laurel complex, 240, 244, 251
Laurentian: culture(s), 229, 230, 232, 235, 245, 253; points, 230, 233
Lauricocha caves, 56–58, 65, 454, 459
Le Paige, Gustavo R. P., 50, 51, 57, 75
Le Plongeon, Augustus, 493
Le Vesconte culture, 253
Leary site, 211, 212
Leather; *see* Skins
Leatherman, Kenneth E., 132, 143
Leavenworth site, 211
Lee, Thomas E., 44, 75
Leechman, Douglas, 107, 111
Legends, 421; Mangarevan, 539; Maya, 350; Totonac, 554
Lehmann, Walter, 312, 327
Lehmer, Donald J., 172, 205, 206, 208, 209, 218
Lehner (Ranch) site, 36, 37, 52, 53, 54, 152; radiocarbon dates from, 52, 55, 197
Leighton, M. M., 18
Lemert, E. M., 62, 73, 123, 141
Leonard, A. Byron, 18, 19
Leonard Rockshelter, 60, 62, 232
Leonhardy, F. C., 133, 143
Lerma complex (phase), 53, 54, 56, 57, 294; points, 32, 36, 298; radiocarbon date for, 57, 294
Lerma River Valley, Mexico, 291, 305, 309, 317, 322–23
Lesser Antilles; *see* Antilles
Levalloisian technique, 87
Levin, M. G., 98, 111
Lewis, T. M. N., 287
Lewis and Clark, 210
Lewisville site, 43, 44, 45; radiocarbon dates for, 44
Lexical similarities, 546
Lexicostatistics, 119, 546–48; divergence, tables of, 550, 551; *see also* Glottochronology
Libby, Willard F., 90, 108, 233, 258
Like-a-Fishhook site, 211
Lillard, J. B., 126, 143
Lima, Peru, 50, 459
Lime; *see* Architectural materials

Lime Creek: complex, 197; sites, 60, 61, 62, 196, 197, 199; sites, radiocarbon date for, 61

Limestone, 334, 352; country, radiocarbon dates for, 239; tempering, 250; tools, percussion-flaked, 343

Lind Coulee site, 60, 62, 151, 167, 169

Lindenmeier, 197; culture, 37, 52, 53, 54; site, 52, 53, 54, 55, 226, site, radiocarbon date for, 55

Linguistic(s), 10, 119, 153, 154, 162, 223, 241, 292, 331, 527–29, 530–39, 541, 542, 544–49, 551–55, 566; *see also* Language(s)

Linguistics, 537, 544, 546, 553

Linne, Sigvald, 310, 327

Lintels; *see* Architectural features

Lions; *see* Felines

Lister, Robert H., 318, 319, 327

Lithic: complexes, 423; evidence, 422, 452, 454; hunters, 167; industries, 121; stage (period), 30, 31, 42, 392, 563–65; workmanship, evolution of, 121; *see also* Stone

Litters, 332, 358, 500

Little Colorado River, 185; drainage, 187; Upper, 184, 187

Little Diomede village, 91

Little Lake site, 158

Little Missouri River, 207

Little Sycamore complex, 64, 123

Liverman, J. L., 296, 326

Llama; *see* Animals

Llano: complex (stage), 37, 162, 196; culture, 37, 38, 52, 53, 54, 151, 152

Llano Estacado, 215

Llanos (Venezuela), 390, 399, 400, 401, 403–4, 406, 407–8, 410

Locale; *see* Ecology

Locarno Beach site, radiocarbon dates for, 134

Lockhart culture, 240

Locust Spring culture, 253

LoDaisKa site, 232; Complex D, radiocarbon date for, 201

Loeb, E. M., 514, 524

Loess; *see* Glacial features

Logan, Wilfred D., 63, 75, 258

Logan Creek site, 196; radiocarbon dates for, 200

Loiza Cave: complex, radiocarbon date for, 398; site, 395

Long, Austin, 63–64, 71

Long Count (Maya), 338, 345, 381, 382

Long Creek site, 201

Long houses; *see* House forms

Long Island Sound, 235

Longacre, Robert E., 556

Longacre, William A., 191

Long-Nosed God, 278, 279, 280, 285, 500; masks, 274–77

Longyear, John M., III, 343, 384

Lorandi, A. M., 50, 78

Los Angeles, California, 117

Los Barrancos: ceramic style, 409, 410, 437; -Guarguapo sequence, 410; site, 402

Los Caros: complex, 428; mound, 430; style, 430

Los Encinos complex, 43, 44

Los Reyes Acozac locality, 293

Los Roques Island, Venezuela, 401, 406

Los Toldos caves, 39, 65–67

Los Tuxtlas region, 377

Loseke Creek focus, 196, 202–3, 248

Lothrop, R. W., 413, 416

Lothrop, Samuel K., 337, 384, 413, 416, 445, 448, 510

Lotus: panels, 504; plants, 506; rhizomes, 360; staffs, 360; thrones, 360

Loud, L. L., 132, 143, 160, 172

Louisiana, 85, 259, 269, 275, 527

Louisville, Kentucky, 251

Loup River, 208

Lovelock Cave, 153, 160, 161, 169, 240, 246

Lovén, Sven, 413, 416

Lowe, 377, 378, 379, 380

Lower California; *see* Baja California

Lower Loup focus, 196, 209, 210; communities, 208

Lower Mississippi Valley tradition, 265, 269, 270, 280; culture, 266, 284, 285; pottery, 272, 273; sites, 270

Lowie, R. H., 118, 144, 153, 212

Lowther, G. R., 107, 112

Lubbock sites, 53, 54, 55, 226

Lucy site, 53, 54

Lumber; *see* Timber

Lumbreras S., Luis G., 469, 485, 486, 522, 524

Lund, Peter, 58

Lundelius, Ernest L., Jr., 44, 75

Mabaruma: phase, 409, 430–31; phase, est. date for, 432; site, 402

McCann, Catherine, 286

McConnell culture, 253

McCorquodale, Bruce A., 203, 217

Macgowan, Kenneth, 27, 28, 75

McKean site, 153, 196, 200

Mackenzie River, 86, 99

McKern, W. C., 136, 144

McKern system; *see* Midwestern taxonomic system

McKusick, Marshall B., 391, 416

MacNeish, Richard Stockton, 54, 57, 62, 63, 75, 76, 85, 87, 112, 164, 172, 203,

204, 218, 235, 242, 257, 258, 291, 294, 296, 297, 298, 299, 302, 327, 399, 416, 522, 525
Machalilla phase (culture), 462, 475; est. dates for, 463, 475
Machinskii, A. V., 98, 112
Macon Plateau culture, 246, 277
Madeira River, Brazil, 420
Madison, Wisconsin, 250
Madisonville culture, 253
Madrid Codex; *see* Codices
Magallanes, Chile, 34, 57
Magdalena Valley, Colombia, 481
Magellan periods, 65, 67
Magic, 249, 262, 269
Maguey; *see* Plants
Maize, 177–79, 182, 186, 195, 202, 203, 205, 207, 213, 214, 237, 248, 249, 250, 251, 273, 279, 294, 296–300, 302, 332, 376, 401, 403, 426, 442, 444, 453–57, 475, 480, 520, 552, 553, 564
Majadas Phase, 366
Makemson, M. W., 345, 346
Malaga Cove site, radiocarbon date for, 123
Malakoff locality, 43, 44, 47
Malamud, C. G., 62, 80
Malcolm I culture, 253
Maldonado, Uruguay, 50
Maldonado-Koerdell, Manuel, 44, 47, 54, 69, 76, 293, 325
Malmo culture, 246
Malpais culture, 122
Mam, Guatemala, 369
Mammoth, 36, 47, 52, 54, 55, 57, 63, 87, 156, 196, 197, 198, 214, 224, 293, 294; dwarf, 44, 46
Mamom phase, 335, 346, 376, 381; ceramics, 335–37, 354, 366, 377; figurines, 336, 350
Mamore River, Bolivia, 420, 441
Manabi, Ecuador, 475–79, 503, 521
Manacapuru culture and site, 428
Manaus, Brazil, 420, 431
Mandan, 196, 208, 210, 211
Mandeville site, 266
Mangelsdorf, P. C., 298, 300, 327
Mangueiras phase, 427, 428, 431
Manicuare: complex, radiocarbon date for, 397; site, 391, 395
Manicuaroid series, 397, 398, 407
Manila Galleon, 508
Manioc, 332, 399, 401, 403, 408, 426, 442; bitter, 400, 401, 403, 430, 431, 433, 434, 435, 441; sweet, 453, 458
Manipiare River, Venezuela, 420, 433
Manitoba, province of, 204, 233, 244, 248; Late Archaic focuses of, 235; mounds, 204; southern, 204, 251

Manitoba focus, 196, 204
Manitoulin Island, Ontario, 44
Mann: culture, 253; site, 244
Mano(s), 32–35, 58–67, 122, 123, 130, 154–59, 165, 178, 179, 182, 344, 368, 401, 456, 516, 517
Mansell Island, Hudson Bay, 86, 107
Manta, Ecuador, 476
Mantaro, the, Peru, 452
Manufacturing, 166, 267, 352
Manzanillo: *barrio* of, 48; complex (culture), 48, 49, 50, 51, 396, 399
Maquixco, Teotihuacán, 308
Maracaibo, Venezuela, 48, 50, 392–93, 396, 399
Marajo, Brazil, island of, 420, 424, 425, 427, 428, 435, 436, 438–39, 440, 441
Marajoara phase (culture), 437–44
Marcos phase, 379
Margarita Island, Venezuela, 391, 402, 407, 409
Marginal areas, 117
Marginal cultures, 425, 443, 451, 514
Marietta, Ohio, 241
Maringer, John, 112
Maritime: adaptation, 134; culture, Early, 134, 564; orientation, 125, 134; relationships, 476
Maritime Provinces, Canada, 233
Markets, 324, 325, 331
Marksville: culture, 240, 265, 266, 269, 280; sites, 241, 265
Marpole culture, 240
Marquina, Ignacio, 359
Marsh, Gordon H., 102, 111
Martin, L., 146
Martin, Paul Schultz, 151, 158
Martin, Paul Sidney, 156, 158, 172, 179, 184, 191
Martinez Hernandez, J., 345
Martinez del Rio, Pablo, 28, 76
Martinique, island of, 392
Martis complex, 131
Masks, 364, 368; fanged, 364; Long-Nosed God, 274–77; pottery, 476, 521; stone, 356, 357; stucco, 336
Mason, John Alden, 100, 112, 377, 378, 483
Mason, Ronald J., 28, 34, 53, 54, 55, 59, 60, 63, 76, 228, 258
Masonry, 373; bench, 315; block-wall, 356; buildings, 183, 339, 343; causeways, 334; Cuzco-style, 473; facing, 369; houses, 307; rough, 363, 480; slab, 302, 356; stone, 371, 378, 458; techniques, 365; temples, 331; tunnels, 348; veneer, 313, 348, 356, 364; walls, 371; worked, 187; *see also* Architectural features
Massachusetts, 231

Massey, William C., 117, 126, 141, 144, 176, 191
Masterson, Dean and Mrs. W. H., vii
Mastodon, 38, 47, 57, 59, 63, 87, 224, 293, 396
Mathematics, 11, 15, 18, 331, 332, 339, 528; *see also* Counting systems
Mathiassen, Therkel, 91, 99, 100, 101, 107, 112
Matting (mats), 154, 155, 161, 186, 248, 456; checker-work, 517; checker-work, impressions on pottery, 516; houses, 163, 212; reed, 455; in tombs, 366, 369; twined, 155, 160, 161, 178, 179
Maudslay, Alfred Percival, 384
Maudslay, Anne Cary, 384
Mauls, 134, 135, 164, 184
Maximilian, reign of, 293
Maxwell, Moreau S., 107, 112
Maya(n), 8, 291, 292, 309, 310, 313, 316, 331–39, 344–48, 351–59, 360–78, 382, 501–4, 538–45, 552, 554, 560, 564
Maya calendar: Long Count, 338, 345; lunar months, 345; Round, 344; Sacred Round (tzolkin), 344, 368; Short Count, 345; system, 345; Vague Year (solar year), 344; weeks, 344; year-bearers, 348
Mayapan, 346, 352, 354, 362–64
Maybe site, 164
Mayer-Oakes, William J., 63, 65, 67, 76, 199, 201, 218, 220, 254, 258
Mazagão phase, 420, 430–32
Meade, Grayson E., 79, 197, 219
Meadowood culture; *see* Point Peninsula
Means, Philip A., 472, 486, 522, 525
Medillin Zenil, 382
Medithermal period, 150, 158; est. beginning date for, 150
Meggers, Betty J., 2, 9, 10, 360, 383, 391, 392, 397, 409, 415, 419, 421, 424, 426, 427, 428, 429, 430, 432, 433, 435, 437, 438, 440, 441, 442, 445, 446–50, 473–78, 485, 503, 508, 510, 511, 520, 521, 523–25, 566
Meighan, Clement W., 31, 36, 54, 59, 76, 124, 125, 126, 129, 130, 135, 136, 144, 152, 172
Meillac site, 402
Meldgaard, Jørgen, 107, 111, 112
Meleen, E. E., 208, 218
Melendrez-Naranjo River, Guatemala, 378
Melita focus, 204
Memphis, Tennessee, 250
Mendocino complex, 130
Menghin, Osvaldo F. A., 28, 29, 42, 50, 51, 65, 76, 120, 144

Mera, H. P., 517, 525
Merchants, 305, 307, 333; Aztec, 310; caravans, 324; class of, 363; guilds, 375; shipping, Southeast Asia, 507
Merriam, John C., 119, 144
Merwin, R. E., 337
Mesa del Guaje phase, est. date for, 299
Mesa Verde: phase (culture), 184, 186, 187; phase, est. dates for, 184; sites, 181, 185
Meserve: points, 32; site, 60, 62
Mesh principle, linguistic, 530, 535, 546, 547
Meso-Indian(s), 29, 39, 392–99, 400, 403, 407, 409, 411, 412, 414
Mesoamerica(n), 4, 8, 9, 10, 175, 236, 242, 262, 273, 274, 277, 279, 285, 291, 292, 295, 299, 300–304, 308, 311, 314, 317–19, 331–37, 343, 360, 366, 367, 380, 381, 389, 390, 400–403, 413, 414, 422, 426, 451, 453, 457, 466, 475–79, 480–82, 496, 497, 500–507, 518–20, 562–66
Mesolithic, 15, 89, 90, 104, 108, 178, 544
Metal(s), 334, 453, 454; objects, 318, 471, 480; ornaments, 318, 502; tools and weapons, 502; zinc, alloys of, 374; *see also* Copper, Gold, Silver, Tin
Metallurgy, 317–18, 374, 480, 519; casting, 465, 470, 481; Colombian, 479; Ecuadorean, 478; Mesoamerican, 501; Old Copper, 233; Peruvian, 453, 465; Tarascan, 319; techniques of, 502; true, 453
Metates, 34, 122, 123, 126, 127, 130, 131, 154, 178, 179, 183, 184, 344, 368, 401, 515, 549, 553
Metcalf, George, 216
Meteorology, 151
Metraux, Alfred, 514, 525
Metropolis, metropolitan; *see* Urban, urban centers
Mexiana, Brazil, island of, 420, 435, 436
Mexico, 23, 36, 37, 39, 53, 54, 62, 63, 117, 129, 155, 156, 167, 176, 179, 180, 183, 186, 223, 291, 292, 293, 296, 297, 318–20, 323, 331, 333, 336, 343, 357, 369, 380, 381, 403, 413, 456, 477, 489, 496, 497, 502, 519, 521, 548, 550, 552, 557, 560, 564; Asiatic influences in, 360; central, 39, 44, 63, 177, 183, 295, 296, 299, 300, 302, 303, 309, 311, 312, 313, 314, 317, 318, 319, 320, 323, 335, 360, 370, 504, 540, 552, 553, 555, 564; central, capitals of, 306, 311, 314, 315, 321, 324–25, 357; central highlands of, 295, 309; central plateau of, 313, 314, 319; city of, 296, 300, 314, 318, 323, 527; northeastern, 36, 294, 296, 300, 317; northern, 34, 168, 540, 550; northwest-

ern, 291, 317; peoples of, 527; peopling of, theory of, 540; southern, 63, 177, 183, 188, 299, 302, 335, 354, 367, 458, 462, 463, 564; Valley of, 4, 46, 47, 54, 57, 299, 301, 304–6, 309, 314, 317, 320–23, 336, 348, 381, 492, 554; western, 318, 319, 323; Western basin of, 293, 295; *see also* individual cultures, sites, and geographical places by name
Miami River, Ohio, 238
Miami (Texas) site, 197
Miccaotli phase, Teotihuacán, est. date for, 306
Michelena site, 395
Michigan, 243–44, 248, 252; eastern, 230, 238; lower peninsula of, 229, 233, 243; southern, 44, 234
Michipicoten River, 251
Michoacan, 182, 316–20
Microblades, 88, 90, 102, 104, 107, 108
Middens (heaps), 90, 92, 94, 96, 99, 102, 128, 164, 165, 166, 266, 271, 273, 274, 397, 429, 444; "burnt rock," 201; dirt (earth), 260; shell, 123, 126, 228, 229, 260, 263, 283, 397, 405, 406, 422, 425, 443, 473, 480, 522
Middle America; *see* Central America, Mesoamerica
Middle East; *see* Near East
Middle Mississippi: -Caddoan axis, 285; ceramics, 264, 275, 277, 280; complex, 206, 277; culture(s), 275, 278, 279, 281–85; influence, 277, 278, 281; sites, 277, 278, 279; *see also* Mississippian
Middle Preclassic stage (period, horizon), 335, 336; Guatemala highlands, 366, 369; southern and western lowlands, 336, 346; Veracruz and Tabasco, 381
Middle Woodland, 239, 243, 244, 245, 252, 255, 256, 338
Midland site; *see* Scharbauer site
Midwestern taxonomic system, 7, 37
Migration(s), 100, 117, 119, 237, 245, 249, 250, 317, 398, 407, 411, 412, 423, 441, 442, 490, 501, 530, 538, 548–52, 566
Militarism, 305, 320, 324, 333, 357, 363, 466, 469, 471, 481, 483
Mill Creek complex, 131, 196, 246, 250–52
Miller, Carl F., 28, 54, 63, 76, 77
Miller, John P., 31, 74, 119, 142
Miller cultures, 267, 275
Milling Stone horizon, 123, 127
Milling stones, 32–35, 58, 59, 61, 63, 64, 65, 154–59, 162, 177, 201, 260, 344, 367, 376, 399; *see also* Manos
Millon, René, 306, 307, 327, 556
Mills, J. E., 132, 141, 144

Milwaukee, Wisconsin, 250
Mimbres culture, 185, 186, 246; est. dates for, 186
Mimbres River, New Mexico, 186
Minas Gerais, Brazil, 57
Mineral(s), 453, 518; amber, 380; biotite, 18; catlinite, 204; chert, 58, 119, 422, 423; diorite, 182; felsite, 422; galena, 164, 235; greenstone, 370; Hematite, 178, 229, 350; jet, 164; lignite, 178; mica, 237, 271, 375; nephrite, 164, 436; Ohio pipestone, 242; quartz, 350, 422, 423, 431; quartzite, 48, 396; red ochre, 165, 225; serpentine, 164, 380; travertine, 131; turquoise, 178, 186, 209, 213, 459, 461; *see also* Basalt, Chalcedony, Flint, Hematite, Obsidian, Steatite
Miniature: jewelry, 479; objects, 493; wheeled animals and vehicles, 494, 495
Minnesota, 59, 204, 228, 236, 243, 244, 247, 248, 251, 252
Minnesota Man, 252; dates for, 228
Minnesota River, 243
Miolithic stage, 29
Miraflores phase, 346, 366, 367, 377
Mirrors: bronze, Chinese, 496; iron pyrite, 377, 496, 521; obsidian, 521
Misiones, Argentina, 50
Missaukee culture, 252
Mississippi, 85, 251, 267
Mississippi River, 231, 237, 244, 248, 249, 266, 274, 283; Delta, 261, 262, 266, 270, 283; lower, 522; Valley, 201, 237, 237, 247, 265, 273; Valley, Central, 267, 269, 273, 274, 281, 284; Valley, Lower, 214, 239, 241, 242, 265–67, 270, 271, 275, 282; Valley, Upper, 224, 228, 233, 242, 250, 251, 255
Mississippian: agriculture, 243; art, 317; centers, 249; ceramics, 249, 250, 264, 274, 278, 281; culture(s), 8, 238, 245, 247–49, 251, 252, 254, 256, 274, 277, 279, 280–83, 338; influence(s), 247, 254, 282, 283; origin, area of, 279; people, 281; sites, 251; *see also* Early Mississippi, Middle Mississippi, Late Mississippi
Missouri, 14, 61, 63, 199, 200, 243–52; central, 228; northern, 248; northwestern, 202; southeastern, 251
Missouri Bluff complex, 248
Missouri River, 196, 199, 202–9, 211, 223, 243, 248; Valley, 202, 214
Mitla, 317
Mixcoatl; *see* Ce Tecpatl Mixcoatl
Mixe(an), 554; divinatory rites, 368; languages, 540; -Zoque dialect, 365, 376

Mixtec(a), 312; connections, 380; divinatory rites, 368; region, 301, 323, 374
Miyowagh site, 92, 93, 94, 96, 106; *see also* Gambell, sites
Moapa, Nevada, cave, 160
Moapa Valley, Nevada, 176
Moats; *see* Defensive works
Mobile Bay, 267, 271
Mobile River, Alabama, 266
Moccasin Bluff culture, 252
Moccasins, 154, 155, 161, 179
Mochica: art (style), 465–68, 471, 482; culture, 454, 457, 465; state, 468, 469
Moctezuma, King, 324
Moctezuma River, Mexico, 291, 317
Modified Florescent (Mexican) stage (period, horizon), northern Yucatan, 356–63; dates for 346, 362
Modoc Rockshelter, 60, 61, 63, 229, 252; dates for, 61, 229
Mogollon: area, 180, 181; culture, 6, 156, 158, 169, 175, 176, 180–85, 240, 564
Mojave Desert, 44
Moldings; *see* Architectural features
Molins Fabrega, N., 322, 328
Mollusks; *see* Seafood
Momil culture, 426
Monagrillo: culture, 400, 404, 426; site, 395, 400
Monangahela: culture, 253, 254; River, 254
Monroe focus, 196, 206; radiocarbon date for, 206
Montana, 210, 212; sites, 200, 201
Montaña, the; *see* Andes
Monte Alban, 301–11, 317, 377
Monte Negro, 301, 303, 304
Montreal, Quebec, 254
Monument Valley, 177
Monuments (monumental), 302, 304, 311, 315, 324, 341, 342, 346, 347, 377, 560; architecture, 336, 339; art, 355, 356; carved, 338, 344, 367, 380, 382; dated, 379; hieroglyphic, 364; Izapa, 377; Maya, 359; Mitla, 317; Monte Alban, 305, 311; sculpture, 303, 325, 372, 381, 480
Morelos, 303, 305, 312, 320, 322
Morgan, Lewis Henry, 8, 195
Moriarty, James R., 62, 77, 123, 146
Morley, Sylvanus G., viii, 342, 361, 384
Morris, A. A., 358
Morris, Earl H., 178, 179, 191, 358
Mortar; *see* Architectural materials
Mortars, 33, 59, 162, 164, 376; stone, 121, 122, 124, 126, 128, 131, 133, 164, 179, 229, 297, 298, 515; wooden, 122, 127; *see also* Pestles
Morton focus, 239, 252

Mosaic(s): breast ornaments, 357; carved stone, 356, 363; geometric, 364; 356, 363; headdresses and turbans, 357; inlaid, 344; jade, 367; plaques, 182; pyrite, 344, 370, 372
Motagua River, Guatemala, 334
Motifs, 497, 503, 504; ceramic, 424, 428 519; ceramic, scroll and step, 436; cross, 498; dragon head, 368; geometric, 317, 349; jaguar, 301; Mexican-influenced, 352, 360; naturalistic and glyphic, 349; Scytho-Siberian, 103; serpent, 301; stepped grecque, 497; tiger, 504; tree of life, 504
Mott, Mildred, 212, 218
Mound(s), 204, 245, 250, 259, 273, 274, 284, 301, 351, 366, 369, 380, 382, 444, 454, 458, 463, 476, 478; Adena, 236, 238; adobe, 366; artificial, 406, 437, 438, 441; assemblages, 371; -building, 205, 236, 407, 414, 478; burial (*see* Burials); ceremonial, 302; complexes, 411; conical, 237, 241, 247, 301; construction, 247; Dakota, 196, 210; earthen, 182, 366, 371, 379; effigy, 247; fill, 369; groups, 263; habitation, 391, 439; linear, 247; Mound 25 (Ohio Hopewell), 239; ovoid, 237, 429; platform, 249, 250, 254, 266, 270, 307, 368, 478; refuse, 182, 183, 429, 433; Serpent, 245; shell, 128, 132, 233, 260, 267, 274 (*see also* Middens); substructure, 186; temple, 266, 270–85, 299, 302, 304, 371, 565; truncated, 301, 302
Moundville, 278, 279, 281, 285; ceramics, 281, 283
Mountain, Bert, 62, 72
Mountain Cow, British Honduras, 338
Mountain-Plains culture, 168
Mousterian culture, 87, 121
Moxeke site, 459, 460
Moxviquil ruin, 379
Muaco site, 57, 395–96
Mud; *see* Architectural materials
Muddy Creek site, 196
Müller-Beck, H., 45, 48, 50, 51
Mullers, 34, 127, 231; *see also* Maños
Mulloy, William, 172, 200, 212, 218
Mural(s), 352, 357–59, 363, 374
Mushroom(s): cult, 368; -shaped stone sculptures, 368, 370, 371, 378
Muskingum River, Ohio, 241
Mussels; *see* Seafood
Mutilation: body, 369; dental, 183, 369
Mylodon Cave, 34, 57, 58, 67
Myths (mythology), 118, 350, 377, 381, 421, 508

Naco, Honduras, 380
Naco (Arizona) site, 36, 37, 52, 53, 54, 152
Napa County, California, 130
Napier ceramic period, 338
Napo complex, 437, 441
Natchez: ceramics, 272; culture, 284; tribe, 273
Navarrete, 380
Navigation, 353, 398, 424, 427, 476, 507–9
Nayarit, 318, 319
Nazca: art style, 465, 468; culture, 457, 469; locality, 456, 459
Near East, 489, 495, 496, 499, 523
Near Ipiutak culture, 88, 91, 103, 104, 105
Nebaj, Guatemala, 369, 371
Nebo Hill culture, 232, 252
Nebraska, 60, 61, 199, 200, 202, 203, 209, 210, 213, 248, 296
Nebraska aspect, 196, 206, 246; est. dates for, 206
Needham, Joseph, 503, 510
Needle(s): bone, 32, 198, 343; cascs, 96, 104
Neill, O. J., 63, 74
Nelson, N. C., 119, 128, 144
Neo-Indian(s), 29, 393, 396–414
Neoamerican stage, 29
Neolithic cultures, 29, 33, 90, 98, 104, 107, 295
Neosho site, 196
Nepeña Valley, Peru, 459, 460
Nericagua: ceramics, 428–30, 433; phase, 428–38, 565; radiocarbon dates for, 429; sites, 420, 428, 430
Net(s), 160, 161, 165, 248; deer, noose, 154; fish, 455; rabbit, 154; sinkers, 164, 165, 260, 477
Netherlands Antilles; *see* Antilles
Netting, 154, 155, 456, 517; impression of, on pottery, 516; knotted, 515; techniques, 519
Neuman, Robert W., 203, 218
Neuquen, Argentina, 67
Nevada, 38, 44, 46, 62, 117, 160, 175–76, 187, 550
New Brunswick, 245
New England, 44, 224, 227, 230–36, 238, 245, 253, 255; *see also* individual cultures, sites, and geographical places by name
New Jersey, 44, 230, 253, 255, 260
New Kingdoms and Empire stage (Peru), 470–73; est. dates for, 470
New Mexico, 37, 52, 57, 88, 181, 197, 213, 215, 297, 550–53; central, 54; eastern, 34, 54, 62, 177, 189; northern, 44, 54, 62, 184, 186, 213; southern, 175–79, 186; western, 158, 176, 186, 187; *see*

also individual cultures, sites, and geographical places by name
New York, 225, 229, 230, 234, 238, 242, 244, 245, 248, 253, 254, 391
Newell, H. Perry, 287
Newfoundland, 107, 233
Newman, T. M., 132, 133, 144
Newtown culture, 253
Nezahualcoyotl, King, 321, 323
Nicaragua(n), 291, 292, 379
Niches; *see* Architectural features
Nicholson, H. B., 392, 398, 414
Niobrara River, 206, 210
Nogales phase, 294; est. dates for, 297
Nopilco, Veracruz, 382
Nopiloa site, 382
Norbeck, Edward, viii, 1, 10, 13, 14, 35, 74, 126, 142, 172
Norbeck, Mrs. Edward, vii
Nordenskiöld, Erland, 441, 449, 514, 525
North America(n): culture areas, 331; early man in, 28, 38; languages, 528, 546. 547; *see also* individual cultures, sites and geographical places by name
North Beach culture, 253
North Carolina, 255
North Dakota, 201, 203, 204, 207, 208
Northeast Woodlands area, 223, 224, 235, 253, 255, 256; historic Indians of, 241
Northern Maritime tradition, 90–101, 102, 103, 105, 106
Northern Plano tradition, 87
Northwest Coast, 118, 135, 180, 240; culture area, 132; cultures, 134–36, 246, 563, 564, 565
Northwest Microblade tradition, 87
Northwest Territories, Canada, 36, 62
Norton culture, 88, 90, 91, 104, 105
Norton Sound, Alaska, 86, 98, 100–105
Nose buttons; *see* Ornaments
Nova Scotia, 224, 245
Nuckoll site, 226
Nuclear America, 490, 519; *see also* Mesoamerica, Andes
Nukleet: culture, 104; site, 98
Numerals (numerical): bar and dot, 381; position, 331, 339; records, 472
Nunagiak site, 98
Nutimik: culture, 246; focus, 196; projectile points, 235

Oak Grove complex, 64, 123, 127, 226
Oak Grove–Topanga–La Jolla–Milling Stone horizon, 127
Oaklawn culture, 253
Oaxaca(n), 292, 301, 303, 304, 306, 309, 311–13, 317–18, 368, 554; capital of central, 311, 317

O'Bryan, Deric, 107, 112
Obsidian, 68, 130, 131, 202, 213, 242, 334; abraders, 344; artifacts, 129, 294; blades, 133, 344, 367, 370, 372, 475; chips, 242; cores, 373; fragments, 294; incised, 341; knappers, 306; knives, 344, 370, 373; mirrors, 521; objects, eccentric, 344; projectile points, 128, 242, 344, 373; scrapers, 344
Ocampo phase, dates for, 294
Ocos ceramic phase, 346, 366, 376
Ocumare: site, 401; style, 406
Ocumaroid series, 405–7
Ohio, 228, 238, 239, 242, 244, 253, 262, 265; central, 254; eastern, 242; northern, 63, 234; River, 223, 229, 231, 236–37, 251, 254, 277; southern, 236, 239, 241; Valley, 201, 223, 229, 230, 235, 236, 238, 244, 247, 254, 255
Ohio Hopewell; *see* Hopewell
Oklahoma, 179, 197, 200–202, 206, 209, 210, 274, 275, 279, 548
Okvik: culture (stage), 93, 96, 98, 100, 101, 102, 105, 106
Okvik–Old Bering Sea culture (stage), 90, 91, 103, 106; radiocarbon date for, St. Lawrence Island, 90
Olcott site, 53, 54
Old Bering Sea culture, 91–100, 106, 240
Old Copper: culture, 85, 105, 232; dates for, 233; points, 88, 233; sites, 233, 234
Old Cordilleran culture, 36, 38, 52, 53, 54, 64, 162, 163, 168, 169; dates for, 36, 55, 57
Old Village complex, 246, 250–52; est. dates for, 250
Old Whaling culture, 88, 105; dates for, 89, 105
Old World, 10, 29, 33, 87, 89, 295, 332, 356, 360, 421, 493, 496, 497, 498, 503, 539; archeologists, 29; civilizations, 489, 491, 566; culture stages, 29; languages, 529, 538, 541; Mesolithic, 89, 90, 104, 108; metallurgy, 502; Neolithic, 104; Paleolithic, 29, 42, 121; traits, absence of in New World, 501
Oliviense complex, 49, 50
Olmec art style, 301, 302, 303, 309, 377, 378, 380, 381, 459, 460, 462, 503, 504, 522
Olmeca-Xicalanca dynasty and state, 311, 312, 320
Olmsted, D., 119, 131, 137
Olson, Edwin A., 131, 138
Olson, Ronald L., 125, 145
Omaha, Nebraska, 202
Oneota culture, 211, 212, 251, 252; sites, 196, 211

Ongamira Cave, 65–67; est. date for, 67
Ontario, 44, 223–24, 229–30, 233–34, 244, 245, 248, 251, 253, 254, 255; *see also* individual cultures, sites, and geographical places by name
Optima focus, 206
Oregon, 54, 62, 88, 132–35, 154, 155, 165, 179; caves, 169; *see also* individual cultures, sites, and geographical places by name
Orient burial complex, 235
Orinoco River, 390–91, 401, 403–4, 407–11, 419–21, 427–34, 437, 446
Oriximina complex and region, 432
Ornaments
  Armlets, 204
  Beads; *see* Beads
  Bells, copper, 182, 515, 519
  Bracelets: bone, 212; copper, 237; jade bead, 333; shell, 179
  Breast, mosaic, 357
  Bronze, 470
  Buttons, 103
  Chains: iron, 103; ivory, 103
  Claus, 166
  Ear, 275, 280, 440; lobes pierced for, 439–40; -rings, gold, 478; spools (*see* Ear spools)
  Gorgets, 164, 235, 237, 333; bar, 234; bone, 245, 247; copper, 234, 237; disk-shape 3-hole, 234; marine shell, mask, 204; rectangular, 234; sandal-sole, 234; stone, 245, 247; *see also* Pendants (*below*)
  Jewelry, 367, 380, 382; gold, 458, 478; gold, miniature, 479; jade, 372; platinum, miniature, 479; Protoclassic, 382; silver, 478
  Labrets, 104, 134, 135, 428
  Nose, 357, 478
  Pendants, 164, 179, 333; disk-shape 3-hole, 234; hoof, 161; horn, 161; shell, 228, 397; steatite, 164, 166; stone, trianguloid, 233; stone, tusk-form, 477; wooden, 179; *see also* Gorgets (*above*)
  Rings, 164, 237
  See also Headdresses
Ornate phase, 310
Orr, Kenneth, 257
Orr, Phil C., 44, 77, 120, 123, 125, 131, 138, 145
Orssich, Adam, 444, 449
Orssich, Elfiede Stadler, 444, 449
Ortoire: complex, 398, 407; site, 395
Osborne, Carolyn M., 126, 144
Osborne, Douglas, 134, 145, 172, 173
Osceola culture, 252
Osgood, Cornelius, 391, 406, 410, 416

Ossuaries, Holmul, 337, 338; pits, 203; Sierran, 131
Osteodontokeratic culture level, 120
Ostiones style, 411, 412
Otomi kingdom, capital of, 322
Otopamean: -Oaxacan dispersal, est. date for, 554; peoples, 554
Ott, Carlos F., 445, 449
Ovens: earth, 154; roasting, 166
Over focus, 196, 206
Overhang locations; *see* Rockshelters
Owasco (Owascoid) culture(s), 245, 246, 248, 253, 254
Oxbow culture, 196, 201
Oxitipan, 322
Oxkintok, 359
Oysters; *see* Seafood
Ozarks, 179, 212
Oztuma, Gerrero, 320

Pachacuti Inca Yupanqui, 471, 472
Pacific Coast(al), 119, 123, 133, 136; Acapulco vicinity, 309; Classic period, 378; of Guatemala, 236, 309, 313, 331, 367, 372, 375, 377, 378, 379, 380, 382; littoral, 48, 64, 135; of North America 117; plain, 375; prehistory, 136
Pacific Eskimo-Aleut: culture, 90, 91, 102, 103; province, 91; tradition, 101
Pacific Ocean, 9, 124, 365, 507, 511, 537, 538, 548, 566; coastal navigation of, 507, 509; direct crossings of, 509; lost continent of, 491; shore of, 508
Pacoval site, 438
Paint, red: on bones, 439; on corpse, 366; on heads, 369; on pottery, 409, 411, 427, 432, 435, 475, 512; on stairways, 371; on walls of burial chambers, 369; *see also* Burials
Painting (of), 102; bark cloth, 332; ceramics (*see* Ceramic decorative styles and techniques); clay relief, 458; codices, 346; columns, 357; figurines, 319; floors, 379; mural, 305, 307; pictographs, 125; stone carvings, 413; stuccoed vessels, 370; walls, 470
Paisley Caves, 60, 62, 153, 232
Palace(s), 304, 306–8, 312, 315, 316, 324, 339, 340, 341, 348, 356, 370, 374
Palavecino, Enrique, 516, 525
Palenque, 336, 343, 504; buildings at, 313, 340, 342, 348, 498; burials, 349; ceramics, 343, 350; figurines, hierarchical, 350, 506
Paleo-Eskimo cultures, 240
Paleo-Indian(s), 27, 30, 32, 33, 37, 39, 51, 64, 177, 197, 396, 399; artifacts, 48, 87; complexes, 38, 39; cultures, 28, 225,

443; cultures, est. terminal date for, 225; epoch (Caribbean area), 392–96; epoch, radiocarbon dates for, 396; hunters, 35, 39; hunting horizon, 422; peoples, 423; Plains, 199; sites, 38, 39, 85; stage (period), 29, 31, 37, 38, 51–59, 61, 68, 133, 252, 421, 422, 423; stage, dating of, 52, 55, 57, 58; stage, est. age of, 31; tradition, 563
Paleoamerican stage, 29, 51
Paleoeastern tradition, 38, 39
Paleolithic, 48, 51, 90, 121; cultures, 10, 29, 88, 89, 177, 224; implements, 43, 44; New World, 121; Old World, 29, 42, 88, 89, 121, 177, 180; sites, 87; stage, 33, 42; stratum in Desert West, 152; traits, 90
Paleonorthern tradition, 38, 39
Paleontology (paleontologists), 13, 45, 47, 293, 490; linguistic, 552, 553, 555
Paleowestern tradition, 38, 39
Palerm, Angel, 23, 321, 328, 329
Palikua River, British Guiana, 422
Palisades; *see* Defensive works
Palisades: culture, 105; site, 87
Palli Aike Cave, 58, 65, 66; radiocarbon date of, 67
Palmatary, Helen Constance, 431, 440, 449, 522, 525
Palmate stones, 313, 371, 382
Palms; *see* Foods, Trees
Palynology, 150, 151; *see also* Pollen
Pampa de los Fosiles, Peru, 459
Pamplona phase, 372
Pan pipes; *see* Pipes
Panama, 395, 400, 404, 426
Panhandle aspect, 206, 207, 232
Pantzac, Guatemala, 373
Panuco: sequence, 299, 302, 399; site, 493, 494; villages, 299
Panuco River, 302
Papantla, Veracruz, 312
Paper, 346, 503
Paracas locality, 456, 463, 464; radiocarbon dates for, 456
Paraguay, 419, 420, 421, 443; southeastern, 445
Parallelism, Parallel(s), 9, 118, 511, 513, 520, 522; California-Polynesia, 124; ceramic, 410; China-Mesoamerica, 504; Ecuador-Japan, 360; forms (types), 513, 514; independently derived, 518; influence, 519; language, 536–41; Mesoamerica–northern South America, 520; Mesopotamia–New World, 360; middle Amazon–lower Mississippi, 522; New World–Asia, 360, 493–96, 518, 538; North Ameri-

Parallelism, Parallel(s)—*Continued*
  ca–South America, 513, 514, 522; Old
  World–New World Paleolithic, 121;
  Olmec-Chavín, 522
Paramonga, Peru, 470
Paraná, Brazil, 50, 420
Paraná River, 419, 420, 421, 443–45, 565
Paria, Venezuela, 403, 407, 408, 410
Paris Codex; *see* Codices
Pasion River, Guatemala, 333, 334, 350
Passages, interior; *see* Architectural features
Patagonia, 39, 50, 58, 64, 67, 68, 443, 513;
  see also Argentina, Chile
Patayan (Hakataya) culture, 181, 185, 189,
  246
Patios; *see* Architectural features
Patricks Point shell mound, est. date for, 132
Pauma complex, 123
Pavon phase, 299, 376; est. dates for settle-
  ments, 299
Payne Bay culture, 240
Payne's Cave, 131
Peake, H. J. E., 121, 145
Peanuts; *see* Plants
Pearls; *see* Ornaments
Peasant(s), 352; cultures, 306; revolution,
  351; society, 309
Pebble(s) (cobbles): choppers, 164, 165;
  cores, 455; hammerstones, 122, 123;
  houses lined with, 455; net sinkers,
  164, 165; notched, axes, 184; tools, 42
Peck, Stuart L., 123, 125, 145
Pecking, 33, 59
Pecos, New Mexico, 185, 188
Pecos River, Texas, 158, 175, 185
Pecos River culture, 232
Pei, W. C., 119, 145
Pendants; *see* Ornaments
Pendergast, D. M., 132, 141, 519, 525
Pennsylvania, 55, 236, 242, 253
Pensacola, Florida, 263, 283
Pensacola culture, 283, 284; est. date for,
  283
Peoples; *see* Populations
Peoria, Illinois, 247, 248, 250
Percussion, 42, 51; chipping, 51, 58; -flaked
  flint and limestone, tools, 231, 343;
  stage, 42; technique, 30
PerPereira, José Anthero, 444, 449
Perforators; *see* Tools
Pericot y Garcia, Luis, 28, 77
Peripheral Big-Game Hunting culture, est.
  dates for, 35
Peru (Peruvian), 50, 57, 65, 175, 292, 296,
  332, 389, 419–26, 436–37, 442, 446,
  451–79, 481–83, 496, 500, 507, 512,
  519, 560; *see also* individual cultures,
  sites, and geographical places by name

Pestles, 33, 59, 162, 166, 229, 231, 376;
  bell-shaped, 234; stone, 127, 164, 399,
  412
Petén, Guatemala, 310, 332–39, 341, 343,
  348, 351, 354, 355, 359, 362, 376–78,
  381
Petersen culture, 253
Petroglyphs, 126, 134, 135, 413
Phallic symbols, 126, 360, 379, 504
Phase(s), 7, 26, 37, 41, 298, 425, 444; *see
  also* individual phases by name
Philippine Islands, 508
Phillips, Philip, 5, 28, 30, 31, 32, 37, 38, 39,
  42, 46, 47, 51, 59, 81, 121, 129, 135,
  136, 148, 279, 287, 392, 394, 417, 479,
  486, 560, 561, 563
Phoenician(s), 421, 494, 523
Phoneme(s), 347, 533, 544; alternation,
  544; archiphonemes, 543; Utanahuan,
  553
Phonetic(s), 539; change, 533; environ-
  ment, 533; similarities, 546
Phonological equations, 533–35, 544
Phylla, linguistic, 527, 528, 531, 532, 534,
  547
Physics, 14, 15, 17, 18
Pic River, Ontario, 251
Pic River I culture, 253
Pictograph Cave: 196, 200, 210; II, 153;
  III, 212
Pictographs: Amazon, 421; painted, 125
Picton: culture, 253; site, 234
Piedra River, 180
Piedras Negras, 336, 343, 348, 360
Pierre, South Dakota, 208, 209
Pillars; *see* Architectural features
Pilling, Arnold R., 128, 145
Pine; *see* Foods, Trees
Pine Lawn Phase, 179, 181, 185; est. date
  for, 179
Pine River, 180
Pinedale, Arizona, 188
Pinnacles; *see* Architectural features
Pinto Basin, 125, 158, 232; cultures, 122;
  points, 160
Pioneer period, 182, 564
Pipes, 280, 407, 497; absence of, 410;
  Adena-Hopewell, 242; clay, 245, 405,
  406; Cherokee, 268; Copena, 267;
  cylinder, 237; effigy, 206, 239, 267;
  elbow, 164, 247, 267, 405, 521; Iroquois, 254; obtuse-angle, 245; pan, 262,
  263, 268, 477, 496; platform, 234, 242,
  245, 247, 262, 265, 268, 405; pottery,
  213, 405; steatite, 128, 204; stone, 161,
  164, 178, 179, 234, 245, 267; tubular,
  128, 154, 161, 164, 166, 204, 234, 235'

237, 428; wooden, with steatite bowl, 132

Pipil: invasion, 369; occupation of Guatemala coast, 376, 378, 379; ruling families, 373

Pit houses, 179–84, 512, 513, 515

Pit River, California, 131

Pits: baking, 213; storage, 178, 179, 183, 198, 202, 205, 209, 365

Pitzer, President and Mrs. Kenneth, vii

Pizarro, Francisco, 472

Plainview: complex, 197, 199; points, 32, 39, 61, 64, 85, 298; site, 60, 61, 62, 196; site, radiocarbon date for, 61

Plano: culture(s), 34, 35, 37, 60–63, 67, 85, 88, 166, 227, 232; dates for, 61, 228; points, 87, 90, 168, 227, 228; sites, 227

Plant(s), 209, 225, 237, 242, 251, 376, 497, 501, 539, 552; achira, 455; amaranth, 296–98, 300, 332; avocados (aguacate), 334, 458; burroweed, 156; cacao, 332, 334; cactus, 176, 515; cattails, 455; chenopodium, 237; coca, 496, 553; creosote brush, 176; cultigens, 297, 299, 300; cultivated, 295, 296, 299, 300, 332, 399, 455, 500; domestication, 294–96, 299, 426, 564; fibers, 456; food (new), 455, 457, 497; fruits, 33, 207, 332, 399, 455; gourds, 178, 237, 296, 297, 298, 332; grain, 518; maguey, 332, 552; peanuts, 453, 457; peppers, 183, 297, 298, 332, 455, 552; pigweed, 237; potatoes, 332, 452, 454, 458; potatoes, sweet, 453, 538, 539, 541; quinoa, 452, 458, 464; ragweed, 237; sagebrush, 149, 176, 515; sunflowers, 237; tomatoes, 552; Tropical Forest, 453; tubers, 165, 454, 455, 458, 464; wild, 294, 295, 297, 298, 302, 422, 454, 455; *Wocas*, 165; yucca, 176, 178; *see also* Beans, Cucurbits, Gourds, Maize, Manioc, Pumpkins, Squash, Tobacco

Planters, planting; *see* Agriculture, Farmers

Plaquemine: culture, 280, 282; period, 284; pottery, 272

Plaster; *see* Architectural materials

Platform(s), 315, 340, 458; adobe, 458; altar, 369, 373, 374; burial, 348, 366; dance, 373; earthen, 182, 249, 339; figurines, caryatid-supported, 352; four-footed, 349; house, 308, 339, 351; long, low, 371; masked human figures on, 368; mounds, 182, 186, 249, 250, 254, 266, 270, 368, 463, 478; pipes, 234, 239, 242, 245, 262, 265, 268; sacrificial, 357, 359; stepped, 301, 377, 466; stone (stone-faced), 377, 379, 458, 476; sup-

porting "apartments," 374–75; thrones, 360

Platinum, 478, 479

Platte River, 208

Playa cultures, 43–44, 53–54, 122–23, 158

Playa Guacuco site, 393

Playa Verde site, 49, 50

Plazas, 188, 249, 254, 277, 302, 307, 312, 315, 336, 339, 341, 363, 366, 369, 371, 373, 374, 413, 427, 429

Pleistocene, 17, 18, 27, 29, 36, 88, 158, 169, 293; fauna, 24, 27, 28, 32, 35, 37, 38, 41, 44, 46, 47, 52, 57, 59, 63, 64, 88, 177, 197, 422

Plumage; *see* Feathers

Plummets; *see* Tools

Plymouth Rock, 255

Point Barrow, Alaska, 86, 98, 99, 100, 101

Point Hope, Alaska, 86, 91, 98, 100, 103, 104, 106

Point Peninsula culture, 234–36, 240, 244–45, 248, 251, 253

Point of Pines, Arizona, 156, 188

Pointed Mountain: complex, 163, 164, 232; site, 60, 62

Pokom phase, 346

Polishing, 33, 45, 59, 68

Pollen, 18; analysis, 15, 233; fossil, 296; profiles, 27

Pollock, H. E. D., 348, 359, 363, 364, 365, 384

Polynesia(n)(s), 118, 124, 507, 508, 538–41

Ponce Sanguinas, Carlos, 464

Poole site, radiocarbon dates for, 239

Pope, Alexander, 13

Popul Vuh, 333, 373, 374

Population(s), 214, 231, 255, 281, 304, 310, 375, 470; Adena-Hopewell, 238, 242; Aztec, 322, 324; centers, 273, 274, 403; Chanchan, 470; concentrations, 243, 437, 457, 519; decline, 283, 284; density, 29, 129, 223, 249, 255, 270, 320, 321, 323, 339, 351, 362, 367, 380, 437, 513; depopulation, 227, 436; dispersal, 285, 548; displacement, 254, 255, 550; expansion, 339, 480; increase (accretions), 117, 125, 127, 178, 180, 183, 214, 237, 238, 256, 262, 269, 270, 274, 275, 456, 463, 465, 466, 478, 552; Indian, 129, 453; Iroquois, 254; Maquixco (Teotihuacán), 308; movements, 29, 100, 101, 117, 133, 134, 207, 209, 210, 227, 235, 238, 239, 243, 248, 249, 250, 251, 255, 269, 277, 317, 324, 412, 426, 427, 433, 434, 435, 445, 456, 457, 490, 529, 548–51 (*see also* Migrations); New World, aboriginal, 490; non-agricultural, 397, 470, 474; sedentary agricul-

Population(s)—*Continued*
tural, 223; stability, 437, 530; Tajin, 312; Tenochtitlán, 308; Teotihuacán, 308; Toltec, 323; units, 29, 35; urban, 305
Portales complex, 34, 60, 62, 196, 198, 199; radiocarbon date for, 198
Porter, Muriel Noé, 521, 525
Porter complex, 267
Portland, Oregon, 134
Porto Alegre, Brazil, 420
Posey County, Illinois, 244
Post-Formative periods, 354, 364
Postclassic stage (period, horizon): Chichén Itzá, 504; Guatemala coast, 379; Guatemala highlands, 372, 374; southern and western lowlands, 350–52 (est. dates for) 507; southern Veracruz-Tabasco, 352, 382; Willey and Phillips, 30
Posthole(s) (post-mold), 160, 182, 198, 231, 237, 238
Potatoes; *see* Plants
Potomac River, 254
Potosi, Bolivia, 50
Potrero Sucio site, 49, 50
Potter Creek Cave, 47, 119
Pottery; *see* Ceramics
Poverty Point, 260
Powder River County, Montana, 201
Powell, Major J. W., 528, 546
Powers-Yonkee bison trap, date for, 201
Pozo de Muaco (La Vela de Coro) site, 49, 50
Prairie: culture, 211; people, 212; *see also* Great Plains
Prairie Provinces, Canada, 195
Pre-Aleut culture, 105
Pre-Cupisnique culture, 426
Pre-Projectile Point stage, 23, 26, 30, 37, 42–51, 57, 58, 68; est. age of, 68
Preclassic (Formative) stage (period, horizon): art, 500; ceramics, 337; Chiapas and Guatemala coast, 376–78; cultures, 367, 496; Guatemala highlands, 365–70, 377; mounds, 366; sequence, 335; southern Veracruz-Tabasco, 380–81; southern and western lowlands, 335, 336, 346, 350, 354, 367, 507
Preformative stage, 30, 129
Prelithic stage, 120, 152
Pressure flaking, 51, 58, 59, 455
Priests, 186, 316, 333, 363, 481
Prince, E. R., 170
Prince William Sound, Alaska, 86, 91, 101, 102, 117, 132, 135
Printing blocks, 503
Projectile points, 23, 26–29, 32, 42, 45–52, 58, 59, 64, 67, 68, 85, 89, 106, 132, 160, 164, 165, 181, 198, 200, 201, 204, 223, 225, 231, 247, 260, 297, 298, 423, 455, 456
Forms (styles), 202, 227, 228, 231; barbed, 182, 233; basally thinned, 67, 130; beveled, 67, 87, 88, 225; blunt-tipped, 127; bunt, 154; chipped, 164, 178, 179, 519; concave base, 130, 228; conical base, 87; contracted base, 423; corner-notched, 32, 59, 61, 202, 231, 233; diagonally-flaked,104; diamond-shaped, 231; eared, 231; flaked, 125; end-notched, 155; fluted (*see* Fluted points); heavy, 126, 130, 260; indented base, 160; lanceolate (*see* Lanceolate points); large, 164, 229, 235, 423; lozenge-shaped (double-pointed),155, 162; medium-sized, 233; notched, 36, 199, 200, 237; parallel-flaked, 177; shouldered, 231; side-notched, 85, 88, 105, 131, 155, 162, 164, 166, 168, 182, 200, 201, 228, 229, 233, 260; small, 154, 231, 515; stemless, 229; stemmed, 36, 52, 55, 58, 59, 67, 131, 161, 164, 208, 227,229, 231, 233, 235, 237, 244, 260, 263, 396, 397, 423, 515; triangular, 65, 67, 155, 161, 163, 164, 168, 182, 208, 231, 235, 245, 248, 396, 397, 423; turkey-tail, 235; unfluted, 32, 37, 55, 59, 64, 197
Materials: antler, 127, 244; argillite, 229; basalt, 131; bone, 87, 88, 127, 225, 233, 263, 397, 398; chalcedony, 242, 422, 423; chert, 422, 423; flint, 161, 229, 344; jasper, 422, 423; obsidian, 128, 242, 344, 373; quartz, 422, 423; shell, 397; slate, 135, 231; stone, 45, 293, 397
Types, 27, 36, 156, 516, 517; Abasolo, 298; Agate Basin, 32, 39, 61, 85, 87, 88, 298; Agate Basin, radiocarbon dates for, 61; Almagré, 298; Angostura, 67, 85, 87–89, 294; Angostura, est. date for in Arctic, 89; Avonlea, date for, 203; Ayampitin, 36, 58, 65; Brewerton Side-Notched, 233; Browns Valley, 32, 85, 88; Caddoan, 269; Cascade, 36, 52, 162, 168; Clovis, 31, 35, 36, 37, 39, 45, 51, 52, 55, 57, 59, 68, 88, 130, 197; Cumberland, 31, 52; Dalton, 228; Deptford, 263; Desert, 131, 162; Eden, 32, 198, 228; El Jobo, 36, 57; Folsom, 31, 36, 38, 39, 51, 55, 57, 59; Gary, 67, 298; Great Plains, 293; Gypsum, 155, 229; Hell Gap, 55; Hidden Valley Stemmed, 229; Hopewellian, 244; Intihuasi, 58; Kent, 298; Kinney, 298; Larter Tanged, 233; Lerma, 32, 36, 37, 298; McKean-Duncan-Hanna series, 200; Midland, 298; Milnesand, 32, 85;

Mousterian, 87; Nutimik, 235; Old Copper, 88, 233; Pinto Basin, 160; Plainview, 39, 61, 64, 67, 85, 298; Plano, 87, 90, 168, 227, 228; Plano, radiocarbon dates for, 61; Sandia, 31, 38, 52, 55, 59, 177; Scottsbluff, 32, 85, 88, 198, 228, 293; Shoshonean, 121; Silver Lake, 160; Solutrean, 87, 88; Southeastern, 260; Sturgeon Triangular, 235; Tortugas, 67, 298

Promontory Cave, 153, 156, 214

Proskouriakoff, Tatiana A., viii, 313, 328, 340, 341, 347, 348, 349, 379, 384, 385

Proto-Formative stage, 335

Proto-Uto-Aztecan culture, 153, 154

Protoarchaic stage, 33, 34, 37, 38, 58, 59–68, 259; est. date for, 31

Protoclassic stage (period, horizon), 335, 337, 338, 367; Guatemala coast, 378; Guatemala highlands, 367, 368, 373; southern Veracruz-Tabasco, 382; southern and western lowlands, 337, 338, 346, 355

Protohistoric stage (period, horizon): Chiapas and Guatemala coast (*see* Late Postclassic); Guatemala highlands, 374, 375; southern Veracruz-Tabasco, 383

Protolithic stage, 29, 42, 120

Providencia phase; *see* Miraflores phase

Pubic coverings: pottery (tangas), 439, 440; textile, 455

Pucallpa, Peru, 420, 425

Pucara: phase, est. date for, 465; site, 459, 465

Puebla: state of, 44, 47, 63, 293, 296–97, 301, 305, 309–12, 320, 322, 370; city, 293, 301

Pueblo(an) culture(s), 158, 176, 181–89, 213–14, 564; Indians, 187–89; influences, 117, 154; *see also* Anasazi, Basketmaker, Mogollon

Puertas Minitas, Baja California, 126

Puerto Cabello, Venezuela, area, 393, 401, 404, 405, 407

Puerto Hormiga site, 395, 400; radiocarbon dates for, 400

Puerto Miranda site, 425

Puerto Rico, 389, 391, 392, 395, 398, 402, 403, 409, 411, 412

Puerto San José, Guatemala, 378, 379

Pulcher site, 250

Pumas; *see* Felines

Pumice falls; *see* Ash falls

Pumpkins, 332; *Cucurbita pepo*, 178, 296–300; *see also* Cucurbits, Squash

Puna, Ecuador, island of, 479

Punctation; *see* Ceramic decorative styles and techniques

Puno, Peru, department of, 65

Punta Arenas, Costa Rica, 292

Punta Arenas (Venezuela) site, 393

Punta Catalina site, 49, 50

Punta Gorda: complex, 397, 409; est. date for, 397; site, 391, 397

Punuk: art style, 94–99; culture (stage), 91, 94, 95, 96, 98, 99, 246; sites, 94, 99

Punuk Island, Alaska, 93, 94, 98, 106

Pure Florescent period (Yucatan), 356, 358, 361, 362, 364; est. dates for, 346

Purron rockshelter, 297, 299

Putnam, F. W., 47, 77, 119, 145

Puuc, the, 313, 356, 357, 364

Pyramid(s), 340, 369; Adivino (Uxmal), 356; Altar de Sacrificios, 337; burial chambers in, 340; burial pits in, 364; Cholol100, 311, 312; E-VII-sub, 336; interior stone-lined passages in, 458; mortuary, 348; Palenque, 342; -platform mounds, 463; Puuc, 356; stepped (terraced), 331; stepped, Kaminaljuyú, 366; stepped, Peruvian coast, 458; stepped, Tollan, 315; stepped, Uaxactun, 336, 337; stone-faced, 378; temples, 340, 502; temples, Maxquixco, 308; temples, Palenque, 348; temples Rio Bec (simulated), 364; temples, Xochichalco, 312; Teotihuacán, 307; Tikal, 337, 340; truncated, 182, 266, 301, 302; *see also* Architecture, Mounds

Pyrite(s): fire-making with, 231, 514; mirrors, 377, 496, 521; mosaic plaques, 344, 370, 372; ornaments, 300

"Q-complex," 337

Quad site, 226

Quadrangles; *see* Architectural features

Qualuyu site, 464; radiocarbon date for, 464

Quarai site, 49, 50

Quartz, quartzite; *see* Minerals

Quebrado de Camarones sites, 56, 57, 58

Queen Charlotte Island, British Columbia, 135

Queen Charlotte Sound, British Columbia, 118, 135

Queretaro, 314

Quetzal: birds, 334, 365; -serpent-jaguar god, 315; -snake; *see* Feathered serpent

Quetzalcoatl, 315–16, 357; cult of, 186, 564

Quezaltenango, Guatemala, 365, 371

Quiché, Guatemala, 367, 373

Quiché: capital of, 374; dialect, 365; kingdom, 374

Quimby, George I., 34, 38, 54, 63, 77, 102, 113, 235, 258, 286

Quimby culture, 252

Quinoa; *see* Plants

Quintana Roo, 334
Quipus, 472, 473
Quirigua, Guatemala, 333, 342
Quito, Ecuador, 65, 471, 479

Rabbit(s), 186; bones, 165; clubs, 154; nets, 154; "stick," 178
Raddatz Rockshelter, 252; est. dates for, 228
Radiocarbon dates, 7, 23, 26, 48, 59, 87, 105, 120, 123, 159, 166, 180, 203, 205, 212, 227, 229, 236, 238, 259, 362, 451, 464; Agate Basin points, 61; American Falls site, 44; Archaic culture in eastern United States, 27; Avonlea points, 203; Ayampitin, 65; Balankanche Cave, 362; Barlovento site, 400; Barrancoid series, 404, 408; Becerra formation, 47; Boyleston Street Fishweir, 230–31; Breeden Island site, 206; Brewster site, 55; Caribbean area, 392; Cazador complex, 61, 63; Cerro Machado style, 405; Chalco complex, 295; Chaluka site, 90, 102; Channel Islands, 124; Chiricahua complex, 61; Choris culture, 89, 104; Cozcatlan complex, 298; Cubagua complex, 397; Danger Cave, 61, 156; Dent mammoth, 55; Dzibilchaltun, 354, 362; Early Horizon, 126–27; El Heneal complex, 397; El Riego complex, 298; Farmington site gravels, 130; Fell's Cave, 34, 67; Fort Rock Cave, 155; Frightful Cave, 63, 156; Graham Cave, 61, 228; Guayabitoid series, 411; Gunther Island site, 132; Gypsum Cave, 61, 155; Hell Gap points, 55; Hopewellian, 239, 241; Horner site, 198; Huaca Prieta, 455; Ievoghiyog site, 99; Infiernillo phase, 294, 297; Intihuasi Cave, 34, 65; Ipiutak, 88, 89, 103; Iyatayet site, 104; Kachemak Bay I, 90, 102; Klamath River, site on, 133; Krum Bay site, 398; Kurigitavik site, 99; La Cabrera style, 404; La Jolla culture, 126; La Venta, 304; Lagoa Santa caves, 58; Lake Mohave, 120; Late period (Northwest Coast), 134; Lauricocha I, 58, 65; Lehner site, 52, 55, 197; Lerma complex 57, 294; Lewisville site, 44, 45; Lindenmeier site, 55; Locarno Beach site, 134; LoDaisKa site, Complex D, 201; Logan Creek site, 200; Loiza Cave, 398; Lubbock site, 55; Malaga Cove site, 123; Manicuare complex, 397; Meso-Indian epoch, 396; Minnesota Man, 228; Missouri River mounds, 205; Moapa, Nevada, cave, 160; Monagrillo site, 400; Muaco site, 57, 396; Mylodon Cave,
34, 58, 67; Naco site, 52; Nericagua phase, 429; Okvik–Old Bering Sea culture stage, St. Lawrence Island, 90; Old Copper culture, 233; Old Cordilleran culture, 55; Old Whaling culture, 89; Oxbow culture, 201; Paleo-Indian epoch, 396; Palli Aike, 34, 67; Paracas, Chilca and Nazca localities, 456; Period III, Cuba, 399; Plainview points, 61; Plano points, 61; Portales complex, 198; Powers-Yonkee bison trap, 201; pre-Dorset sites, 107; Puerto Hormiga site, 400; Qualuyu pottery, 464; Rancho Peludo site, 396, 399, 400; Rio Napo sites, 441; Saladero site, 408; Saladoid series in Antilles, 409; San Dieguito, 123, 159; San Francisco Bay shell mounds, 128; Sandia Cave, 52; Santa Rosa Island, 44, 123; Scripps Campus (Estate) site, 44, 123; Serpent Mound, 245; Sierran ossuaries, 131; Signal Butte I, 201; Simonsen site, 61, 199, 200; Site Cs-23, Oregon, 132; Site Ti-1, Oregon coast, 133; Sulphur Spring stage, 61, 63, 156; Tl site, Dorset culture, 90, 91; The Dalles, lowest level, 163; Thomas Riggs focus, 206; Tlapacoya, Mound 1, 301; Tocuyano style, 405; Tule Springs site, 44, 46; U. P. Mammoth kill, 197; Valencia style, 406; Valley focus, 202; Venezuela, 392; Ventana Cave, lower level, 64; Wales beachmidden, 99; Washita River focus, 206; Whalen Farm site, 134; Willow Creek midden, 128; Wisconsin glacial period, 27; Zuma Creek site, 123
Radiocarbon dating, 14, 15, 16, 17, 24, 27, 154, 215, 243, 345, 354, 392; black carbon, 233; carbon dioxide, 63
Rafts, 225; balsa, 539; Formosan, 508; South American, 507, 508
Rainey, Froelich G., 62, 77, 85, 87, 88, 90, 91, 93, 94, 99, 103, 104, 105, 106, 109, 111, 113, 391, 411, 416
Rainy River aspect, 252; est. date for, 244
Raisch-Smith culture, 253
Ralph, Elizabeth K., 90, 91, 99, 103, 113, 385
Ramos phase, 188
Ramps; *see* Architectural features
Rampton, Mrs. Lucybeth, vii
Rancho Peludo site, 392, 393, 395, 399, 400; radiocarbon date for, 396, 399, 400
Rands, Barbara C., 336, 343, 350, 352, 365, 384
Rands, Robert L., 336, 343, 350, 352, 365, 384

Rasps, musical, 208
Rattles, 248; bone-handled, 154; copper-covered, 280; deer-hoof, 155, 161
Raw materials, 225, 242, 422
Rawlins, Wyoming, 197
Raymond complex, 248, 252
Reagan culture, 253
Red Cedar River culture, 252
Red ocher; *see* Burials, Minerals
Red Ocher culture, 252; burials, 234, 235, 236; mounds, 234
Red River, 265, 266, 270
Red Smoke site, 60, 62
Red Valley culture, 253
Redfield, Robert, 295
Redondo Beach, California, 123
Reduplication, linguistic, 542, 543
Reed, Erik K., 1, 6, 175, 176, 181, 189, 191, 563, 564
Refuse (debris, trash), 295, 297, 298, 299, 365, 465; burials in, 249; from habitation mounds, 439; shell-midden, 425; village, 243, 424, 427, 431, 436, 476; village, as indicator of settlement pattern, 424, 427, 428–29, 431, 434, 437
Regional Classic stage, 465
Regional Developmental period (Ecuador), 476–78; est. dates for, 476
Regional States (Peru): Florescent stage, 465–68, 476; Formative stage, 463–65, 476
Regionalism, 463–68, 470, 471, 476, 478, 481
Reichel-Dolmatoff, Gerardo, 50, 453, 480, 481, 486
Reigh culture, 252
Religion(s) (religious), 262, 265, 277, 357, 489, 502, 545; activities, 249; ancestor worship, 364; architecture, 301; bases, 278; beliefs, 332; centers, 333, 480; ceremonialism, 271; concepts, 514; control, 304; cults, 186, 357, 468; development, 475, 476; expressions, 502; functions of, 367; ideas, 265, 303, 463; life, 242, 481; manifestations, 269; Mesoamerican, 303; organization, 280, 339; rituals, 242, 303, 331, 344, 368–69, 514–15; sanctuaries, 476; state, 472; strife, 316; structures, 186, 266, 285, 301, 378, 481; symbolism, lack of, 464, 468; systems, 262, 265, 273, 285, 304; traditions, 267; transformation, 281; unity, 460
Renaud, E. B., 44, 77
Renier: culture, 252; site, 228
Renner site, 243
Repoussé; *see* Techniques
Reptiles, 201, 368; *see also* Serpents

Requena, Antonio, 391
Requena, Rafael, 391, 406, 416
Research Cave I, 252
Reserve (District), New Mexico, 179, 185
Reservoirs, 334, 476
Resist painting; *see* Ceramic decorative designs and techniques, painting
Rex Gonzalez, Alberto, 28, 34, 50, 51, 57, 58, 65, 66, 67, 77, 78, 515, 519, 524
Ricketson, E. B., 341
Riddell, F. A., 162, 173
Riddell, Harry S., 173
Riley, Carroll L., 522, 525
Rinaldo, John B., 172, 191
Rings; *see* Ornaments
Rio Aguarico, Ecuador, 420, 438
Rio Asa, Venezuela, 423
Rio Bec, 364; architecture, 364; area, 359, 364, 365; sites, 364
Rio Branco, Brazil, 420, 433; territory of, 434
Rio Chico, Venezuela, 393, 401, 403, 406
Rio Chiguano, Venezuela, 423
Rio Gallegos I complex, 49, 50
Rio Grande, 185, 187, 188, 189, 193, 204; Valley, 156; upper, 213, 214
Rio Grande do Sul, Brazil, 50
Rio Guas, Venezuela, 399
Rio Icabaru, Venezuela, 423
Rio de Janeiro, Brazil, 420, 444
Rio Kukenan, Venezuela, 423
Rio Los Esclavos, Guatemala, 378
Rio Mapuera, Brazil, 420, 433, 434, 435
Rio Maraca, Brazil, 420, 431
Rio Napo, Ecuador, 420, 424–26, 438, 440–42, 446
Rio Negro, 420, 428, 434
Rio Negro, Argentina, 50
Rio Paragua, Venezuela, 420, 423
Rio Paraná; *see* Paraná River
Rio Pedernales, Venezuela, 396
Rio Putumayo-Aguarico, Colombia, 442
Rio Solimoes, Brazil, 420
Rio Tapajos, Brazil, 420, 428, 430, 431
Rio Trombetas, 430, 432
Rio Tuy Venezuela, 401
Rio Ucayali; *see* Ucayali River
Rio Uruguay, 420, 443
Ritchie, William A., 54, 78, 229, 230, 235, 238, 258
Rituals; *see* Religions, rituals
Ritzenthaler, Robert E., 235, 258
River(s), 353; banks, 428; terraces, 15
River Basin Surveys (Missouri River), 204, 205
Riverine: mounds, 439; specialization, 163, 167
Riverton culture, 252

Rivet, Paul, 537, 538
Roads: Inca, 472; jungle, 334; pre-Inca, 469
Roaring Spring Cave, 60, 62, 153, 155
Robbins, Maurice, 231, 258
Roberts, Frank H. H., Jr., 27, 34, 54, 55, 61, 62, 78, 145, 180, 191, 197, 219
Robes; *see* Clothing
Robinson, E., 125, 145
Rockport culture, 246
Rockshelters, 32, 33, 36, 41, 154; Lagoa Santa, 58; Sierra de Tamaulipas, 297; Tehuacán, 294, 296, 297, 298, 422, 434
Rocky Mountains, 34, 35, 38, 39, 117, 149, 162, 189, 193, 202
Rogers, D. B., 123, 124, 145
Rogers, Malcolm J., 44, 54, 62, 78, 120, 122, 123, 124, 125, 145, 159, 173
Rogue River, Oregon, 133
Rohr, Alfredo, 444, 449
Rohr I culture, 253
Roman: coastal shipping, 509; ports, 507
Romer, Alfred S., 15
Romero, Javier, 44, 54, 63, 72, 294, 326
Romney, A. K., 173
Ronquin Site, 391, 401, 408
Roofs; *see* Architectural features
Rooms; *see* Architectural features
Roosa, William B., 54, 78
Root(s), 33, 201, 207, 422; agriculture, 403; crops, 332, 423, 426, 452, 480; linguistic, 541–45
Rose Mound, 282
Rosenkrans culture, 253
Rosetta stone, 346
Rouse, Irving B., viii, 2, 9, 17, 29, 48, 57, 71, 78, 389, 390–99, 404–8, 411–17, 421, 430, 432, 442, 447, 449, 565
Rowe, John Howland, 42, 78, 470, 471, 472, 483, 486
Rowley, Graham, 107, 113
Royo y Gomez, José, 50, 57, 78
Roys, Lawrence, 313, 328
Roys, Ralph L., 384
Rubber, 334, 369; ball(s), 497; ball game 522; syringes, 497; waterproofing, 497
Rubbing stones; *see* Manos
Rubble; *see* Architectural materials
Rubin, Meyer, 67, 78
Rudenko, S. I., 98, 106, 113
Ruiz site, 379
Rulers, 331, 333, 348, 483; Guatemalan, 373; Inca, 471, 472; kings, 316, 322, 323, 333, 500; Mochica, 466; Peruvian kingdoms, 470; princes, 307, 322; Valley of Mexico, 321–23; *see also* Priests
Ruppert, Karl, 363
Rupununi: district of (British Guiana), 422,

423, 434; phase (complex), 434; River, 420
Russell Cave, 60, 63
Russia(n); *see* Soviet
Ruz Lhuillier, Alberto, viii, 313, 328, 341, 342, 348, 384

Sacatepequez, Guatemala, 365
Sacaton (Sedentary) period, 182
Sacramento, California, 127
Sacramento River, 129
Sacramento Valley, California, 126–31
Sacrifice(s): burned grave offerings, 128; cardiac, 315, 324, 360; human, 331, 341, 357, 359, 363, 366, 481; platforms for, 357, 359; rites of, 369; retainer, 366
Saginaw Valley, Michigan, 243
St. Johns cultures, 240, 261
St. Johns River, Florida, 261
St. Joseph Valley, Michigan, 243
St. Lawrence: culture(s), 94, 98; Eskimos, 94, 98
St. Lawrence Island, Alaska, 86, 90–100, 106; radiocarbon date for, 90
St. Lawrence Valley, 230, 231, 234, 248, 255
St. Louis, Missouri, 229, 243, 244, 248–49, 251, 278
St. Lucia, island of, 391, 392
Saladero site, 391, 402, 408; radiocarbon dates for, 408
Saladoid series, 397, 408–12; est. dates for, 408; radiocarbon dates for diffusion into Antilles, 409
Salt, 121, 334, 380
Salt River, Arizona, 188
Salto Grande, Uruguay, 420
Salto Grande pottery, 444
Salvador, Brazil, 420
Sambaqui(s), 425, 443, 444; *see also* Middens
San Agustin site, est. date for, 480
San Andres Sajcabaja, Guatemala, 373
San Clemente Island, California, radiocarbon date for, 124
San Diego, California, 31, 46, 121, 123, 124, 126
San Dieguito complexes, 53, 54, 122, 159, 167, 169; dates for, 123, 159
San Francisco Bay, California, 128–30
San Francisco de Yarinacocha, Peru, 425
San Joaquin Valley, California, 126–30
San Jon site, 34, 60, 62
San Jose complex (phase), 60, 62, 232, 310, 335
San José, Costa Rica, 511
San Juan complex (industry), 53, 54, 57
San Juan Islands, British Columbia, 134

San Juan River, Utah and Colorado, 178, 180, 182, 185, 186, 187
San Juan River Valley, Mexico, 308
San Lorenzo site, 303
San Luis, Argentina, 34, 65
San Luis Potosi, 314
San Marcial, New Mexico, 188
San Marcos, Guatemala, 365
San Marcos rockshelter, 297, 298, 299
San Martin Mountains, Veracruz, 380
San Miguel Island, California, radiocarbon date for, 124
San Nicholas Island, California, dates for, 124
San Pablo, Ecuador, 459
San Pedro Buenavista, Chiapas, 379
San Pedro stage (complex), 61, 169, 178
San Pedro Zacachimalpa's barranca, Puebla, 293
Sandals, 154, 155, 160, 176, 181, 186, 332; est. age of, in Southwest, 176; fiber, radiocarbon date for, 155; leather, 179; Maya, 349; wickerwork, 179; woven, 156, 178
Sanders, William T., 305, 307, 308, 311, 312, 321, 328
Sandia: artifacts, 38; Cave, 52, 53, 54, 152, 177; radiocarbon dates for, 52; points, 31, 38, 52, 55, 59, 177 (*see also* Projectile points)
Sandy Creek site, 196
Santa Barbara, California, 123, 124, 125, 128; Channel, 129
Santa Catalina Island, California, dates for, 124
Santa Catarina, Brazil, 420, 445
Santa Clara phase; *see* Miraflores phase
Santa Cruz, Argentina, 50, 65
Santa Cruz (Colonial) period, 182
Santa Elena Poco Uinic, Chiapas, 379
Santa Fé, Argentina, 50
Santa Isabel Iztapan sites, 53, 54, 57, 293, 294
Santa Marta complex, 60, 63
Santa Rita, British Honduras, 352, 363
Santa Rosa cultures, 240
Santa Rosa Island: cultures, dates for 44, 46, 120, 123; sites, 43, 44, 46, 120, 121
Santa Valley, Peru, 459
Santarem culture and sites, 420, 430–32
Santiago Tuxtla, Veracruz, 382
Santo Domingo, 389
São Paulo, Brazil, 420
Sapir, Edward, 101, 113, 546, 547, 556
Sarcophagi; *see* Burials
Saskatchewan, province of, 201–4
Saskatchewan River, 193

Satchell complex, 252
Satellite communities, 306, 307, 308
Sato, Hisashi, 485
Satterthwaite, Linton, Jr., 62, 73, 78, 385
Sauer, Carl O., 403, 417, 427
Savagery, cultural stage of, 300, 317
Savanna(s), 292, 314, 334, 353, 375, 380, 403, 422, 428, 439; Brazilian, 419, 434; climate of, 291, 317; Gran Sabana, 420, 423; movement of Macusi Indians to, 434; Rupununi, 422, 423, 434; Venezuelan, 419, 423
Savannah River, Georgia, 261, 263, 284
Sawmill culture, 253
Sayles, E. B., 52, 54, 61, 62, 73, 79, 123, 146, 156, 173, 181, 190
Scalp Creek complex, 248
Scapula(r): awls, 155; cutters or harvesters, 155; hoes, bison, 205, 211
Schaedel, Richard P., 470, 486
Scharbauer (Midland) site, 53, 54
Schenk, W. Egbert, 128, 139, 146, 173
Schmidt, Max, 445, 449
Schmidt, W., 514, 525
Schmitt, Karl, 16
Schmitz, Ignacio, 444, 445, 449
Schroeder, A. H., 213, 219
Schroeder, Gerd, 65, 76
Schuetz, Mardith K., 173
Schuiling, W. C., 146
Schultz, C. Bertrand, 61, 62, 69, 72, 79
Schumacher, Paul, 132, 146
Schurz, William Lytle, 508, 510
Scoops: bison frontal, 210; wooden, 178
Scottsbluff: complex, 198, 199; points, 32, 85, 88, 198, 228, 294; site, 60, 62, 196
Scraper-Maker culture, 122
Scraper(s), 36, 45, 47, 64, 96, 104, 131, 152, 154–56, 158, 161, 164, 176, 178, 179, 197, 198, 201, 224, 225, 229, 231, 233, 260, 293, 422; cannon-bone, 103; core, 231; El Jobo, 57; end, 103, 122, 197, 198, 208, 211, 212, 225; flake(d), 87, 122, 123, 125, 130, 165; flint, 225, 344; hide, 210; ivory, 103; keeled, 122; obsidian, 344; percussion flaked, 231; planes, 122, 123, 130; plano-convex, 51, 202, 423; quartzite, 396; side, 103, 122, 198; side-notched, hafted, 229; snubnose, 122, 211; sweat, 127
Scripps Campus (Estate) site, 43, 44, 46, 123; radiocarbon date from, 44, 46, 123
Sculpture(d) (s), 165, 314, 332, 348, 358, 358, 360, 369; bas-relief, 313, 315, 348, 349, 357, 359, 379, 458, 470; boulder, 368; bowls, 134; Classic, 368; clay relief, 458; La Venta, 380, 381; Late

Sculpture(d) (s)—*Continued*
  Classic, 349; Maya highlands, 367, 368, 370, 374, 377, 379; Maya lowlands, 341, 349; Mitla, 317; monumental, 303, 325, 372, 381, 480; mushroom-shaped stone, 368, 370, 371, 378; Olmec (Izapan) style, 377, 381; Pacific slope, Guatemala, 379; panels, 315, 360; pedestal, 368, 377, 379; phallic, 504; Postclassic, 374; Preclassic, 368, 377; reliefs, 341, 349; in the round, 303, 359, 368; sculptors, 306; stone, 134, 249, 331, 371, 378, 379, 480; stucco relief, 349; styles, 378; Tajin, 313; terra-cotta, 319; theriomorphic friezes, 315; Tiahuanaco, 469; Tollan, 315; zoömorphic, 164; *see also* Chac mools, Parallelism, Stelae

Seafaring, 398, 409, 508–9, 523, 538

Seafood, 375, 376, 396, 398; crabs, 411; mollusks, 128, 133, 375, 422; mussel(s), 165, 239, 376; oysters, 376; shellfish, 123, 125, 260–63, 399, 455, 473, 474, 476; shrimps, 375

Sea mammals, 94, 105, 107, 128, 133, 455

Seals, clay; *see* Stamps, clay

Sears, William H., 2, 8, 9, 259, 287, 496, 500, 563, 564

Seed(s), 33, 121, 162, 165, 200, 224, 501; agriculture, 403, 442; beads and ornaments, 178; -beaters, 154; buffalo gourd, 296; crops, 156, 332, 423, 426; -gathering, 123, 131; -grinding tools, 122, 125, 127; grass, 162; -harvesting tools, 155; milling of, 552, 553; -planting complex, 300; squash and pumpkin, 178; sunflower, 237, 332; -using cultures, 130; wild-plant, 176, 422, 518, 552; *Wocas*, 165

Seinfeld, Mrs. Deni, vii

Seklowaghyaget site, 92, 93, 94; *see also* Gambell, sites

Selkirk focus, 196

Sellards, E. H., 28, 34, 37, 44, 45, 47, 54, 55, 62, 79, 120, 146, 197, 198, 219

Sequences, *see* individual cultural sequences by name

Sergeev, D. A., 98, 111, 113

Series, *see* individual cultural series by name

Serpent(s), 460, 462; balustrades, 357, 360, 363; columns, entrance, 357, 359; cult, 500; Feathered (plumed), 312, 315, 316, 377; fire-, 360; heads, 370; -jaguar-quetzal god, 315; motifs, 301, 356, 368; mouths, profiled, 364, 365; on pottery, 405; symbolism of, 303, 369

Serpent Mound: culture, 253; radiocarbon date for, 245

Serrano, Antonio, 449, 516, 525

Seward Peninsula, Alaska, 98

Shabik'-eschee site, 181

Shaft wrenches; *see* Tools

Shakimu complex, 436, 437

Shamans: figurines of, 301; regalia, at Ipiutak, 103; Siberian, 103

Shang dynasty; *see* China

Shannon focus, 208

Shasta County, California, 130

Shasta Dam, California, 131

Sheguiandah site, 43, 44, 228, 231; I, 253; V, 44

Shell(s), 154, 399, 411, 455; abalone, 127, 128, 154; artifacts, 38, 204, 205, 397, 398; beads, 125–28, 132, 161, 162, 166, 178, 209, 213, 234, 271, 344, 397; bracelets, 179; *Busycon perversa*, 228; carved, 182; celts, 397; charred, 46; *Chione*, 123; conch, 263–65, 271, 279; cups, 397; dentalium, 213; dippers, 271; engraved, 249, 264; etched, 182; fishhooks, 51, 118, 123–25, 128, 422, 456; gastropod, 18; gouges, 397, 398; haliotis, 161; hammers, 397, 398; heaps (*see* Middens); industries, 26, 129; inlays, 413; marine (ocean), 166, 204, 228, 234; marine, radiocarbon date on, 239; mask gorgets, 204; middens, radiocarbon dates for, 123, 126 (*see also* Middens); mounds (*see* Mounds); mussel, 120, 239; olivella, 154, 155, 161, 209, 213; ornaments, 125, 126, 178, 182, 333, 337, 344; ostracodes, fresh-water, 18; pendants, 228, 397; pond-snail, 55; projectile points, tempering, 206, 211, 277, 278, 280, 281, 282, 285; trumpets, 182; -work, 412, 413

Shell Fishhook culture, 51

Shell Midden culture, 122

Shelter(s), 208, 260, 295, 296, 518; rock, 32, 33, 36, 41, 154, 294, 296; sites, 126; skin, 225; temporary, 225, 435; wickiups, 162; wigwams, 248, 254

Shields; *see* Weapons

Shiner, Joel L., 165, 173

Shiprock, New Mexico, 177

Ships; *see* Boats

Shoenwetter, James, 172, 191

Shook, Edwin M., viii, 310, 326, 340, 371, 376, 378, 379, 384, 385

Shoop site, 226

Shore lines; *see* Beach, lines

Shoshoni (Shoshonean), 121, 196, 212, 548;

Basin, 196; -Comanche language, 550; Death Valley, 121; Puebloized, 187; -speakers, 131, 162, 459; -type arrow points, 121

Shoshoni Basin site, 200

Showlow, Arizona, 188

Shrimps; *see* Seafood

Shrines; *see* Ceremonial structures

Shroeder, A. H., 219

Shumway, George, 62, 77, 123, 146

Shutler, Dick, Jr., 131, 143, 172

Siberia(n)(s), 90, 98, 100, 490, 531; East Cape, 86, 98; eastern, 230; miniature wheeled animals in, 495; Neolithic, 98, 104; northeastern, 91, 98; northern, 105; Okvik and Old Bering Sea sites in, 106; shamans, 103; sites, 98; Yuit, 98; Yukaghir, 105

Side blades; *see* Blades

Side-blading, 90

Sierra de Tamaulipas, 297; sequence, 294, 302; sequence, est. dates for, 294, 297

Sierra Madre, 178, 302; del Sur, 318; Occidental, 291, 314; Oriental, 297, 302; Oriental, dates for, 294, 299; Oriental, sequence, 294

Sierra Nevada, 118, 126, 130–31, 149

Signal Butte site, 153, 196, 200–201, 240; dates for, 201, 240

Silva, F. Altenfelder, 444, 445, 450

Silver, 319, 453, 465; alloys of, 374, 465; jewelry, 478–79

Silver Lake site, 158; points, 160

Simonsen site, 60, 61, 62, 196, 199, 200; radiocarbon date for, 61, 199

Simonson, Roy W., 18

Simpson, Ruth DeEtte, 44, 46, 73, 79, 121, 146

Sinagua culture, 184–88, 246; est. dates for, 186

Sinaloa, state of, 317–19

Sinaloa River, 291

Sinclair, W. J., 47, 79

Sinkers; *see* Tools

Sisters Hill site, 60

Sizer wrenches; *see* Tools

Skarland, Ivar, 85, 93, 113

Skin(s): animal, 186; artifacts, 100; bedding, 225; boats, 134, 225; buckskin, 154; clothing, 225, 518; embroidered, 514; houses, 94; jaguar, 332, 453; sandals, 179; shelters, 255; vicuña hides, 456

Skin-working, 231; techniques, 198; tools, 201, 210

Skirts, 553; words for, 549

Skull(s): burials, 360, 369; caches of, 363; with clay-filled sockets, 244; Ipiutak, 105; split and preserved, 364; trophy, 369; Yukaghir, 105

Skunk Run culture, 253

Slab(s): carved, 315, 458, 459, 461; doors, 349; grinding, 164; -lined tombs, 369; metates, 126, 127, 131; profile, 313; roofs, 313; stone, 340, 348, 413; vaults, 355

Slash-and-burn; *see* Agriculture

Slate: blades, 102, 103, 134–35; chipped, 102; clubs, 132; forms, Northeastern, est. dates for, 234; implements, burinlike, 103; knives, 134, 135; palettes, 182; projectile points, 135, 231; rubbed, 96, 98, 102–4; scraped and ground, 104, 134, 135

"Slavekillers"; *see* Clubs

Sleight, F. W., 392

Slings; *see* Weapons

Sloth, giant; *see* Fauna, extinct

Smith, A. G., 29, 79

Smith, A. Ledyard, 363, 371, 373, 375, 384, 385

Smith, C. E., 130, 131, 146, 147

Smith, Carlyle S., 208, 219

Smith, David B., 459, 460, 485, 486, 522, 524

Smith, Elmer R., 62, 79

Smith, G. A., 125, 145, 146

Smith, Harlan I., 133, 146

Smith, Marian W., 134, 135, 136, 146, 173

Smith, Robert E., 341, 343, 349, 350, 365, 385

Smoke signaling, 514

Smoky Hill complex, 196, 206

Snakes; *see* Serpents

Snaketown: phase, 181; site, 180–82, 185, 564

Snow goggles; *see* Clothing

Sobanski, A., 447

Social organization (structure, systems), 153, 167, 266, 277, 279, 280, 489, 513, 530, 545; bands, 35, 156, 178, 223, 225, 235, 422, 423; Hopewellian, 241; Maya, 333, 348; Natchez, 284; sedentary agricultural, 249; Tarascan, 320

Social stratification (classes), 186, 207, 238, 241, 273, 299, 333, 367, 427, 437, 439, 471, 478, 481; artisans, 306, 333, 363; artists, 333; bureaucrats, 472, 483; caste systems, 284; farmer-peasant (rural), 306, 308, 333; intelligentsia, 305, 307; middle, 333, 363; priestly, 370, 462; rank, insignia of, 500;

Social stratification (classes)—*Continued*
    royal(ty), 333, 334; slavery, 481, 513;
    upper (elite, patriciate), 273, 306, 308,
    332, 333, 358, 370, 470, 471
Soconusco district, Chiapas, 377, 380
Soil(s), 207, 319; alluvial, 243, 250, 321,
    375; depletion, 254, 351; experts, 442;
    lateritic, 428; organic, 63; solifluction,
    87; studies, 166; volcanic, 365, 375
Solberg, O., 113
Solecki, Ralph S., 85, 113
Solola, Guatemala, 365
Sonora, 175, 180, 188
Sonoran Desert, 117
Sorenson, John L., 385
Soto la Marina River, Mexico, 291
Souris-Antler Creek district (junction), 204
South America(n), 3, 8, 9, 23, 24, 26, 31,
    33, 37, 38, 40, 41, 48, 49, 50, 56, 57,
    59, 68, 389, 403, 422, 445, 451, 453,
    504, 511–23, 531, 537, 565, 566; an-
    thropology, 446; archeology, 419, 421,
    426, 432, 445; culture areas, 331, 479;
    cultures, 451; early man in, 28; lan-
    guages, 531, 546, 547; *see also* individu-
    al cultures, sites, and geographical
    places by name
South Appalachian: ceramics, 265, 267, 268,
    271, 280; culture area, 266, 271; cul-
    ture, 277, 279, 281, 285; tradition, 262,
    265, 269, 270, 275, 279, 280, 284
South Carolina, 255, 261
South Dakota, 61, 197, 203, 250; Black
    Hills of, 200; eastern, 210, 248
Southampton Island, Hudson Bay, 86, 90,
    91, 107
Southern Cult, 238, 242, 249, 254, 264, 274,
    278–85, 565
Soviet archeologists, 98
Soviet scholars, 347
Spanish (Spaniards), 188, 189, 323, 324,
    353, 356, 373, 472; cedar, 334; Con-
    quest, 35, 291, 292, 308, 311, 318, 333,
    346, 351, 376, 379, 451, 470, 508; con-
    quistadores, 306, 324; documents, 213,
    311, 470, 473; explorers, 125; lan-
    guage, 421, 527; missionaries, 125;
    -speaking archeologists, 563
Spanish Fort site, 196
Spaulding, Albert C., vii, 102, 113, 202, 209,
    219
Spear(s), 47, 179, 260, 261; -heads, 204,
    210, 213; salmon, barbs, 103; -throw-
    ers, 135, 176, 375 (*see also* Atlatls);
    throwing, 176, 178, 181; thrusting,
    396; wooden, 44, 396
Spear points, 231, 261, 422; barbed, 204;

chalcedony, 242; notched, 199; obsidi-
    an, 242
Specialization (specialists), 165, 186, 256,
    306, 332, 333; art(s), 207, 304;
    craft(s), 129, 207, 304, 438, 462, 483;
    environmental, lacustrine and riverine,
    163, 167, 168; food, 165; industrial, 471
Speech communities, 535
Spicer, E. H., 189, 191
Spinden, Herbert J., 385; correlation, 345,
    346, 362
Spindle whorls, 344, 477, 516; biconical,
    183; diamond-shaped, 433; disk-shaped,
    435; wooden, 517
Spiro site, 279, 280, 282
Spoon River complex, 251, 252
Spouts; *see* Ceramic forms
Spring Creek culture, 252
Squash, 178, 207, 237, 295–300, 332, 444,
    455, 458, 552; *see also* Cucurbits
Squier, Robert J., 304, 326
Stage; *see* individual cultural and archeologi-
    cal stages by name
Stahl site, 153, 160, 169; est. date for, 160
Stairways; see Architectural features
Stallings Island Culture, 232
Stamped pottery; *see* Ceramic decorative
    styles and techniques
Stamps, clay, 429, 476, 496, 521; cylindrical,
    301, 367, 429; flat, 301, 433; in Near
    East and India, 496
Stanislawski, Dan, 320, 328
Stanley focus, 196, 208, 210
Stansbury Cave, 156
Stanton site, 211
Starved Rock site, 60, 63, 232
State(s), 270, 279, 314, 322, 324, 471–72,
    481; city-, 320, 322, 339, 348, 351;
    conquest, 331, 466, 467; incipient, 305
Stearns Creek complex, 248
Steatite, 125; beads, 164; bowl forms, 236;
    bowls in wooden pipes, 132; pendants,
    164, 166; pipes, 128, 204; rings, 164;
    vessels, 212
Stecker, Oklahoma, 197
Steed-Kisker culture, 252
Stefansson, Vilhjalmur, 101, 114
Stela(e), 304, 339, 344, 372, 377–79, 382;
    carved, 303, 341, 343, 345; cult, 331,
    352, 363, 368, 370; fragments, reset,
    352; free-standing, 458; hieroglyphic,
    502; inscriptions on, 348; lowland, 368;
    plain, 370
Stephens, John Lloyd, 385, 491
Steppe(s), 149, 193, 314–17; climate of, 291,
    317
Stern, Theodore, 522, 526

Sterns Creek focus, 202, 252
Steward, Julian H., 62, 79, 121, 146, 149, 150, 154, 173, 211, 292, 328, 413, 414, 417, 433, 446, 451, 522, 526
Stewart, T. D., 42, 44, 54, 63, 72, 80, 81, 294, 326
Stick(s), 541; dice, 154, 164; digging (*see* Digging sticks); figure-4, 154
Stirling, Matthew W., 303, 328, 377, 493, 510
Stockades; *see* Defensive works
Stocks, linguistic, 119, 162, 223, 241, 331, 530–37
Stone(s), 211, 313, 424, 431; *see also* Basalt, Blades, Chalcedony, Chipped stone, Cores, Flakes, Flint, Ground stone, Minerals, Obsidian, Scrapers, Slate, Steatite, and types of stone artifacts by name
Stools: pottery, 440; wooden, 413
Storage pits (cists); *see* Pits, storage
Straits of Juan de Fuca, 133
Straits of Mackinac, 250
Straits of Magellan, 38, 67
Strand lines; *see* Beach lines
Stratigraphy (stratigraphic), 16, 26, 52, 60, 63, 66, 87, 92, 94, 99, 153, 158, 159, 200, 202, 239, 298, 318, 335, 338, 354, 362, 374, 380, 381, 396, 422, 427, 451, 560; archeology, 437, 446; control, 87, 372; evidence, 251, 445; excavations, 429, 431, 440, 441, 481, 559; research, 392, 436; sequences, 94, 319, 371, 406, 425
Streets; *see* Architectural features
Strong, Emory M., 134, 147
Strong, W. Duncan, 13, 14, 19, 173, 200, 202, 206, 213, 219, 486
Strongholds; *see* Fortresses
Structures, 250, 263, 277, 279, 280, 341, 366, 454, 465; long, single-room, 374; multistage burial, 236; religious, 186, 465, 470, 481; remains of, 198; ceremonial, 263, 301, 405, 476, 480; *see also* Architecture, Houses, Palaces, Pyramids, Temples
Stucco: carvings, 355, 356; decoration, 341, 348, 349, 363; masks, 336; -painted wares, 370, 377, 382; relief figures and glyphs, 349; -surfaced earthen mounds, 379
Stuiver, Minze, 398
Sturtevant, W. C., 414, 417
Style(s); *see* Architecture, Art, Ceramics, and individual cultures by name
Sub-Andean cultures, 421, 427, 437–42, 479–81, 565

Subsistence: dual, 205; economy, 195, 198, 199, 203, 211, 424, 457, 514; patterns, 153, 294, 299, 332, 437, 476; *see also* Agriculture, Economy, Fishing, Gathering, Hunting
Substructures; *see* Architectural features
Suburbs, 307, 308, 312; *see also* Satellite communities
Suchiate River, Guatemala, 378
Suhm, Dee Ann, 29, 51, 67, 80, 201, 219
Sulphur Spring complex (stage), 60–63, 169, 226; dates for, 61, 63
Sumidero site, 379
Sun God, 324, 359
Sundisks, 360
Superstructures, 340; basal zone, 357; perishable, 366, 371; *see also* Palaces, Temples
Surinam, 420
Swadesh, Morris, 2, 9, 119, 147, 515, 526, 527, 556, 566
Swanson, Earl H., Jr., 36, 39, 54, 80, 168, 169, 173, 174
Swanton, John R., 287
Sweat houses, 357, 514; stone, subterranean, 371
Sweet manioc; *see* Manioc
Sweet potatoes; *see* Plants
Swift Creek period, 240, 244, 266–69
Symbolism, 279, 313, 368; in art, 331, 343; of ceramic motifs, 319; Chavín, 463; in glyphs, 347; jaguar and ophidian, 369; religious, 468; religious, absence of, 464; Tiahuanaco-Wari, 473
Symbols: calendrical, 301; cult, 281; of Kukulcan, 357; phallic, 360

T1 site, 90, 107, 240; dates for, 90–91
Tabasco, 303, 333–34, 348–52, 360, 369, 380, 382
Tabatinga River, British Guiana, 422
Taborda ceramic style, 404
Tacamichapa Island, Tabasco, 303
Tacubaya (Mexico City), 293
Tajin, 309, 312, 313; art style, 313, 370, 498, 504; art style, est. dates for, 498
Takutu River, 420, 434
Taltal site, 49
Tamaulipas, state of, 54, 57, 237, 292, 294 296–99, 302
Tamazula district, Jalisco, 319
Tamesi River, Mexico, 291, 302
Tamuin River, Mexico, 291
Tandilense complex, 49, 50
Tanganhuato site, 309
Tangas; *see* Pubic coverings
Taos, New Mexico, 185, 188, 214

Tapajos River; *see* Rio Tapajos
Tarapaca, Chile, 57
Tarascan(s), 318–20, 323
Tariacuri, 320
Taruma, 434, 435
Tayasil, British Honduras, 352
Taylor, Edith S., 133, 148
Taylor, Walter W., 37, 62, 63, 80, 119, 128, 147, 156, 162, 174, 556
Taylor, William E., 107, 114
Taxonomy, 7, 292
Tchefuncte, 262, 263, 265, 266; ceramics, 261, 263, 265, 269, 272; culture, 262, 265, 270, 275, 280
Tchula culture, 269
Tecolpan stage, 350, 352
Teeth: beaver, 233, 244; bison, 293; bone bear, 202; eastern timber wolf, 228; inlaying of, 521; ornaments of, 166; sharks', 245
Tehachapi, California, 126
Tehama County, California, 131
Tehuacan: area, 299; caves, 294, 296, 297, 309; complexes, 298; est. dates for appearance of cultivated plants in, 295, 298; rockshelters, 297; sequence, 301; Valley, 399, 426
Tehuantepec, Isthmus of, 292, 296, 299, 310, 331, 380
Tejar phase, 377
Telamones; *see* Architectural features
Tempering; *see* Ceramics, tempering
Temple(s), 207, 249, 304, 306, 307, 308, 312, 315, 324, 335, 339, 340, 341, 357, 360, 363, 374, 378, 458, 464, 480; Angkor, Cambodia, 501; -building 369; of the Cross (Palenque), 498; Cuicuilco, 301; cults, 460, 480, 482; of the Foliated Cross (Palenque), 498; the Inscriptions (Palenque), 348; the Jaguars (Chichén Itzá), 357; masonry, 331; miniature, 356, 363; of the Moon (Teotihuacán), 554; mounds (*see* Temple mounds); -palace compounds, 304, 315; -priest-idol cults, 481; pyramid(s) (*see* Temple pyramids); sanctuaries, 349; single-room, 369, 373; of the Sun (Teotihuacán), 554; towns, 300, 304; towns, est. beginning date for, in Mexico, 292, 300; towns, stage, 309; twin, on single substructure, 374; of the Warriors (Chichén Itzá), 357, 359; wattle-and-daub, 302; for zemis, 413
Temple mound(s), 266, 270, 271, 273, 274, 277–85, 299, 302, 304, 565; communities, 282; mortuary, 371; -and-plaza complexes, 282; and village patterns, 302

Temple Mound periods: I, 270; I, est. dates for, 270; II, 279
Temple pyramid(s), 340, 502; Cholollan, 311; Maquixco, 308; Palenque, 348, 349; Rio Bec (simulated), 364; Tollan, 315; Xochichalco, 312
Tenam, Chiapas, 379
Tenayocan, 322
Tennessee, 234, 250, 254, 259, 277
Tennessee-Cumberland: area, 281; varieties of Mississippian, 251
Tennessee River, 260, 261, 277, 279; Valley, 275, 277
Tennessee Valley, 228; Mississippian cultures of, 281
Tenochtitlán, 306, 322, 323, 324, 325, 348; population of, 308, 321
Teosinte (teocentli), 300
Teotihuacán, 304–15, 369, 370, 373, 378, 382, 501, 504, 554, 555; est. date for, 304; est. date of destruction of, 311
Teotlalpan, Mexico, 314, 322
Tepanec(s), 322, 323
Tepeu ceramic phase, 346, 349, 350, 355, 362, 379
Tepexpan: area, 293, 294; man, 294
Tequixquiac, 43, 44, 46, 293; est. date for artifacts from, 47
Terra-cotta: figurines, 300, 302, 303; figurine, "Smiling Face," 314; sculptures, Colima burnished, 319; sculptures, Nayarit painted, 319
Terrace(d) (s), 340, 369; agricultural, 332, 478; alluvial, 243; ball-court walls, 375; buildings, two-story, 364; fossil, 159; funeral chambers in, 348; hill slopes, 305, 312, 320, 378; lava, 365; platforms, 377; pyramids, 336; at Rio Pedernales, Venezuela, 396; roofs, 307; roughly modeled, 366; sloping, 369
Tetrapod; *see* Ceramic forms
Tetzcoco, 321–23; est. date for irrigation system of, 321
Texas, 29, 67, 158, 176, 179, 197, 212, 548, 552; central, 36, 37, 44, 45, 201; eastern, 67, 269; Gulf, 155; northern, 207; Panhandle, 37, 54, 55, 62, 177; western, 36, 37, 54
Texas Street site, 31, 46
Textiles, 181, 332, 427, 462, 465, 469, 470, 471, 479; agave, 332; beaded, 479; cotton, 332; Hohokam, 183; ikat, 479; mass production of, 471; patterns in, 455, 479, 497; twined, 455, 458; *see also* Weaving
Tezozomoc, 322, 323
The Dalles, Columbia River, 133, 163, 164, 169; radiocarbon date for, 163

Theocratic: authority, 351, 466; caste systems, 284; class, 333; organization, 339; orientation, 273; tendencies, 316

Thomas, A. B., 213, 219

Thomas, Tully H., 62, 81

Thomas Riggs focus, 196, 206, 210; dates for, 206

Thompson, D. G., 120, 147

Thompson, Howard A., vii

Thompson, J. Eric S., viii, 333, 334, 338, 341, 342, 344–50, 352, 358, 373, 378, 385, 510

Thomson, Jack, 54, 80

Thrones: lotus, 360; platform, 360; tiger, 360, 504

Throwing stick (boards); *see* Atlatl

Thule culture (stage), 88, 91, 98–100, 104, 107; Eskimos, 100, 106, 107; pre-, 91; radiocarbon dates for, 99; Western, 246

Thunder Creek site, 196

Tiahuanaco, 459, 464, 465, 468, 469, 471, 480; Bolivian, 469; ceramics and sculpture, 469; Classic, 465, 469; Coast, 469; -Wari expansion, 482

Tiburtius, G., 444–47, 450

Ticoman ceramics and tradition, 306

Tierra Blanca, Veracruz, 314

Tierra del Fuego, 34, 37, 48, 50, 68, 415

Tiger(s): motif, 504; seated, 360; thrones, 360, 504; *see also* Felines, Jaguars

Tikal, 336, 337, 340, 341, 352, 505

Timber; *see* Wood

Time: lag, 463; levels, 553; -markers, 165, 277, 310, 319, 409; Maya concepts of 333, 344, 345, 368; scales, 392, 393, 394, 451; scales, linguistic, 545

Tin, 453, 470; alloys of, with gold and copper, 374

Tiputini, Ecuador, 425

Titicaca; *see* Lake Titicaca

Titicut culture, 253

Tlachco (Taxco), Mexico, 323

Tlacopan (Tacuba), Mexico, 323

Tlapacoya, 302, 304; est. dates for, 301

Tlatelolco, 322, 324, 348

Tlatilco, 300, 301, 381

Tlaxcala, 305, 309, 312, 323

Tobacco: cigarettes, cigars, 497; *Nicotiana rusticum*, 178, 179, 186, 242, 553; *Nicotina attenuata*, 154; smoking, invention of, 497; words for, 549

Tocuyano, Venezuela, 391, 401

Tocuyano style, radiocarbon date for, 405

Tocuyanoid series, 404, 405

Tohil ceramic phase, 346; Plumbate ware, 372, 374

Toilets; *see* Architectural features

Tolchaco complex, 31, 43, 44

Toldense complexes, 65, 66

Tollan, 311, 312, 314, 316, 317; est. date of fall of, 316

Tollantzinco, 323

Tollocan, 323

Tolstoy, Paul, 306, 328

Toltec(s), 311, 314–17, 319, 353, 356–59, 360, 364, 382; population, 323

Toluca, valley of, 320, 322

Tomatoes; *see* Plants

Tomb(s), 319, 360, 369, 373; brick (Han period, China), 501; -building, 369; chamber, 521; cruciform, 364; floor, 301; royal, 369, 371; pyramid, rectangular, 342, 366, 369; sepulchers, 304; shaft, 521; slab-lined, 369; stone-covered, 480; subterranean, 348; vaulted, 373, 378; vaulted, Altar de Sacrificios, 337, 338; vaulted, Central Depression (Chiapas), 378; vaulted, Holmul, 338; vaulted, Mountain Cow, 338; walls, 349; *see also* Burials

Tombigbee River, Alabama, 266, 267

Tommy Tucker Cave, 161

Tonala, Chiapas, 377, 378

Tonala River, Tabasco, 303

Tonto Basin, Arizona, 183, 185, 188

Tools, 224, 231, 364, 456; barbs, 103, 127, 182, 204, 210, 213, 233; beamers, 202; bone, 133, 186, 202, 456; bronze, 470; core, 42, 343; conchshell, 263; copper, 233, 465, 478; cutting, 52, 197, 198, 201, 260; diffusion of, 227; flake, 42; flint, 343; grinding, 122, 518 (*see also* Manos, Metates, Mortars, Pestles); hammers, 103, 165, 399; hammers, shell, 397, 398; hammerstones, 58, 64, 122, 123, 161, 224, 229, 231, 422, 455; limestone, 343; marlinspikes, 103; mattocks, 103, 107; metal, 502; pebble, 42; pecking, pounding, 344; perforators, 32, 229, 344; picks, 103; plummets, 127, 231; scraping, 52; shaft smoothers, 32, 164, 166, 212; shovels, 103, 107; sickles, 160, 161; sinkers, 132; sinkers, bolas, 198; sinkers, fishline, 96, 103; sinkers, fish net, 102, 104, 165, 260, 455; sinkers, pebble, 164, 165; snares, cordage, 160; traps, 154; whetstones, 164; wound plugs, 103; wrenches, antler, 155; wrenches, horn, 154, 155, 178; wrenches, shaft, 154; wrenches, sizer, 154; *see also* Blades, Celts, Drills, Gravers, Harpoons, Hoes, Knives, Projectile points

Topa Inca Yupanqui: 471, 472, 479

Topanga: culture (complex), 31, 59, 60, 62, 64, 127; est. date for, 64; site, 123

Topo: site, 401; style, 407
Topoxte, British Honduras, 352
Totonicapan, Guatemala, 365
Toulouse, Joseph H., Jr., 62, 70
Towers; *see* Architectural features
Towns, 320, 333, 463, 465, 476, 481, 515; agglutinated, 466; large, 470; small, 285; temple, 300, 304, 309; words for, est. age of, 552
Toy(s), 495; Mexican wheeled, 493, 495, 499, 504; objects, 493
Toynbee, Arnold, 562
Tozzer, Alfred M., 357, 385, 386
Trade (trading), 106; barter, words for, est. age of, 552; Egyptian, 499; expeditions, 523; goods, 131, 209, 211, 237, 238, 255, 262, 319, 334, 339, 354, 355, 376, 432, 465, 476; goods, European, 166, 205, 432, 435, 436; interareal, 519; long-distance, 306; objects, 500, 522; Ohio Hopewell, 242; pottery, 267, 302, 349–50, 355, 374, 375, 397, 409; in prehistoric Peru, est. dates for, 453; relations, 202, 211, 265, 499; units, 305; voyages, 477
Traders; *see* Merchants
Traditions, 26, 32, 39, 91, 209, 256, 281, 355, 394; *see also* individual cultures and elements of culture by name
Trail Creek site, 60, 62
Tranquillity site, 127
Transitional culture (Northeastern United States), 228, 235, 253
Transitional period: Intermontane tradition, 157, 167, 169; (stages) Northern Yucatan, 355, 362, 364; est. dates for, 346
Transpacific: contacts, 360, 489–510, 511, 522; diffusion, 118, 541; introduction of pottery, Ecuadorean coast, 474, 477; linguistic relationships, 537–41; voyages, 502, 507–9
Transportation, 117, 434, 501, 502; of artifacts by animals, 124; canal, 324; canoe, 332; dugouts, logs, rafts, skin boats, 225; facilities, 351; foot, 332; lagoon and sea, 376; lake, 321; water, 38, 225; by wheel, 499; *see also* Travel
Trappist phase, 251, 252
Trash; *see* Refuse
Travel: in boats, 456; by canoe, 332; by dugout, 135; on foot, 332, 456; by litter, 332, 334; overland, 507, 509; routes, 403, 404; by sea, 396; *see also* Transportation
Tree(s), 334, 541; allspice, 334; juniper, 149, 176; of life, 504; mahogany, 334; mamey, 334; marsh elder, 237; palm,

334; piñon pine, 149, 176; -ring studies (*see* Dendrochronology); sapodilla (zapote), 334; scarcity of, 518; spruce, 149; stylized or celestial, 360; vanilla, 334
Treganza, Adan Eduardo, 31, 44, 62, 80, 123, 128, 130, 131, 139, 147
Trempealeau complex, 243, 252
Trenton, New Jersey, 44
Tres Zapotes site, 304, 368, 380–82, 493–94; est. date for, 381
Tribal: councils, 189; groupings, 254
Tribes; *see* individual Indian tribes by name
Tribute, 331, 324
Trickster, 514
Trik, Aubrey S., 386
Trinidad, island of, 390–92, 395, 396, 398, 402, 403, 407–10, 413
Trinidad Bay, Oregon, 132
Trinity culture, 232
Tripod; *see* Ceramic forms
Tripsacum grass, 300
Trombetas River; *see* Rio Trombetas
Tropical forest, 453; agriculture, 442, 443; area, 441; complexes, 432–37; conditions, 442; cultural development, 433; culture(s), 425, 429, 435, 451; cultures, origins of, 433–34; lifeway, 435, 437, 453; peoples, 434–35, 455; plants, 453; products, 453, 454; sequence, 436; sites, 430; traits, 431
Tropical Forest slash-and-burn agricultural stage (complex): Amazon-Orinoco drainages, 421, 424, 426–37; Guiana variety of, 435; Paraná drainage, 444–45
Troyville: ceramics, 266, 267, 269, 271; culture, 266, 267, 285; period (stage), 266, 267, 270–71, 273, 274, 277
True, D. L., 54, 62, 64, 80, 121, 122, 123, 125, 147, 148, 158, 174
Tschopik, Harry, Jr., 65
Tsurai site, est. date for, 132
Tubers; *see* Plants
Tucacas, Venezuela, area, 393, 397
Tucker, H., 296, 327
Tula, Hidalgo, 314, 357, 359, 360, 373
Tula-Mazapan: horizon, 183; horizon style, 319
Tularosa Cave, 158, 169, 179, 185, 186; est. dates for, 179, 186
Tularosa River, 184, 187
Tule Springs site, 43, 44, 46; radiocarbon date for, 44, 46
Tulum, 363, 364
Tumplines; *see* Clothing
Tundra (North America), 223, 230
Tunnels; *see* Architectural features

Tuohy, Donald R., 170, 174
Tupi-guarani: ceramics, 444; complex (culture, tradition), 443–45, 522
Turbans; *see* Clothing
Turin culture, 252
Turkey(s): eating of, 184, 187; domesticated, 179, 181, 182, 184, 187, 332; feathers, 187; -tail projectile points, 235; wild, 187
Turquoise; *see* Minerals, Ornaments
Turtle shell, 228; engraved, 382
Tuthill, Carr, 124, 147
Tutischcainyo complex and site, 420, 424–25, 436; est. date for, 426
Tuxtla Mountains, Veracruz, 304, 380, 381
Tuzigoot pueblo, 187
Twin Rivers culture, 253
Twined: bags, 154, 160, 161, 178, 179; basketry, 154, 155, 160, 161; matting, 155, 178, 179
Typology (typological), 85, 88, 90, 99, 102, 121, 158, 159, 160, 293, 560; analysis, 176; ceramic, 301, 381; evidence, 259, 302, 312
Tzacualli phase, 306
Tzakol: ceramics, 310, 341–43, 349; phase, 310, 338, 346, 355, 362, 378
Tzintzuntzan (Tarascan capital), 320
Tzolkin; *see* Calendars
Tzutzuculi, 377

U. P. Mammoth kill, radiocarbon date for, 197
Uaxactun, 310, 335–39, 341, 361; Pyramid E-VII-sub, 336, 340
Ucayali River, Peru, 420, 424–26, 436, 437, 446
Uelen, East Cape, Siberia, 98, 106
Uhle, Max, 51, 80
Ulua River, Honduras, 292
Ulua valley ceramics, 337, 343; est. date for bichrome wares, 376
Umbrellas, 500
Umnak Island, Aleutians, 90, 102
Uncompahgre culture, 232
Upper Becerra formation, 293
Upper Lithic stage, 30, 31, 37, 38, 51, 59
Upper Mississippi Valley; *see* Mississippi Valley
Upper Paleolithic; *see* Paleolithic
Upper Republican aspect, 196, 206, 207, 210, 246; est. date for, 206
Urban: axis at Teotihuacán, 307; characteristics, 306, 333; core, 306, 307, 315; culture(s), 306, 308, 375; density, 307; development, 304, 306; elite, 306, 309; intelligentsia, 305; -life stage, 29; living, 363; markets, 321; patterns, 306, 312; population, 305, 306; revolutions, 295
Urban centers, 278, 295, 305, 306, 320, 322; absence of, 480; Ecuadorean coast, 478; elite, 470; Monte Alban, 304, 305, 309; lay, 470; Peruvian coast, 467 ff.; Tajin, 312; Tenochtitlán, 324–25; Teotihuacán, 304, 309, 311; Tollan, 315; Xochichalco, 312
Urban (Temple) Formative period, 335, 366
Urbanization (urbanism), 186, 295, 304, 320, 362, 470
Uren culture, 246, 253
Urns; *see* Ceramic forms
Uruguay, 50, 419, 420, 443, 444
Usumacinta, Guatemala, 332, 348, 351, 355, 359, 360; cities, 336, 340–43; River, 333, 334, 343
Utah, 550; caves, 54, 60–62, 154, 156, 158, 214; central, 175; southeastern, 181, 184; southern, 176, 177; southwestern, 187; western, 176
Utatlan, Quiché area, Guatemala, 374, 375
Utility wares; *see* Ceramic wares, utility
Utonahua(n) (Utoaztecan): continuum, 550; culture, 549, 552–53; divergence, 550; expansion, 553, 554; languages, 548–52; languages, center of dispersal of, 549; peoples, 539, 548–50, 553, 554, 555; phonemes and words, 553; Proto-, 549; -Tanoan interrelations, 551; territory, 552–54
Uxmal, 354, 356, 359

Vahki phase, 180
Vaillant, George C., 35, 80, 337
Valders substage; *see* Glacial, stages
Valdivia culture (phase), 426, 459, 474–75; ceramics, 437, 474, 496, 503, 522; figurines, 474, 475
Valencia: Basin, 390, 399–410, 413; ceramic style, 406; radiocarbon dates for, 406
Valencioid series, 406, 407
Valle de Bravo site, 309
Valley focus, 196, 202, 203; radiocarbon date for, 202
Valley of Mexico; *see* Mexico, Valley of
Valley Woodland, 240
Valliserrana region, Argentina, 515
Valsequillo: localities, 43, 44, 293; reservoir, 47
Van Stone, James W., 114
Vancouver Island, British Columbia, 118, 135, 527
Varves; *see* Glacial, features
Vashion retreat; *see* Glacial, stages

Vaults; see Architectural features, arches
Vegetable(s) (vegetal), cultivated, 332; fibers, 160; foods, 33, 63, 201, 294, 297, 399; materials, 34, 229; products, 58; quids, 154; remains, 297; wild, 399; see also Foods, Plants, Trees
Veneer; see Architectural features
Venezuela(n), 36, 48, 50, 51, 57, 389–434, 451; radiocarbon dates for, 392; see also individual cultures, sites, and geographical places by name
Ventana: Cave, 60, 62, 64, 152, 156, 158, 169, 185, 226; complex, 64
Ventuari River, Venezuela, 420, 428, 433
Venus, planet; see Astronomy
Veracruz (city), 314
Veracruz (state of), 117, 492, 494, 499, 554; central, 303, 313, 314, 321; coastal, 369; Early Classic tradition, 313; northern, 554; southern, 304, 380, 382
Verde Valley, Arizona, 183–85, 188
Vessel(s), 262, 337; bark, sewed, 514; bronze (Chinese), 504, 505; burials in, 363; clay, unfired, 178, 179; "comal," 372; conoidal, 248; cylindrical and comal-like, 371; doughnut-shaped, 265; effigy, 268, 367; killed, 273; large, 410; marble, 352, 367, 382; pottery, 234, 248, 300, 461; shapes (forms), 249, 261, 267, 271, 278, 281, 349, 424, 428, 433, 438, 512, 518, 520, 522; small, 261; steatite, 212; stirrup-spouted, 462; stone, 135, 164, 461; stucco-painted, 377; see also Ceramics
Vicksburg, Mississippi, 248, 250
Vieques Island, Puerto Rico, 402
Vignati, M. A., 50, 80
Village(s), 92, 125, 208, 209, 248, 249, 254, 300, 302, 333, 423, 456; Ananatuba, 424; Bennett focus, 208; circular, 464; clustered, 179; debris (middens, refuse), 202, 203, 243, 271, 424–29, 431, 434; -dwelling cultures, 214; duration (permanency), 424–27; earth lodge, 211; farming (rural), 300, 371; federations, 481; fishing, 454; fortified, 480; frequently moved, 425; Glacial Kame, 234; Hohokam, 182; Hopewellian, 202, 239, 242; Hopi, 185, 188; Indian, modern, 368, 425, 437; Iroquois, 254; large, 129, 186, 437, 466; life, 179, 333, 520, 552; location, 424; long-rectangular-house, 207; loosely arranged, 260, 207; Mangueiras, 427; Maquixco (Teotihuacán), 308; Maya, lowland, 339; Mexican, est. beginning dates for, 299; Middle Missouri, 208; Mogollon, 181;

Mississippian, 278; northern Mesoamerica, beginning date for, 299; number of, 256; Panuco, 299; permanent, 179, 205; planned, 206; pre-Monte Alban, 301; Rupununi phase, 433; satellite, 277, 375; "scattered house" (unplanned, random), 366, 376, 458, 463; settlement, 292, 300; Shannon focus, 208; sites, 91, 92, 104, 122, 162, 202, 204, 231, 233, 247, 299, 308, 405, 435; size of, 249, 256, 426; small, 186, 480; Stanley focus, 208; stockaded, 211, 248; -temple-mound pattern, 301; Tupi-guarani, 444; Urban (Temple) Formative, 335; Village tribes, 195
Village Formative period, 335
Village Indian period (stage), 206 210; see also Plains Village Indians
Virgin Islands, 391, 392, 398, 403, 411, 412
Virgin River, Nevada and Utah, 176, 185
Virginia, 254, 255
Viru Valley, 459, 463, 468; Project, 482
Viscanchani: complexes, 49, 50, 51, 65, 66 (see also Copacabaña complex); site, 459
Vowels (vocalic), 542; alternation of, with consonants, 542, 544; back, 543; change, 542; front, 543
Voyages: drift, 508; Polynesian, 507; trans-pacific, 502, 507, 508

Wai Wai complex sites, 435
Wakemup mound series, est. beginning date for, 165
Wales beach midden, radiocarbon date from, 99
Walker, Edwin F., 123, 128, 147
Wall(ed) (s), 340, 348, 520; adobe, 374, 470; basal batter on, 363; block, 355; cities, 362, 363, 469, 470; concrete, 313; defense, 363, 515; end zone (ball court), 373; high, around ball courts, 375; -inclosed religious precincts, 378; lime plastered, 307; masonry, 371; mud-daubed, 366; paintings on, 466, 470, 504; openings, trapezoidal, 473; playing (ball court), 371, 373, 375; retaining, 340, 455; screen, 315; sites, fortress, 374; sloping elements at base of, 369, 373; sloping summit platform, 369; stone, 433, 515; stone, carved and painted, 315; substructure, battered, 357; tomb, 349; tomb, red-painted, 369
Walla Walla, Washington, 543
Wallace, William J., 54, 64, 80, 121, 122–25, 131, 133, 148, 158, 174
Wallula site, 166
Walnut River, 208

Wapanucket culture, 231, 253
Wares, ceramic; *see* Ceramic wares
Warfare, 126, 127, 129, 249, 322, 324, 380, 462, 464, 468; absence of, coastal Ecuador, 478; Colombian highlands, 481; Guatemala, 376; Mochica, 466–68
Wari: ceramics, 469, 470; expansion, 470, 482; influence, 469–70, 471; site, 459, 468, 469, 482; textiles, 469, 470; Tiahuanaco designs of, 469, 473
Waring, A. J., Jr., 278, 279, 287
Warren, Claude N., 54, 62, 64, 77, 80, 121, 122, 123, 148, 159, 174
Warrior(s): Aztec, 324; camps, 308; depictions, 360; eagle- and jaguar-societies, 378; figures, 315, 521; figurines, 301, 363; Maya, 357; Mochica, 467, 468; Temple of the, Chichén Itzá, 357, 359; Toltec, 357, 358
Washington (state), 23, 55, 62, 543; eastern, 55, 62; upper coast of, 133, 135; western, 54
Washita River focus, 196; radiocarbon dates for, 206
Wasley, William W., 52, 54, 73
Watanabe, H., 119, 148
Water: conservation of, 518; -courses, 150, 159, 434; hole(s), 121, 339, 425; level, 334, 406; -proofing, 497; runoff rates (patterns), 150, 151; storage, 334, 476; supply, 334, 351, 353, 452; transportation of, 518; underground, 353; -ways, 208, 321, 365
Wattle-and-daub, 188, 249, 299, 302, 376, 424
Wauchope, Robert, vii, viii, 2, 8, 9, 303, 310, 331, 346, 373, 386, 491, 510, 523, 526
Wealth: accumulation of, 126, 127, 324, 520; consciousness, 129, 367; differences in, 300; objects, 132
Weapons, 224, 231, 260, 455, 468, 539, 541; blowguns, 365, 496, 522; bolas, 397; bolas, bird, 94; bolas, grooved-stone, 163, 231; bolas, weights or sinkers, 94, 198; bow and arrow, 125, 127, 128, 131, 161, 178, 179, 181, 186, 247, 248, 365; copper, 465; crossbow, 503; hunting, 455; metal, 502; Peruvian, 455; shields, 357, 467; slings, 161, 397, 455; *see also* Blades, Clubs, Darts, Knives, Projectile points, Spears
Weaver site (focus), 239, 248; radiocarbon date from, 239
Weaving (weaves, woven), 102; bags, 178; cloth, 238; ikat decoration, 479; industries, 183; over-and-under, 455; sandals, 156, 178; straps or sashes, 178; techniques, 158; true, 458; twined, 455, 458; *see also* Textiles
Webb, Clarence H., 287
Webb, Walter P., 193, 219
Wedel, Mildred M., 212, 220
Wedel, Waldo R., vii, 1, 6, 7, 127, 128, 148, 193–95, 202, 203, 206, 208, 211, 213, 217, 220, 317, 329, 560
Weeden Island: area, 271, 273; ceramic complex, 262, 268, 271; ceremonialism, 271; communities, 283; culture, 246, 271, 275, 277, 280, 282, 283, 285; period, 271; sites, 273
Weights: atlatl, 131, 164; bolas, 94, 198
Weiser River, Idaho, 54
Weitlaner, 318
Weller, J. Marvin, 17, 19
Wells (cenotes), 353, 376; at Chichén Itzá, 359, 360
Wendorf, Fred, 54, 61, 62, 81
West, Robert C., 321, 329
West Indies, 389, 396, 398, 399, 411, 413; central, 403; *see also* Antilles
West Mound, radiocarbon dates from, 241
West Virginia, 236, 238, 253, 254
Western Hunting culture, 122
Wettlaufer, B., 201, 220
Weymouth, W. D., 130, 131, 146, 147
Whalebone: clubs, 133, 165; mattocks, 107; roofs, 455; *see also* Baleen
Whalen Farm site, radiocarbon dates for, 134
Whaling, 94; harpoon heads, 94, 104; with poisoned lance, 102; in Punuk culture, 94
Wheat, Joe Ben, 184, 191
Wheel(ed) (s): absence of, 501, 502; clay, 493; history of the, 493; idea of, 499; origin of the, 493; toys, Mexican, 493, 495, 499, 504; vehicles, 332, 494, 495, 522
Wheeler, S. M., 62, 81
Whistles, 204; anthropomorphic, 382; birdbone, 155, 212; bone, 127; effigy, 352, 366, 370; Mamom, 336, 337; pottery, 435
Whitaker, Thomas W., 296, 326
Whitcomb, Mr. and Mrs. Gail, vii
White, Leslie A., vii, 195, 220
White Mountains, Arizona, 188
White potatoes; *see* Plants
White River Terrace sites, 196
Whiteshell focus, 196
Whittlesey culture, 253
Wicke, Charles R., 309, 329
Wickiups; *see* Shelters
Wigwams; *see* Shelters

Wike, Joyce, 62, 73, 197, 217
Will, George F., 208, 220
Willamette Valley, Oregon, 133
Willey, Gordon R., vii, 5, 28, 29, 30, 31, 32, 37, 38, 39, 42, 46, 47, 51, 59, 81, 121, 129, 135, 136, 139, 148, 287, 339, 363, 386, 392, 394, 398, 400, 404, 414, 417, 421, 426, 428, 444, 445, 450, 463, 465, 466, 468, 479, 486, 521, 526, 560, 561, 563
Williams, Howel, 170
Williams, Stephen, 38, 63, 81
Williams, Mr. and Mrs. Willoughby, vii
Williamson site, 226
Willie, Mrs. Roy E., vii
Willis, Roger, 257
Willman, H. B., 18, 19
Willow Creek midden, radiocarbon date from, 128
Wilmington culture, 275
Wilson Butte Cave, 60, 62, 166, 169; est. time for, 166
"Winged objects"; see Harpoons
Winona, Arizona, 183, 185
Wintemberg, W. J., 107, 114
Wisconsin, 59, 228, 234, 242, 243, 247–48, 250, 252
Wisconsin glacial period, 27, 45, 68; fauna, 45; last major moraine of, 224; radiocarbon dating for, 27; see also Glacial stages
Wissler, Clark, 100, 114, 125, 193, 223, 258
Wissler, Mildred, 148
Witthoft, John, 54, 55, 81
Wittry, Warren W., 228, 250, 258
Wolf, Eric R., 321, 329
Wolfe, M. K., 296, 325
Wood(en) (s), 207, 208, 334, 353, 453; artifacts, 100; beads, 178; boxes, 178, 179; burial platforms, 366; -carving, 134, 135, 163, 165, 413, 479, 499; clubs, 154; fire-drills, 160; foreshafts (arrow and dart), 160, 161; fossil, 50, 396; fragments, 92; hard tropical, 422; hearths, 155, 160; houses, 166; knife handles, 155, 160; implements, 176, 181; mortars, 122, 127; ornaments, 178; palisades, 254; pendants, 179; petrified, implements of, 50; pipes, with steatite bowl, 132; prototypes for copper tools, 234; scoops, 178; shafts, 96; spears, 44, 396; spindle whorls, 517; statues, 413; stools, 413; utensils, 176; -working, 102, 125, 166, 225, 230
Woodbury, Richard B., 386
Woodland: Arctic hunters, 240, 246; Coastal, 240; complexes, 202, 203, 205, 256; culture(s), 16, 203, 212, 214, 225, 275, 564; Eastern, 215; Northern hunters, 240; Plains, 7, 195, 201–5; Plains, est. dates for, 202; pottery, 131, 201, 203, 212, 250, 496; pre-Woodland groups, 203; Valley, 240
Woodstock ceramic period, 338
Wool, 452–54
Word(s), 531, 533, 534, 537, 539, 541; abstract, 539; cognate, 535, 552, 553; common, 533; comparison of, 552, 553; diagnostic lists of, 534; Gothic, 545; Greek, 541, 545; Hebrew, 539; Indo-European, 545; Latin, 533, 541, 545; loan, 538–41; Maya, 347; meanings of, 534, 539, 541, 544; Nahuatl, 539, 541, 544, 545, 553; number, 544; Nutka, 541, 544, 545; pairs, 551; Russian, 545; similar, 537; stems, 539; triconsonantal, 539
Workshops, 121, 306, 422
Wormington, H. M., 27, 28, 38, 39, 51, 53, 54, 62, 81, 89, 114, 121, 148, 176, 191, 197, 220, 417
Wrenches; see Tools
Writing, 332; hieroglyphic, 304, 331, 339, 343, 345, 346, 347; ideographic, 347; rebus, 347; syllabic, 347; systems, 496
Wyoming, 44, 55, 60–62, 197, 200–201, 212–14

Xaltocan, 322
Xicco, 322
Xingu River, Brazil, 420, 431
Xochichalco, 312, 315, 359; est. dates for, 312
Xolalpan phase, 306, 309; est. date for, 306

Yadkin culture, 246
Yale site, 53, 54
Yankeetown culture, 253
Yaqui ceramic phase, 346
Yaracuy Valley, Venezuela, 404, 405
Yarinacocha, Peru, 436, 437
Yarumela site, 376
Yasuni: complex, 425; site, 420, 424
Yazawa, Taiji, 485
Yazoo Basin, 266, 270
Yoder, Hatton, 15
Yojoa: monochrome wares, 376; site, 335
Yokes, 313, 371; coolie, 477; stone, 352, 378, 382
Young site, 246, 252
Yucatan, 4, 297, 302, 310–16, 331–33, 345–64, 375, 387; see also individual cultures and sites by name

Yucatec(an): changes, 357; dialect, 334, 347, 353; Maya, 373; north, 351; slate-wares, 349
Yucca; *see* Plants
Yucuñudahui, Oaxaca, 309
Yukon Island, Cook Inlet, Alaska, 90
Yukon Territory, Canada, 36; northern, 54; southern, 54
Yuma(n) (s): culture, 122, 185; language, 550; proto-, 181; -speaking tribes, 181, 182, 189, 549

Zaachila site, 317
Zacatecas, 183, 293, 314
Zacatenco, 299, 381; est. dates for, 299
Zacualpa, Guatemala, 338, 371, 373; ceram-
ic phases, 309, 367, 372, 374; Early Classic, 370
Zaculeu, Guatemala, 309, 369, 371
Zapote; *see* Trees
Zea mays; see Maize
Zemis; *see* Gods
Zingg, Robert Mowry, 153–55, 174
Zoömorphic (zoöform): ceramic designs, 430; cover handles, 343, fillets (ceram-ic), 433; lizard-man, Mochica, 467; lugs on pottery, 406, 410, 411; sculp-ture, 164; "slavekiller" clubs, 132, 134; *see also* Animals, Effigy
Zulia, Venezuela, 50
Zuma Creek site, radiocarbon date for, 123
Zuniquena sites, 56, 57, 58
Zutuhil kingdom, 374